The Economic Approach to Environmental and Natural Resources

Third Edition

James R. Kahn

Washington and Lee University
and
Universidade Federal do Amazones

THOMSON
SOUTH-WESTERN

Australia Canada Mexico Singapore Spain United Kingdom United States

THOMSON
SOUTH-WESTERN

The Economic Approach to Environmental and Natural Resources, Third Edition
James R. Kahn

VP/Editorial Director:
Jack W. Calhoun

VP/Editor-in-Chief:
Michael P. Roche

Publisher:
Michael B. Mercier

Acquisitions Editor:
Michael Worls

Developmental Editor:
Sarah K. Dorger

Marketing Manager:
Jennifer Garamy

Production Editor:
Robert Dreas

Sr. Technology Project Editor:
Peggy Buskey

Sr. Media Editor:
Pam Wallace

Manufacturing Coordinator:
Sandee Milewski

Production House:
Argosy Publishing

Printer:
Courier-Westford
Westford, Massachusetts

Design Project Manager:
Rik Moore

Internal Designer:
Lisa Albonetti

Cover Designer:
Rik Moore

Cover Images:
© Monte Nagler, Digital Vision

Printed in the United States of America

1 2 3 4 5 07 06 05 04

ISBN: 0-03-031454-2 package
0-324-20275-X book

Library of Congress Control Number:

2004106716

For more information contact South-Western, 5191 Natorp Boulevard, Mason, Ohio 45040.

Or you can visit our Internet site at: http://www.swlearning.com

To Jerry, Steve, and Bari, who share my love of learning.

preface

> *If it's wild to your own heart, protect it. And fight for it, and dedicate yourself to it, whether it's a mountain range, your wife, your husband, or even (heaven forbid) your job.*
>
> *It doesn't matter if it's wild to anyone else: if it's what makes your heart sing, if it's what makes your days soar like a hawk in summertime, then focus on it. Because for sure, it's wild, and if it's wild, it'll mean you're still free. No matter where you are.*
>
> Rick Bass, *Wild to the Heart*

The question of why study environmental and resource economics is posed in Chapter 1. A more basic question is, "Why write a book about environmental economics?" The answer to the second question is much more complex than the first, but it revolves around the sentiments expressed in the above quotation by Rick Bass. Quite simply, the environment matters and the field of environmental economics offers a unique way of thinking about the environment. A former colleague of mine, a biologist, used to kid me that *environmental economics* is an oxymoron. That always provoked a reaction from me. I believe very strongly that it is possible to be passionate about both the environment and economics, and this book tries to reflect these two passions and show that they are not mutually exclusive.

Organization of the Book

This book does several things differently from other textbooks in this area. The first is the division into theory (Chapters 1 to 6) and application (Chapters 7 to 19). The second organizational difference that distinguishes this textbook from others is the integration of environmental and resource economics.

The theory of environmental and resource economics is initially presented in the dedicated theory chapters but is constantly revisited in the application chapters to reinforce the theoretical concepts and to demonstrate their practical importance. For example, the theory of marketable pollution permits is extensively developed in Chapter 3, but applied to specific environmental problems in many different chapters such as Chapter 7 (global change), Chapters 8 and 9 (energy), Chapter 14 (water resources), and Chapter 18 (environment and development in Third World countries).

The second organizational difference between this book and most others is the integration of environmental and natural resource economics. This integration is important because the pressing environmental and resource issues of the current time all have to do with the environmental implications of resource production and use. Although traditional resource economic issues (e.g., the optimal rotation of a forest, the optimal amount of effort in a fishery, and how the market allocates an exhaustible resource over time) are all covered, more emphasis is placed on the interaction of resources with the environment. For example, Chapter 10 discusses exhaustible resources, but it places the discussion in the context of materials policy and the environmental impacts of mining. The chapter looks at the problem from the perspective of extraction of minerals to the disposal of the materials that are made with minerals. Similarly, the forestry chapters look not only at the question of harvesting, but also focus on the questions of the causes and consequences of deforestation and whether old growth forests should be harvested or preserved. Chapters on global warming, energy, biodiversity, agriculture and the environment, the environment and the macroeconomy, tropical forests, and issues relating to the environment in developing countries also distinguish this from other existing textbooks.

Level

The theory chapters present the economic theory of environmental and resource economics in a format useful to students with varied backgrounds in economics. Environmental and resource economics is a required course for students from many different majors, yet intermediate microeconomic theory is usually taken only by economics students. Consequently, this book does not require an intermediate microeconomics prerequisite. New economics concepts such as consumers' and producers' surplus, demand and supply analysis, opportunity cost, and marginal analysis are thoroughly explained as they are encountered, providing a review for economics students and a foundation for students with less experience in economics. The presentation is designed to give economics majors an opportunity to apply their economic learning to an interesting and topical area, whereas non-economics students will find the new perspective an interesting and different approach from other perspectives, such as ecology. The key vehicle for maintaining student interest and providing intellectual challenge are the application chapters. The material from the theory chapters is pulled into the application chapters in a manner specifically tailored to the applications. The student thus learns how economic theory can be used to understand both the causes of specific environmental problems and the process for developing specific solutions for each environmental problem.

One of the important features of the book is the boxed application, which contributes to the understanding of how to use environmental and resource economics to solve real-world problems. The main goal of the boxed application is to show how the principles of environmental and resource economics are applied in specific situations. For example, boxed applications include gold mining in the Amazon, the protection of elephants in Africa, the pollution of fisheries in Europe, and water allocation in New York City. The book contains a total of 45 boxed applications.

Orientation

Another feature of this textbook that distinguishes it from other textbooks in the market is its orientation. Many textbooks take the perspective that environmental and resource economics are a subset and straightforward application of microeconomics. Although microeconomics is extremely important in studying environmental and resource issues, other perspectives must also be utilized. The macroeconomic perspective also generates important insights into these issues. In addition, one must understand the basic principles of the natural and physical sciences that govern the natural world to properly apply economic principles that also govern the human-environmental interaction.

Part of developing an appropriate economic perspective on an environmental problem is understanding the underlying natural and physical science. In an effort to place economics in an interdisciplinary context, the applications chapters of this book include basic information on the natural and physical science dimensions of each application topic. The emphasis, however, is on the economics and its role in the development of environmental policy. Students who desire more in-depth understanding of the physical and natural sciences should take a course or read a book that directly emphasizes the physical and natural sciences component of environmental studies.

What's New in the Third Edition

The most important revisions made in the third edition were to incorporate the many changes in the environment and in environmental policy that have occurred since the second edition was written. For example, Chapter 7, *Acid Rain*, and Chapter 8, *Energy*, have been completely rewritten into two chapters (8 and 9) that focus on energy and the environment.

Another important feature has been the rewriting of Chapter 4 into two new chapters. The new Chapter 4 focuses on valuation issues, and the new Chapter 5 focuses on decision-making criteria and how to use them in decision-making processes. In addition, a theme about the importance of ecological services to the economic process has been added to the text and woven throughout the theory and application chapters.

Learning Tools

Each chapter contains many tools to help students better understand and master environmental economics. Throughout both the theory and application chapters, boxed applications pose environmental questions and issues with analysis relevant to the topics being discussed. Each chapter ends with a *Summary* recapping the main topics, concepts, and current debates. The *Review Questions* help to test student's comprehension of the material presented in the chapter, and the *Questions for Further Study* provide a more general framework for reviewing material, tying the material in the current chapter to broader themes and to material presented in earlier chapters. The *Suggested Paper Topics* are offered to help the student with the difficult task of getting started on a research paper. In addition to suggesting topics revolving around different approaches to issues, policies, problems, effects, and consequence; both electronic and print resources are listed to help the students begin their research. *Works Cited and Selected Readings* provide a sample of writings on current issues, as well as a listing of established sources.

Instructor and Student Resources

Instructor's Manual and Test Bank

Joy Clark at Auburn University in Montgomery, Ala. has authored an instructor's manual with test bank (IM/TB) to accompany the text. The IM/TB includes chapter summaries, additional sources, key concepts and definitions, and answers to the end-of-chapter review questions. The IM/TB also includes 500 test questions with 10 short-answer questions for every chapter. This resource is available to qualified instructors in a print version and in downloadable Microsoft® Word files from the book's web site at http://kahn.swlearning.com. For assistance, contact your Thomson Business and Professional Publishing representative or Academic Support at (800)423-0563.

Microsoft PowerPoint Slides

PowerPoint slides, also created by Joy Clark, are available for use by students as an aid in note taking and by instructors for enhancing their lectures. The slides are available for download from the book's web site at http://kahn.swlearning.com.

e-con @pps

I am pleased to introduce an improved technology supplement with this edition-the ***e-con @pps*** web site (http://econapps.swlearning.com). This site offers dynamic web features including EconNews Online, EconDebate Online, and EconData Online. Organized by pertinent economic topics, and searchable by topic or feature, these features are easy to integrate into the classroom. EconNews, EconDebate, and EconData deepen a student's understanding of theoretical concepts through hands-on exploration and analysis of the latest economic news stories, policy debates, and data. These features are updated on a regular basis. The ***e-con @pps*** web site is complimentary through an access card included with each new edition of *The Economic Approach to Environmental and Natural Resources*. Used book buyers can purchase access to the site at http://econapps.swlearning.com.

Acknowledgments

This book could not have been written without the help of many people to whom I owe immeasurable thanks. The many students I taught at Washington and Lee University, the University of Tennessee, the Universidade Federal do Amazonas, and SUNY-Binghamton helped shape my approach to teaching environmental and resource economics and have substantially influenced the book. My approach to environmental economics has also been influenced by my colleagues at these institutions, as well as my colleagues throughout the profession. I would especially like to thank John Cumberland, Wallace Oates, and Kerry Smith who have been my mentors throughout my career and who continue to encourage and guide me even as I enter middle age. I owe special thanks to John Cumberland for his constant and continual support. When I was a graduate student, it was John who taught me that it is possible to be passionate about the environment and still be a careful economist. I also would like to thank my many research collaborators who have taught me so much about the relationship between the environment and the economy. In particular, I would like to thank Amit Batabyal, Jim Casey, Amy Farmer, Jill Caviglia-Harris, Dina Franceschi, Judy McDonald, Bob O' Neill, Alexandre Rivas and Steve Stewart.

Many people reviewed the book and used drafts in their classes. They all made substantial contributions to the development of the book. Without the help of these colleagues, the book would not have progressed as quickly or as well as it did. The reviewers include Mark Ashe, Westminster College; Rebecca Lee Harris, University of South Florida; Zhao Jinhua, Iowa State University; Lynne Lewis, Bates College; Jeffrey Sundberg, Lake Forest College; and Joy L. Clark, who wrote the IM/TB and created the PowerPoint slides. In addition to the contributions of the reviewers, many professors and students who used the second edition made valuable suggestions to improve the third edition, including Peter Lyneis.

I would like to thank my colleagues at Thomson Business and Professional Publishing who guided my efforts and graciously tolerated many missed deadlines. First, I would like to thank Sarah Dorger, my developmental editor, who was always positive and who improved the quality of the third edition in numerous ways. Her guidance was always on the mark and much appreciated. I would like to thank Mike Worls, Acquisitions Editor, whose enthusiasm for the project was appreciated. I would also like to thank Bob Dreas, Production Editor; Rik Moore, Design Project Coordinator; Jenny Fruechtenicht, Senior Marketing Coordinator; and John Carey, Senior Marketing Manager, for their efforts.

People who have not written a book may not be aware of the tremendous costs that the author's family bears. I thank my sons, Steve and Jerry, for tolerating my preoccupation and for encouraging me rather than complaining. Last and most importantly, I thank my wife Bari, whose patience, support, and encouragement was much appreciated. Bari not only helped create the time for me to complete this book, but she went above and beyond the call of spousal duty by reading every single word I wrote. She provided the first edit of the book, which substantially speeded the project and improved the quality of exposition.

James R. Kahn

about the author

James R. Kahn received his doctorate in 1981 from the University of Maryland, concentrating on environmental economics. From 1980 to 1991, he served on faculty in the economics department at the State University of New York at Binghamton (now Binghamton University), where he taught both graduate and undergraduate environmental and resource economics. From 1991 to 2000, Dr. Kahn had a joint appointment as a professor in the economics department at the University of Tennessee and as a collaborating scientist at the Oak Ridge National Laboratory. He returned to Washington and Lee University (his alma mater) in 2000 as the Director of the Environmental Studies program and the John F. Hendon Professor of Economics. He also has an appointment as collaborating professor at the Federal University of Amazonas in Manuas, Brazil and is the U.S. director of the United States/Brazil Consortium for Environmental Studies, a consortium of four universities that is funded by a bilateral agreement between the United States and Brazil. Dr. Kahn has published more than 90 journal articles, books, and book chapters. Lately, his research interests have focused on the relationship between the environment and economic development in tropical countries, with a special interest in rain forest and coastal issues. He also continues his work looking at the interaction between ecosystems and economic systems, valuation, and the development of economic incentives for environmental preservation.

Dr. Kahn has had an interest in the environment since he was a young child. He enjoys hiking, camping, fishing, landscape gardening, golf. and playing with his chain saw. He is a former soccer player and has become a compulsive distance runner. James R. Kahn has been married to Bari Kahn for 28 years. The couple has two children, Steven, 24 and Jerry, 18.

brief contents

contents

PART I

theory and tools

of environmental and resource economics

This textbook develops an economic approach to environmental and natural resources in an interdisciplinary context. Part I is designed to develop the economic theory and analytical tools that are necessary to understand this approach.

chapter 1
Introduction

In the space of a single human lifetime, society finds itself suddenly confronted with a daunting complex of trade-offs between some of its most important activities and ideals.

Gretchen Daily, *Nature's Services: Societal Dependence on Natural Ecosystems*

Introduction

The quotation from Gretchen Daily has great significance for the study of environmental and resource economics. Economics has often been described as the study of how to make trade-offs, or as the science of the allocation of scarce resources. Although that has always been the focus of environmental and resource economics, Daily's quotation implies that we have difficulty in confronting these trade-offs between environmental preservation and other economic and social activities. Note that the decision need not be giving up environmental quality to have a better economy or giving up economic benefits to have better environmental quality, but rather how both can be better managed to improve social welfare. Many decision makers, however, have avoided confronting difficult decisions, particularly when the decision involves current costs and future benefits.

As we defer these decisions into the future, though, the trade-offs become increasingly stark. A good example of this is the Everglades ecosystem, which has been assaulted from the north by agriculture that diverts water flows and contaminates the water with fertilizer, animal wastes, and pesticides. At the same time, the population of Miami and the rest of southern

Florida continues to grow, drawing more and more water from the aquifers, shrinking both the aquifer and the wetlands.

Can the Everglades continue to exist if we continue our current behavior? Can maintaining the level of activities but looking toward a "re-engineering" of water flows provide an effective solution, or do we need to think about a fundamental change in economic and social activities in this region?

The Everglades, unfortunately, is not an isolated example. These trade-offs occur at every geographic scale, from that of the individual landowner to the earth's global systems. For example, we are experiencing great losses of habitat and the collapse of many renewable resource systems, including

- The majority of our most important global fisheries
- Massive losses of tropical forests
- Rapid die-off of coral reefs
- Extensive losses of wetlands
- Conversion of grassland and other ecosystems to desert at an alarming rate

Polluted drinking water leads to the death of one in five children in rural Africa. Acid rain still creates problems in North American and European ecosystems. Children in the United States are experiencing unprecedented levels of asthma, with air pollution suspected to be a major contributor to this problem. Of course, the list would not be complete without mentioning what many view to be the most significant potential global environmental problem, that of global climate change.

In the face of these environmental problems, how can we modify our activities to protect the environment and provide a high standard of living for the world's growing population? That is the question this book addresses, but not in the sense that the book provides the answers. Rather, the goal of this book is to help the students develop a framework both for thinking about the significance of an environmental problem and about what constitutes a set of feasible solutions to the problem.

Because this book is intentionally focused on environmental and resource economics, the insights from economics play an important role in the process. Economics alone, however, is not capable of generating either understanding of or solutions to environmental problems. Our insights from ecology, business administration, physics, chemistry, philosophy, sociology, and many other scientific disciplines and the humanities must be integrated with the economic perspectives so as to develop an appropriate framework to develop robust solutions to these problems. The book attempts to show how economics can be a part of this framework.

A Taxonomy of Resources

The title of this book indicates that both environmental and resource issues are examined. Most economics courses in this area are entitled "Environmental and Natural Resource Economics." Does the presence of the words *environmental* and *natural resource* imply a dichotomization, or are these terms synonyms, merely representing a redundancy?

It is difficult to answer this question in a universal sense, as definitions are in themselves quite arbitrary. Yet, it is important to develop a consistent categorization, as resources with different properties must be analyzed with these distinctions in mind. The three categories of resources defined in this book are natural resources, physical resource flows, and environmental resources.

Natural Resources

Natural resources are those resources provided by nature that can be divided into increasingly small units and allocated at the margin. Examples of such resources are barrels of oil, cubic meters of wood, kilograms of fish, and liters of drinking water. Although these resources are provided by nature in the sense that they are found in or on the earth, they cannot be utilized without the provision of other inputs, such as capital and labor.

The stocks of natural resources may be fixed or may have regenerative capability. This characteristic is used to divide natural resources into renewable resources and exhaustible resources. Resources such as oil, minerals, and coal are generally included among exhaustible resources, whereas living resources such as plants and animals are generally included among renewable resources. Although new deposits of oil and coal are currently being formed, this regeneration does not meet the definition of renewable for two reasons. First, the rate of regeneration of oil is so small relative to the consumption of oil that, for practical purposes, it can be regarded as being equal to zero. Second, and more importantly, the regeneration is not due to the current stock but due to new deposits of organic materials subject to pressure. It is this property of the stock being responsible for the growth or regeneration that characterizes a renewable resource, and this property also makes for extremely interesting management decisions. (How many fish should we catch today, and how many should we leave to produce new fish for tomorrow?)

Physical Resource Flows

Solar energy, wind power, and similar resources are often called renewable resources, but they do not fit the above definition of a renewable resource, for even though they cannot be exhausted, they do not have regenerative capabilities. Solar energy may be naturally stored by trees, fossil fuels, or algae, and solar energy may be artificially stored by batteries or hot water tanks, but the stock of solar energy is the sun itself. Our consumption of solar energy has no effect on the stock or on our ability to consume solar energy in the future. These resources, which do not exist as a stock but which have never-ending flows, will be called physical resource flows to differentiate them from renewable resources. The term *physical resource flows* is used to differentiate them from the flows of ecological services, which are discussed in the following section. Wind power, tidal power, and geothermal power from the earth are among the other physical resource flows that we currently utilize.

Environmental Resources

Environmental resources are those resources provided by nature that are indivisible. For example, an ecosystem, an estuary, the ozone layer, and the lower atmosphere cannot be allocated unit by unit in the same fashion that you could allocate barrels of oil or tons of copper. These environmental resources can be examined at the margin in terms of quality but not in terms of quantity. For example, if one is formulating environmental policy for an estuary such as the Chesapeake Bay, the marginal units are not quantity units such as volume of water, but quality units such as dissolved oxygen levels, concentrations of herbicides, or the overall health of the ecosystem. Another distinguishing property of environmental resources is that the resources are not consumed directly, but that people consume the services these resources provide. These services include a very broad spectrum of ecological services, from basic biological life support services to aesthetic benefits.

It is possible that some resources may be classified into more than one category. For example, trees can be viewed as a renewable resource that can be harvested, but the forest ecosystem should be viewed as an indivisible environmental resource. Similarly, salmon swimming up a river can be viewed as a harvestable renewable resource, but the riverine ecosystem and the existence of salmon in the river can be viewed as an environmental resource.

One of the reasons this book separates environmental resources from natural resources is the importance of ecological services. As emphasized earlier, ecological services are a flow from the environmental resources. These environmental resources, which can be viewed as a type of capital, consist primarily of living ecological systems such as forest, wetlands, coral reefs and lagoons, mangroves, savannahs, lakes, rivers, estuaries and oceans. Physical systems, such as the atmosphere, also are important environmental resources that both influence and are influenced by the ecological systems. An extremely important aspect of the provision of these ecological services is that the level of the flow is a function of the quality of the environmental resource. As stresses from human activity accumulate and negatively affect the quality of the ecosystem, the ecosystem is generally reduced to producing a less comprehensive set of ecological services.

Ecological services are provided to both ecosystems and social systems. The importance of their direct provision to social systems is quite apparent. People need clean air, clean water, flood protection, fertile soil, and other ecological services to support basic biological functions. In addition, these ecological services contribute to an individual's quality of life in many other ways. Ecological services create important recreational and aesthetic benefits.

In addition, ecological services are important to economic production processes. For example, soft drinks can be produced more cheaply if the manufacturer has a source of clean water. The production of microchips, which requires a "superclean" production environment, is less expensive in an area with clean air than an area that has many particulates and other types of pollution in the air.

Ecological systems also contribute to social systems indirectly, because a high level of ecological services promotes the health of the ecosystem itself as well as promoting the health of other ecosystems to which ecological services are exported. For example, a coastal wetland provides habitat for juvenile species that spend their adult life in the ocean. Without the wetland to support and protect the development of the juvenile fish, the oceanic ecosystem would be less productive.

Ecological services promote the stability and resilience of the ecosystem that generates them and the other ecosystems to which it is connected. There are very complex definitions of stability and resilience, as well as some controversy in the scientific literature about exactly what these two terms mean. It is possible, however, to formulate some simple definitions that incorporate the general thrust of the more complex definitions. In this context, we can define stability as the ability of an ecosystem to withstand a shock or stress without alteration of the ecosystem. Resilience refers to the ability of an ecosystem to recover from a shock or stress that has caused alterations. In other words, it refers to the ability of the ecosystem to repair the damage and undo the alterations that have occurred as a result of the shock.

It is critically important to be aware that there is more to environmental quality than reducing the types of pollution that affect the health of humans. It is important to develop environmental policy that not only reduces the direct impact of pollution on humans, but also protects our environmental resources and the flow of ecological services. It is interesting to note that in the United States the Clean Air Act and the Clean Water Act and associated amendments focus primarily on protecting human health.

The importance of ecological services are further discussed in Chapters 5 and 6 and almost all the application chapters (forests, fisheries, biodiversity, and so on). For further readings about the importance of ecological services, see Yvonne Baskin's *The Work of Nature* and Gretchen Daily's *Nature's Services: Societal Dependence on Natural Ecosystems*.

Why Study Environmental and Resource Economics?

The question of why one should study environmental and resource economics hinges on whether existing academic disciplines are adequate for examining the environmental problem. One can look toward conventional economics and other social sciences and one can look toward the natural sciences, but none of these disciplines is independently capable of analyzing and developing solutions to environmental and resource problems.

Study of natural sciences, such as ecology, is not sufficient to completely analyze the problem, because these sciences do not include analysis of human behavior. Although understanding the natural sciences is essential to the understanding of the impacts of human activity, natural science studies do not include how human activity responds to changes in the economic and natural environment.

On the other hand, economics is often defined as the study of the allocation of scarce resources. If so, why do we need to study environmental and natural resources separately? Aren't the guiding principles developed in microeconomics sufficient to correctly allocate our environmental and natural resources?

The answer is that there are important differences between environmental resources and conventional goods, which need to be examined differentially. For example, the rules that define optimality in the allocation of private goods are essentially static in nature. Today's decision of how many DVDs to produce in the current period does not substantially affect the ability to produce DVDs in some future period. The decision of how much oil to produce and consume in the current period, however, has important implications for the future. First, the amount of oil taken out of the ground today affects our ability to take oil out of the ground in the future. Also, the amount of oil consumed today affects the level of carbon dioxide in the atmosphere, which will lead to a future warming of the earth's climate. The answer goes far beyond this dynamic issue, however.

That many decisions regarding environmental resources are irreversible further complicates analysis, particularly when viewed in the context of the dynamic issues already discussed. For example, the market producing insufficient DVDs in one period would not interfere with the ability to produce DVDs or enjoy using DVDs in the future. Any loss in social welfare that was created by that production decision need not be carried forward to future periods. Let's assume, however, that the current demand for preserving giant redwood forests (each redwood tree is several hundred to more than a thousand years old) is low, so we decide to cut them for export to Japan. This action is irreversible. Once these forests are cut, it will take many hundreds of years for them to become reestablished, and there is a significant probability that they will never become reestablished. No matter how high the future demand is for intact giant redwood forests, it is impossible to provide the forests. Other examples of irreversible events or actions include the generation of nuclear wastes (which retain their radioactivity for hundreds of thousands of years), the destruction of tropical rain forests, global warming, the extinction of species, and the release into the environment of toxic substances such as dioxins (toxic chemicals) and DDT (a persistent pesticide).

In addition, another critical factor differentiates environmental and natural resources from typical goods. Market failure, which is assumed not to exist in the basic market models, is obviously important, because pollution is a form of market failure and because environmental and natural resources may be public goods or open access resources. The importance and pervasiveness of market failure is discussed in depth in Chapter 3 and reinforced in every application chapter. For example, Chapter 13 examines the type of market failures that generate excessive clearing of tropical forests by subsistence farmers in countries such as Indonesia, Brazil, and Mexico; Chapter 11 examines the market failures that have lead to the global collapse of fisheries; and Chapters 7, 8, and 9 look at the suite of market failures associated with the production and use of energy.

Finally, and most importantly, environmental and natural resources require separate examination, because optimal allocation requires an understanding of more than just economic behavior. It also requires an understanding of the whole ecological system and how the ecological system responds to changes in both the economic system and the ecological system. The interrelationships between these two systems are some of the keys to understanding environmental and resource economics.

Figure 1.1 represents a schematic diagram of all relationships between the economic system, the physical environment, and the ecosystem. It may seem surprising to see separate demarcations for the physical environment and the natural environment, as these two systems are obviously very closely intertwined. They have been separated for the purposes of the discussion to allow more precise focus on these intertwining relationships. The physical environment includes all the nonliving aspects of the environment, such as the climate, the chemical composition of air, soil, and water and the mechanical systems (wind, evaporation, tides, earthquakes, and so on), that influence these nonliving components of the environment. The natural environment, as defined for the purposes of this book, includes all the living components of the environment. As stated earlier, the two are closely intertwined, as climate, soil, and water have an effect on the living components of the ecosystem, and, in turn, the living components alter the physical systems. Of course, the living components have effects on each other, as do the physical components.

Now, let's assume that we want to figure out the effects on social welfare of an environmental problem such as acid rain, which is caused by the emission of sulfur dioxide and nitrogen oxides during the combustion of fuels such as oil, gasoline, and coal. Figure 1.2 shows just some of the relationships that must be determined to make this assessment. Traditional economics has only been concerned with relationships within the economic systems; environmental and resource economics directly focus on relationships B, C, D, and E (relationships between the economic system and the natural and physical environment).

The purpose of the illustrations in Figures 1.1 and 1.2 is to show that one must also understand the importance of relationships within the natural environment, within the physical environment, and between these interacting systems. At another level, however, the depiction of the systems in these figures as standing apart can lead to erroneous thinking. In reality, the social and economic systems are not separate from the physical and natural environment, but contained within in it, as depicted in Figure 1.3. This approach yields additional insights. If the economic and social systems are contained within the larger physical and natural systems, then the processes

Figure 1.1 Environmental, Economic, and Social Systems

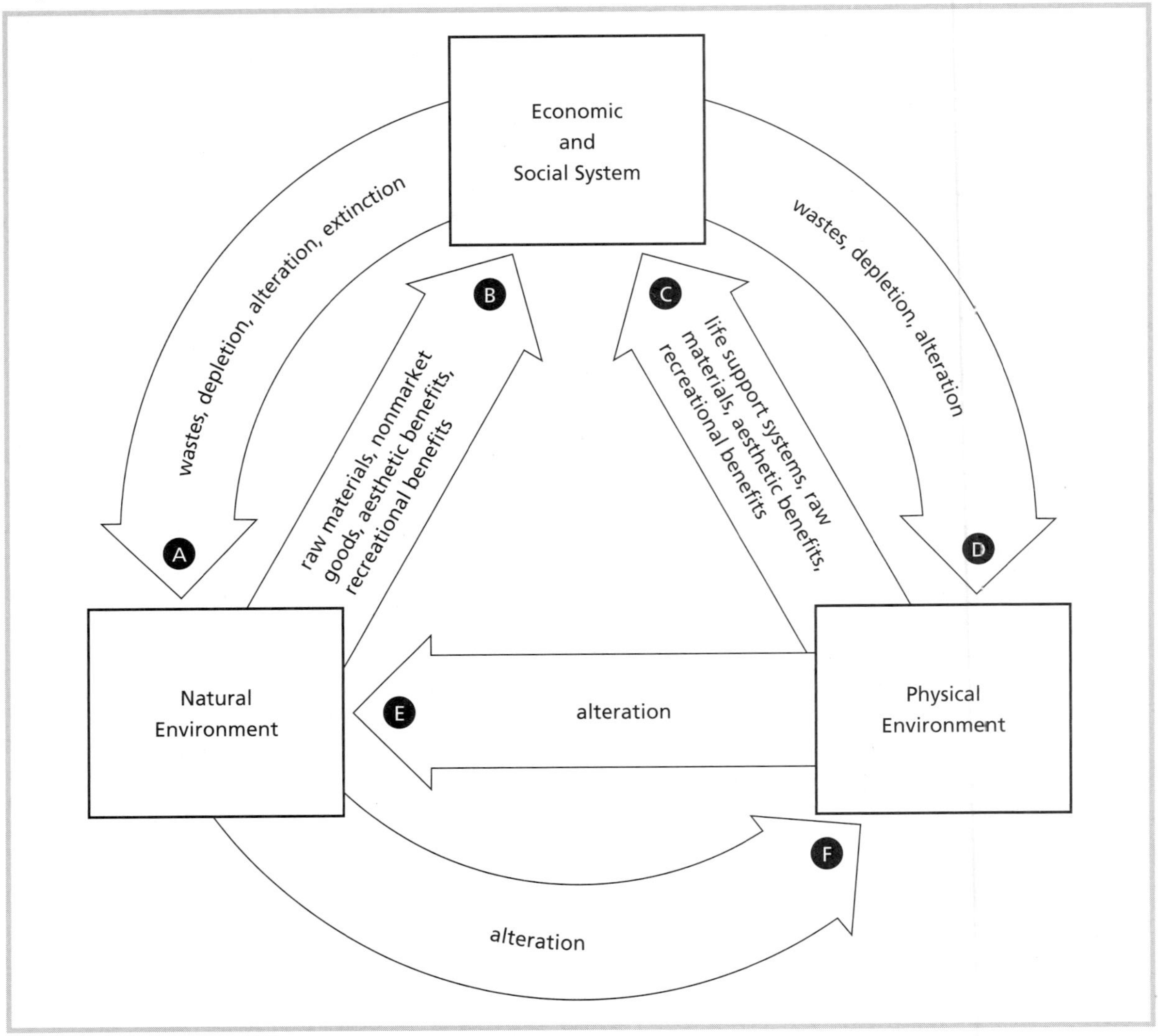

that govern the behavior of the physical and natural systems must ultimately govern the behavior of the human systems. Furthermore, the collapse of the larger physical and natural system must imply the collapse of the economic and social systems. History is filled with examples of how environmental degradation led to social collapse, including ancient examples such as the collapse of the Mayan civilization and the disintegration of society on Easter Island. More recent examples include the southern movement of the Sahara desert into the Sahel region of Africa, impoverishment due to deforestation in areas such as Haiti, and the impact on Lake Victoria

Figure 1.2 **Effect of Acid Rain on System Relationships**

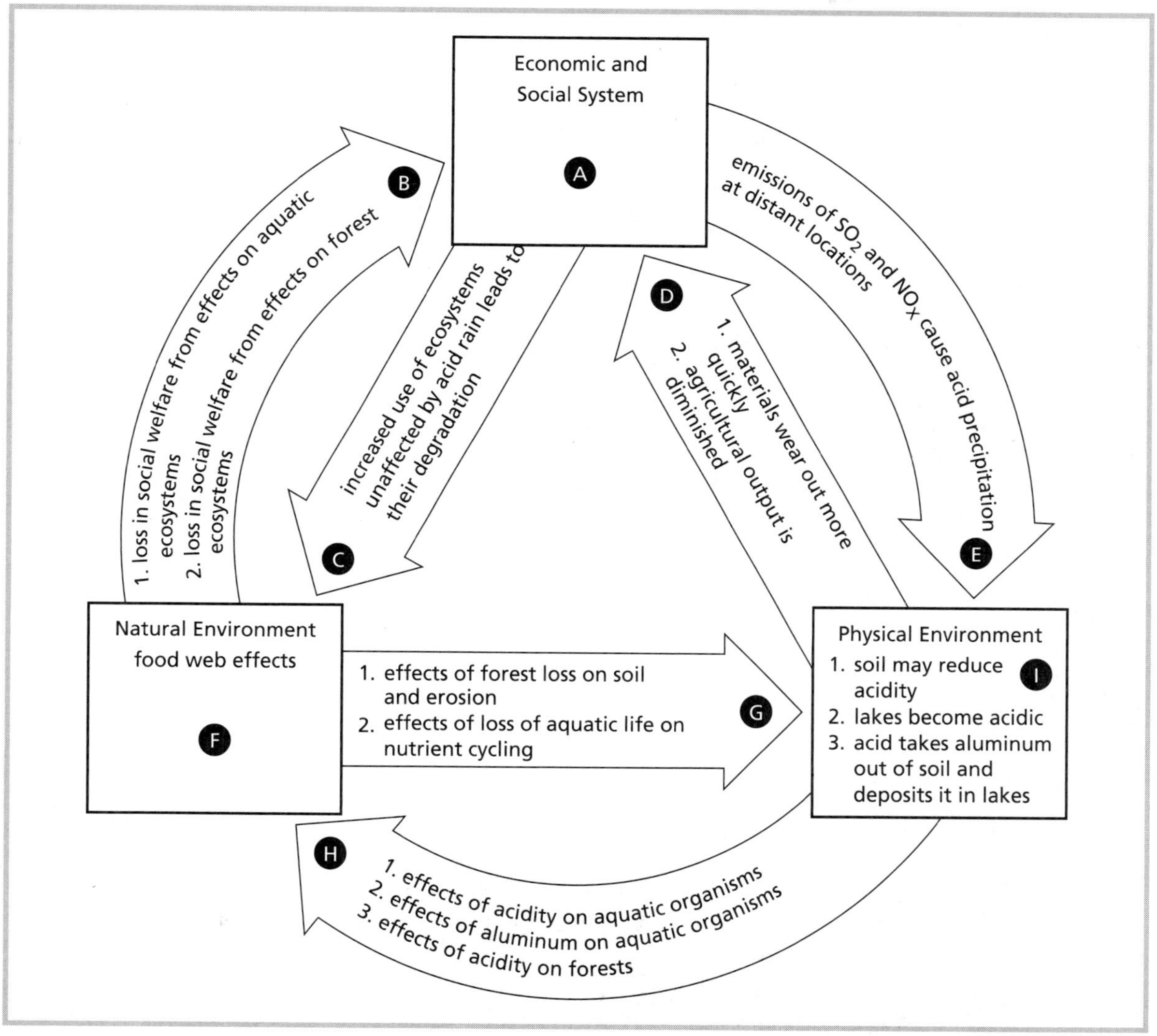

fishing villages of fish species decline due to the invasion of exotic species such as the Nile perch.

To develop a good understanding of environmental and resource economics, one does not need to become an expert in the natural and physical sciences, but one must develop an understanding of the contributions of other disciplines. For example, to understand how pollution affects an individual's utility function, some knowledge of the role of nutrient cycling must be obtained. To be able to talk to scientists in these fields, an environmental and resource economist, particularly if anticipating a career in the public policy

Figure 1.3 **Economic and Social Systems Embedded within the Natural and Physical Environment**

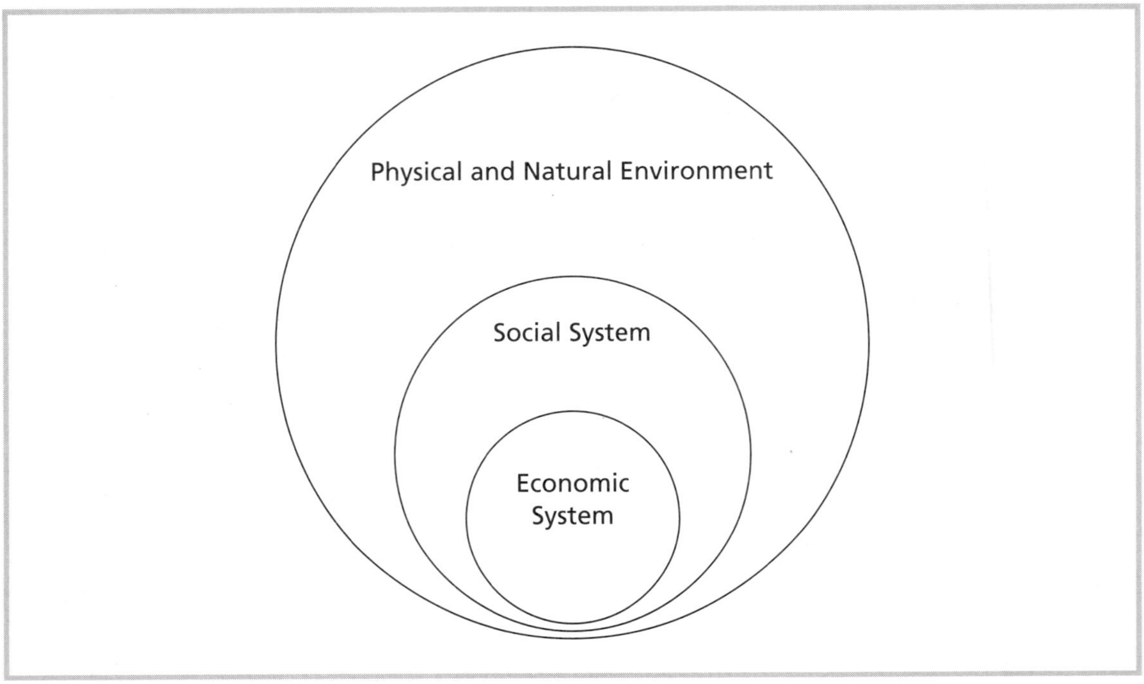

area, must be somewhat interdisciplinary and understand enough of how the physical and natural environment works. The same thing can be said for people who wish to make a contribution in other areas of environmental study. To be a good ecologist, political scientist, resource manager, and so on, one must develop an interdisciplinary perspective, including an understanding of environmental economics.

Economics has some very important contributions to make to the solution of our environmental and resource problems, contributions that become even more significant when integrated into an interdisciplinary overview. It is hoped that this book will not only help the reader develop an understanding and appreciation for the theory and application of environmental and resource economics, but also help develop an insight into how other disciplines can be integrated with economics to find solutions to our most pressing environmental and resource problems.

The first section of the book (Chapters 2–6) outlines some basic principles of economic theory and applies them to environmental and natural resources to develop a foundation for the study of environmental and resource economics. Part II (Chapters 7–10) uses the theory to look at the problems associated with exhaustible resources and the environment with a particular focus on energy. Part III (Chapters 11–15) looks at the relationship between renewable resources and the environment, and Part IV (Chapters 16–19) looks at additional topics such as the relationship between agriculture and the environment, Third World environmental problems, toxins in the ecosystem, and prospects for the future.

Suggested Paper Topics

1. Trace how our perception of environmental problems has changed over time. Begin at a distinct point in time such as when the American conservation movement became active in the late nineteenth century (see authors such as George Perkins Marsh, John Muir, and Gifford Pinchot). Look at the literature through the current day. Identify general trends and hypothesize why you think these changes in perception have occurred.
2. Compare the way two different societies (or groups of people) view the environment. For example, compare the perspectives of Native Americans with the Judeo-Christian tradition. What do you think are the underlying factors that lead to such different attitudes? What are the implications of the different perceptions for the development of solutions to environmental problems?

Works Cited and Selected Readings

1. Baskin, Y. *The Work of Nature: How the Diversity of Life Sustains Us.* Washington, DC: Island Press, 1997.
2. Brown, L. *State of the World.* New York: W. W. Norton, annual editions are available beginning in 1984.
3. Cahn, M. A., and R. O'Brien (eds.). *Thinking About the Environment: Readings on Politics, Property, and the Physical World.* London: M. E. Sharpe, 1996.
4. Daily, G. (ed.). *Nature's Services: Societal Dependence on Natural Ecosystems.* Washington, DC: Island Press, 1997.
5. Gore, A. *Earth in the Balance.* New York: Houghton Mifflin, 1991.
6. Kahn, H., and J. Simon. *Global 2000 Revised.* Washington, DC: Heritage Foundation, 1982.
7. Krutilla, J. Conservation Reconsidered. *American Economic Review 57* (1967): 777–787.
8. Marshall, P. (ed.). *Nature's Web: Rethinking Our Place on Earth.* London: M. E. Sharpe, 1996.
9. Myers, N. *Population, Resources, and the Environment: The Critical Challenge.* New York: United Nations Population Fund, 1991.
10. Pearce, D., E. Barbier, A. Markandya. *Sustainable Development: Economics and Environment in the Third World.* London: Edward Elgar, 1990.

chapter 2

Economic Efficiency and Markets: How the Invisible Hand Works

. . . and by directing industry in such a manner as its produce may be of the greatest value, he intends only his own gain and he is in this, as in many other cases, led by an invisible hand to promote an end which was no part of his intention. Nor is it always the worse for society that it was no part of it.

By pursuing his own interest he frequently promotes that of society more effectually than when he really intends to promote it.

Adam Smith, *The Wealth of Nations*, 1766

Introduction

The above passage is the famous excerpt from Adam Smith's *The Wealth of Nations* in which he describes why markets lead to a socially efficient allocation of resources. His argument is very simple: People acting in their own best interests tend to promote the social interest. By allocating the resources under their control in a fashion that maximizes their well-being, individuals maximize society's well-being.

There has been an increasing reliance on the free-market system, beginning in the 1980s with the Reagan administration in the United States and the Thatcher administration in England. This free-market "revolution" caught fire and became established in many countries in Latin America and Asia, particularly during the 1990s. The recent (and oftentimes violent) antiglobalization protests, however, show that not everyone is enamored of free markets. These protestors argue that free markets are the root of all social evils, particularly with respect to environmental quality. Who is right, the people who think free markets are our salvation or the people who think free markets are our damnation?

As usual, when contrasting extreme positions are formulated, the truth probably lies somewhere in between. The author of this textbook believes that markets have desirable properties, but they cannot do everything. In particular, they fall short in terms of promoting a level of environmental quality that maximizes the well-being of society. This position, however, has merely been asserted at this point, and the book has not yet offered evidence to support this position. The remainder of this chapter examines the invisible hand of the market to see exactly how it works and whether or not either of the extreme positions are justified, or if the truth lies somewhere in between.

The functioning of the invisible hand as an efficient allocator of resources will seem obvious to some students and an impossibility to other students. The divergence of the two views will become more clear as the invisible hand is further examined. The key to understanding the problem is understanding what kinds of costs and benefits are generated by the good or activity in question. Even though our ultimate interest is the study of the environment, we begin our examination of the way the market works with an everyday private good. After examining how the market works in this simple case, we can add the complexity associated with the impact of market activity on the environment, and the impact of the environment on market activity and society in general.

Let us assume that the good we are talking about is blue jeans. The marginal costs of blue jeans can be represented by the upward sloping function in Figure 2.1. These consist of the costs of production such as labor, energy, capital, and materials. The marginal cost function is upward sloping to reflect the increasing costs of production. The demand curve represents how much people are willing to pay for an additional pair of blue jeans, given a level of consumption. The demand or willingness to pay function is downward sloping to reflect that the greater the level of consumption of the good, the less people are willing to pay for an additional unit of the good. We also know that the market will arrive at equilibrium, with quantity demanded equal to quantity supplied at Q^*.

The equilibrium properties of a free market can be examined by imagining that for some reason, the market was not in equilibrium because the market price was less than P^*. With a market price of less than P^*, the quantity demanded would be greater than the quantity supplied, so there would be unsatisfied demand. The unsatisfied demand would create pressure for price to rise, and suppliers would respond to a rising price by producing more. This process would continue until there was no longer any upward pressure on

Figure 2.1 Market Equilibrium

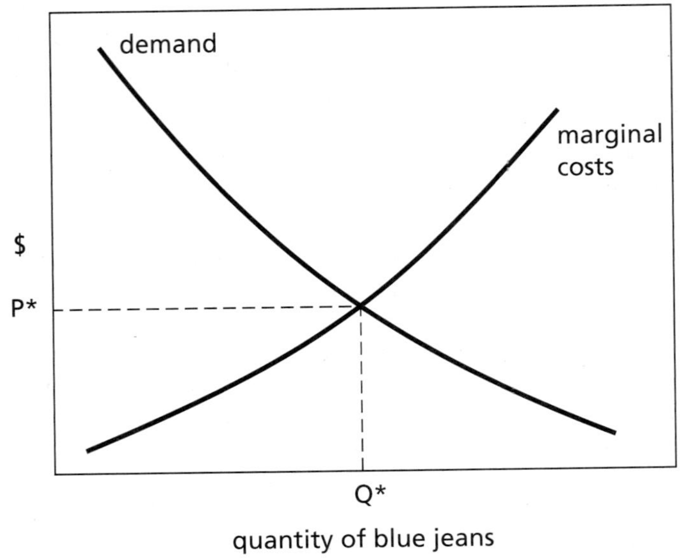

price, at the point where quantity demanded equaled quantity supplied at Q*. Conversely, if for some reason the initial price was above P*, producers would want to produce more than consumers were willing to buy. Inventories would accumulate, which would create a downward pressure on price. As price fell, consumers would purchase more. This process would continue until quantity demanded equaled quantity supplied.

We start by making two simplifying assumptions that will later be relaxed. These assumptions are that all the costs associated with blue jeans are incorporated into the supply function and that all the benefits associated with blue jeans are incorporated into the demand function. Thus, it is implied that the market forces that equate quantity demanded and quantity supplied also equate marginal benefits and marginal costs.

A basic microeconomic principle is that the equating of marginal benefits and marginal costs will maximize total net benefits.[1] If marginal costs are greater than marginal benefits (quantity is greater than Q* in Figure 2.1), then reducing quantity reduces costs by more than it reduces benefits, so total net benefits would increase. On the other hand, if quantity is less than Q*, then increasing quantity increases benefits by more than it increases costs (marginal benefit is greater than marginal cost), so total net benefits would

[1] Net benefits are equal to total benefits minus total costs. When used without a qualifier, the term *benefits* is used to signify benefits before costs have been subtracted. If benefits minus costs are being discussed, the adjective *net* will always appear in this text.

increase. It is only at Q^*, where marginal costs and marginal benefits are equal, that it is impossible to increase net benefits by changing quantity. If it is impossible to increase net benefits, then net benefits must be at their greatest.[2] Although this argument has been developed for the market for an output, similar arguments could be constructed for the market for an input, such as the cotton that is used to make the blue jeans.

This discussion shows how the market can maximize net benefits by equating marginal benefits with marginal costs. What has not been discussed is the nature of the costs and benefits that comprise these net benefits that have been maximized. To understand this concept, one must examine the behavioral forces that give rise to the demand and supply curves. As stated earlier, the demand curve can be viewed as a marginal value function that is based on willingness to pay for an additional unit of consumption. Because the market demand curve is the sum of every individual demand curve, marginal value is ultimately based on individual willingness to pay, which is based on how much an individual thinks the particular good or service will contribute to his or her utility in comparison with other goods and services. Thus, the demand curve reflects private benefits.

The supply curve, as stated previously, reflects the costs of producing the good or service. These costs are those incurred in production, such as labor, capital, energy, and materials, and they can also be viewed as private in the sense that all these costs of production are borne by the suppliers. Because the demand curve embodies private benefits and the supply curve embodies private costs, it follows that the net benefits that are maximized by market forces are private net benefits. For social net benefits to be maximized, it is necessary that private marginal benefits be identical to social marginal benefits and that private marginal costs be equal to social marginal costs. Then, market forces that equate marginal private cost (MPC) with marginal private benefit (MPB) will also equate marginal social benefit and marginal social cost.

This discussion is highlighted in the concept map of Figure 2.2. The first rectangle in this map begins with the concept that individuals respond to markets by choosing a quantity of the good that equates marginal private benefit and marginal private cost. This conclusion follows directly from the assumption that individuals endeavor to maximize their well-being. The second rectangle illustrates the concept that the equating of marginal private cost and marginal private benefit maximizes individual net benefits. The concepts of these first two rectangles must be accepted if one accepts the

---

[2] Readers who are familiar with calculus can see this quite readily. Let *NB* represent net benefits, *TC* represent total costs, and *TB* represent total benefits, all of which are functions of *Q*. Then

$$NB(Q) = TB(Q) - TC(Q)$$

To maximize *NB*, take the derivative (dNB/dQ) of net benefits and set it equal to zero:

$$dNB/dQ = dTB/dQ - dTC/dQ = 0$$

Since $dTB/dQ - dTC/dQ = 0$, then $dTB/dQ = dTC/dQ$. Since dTB/dQ = marginal benefits and dTC/dQ = marginal costs, then net benefits are maximized when marginal benefits and marginal costs are equal.

Figure 2.2 Concept Map of the Invisible Hand of the Market

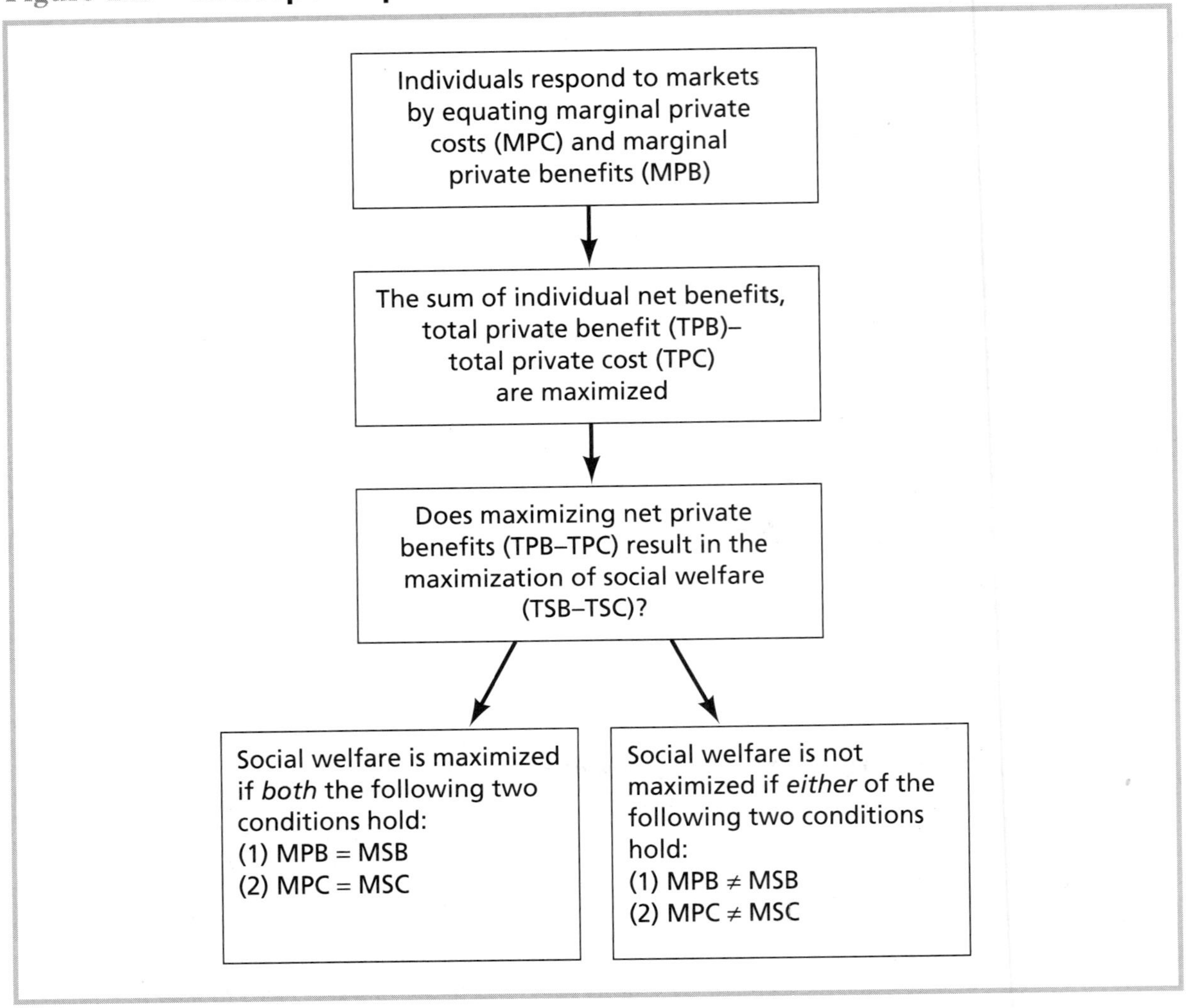

basic assumptions underlying market behavior. The essential question, however, is framed in the third box; that is, does the maximization of private net benefits imply the maximization of net social benefits? The answer is yes if all private values are equal to social values and no if there is a disparity between private values and social values.

Returning to the quotation by Adam Smith at the beginning of this chapter, it appears obvious that although Smith never explicitly stated it in these terms, he believed that private costs were identical to social costs and that private benefits were identical to social benefits. In a somewhat tautological fashion, that is how economists define a perfectly competitive market, and perfectly competitive markets automatically allocate resources efficiently.

The critical questions are to what extent does this type of market exist in the real world and to what extent do deviations from this type of market impact the environment and lead to losses in social welfare.

Market Failure: When the Invisible Hand Doesn't Work

An inability of the market to allocate resources efficiently is called a market failure. "Failure" does not imply a barrier to market clearing (quantity demanded equaling quantity supplied); rather, it means that the market clearing forces do not maximize social net benefits by equating marginal social benefits with marginal social costs. A market failure may create a divergence between private costs and social costs. For example, the production of steel generates labor, land, capital, and material costs for the producers, which are costs to both the steel producer and society as a whole. Hence, these land, labor, capital, and material costs are components of both private (producer's) costs and social costs. In addition, there is a set of costs attributable to the pollution generated by the steel production that is borne by society as a whole and not by the individual steel producers. This situation creates the disparity between private costs and social costs in Figure 2.3. Social costs are greater than private costs because both types of cost include the private costs of production (land, labor, capital, and so on), and social

Figure 2.3 **An Example of Market Failure**

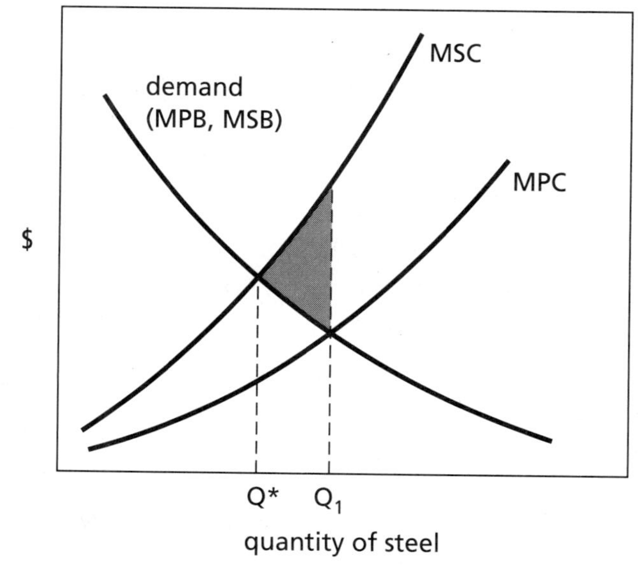

costs include additional costs consisting of the damage generated by pollution. (In this case, nothing has happened to create a gap between private benefits and social benefits.)

The steel producers respond to private costs and price; the steel consumers respond to private benefits (which in this example are equal to social benefits) and price. Thus, the market forces will generate an equilibrium where marginal private cost is equal to marginal private benefit at a level of output equal to Q_1. This level is greater than the socially optimal level of output that is equal to Q^*, where marginal social cost is equal to marginal social benefit. Note that for the output between Q^* and Q_1, the benefits of the good are less than the costs associated with the good. This excess cost is the shaded area in Figure 2.3 and represents the costs to society of having this higher than optimal level of output. Pollution is not the only phenomenon that creates a disparity between social costs and private costs. There are five categories of market failure, all of which have some importance for environmental and natural resources: imperfect competition, imperfect information, public goods, inappropriate government intervention, and externalities.

Imperfect Competition

Imperfect competition is the term used for markets where the individual actions of particular buyers or sellers have an effect on market price. The importance of imperfect competition is that in such markets the marginal revenue of the firm becomes different from market price, which tends to generate an equilibrium where marginal social cost is not equal to marginal social benefit. Figure 2.4 contains a market equilibrium for a market characterized by an extreme form of imperfect competition, monopoly (only one seller). In this case, the monopolist chooses the level of output that will maximize profit. In contrast, output in a competitive market is determined by market forces. The profit maximizing level of output for the monopolist is lower than the competitive market level of output, and it occurs at the point where marginal costs are equal to marginal revenues. Marginal revenue measures how much more money the monopolist receives from an additional unit of output. Market failure occurs because, in the case of monopoly, marginal revenue is different from marginal social benefit. The marginal revenue function is below the average revenue function (the average revenue function is the same as the demand function and the marginal social benefit function). The monopolist's marginal revenue function is below the demand function because when the monopolist increases output, the price it receives for output becomes smaller. In contrast, in perfect competition, an individual firm's output level has no effect on the price the firm receives.[3] In the case of monopoly, the market output (Q_1) is less than the

[3] A more detailed explanation of this point can be found in any principles of economics textbook.

Figure 2.4 **Market Failure Due to Monopoly**

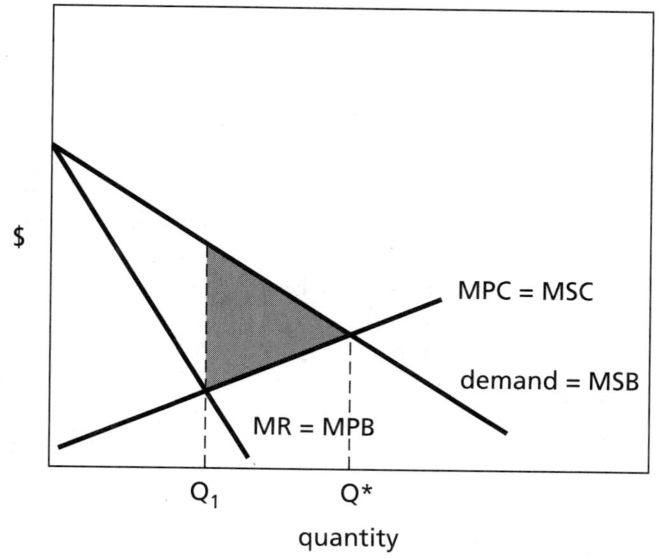

socially optimal level of output (Q*) and the cost of the market failure is equal to the shaded area. The market failure of imperfect competition is important in the study of environmental and natural resources, because many extractive industries may be characterized by imperfect competition. Some industries, such as oil and coal, are regarded by the general public as oligopolistic (only a few sellers who have price-setting ability). Other industries, such as electric power and natural gas distribution, are regulated monopolies, but in many states in the United States and in many countries throughout the world, there is an increasing movement toward deregulation and competition. In many cases, such as in southern California and the Rio de Janeiro area of Brazil, the movement toward deregulation has created some important disincentives and has led to problems with shortages of supply. Such issues associated with imperfect competition in the energy industry are further discussed in Chapter 8.

Imperfect Information

Imperfect information means that some segment of the market—consumers or producers or both—does not know the true costs or benefits associated with the good or activity. If that is the case, then one would not expect the forces of supply and demand to equate marginal social benefits with marginal social costs. The importance of imperfect information to the study of natural and environmental resources cannot be understated. For example, labor markets may efficiently allocate the on-the-job exposure to toxic substances if wage differentials between high-exposure jobs and low-exposure jobs adequately reflect the cost to workers of increasing their probability of contracting cancer or other health risks. The prospect of paying these compensating differentials will lead employers to pursue risk reduction measures that are less costly than making compensating payments for the higher risk, and an optimal level of on-the-job safety should be achieved. This market for risk, however, will not give the optimal amount of risk if workers do not adequately understand the health consequences of exposure to toxic substances. If they do not understand the true nature of the risk, they will require too much or too little compensating payment and the market mechanism will generate too much or too little risk. This subject is further discussed in Chapter 4.

One can think of many other instances in environmental and natural resource economics in which imperfect information may be an important factor, including global warming, acid rain, the effect of exposure to radon in the home, and the hazards of using chemicals in the home (pesticides, solvents, and so on). One must be careful, however, to distinguish between imperfect information involving a public good or an externality and imperfect information involving a private good. The first two examples, global warming and acid rain, involve public goods and externalities. There is already a market failure in the global warming problem in that carbon dioxide is emitted into the atmosphere based on comparisons of private costs and benefits, not social costs and benefits. There is also imperfect information in that the exact relationship between atmospheric build-up of carbon dioxide and global warming is not known; there is further uncertainty concerning the societal implications of global warming and the responsiveness of emissions to regulatory steps (see Chapter 7). This imperfect information does not cause the market failure but does make it more difficult to develop public policy dealing with the market failure. On the other hand, radon (radioactive gas caused by the decay of naturally occurring uranium in the soil) leaks into homes, but that is not an externality; it is a natural feature in certain geographic regions of the United States and elsewhere. The market failure occurs if people do not understand the true health consequences associated with radon leaks and do not take proper mitigative measures (sealing cracks in foundations, ventilating basements, moving to another location). If people understood the health consequences of radon leaking into their homes, in the long run there would be an adjustment of housing prices and institution of mitigative measures to generate the optimal level of exposure to radon.

Imperfect information is also a problem in environmental degradation in developing countries. For example, much of the deforestation that occurs in tropical countries occurs as the result of small farmers cutting and burning the forest to clear fields to plant crops. Agricultural methods are available whereby the farmers could produce more food and more income without destroying the forest, yet farmers do not employ these methods because they are not aware of them (see Chapter 13).

Public Goods

The third class of market failure deals with public goods. Although one tends to think of goods and services provided by the government when thinking of public goods, government provision merely implies that goods are classified as collectively provided. These goods are not necessarily public goods, because public goods may be collectively or privately provided, whereas private goods may be privately or collectively provided. The market failure exists because the market fails to provide the socially optimal level of public goods.

Public goods are distinguished from private goods by two primary characteristics: nonrivalry and nonexcludability in consumption. Nonrivalry means that one individual's consumption of the public good does not diminish the amount of the public good available for others to consume. Nonexcludability means that if one person has the ability to consume the public good, then others can't be excluded from consuming it. These properties can be more easily understood by looking at national defense, one of the most frequently cited examples of a public good. The property of nonexcludability holds for national defense because, in protecting one citizen in a region from a missile attack, every citizen is simultaneously protected. The property of nonrivalry or nonexhaustibility also holds, because one citizen's consumption of protection does not reduce the amount of protection available to other citizens in the same geographic region.

National defense also is an example of a pure public good. A pure public good enjoys these properties completely. In contrast, a pure *private* good is completely exhaustible and completely excludable. An environmental resource that has pure public good characteristics is climate. All people in a geographic location experience the same climate, and none can be excluded from experiencing it.

Most of what we think of as public goods are not pure public goods because they have some degree of exhaustibility and excludability. For example, the Grand Canyon is often thought of as one of our environmental resources that is a public good. Although it is true that it has a high degree of nonrivalry and nonexcludability, these properties are not present to the same extent as with national defense or climate. For example, it would be technically possible to exclude a subset of the population by building a fence (albeit a long and expensive one) around the canyon. Also, as the use of the canyon increases, the quality of the experience in the canyon declines (because of congestion and environmental degradation, such as erosion and littering), so the Grand Canyon is not completely nonrival in consumption.

Rather than trying to categorize a particular good as strictly a pure public good or strictly a pure private good, one should look at where it lies on a spectrum with pure public goods and pure private goods at the extremes. Figure 2.5 illustrates a two-dimensional spectrum, with the degree of nonrivalry on the vertical axis and the degree of nonexcludability on the horizontal axis. Goods such as national defense and climate, which are pure public goods, are in the upper right corner. This location signifies complete nonri-

Figure 2.5 **The Spectrum of Public and Private Goods**

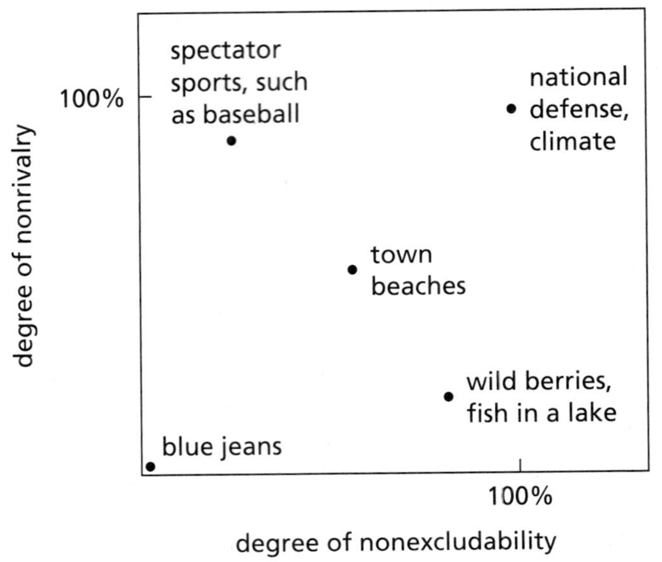

valry and nonexcludability. Goods such as blue jeans are pure private goods and are at the origin, signifying no public good characteristics. Spectator sports, such as major league baseball, are mixed goods in that they have some public good properties. These spectator sports are nonrival in the sense that one spectator's consumption of the game does not diminish the quantity of the good available to other spectators. Note that this good is not located at a position of complete nonrivalry, because congestion can diminish the quality of the consumption available to spectators. Note also that spectator sports are located in a position of a low degree of nonexcludability. Fans can be easily excluded from stadium attendance (they need one of a limited number of tickets for admission). If one was looking at spectator sports in a broader perspective, including television consumption of spectator sports, then these sports would have a higher nonexcludability score, because spectators cannot be excluded from network (non–pay TV) broadcasts of the game. Other goods are mapped on this spectrum to show their public good properties.

Inappropriate Government Intervention

Another example of market failure is inappropriate government intervention. In many textbooks, inappropriate government intervention is not included as a market failure, because it represents constraints imposed on buyers and sellers rather than direct actions of the buyers and sellers themselves. In this book, however, it is included as market failures because the government intervention is a source of disparity between private and social values, which is the particular focus on market failure here. An inappropriate government intervention means that the government intervenes in the economy not to correct a divergence between private costs and social costs, but for some other purpose, which can cause a divergence between private and social costs. A prime example, examined in greater detail in Chapter 12, is the U.S. Forest Service (USFS) policy concerning the leasing of timbering (wood-harvesting) rights in national forests. In this case, the USFS is treating the forests as private goods (ignoring their public good characteristics, such as recreation sites, wildlife habitat, and wilderness). For the time being, let's assume that it is wise to treat at least a portion of national forests as private goods for use in wood production. Then the appropriate policy for the USFS would be to lease the rights to the highest bidder, allowing timbering if the bid is positive (which assumes that there is no opportunity cost to cutting down the forest). What the USFS does, however, is to make roads through the forest at no cost to the companies who are leasing the cutting rights. Figure 2.6 shows how this distorts the market. The higher marginal social cost function contains all the costs of cutting wood, including road building. Because the timber companies do not pay the cost of road building, however, their marginal private costs are lower. Although the socially optimal level of cutting is Q*, the market solution based on the lower costs (MPC) to the harvesters generates an inefficiently high level of harvests (Qm). Of course, if there are additional social costs associated with cutting

Figure 2.6 **Inappropriate Government Intervention**

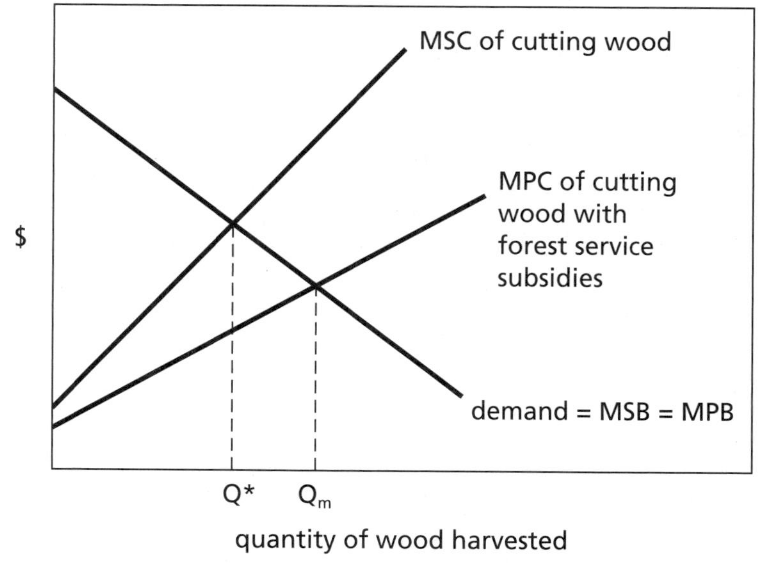

trees (such as loss of ecological services), then the socially optimal level of harvest will be even lower.

Sometimes, the inappropriate government intervention is part of the attempt to correct a market failure, such as pollution. Chapter 3 discusses China's pollution taxes, which have a strange refund component that actually gives polluters an incentive to pollute more instead of less.

Externalities

Externalities are perhaps the most important class of market failures for the field of environmental and resource economics. In fact, pollution is probably the most often cited example of an externality in principles of microeconomics textbooks. In these textbooks, externalities are probably described as spillover costs or benefits, unintended consequences, or unintended side effects (either beneficial or detrimental) associated with market transactions. If there is an unintended detrimental consequence (such as pollution) associated with a good or an activity, then its marginal private cost function will be below its marginal social cost function, generating a market failure of the type analyzed in Figure 2.3. As explained when this graph was introduced, the market failure (in this case a detrimental externality) creates a disparity between marginal social costs and marginal private costs, so that when the invisible hand equates marginal private benefits and marginal private costs, it generates an excessive level of the activity of Q_1, rather than a socially optimal level of Q^*.

Most people think of externalities as detrimental, but it is also possible for externalities to be beneficial. For example, when parents have their child vaccinated against measles, they also protect other children, since their vaccinated child can't spread the disease. In other words, the private benefits of vaccination are less than the social benefits. Similarly, when suburban landowners generate private benefits by planting trees, they also generate social benefits by reducing erosion, increasing air quality, reducing global warming, and improving neighborhood aesthetics. Because landowners make the tree-planting decision by equating marginal private cost and marginal private benefits, the market level of suburban trees will be Q_1 in Figure 2.7, whereas the optimal level is Q^*.

Although the above discussion does give some insight into what is meant by an externality, a more complete definition would help specify exactly what is meant by the term *externality*. The definition that will be employed in this textbook is that of Baumol and Oates (1988, p. 17):

> An externality is present whenever some individual's (say A's) utility or production relationships include real (that is nonmonetary) variables, whose values are chosen by others (persons, corporations, governments) without particular attention to the effects on A's welfare.

Baumol and Oates have chosen the words in this definition very deliberately. The key points are production and utility, real variables, and unintended

Figure 2.7 **Optimal Quantity of a Good with Partial Public Good Characteristics**

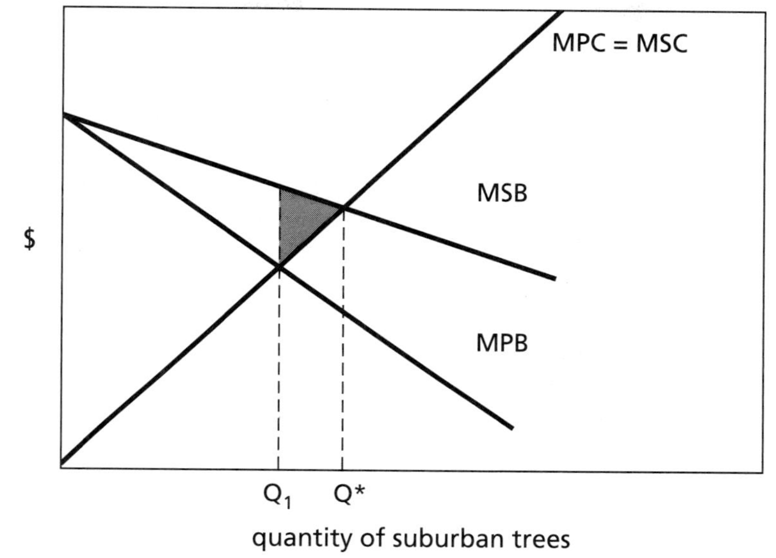

effects. The first point to examine is that Baumol and Oates are talking about unintended effects. If you were to intentionally blow cigar smoke in someone's face, then that is not an externality, as you are doing it with the purpose of lowering that person's welfare. If your cigar smoke drifts from your restaurant table to another, however, then that would be an externality, as you are disregarding the utility of the affected people rather than making your decisions based on your effects on their utility.

The second point to examine is that they are talking about real variables, not prices, which rules out an unintended price change as an externality. For example, assume that the demand for blue jeans increases, which increases the price of cotton (from which blue jeans are made). That will increase the price of flannel shirts (also made of cotton), which hurts people who like to wear flannel shirts. Note, however, that nothing has been done to interfere with the ability to produce or enjoy flannel shirts; they are simply more expensive.

Although this type of price effect is not regarded as an externality, it is generally called a pecuniary externality. The adjective *pecuniary* indicates that it has to do with money variables and not real variables. A pecuniary externality is not considered an externality despite the term *externality* appearing in its name. Although this jargon is unnecessarily confusing, it is widely used in the literature, so new terms will not be developed in this case.

The third point to examine is the focus on the effects on production and utility relationships. If we examine air pollution, which we suspect might be an externality, several effects on production and utility functions can be specified. First, certain types of air pollution lead to reduced yields of agricultural crops. The presence of air pollution in a cotton-growing region implies that it now takes more resources (land, labor, fertilizer, and so on) to grow cotton than it did in the absence of the pollution. This reduced capability to grow cotton can be contrasted with the mere price increase of the blue jean/flannel shirt example. In addition to interfering with the production of goods, air pollution may interfere with the production of utility. For example, a person will get less utility from an outdoor sport, such as jogging or tennis, in a polluted environment than in a clean-air environment. This type of externality (which affects production of goods or utility) is called a technological externality.

An ideal way to distinguish between a technological externality and a pecuniary externality is to examine their differential effects on the production possibilities frontier. The production possibilities frontiers in Figure 2.8 are based on the assumption of an economy based on only two goods, in this case, cotton and steel. The production possibilities frontier labeled p_1 in Figure 2.8 shows the set of all feasible production points. These feasible

Figure 2.8 Technological Externality Shift in Production Possibilities Frontier Due to Pollution

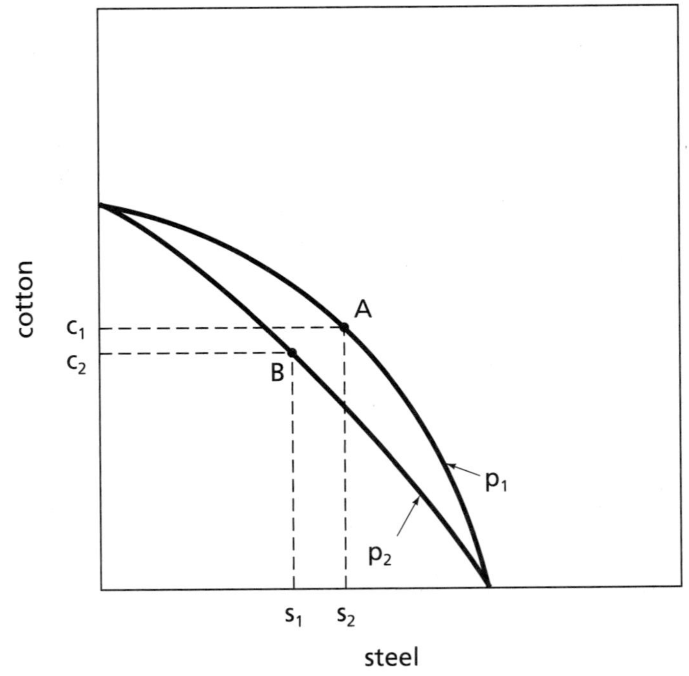

points are all the combinations of levels of cotton and steel that it is possible to produce with the economy's endowment of resources, and they include all the points on or below the production possibilities frontier p_1. In Figure 2.8, the production possibilities frontier p_1 represents the case where there are no externalities.

The actual combination of goods that are produced is determined both by the production possibilities frontier and consumer preferences. The production possibilities frontier determines what is possible to produce, whereas consumer preferences determine which of the possible combinations is actually produced. For example, if the current combination of cotton and steel leaves consumers unsatisfied and wanting more cotton, the price of cotton will be bid up as consumers try to buy more cotton, which will encourage more production of cotton and less production of steel. Let's assume that the level of steel and cotton that maximizes society's well-being is represented by point A.[4]

Now, instead of assuming a world of no externalities, let's assume that the production of steel generates air pollution that reduces the yield per acre of cotton. Thus to produce as much cotton as before, more resources (land, labor, energy, and so on) will have to be devoted to growing cotton. If these resources are devoted to cotton, then they cannot be devoted to steel, which means that steel production must fall. Alternatively, some resources could be devoted to reducing pollution so that the effects on cotton would be mitigated, but then there would still be fewer resources available for either cotton or steel. The end result is that because the pollution adversely affects the production of cotton, the economy can no longer produce as much cotton as before, or as much steel as before, or as much of both as before. The only exception, as pointed out by Baumol and Oates, is when the economy specializes in the production of only cotton or only steel. If the economy is only producing cotton, then there is no pollution from steel production, so as much cotton can be produced as before. If the economy is producing only steel, then there is pollution, but nothing to be adversely affected by pollution (remember that in this model there are only two goods in the economy), so as much steel can be produced as before.

The negative effect of pollution on the production possibilities of an economy is represented by the downward shift of the production possibilities frontier from p_1 to p_2 in Figure 2.8.[5] This shift will result in a new equilibrium at a point such as B. In this example, point B is clearly inferior to point A, because point A is associated with more of both goods.[6]

---

[4] A more comprehensive understanding of this point can be gained by indifference curve analysis, which models the consumer preference side of the adjustment process. Indifference curve analysis is a topic that is generally covered in intermediate microeconomic courses.

[5] In this simple example, utility has been lowered because the pollution has reduced society's ability to produce manufactured outputs. Obviously, pollution can have other types of effects on society's welfare, such as loss of ecosystem productivity, biodiversity, and recreational opportunities.

[6] A beneficial externality would shift the production possibilities frontier upward instead of downward and move society to a higher indifference curve and a higher level of utility.

In contrast, a pecuniary externality represents a movement along a production possibilities frontier rather than a shift of it. Figure 2.9 shows a shift in preferences toward blue jeans that is represented by the equilibrium shifting from point A to point B. The number of blue jeans demanded and produced increases from j_1 to j_2, and the number of flannel shirts produced decreases from s_1 to s_2. This new allocation of resources has not decreased society's welfare; rather, the change in prices results in a transfer from one segment of society to another. It is important to understand the difference between a true externality (technological externality) and a price effect (pecuniary externality). Figure 2.10 summarizes the important differences between a pecuniary externality and a technological externality.

Many externalities have public good characteristics. Called nondepletable externalities, they are characterized by the public good property of nonrivalry in consumption. Thus one person's consumption of the externality does not reduce the amount of the externality available to others to consume. The pollution of drinking water supplies is a good example of a nondepletable externality, because one person's consumption of the water pollution does not reduce the amount of the water pollution to which other people are exposed.

Figure 2.9 **Pecuniary Externality: Movement Along Production Possibilities Frontier Due to Changes in Preference**

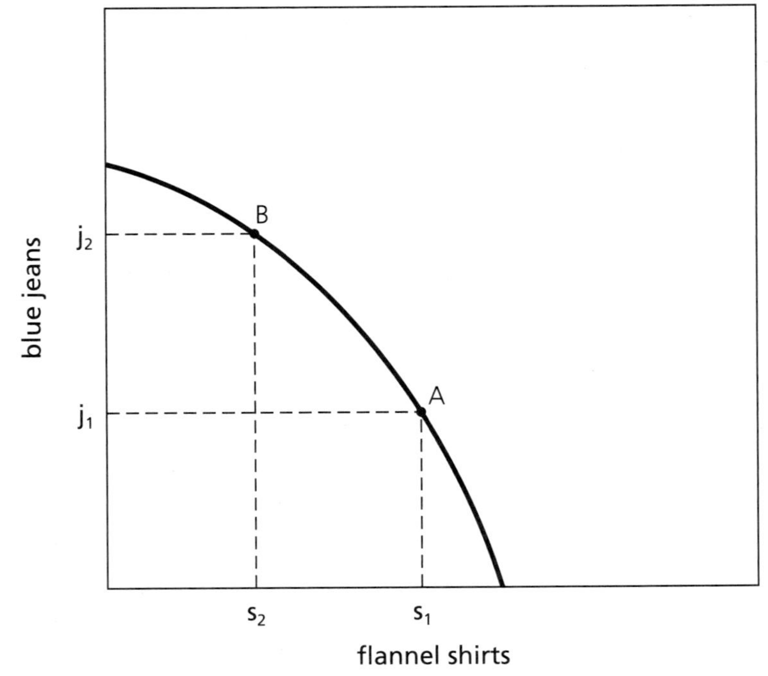

Figure 2.10 **Summary of Differences Between Pecuniary and Technological Externalities**

Type of Externality	Types of Variables Affected	Effect on Production	Effect on Social Welfare
Pecurniary externality (not a real externality)	Prices	Movement along frontier	Transfer from one segment of society to another
Technological externality	Ability to produce goods or utility	Shift of frontier (downward in the case of detrimental externalities)	Net change in welfare (loss in the case of detrimental externalities

Market Failure and Property Rights

Although the process by which externalities are generated by a disparity between social costs and social benefits has been discussed, the reasons for the existence of this disparity have not been examined. One important reason has to do with the existence and enforcement of property rights.

For example, no one has property rights to clean air, unless environmental legislation specifically defines these property rights. Consequently, a person who suffers from air pollution has no legal recourse to prevent someone from polluting the air or to collect damages from someone who does pollute the air. In contrast, a homeowner has the legal right to prevent another person from using the homeowner's front yard as a garbage disposal site. The difference between the two situations is that property rights to front yards are well defined, whereas property rights to air are not well defined.

A special class of externality that is generated by a lack of property rights (or an inability to enforce property rights) is the open-access externality. An open-access externality exists when property rights are insufficient to prevent general use of a resource and when this uncontrolled use leads to destruction or damage of the resource. For example, if access is not controlled to a fishery, then anybody who so desires can pursue the fish, diminishing the availability of future fish and increasing the cost of harvesting fish (see Chapter 11).

Even if property rights exist, a lack of ability to enforce them might lead to destruction of the resource. For example, many rain forest areas are communally owned by indigenous people who manage the forests in a sustainable fashion. Yet even though the indigenous people have property rights that may be legally recognized by the national government, the indigenous people may not have the ability to enforce the property rights when outsiders migrate to the region. If the outsiders have no legal right to the forest, then they have no incentive to preserve it and destructive deforestation results (see Chapter 13).

The Invisible Hand and Equity

It has been shown that, absent of market failure, the invisible hand of the market is an efficient allocator of resources. As discussed at the beginning of the chapter, *efficient* means maximizing the difference between social benefits and social costs. Nothing has yet been said about how those costs and benefits are distributed among the members of society, however.

Many critics of the market system criticize it on these distributional grounds rather than for efficiency reasons. There is nothing inherently superior in how the market distributes costs and benefits across society. The market distribution of net benefits is only one of many possible distributions. The "best" distribution depends on what view of equity and fairness is held. There is extensive discussion of equity issues in Chapter 5 as well as in the application chapters. In Chapter 5, additional criteria for decision making such as sustainability, environmental justice, and ecological stewardship are also introduced.

The Invisible Hand and Dynamic Efficiency

The discussion in the first half of this chapter showed how the market can be an efficient allocator of resources and under what circumstances the market fails to do so. This discussion, although appropriate for most markets, is not a complete discussion of efficiency because it has been examining efficiency in a static sense.

A static analysis is an analysis that is only concerned with one time period. Although one might initially think that a one-period analysis has limited basis in reality, that is certainly not the case because most multiperiod analyses are actually a series of independent one-period analyses. That will be true as long as the optimizing decisions in one period are independent of the optimizing decisions in other periods. If the optimizing decisions are independent across periods, then a static analysis is sufficient. If the optimizing decisions of one period depend on the optimizing decisions of past or future periods, however, then a dynamic analysis must be employed.

The difference between the types of markets that can be examined statically and the types that must be examined dynamically can best be illustrated by example. Let's look at a small farmer who has 100 acres of cropland. The farmer looks at market conditions today and decides that corn is the best crop to grow this year. Then, the next year at planting season, the farmer is faced with the same decision as last year, but the answer may turn out to be something different from corn if market conditions have changed. Each year the farmer makes choices that are, for the most part, independent of the decisions that were previously made.

Let's now assume that the farmer has 100 acres of forest instead of 100 acres of cropland. If the farmer decides to cut the trees today and plant corn, then in the next period the farmer cannot decide to have trees again.

An important and often cited example of dynamic optimization is the investment decision. Today's decision of how much output to consume and how much output to invest will affect these decisions in future periods because investment determines the capital stock that is used to produce output. Social and private efficiency of possible time paths of investment are examples of one area where dynamic, or intertemporal, considerations must be taken into account.

Dynamic Efficiency and Exhaustible Resources

Because decisions today can influence the quality of the environment and the stock of a resource far into the future, one would expect dynamic considerations to be important in the study of environmental and resource economics. For example, the decision of how much oil to take out of the ground today affects our ability to take oil out of the ground in the future. As is illustrated next, the decision of how much oil to take out of the ground today is also dependent on how much people are willing to pay for oil in the future.

To examine the ability of the market to generate intertemporal efficiency, let's assume that you are an oil producer who has to decide how much of your oil to sell today and how much to sell in the future. As you might expect, efficiency requires that you continue to sell oil today until the point where marginal cost equals marginal revenue. For the time being, we will assume that there are no market failures associated with oil, such as imperfect information, imperfect competition, externalities, public goods, or inappropriate government intervention. This assumption is not realistic, as is documented in Chapters 8 and 9, but it will allow us to examine to what extent the market is capable of generating a dynamically efficient allocation of resources, independent of the types of market failures discussed earlier.

As an individual owner of oil, you will maximize your profits by setting private marginal cost equal to private marginal benefits, which in the absence of the market failures discussed earlier also generates marginal social cost equal to marginal social benefit. So far, nothing is different from the static case, and we have done nothing to show how the market takes intertemporal considerations into account. The way in which the future is considered by the market is that individual owners of oil, in deciding whether to sell their oil today or wait and sell it in the future, incorporate an additional opportunity cost in their decision making. The opportunity cost of not having the oil available in the future is sometimes known as user cost or rent.

As one might expect, the interest rate has an important influence in the process of intertemporal allocation of oil, because the individual oil owner has two choices for producing income into the future. First, the oil producer can sell all his or her oil and invest the money and earn interest income, or the oil producer can hold the oil and sell it in the future at a higher price. The oil producer will make a choice that will maximize the sum of the present values of the earnings potentially received in each period. (See Appendix 2.a if you need review on the concepts of discounting and present value.)

To illustrate the intertemporal allocation process, let's assume that this particular oil producer, as well as the other oil producers, believes that the future price will be too low, so he or she is better off selling the oil now. Thus more oil is sold in the present, so less will be available for the future, so the expected future price will rise. The sale of more oil in the present will cause present prices to fall. The combination of the higher expected future prices and the lower present prices will make holding oil for future sale a more attractive alternative.

On the other hand, if the initial conditions are such that the current price of oil is perceived as low relative to the future price, oil producers might initially view selling in the future to be the more attractive option. Production in the present will be withheld, which will drive up the present price. At the same time, the expected future price will fall as oil owners and oil consumers realize that too much oil is being held for future use. The combination of the rising present price and the falling future price will cause selling in the present to become a more attractive option.

As long as one option (selling in the present versus selling in the future) appears to be a more attractive option than the other, prices will adjust. This process of price adjustment will continue until owners of oil are indifferent between the options of selling in the present and selling in the future.

Because the present price is dependent on the future price and the future price is dependent on the present price, there is an opportunity cost for using a barrel of oil at any particular point in time. This opportunity cost is the cost associated with not having the barrel of oil available in another time period. Note that this opportunity cost would not exist if there were an unlimited amount of oil.

This opportunity cost is a social cost, but at the same time, it is a private cost to the owner of the barrel of oil. This particular type of opportunity cost is often referred to as user cost. As a private cost, it is incorporated into price, and so the intertemporal dimension does not necessarily introduce a market failure, although Chapters 8 and 9 discuss how the intertemporal dimension can cause a market failure in conjunction with imperfect information about the future. For now, however, we will assume perfect information about the future, which means that the marginal user cost of a barrel of oil is known.

The price of oil at any particular time can be represented by equation 2.1.[7] In this equation, MUC refers to marginal user cost and MEC refers to marginal extraction cost.

---

[7] A short mathematical and graphical derivation is presented in Appendix 2.b. For a complete mathematical discussion of the notion of user cost and how the time path of the price of an exhaustible resource is determined, three references are suggested, in order of level of difficulty: J. M. Griffen and H. B. Steele, *Energy Economics*. New York: Academic Press, 1980. P. Dasgupta and G. Heal, *Economic Theory and Exhaustible Resources*. London: Cambridge University Press, 1979; and H. Hotelling, The Economics of Exhaustible Resources, *Journal of Political Economy* 39 (1931): 137–175.

$$P_t = MUC_t + MEC_t \qquad 2.1$$

The most important thing to be noted about this equation is that one can predict changes in the price of oil by predicting changes in the marginal extraction cost and the marginal user cost. In particular, looking at marginal user cost can be especially informative. For example, one can explain how the Persian Gulf War generated changes in the price of oil by looking at marginal user cost.

When Iraqi forces invaded Kuwait in early August 1990 and it looked as if Iraq might also gain control of (or destroy) Saudi oil fields, the price of a barrel of oil immediately rose about 50 percent. Although many people attributed this rise to "price gouging", it could also be explained by changes in marginal user cost. Marginal user cost rose dramatically as the taking of Kuwait and threats to Saudi Arabia dramatically changed the opportunity cost of using a barrel of oil at that point in time. When the United States and coalition forces began their air attacks on January 16, 1991, and rapidly achieved air superiority and then air supremacy, however, it became apparent that Iraq could not damage Saudi oil fields or affect Persian Gulf exports in the long run. People's perceptions of the opportunity cost of using a barrel of oil at the point in time lowered (lowered marginal user cost), and the price of oil fell almost as rapidly as it had risen. By the beginning of the ground campaign (late February 1991), the price of oil was approximately at its prewar levels. It is easy to see how marginal user cost serves as a vehicle for other phenomena to affect price. For example, if you wake up tomorrow morning and read in the newspaper that an engineer has developed an inexpensive and efficient cell for converting sunlight into electricity, the opportunity cost of using a barrel of oil today would be lowered and the price would fall.

Two other important observations can be made with respect to marginal user cost. First, the existence of marginal user cost implies that price will be different from marginal extraction cost. Thus, that price is greater than the marginal cost of extraction is not in itself an indication of the existence of monopoly profits. Although marginal user cost accrues to the owner of the resource, it is a scarcity rent rather than a monopoly profit. Second, for an owner of oil to be indifferent as to the period in which he or she sells the oil, the present value of the marginal user cost of oil must be the same in all periods. Thus means that, *ceteris paribus*[8] the marginal user cost of an exhaustible resource will increase at the discount rate.

---

[8] *Ceteris paribus* is a Latin phrase meaning "everything else remaining the same." It is often used in economics to mean that all the other factors that could influence the outcome are being held constant so that they do not influence the outcome. In this example, factors that could influence the values of marginal user costs in the future include unforeseen changes in demand (such as those caused by technological innovation in solar energy) and unforeseen changes in supply (such as unexpected discoveries of large amounts of low-cost oil).

Other Examples of Dynamic Problems in Environmental and Resource Economics

Market failures can also have a dynamic dimension. For example, the decision of how much to pollute has intertemporal dimensions when pollutants

Box 2.1 Marginal Analysis and Decision-Making

Those students who have not taken an economics course may be unfamiliar with the concept of marginal analysis. It is a relatively simple but critically important concept in the economic approach to decision making.

The fundamental tenet underlying marginal analysis is that we should never make decisions of how much of a good, service, or activity to produce or consume by comparing total benefits and total costs, but by comparing marginal costs and marginal benefits. Marginal costs are the costs associated with a small change in the level of the good, whereas marginal benefits are a corresponding measure of benefits. To illustrate let's look at a university student's decision to drink coffee.

Let's say that in the past, the student has been drinking 10 cups per day. He or she realizes that the coffee consumption is causing problems in the student's life. The student measures the costs associated with 10 cups of coffee (monetary costs, difficulty sleeping, irritability, and so on) and the benefits (the pleasures of drinking coffee, its ability to get the student going in the morning, its ability to allow the student to stay awake in boring classes, and so on). The student realizes that the costs of 10 cups of coffee per day exceed the benefits of ten cups of coffee per day.

Does that mean that the student should stop drinking coffee? Of course not, but he or she should adjust the level of cups per day to maximize his or her well-being. This adjustment process is a classic example of marginal analysis. In this process, the student asks the question, "Should I reduce consumption by one cup per day to nine?" If the costs that are eliminated by this reduction are greater than the benefits that are sacrificed, the answer to the question is yes. The decision is then confronted—should reduction continue from 9 cups to 8—and the answer is the same. If the costs that are eliminated by this reduction are greater than the benefits that are sacrificed, then reduction should continue to 8 cups. The student keeps comparing the costs and benefits of further reduction.

Eventually, the student will reach a point at which the benefits of reducing coffee consumption are exactly equal to costs. At this point, the student's net benefits (benefits minus costs) from coffee consumption are maximized. If further reductions are contemplated, the costs that are eliminated from further reduction will be less than the benefits that are sacrificed, so welfare will be diminished by further reductions in coffee consumption.

accumulate in the environment without breaking down. Such pollutants are referred to as persistent pollutants, chronic pollutants, or stock pollutants. Some examples include heavy metals (such as lead, mercury, and cadmium) certain classes of pesticides, radioactive wastes, PCBs, and chlorofluorocarbons. Because today's decision to generate a stock pollutant (such as radioactive waste) has an effect on environmental quality far into the future, the present value of future social costs must be considered when deciding on today's pollution standards.

Another important example of dynamic dimensions of environmental problems is that of changes in land use. Many changes in land use generate changes in environmental resources that can never be restored or that can only be restored over hundreds of years of time. For example, overgrazing of livestock by nomadic groups in the Sahel region of Africa has destroyed the grasslands and allowed the Sahara desert to move south at an alarming rate. Once the grassland is destroyed and desert scrub vegetation is established, the grassland cannot re-establish itself. The same is true when tropical forests are clear-cut. Changes to the soil and losses of nutrients prevent the forest from recovering for very long periods, and under some conditions the deforestation will be permanent (see Chapter 13).

Summary

Although the focus of this book is environmental and natural resources, which are often nonmarket goods, the bulk of this chapter focuses on markets, how they work, and their significance in the promotion of social welfare. This focus on markets is an important first step in the understanding of environmental and natural resource issues, because the primary reason we need to study environmental and natural resource economics is that the market often fails with respect to generating the socially optimal utilization of these resources.

For market goods, the market can be very effective in allocating resources, because the market can equate marginal social costs and marginal social benefits. The market mechanism, however, fails to allocate resources efficiently when private costs are not equal to social costs or when private benefits are not equal to social benefits. When marginal private cost is not equal to marginal social cost, or when marginal private benefit is not equal to marginal social benefit, then the market is characterized by failure. Market failures are caused by phenomena such as externalities, public goods, imperfect competition, imperfect information, and inappropriate government intervention.

One of the most important types of market failure, from the perspective of the study of environmental and resource economics, is the externality. An externality occurs when one person (or firm or agency) chooses values of variables in another person's (or firm's or agency's) production or utility function. Externalities are the source of most of our most important environmental problems. For example, when persons use a fossil fuel such as oil or coal, they make their decision of how to use the fuel based on a comparison of private costs and private benefits, and they do not consider the social costs associated with the fuel, such as its impact on air quality, acid rain, and global warming.

This chapter has highlighted the sources of market failure with a focus on the disparity between marginal social cost and marginal private cost that a market failure such as an externality can create. Aspects of the focus of the following chapters of the book illustrate that market failures are pervasive and that we need to develop policies to correct these market failures. The next chapter features a discussion of the different strategies with which society can mitigate the social losses associated with market failure. With the critical emphasis that we have placed here on market failure and the disparities between marginal social cost and marginal private cost, it will not be surprising when in Chapter 3 we discuss policy tools that can help to eliminate that disparity.

appendix 2.a

Discounting and Present Value

The concepts of discounting and present value are based on a type of behavior called time preference, which suggests that people prefer to realize benefits sooner rather than later (and realize costs later rather than sooner). Because people prefer benefits in the present, the individual is not indifferent between one dollar of benefits today and one dollar of benefits sometime in the future.

Discounting is a procedure by which dollars of benefits in different periods can be expressed in a common metric. The common metric is called present value, whereby all future values are converted to a value in today's dollars with the conversion constructed so that the individual is indifferent between the dollars in the future and the present value of those dollars today.

One can obtain an informal idea of the process of constructing present values by playing the following game. Suppose that you are given the option of buying a bond for \$100 with complete certainty of payoff 1 year from now. What is the minimum amount of money that the bond would have to pay 1 year from now to make you willing to buy it today? Let's say that your answer is \$110. That means that you are indifferent between \$100 today and \$110 a year in the future or that you view the present value of \$110 a year from now to be \$100. From your response to the question, we can observe that your rate of time preference, or your discount rate, is 10 percent.

This process of obtaining present values by discounting future values can be formalized into the mathematical expression of equation 2a.1, where

FV refers to the value that occurs *t* periods into the future, *r* is the discount rate, and *PV* is the equivalent present value:

$$FV = PV(1+r)^t \qquad 2a.1$$

In our example, $t = 1$, $FV = \$110$, and $r = 0.1$. Performing the calculations indicated by equation 2a.1, we see that

$$\$100 = \frac{\$110}{(1+0.1)} \qquad 2a.2$$

The formula can be better understood by looking at another example. What is the present value of $1000 payable in 10 years if the discount rate is 8 percent (0.08 in decimal terms)? Using our formula of equation 2a.2, with the values of $t = 10$, $r = 0.08$, and $FV = \$1000$, the present value can be calculated as

$$PV = \frac{\$1000}{(1+0.08)^{10}}$$
$$PV = (0.463)(1000) = 463 \qquad 2a.3$$

which indicates that the present value of $1000, payable 10 years from today, is $463. In other words, a person with a discount rate of 8 percent is indifferent between receiving $463 dollars today and $1000 ten years in the future.

In our examination of environmental and resource economics, it will be necessary to examine slightly more complex formulations. For example, let's say that we wanted to examine the desirability of a project to upgrade New York City's sewage treatment plant to protect area beaches and other marine resources. In each year of the project, there will be costs and benefits. In some years, the costs might exceed the benefits; in other years, the benefits might exceed the costs. To determine if the project is a good idea, one must take the present value of the benefits and costs in each year and then determine if the present value of the benefits minus the present value of the costs (present value of the whole time stream of net benefits) is positive or negative. If we let B_t refer to the benefits (measured in dollars of year t), *Ct* be the corresponding measure of costs in each year, and *T* be the number of periods in which the project will be yielding either costs or benefits, then the present value (*PV*) of the total net benefits (*TNB*)of the project is

$$PV \text{ of } TNB = \sum_{t=1}^{T} \frac{(B_t - C_t)}{(1+r)^t} \qquad 2a.4$$

An analogous process can be used to show the extent to which amounts in the present will grow through some future date. Note that if equation 2a.1 were solved for *FV*, then the result would be

$$FV = PV(1+r)^t \qquad 2a.5$$

For example, if \$100 was invested for 10 years at an annually compounding interest rate of 10 percent, then the future value of this \$100, 10 years in the future could be calculated by substituting the appropriate values into equation 2a.6:

$$\begin{aligned} FV &= PV(1+r)^t \\ &= \$100(1+0.01)^{10} \\ &= \$2.50(100) = \$250 \end{aligned} \qquad 2a.6$$

In this example, the interest was compounded annually, meaning that after each year, the interest would be earned on the previous year's interest. Although this example is an adequate representation of some types of interest growth, it is not an adequate representation of many types of growth, either economic or biological. For many assets, interest compounds instantaneously, which means that there is no waiting period for earning interest on the interest previously earned. That is certainly the case for measuring the growth of the populations of most organisms, including human beings. Equation 2a.7 illustrates a growth function with continuous compounding, whereas equation 2a.8 represents the analogous discounting process. Equation 2a.9 is the continuous analog of equation 2a.4.

$$FV = PVe^{rt} \qquad 2a.7$$

$$PV = FVe^{-rt} \qquad 2a.8$$

$$PV \text{ of } NB = \int_{t=1}^{T} [(B(t) - C(t)]e^{-rt}dt \qquad 2a.9$$

One convenient mechanism for looking at growth and discounting without the aid of a calculator is the "rule of 70." The rule of 70 states that if you take the growth rate, multiply it by 100, and divide it into 70, the answer is the number of years that it will take the sum to double when growing at that rate (or the number of years it would take to shrink to half its value when discounted at the given rate). For example, if you invest your money at 10 percent (0.1 in decimals) interest, it would double every $70/(0.1 \times 100) = 7$ years.

The rule of 70 can be derived from equation 2a.7. Let the quantity that is growing be represented by the variable X. Then the length of time it would take for X to grow to $2X$ would represent the doubling time. Let $2X$ represent FV and let X represent PV in equation 2a.7. Then equation 2a.7 can be rewritten as equation 2a.10 and then solved for t:

$$2X = Xe^{rt} \qquad \text{2a.10}$$

Divide both sides by X:

$$2 = e^{rt}$$

Take the natural logarithm of both sides:

$$1n(2) = rt$$

$$0.693 = rt$$

$$\frac{0.693}{r} = t$$

$$\frac{0.693}{100r} = t$$

Therefore, t is approximately equal to $\dfrac{70}{100r}$

appendix 2.b
Dynamic Efficiency

The concepts of present value developed in Appendix 2.a can be used to look more precisely at the question of the dynamically efficient allocation of an exhaustible resource. Assume that there are 100 tons of coal, that marginal extraction costs are zero, and that time consists of two periods, period 1 and period 2. This two-period model is a convenient way of collapsing continuous time into a tractable model. Period 1 can be viewed as the present, and period 2 can be viewed as the rest of time. Assume that the demand curve in each period is equal to $P = 500 - 0.5q$. In any period, people are willing to purchase the whole 100 tons (at 100 tons, the price people would be willing to pay is \$450). How, then, will the 100 tons be allocated over the two periods?

The answer is that the owners of the coal would try to maximize the present value of the income they would receive in each period. The income they would receive in period 1 is equal to the price they would receive multiplied by the quantity that is sold, or $(500 - 0.5q_1)\,q_1$. The income they would receive in period 2 is equal to $(500 - 0.5q_2)q_2$. Since $q_1 + q_2$ must equal 100, the income received in period 2 can be written as $[500 - 0.5(100 - q_1)](100 - q_1)$. If the discount rate is equal to 5 percent, then the present value of the income received in period 2 can be rewritten as $[500 - 0.5(100 - q_1)](100 - q_1)/1.05$ or as $[476.2 - 0.4762(100 - q_1)](100 - q_1)$.

Present value of the income from the two periods can be computed as

$$PV = (500 - 0.5q_1)q_1 + [476.2 - 0.4762(100 - q_1)](100 - q_1)$$

To maximize PV, set $dPV/dq_1 = 0$ and solve for q_1. The solution is $q_1 = 60.97$ and $q_1 = 39.02$, with $p_1 = 469.5$ and $p_2 = 480.5$.

Two points are important:

1. Although marginal extraction cost is equal to zero, price in both periods is positive. The price is composed exclusively of user cost, the opportunity cost of not having the coal available in another period.
2. Price is higher in period 2 than in period 1; the difference between the two reflects the positive rate of time reference.

Figure 2.11 contains a graphical analysis of this issue. The horizontal axis of this graph is equal to 100 tons of coal. As one reads from left to right, the quantity in period 1 gets larger. As one reads from right to left, the quantity in period 2 gets larger.

Demand 1 is the demand curve in period 1. Demand 2 is the present value of the demand in period 2 (which is read from right to left). The present value of total income is maximized where the two demand curves intersect. To the left of the intersection, PV can be increased by allocating more coal to period 1, since the price that people are willing to pay in period 1 is greater than the present value of the price in period 2. To the right of the intersection, present value can be maximized by allocating more coal to period 2, since the present value of the price that people are willing to pay in period 2 is greater than the price in period 1.

Figure 2.11 **Summary of Differences Between Pecuniary and Technological Externalities**

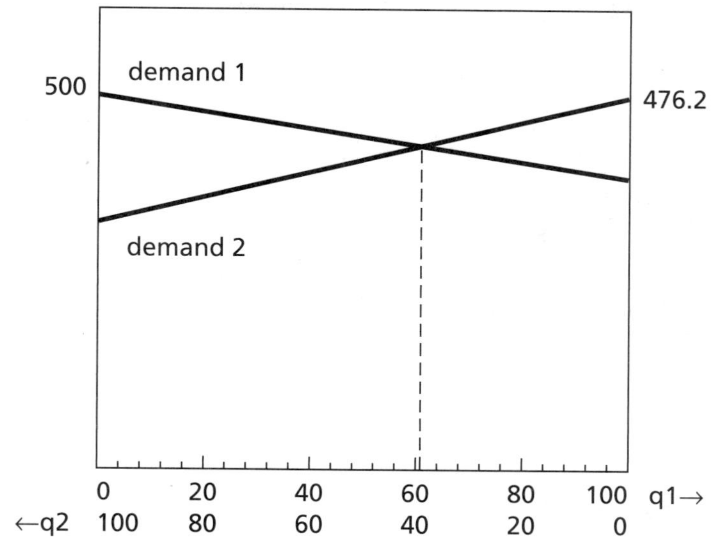

Review Questions

1. When does the invisible hand fail to maximize net social benefits?
2. Place the following goods on the two-dimensional privateness/publicness spectrum of Figure 2.5:
   a. elementary education
   b. secondary education
   c. undergraduate education
   d. a metropolitan opera company
   e. health care
   f. Yosemite National Park
   g. indoor air quality
   h. outdoor air quality
   i. the ozone layer
   j. biodiversity
   k. urban parks
   l. hiking trails
3. Distinguish between a pecuniary and technological externality.
4. Assume that the demand curve for a particular good is fully coincidental with the marginal social benefit function and can be described by MSB = MPB = 24 – 2q, where q refers to the quantity of the good. Assume that the marginal private cost function can be described by MPC = q and that marginal social costs are always double the marginal private cost. Graph the functions and algebraically determine the market level of output and the optimal level of output.
5. Assume that a dam costs $20 million to build in one year and that, beginning in the second year, the dam yields net benefits of $2 million per year for 30 years. If the discount rate is equal to 5 percent, what is the net present value of the dam?
6. Define *user cost*.

Questions for Further Study

1. Discuss the process by which the invisible hand efficiently allocates resources. List the market failures that may lead to inefficiency. Show how each market failure causes a loss in social benefits.
2. Derive the "rule of 70" discussed in the appendix.
3. Discuss the process by which an exhaustible resource is efficiently allocated over time.
4. If the price of oil is observed to be greater than the marginal extraction cost, can one infer that monopoly profits are being generated in the oil industry? Why or why not?
5. Do you believe that markets promote social welfare? Why or why not?

Suggested Paper Topics

1. Write a paper that discusses the development of economic thought on externalities. Start with early work by Arthur Pigou, Ronald Coase, Francis Bator, and their contemporaries and move forward to the work by Anthony Fisher and Frederick Peterson, William Baumol and Wallace Oates, and others.
2. Trace the development of the concept of user cost. Start with the work of Ricardo, who was one of the first to be concerned with the scarcity of exhaustible resources, and examine the work by Harold Hotelling and more contemporary authors. Textbooks by Anthony Fisher, Partha Dasgupta and Geoffrey Heal, and James Griffen and Henry Steele may be useful. Also, consult the survey article by Frederick Peterson and Anthony Fisher.

Works Cited and Selected Readings

Bator, F. M. The Anatomy of a Market Failure. *Quarterly Journal of Economics 72* (1958): 351–379.

Baumol, W. J., and W. E. Oates. *Theory of Environmental Policy*. London: Cambridge University Press, 1988.

Coase, R. H. The Problem of Social Cost. *Journal of Law and Economics 3* (1960): 1–44.

Dasgupta, P., and G. Heal. *Economic Theory and Exhaustible Resources*. London: Cambridge University Press, 1979.

Dorfman, R., and N. S. Dorfman. *Economics of the Environment: Selected Readings*. New York: W. W. Norton, 1993.

Fisher, A. C., and F. M. Peterson. The Environment in Economics: A Survey. *Journal of Economic Literature 14* (1976): 1–33.

Griffin, J. M., and H. B. Steele. *Energy Economics*. New York: Academic Press, 1980.

Hotelling, H. The Economics of Exhaustible Resources. *Journal of Political Economy 39* (1931): 137–175.

Meade, J. E. *The Theory of Economic Externalities*. Geneva: Institute Universitaire de Haustes Etudes, 1973.

Peterson, F. M., and S. C. Fisher. The Exploitation of Extractive Resources: A Survey. *Economic Journal 87* (1977): 681–721.

Pigou, A. C. *The Economics of Welfare*. London: MacMillan, 1938.

Ricardo, D. *Principles of Political Economy and Taxation*. London: Everyman, reprint 1926.

Smith, A. *The Wealth of Nations*, vol. 1, 1776. Chicago: University of Chicago Press, reprint 1976.

chapter 3
Government Intervention in Market Failure

"Since its creation three decades ago, EPA has made great strides in protecting the environment. For the most part, these environmental improvements were made through the use of command-and-control regulation; that is, promulgation of uniform, source-specific emission of effluent limits.

It is becoming increasingly clear that reliance on the command-and-control approach will not, by itself, allow EPA to achieve its mission. . . .

To maintain momentum in meeting environmental goals, we must move beyond prescriptive approaches by increasing our use of policy instruments such as economic incentives. Properly employed, economic incentives can be a powerful force for environmental improvement."

William K. Reilly, Administrator's Preface

Introduction

The quotation from former U.S. Environmental Protection Agency (EPA) Administrator William K. Reilly and the actual existence of an agency such as the EPA are based on the supposition that government intervention to correct environmental externalities improves society's well-being. The issue to which the quotation relates is not whether the government should intervene, but rather, what form government intervention should take. In virtually every high-income country and in many developing countries, the necessity for environmental policy is accepted by the majority of the citizens, and the focus of the debate is how policy should be formulated, both in terms of methods of environmental protection and intensity of environmental protection. Despite economists' enthusiasm about the potential of economic incentives, they have not been a magic bullet and have not been widely adopted by governments. Systems were originally based in command and control methods, and forces of inertia slowed the transition to economic incentives. In addition, in a large portion of the limited cases in which economic incentives have been implemented, the economic incentives have been poorly constructed and have had undesirable results, in some cases giving polluters an incentive to pollute even more. This chapter shows, however, that correctly structured economic incentives have great potential for improving the environment at the lowest possible cost, and throughout this book real-world examples of well-structured economic incentives are discussed. In keeping with this theme, the major thrust of this chapter is a discussion of how policy should be structured and the relative merits of alternative policy instruments. This chapter begins, however, by taking a step back to examine the intellectual arguments that would support or refute the necessity of government intervention.

In Chapter 2, market failures and their implications for social welfare were discussed. It was shown that market failures lead to inefficient allocations of resources, because marginal social costs (MSC) and marginal social benefits (MSB) are not equated by market forces. Because the existence of market failures implies losses in social welfare, the natural question to investigate is whether the mitigation of market failures can lead to improvements in social welfare. In other words, can we make ourselves better off by correcting the problem, or is the solution more costly than the problem it seeks to address? The answer to this question may seem rather obvious to many readers, but it will be examined thoroughly, because the development of the answer to this question was an important step in the evolution of environmental economics.

Because externalities are such an important component of environmental market failures, this discussion of whether to intervene to correct market failures focuses on externalities and leaves the discussion of monopoly, for example, to industrial organization courses. Specifically, should society, through collective action, actively intervene to correct market failures associated with such environmental externalities as pollution?

This question has been addressed by many economists in past writings, with arguments on both sides. The early work of greatest significance arguing for government intervention was by A. C. Pigou. The counterpoint argument was provided by Ronald Coase, who argued that government intervention was not only unnecessary, but counterproductive. The next section of this chapter focuses on their arguments and on critical analysis of their work by subsequent authors.

Once the issue of whether the government should intervene is resolved, then the question of how it should intervene must be examined. Different sets of policies will have different effects on efficiency and on how social welfare is distributed among the members of society. These issues are analyzed in the remaining sections of the chapter.

Should the Government Intervene to Correct Environmental Externalities?

The question of whether governments should intervene to correct market failures is not a new question. Although it is constantly re-examined, arguments on either side of the issue usually begin with the writings of A.C. Pigou and Ronald Coase.

A. C. Pigou

The discussion of this issue begins with the work of A. C. Pigou (1938), who was among the first to recognize the existence of externalities and the associated divergence between private costs and social costs and between private benefits and social benefits. Pigou argues that the externality cannot be mitigated by contractual negotiation between the affected parties and recommends either direct coercion on the part of the government or the judicious uses of taxes against the offending activity. These externality taxes are often referred to as Pigouvian taxes, after the economist who first proposed them.

The basic principle behind the use of externality taxes is that the tax eliminates the divergence between marginal private cost (MPC) and marginal social cost (MSC). This principle is illustrated in Figure 3.1, which reproduces the graph contained in Figure 2.2. In this graph, MPC represents the marginal private cost function; Q_1 represents the market equilibrium, where MPC = MPB; and Q^* represents the optimal level of output, where marginal social cost = marginal social benefit. If an externalities tax equal to the divergence (measured at Q^*) between MPC and MSC were charged, then it would raise the steel firms' private costs, because they would have to pay the tax on each unit of output. This tax would be equal to the vertical distance from a to b in Figure 3.1. The tax would shift the marginal private cost curve by a corresponding amount, from MPC' to MPC''. This new higher level of marginal private costs would force marginal private costs to become equal to

Figure 3.1 **An Externality Tax on Output**

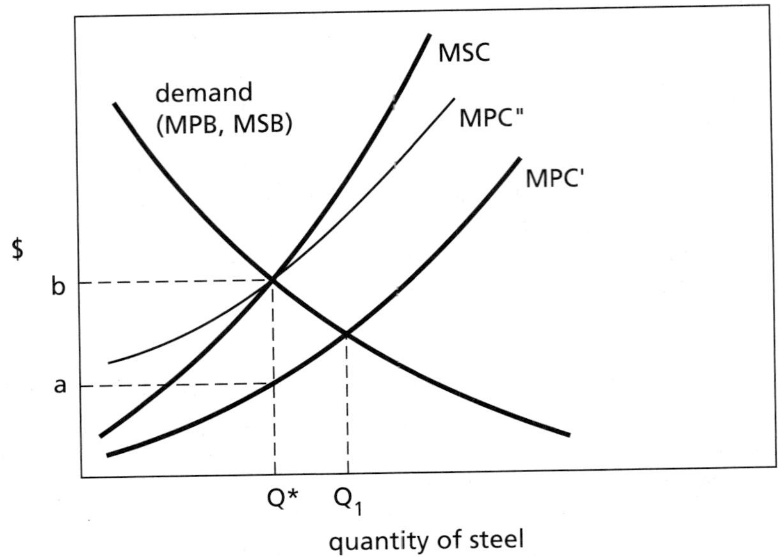

marginal social costs, and thus the market would arrive at the optimal equilibrium of Q*. This process is sometimes known as internalizing the externality. Subsequent examination of externalities taxes has shown that the tax should not be placed on the output (such as steel) but on the externality (such as emissions of sulfur dioxide), because the output should not be directly discouraged, as it yields benefits.[1] It is the externality that generates the additional social costs, and so it is the externality that should be taxed. The important differences between a tax on emissions and a tax on output are discussed in more detail when pollution taxes are analyzed later in the chapter.

Ronald Coase

Ronald Coase (1960) argues that not only is such an externality tax unnecessary, but it is often undesirable. The reason, Coase believes, is that a market for the externality will develop without government intervention. Coase makes two major arguments: the market will automatically generate the optimal level of the externality, and this optimal level will be achieved regardless of the definition of property rights. The definition of property rights refers to whether the generator of the externality has the legal right to

[1] This statement would not be true if the only way of reducing the externality were to reduce the output.

generate the externality or whether the victim of the externality has the legal right to be free from exposure to the externality. In other words, do steel mills have the right to dump their emissions in the air, or do citizens have the right to clean air? Coase's supposition that the market will generate the optimal level of the externality, regardless of the definition of property rights, has come to be known as the Coase theorem. The Coase theorem is often the point of embarkation for discussion of the necessity of government intervention to correct externalities.

Coase's example, which forms the primary conceptual evidence for the Coase theorem, is based on the interaction of a cattle rancher and a crop farmer. The interaction occurs because the cattle occasionally leave the rancher's property, venture to the farmer's property, and damage the farmer's crops. Coase uses an arithmetic example to show that if reducing the number of cows by one animal is in the social interest, it will actually happen without the need for government intervention, regardless of the direction of definition of property rights. For example, let's say that if the rancher were to increase his herd by one unit, he would receive profits of $3, but the farmer would suffer damages to his crops equal to $10. Let's also say that the farmer does not have the right to sue for damages; in other words, the rancher need not be concerned about the damages his cow imposes on the farmer. Clearly, it is not in the social interest for the rancher to add that cow to his herd, because the damages to the farmer are greater than the benefits to the rancher. Will the rancher pursue his private benefit and add the cow to the herd?

The answer that Coase gives is no; the farmer and the rancher will negotiate, because an agreement can make them both better off. The farmer would be willing to pay the rancher an amount less than $10 to forgo adding the cow. The rancher would be willing to accept an amount more than $3 to forgo adding the cow. Obviously, there is room for an agreement here. The same type of argument could be made if the farmer had the rights to recover damages and the damages of the cow to the farmer were less than the benefits to the rancher. Coase uses this type of arithmetic example to show that a negotiation process will develop, regardless of the direction of the definition of property rights that leads to the optimal level of cattle. Coase also shows that if some other strategy, such as building a fence, were optimal under one property right regime, it would be optimal under the other property right regime.

Because Coase believes that the market automatically generates the correct level of an externality, he argues against the imposition of interventions such as the externalities tax Pigou suggested. In fact, he argues that a Pigouvian tax is not only unnecessary but counterproductive, because it will encourage people to locate in the vicinity to collect the compensation. Before addressing this issue, let's examine whether Coase's primary assertion (the market will automatically generate the optimal amount of the externality) is correct.

One critical assumption Coase makes is that transaction costs are insignificant. Transaction costs are those costs borne by the victim and the generator of the externality in negotiating an "agreed-upon level" of the externality, with compensation to one party or the other as part of this agreement. In the case of the rancher and the farmer, it is an appropriate assumption, as the two can get together over a cup of coffee to discuss who is going to make an adjustment and at what level of compensation. If the externality in question is sulfur dioxide emissions in North America, however, then one must consider that there are hundreds of millions of generators of the externality (everybody who burns a hydrocarbon-based fuel) and hundreds of millions of victims of the pollution. In addition, the pollution generated in one part of the continent affects environmental quality in other parts of the continent, with significant amounts of pollution migrating across the U.S.-Canada border. Even more difficult is the situation in which the pollution externality is global, as in the case of the emission of greenhouse gases. In all these cases, as in most contemporary environmental problems, transaction costs would be significant.

The polar examples of the rancher-farmer interaction and the sulfur dioxide pollution or greenhouse gas emission problems illustrate the relevance of the number of participants to the importance of transaction costs. Not only are transaction costs likely to be positively related to the number of participants, but they are likely to be increasing at an increasing rate. In Figure 3.2, schematic drawings show the number of participants and the lines of communication among the participants. As shown in the accompanying chart, as the number of participants increases by a constant of 1, the number of lines of communication among the participants increases according to the progression {1, 3, 6, 10, 15, 21, . . .}.

One way to reduce transaction costs is to appoint an agent who acts in behalf of a large number of people. For instance, the Sierra Club acts as an

Figure 3.2 **Difficulty of Communication**

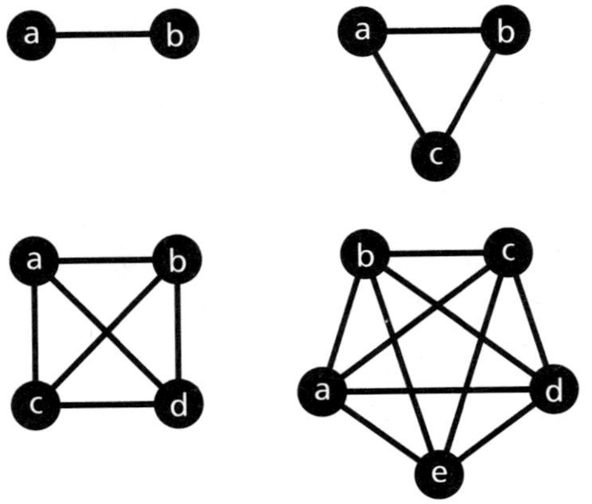

number of people	number of lines of communication
2	1
3	3
4	6
5	10
6	15
7	21

agent for many thousands of its members in making their positions known (or potentially negotiating in their behalf) on environmental externalities such as sulfur dioxide pollution. Not everybody who desires lower sulfur dioxide levels, however, contributes to the Sierra Club for this goal. This phenomenon may be due to what economists call the *free rider problem*. This problem occurs in the case of a public good, when *an individual may decline to share in the costs* knowing that he or she *cannot be precluded from sharing the benefits*. If the Sierra Club is successful in reducing sulfur dioxide emissions, all people who prefer cleaner air benefit, not just the dues-paying members of the Sierra Club, because clean air is a public good. A similar problem can occur in terms of taking collective action in a Coasian negotiation framework. Another significant problem to developing a negotiated solution with the help of agents is the information problem associated with choosing an agent, because it is costly for an individual to acquire information about which agent would best represent him or her. In other words, should this individual join the Sierra Club, the Environmental Defense Fund, Greenpeace, Earth First!, The Nature Conservancy, the Natural Resources Defense Council, or one of the many other different environmental nongovernmental organizations (NGOs).

Although recognizing the relevance of transaction costs, many economists in the 1960s and early 1970s still argued the general applicability of the Coase theorem, because most of the externalities that economists discussed were of the one generator/one victim format of Coase's example. Examples of externalities that were cited in this early literature included a factory located next to a dentist's office, a beekeeper and an orchard owner, and several more pastoral examples of the Coasian genre. These economists did not refer to externalities where transaction costs would immediately be recognized as important, such as the collapse of global fisheries or air pollution. Nonetheless, the Coase theorem may not hold even if zero transaction costs are assumed. William Baumol and Wallace Oates derive a result that shows that the Coase theorem breaks down even if zero transaction costs are assumed. Their result is that optimality (maximizing social welfare) requires that the generator of a negative externality be charged a price, while the victim remains uncompensated. Optimality requires a different price for the victim and the generator (asymmetric prices), so an efficient market cannot develop, because a market requires the same price for the buyer and the seller.

The intuition behind the need for this asymmetric pricing is that because the victim does not control the amount of the externality to which he or she is exposed, an externality price is superfluous to that individual's decision-making process. The inability of an efficient market to develop is a critically important flaw in the Coase theorem. This flaw exists regardless of the presence or absence of transaction costs.

One of the problems with the Coase example (and the same argument can be applied to the writings of many of Coase's contemporaries) is that if the example only has one victim of the externality, then the externality may quickly cease to be an externality. The reason is that in the one-versus-one case, the total amount of the externality is identical to the amount to which the victim is exposed, and the negotiation process therefore allows the victim control over how much of the externality to which he or she is exposed. It is very tenuous logic to develop an example for a one-versus-one situation and then generalize to large numbers.[2]

Another problem with the generalization from the one generator/one victim example to the large-numbers case is that focusing on one generator and one victim also misses an important dimension of the problem, because focusing on this one-on-one interaction masks the importance of entry and exit. The entry and exit of firms into or out of the market will affect both the number of generators and the number of victims. If the ranchers have the right to let their cattle roam without worrying about the damages to farmers, then there will be more ranchers than in a society in which they are responsible for their damages. An analogous statement can be made about the number of farmers. If that is the case, then in a multiple generator/multiple victim world the definition of property rights will have a critically important impact on the outcome, because it will have an impact on the relative numbers of generators and victims.

Finally, property rights might matter because there may be important differences between the victim's willingness to pay for reducing the detrimental externality and the victim's willingness to accept compensation to allow increases in the level of the externality. Part of the difference may be due to the existence of *income effects*, which would imply that *the higher an individual's standard of living, the greater his or her marginal valuation of a normal good or service*. Because being exposed to detrimental externalities such as pollution lowers an individual's standard of living and being free from a detrimental externality raises an individual's standard of living, the marginal valuation of the damages of an externality depends on the definition of property rights. If the value of the externality depends on the definition of property rights, then the way property rights are defined must have an effect on the negotiated level of the externality.

In summary, the Coase theorem suggests that there is no need for government intervention to correct market failures due to externalities. This theorem, however, suffers from four important flaws:

1. The Coase theorem assumes zero or insignificant transaction costs, an assumption inappropriate for environmental externalities, because it is likely that there are large numbers of generators and victims.

---

[2] This problem is one of two very important logical errors that Coase made in his widely cited paper. First, he derives a proof for the Coase theorem based on an arithmetic example. In fact, you cannot prove the existence of a theorem with an arithmetic example, because you must show it to be true in all cases, not just in the particular example. Although it is possible to disprove something by showing one case where it does not work, you cannot prove a proposition by showing one case where it does work. Second, normally it is not possible to generalize from the small-numbers case to the large-numbers case.

2. Even if one assumes zero transaction costs, the theorem cannot generate an efficient market, because efficiency requires asymmetric prices.
3. The definition of property rights will have an effect on the outcome, because this definition affects the number of potential participants in the market for the output and the market for the externality associated with the output.
4. The definition of property rights may be important due to the existence of income effects, which may affect the marginal value of the externality.

Resolution of the Issue of Government Intervention

In Chapter 2, it was shown that market failures, such as environmental externalities, can lead to losses in social welfare. In the economic literature, many economists, such as Pigou, suggest that government intervention to correct market failure would lead to improvements in social welfare. Other economists, most notably Coase, argue that government intervention is unnecessary, because a market for the externality would develop that would lead to the socially optimal level of the externality being chosen. It was shown in the previous section, however, that under most circumstances, and certainly under the circumstances surrounding most environmental externalities, the Coase theorem is not applicable, and consideration must be given to the option of government intervention. Of course, the costs of government intervention must be compared with the benefits of government intervention before deciding that government intervention is desirable. This comparison cannot be done for externalities in general, but must be done on a case-by-case basis for the externalities of greatest concern. Also, it should be recognized that the costs and benefits of government intervention are a function of the type of intervention. For example, one way to control the externalities associated with littering is to execute all people who are found littering. Most people, however, would regard such a policy as having costs far in excess of its benefits.

Types of Government Intervention

There are five broad classes of government intervention to correct market failures associated with externalities: moral suasion, direct production of environmental quality, pollution prevention, command and control regulations, and economic incentives. Each of these classes of intervention or policy instruments represents a different philosophy toward the role of government in society, generates different behavioral incentives for those who are generating externalities, and leads to different levels of costs and benefits. These different instruments should not be viewed as mutually exclusive methods; an appropriate environmental policy may have elements of all five classes of policy instruments.

Moral Suasion

Moral suasion is a term used to describe governmental attempts to influence behavior without actually stipulating any rules that constrain behavior. Governmental leaders, usually the chief executive of the jurisdiction, make public announcements that detail the way in which they would like people to behave. To be effective, the statements of the government officials must convince the public that the benefits of behaving in the desired fashion are substantially greater than the costs. Such federal government programs as Woodsy Owl's "Give a hoot, don't pollute" and Smokey Bear's "Only you can prevent forest fires"[3] are examples of relatively successful moral suasion programs aimed at environmental problems. Currently, many levels of government as well as corporate and not-for-profit organizations are engaged in moral suasion programs aimed at reducing the volume of waste, increasing recycling, reducing energy use, protecting local streams, and preventing littering, among other programs.

The effectiveness of moral suasion programs depends on the extent to which the people (household, firm, or organization members) who are being asked to change their behavior believe that it is in their individual and collective interests to do so. A change in their behavior may be in their individual or collective interests because of the relative magnitudes of the direct costs and benefits of the program. This change may also be in their private interests if the people believe that if they do not voluntarily adopt the behavior advocated by the moral suasion program, then more severe restrictions on their behavior will be adopted as permanent law.

Moral suasion can be an effective method for generating environmental improvement, as the success of voluntary recycling programs indicates; it may not, however, be practical in many circumstances. In particular, the free rider problem (defined on page 51) can inhibit the effectiveness of moral suasion.

Direct Production of Environmental Quality

The direct production of environmental quality is another way in which the government can mitigate environmental market failures. At first, it might seem unrealistic to say that government programs could undo environmental degradation, but reforestation, breaching of dams, stocking fish, creating wet-

[3] Although the Smokey Bear program has been effective in reducing accidental forest fires, many forest ecologists believe that fire is a natural element in the forest and that fire reduction programs are counterproductive in the long run. Chapter 12 discusses this issue.

lands, treating sewage, and cleaning up toxic sites are all examples of this type of activity. As one might suspect, government production of environmental quality is largely an ameliorative action, and in many cases it would have been better for society if the environmental degradation had been prevented in the first place.

Although both moral suasion and direct production of environmental quality are important features of the policy arsenal, they have limited applicability to environmental problems in general. In particular, it is unlikely that such pressing problems as air pollution, global warming, water pollution, global fisheries collapse, tropical deforestation, and the depletion of the ozone layer are likely to be adequately addressed by either of these types of policies. As a consequence, more comprehensive types of government intervention must be considered.

Pollution Prevention

Pollution prevention programs are not designed to control the externality itself, but, rather, to address a related market failure of imperfect information. These programs are partnerships of business and government agencies designed to increase the profitability of reducing pollution by developing technologies that are both more profitable and cleaner. The basic premise underlying pollution prevention programs is that the knowledge to develop these cleaner and more profitable technologies is beyond the capability of an individual firm to develop. The combined efforts of government agencies, national laboratories, universities, and private firms, however, can lead to the development of these innovative and beneficial technologies. Pollution prevention programs emphasize being proactive in reducing pollution rather than waiting to react to new regulations. A proactive policy can lead to lower costs of abatement in the long run, especially because one way of reducing pollution outputs is to reduce the use of inputs. For example, if a firm lowers emissions by using more energy-efficient equipment, the firm also reduces its energy costs. These types of programs need not be confined to industry. For example, similar types of information programs can help small farmers in developing countries learn to use agricultural techniques that have minimal impact on the environmental. This issue is further discussed in Chapter 13.

Command and Control Regulations

Command and control regulations are a class of policy instruments that have greater ability to modify environmentally degrading behavior. In many textbooks and articles, these regulations are also referred to as direct controls. Command and control regulations are distinguished from other policy instruments, in that they place constraints on the behavior of households and firms (and any other generators of externalities). If behavior remains within these boundaries, then the household or firm is behaving lawfully. If behavior violates these boundaries, however, then the firm or household is behaving illegally and suffer penalties specified by the rule or law that established the direct control. These constraints generally take the form of limits on inputs or outputs to the consumption or production process. Examples of command and control restrictions that constitute restrictions on inputs include requiring sulfur-removing scrubbers on the smokestacks of coal-burning utilities, requiring catalytic converters on automobiles, and banning the use of leaded gasoline. Command and control regulations that take the form of restrictions on outputs include emissions limitations on the exhaust of automobiles, prohibitions against the dumping of toxic substances, and prohibitions against littering.

Economic Incentives

Economic incentives are based on a different philosophy than command and control regulations. Rather than defining certain behaviors as legal or illegal and specifying penalties for engaging in illegal behavior, economic incentives simply make individual self-interest coincide with the social interest. Examples of economic incentives include pollution taxes, pollution subsidies, marketable pollution permits, deposit-refund systems, performance bonds, and liability systems.

Choosing the Correct Level of Environmental Quality

Whether one employs command and control techniques or economic incentives, a crucial issue involves determining the desirable level of pollution or environmental degradation. At first, this question might seem to be illogical, because the desirable level of something that is bad (like pollution) should be zero. Some reflection, however, will reveal that this assumption is not likely to be true because the reduction of pollution will have opportunity costs. In actuality, a zero level of pollution is impossible to achieve due to a principle of physics known as the law of mass balance.

The law of mass balance is based on the proposition that an activity cannot destroy the matter in the reaction; it can only change its form.[4] The law of mass balance states that the mass of the outputs of any activity are equal to the mass of the inputs. For example, if 10 pounds of wood are burned in a fireplace, 10 pounds of matter are not destroyed. The 10 pounds of matter still exist, although the form of the matter may have been altered to carbon dioxide, water vapor, smoke, and ash. The law of mass balance directly indicates that any production or consumption activity will be associated with waste. Eliminating all pollution means eliminating all production and con-

[4] Of course, fusion and fission reactions are exceptions to this law, where the mass of the materials that are inputs to the reaction is different than the mass of the materials after the reaction. The difference in mass becomes converted to energy.

sumption activities, as all consumption and production activities must produce waste. A society whose sole economic activity consisted of organic agriculture would still be a polluting society.

The discussion suggests that some pollution is inevitable and that zero pollution is neither desirable nor achievable. The discussion in Chapter 2 suggested that the unregulated market level of pollution is likely to be excessive, because the market failure implies that social welfare is lower than it could be with less of the externality. If zero pollution is likely to be too costly or unattainable and if the unregulated level is excessive, then some level of pollution between zero and the unregulated market level should be the target or desired level of pollution.

The desired level of pollution will be a function of the social costs that are associated with the pollution. There are two such categories. The first is the damage that pollution creates by degrading the physical, natural, and social environment. These damages include effects on ecosystems, human health effects, inhibition of economic activity, damage to human-made structures, and aesthetic effects. The second type of cost is that of reducing pollution; it includes the opportunity costs of the resources used to reduce pollution and the value of any forgone outputs.

The Marginal Damage Function

The damages that pollution generates by degrading the environment are represented in the marginal damage function of Figure 3.3. The emissions of pollution are specified on the horizontal axis, and dollar measures of the damages pollution generates are specified on the vertical axis. Many people question the ability to derive dollar measures of the damages from pollution (such as human health or ecosystem effects). Investigation of this issue will be postponed, however, and for now it will be assumed that these effects are quantifiable. Even if they are not, the marginal damage function is useful for thinking about the relationship between environmental change and social welfare, and how environmental policy can change that relationship. The issues associated with the measurement of the value of environmental resources and the damages from environmental degradation are examined in Chapter 4.

The damage function presented in Figure 3.3 is a marginal damage function that specifies the damages associated with an additional unit of pollution. For example, if the level of emissions is equal to E_1, then the damage of an additional unit of emissions is equal to D_1. The total damages generated by a particular level of pollution can be examined by looking at the area under the marginal damage function. For example, the total damages associated with E_1 units of pollution are equal to the shaded area $0AE_1$. Several other characteristics of the marginal damage function in Figure 3.3, concerning the slope and the intercept of the marginal damage function, warrant discussion. The marginal damage function in Figure 3.3 has a slope that increases at an increasing rate. Thus as the level of pollution becomes larger,

Figure 3.3 **The Marginal Damage Function**

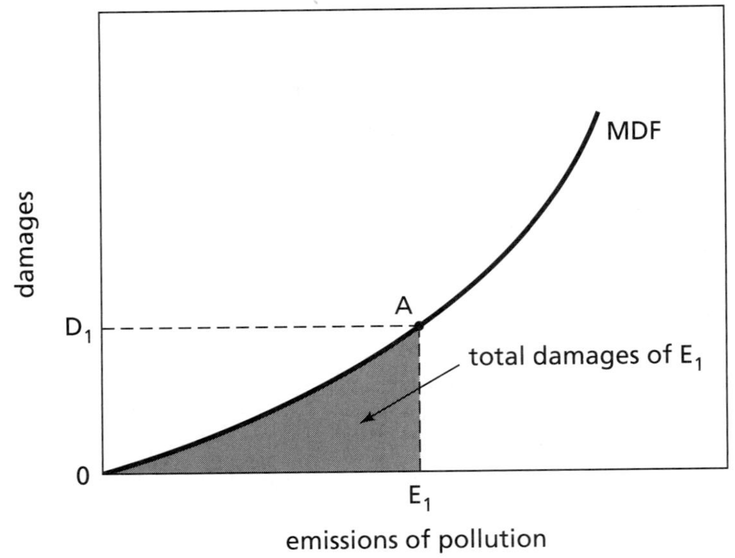

the damages associated with the marginal unit of pollution becomes larger and the rate at which they become larger is increasing. Although there has not been enough study of marginal damage functions to say that this conclusion is true for pollution in general, the author of this book believes it to be likely for many types of pollution, particularly those that have human health effects or large-scale impacts on ecosystems, or those that have global effects. Evidence concerning the shape of the marginal damage function is presented in Chapter 5, along with a discussion of the relevance of the shape of the function for environmental policy.

The Marginal Abatement Cost Function

As mentioned, damages are only part of the social costs associated with pollution. The other cost is the cost of abating (reducing) pollution to a lower level so that there are fewer damages.[5] Such costs include the costs of the labor, capital, and energy needed to lessen the emissions of pollution associ-

---

[5] An additional cost is the cost of avoiding pollution damages. For example, some of the damages from air pollution can be avoided by filtering air as it passes though air-conditioning and heating systems. Another example is that some of the damages from the depletion of the ozone layer can be avoided by the wearing of sunblock. The marginal damage function presented here can be viewed to be incorporating this type of avoidance cost.

ated with particular levels of production or consumption; or the costs may take the form of opportunity costs from reducing the levels of production or consumption.

Figure 3.4 contains a marginal abatement cost function, where E_u represents the level of pollution that would be generated in the absence of any government intervention. At this level of emissions, the marginal cost of abatement is zero because polluters have not yet taken any steps to reduce the level of pollution below the level they each privately regard as optimal. As pollution is reduced below E_u, the marginal cost of abatement (the cost of reducing pollution by one more unit) increases because the cheapest options for reducing pollution are the first to be employed. As the cheaper alternatives are exhausted, more expensive steps must be taken to further reduce pollution, so marginal abatement costs rise as the level of emissions moves from E_u to the left. For example, the cheapest way to remove sulfur dioxide (SO_2) from the effluent gases of a coal burning power plant may simply be to buy coal with a lower sulfur content. How, though, does the power company reduce emissions of SO_2 even more after it has already switched to low sulfur coal? It would have to buy and install equipment that removed the SO_2 before it exited the smokestack, which would entail a much higher cost. As firms utilize the cheapest techniques first, the marginal cost of abatement will continue to rise as they attempt more and more emissions reduction. At E_1, the marginal abatement cost is equal to C_1, and the total abatement cost

Figure 3.4 **Marginal Abatement Cost Function**

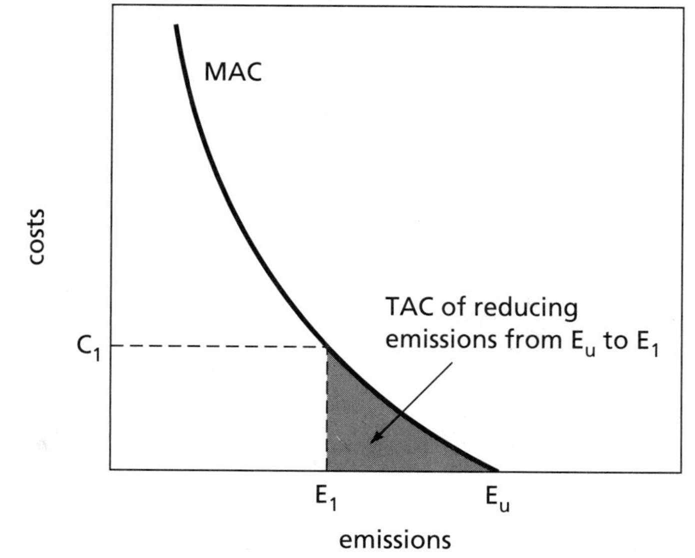

(TAC) is equal to the shaded area under the marginal abatement cost function between E_u and E_1.

As was the case with the marginal damage function, it is important to discuss the nature of the slope and intercept of the marginal abatement cost function. The marginal abatement cost function in Figure 3.4 has a slope that decreases at a decreasing rate. Thus, as one abates emissions from a starting point of E_u (as one moves in the direction of zero pollution), the costs of further reducing pollution increase at an increasing rate. This increase is consistent with an extremely high vertical intercept or with the case in which the marginal abatement cost function approaches an asymptote as in Figure 3.4. The extreme magnitude of the intercept implies that the cost of eliminating the last few units of pollutants is extremely high. That would most likely be the case for pollutants, such as sulfur dioxide and nitrogen oxides, that result from the burning of fossil fuels, such as coal, oil, and gasoline.

On the other hand, there are many pollutants for which the slope and intercept would have the shape of the marginal abatement cost function in Figure 3.5. This function is decreasing at an increasing rate, implying that the costs of reducing pollution increase at a decreasing rate as one abates from the unregulated level of emissions (E_u). The marginal abatement cost function of Figure 3.5 also has a relatively low intercept, indicating that the cost of eliminating the last few units is not that much higher than the cost of eliminating the first few units. The release of lead emissions into the air

Figure 3.5 **Marginal Abatement Costs that Decrease at Decreasing Rate**

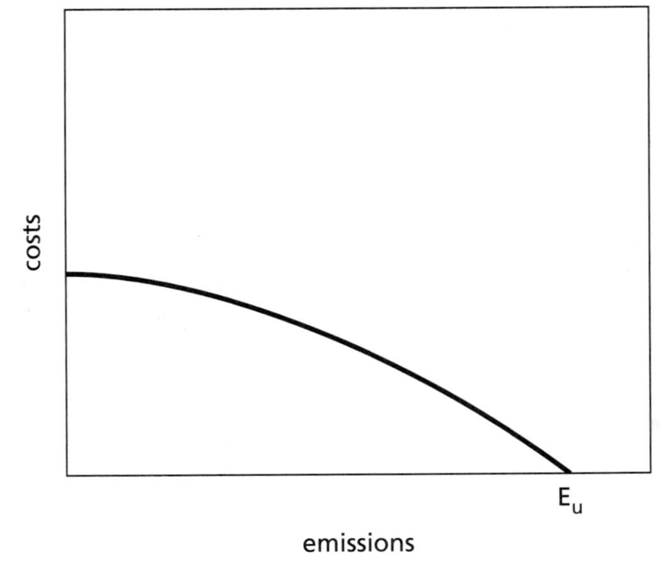

through automobile exhaust is a good example of this type of pollution.[6] Because the presence of lead allows gasoline to be made with fewer of its higher octane components, lead was added to gasoline to reduce refining costs. Simply stated, removing lead means that more of other inputs need to be used in producing gasoline. The cost of not adding lead to the last few gallons of gasoline is not likely to be significantly larger than the cost of not adding lead to the first few units of gasoline. In fact, these costs would even be decreasing if economies of scale could be realized in refining.

Marginal Damages, Marginal Abatement Costs, and the Optimal Level of Pollution

Now that the two costs of pollution (abatement costs and damages) are fully understood, it is possible to determine the optimal level of pollution emissions. The optimal level of emissions is the level that minimizes the total social costs of pollution, which is the sum of total abatement cost and total damages. This level occurs at the point where marginal abatement costs are equal to marginal damages, which is E_1 in Figure 3.6.

Figure 3.6 **The Optimal Level of Pollution**

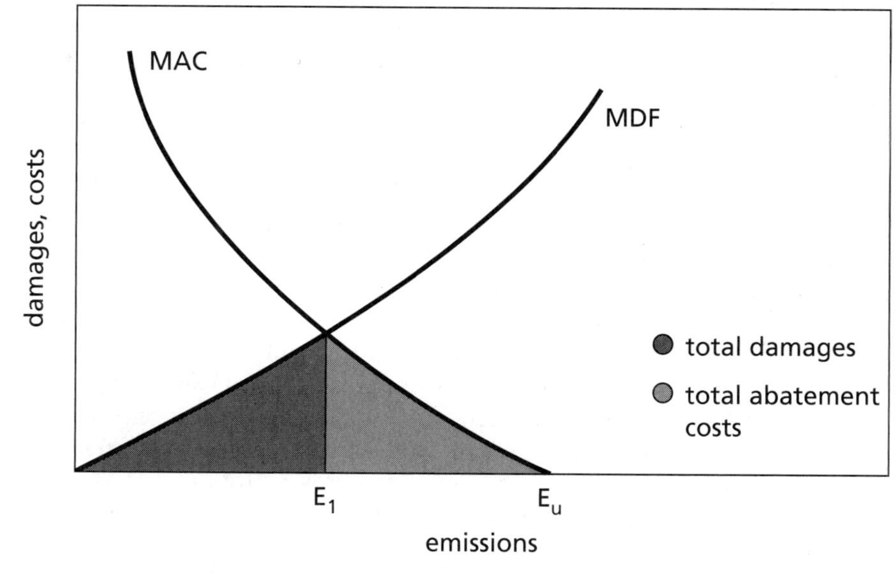

[6] Lead is an extremely toxic (especially to children) heavy metal that was extensively used as an additive in gasoline and emitted in automobile exhaust. Although small amounts of lead are still added to gasoline, recent regulations have reduced the use of lead in gasoline to a trace of past levels.

It is relatively easy to demonstrate that equality of marginal abatement cost (MAC) and marginal damages is the condition for determining the optimal level of emissions. If the level of emissions is less than E_1 (to its left), then marginal abatement costs are greater than marginal damages. Thus the cost of eliminating the marginal unit of pollution is greater than the damages the unit of pollution would have caused, and therefore, it would be beneficial to have more pollution. This statement would be true as long as the level of pollution is less than E_1. On the other hand, if the level of emissions is greater than E_1, then marginal damages are greater than marginal abatement costs. Because the damages caused by the marginal unit of pollution are greater than the costs of eliminating that unit of pollution, then society is better off eliminating it. That will be true as long as the level of emissions is greater than E_1.

At E_1, where marginal abatement costs are equal to marginal damages, the total social costs of pollution cannot be lowered by changing the level of emissions. This minimized total social cost is shown as the shaded triangular area in Figure 3.6. Figure 3.7a and 3.7b more graphically illustrate the excess social costs associated with a level of pollution different from E_1. In Figure 3.7a, the actual level of emissions (E_2) is above the optimal level (E_1). In the range of emissions between E_1 and E_2, marginal damages are greater than marginal abatement costs, generating excess social costs of area abc. Similarly, in Figure 3.7b, the actual level of pollution (E_3) is lower than the optimal level (E_1), leading to excess social costs of area ade. The optimal level of pollution need not be static but may change over time. For example, if an engineer developed a new device for cars that enabled them to get substantially better gas mileage (which would reduce the pollution per mile), then the marginal abatement cost function would shift downward, as in Figure 3.8. The optimal level of pollution would decrease from E_1 to E_2, and the unregulated level of pollution would decrease from E_u' to E_u''. It may appear strange that the unregulated, or market level, of pollution would decline, but many people would desire the new device on their cars—independent of environmental regulations—because better gas mileage reduces their operating expenses.

Knowledge of the marginal abatement cost function and marginal damage function is not always available to policy makers. When that is the case, a target level of pollution is chosen that usually corresponds to some sort of legislative goal, such as a level of air pollution that is consistent with "protecting the public health" or a level of water pollution that is consistent with "fishable/swimmable waters." The implications of imperfect information for the development of environmental policy is discussed later in this chapter and in many of the applications chapters, such as the chapters on global environmental change (Chapter 7) and energy (Chapters 9 and 10).

Figure 3.7A **Social Costs When Pollution Is Greater Than Optimal**

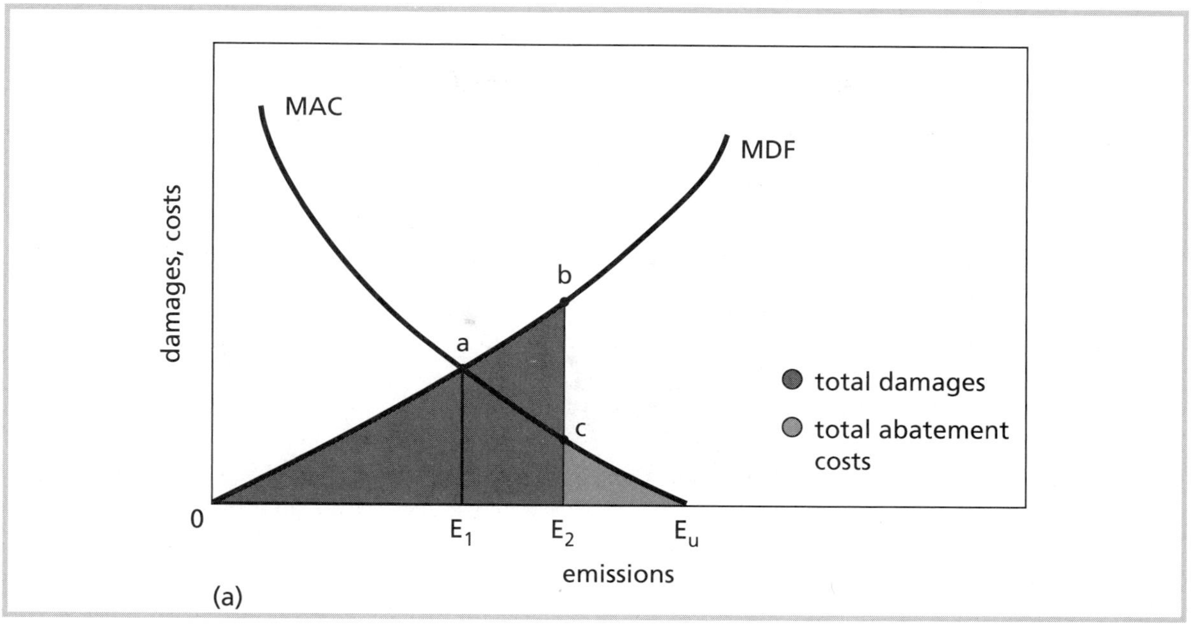

Figure 3.7B **Social Costs When Pollution Is Less Than Optimal**

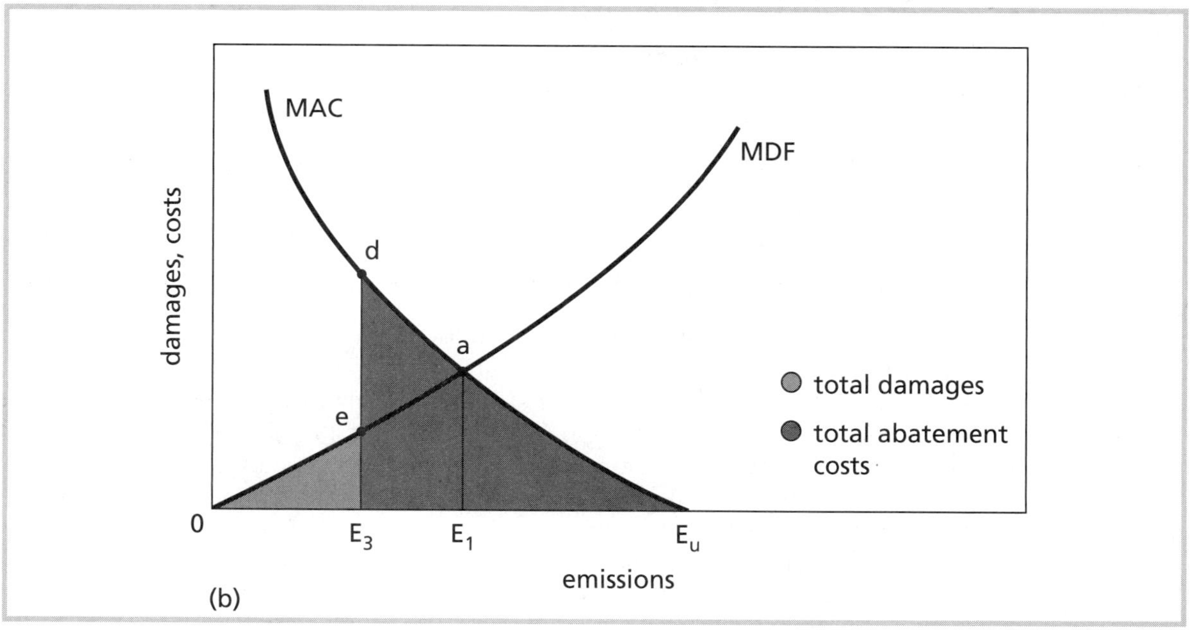

Figure 3.8 **Technological Innovation That Lowers Abatement Costs**

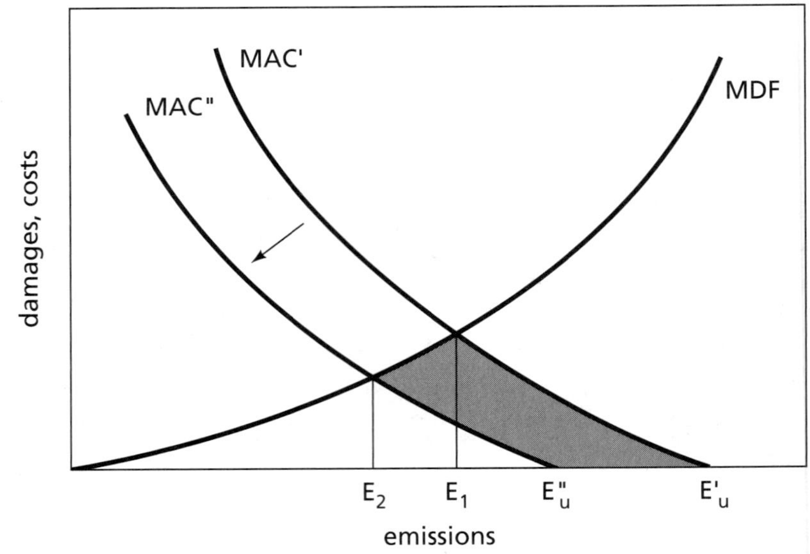

Pursuing Environmental Quality with Command and Control Policies

One potential way of achieving the optimal level of pollution is through use of command and control polices. If the optimal level of pollution is known to be E_1, then E_1 units of pollution could be allocated among all the polluters. For example, if the optimal level of pollution is equal to half of the unregulated level, then a regulation could be imposed that would require each polluter to reduce his or her level of pollution by 50 percent.

Command and Control Policies and Excess Abatement Cost

Command and control regulations have been criticized as generating more abatement costs than necessary to achieve a given level of emissions. This point can best be illustrated by assuming that there are only two polluters in society and then looking at the marginal abatement cost functions of the individual polluters. Figure 3.9 contains the marginal abatement costs for two polluters and for society as a whole. The aggregate marginal abatement cost function (societal marginal abatement cost function) is derived by horizontally summing the marginal abatement cost functions for all polluters. In this example, there are just two polluters, polluter 1 and polluter 2. For example, if there are no environmental regulations, then polluter 1 will emit 8 units of pollution and polluter 2 will emit 6 units. The total for society, therefore, will

Figure 3.9 **Aggregating Marginal Abatement Cost Functions**

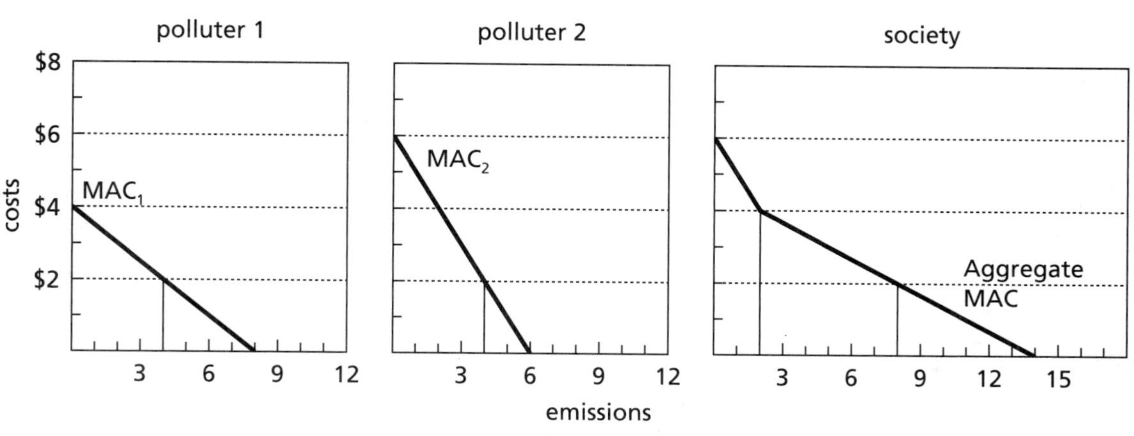

be 14 units, which becomes the horizontal intercept for the aggregate marginal abatement cost function. Other points on the aggregate marginal abatement cost function may be derived in similar fashion. For example, if each polluter reduced his or her level of pollution to the point where marginal abatement costs were \$2, then polluter 1 would be emitting 4 units and polluter 2 would be emitting 4 units, so when marginal abatement costs are equal to \$2, society is emitting a total of 8 units. Notice the kink that occurs in the aggregate abatement cost function at a marginal abatement cost of \$4, since polluter 1 has eliminated all emissions at this level of marginal abatement costs.

The effects of a command and control regulation that requires all polluters to reduce pollution by 50 percent can now be analyzed with the aid of a similar graph, shown in Figure 3.10. In this example, the unregulated level of pollution is 10 units for polluter 1 and 6 units for polluter 2. If pollution is cut by 50 percent for each polluter, then polluter 1's pollution declines from 10 to 5 units, polluter 2's from 6 to 3, and society as a whole's from 16 to 8. Although each polluter has cut his or her pollution by half, their marginal abatement costs are not equal. Polluter 2 incurs a higher cost (\$3) than polluter 1 (\$2) for reducing the marginal unit of pollution. This higher cost represents a misallocation of resources from society's point of view, because the total costs of obtaining any particular level of emissions will occur when the marginal abatement costs are equal across all polluters.

This point is illustrated in Figure 3.11, which shows how society's total abatement costs can be lowered by keeping the total emissions constant but changing the allocation of emissions across the two polluters so that one polluter pollutes more, the other pollutes less, and the total remains constant.

Figure 3.10 **Reduction in Pollution through Equal Percentage Reduction by Each Polluter**

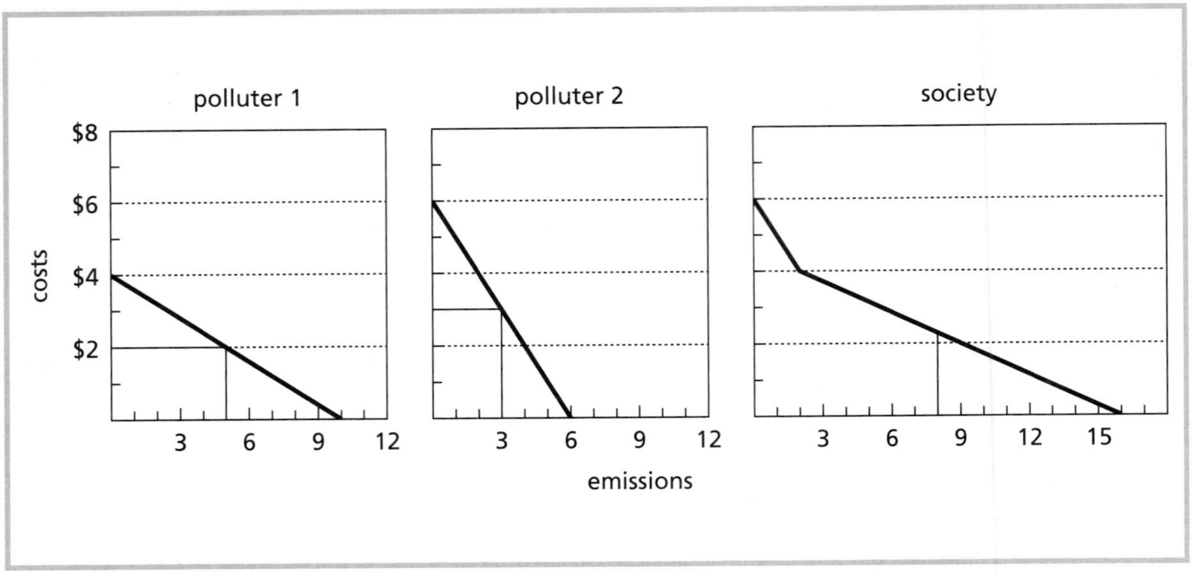

Figure 3.11 **Minimizing Total Abatement Cost by Equating Marginal Abatement Cost**

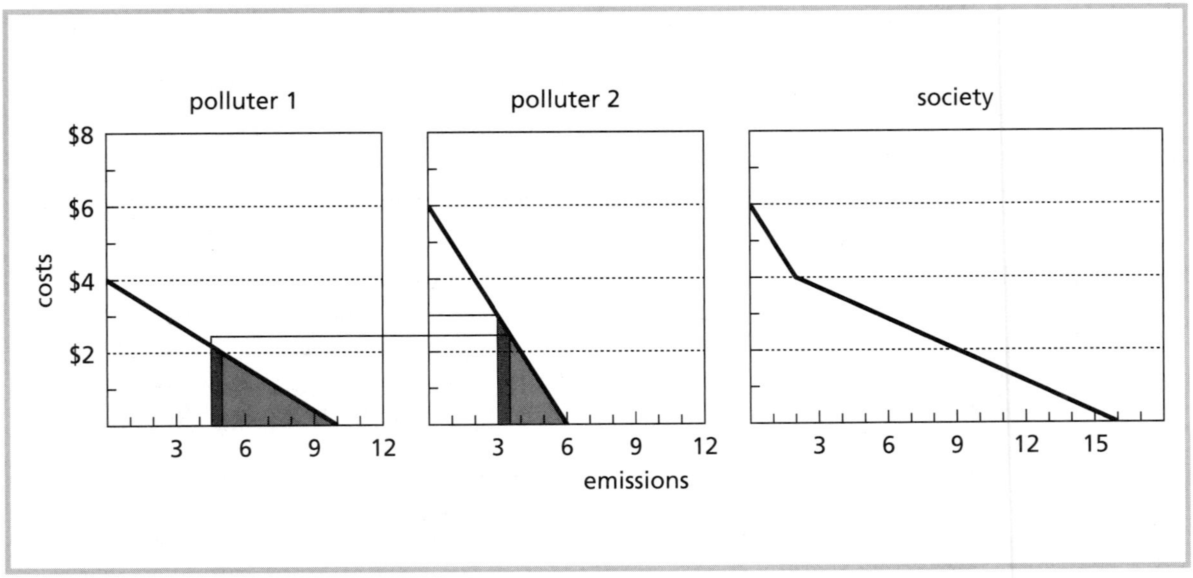

Because polluter 2 has higher marginal abatement costs, polluter 2 will be allowed to emit more and polluter 1 will be required to pollute less. In this case, polluter 1 reduces pollution by one half unit (to $4\frac{1}{2}$) and polluter 2 increases pollution by one half unit (to $3\frac{1}{2}$).

The heavily shaded areas in Figure 3.11 show the changes in each polluter's abatement costs, which arise from the marginal reallocation of one-half unit of pollution. Polluter 1's abatement costs increase as a result of the reallocation, whereas polluter 2's abatement costs decrease. Because the decrease in polluter 2's abatement costs is greater than the increase for polluter 1's, the reallocation reduces costs for society as a whole. Only when the marginal abatement costs are equal for each polluter will there be no possible cost-saving reallocations of emissions. The principle that total abatement costs are minimized when marginal abatement costs are equalized across polluters is fundamental to understanding the differences among pollution control policies.

Command and control regulations that have the property of assigning pollution levels to different polluters are not likely to result in achieving the minimum abatement costs of obtaining the target levels of pollution, unless, of course, the assignment was made in such a fashion as to equate these marginal abatement costs across all polluters. This assignment is only feasible under two conditions. The first is the unlikely condition that all polluters face the same marginal abatement cost function. If so, equalizing emissions across polluters (or requiring each polluter to reduce emissions by the same percentage amount) will equalize marginal abatement costs. Because many different types of producers and consumers emit the same pollutants, however, it is highly unlikely that all polluters will have the same marginal cost functions. For example, steel factories, electricity generation plants, and automobiles all emit sulfur dioxide pollution, yet they have very different production or consumption technologies. The second condition is that if the regulating authority knew the marginal abatement cost function for each polluter, then it could choose an allocation across polluters in which the level of marginal abatement costs were equal for all polluters. The same technological diversity that makes the first condition unlikely, however, makes the second condition prohibitively expensive. Because there are literally thousands of types of polluters for the more common pollutants, it would be prohibitively expensive to develop even rough estimates of the marginal abatement cost function of each polluter.

An assignment of pollution levels to the various polluters cannot generally equate the marginal abatement costs across the various polluters, so this type of command and control policy will result in higher abatement costs than necessary for any target level of pollution. Other types of command and control regulations that have the property of specifying the specific abatement technologies that must be employed may be even worse. For example, the least expensive way to deal with sulfur dioxide pollution from electric utilities may be to burn a low-sulfur fuel. Regulations that require more expensive scrubber stacks, however, do not allow firms to use lower-cost technologies. Even worse from an efficiency standpoint, such regulations reduce the profit motive for research and development of lower-cost methods of reducing pollution.

Many critics of environmental policy in OECD countries[7] believe that the expenditures on pollution control are excessively high. Other critics of these environmental policies argue that current levels of pollution are much higher than optimal. In what might appear to be a paradox, both may be right.

What makes this apparent paradox nonparadoxical is that environmental policies in the United States and many other nations, which are primarily of the command and control method, move society onto a higher marginal abatement cost curve than is necessary. For example, in Figure 3.12, MAC_2 represents the lowest-cost means for abating pollution, but MAC_1 is the higher-cost function that inefficient and ill-advised policies would force upon society. Because of the high abatement costs, it is likely that the target level of pollution chosen will be greater than the optimal level of pollution (E_1).

Figure 3.12 **Excess Social Costs from Inefficient Regulation**

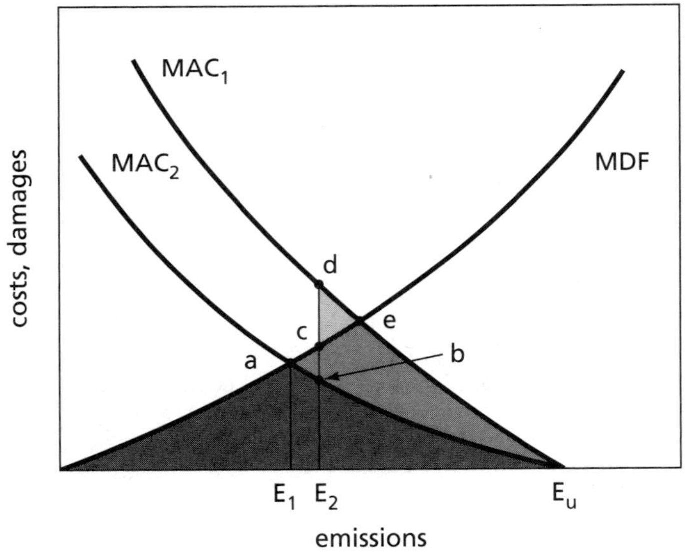

[7] The Organization for Economic Cooperation and Development (OECD) is a group of high- and middle-income nations designed to find common solutions to economic and social problems. It consists of 30 members, the original 20 from Western Europe and North America, plus newer members from Eastern Europe and the Pacific Rim.

Let's assume that E_2 is the target level of pollution. The excess social costs that inefficient regulations force upon society are diagrammed in Figure 3.12. Area $E_u$ecb plus area cde represents the extra abatement costs associated with using inefficient policies to reduce pollution from E_u to E_2. Area acb represents the excess social costs from having a level of pollution that is higher than optimal.

The Role of Command and Control Policies

In the next section of this chapter, it will be shown that economic incentives such as pollution taxes and marketable pollution permits do equate the marginal abatement costs across polluters. Because marginal abatement costs will be equated across all polluters with these policies, they will achieve the target level of pollution with the minimum total abatement costs for society. Before beginning the discussion of these policies, several circumstances for which command and control regulations may still be the most desirable policy instrument, despite their inability to equate marginal abatement costs across polluters, are considered. The three sets of circumstances that may call for the use of direct controls are

1. When monitoring costs are high
2. When the optimal level of emissions is at or near zero
3. During random events or emergencies that change the relationship between emissions and damages

Many types of command and control regulations, particularly those that set allowable levels of pollution for each polluter, require just as extensive a monitoring effort as pollution taxes or marketable pollution permits. In all these cases, the pollution control authority must know the exact (or estimated) amount of pollution each polluter emits. Yet, consider an environmental problem such as littering, where the optimal amount of emissions is some nonzero amount. For the sake of the example, say that the optimal level is 1000 units of litter per week in a society of 1000 people. One could achieve this level through a direct control that specified that each person could litter 1 unit per week, or one could set a tax designed to achieve this. To implement either policy, however, one would need "litter police" constantly observing the actions of all individuals to measure the amount of litter being released into the environment. Obviously, these monitoring costs would be so high that the policies would not be workable.

An alternative would be to institute a command and control policy that only requires sporadic, rather than continuous, monitoring. That could be done by making all littering illegal and stipulating that anyone caught littering must pay a punitive fine. The fine multiplied by the probability of being caught is the expected private cost of littering to the individual who litters. Potential litterers would compare the expected private cost of littering with the private benefits of littering (that is, not having to carry the dirty trash around in their pockets) when deciding whether to litter. The higher the fine and the greater the probability of being caught, the greater the expected cost of littering; thus, less littering will take place. If monitoring is relatively easy, so that the probability of being caught is near 1, the fine could be very low and still generate compliance. Under these circumstances, the system more resembles a per unit pollution tax. If the cost of monitoring is extremely high, however, then the best way to maintain the expected cost is with a relatively high fine. Care must be taken, however, that the fine is not so high that authorities are reluctant to support it. For example, a fine of $100,000 for throwing a gum wrapper on the ground is not likely to be enforced, so it does not constitute a credible threat.

The second set of circumstances in which direct controls are advantageous is when the optimal level of release into the environment is zero or a level close to zero. When one casually lists pollutants for which the optimal level seems to be at or near zero, extremely dangerous pollutants—such as heavy metals and radioactive waste—immediately come to mind. These pollutants are ones for which initial marginal damages are likely to be quite high relative to marginal abatement costs, because the damages associated with them are quite severe (and because they persist in the environment without decomposing to more innocuous substances). Another class of pollutants for which the initial marginal damages are likely to be quite high relative to marginal abatement costs are pollutants for which the costs of abating the last few units of the pollutant are quite low. This class generally includes all pollutants for which there are good substitutes that create less damage. For example, chlorofluorocarbons (CFCs), which were used as propellants in spray cans (such as hair spray or deodorant), depleted the ozone layer (see Chapter 7). Because there are extremely good substitutes for CFCs as a propellant in toiletries (roll-on deodorants, mechanical pumps, and so on), the marginal cost of reducing CFC pollution from this source was believed to be extremely low. Figure 3.13a contains representations of marginal abatement and marginal damage functions for which the optimal level of emission is zero, because the marginal damages are always greater than the marginal abatement costs. Although pollution could always be reduced to zero with an appropriately high pollution tax, it is simpler and less expensive to simply ban it. For example, the use of CFCs as a propellant in toiletries has been banned.[8] Another example is banning the use of lead shot (steel is the substitute) for hunting ducks and geese, although many hunters remain passionately opposed to steel shot.

A ban may also be cost effective when the optimal level of pollution is near zero, as in Figure 3.13b. Here, a positive level of pollution, E_1, is optimal. If emissions were reduced to zero, excess social costs in the shaded area would be generated. These excess social costs, though, may be small relative

---

[8] Chapter 7 discusses the Montreal Protocol, an international agreement for reducing and eventually eliminating the use of CFCs.

Figure 3.13 A and B **Optimal Level of Emissions at or near Zero**

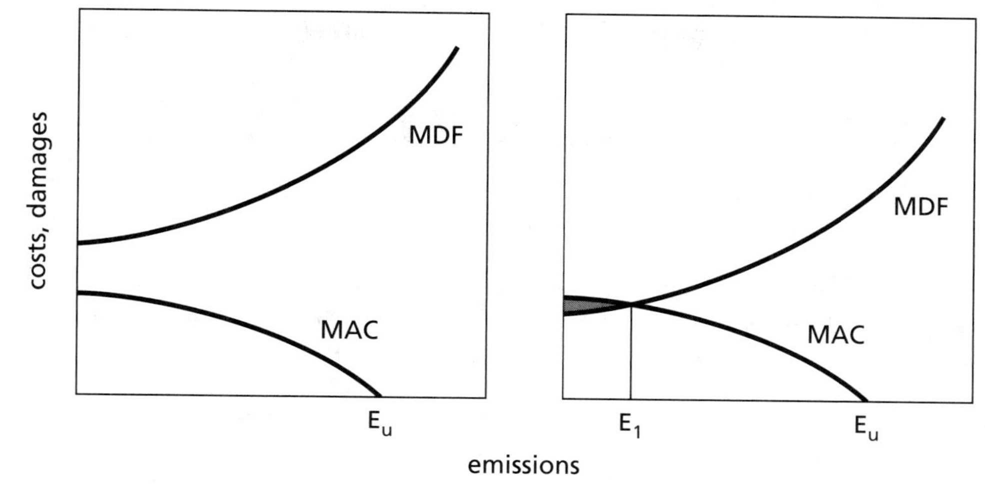

to the costs of implementing a government program (such as pollution taxes) designed to bring society to the optimal level of E_1. Because the costs associated with reducing pollution from the optimal level to zero are relatively small, the cost-minimizing action may be to ban the pollution entirely and not expend the resources needed to achieve the optimal level. This scenario may describe the situation for lead additives in gasoline, which were banned by the U.S. EPA in 1986.

The last set of circumstances in which direct controls may be the preferable policy instrument is in dealing with emergency situations such as smog alerts or droughts. The problem generated by these events is that they temporarily change the nature of the relationship between emissions and damages. For example, if there is a drought that reduces the volume of water in a river, then each unit of pollution that is emitted into the river is less diluted and causes greater damages. Similarly, when a thermal inversion over southern California (or Santiago, São Paulo, or Beijing) traps pollutants in the lower atmosphere, the damages associated with each unit of air pollution increases. In these events, which may occur in a random or unpredictable fashion, taxes may not provide enough flexibility to deal with the new set of circumstances adequately. The nature of the relationships between emissions and damages has changed so much as a result of random events that immediate and drastic action is often warranted. For example, during smog alerts, the Los Angeles area prohibits single-person commuting, requiring carpooling or the use of mass transit. Also, some factories and schools are required to close until the emergency passes.

Pursuing Environmental Quality with Economic Incentives

Command and control policies may be preferable when monitoring is particularly difficult,[9] when the optimal level of pollution is near zero, or during unpredictable emergency events. Most economists, however, advocate general policies based on economic incentives for two primary reasons:

1. Economic incentives minimize total abatement costs by equating the marginal abatement costs across polluters and encouraging a broader array of abatement options.
2. Economic incentives encourage more research and development into abatement technologies and alternatives to the activities that generate the pollution.

Economic Incentives and Minimized Total Abatement Cost

Several times it has been mentioned that economic incentives can equate the marginal abatement costs across all polluters, but this assertion has not yet been demonstrated here. The proof is actually quite simple and can be easily visualized by referring to Figure 3.14.

Assume that a polluter is polluting at the unregulated level of 10 units and the government imposes a tax equal to t dollars per unit of pollution (not per unit of the economic good that the firm produces). If the polluter continues to pollute 10 units, he or she will be liable for 10t dollars in total taxes. The polluter, however, will not continue to pollute 10 units, because he or she will realize that costs can be reduced by reducing the level of pollution. For example, the polluter will consider whether to reduce pollution to 9 units. The cost of the tax on that tenth unit can be visualized graphically as the shaded rectangle with its base between 9 and 10, and its height equal to t. Notice that the cost of abating the tenth unit is the area underneath the marginal abatement cost function between 9 and 10. As visual inspection clearly shows, this abatement cost is less than the cost of the tax, so the polluter saves money by reducing pollution from 10 units to 9 units. This situation will be true as long as the per unit pollution tax is greater than the marginal abatement costs. Conversely, if the tax is less than the marginal abatement cost, the polluter can reduce costs by increasing pollution and paying the lower tax rather than the higher abatement costs. The only level of pollution for which a change cannot reduce total costs (total abatement costs plus tax payments) is when the tax is equal to the marginal abatement costs.

---

[9] For most types of conventional pollution, such as air pollution from factories, the monitoring costs associated with command and control are the same as for economic incentives. When the pollution is sporadic, nonstationary, or emitted by large numbers of small polluters, monitoring becomes more difficult.

Figure 3.14 **Polluter Behavior in the Presence of a Pollution Tax**

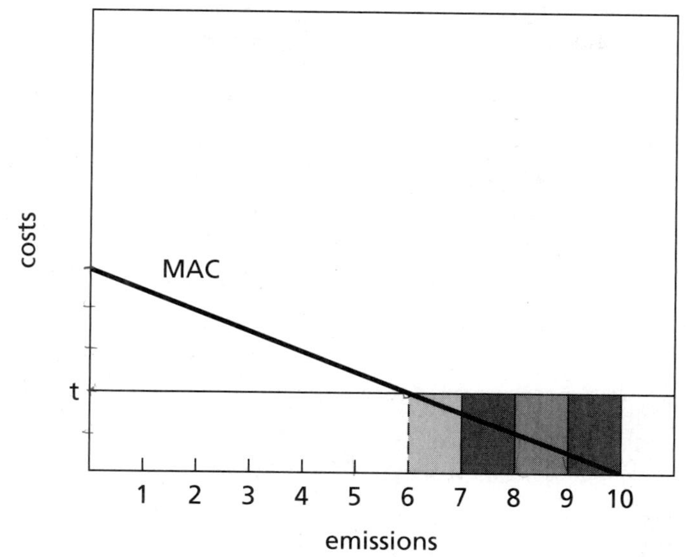

Because any individual polluter will adjust his or her level of emissions to the point where marginal abatement cost is equal to the per unit tax, all polluters will adjust to the point where their marginal abatement costs are equal to the tax. In other words, as long as all polluters face the same tax, a tax will equate the marginal abatement costs across polluters. Thus, a tax on each unit of pollution will minimize the total cost of obtaining the target level of pollution.[10]

---

[10] Mathematically, the proof is quite simple. The proof is set up as if there were only two polluters, but Langrandian optimization can be used to prove the same thing with any number of polluters. Let TAC_1 = the total abatement cost of polluter 1, and let TAC_2 = the total abatement cost for polluter 2. Then the total abatement cost for society is equal to the sum of the total abatement cost of the two polluters. If E* is the target level of pollution, then E can be defined as the level of pollution emitted by polluter 1, and polluter 2's level must be E*–E.

The formal problem is to minimize $TAC = TAC_1(E) + TAC_2(E^*-E)$, by choosing E (which also chooses E*–E since E* is constant.)

To maximize, take the derivative of TAC with respect to E and set equal to zero:

$$dTAC/dE = d\,TAC_1/dE - dTAC_2/dE = 0 \text{ or } dTAC_1/dE = dTAC_2/dE$$

Since $dTAC_1/dE$ is equal to the marginal abatement cost of polluter 1 and $dTAC_2/dE$ is equal to the marginal abatement cost of polluter 2, the maximization condition requires that the two be equal.

Box 3.1 Cigarette and Alcohol Taxes as Externality Taxes

From time to time, there is increased discussion about raising the taxes on cigarettes and alcohol to pay for the cost of health care, programs to reduce cigarette usage by children, driving while driving intoxicated, and so on. Cigarette and alcohol taxes (also called "sin taxes") are often advocated as revenue sources since the demand functions of both goods are inelastic. This inelasticity implies that if price increases, the associated reduction in the quantity demanded is proportionately smaller. Because quantity demanded is relatively insensitive to price increases, increasing the tax will lead to an increase in revenue.

Although these taxes are often viewed simply as revenue raising devices, they can also be interpreted as externality taxes. Cigarette smoking generates externalities associated with secondhand smoke and increased health care costs. Alcohol is associated with many externalities, including driving while intoxicated which is responsible for tens of thousands of traffic fatalities each year. Because both alcohol and cigarettes are associated with external costs, it makes sense to tax them to reduce the external costs. Yet because the demand for these goods is inelastic, large increases in taxes will be necessary to reduce the use of these goods.

Economic Incentives and the Certainty of Attaining the Target Level of Pollution

Although a tax can modify polluters' actions so that the target level of pollution is achieved at minimum total abatement costs, the question of what tax level will induce the target level of pollution is a much more difficult problem to address. If the aggregate marginal abatement cost function is known, the problem becomes trivial. If E_1 in Figure 3.15 is the target level, then t_1 is the tax that will achieve the target level. The problem is determining what tax level should be chosen when the aggregate marginal abatement cost function is not known.

This problem is examined in Figure 3.16, where it is assumed that evidence suggests that the true marginal abatement cost function lies between the upper and lower bounds of MAC_{ub} and MAC_{lb}. Let's further assume that policy makers choose a target level of pollution of E_1 based on this uncertain knowledge of the position of the marginal abatement cost function. Let's also assume, however, that policy makers think that the true marginal abatement cost function is MAC_{lb} and therefore choose a tax of t_1, which would generate a level of emissions of E_1 if MAC_{lb} were the true marginal abatement cost function. If MAC_t describes how polluters actually respond to the tax, however, the level of pollution t_1 would generate would be E_2. Notice that E_2 is

Figure 3.15 **Choosing the Tax When the Aggregate Marginal Abatement Cost Function Is Known**

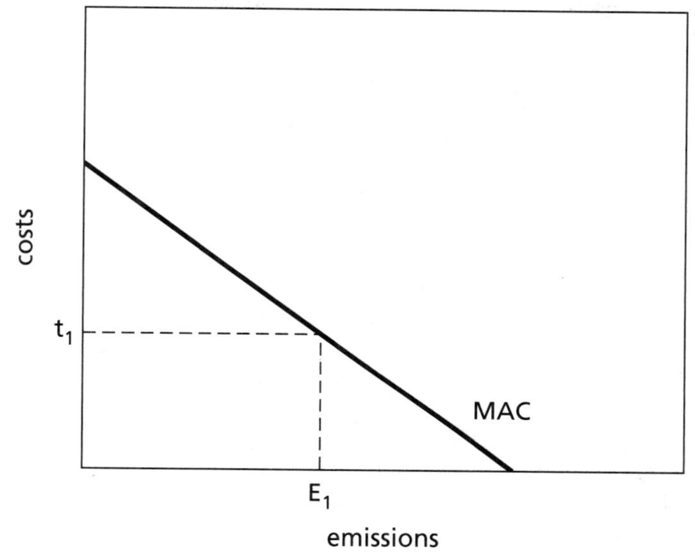

Figure 3.16 **Choosing the Tax when the Aggregate Marginal Abatement Cost Is Not Known**

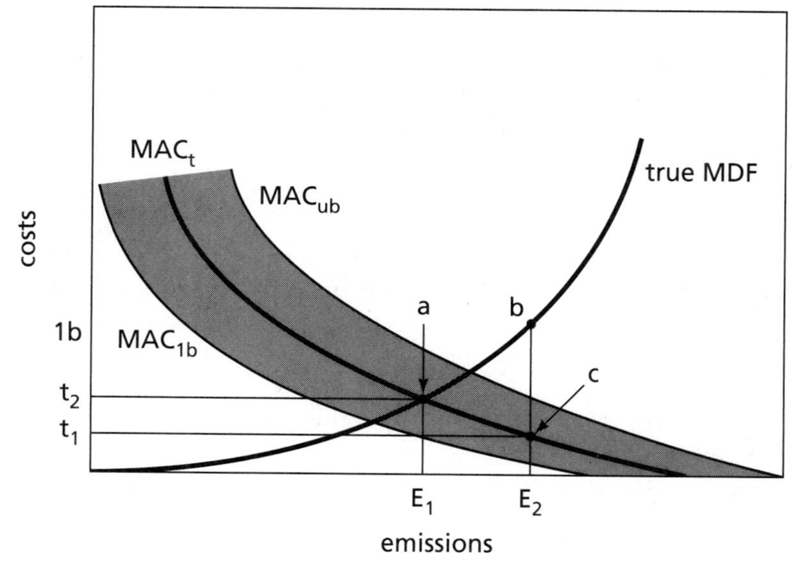

higher than the true optimal level of pollution (E_1) and would generate the excess costs of area abc. In reality, policy makers would have chosen the higher tax (t_2) if they had known how polluters would react to the tax. In an interesting (but somewhat technical) article, Martin Weitzmann (1974) shows that the flatter the marginal abatement cost function, the greater the disparity between the "arrived at" level of pollution and the target level of pollution. Weitzmann also shows that the steeper the marginal damage function, the greater the social losses associated with the disparity between the "arrived at" level of pollution and the target level of pollution. He suggests that with appropriate slopes of the marginal abatement cost and marginal damage functions, quantity restrictions (command and control) may be preferable to price restrictions (pollution taxes). This suggestion represents another apparent argument in favor of command and control policies. Command and control techniques can achieve the target level of pollution with greater certainty than can taxes, because policy makers seldom have perfect prior information on the responses of polluters to the taxes.

In the past, it has been argued that errors in the choice of the pollution tax are not important, because one can iterate toward the correct tax rate: If a tax is chosen that leaves the level of emissions too far above the target level, simply raise the tax in the next period. If a tax is chosen that reduces the level of pollution too far below the target level of pollution, simply lower the tax in the next period. This argument may seem to have some appeal, but it should be realized that pollution control is not generally achieved by changing the level of easily variable inputs such as labor, materials, and energy. In fact, pollution control is relatively capital intensive. Pollution abatement and production technologies that are optimal under one set of taxes would not be chosen under a different set of taxes.

For example, if a carbon tax (to control greenhouse gas emissions) was instituted, the price of gasoline would increase. Let's assume that the price increased from $1.60 to $2.50 per gallon. Consumers would be willing to pay more money for cars that offered better gas mileage, which would be reflected in their purchases. If, however, the pollution control authority then decides that there is still too much carbon dioxide pollution and increases the tax so the price of gasoline rises to $4.00 per gallon, then consumers would want even more efficient cars. Yet they are stuck with their purchasing decisions of the past period. If they sell their existing cars, they will suffer losses on resale value; if they keep driving these cars, they will pay high taxes. Their ability to react to the new situation in a cost-minimizing fashion is constrained by their previous purchase of a capital good. Consumers would have preferred to know about the higher taxes before they made their purchases. The same thing would be true for firms in respect to their capital purchases.

Marketable Pollution Permits

A summary of this discussion of potential policy instruments suggests the following:

1. Pollution taxes are preferable to command and control techniques because they minimize abatement costs and provide other desirable incentives.
2. Under certain conditions, pollution taxes are less proficient than command and control techniques in achieving the target level of pollution.

Because pollution taxes are preferable on one count and command and control techniques are preferable on the other, the choice between the two appears to be a difficult one. Yet it is a choice that does not have to be made, because an instrument exists that can both minimize the total abatement cost and achieve the target level of pollution with a high degree of uncertainty.[11] This instrument is known as the marketable pollution permit.[12]

Marketable Pollution Permits and Efficiency. The institution of a system of marketable pollution permits begins with the determination of the target level of pollution. For the purposes of this discussion, it is assumed that there are 100 polluters and that the target level of pollution is 1000 units. The next step is to determine the allocation of pollution across polluters. For example, one could authorize each polluter to pollute 10 units. So far, that is exactly the same as a command and control policy that specifies the legal amounts of pollution for each polluter. The major difference between a command and control system and a system of marketable pollution permits, however, is that once the initial allocation of pollution is made, polluters are free to buy and sell the rights to pollute.

At first, this ability to buy and sell the rights to pollute may seem to be unimportant, but it is this feature that equates the marginal abatement costs across polluters. Marketable pollution permits (MPPs) equate the marginal costs across polluters because each polluter compares his or her marginal abatement costs with the price of a permit in deciding whether to reduce (increase) pollution by one unit and sell (buy) another permit. For polluters whose marginal abatement costs are greater than the price of a permit, total costs can be reduced by buying more permits and polluting more. For polluters whose marginal abatement costs are less than the price of a permit, profits can be increased by selling permits and polluting less. Polluters will have an incentive to buy or sell permits as long as the price of permits is different than the individual polluter's marginal abatement costs. Because our knowledge of competitive markets tells us that there can be but one equilibrium price for the permits, marginal abatement costs for all polluters will be

[11] Command and control techniques will still be an essential part of environmental policy when monitoring is difficult, when the optimal level of emissions is at or near zero, or in the presence of unpredictable emergency events.

[12] Marketable pollution permits are also referred to as transferable discharge permits, pollution allowances, tradable credits, offsets, and tradable pollution quotas.

equated when the market for permits is in equilibrium. This result is independent of the method that is used to initially distribute the permits. The permits could be given to existing polluters proportional to historic pollution levels, auctioned to the highest bidder, distributed by lottery, or allocated by some other scheme or combination of schemes. One method of distributing permits that is increasingly viewed as a desirable process is to distribute permits based on historical (the level in some base year) economic outputs. For example, if this type of system was applied to the electric utility industry, then a firm that produced 5 percent of the total electricity production would receive 5 percent of the permits. As long as the permits are marketable, polluters' attempts to minimize their total pollution costs (the cost of abatement for pollution that is eliminated plus the cost of permits for pollution that is still emitted) will result in marginal costs being equated across all polluters and the minimization of the total abatement costs of achieving the target level of pollution.

Although the method for the initial allocation of MPPs is irrelevant from an efficiency viewpoint, it is controversial because there are important equity considerations. If permits are auctioned, then a substantial initial cost for polluters (and revenue for the government) is created, but if permits are allocated based on historical levels or lotteries, then an asset for polluters is created.

Marketable Pollution Permits and Geographic Considerations. So far, the discussion of pollution policy has proceeded as if a unit of pollution has the same importance regardless of the location at which it is emitted. For some types of pollution, such as the emission of greenhouse gases or chemicals that deplete the ozone layer, this statement is true. For other types of pollution, however, the geographic location of the emissions can have a profound effect on the damages the pollution generates. For example, air pollution generated in the vicinity of large numbers of people will generate greater health effects, because more people are exposed to the pollution. On the other hand, air pollution emitted downwind from population centers will have very little effect on the health of people in the population centers. In general, if the marginal damage function is increasing at an increasing rate, then geographical concentration of emissions will increase total damages.

Central to the importance of the location of the emissions is the manner in which the pollution disperses when it enters the environment. For example, air pollution tends to disperse in all directions when emitted from a smokestack, but there is a tendency for the pollution to move from west to east, which is the prevailing wind direction in much of North America. For water pollution, the dispersion is downstream, with tidal fluxes, and with wind patterns. As mentioned, geographic location is not relevant for all types of emissions. Pollutants that generate their damages in the upper atmosphere (greenhouse gases and chemicals that deplete the ozone layer) have the same effect regardless of the location of emissions. Thus the establishment of a system of marketable emissions permits is more straightforward, because only one market for emissions need be established.

In contrast, the release of carbon monoxide (from automobile exhaust) in California does not affect air quality in Manhattan, although the release of carbon monoxide in northern Virginia does affect air quality in Washington, D.C. A unit of carbon monoxide released in Raleigh, North Carolina, would create more damages than a unit released in Wilmington, North Carolina (where most of it would blow out over the ocean). For any set of pollution controls to be effective, they must take into consideration the geographic variation in the effect of pollution on society. This consideration is necessary whether one is using taxes or marketable pollution permits.

A tax system would take this variation into account by charging higher taxes in areas where emissions are more damaging. One would expect higher taxes in metropolitan areas, such as Los Angeles, Atlanta, St. Louis, and Chicago, and lower taxes in more rural areas like Wyoming, Alaska, and South Dakota. The policy would consider the effects of one region's pollution on the welfare of other regions. For example, sulfur dioxide taxes in the Midwest should be set with consideration of the effects of these emissions on acid rain in the Northeast.

It is slightly more complex to adapt a marketable pollution permit system to deal with the geographic variability in the effects of emissions. Generally, it must be done by dividing the overall region into subregions. Then, the subregions can be used to account for geographic variability in one of two ways. First, receptors (pollution measurement locations) can be located across the region. They are denoted by the lettered points in Figure 3.17, where the location of a particular polluter is denoted by the circled star. Under this type of receptor-based system (which is often called an ambient-based system), the

Figure 3.17 **Ambient-Based Permit System Marginal Abatement Cost Is Not Known**

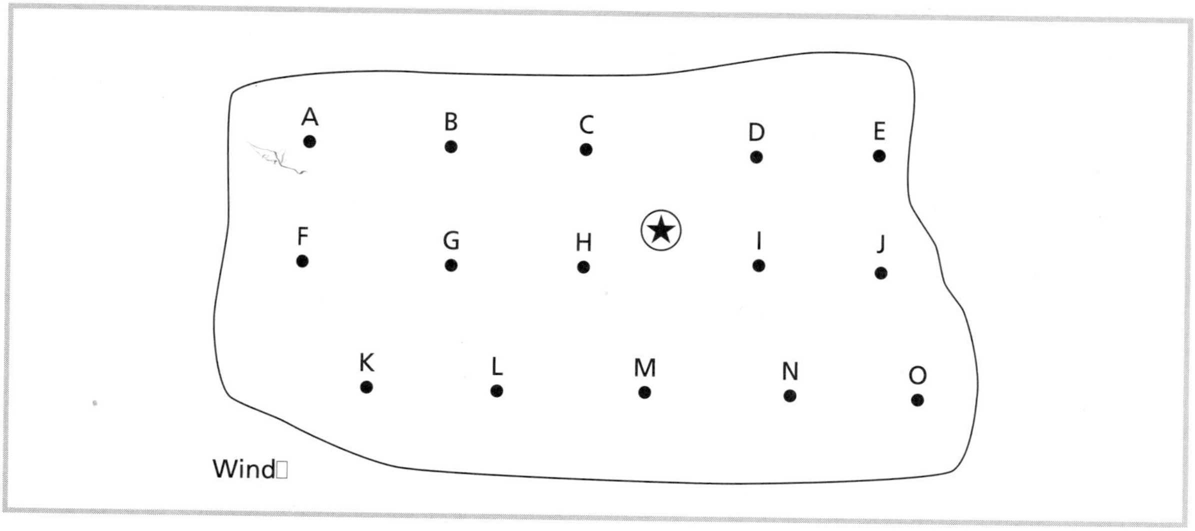

polluter would need to purchase marketable pollution permits based on the effect of his or her pollution on each receptor in the region. Because receptor "I" is relatively close to, and downwind from, the polluter, the polluter would need to purchase more "I" permits than "A" permits, which is farther away and upwind. The effect of a polluter's emissions on the concentration of pollution receptors is determined by dispersion coefficients. Dispersion coefficients are derived from mathematical models of wind, topography, and other factors, and measure the way pollution spreads from its source to other locations. These dispersion coefficients can be used to help define the terms of trade in a marketable pollution permit market. For example, for each unit of pollution that the polluter at the circled star emits, he or she may need to purchase one "I" permit but only one quarter of an "A" permit. The polluter would have to buy 15 different types of permits (one for each receptor, A through O). Although this system does a good job in dealing with the geographic variability in the effect of pollution, it has high administrative and transactions costs associated with it due to the many different markets in which each polluter must participate.

An alternative to the ambient-based system is to establish separate markets for each subregion, where the total number of permits available in each subregion is set with consideration of the effect of pollution from the subregions on the overall region. The polluter need only purchase permits for the subregion in which he or she is located. This emissions-based permit system is illustrated in Figure 3.18. A polluter located at the star would only have to buy permits for subregion L. Although this system greatly reduces transaction costs by limiting the number of markets in which the polluter must

Figure 3.18 **Emissions-Based Permit System**

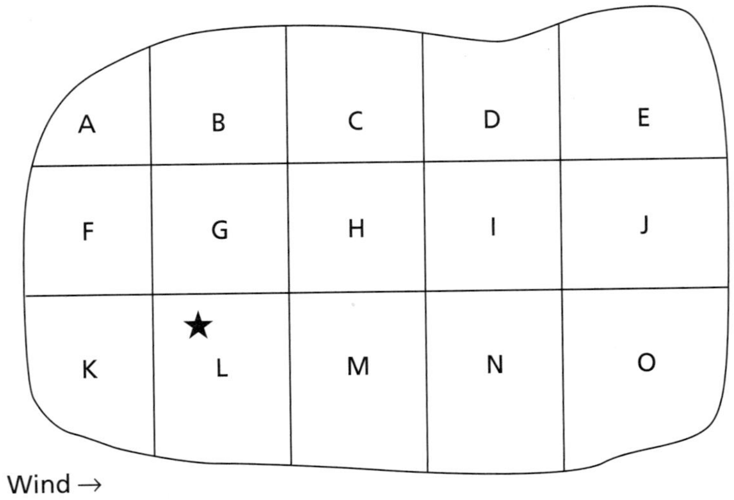

Box 3.2 Disincentives of Economic Incentives in China

China, like many developing countries, has very high levels of air pollution. These high levels of pollution have persisted despite the existence of a pollution tax system for more than two decades. The failure of the Chinese system is a good example of the importance of understanding the incentives associated with the indirect impacts of a system, because the indirect impacts of the system doomed it to failure.

The Chinese system was not established until the nation's first environmental protection law was passed in 1979. This system was based on a command and control system (emissions standards), with an emissions tax that was charged only on emissions that were in excess of the emissions standards. Firms that exceeded the standard for three consecutive years received tax increases of 5 percent per year. Other important features of this system, noted by Blackman and Harrington (1999), include the following:

- Fees are twice as high for new plants to encourage them to install high-quality pollution control equipment.
- New firms that are noncompliant will have their fees increased by 100 percent instead of 5 percent per year.
- Although fees are set by the federal government, local governments are free to increase the fees.
- Fees are charged on 20 different pollutants, but if a firm is noncompliant for more than one pollutant, it only pays fees for the pollutant that generates the largest fee payment.
- The national fee for particulate matter is \$280 to \$700 and is roughly \$280 per ton for most other pollutants, including carbon monoxide, sulfur dioxide, and nitrogen oxides.

Although pollution is somewhat better than before the system was established in 1979, the improvement has not elevated environmental quality to a level that most nations (developed or developing) would regard as acceptable. According to Blackman and Harrington (1999), the improvement that has taken place cannot be attributed to the fee system, and the lack of significant improvement can be blamed on faults of the system.

The first major problem of the system is that the fees are too low. Blackman and Harrington (1999), Florig et al. (1995), Yang et al. (1997) and Yun (1997) all indicated that the emissions fees are well below marginal abatement cost and consequently do not provide much of an incentive for abatement. Fees have only been increased once during the 20-year life of the program; therefore, their effectiveness has been further eroded by inflation. The problem of fees being too low is so bad that in a statistical study of firm-level data, Yang et al. (1997) found that fees are so low in comparison to marginal abatement costs that even firms that have already installed abatement equipment have little incentive to limit their emissions.

(continues)

Box 3.2 (continued)

This problem is not even the biggest one associated with the Chinese system. As stated earlier, provisions of this system generate a set of indirect impacts that doom the system to ineffectiveness. As Blackman and Harrington (1999) argue, these provisions create incentives for both firms and the local pollution control boards that perpetuate noncompliance. The first problem is that the firms are allowed to include emission-fee-payments as production costs. This provision further erodes the fee's effectiveness because of the savings on profit taxes that the deductibility of the fees generates. The second and even greater problem is that 80 percent of the fees a firm pays are returned to the firm for the alleged purpose of investing in pollution control. Of course, difficulty in monitoring and the lack of political will by local pollution boards to enforce the law means that much of the rebated pollution fees are used for purposes other than pollution control. With a 33 percent tax rate on profits, if all emissions fees can be counted as production costs and if 80 percent of the fees are rebated, noncompliance can actually increase the profitability of firms. This point was echoed by Yun (1997), who found that many firms actually view the fee as "depositing money in a bank" and often intentionally overpay their pollution taxes so as to reduce their general tax liabilities. The local pollution boards also have an incentive to perpetuate noncompliance, because they receive their entire operating budget from the pollution fees. No fees are paid for pollution levels below the standard, so these governmental bodies only have funds if there is noncompliance.

The return of the emissions fees to the firms erodes most of the incentive to comply, because the fees are returned in direct proportion to the amount of fees they pay, which is in direct proportion to how much they pollute. Therefore, the more a firm pollutes, the more money is returned to the firm. If the government is going to return tax payments to the firm (which makes the tax system much more politically acceptable to industry), it must return the taxes in a fashion that is independent of how much pollution a firm generates. Chapters 8 and 9 present discussion of some systems from Sweden and other places that work well.

participate, it does have an important shortcoming: a polluter located in one subregion cannot trade with a polluter located in another subregion. This restriction is bothersome, because there could be polluters in one subregion with a relatively low abatement cost function and polluters in another subregion with a relatively high marginal abatement cost function. Even though it would be in both the public and private interest for the high-cost polluter to buy permits from the low-cost polluter (and for the high-cost polluter to pollute less and the low-cost polluter to pollute more), this scenario would not be permissible under an emissions-based system. More trades could take place if each subregion constituted a larger fraction of the overall region, but if the subregions become larger, then the division into subregions does not do as good a job accounting for the geographic variability in the effect of emissions.

Alan Krupnick, Wallace Oates, and Eric Van de Verg (1983) suggest a compromise system that allows more trades but with lower transaction costs. Many different receptors would be defined, as in the ambient-based system. There would, however, be only one type of permit for the overall system, and any polluters could trade emissions (buy and sell marketable pollution permits) provided that their trade does not result in the ambient air quality standards being violated at any receptor point. Although this system has some important advantages, it treats increases in pollution at a particular receptor that do not result in the violation of the standard as having no social cost.

Other Types of Economic Incentives

Although pollution taxes and marketable pollution permits receive most of the attention of policy analysts, they cannot be applied to all environmental problems. However, even when taxes or permits cannot be successfully implemented, economic incentives for environmental performance can be created through the implementation of deposit-refund, subsidy bonding, and liability systems.

Deposit-refunds. Many students are familiar with deposit-refunds as a means of controlling environmental externalities. Many countries and states or provinces within a country now have deposit-refund regulations in place for beverage containers (primarily beer and soda). Deposit-refund systems are a good way of employing economic incentives when monitoring costs are high.

For example, the monitoring costs of making sure that everyone properly disposed of their soda cans are extremely high. The social costs associated with improper disposal are not likely to exceed several cents a can. In most cases, the private benefits of improper disposal are likely to be several cents per can as well. Figure 3.19 shows the hypothetical social cost associated with improper disposal as well as the hypothetical private benefits of improper disposal. Let's assume that proper disposal means that the beverage containers are collected for recycling. In this case, the social costs could include aesthetic values associated with reduced littering as well as the costs of landfill space and the environmental externalities associated with the use of energy to produce containers from new metal, glass, or plastic. The private benefits of improper disposal are the inconvenience and other costs that the consumer avoids with improper disposal. In this illustration, the optimal amount of improper disposal is about 40 percent of total beverage containers.

One way to achieve the optimal level of improper disposal is to set a tax equal to five cents for each container that is not disposed of properly. Because

Figure 3.19 **Costs and Benefits of Improper Disposals**

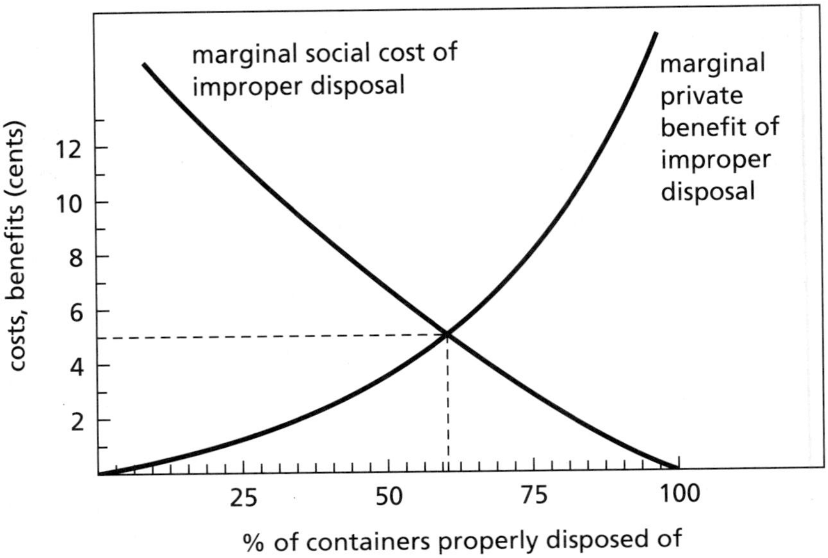

the marginal private benefits of improper disposal are less than five cents for 60 percent of the containers, the consumers would suffer the lost benefits rather than pay the tax, and 60 percent of the containers would be disposed of properly. A tax such as this one, however, would be difficult to enforce because there are virtually unlimited opportunities for improper disposal, making monitoring costs high.

A deposit-refund system is similar to a tax, but instead of making the individual pay for undesirable acts as they occur, the individual pays up front and then is rewarded if he or she acts properly. A five-cent deposit would be collected upon purchase and is refunded when the container is returned. Although the most apparent example of the deposit-refund system is beverage containers, it has been used on cars in Scandinavia and batteries in many countries, especially in Europe. It has also been suggested for use with tires, CFCs in refrigerator coils (see Chapter 6), and containers of toxic household products (such as pesticides or paints; see Chapter 16).

Bonding Systems. Bonding systems are closely related to deposit-refund systems. With bonding systems, a potential degrader of the environment is required to place a large sum of money in an escrow account. The money will be returned if the environment is left undamaged (or returned to its original condition); otherwise, it will be forfeited. The size of the bond should be large enough to ensure appropriate safeguards by those posting the bond or large enough that the government can use the funds to clean up damage if it occurs. Bonds are employed in strip-mining areas, whereby mining companies forfeit the bond if the land is not returned to its original condition. Bonds have also been suggested for companies that have leases to cut trees in public forests (see Chapter 13) and for companies that transport oil or toxic substances (see Chapters 8 and 16).

Liability Systems. Liability systems are based on defining legal liability for the damages caused by certain types of pollution discharges and facilitating the collection of these damages. The Comprehensive Environmental Response, Compensation and Liability Act of 1980 (CERCLA) defines legal rights to natural resources for local, state, and federal governments and specifies methods by which damages may be measured. The provisions of this act provide a means for facilitating the incorporation of the expected social cost of spills into the private cost calculation by potential polluters or internalizing the expected damages of spills. CERCLA increases the probability that the firm will have to pay the social cost of its spills, so the firm is more likely to take appropriate safety measures.

A related system is to define legal liability as above and then require potential polluters to obtain full insurance against any damages they might generate. The idea behind this system is that the insurance industry would then require appropriate safety measures on the part of potential polluters. This type of system has been suggested for generators, haulers, and disposers of toxic waste.

One potential problem with insurance is the problem of moral hazard. In this case, moral hazard would exist because people with insurance are more likely to engage in risky behavior. For example, a person with theft insurance for his or her car is more likely to park the car in a high car-theft area than someone with no auto insurance. The implications of moral hazard for environmental liability systems is that mining companies, toxic waste haulers, or oil transport companies might take fewer safety measures if the insurance company protects them against losses associated with their activities. Moral hazard is not a problem, however, if the insurance companies can detect risky behavior and incorporate it into insurance premiums, so the riskier the behavior, the higher the insurance premiums. For example, people with speeding tickets pay more for auto insurance than safer drivers. For this reason, insurance companies often send inspectors to ensure that their policyholders are using the appropriate methods.

Pollution Subsidies. The last type of economic incentive to be discussed is the per-unit pollution subsidy, which pays the polluter a fixed amount of money for each unit of pollution that is reduced. This type of incentive is depicted in Figure 3.20, where s is the amount paid per unit of pollution that is reduced. In this example, the polluter pollutes 10 units in an unregulated environment. If the subsidy system is imposed, the polluter will evaluate his or her tenth unit of pollution and discover that the cost of abating it is less than the payment that would be received for abating it. Thus, the polluter

Figure 3.20 **Polluter Behavior in the Presence of a Per-Unit Pollution Subsidy**

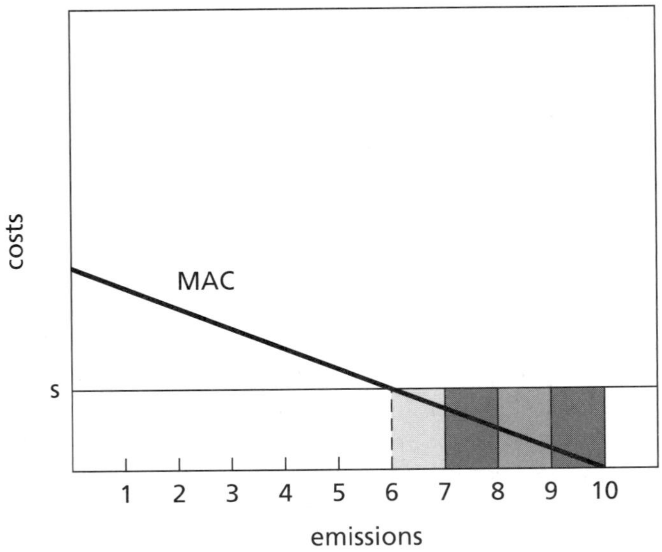

would make a net profit by reducing pollution from 10 units to 9 units. This situation would be true as long as the per-unit subsidy is greater than the cost of abatement. The polluter will reduce pollution to the point where the subsidy is equal to the marginal cost of abatement. Remember that under the tax system, pollution was reduced until the point where the tax was equal to marginal abatement cost. Therefore, if the amount of the per-unit subsidy is equal to the amount of the per-unit tax, the two systems will generate identical behavior on the part of an individual polluter.

For many years, economists argued that tax and subsidy systems had equivalent efficiency effects although different distributional effects, the most notable being that the subsidy system transfers resources toward polluters because they are receiving a payment rather than making a payment. Other potential problems with subsidies include lack of political acceptability (politicians would be reluctant to support a system that paid polluters, due to potential adverse reaction by voters) and the possibility of strategic behavior (increasing the initial amount of pollution before the system goes into place so that a larger subsidy can be obtained). An additional problem was articulated later in the discussion (Baumol and Oates, 1988, pp. 211–234): Although taxes and subsidies have equivalent effects on an individual polluter, they have quite different effects on the number of polluters. Quite simply stated, subsidies make firms more profitable, so although both reduce the amount of pollution per polluter, there will be more polluters under a subsidy system than under a tax system. A subsidy system that reduced the amount of pollution per polluter could actually result in an increase in the amount of pollution if enough new firms entered the market due to the increased profitability generated by the subsidy. This situation is very similar to the one discussed with the Coase theorem, where the definition of property rights had an important effect on the number of polluters.

Hence, a powerful argument that subsidies may be an inferior policy instrument, especially in comparison with per unit pollution taxes, has been established. In the case of small firms or farmers in the informal sector of the economy in developing countries, however, subsidies could play an important

Box 3.3 The Movement Toward Economic Incentives

The first 30 years of environmental policy saw little in the way of economic incentives, but we are increasingly moving in this direction throughout the world. The United States has moved primarily in the direction of marketable pollution permits, with permit systems established to help control sulfur dioxide emissions. This program is relatively young but has generally had good results and is discussed further in Chapters 8 and 9. Europe has moved more in the direction of pollution taxes, with very innovative systems developed in Sweden and other countries.

Some countries have developed economic incentives that have not worked well. Box 3.2 discusses China's experience with pollution taxes, which have not been effective. Poland and other Eastern European countries have had similar problems with ineffectively designed systems.

A very interesting situation is developing with many countries in South America that are privatizing formally state-owned enterprises, such as electric power companies, mining companies, and petroleum production and refining companies. As state-owned enterprises, environmental regulation was often internal. As these enterprises are sold to private firms or as competition from private firms is invited, however, there is a need for the development of formal environmental policy. Given that the move for privatization has emerged from the growing "market economy" movement in South America, it is not surprising that many countries are discussing the idea of economic incentives to control emissions from these newly privatized industries. It would be a mistake, however, to think that this movement is solely driven by ideological perspective. In reality, these countries have seen the inefficiencies created by the old systems of command and control in developed countries, how developed countries are moving away from these systems, and the opportunity to avoid making some of these same mistakes.

role. The reason is that these types of activities are difficult to monitor because of their mobility. In addition, the participants generally have few assets with which to pay a tax (or penalty, in the case of direct controls.) In these cases, a carefully constructed subsidy system might be effective, but caution must be exercised to avoid the problem of entry. Examples of this type of subsidy system are more fully discussed in Chapters 13 and 18.

Summary

The market failures associated with environmental externalities generate losses in welfare. Despite the arguments advanced by Ronald Coase, government intervention may be necessary to reduce the magnitude of these social losses.

Command and control policies form the basis of current environmental policy in the United States and in many other nations. Although these policies may be preferable under certain conditions (the presence of high monitoring costs, the possibility of unpredictable emergency events, or the case when the optimal level of release is at or near zero), command and control policies do not equate the marginal abatement costs across polluters. They also restrict the options available to control pollution. Consequently, command and control policies do not minimize the costs of obtaining the target level of environmental quality.

Economic incentives, such as taxes and marketable pollution permits, do equate the marginal abatement costs across polluters and therefore minimize the costs of obtaining the target level of environmental quality. Taxes have a shortcoming in that the response of polluters to the taxes is not known in advance, so the level of pollution induced by the taxes may differ substantially from the target level of pollution. The more elastic the marginal abatement cost function, the more likely it is to be a problem. Marketable pollution permits, however, do not suffer from this problem and generate the target level of pollution with much more certainty. In addition, economic incentives create additional motivation for technological innovation in developing better ways to reduce pollution.

In conclusion, this chapter demonstrated important social benefits that can be realized by the use of economic incentives in environmental policy, but current environmental policy (both in the United States and elsewhere) tends to be based almost entirely on direct controls. There is, however, increasing movement towards economic incentives.

Although this chapter has reached its conclusion, the examination of these issues has not. In future chapters, problems such as the use of fossil fuels, global warming, the depletion of the ozone layer, water pollution, deforestation, loss of biodiversity, and depletion of marine resources are discussed in the context of the different types of environmental policy instruments. In particular, how economic incentives and command and control policies are currently used to control these problems and how they can be used more effectively are examined.

Review Questions

1. What types of environmental problems are best handled with deposit-refund systems?
2. What are the five broad classes of policy instruments available to the government to correct market failures associated with externalities?
3. Describe how the various policy instruments give differential incentives for research and development of new production and abatement technologies.
4. What is the Coase theorem? Does it have important implications for environmental policy?
5. Show how an economic incentive system can minimize total abatement costs.
6. Assume that a society is composed of two polluters, with the marginal abatement costs of polluters 1 and 2, respectively, equal to

$$MAC_1 = 18 - E_1$$
$$MAC_2 = 12 - 2E_2$$

where MAC_c refers to the marginal abatement costs of $polluter_c$ and E_c refers to the level of emissions of $polluter_c$. What is the unregulated level of pollution for each polluter? Find the total slevel of emissions that would be generated if a per-unit pollution tax of $4.00 were imposed. Perform the same exercise for taxes of $6.00 and $8.00.

7. Given the same two marginal abatement cost functions in question 6, find the market price of a marketable pollution permit if pollution is limited to 18 units through the issuance of marketable pollution permits.
8. Given the same two marginal abatement cost functions in question 6, find the marginal abatement cost of each firm if both were to reduce its pollution levels by 50 percent from the unregulated levels of emissions.
9. Given a societal marginal abatement cost function of:

$$MAC = 100 - 3E$$

and a societal marginal damage function of

$$MD = 2E$$

find the optimal level of pollution and the per-unit pollution tax that would achieve it.

MAC < tax
abate more

10. MAC_1 and MAC_2 are two different societal marginal abatement cost functions:

Which is more likely to be associated with an optimal level of pollution that is at or near zero? Why?

$$MAC_1 = 10 - 0.2E$$
$$MAC_2 = 1/E$$

Questions for Further Study

1. What issues must be considered in the development of marketable pollution permit systems?
2. How would you counter the argument that economic incentive systems (such as pollution taxes and marketable pollution permit systems) are immoral because they sell the right to do something that is bad for society?
3. Use what you have learned about environmental policy to develop a policy for the parking problem on your campus.
4. Use what you have learned about environmental policy to develop a policy for the problem of large numbers of students being closed out of classes. (Assume that you cannot hire more professors and cannot make professors teach more or larger classes.)
5. Under what conditions would per-unit pollution taxes be preferable to marketable pollution permits?
6. Why are pollution subsidies not given serious attention as environmental policy instruments?
7. What issues must be addressed when establishing a system of marketable pollution permits?
8. Are economic incentives likely to be effective in controlling environmental degradation arising from nonmarket activities, such as subsistence farming or fishing in developing countries?
9. Compare the advantages and disadvantages of marketable pollution permits and per-unit pollution taxes.

Suggested Paper Topics

1. Choose a local or regional pollution problem and develop a system of controls (economic incentives, command and control policies, or a combination of both) that best deals with the problem. Make sure to look at the literature (*Journal of Environmental Economics and Management, Land Economics, Journal of Environmental Management*) to see what others have suggested or done in analogous circumstances. Discuss the implications of your choices and justify them over alternatives. Check local newspapers, environmental groups, or your professors for suggested problems. Develop background information from newspapers and local authorities. Then, develop your plan by comparing your problem to others that have been analyzed in the literature.
2. Analyze the marketable pollution permit provisions of Title IV (Acid Precipitation) of the 1990 Clean Air Act Amendments. Look at issues such as how markets are defined, who participates, the initial allocation, and local emissions effects. Suggest changes that could improve the way the market is established. Check the references to Chapters 8 and 9 for more information on these amendments. Also, look at recent issues of the *Journal of Environmental Economics and Management, Land Economics*, and the *Rand Journal of Economics*. Search bibliographic databases using *pollution trading, sulfur dioxide, acid rain*, and *1990 Clean Air Act Amendments* as keywords.
3. Write a survey paper about the use of deposit-refund systems to control environmental externalities. The article by Porter and the book by Bohm (see Works Cited and Selected Readings) are a good place to start your search for references.
4. Investigate the role of property rights in mitigating environmental externalities. Search for references in the *Journal of Economic Literature* and in the bibliographic databases, using *environment, pollution*, and *property rights* as keywords.
5. Look at the use of economic incentives in developing countries. Focus on a particular country and discuss the incentive properties of its systems. Compare this system to other systems in developing and developed countries. The article by Blackburn and Harriman is a good place to start.

Works Cited and Selected Readings

Anderson, F., A. Kneese, P. Reed, S. Taylor, S.T. Taylor. *Environmental Improvement through Economic Incentives*. Washington, DC: Resources for the Future, 1977.

Barde, J. Environmental Taxation: Experience in OECD Countries. 223–227 in EcoTaxation, edited by T. O'Riordan, London: Earthscan, 1997.

Baumol, W. J., and W. E. Oates. *The Theory of Environmental Policy*. London: Cambridge University Press, 1988.

Blackman, A., and W. Harrington. The Use of Economic Incentives in Developing Countries: Lessons from International Experience with Industrial Air Pollution. Discussion Paper 99-39. Washington, DC: Resources for the Future, 1999.

Bohm, P. *Deposit-Refund Systems: Theory and Applications to Environmental Conservation and Consumer Policy*. Washington, DC: Resources for the Future, 1981.

Burrows, P. *The Economic Theory of Pollution Control*. Cambridge, MA: MIT Press, 1980.

Coase, R. H. The Problem of Social Cost. *Journal of Law and Economics 3* (1960): 1–44.

Dales, J. H. Land, Water and Ownership. *Canadian Journal of Economics* 1968. Reprinted in R. Dorfman and N. S. Dorfman, *Economics of the Environment*. New York: W. W. Norton, 1993.

Florig, H. K., W. Spofford, Z. Ma, X.Y. Ma. China Strives to Make the Polluter Pay: Are China's Market-Based Incentives for Improved Environmental Compliance Working? *Environmental Science and Technology* 29 June (1995): 268–273

Freeman, A. M. Depletable Externalities and Pigouvian Taxes. *Journal of Environmental Economics and Management* 11 (1984): 173–179.

Hahn, R. W. Economic Prescriptions for Environmental Problems: How the Patient Followed the Doctor's Orders. *Journal of Economic Perspectives* 3 (1989): 95–114.

Joeres, E. F., and M. H. David. *Buying a Better Environment: Cost—Effective Regulation through Permit Trading*. Madison: University of Wisconsin Press, 1983.

Krupnick, A., W. E. Oates, and E. Van de Verg. On Marketable Pollution Permits: The Case for a System of Pollution Offsets. *Journal of Environmental Economics and Management* 10 (1983): 233–247.

Oates, W. E., Markets for Pollution Control. *Challenge* (1984): 11–17.

Organization for Economic Cooperation and Development (OECD). Evaluating Economic Instruments for Environmental Policy. Paris: OECD, 1997.

Pearce, D. and K. Turner. *Economics of Natural Resources and the Environment*. Hertfordshire, UK: Harvester Wheatsheaf, 1990.

Pigou, A. C. *The Economics of Welfare*. London: Macmillan, 1938.

Porter, R. C. A Social Benefit-Cost Analysis of Beverage Containers: A Correction. *Journal of Environmental Economics and Management* 10 (1983): 191–193.

Portney, P. R., and R. C. Dower. *Public Policies for Environmental Protection*. Washington, DC: Resources for the Future, 1990.

Reilly, W. K. Administrator's Preface. In A. Carlin, *The United States Experience with Economic Incentives to Control Environmental Pollution.* Washington, DC: U.S. Environmental Protection Agency, 1992.

Spence, A. M. and M. L. Weitzman, Regulatory Strategies for Pollution Control. in *Economics of the Environment: Selected Readings*, edited by R. Dorfman and N. Dorfman. New York: W.W. Norton, 1994.

Stavins, R. and B. Whitehead. The Greening of America's Taxes. Progressive Policy Institute Policy Report, February 1992.

Tietenberg, T. H. *Emissions Trading: An Exercise in Reforming Pollution Policy*. Washington, DC: Resources for the Future, 1985.

Weitzman, M. L. Prices vs. Quantities. *The Review of Economic Studies* 41 (1974): 477–499.

Yang, J., D. Cao, and D. Want. The Air Pollution Charge System in China: Practices and Reform. 67–87 in *Applying Market-Based Instruments to Environmental Policies in China and OECD Countries*. Paris: OECD, 1997.

Yun, P. The Pollution Charge System in China: An Economic Incentive? Working paper. Beijing: Renmin University, 1997.

chapter 4

Valuing the Environment

> *The same thing is good and true for all men, but the pleasant differs from one and another.*
>
> *Democritus (c. 460–370 B.C.), in Henry Spiegel,* The Growth of Economic Thought

Introduction

Chapter 3 looked at the question of how the proper development of environmental policy can efficiently and effectively help us achieve our environmental objective. This chapter (and Chapter 5) pursues the question of how we should identify our environmental objectives. One aspect of this process is the measurement of both the value of environmental resources and the value of changes in the level of environmental quality. This kind of information is essential in determining the benefits of environmental policy, which must be compared to the costs of obtaining these environmental goals.

For example, in the late 1980s, substantial problems resulted from debris washing ashore on Atlantic Ocean beaches, particularly in the New York/New Jersey area. Beaches closed, marine recreational activity dropped off precipitously, and seafood sales fell because people were afraid to eat seafood. As it turned out, a major source of the debris problem was, and still is, the New York City combined sanitary and storm sewer system, which overflowed and bypassed the treatment facilities whenever there was significant rainfall.

For there to be significant improvement in beach and water quality, New York City must overhaul its sewer system at a cost that is likely to exceed $15 billion. Is it worth it? Not only is it important to measure value for the evaluation of a particular project, it is important to measure value when comparing alternative projects. For example, it has been estimated that the costs of completely cleaning one former weapons production facility in eastern Washington (Hanford) is roughly $50 billion. Should we spend $50 billion to clean up the coastal environment all along the Atlantic Coast, should we invest the money in preserving tropical rain forests, should we spend $50 billion to clean up a contaminated, but isolated, former weapons facility, or should we not do any of these projects? Is it worth higher energy costs to have less air pollution? Should we forgo oil production to protect the Artic National Wildlife Reserve? Should we accept energy taxes to reduce the global warming problem? As might be expected, questions of how much we should spend on improving environmental quality, and what areas of environmental quality should be emphasized, cannot be resolved unless the value of clean beaches, healthy ecosystems, clean water, and all the other environmental resources is clearly understood.

Some of the biggest environmental policy questions focus on this valuation issue. For example, how aggressive should the nations of the world be in reducing greenhouse gas emissions? The answer to this question is a function of the magnitude of social losses associated with climate change, but how do we measure these losses? Similar points can be made about protecting the rain forest, preserving habitat, or any other environmental issue.

Chapter 3 focused on alternative policies for achieving a target level of environmental quality. Chapters 4 and 5 focus on how a society might choose its environmental policy goals. This process begins in this chapter, which focuses on methods for measuring the change in social welfare associated with a change in environmental quality. Chapter 5 looks at how this information can be combined with other types of information in the environmental decision-making process. This chapter is only a short introduction to the valuation question. Even a two-semester course sequence could not address all the important aspects of this topic.

Before discussing methods for the measurement of value, it would be useful to define value. Value is used in two ways in social and economic analysis. First, it is used as a concept to express the benefit that a good, service, or activity generates. For example, one measure of the value of a college education is the increase in your future income that will be generated as a result of the education. Second, value is used to reflect an individual's or society's norms or guiding principles of behavior. One of the reasons that you went to college was because you and your family value higher education; that is, higher education is an objective in itself, independent of any other benefits it might generate.

In this chapter, the focus is on the first concept of value, the benefits that an individual or society obtains from a good or service. This concept of value provides the opportunity to develop a criterion for evaluating policy choices. This concept is that of economic efficiency, which seeks to maximize social welfare as measured by this notion of value as benefits to individuals or communities of individuals. The other notion of value is further discussed in

Chapter 5, where a broad range of additional decision-making criteria will be discussed. These criteria include equity, ethics, environmental justice, and sustainability. For now, however, the focus is on an economic perspective of value and the associated decision-making criteria of economic efficiency.

What Is Value?

The first point that distinguishes the economic view of value from other perspectives is that it is an anthropocentric concept. In the economic perspective, value is determined by people and not by either natural law or government. Although government representatives may have their own values and may incorporate these values into policy, their values do not necessarily reflect society's values. Here, the distinction between the first notion of value (the benefit of a good or service) and the second notion of value (norms or guiding principles of behavior) is very useful.

The second point is that value is determined by peoples' willingness to make trade-offs, as best seen with market goods, where the willingness to make trade-offs is reflected in peoples' willingness to pay a monetary price for the good. In other words, when an individual spends money on one good, there is less money available to spend on other goods. First, how value is measured for market goods is examined, followed by the measurement of value for nonmarket goods, with an emphasis on environmental resources and environmental quality.

For market goods, the inverse demand curve represents a marginal willingness to pay function. For example, in Figure 4.1, P_1 represents how much people are willing to pay for an additional unit of the good, given that Q_1 units are already being consumed. The total willingness to pay for Q_1 units is represented by the shaded area. Although the shaded area represents the total value or the total benefit associated with the Q_1 units of the good, total benefit is not usually an appropriate measure of the contribution of the good to society's well-being, because the cost of producing the good is not taken into account. The resources that are used to produce this good could be used to produce other goods that would benefit society, so these resource costs must be subtracted from total value to yield net value.

Total resource costs can be examined with the aid of the marginal cost function. In Figure 4.2, the relevant resource cost associated with Q_1 units of the good is given by the area under the marginal cost function, or the shaded triangle $0BQ_1$. This notion of cost may be somewhat confusing to students who are aware that total revenue is equal to area $0P_1BQ_1$. Because total revenue must equal total cost in a perfectly competitive market, it seems as if total costs should be area $0P_1BQ_1$ and not $0BQ_1$. The resolution to this apparent contradiction is that area $0P_1BQ_1$ contains producers' surplus (sometimes referred to as economic rent), which represents the benefit gained by society from having these resources utilized in their most productive application. Only the opportunity cost (the productivity of these

Figure 4.1 **Marginal and Total Willingness to Pay**

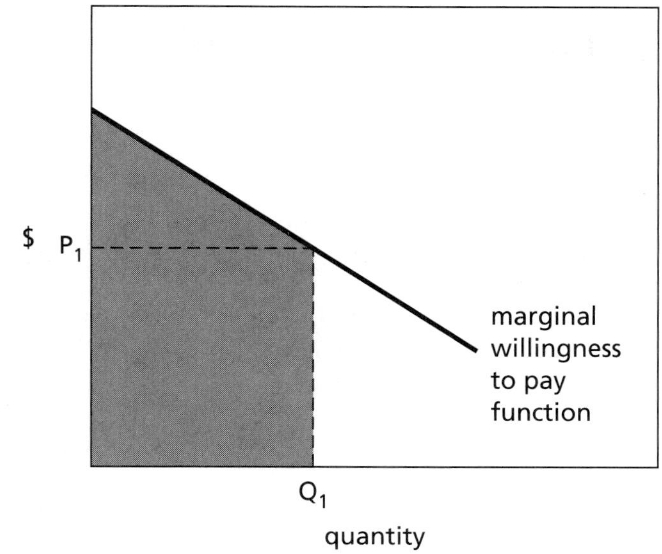

Figure 4.2 **Opportunity Cost, Consumers' Surplus, and Producers' Surplus**

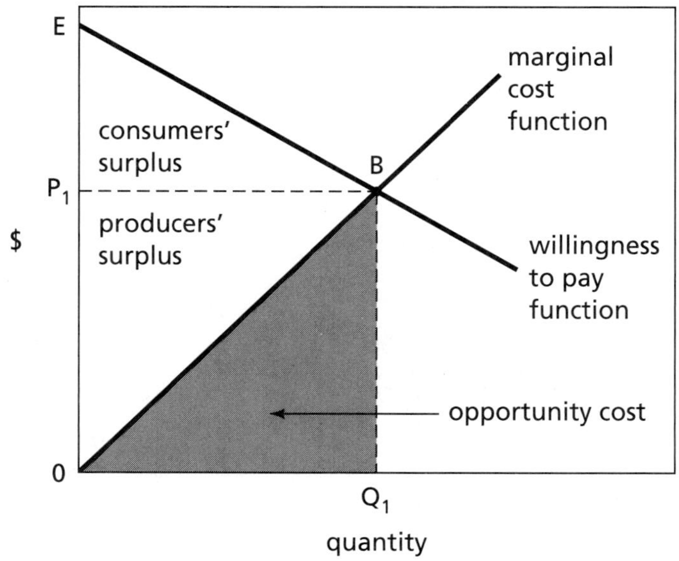

resources in their next most productive application) is subtracted from total value. Opportunity cost is represented by the area under the marginal cost function, which is the shaded area in Figure 4.2. Net value is therefore equal to area 0BE, which for market goods is equal to the sum of consumers' surplus (EP_1B) and producers' surplus (P_10B).

This concept of the measurement of net benefits can be applied to some environmental problems in a rather straightforward fashion. For example, one of the impacts of air pollution is to reduce the productivity of both agriculture and forestry. In other words, both agricultural crops (such as soybeans, cotton, or corn) and tree crops (such as southern pine, oak, or maple) produce less economic output per acre in a more polluted environment than a less polluted environment.

Figure 4.3 shows this process, where the loss in productivity is reflected by the leftward shift of the marginal function from MC_1 to MC_2. The loss in net economic benefits associated with the reduced productivity generated by the pollution is equal to area ABCD. In actuality, the measurement process is more complicated than this one, because the market for soybeans is connected to the market for other grains such as corn through both the demand and the supply sides of the market. Farmers may elect to plant a different crop, or they may plant more or less acres as a result of the loss of productivity. Economists use complicated models that show the connectivity of markets when analyzing this type of issue, but the basic concept is the same as in

Figure 4.3 **Loss in Economic Benefits from Soybeans Associated with an Increase in Pollution**

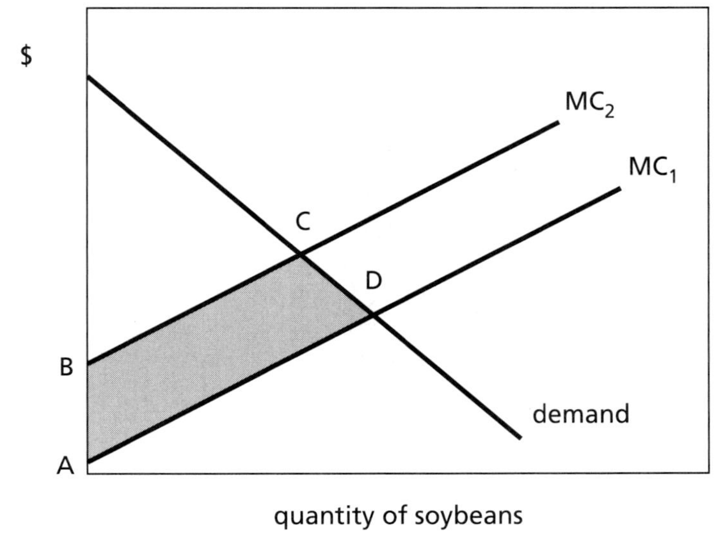

Table 4.1 Effect on Agricultural Sector of Changes in Tropospheric Ozone and Atmosphere Deposition of Nitrogen

	Change in Surplus (updated to billions of 2003 dollars)		
% Changes in ozone	**Consumers**	**Producers**	**Total**
–10	1.15	–0.067	1.08
–25	2.4	0.14	2.54
+10	–1.53	0.31	–1.21
+25	–3.90	0.66	–3.23

	Change in Surplus (updated to billions of 2003 dollars)		
%Changes in nitrogen	**Consumers**	**Producers**	**Total**
Yield based analysis: –50	–0.24	0.0044	–0.24
Yield based analysis: +50	0.33	0.020	0.35
Cost based analysis: –50	–0.017	–0.80	–0.10

Source: *1990 Integrated Assessment Report*, p. 401–402.

Figure 4.3. An example of this type of analysis can be seen in the research that was conducted for the National Acid Precipitation Assessment Program (NAPAP) in the 1980s and was the research upon which the 1990 Clean Air Act Amendments (CAAA) were based. Table 4.1 looks at increases and decreases in different types of pollution and shows the changes in consumers' and producers' surplus.

Unfortunately, this process is not as easy for nonmarket goods as for market goods. Because we do not observe prices for nonmarket goods, we cannot estimate demand and supply curves in a straightforward fashion. Nonetheless, we can use a variety of techniques to look at the willingness to pay or willingness to make trade-offs (such as expenditures of time) to obtain a nonmarket good or to attain access to a nonmarket good associated with higher environmental quality.

Value and Nonmarket Goods

Although money is one thing people give up or trade to obtain goods, it need not be the only thing that people sacrifice to obtain more of a market or nonmarket good. Time or other opportunities are sacrificed to obtain both market and nonmarket goods,[1] and an examination of these trade-offs can serve as a basis for valuing goods that have no market price.

Nonmarket goods may have both direct use and indirect use values. Direct use values are those associated with tangible uses of environmental resources, such as when clean water is used as an input in the manufacturing process, when environmental resources are used in recreational activities, or when environmental quality affects human health. Indirect use values are those associated with more intangible uses of the environment, such as aesthetic benefits or the satisfaction derived from the existence of environmental resources. Indirect use values are also called passive use and nonuse values. In addition to existence value, indirect use values also include bequest value, altruistic value, option value, and the value of ecological services.

Of all the indirect case values, option value is the closest to use value. Option value means that an individual's current value includes the desire to preserve the option to use a resource in the future. For example, a 20-year-old student may have no current desire to visit the Grand Canyon but may wish to preserve the option to take his or her future children to visit the Grand Canyon.

Bequest value refers to an individual's value for having an environmental resource or general environmental quality available for his or her children and grandchildren to experience. It is based on the desire to make current sacrifices to raise the well-being of one's descendants. Existence value means that an individual's utility may be increased by the knowledge of the existence of an environmental resource even though the individual has no current or potential direct use of the resource. For example, an individual may have a positive willingness to pay to preserve whales even though that individual may get so hopelessly seasick that he or she would never want to go on a whale-watching trip under any circumstances.

Altruistic value occurs out of one individual's concern for another. A person values the environment not just because that person benefits from environmental quality but because the person values the opportunity for other people to enjoy high environmental quality.

These values are not mutually exclusive. A person who has a direct use value for preservation of old-growth forests (such as a backpacker) may also have option, bequest, altruistic, and existence values for old-growth forests.

The value of ecological services (which include nutrient cycling, atmospheric processes, carbon cycling, clean air, clean water, and biodiversity, among other services) are unique among indirect use values in that people do not always know that these services positively affect their well-being. For example, although people recognize the value of clean water, ecological services such as biodiversity and nutrient cycling affect their well-being through

[1] Market goods are goods for which the invisible hand of the market generates a market price that is paid by consumers to suppliers. Nonmarket goods are not traded and have no corresponding market price. Nonmarket goods include environmental resources, ecological services, outdoor recreation, and many other amenities.

a less obvious path than many other types of indirect use values. Because these paths are less obvious, the valuation process for these very important contributions of the environment to social welfare is more difficult.

V. Kerry Smith (1993) reiterates and argues persuasively the point made by Charles Plourde (1975) and Kenneth McConnell (1983) that these indirect use values are not really values that are unique to environmental resources. Indirect use values are the values from the pure public good aspects of environmental resources, whereas direct use values are the private good or mixed good (part public and part private) values of environmental resources (see Chapter 2 for a discussion of private and public goods). The value of ecological services would also fit into this public good category. Smith's 1993 article provides an accessible and insightful perspective on the measurement of direct use and indirect use values associated with environmental resources.

Techniques for Measuring the Value of Nonmarket Goods

There are three major classes of techniques for measuring the value of nonmarket goods: revealed preference, stated preference techniques, and benefit transfer techniques. Revealed preference approaches look at decisions people make regarding activities that utilize or are affected by an environmental amenity to reveal the value of the amenity. These approaches focus on measuring direct use value and are not particularly useful in measuring indirect use value. Stated preference techniques elicit values directly from individuals through survey methods. These methods can be used to measure both direct use and indirect use values. The third approach is the benefit transfer approach. Rather than conduct a new valuation exercise, the benefit transfer approach looks to existing studies for values of analogous environmental change and then adapts these estimates to the problem at hand. Benefit transfer approaches will use estimates derived from both revealed preference and stated preference methods.

Revealed Preference Approaches

At first, one might expect it to be very difficult, if not impossible, to measure the value of an environmental amenity. How can one put a value on an unpriced resource such as clean air? In fact, it can be done, and a process for doing so can be illustrated by an example. Imagine a neighborhood composed of identical houses. Assume that the neighborhood is featureless (it has no attractive facilities, such as parks, and no noxious facilities, such as slaughterhouses). Further, assume that everyone works in his or her home. Under these conditions, all the houses will have identical prices.

Now, imagine that a factory is built in the eastern part of the neighborhood, which emits air pollution and creates smog over the eastern half of the city. People will now prefer to live in the cleaner western part of the city. As

Box 4.1 Natural Resource Damage Assessment and Valuation Methodologies

The Comprehensive Environmental Response, Compensation and Liability Act of 1980 (CERCLA) establishes the legal right of the trustees of natural resources (local governments, state governments, the federal government, and Native American nations) to collect damages from firms or individuals who release hazardous substances that then damage or destroy environmental resources.

These liability cases are often settled out of court, but many times the cases go to trial. To collect damages in court, the trustees must establish the existence of damages. The federal government, under the provisions of CERCLA, has established guidelines for the methodologies that have legal standing in these proceedings. Both the travel cost technique and the contingent valuation method have attained this status, and the use of these methodologies may not be challenged by the parties to the dispute (although the specifics of how they are used may certainly be challenged in court). One of the most prominent cases in which these techniques were used was the measurement of damages in the *Exxon Valdez* oil spill, which was eventually settled out of court. Because this case was settled out of court, many of the estimated values have not been made public.

Because there is such controversy surrounding the use of contingent valuation in natural resource damage assessment, the National Oceanic and Atmospheric Administration (NOAA) commissioned a blue-ribbon panel of experts to investigate contingent valuation and make recommendations about the best ways it could be employed in assessing the monetary value of damage from oil spills and other compensable environmental accidents. These findings have been published in the *Federal Register* (see U.S. Department of Commerce, 1993). Many articles have been published in response to this report. To access the latest research, search *EconLit* (if available among your library's databases) and the Internet on using the keywords NOAA Blue Ribbon Panel.

people try to move from the eastern part of the city to the western part of the city, housing prices will fall in the east and increase in the west, which reflects the increase in demand for houses in the cleaner west and the fall in demand for the dirtier east. There will always be upward pressure on western prices and downward pressure on eastern prices as long as people prefer living in the west over living in the east. The price movement will cease when the price differential is large enough to make people indifferent between living in the clean west and living in the dirty east. Because the only difference between the two areas is the higher air pollution in the east, the price differential reveals people's willingness to pay to avoid the air pollution.

Housing is just one area in which people's willingness to pay for environmental quality can be observed. Many other types of behavior can also reveal an individual's willingness to pay for environmental quality. For example, recreationists will travel farther for higher-quality outdoor recreational sites (cleaner beaches, better fishing, and so on). Other types of observable behavior include the choice of location among cities, the choice of jobs, and the choice of consumer goods.

Hedonic Pricing Techniques. The prior discussion of air pollution is an example of a hedonic pricing technique, which is one methodology for revealing willingness to pay. Hedonic price techniques are based on a theory of consumer behavior that suggests that people value a good because they value the characteristics of the good rather than the good itself. According to this theory, an individual would not value a car because the car directly gives him or her utility, but because the characteristics of safety, transportation, operating cost per mile, luxury, comfort, and status provide utility. If that is the case, an examination of how the price of a car varies with changes in the levels of these characteristics can reveal the prices of the characteristics.

These techniques were first developed to help measure inflation properly. If the price of a good increases, it could be due to inflation or because the quality of the good increases. Thus there could be a problem with measuring the true level of inflation. If the price of a car increases solely because it has become safer (air bags, ABS brakes, crumple zones, and so forth), then we do not want to attribute this price increase to inflation. If the influence of price changes on the level of quality characteristics can be measured, then the impact of inflation on prices can be measured separately, because the residual is not caused by quality changes.

To illustrate this process in an environmental context, let's return to the housing price and air pollution model. Housing prices will be related to a variety of characteristics including attributes of the house itself (number and size of rooms, size of lot, number of bathrooms, quality of construction, and so on) and attributes of the neighborhood (distance to employment centers, level of crime, quality of schools, air quality, and so on).

For the time being, let's assume that all characteristics of houses and neighborhoods except air pollution, which varies with location, are the same throughout the city. Then, houses in the areas with higher air quality will have higher prices. This relationship is reflected in Figure 4.4, where each dot represents the housing price and air quality levels associated with each individual house in the city.

The general upward sloping constellation of these points suggests a positive relationship between air quality and housing prices, which can be formalized through regression analysis. Regression analysis is a statistical process for fitting a line through the cluster of points. In this case, the line describes the fashion in which improvements in air quality lead to increases in housing prices. For example, an ordinary least-squares regression fits the line by

Figure 4.4 **The Relationship between Air Quality and Housing Price**

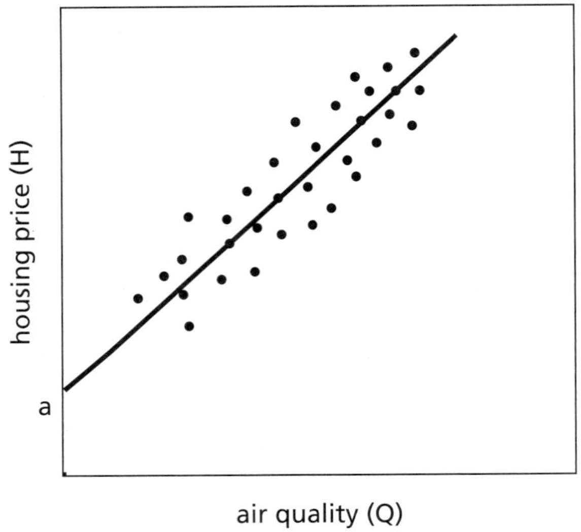

minimizing the sum of the squared values of the distances between each point and the line, as in Figure 4.4.

If H represents the housing price and Q represents air quality, then the regression will draw the line by choosing the intercept and slope of equation 4.1:

$$H = a + bQ \qquad 4.1$$

The estimate of b tells the researcher how many units H will increase for each unit of increase in air quality. The estimate of b can be interpreted as the slope of the regression line.

Of course, in reality the prices of houses are dependent on many different characteristics that the researcher must consider. For example, the size of the house (S) is likely to have an effect on the price of housing, so equation 4.2 might better explain the variation in housing prices that one observes when looking at the spectrum of housing prices in a city:

$$H = a + bQ + cS \qquad 4.2$$

A regression analysis chooses a, b, and c by fitting a surface to a cluster of points in three-dimensional space, with each point corresponding to the price, air quality, and size of a particular house. It is conceptually identical to the process depicted in Figure 4.4, but performed in three-dimensional space.

Although it is difficult for a person to conceptualize more than three dimensions, the formulas for computing distance in multidimensional space are relatively simple. The regression analysis can be expanded to include many right-hand-side variables, such as the characteristics of the house and the characteristics of the neighborhood. The regression can also be estimated in a fashion that represents a nonlinear relationship among the variables. For example, housing price is likely to increase with air quality but not necessarily at the constant rate of a linear relationship. Housing prices could increase with increased air quality at either an increasing rate (Figure 4.5) or a decreasing rate (Figure 4.6).

Two basic types of variables, the characteristics of the house itself and the characteristics of the neighborhood in which the house is located, are included as explanatory variables in the hedonic housing price function. Real estate transactions databases form the basic database for this type of analysis, as these computerized databases usually contain both the price at which the house is sold and the characteristics of the house. Such databases will also have the address, which can be used to define neighborhood variables. Geographic information systems (GIS) computer software and databases increase the ease of associating neighborhood variables with an address.

Because researchers and policy makers were anxious to measure the benefits associated with the Clean Air Act and subsequent amendments, the early hedonic housing price literature focused on air quality. Table 4.2 contains

Figure 4.5 **Housing Price Function, Increasing at an Increasing Rate**

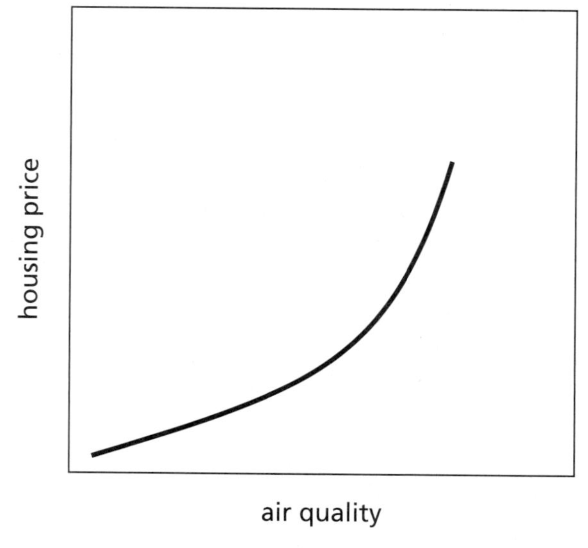

Figure 4.6 **Housing Price Function, Increasing at a Decreasing Rate**

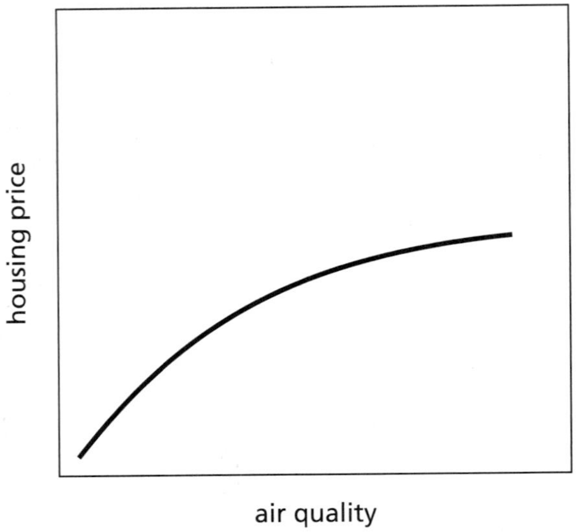

Table 4.2 **Hedonic Estimates of the Willingness to Pay for Reductions in Air Pollutants (updated to 2003 dollars)**

Study	Pollutant	Household Willingness to Pay per Unit of Air Quality Change
Ridker and Henning (1967)	Sulfur particles	\$53.31 per mg/m^3
Nelson (1978)	Average summer ozone concentration	\$42.27 per ppm
Nelson (1978)	Average monthly particulate concentration	\$193.25 per mg/m^3
Harrison and Rubinfield (1978)	NO_x	\$4495.00 per ppm
Harrison and Rubinfield (1978)	Particulate concentration	\$50.16 per ppm
Brookshire et al. (1982)	NO_2	\$86.46 for poor to fair
		\$111.13 for fair to good[a]
Blomquist et al. (1988)	particulates	\$552.96 per mg/m^3

[a] poor > 11 parts per hundred million (pphm), fair = between 9 and 11 pphm, good < 9 pphm

some examples of studies that have related housing prices to air quality to measure the value of air quality improvement. The air quality variable examined is listed in the second column, and the willingness to pay for improvement in air quality is listed in the third column. More recently, the hedonic housing price literature has focused on the social costs associated with "LULUS" (locally undesirable land uses) such as toxic waste sites, giant hog farms, and nuclear power plants.

Hedonic Wage Studies. An analogous technique to the hedonic housing price approach is the hedonic wage approach. This approach is based on the idea that an individual will choose the city in which he or she resides so as to maximize his or her utility. The individual will consider the wage that can be earned in a particular city as well as a host of other factors including negative characteristics (such as crime, pollution, high cost of living, extreme climate, and congestion) and positive characteristics (such as educational opportunity, recreational opportunity, fine arts, social life, sports, and mild climate). One might question why these market wages will reveal information about people's valuation of nonmarket goods, but a simple example will show how wages adjust to compensate people for differential city characteristics. This compensation will be positive for negative characteristics or disamenities and negative for positive characteristics or amenities.

In this example, assume that a person has two job offers, one in a cold-weather city (such as Buffalo) and one in a warm-weather city (such as Atlanta). Let's also assume that in both cities the person is offered a job with the same characteristics and the same pay. Which job will the person accept? If we assume that Buffalo and Atlanta are identical in all aspects but weather, then the person will choose Atlanta if he or she prefers warm weather to cold weather. If everybody prefers warm weather to cold weather, then they could make themselves better off by moving to warm weather cities such as Atlanta, yet that will increase the supply of labor in warm-weather cities and decrease the supply of labor in cold-weather cities. Wages will fall in warm-weather cities and increase in cold-weather cities until people can no longer make themselves better off by moving. The difference between the wage in a warm-weather city and the wage in a cold-weather city will be just sufficient to compensate people for the disutility associated with the colder weather. Notice that although some people may prefer cold weather to warm weather, there will still be a positive differential associated with cold weather if the marginal worker prefers warm to cold. As mentioned, many different characteristics will affect people's choice among cities.

Many city characteristics are associated with city size. Disamenities such as crime, pollution, congestion, and cost of living tend to increase as city size increases. Similarly, some amenities are associated with city size, such as cultural opportunities, spectator sports, and social activities.

The use of this model to estimate willingness to pay or environmental amenities requires one to be satisfied with the underlying assumption that people will move among cities to maximize their utility. In highly mobile societies such as the United States, Canada, and Australia, that is probably a good assumption. In many developing countries and some European countries, however, labor is not mobile to this degree, perhaps due to cultural reasons, difficulty in finding information about labor markets in other cities, or high transaction costs of changing locations. Under these circumstances, the hedonic wage model will not yield satisfactory results and could give either overestimates or underestimates of the true willingness to pay.

The hedonic wage model (also called the compensating wage differential method) originated in the labor economics literature to measure the impact of education on wages. Later, it was used to test to determine if black/white and male/female income earnings gaps existed. Another application in the labor economics literature was to evaluate people's willingness to pay to avoid risks of mortality in the workplace. This model obviously has direct implications for environmental valuation, because air pollution and other types of environmental problems can increase the incidence of cancer and other fatal diseases.

It is easy to explain how the hedonic wage method can also be used to gain information about the value of human life. If two jobs are identical in all respects except the risk of accidental death, then the wage in the riskier job must be higher to induce people to accept that job. The estimation of a hedonic wage function, with the degree of risk as an explanatory variable, can be used to quantify this relationship between risk and the willingness to accept higher wages to be exposed to greater risk.

If a study revealed that an individual must be compensated \$1000 per year to accept an additional 0.1 percent (1 in 1000) annual risk of dying, then the value of saving a life can be computed in the following fashion:

1. Each individual is willing to receive \$1000 to accept an increased 1/1000 risk of dying.
2. The size of the population for which one would expect exactly one person to die is 1000 people.
3. These 1000 people have a collective willingness to accept \$1 million (\$1000 multiplied by 1000 people) to be exposed to this risk, which would be expected to lead to the death of one individual.
4. The collective willingness to be compensated to accept a loss of one life is therefore equal to \$1 million.

In empirical studies of willingness to pay for reduction in risk, there is considerable variation in the estimates. An informal examination of these studies suggests an average willingness to pay between \$1 million and \$12 million per life saved (see Table 4.3 and Box 4.2). However, caution must be exercised when utilizing this type of measure of the value of a human life, because it measures the value of saving a statistical life and not the life of a specific person. If a specific person is faced with the certain prospect of death, then that person and his or her family and friends would be willing to pay a near infinite sum to keep that specific person alive. This discrepancy also explains why we as a society are willing to pay tens of millions of dollars to save the

Table 4.3 Values of Human Life

Author	Date	Values (2001 dollars)
Fisher, Chestnut, and Violette	1989	$2.3 million to $12.2 million
Johannesson, Johansson, and O'Conor	1996	Two estimates based on values of reducing traffic accidents ($10.1 million and $8.4 million per life)
Viscusi	1993 (1990 dollars)	$0.95 to $5.54

NOTE: These values are based on the summaries provided in Professor John Whitehead's web site on valuing statistical life at http://john-whitehead.net/ecu/5000/ch10b/vsl.htm. Values have been updated to 2001 dollars. See this web site for more information on procedures for valuing a statistical life.

Box 4.2 The Politics of the Value of a Saved Life

Many noneconomists criticize willingness to pay techniques as inherently inequitable, because willingness to pay is most definitely a function of ability to pay. If policy decisions are based on willingness to pay, then, they argue, people with higher incomes will have a greater weight in the decision-making process. Their argument is that the principle of "one person, one vote" is transformed into "one dollar, one vote."

This type of argument spilled into the pages of the popular press when the Economics Working Group of the Inter-Governmental Panel on Climate Change released a set of results on the costs of global warming that used willingness to pay based on value of life, in which the value for a person in North America or Europe was approximately 15 times greater than the value of life of a person in India or Africa. A logical extension of this argument is that it is better to prevent the death of one European (or North American) than 14 people from India. Of course, this report triggered fierce international debate about the appropriateness of valuation methods and cost-benefit analysis in general. Much of this debate is summarized and linked in a Global Commons Institute web site at (http://www.gci.org.uk).

Should cost-benefit analysis and valuation be abandoned in the face of this very powerful equity argument? The answer to this question, which is discussed in greater detail and broader application in Chapter 5, is that valuation estimates and cost-benefit analysis should not be viewed as decision-making tools but as information organizing tools. Economic efficiency is but one type of information, one

(continues)

Box 4.2 (continued)

criterion that must be balanced against other criteria such as equity, sustainability, and environmental stewardship.

In addition to talking about multiple criteria, Chapter 5 stresses the importance of sensitivity analysis in cost-benefit analysis. Sensitivity analysis is a method for testing the results of cost-benefit analysis with variation in the level of variables that are difficult to measure (or values are not universally accepted). For example, in the global warming study, the value of human life in developed and developing countries could be set equal to the measured level of the value that was in the respective category of countries, and the cost-benefit analysis performed. Then, the results could be recalculated with all life valued at the high willingness to pay that was measured in developed countries. In addition, the same exercise could be conducted by valuing all life at the low value measured in developing countries. Sensitivity analysis is examined in greater detail in Chapter 5.

life of a specific little girl who has fallen into a well or the life of a specific coal miner who is trapped in a mine, but we will not pay the same (or even lesser amounts) for highway improvements that would save the lives of more (but unidentified) individuals.

Both the hedonic housing price model and the hedonic wage model are powerful tools in estimating the health costs associated with air and water pollution. As long as people are aware of the health consequences of living in polluted areas, housing prices and wages should reflect their willingness to pay to avoid the health risk. Even if this information requirement is not met for some pollutants, one can value the benefit of a reduction in these pollutants by looking at an analogous risk for which people are better informed.

Three basic types of variables are included on the right-hand side of the hedonic wage equation. These variables include the characteristics of the individual (such as age, education, and occupation), the characteristics of the job (such as risk of accidental death), and the characteristics of the city (such as air pollution, crime, congestion, climate, and proximity to the coast). Census of population data forms the primary data set for the creation of these variables and the estimation of this model. Many countries make a subset of the census of population data available. This subset usually has data on a large number of individuals, but the identity of the individual is removed for obvious privacy reasons. These data sets often list the individual's income, age, education level, occupation, and other socioeconomic variables. Another important aspect of these data sets is that they list the city in which the individual lives, so that city characteristics can be obtained from other databases and matched to the individual's location. In the United States, the subset of the census of population is called the Public Use Microdata Set, (or PUMS) and is available at http://www.census.gov/main/www/pums.html.

Travel Cost Model. The travel cost model is a method for valuing environmental resources associated with recreational activity. This method was first proposed by Harold Hotelling in 1947. The basic premise behind the model is that the travel cost to a site can be regarded as the price of access to the site. If recreationists were asked questions about the number of trips they take and their travel cost to the site, enough information would be generated to estimate a demand curve. Just as the implementation of the Clean Air Act spurred the development of the hedonic pricing methods, the Clean Water Act (CWA) spurred the development of the travel cost method because recreational benefits were likely to be a large component of the benefits of water quality improvement.

Figure 4.7 contains a collection of such observations on travel cost and number of trips. In this figure, each point represents the combination of travel costs and number of trips reported by an individual. Using regression analysis, a line is fitted through these points, and that line represents an individual demand curve. The value of the site to an individual can be estimated by computing the consumer surplus for each individual in the survey, averaging the consumers' surplus, and then multiplying by the estimated number of recreationists. Consumers' surplus is the area under the demand curve and above the price (the travel cost) that the individual actually incurred. For example,

Figure 4.7 **Estimation of Travel Cost Demand Curve**

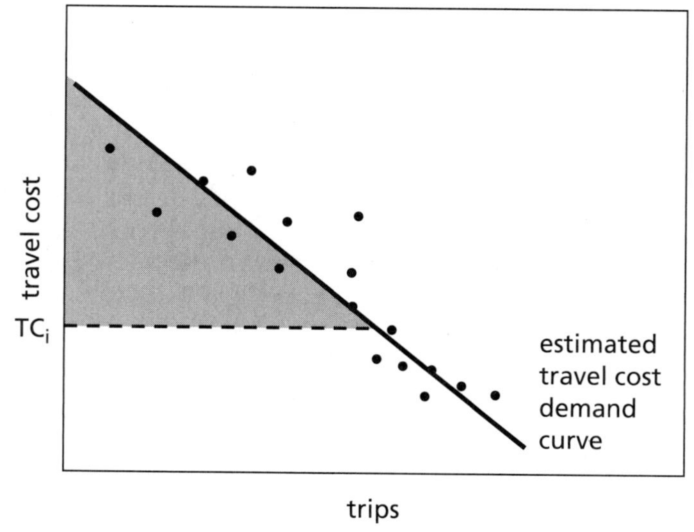

if TC_i is the travel cost paid by the individual, the individual consumer's surplus is equal to the shaded triangle in Figure 4.7. The travel cost demand curve is often expanded to include other explanatory variables, such as age, income, family size, educational level, and other socioeconomic variables.

Table 4.4 lists annual consumers' surplus associated with different types of recreational activities for a selected group of studies. For a comprehensive discussion of how and why consumers' surplus estimates vary across studies, see Smith and Kaoru (1990b). The studies listed in Table 4.4 give the value of the recreational activity or the value of the sites that provide the opportunities. They do not give information about the value of changing the quality of the activity, which is the information one would need to determine the value of environmental improvement. For example, increased water quality will increase fish populations, which will increase recreational fishers' utility. How can the travel cost method be used to measure their willingness to pay for this increased water quality?

Table 4.4 **Consumers' Surplus Estimates from Selected Studies (updated to 2003 dollars)**

	Study	Region and Activity	Consumers' Surplus
Saltwater Fishing	Bockstael, Hannemann, and Strand	Chesapeake Bay and Ocean City, MD	\$5724 to \$7146
	Bockstael, McConnell, and Strand	Southern California private boat fishery	\$2703 to \$4148
	Bell, Sorenson, and Leeworthy	Florida resident saltwater fishing	\$884 to \$2278
Freshwater Fishing	Kealy and Bishop	Lake Michigan fishery (Wisconsin side)	\$1750
	Kahn	Great Lakes fishing	\$661 to \$1544
Hunting	Balkan and Kahn	U.S. deer hunting	\$2300
Beach Use	Bockstael, Strand, and Hannemann	Chesapeake beaches	\$2381 to \$6079
	Bell and Leeworthy	Florida tourist beach users	\$335
		Florida resident beach users	\$636
Other	Rockel and Kealy	Nonconsumptive wildlife-associated recreation	\$2827 to \$5300

Source: Kahn, 1991.

Two travel cost demand curves are shown in Figure 4.8. The lower one (D_1) represents an individual's willingness to pay for recreational fishing trips at the current lower level of water quality. The upper one (D_2) reflects willingness to pay for recreational fishing trips with an improved level of water quality. If P_1 represents the travel cost actually incurred by the typical recreational angler, then the area ABCE represents the value of the improvement in water quality to that person. Note that the improvement in water quality would generate an increase in the number of trips from Q_1 to Q_2.

To measure how the travel cost demand curve shifts as environmental quality shifts, the travel cost demand curve must be estimated with quality as an explanatory variable. For example, in the recreational fishing context, the travel cost demand curve could be estimated using the number of trips as the dependent variable and travel cost, socioeconomic variables (age, income, family size, and so on), and the average catch per day at the fishing site or sites as the explanatory variables. Then, fishery biologists would be asked to help establish the relationships among water quality, catch, and fish populations to establish the links between water quality and value. Table 4.5 contains information from empirical studies of recreational activities, showing how consumers' surplus varies with quality.

Although the travel cost procedure has been widely used and holds great promise for further understanding the way that environmental quality affects

Figure 4.8 **Increase in Consumers' Surplus Associated with Improvement in Water Quality**

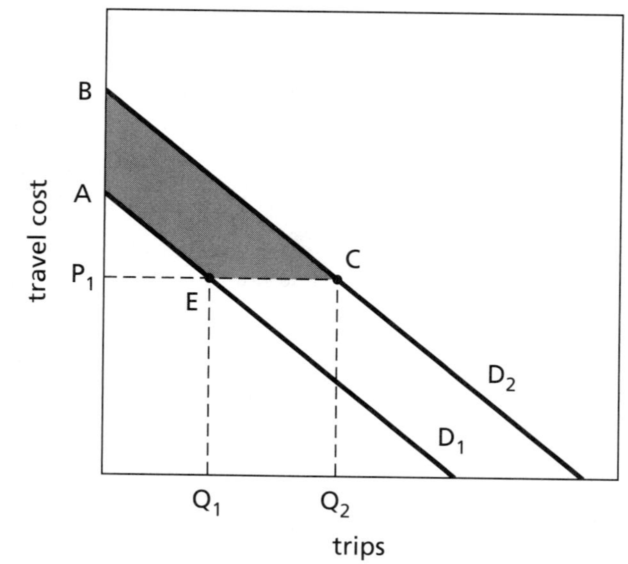

Table 4.5 Cross-Study Comparison of Benefit Estimates of Changes in Sport Fish Catch Rates (updated to 2003 dollars)

Study	Date	Location	Species/Type	Model[a]	Catch Rate % Value
Bockstael, Mcconnell, and Strand (1988)	Nov–Dec 1987	Florida (Atlantic Coast)		RUM Nested Logit	+(20%)
			Big game		$2.49
			Small game		$0.52
			Nontargeted small game		$0.51
			Bottom fish (from boat)		$2.03
Smith and Palmquist	Summer 1981 and and1982	Albermarle/ Pamlico Estuary	All species	RUM Nested Logit	+(25%)
					(per choice occasion)
		All sites	All species		$4.85
		Closest 4 sites			$1.19
		Outer banks range	All Species	CTC	$1.74 to $76.11
		Across most sites			
		Pamlico range	CTC		$3.98 to $28.47
Huppert (1977)	July 1975–June 1986	San Francisco Bay and Ocean Area	Anadromous Fish runs (Salmon and Striped Bass)	CVM	–(50%) (per year)
				EV	$63.60
				CV	$141.39
					+(100%)
				CV	$72.71
				CTC	–(50%)
				EV	$214.00
				CV	$215.00
					+(100%)
				CV	$117.52
Morey and Shaw	1986/87	Adirondacks (Saranac, Raquette, Lake Placid, and Piseco)	Brook and Lake trout (average)	SHR	+(25%) (per season)
					$14.39
					+(50%)
					$25.72
Bockstael (1988b)	1980	Chesapeake Bay	Striped bass	CTC	+(20%) (per trip)
					$4.41 to $13.89

(continues)

Table 4.5 (continued)

Study	Date	Location	Species/Type	Model[a]	Catch Rate % Value
Milon (1988a, 1988b)	1981 and 1986	Gulf of Mexico	King mackerel average for 4 sites	RUM	+(25%) (per trip) $10.79 +(50%) $33.38

Source: Brown, et al. 1990

[a] The guide to symbols is RUM for Random Utility Model; CTC for Conventional Travel Cost (includes Simple Travel Cost and Varying Parameter/Regional Travel Cost Models); CVM for Contingent Valuation Method (EV for Equivalent Variation and CV for Compensating Variation); and SHR for Share Model.

the value of recreational activities, many methodological issues remain unresolved. They include the following:

1. How to incorporate the opportunity cost of travel time into the measure of travel cost
2. How to properly account for substitutes (multiple sites) in estimating a travel cost demand curve
3. How to account for a variety of sampling biases that arise when data is collected by interviewing recreationists at recreation sites
4. How to properly measure recreational quality and relate recreational quality to environmental quality

Data with which to estimate travel cost demand curves are generally collected through the means of "intercept surveys" conducted by researchers at sites where recreationists pursue their activities. In an intercept survey, recreationists are asked to complete surveys containing questions about the number of trips, the recreationists' perception of the quality of the site, the socioeconomic characteristics of the recreationist, the distance traveled, and other relevant travel costs. Many insightful studies have been implemented in this fashion, and it is a very cost-effective method for collecting data.

One potential drawback of the method is that the intercept process creates a bias in the sample of data. One reason for this bias is that the more trips per year that a recreationist takes, the more likely he or she is to be included in the sample. Therefore, recreationists who take a large number of trips per year are overrepresented in the sample compared with people who take few trips. Moreover, people who take no trips are not included in the sample at all. A number of statistical procedures exist that can adjust for these biases. In addition, data could be collected by a random method, such as a random telephone survey. This process, however, can be more expensive.

Students who are interested in exploring the travel cost method in a research paper are unlikely to be able to collect their own data given the associated cost and the small amount of time available during a semester. Travel cost data are available, however, from a number of sources. One important and comprehensive source of data is the U.S. Fish and Wildlife Service's *National Survey of Fishing, Hunting and Wildlife-Associated Recreation.* (Available at http://fa.r9.fws.gov/surveys/surveys.html). Also, many researchers make the data from their published studies freely available. Authors can be identified in journals such as the *Journal of Environmental Economics and Management*, *Ecological Economics*, *Land Economics*, and *American Journal of Agricultural Economics*. The authors' web sites can then be examined to see if such data are available.

Stated Preference Techniques

Stated preference valuation techniques are somewhat different than the revealed preference techniques already discussed. The indirect techniques are designed to measure the value of environmental resources by looking at how people's actual behavior (choice of city, house within a city, job, recreational activities) changes as the level of environmental quality changes. Stated preference techniques do not have this link to actual behavior. Instead, they solicit value measures directly by asking individuals hypothetical questions.

Contingent Valuation. The most widely used stated preference valuation technique is the contingent valuation method. The contingent valuation method ascertains value by asking people their willingness to pay for a change in environmental quality. One reason many researchers are enthusiastic about contingent valuation is that it enables them to measure values that are not related to a direct use of the resource.

The contingent valuation method is based on asking an individual to state his or her willingness to pay to bring about an environmental improvement, such as improved visibility from lessened air pollution, the protection of an endangered species, or the preservation of a wilderness area. Questions have been asked in a variety of ways, using both open-ended and close-ended questions. In open-ended questions, respondents are asked to state their maximum willingness to pay. In close-ended questions, respondents are asked to say whether or not they would be willing to pay a particular amount to preserve the environmental resource.

In addition to the hypothetical question of willingness to pay, the contingent valuation procedure must specify the mechanism by which the payment will be made. For the question to be effective, the respondent must believe that if the money was paid, whoever was collecting it could affect the specified environmental change. An example of such a question, which specifies a payment mechanism (or vehicle, as it is known in the contingent valuation literature) is as follows:

> Water quality in the Tennessee River is adversely affected by problems of contamination from combined sewage outflow. This problem is caused by the connection between storm sewers and sanitary sewers, which causes the sewer system to overflow when there are heavy rains and spill untreated sewage into the Tennessee River. If the storm runoff was handled through a separate system, it would eliminate the spillage of untreated sewage, significantly improving water quality. The water, which is currently too polluted to swim in, would become safe for swimming. Would you be willing to pay an additional $X per year in your sewer and water bill if the money was used to correct this problem?

Several aspects of the structure of this question are important. First, information was provided about the cause and significance of the environmental problem. Second, the payment vehicle was appropriate to the particular problem. The payment question was structured as a close-ended question, where different values of $X are specified for different individuals. Although these close-ended questions only let us know that the individual is willing to pay at least the particular amount, appropriate statistical techniques exist to derive willingness to pay measures from these responses.

Care must be taken that the contingent valuation exercise does not become a referendum on the payment vehicle. For example, in some communities high property taxes are a subject of political contention. If a researcher was to use a property tax payment vehicle in a contingent valuation questionnaire, then respondents' stated values might be biased because people already think property taxes are inappropriately high and they may react to the tax rather than the environmental issue. In other areas, income, value-added or sales taxes may be a source of contention, as could be the high cost of utilities such as electricity or water/sewage.

A very controversial aspect of the process of measuring the value of nonmarket goods such as environmental resources has to do with whether the researcher or policy analyst should use a measure based on willingness to pay for access to an environmental resource or on willingness to accept a payment to forgo access to the resource. One would expect willingness to accept a payment to be larger than willingness to pay because the latter is constrained by the individual's income, whereas the former is unconstrained, and one could imagine cases where it would be infinitely large.

It is difficult to specify which is the better measure to use in policy analysis, because in many ways it is an ethical issue. For example, if one believes that people have the right to clean air, then a better measure of the value of clean air would be willingness to accept a payment to allow the deterioration of air quality, rather than willingness to pay to prevent a deterioration of air quality.

Although the contingent value method has been widely used since the late 1970s, there is considerable controversy over whether it adequately measures people's willingness to pay for environmental quality. That is less so for the measurement of use values than indirect use values or the values of ecological services. These arguments are based on informational issues and because people may be indicating their value of something other than the particular environmental issue that is the subject of the questionnaire.

The informational issue revolves around experience with the good in question. With market goods, people have practice making choices, so their purchasing decisions are likely to reflect their true willingness to pay. Consumers buy clothes frequently, so when they see a clothes item for a given price, they are likely to know if their true willingness to pay is greater than the price. We do not, however, have practice valuing threatened species, so if persons are asked if their willingness to pay to save the black-footed ferret from extinction is greater than $40 per year, they are not certain that their true willingness to pay is greater than $40. Information is a big problem as well, because persons may not know why black-footed ferrets are important to biodiversity or how biodiversity affects ecosystem stability, the production of ecological services, and their utility function.

The second issue involves the potential existence of a bias generated because the expressed answers to a willingness to pay question in a contingent value format may not reflect true value because the respondent actually answers a different question than the surveyor intended. For example, the respondent may state a positive willingness to pay because the respondent wants the surveyor to think he or she is a good person. Alternatively, the respondent may express a willingness to pay because he or she feels good about the act of giving for the social good, and the social cause itself is unimportant. Finally, a respondent may just be trying to signal that he or she places importance on improved environmental quality by stating a positive willingness to pay. These biases are being discussed as potential sources of bias, rather than proven sources of bias. The biases are more likely to occur in poorly implemented surveys than well-implemented surveys.

Another problem is that the respondent may make associations between environmental goods that the researcher had not intended. For example, if the question asks for the willingness to pay for improved visibility through reduced pollution, then the respondent may actually answer based on the health risks that he or she associates with dirty air. This answer may seem appropriate, but a big problem of double counting may develop if health risks are examined separately. Similarly, researchers have found that there is very little difference between stated willingness to pay for a more encompassing set of environmental resources and a less encompassing set. For example, researchers have found that the willingness to pay for improved air quality in a system of Rocky Mountain parks is not too different from the willingness to pay for improved air quality in one Rocky Mountain park (Schultze et al., 1990). This similarity may occur for some of the reasons stated previously or because people do not believe that it is possible to increase air quality in one park without increasing air quality in another.

Some researchers argue that there is a fundamental difference in the way people make hypothetical decisions relative to the way they make actual decisions. A series of experiments looked at hypothetical versus actual decision making. Some experiments (Kealy, Montgomery, and Dovido, 1990; Cummings and Harrison, 1992; Cummings 1996) ask the hypothetical willingness to pay for a private good (candy, electric juicer, calculator) and then offer respondents the opportunity to purchase at the stated willingness to pay. Many of the survey respondents do not elect to purchase at that price. Similar experiments have been conducted with public goods with similar results. (Duffield and Patterson, 1992; Seip and Strand, 1992).

Although these experiments provide some evidence that hypothetical values exceed actual values, one cannot conclude that this result is definitely true. So few experiments have been conducted that it is difficult to determine if the differences between hypothetical and actual values are a result of the experimental method or if they truly reflect the way people behave. As with many issues in nonmarket valuation, the answers await further research.

The significance of the problems mentioned above is highly debated. Although some researchers hypothesize the existence and insurmountability of these problems, other researchers believe that these are technical issues that can be resolved by proper survey design. Contingent valuation remains an important technique in the researcher's valuation arsenal. Many of these issues, however, need to be resolved for researchers and policy makers to have more confidence in the value measures resulting from these techniques. Research has been proceeding at a rapid pace, and many studies have taken great care to minimize the magnitude of the problems discussed above. Yet many questions still must be answered before contingent valuation receives general acceptance among environmental economists, scholars from other disciplines, and environmental decision makers.

Conjoint Analysis. Conjoint analysis is a technique employed by researchers in marketing, transportation, psychology, and increasingly in economics for determining individual preference across different levels of characteristics of a multiattribute choice. For example, a marketing study might ask potential consumers to state which of two hypothetical cars they prefer, with each car having a stated level of different characteristics such as price, roominess, reliability, safety, fuel economy, and power. These choices can be made in a pair-wise fashion or by ranking a number of alternatives, although economists generally prefer the pair-wise choices. Statistical techniques are then used to establish a relationship between the characteristics and preference. As long as one of the characteristics is price, it is possible to use the preference function to derive the willingness to pay for changes in the levels of the other characteristics. The probability function is estimated using a technique called logit analysis. Daniel McFadden, Jordan Louviere, and others have shown that consumers' surplus can be derived from the parameters that are estimated by the logit method. It should be noted that conjoint analysis can be viewed as a hedonic price technique, where hypothetical price substitutes for actual market price.

The applications of conjoint analysis to valuing other types of environmental resources can be seen immediately. For example, if one were trying to value forest quality, one could define characteristics such as the age of trees, the diversity of trees, the diversity of other organisms, soil productivity, water quality, and so on. Then one could use conjoint analysis to determine the importance of the various characteristics.

Alternatively, one could use conjoint analysis to directly value alternative national environmental policy scenarios. For example, respondents can be asked to compare alternative scenarios with different levels of cleanup of toxic waste sites, different levels of acid precipitation, different levels of global warming, different levels of ambient air quality, different levels of old-growth forests, and most importantly, different tax burdens for the respondent. The respondents' preference ordering will then allow a determination of the willingness to be taxed so as to obtain different levels of the environmental variables.

One advantage of conjoint analysis over contingent valuation is that it does not ask respondents to make a trade-off directly between environmental quality and money. Rather, it asks respondents to state a preference between one bundle of environmental characteristics (at a given tax burden) and another bundle of environmental characteristics at a different tax burden. Although environmental characteristic/money trade-offs can be statistically derived from conjoint analysis, respondents do not perceive the ranking as a direct trade-off between environmental quality and money. More importantly, conjoint analysis presents a type of choice with which respondents are more familiar. In contingent valuation, respondents are asked to state their willingness to pay for a nonmarket good. As mentioned earlier, this type of decision is one with which the individual is not typically familiar. Conjoint analysis, however, asks respondents to choose between two states of the world, which have different levels of both market and nonmarket goods. This method is a choice process with which we are all familiar and practiced. We engage in this type of choice process when we are faced with voting Democratic or Republican, getting married or staying single, choosing a major in college, or choosing which college to attend. Because conjoint analysis is based on a more familiar choice process, it should therefore reduce problems with protest bids, signaling, and some of the other sources of potential bias associated with contingent valuation. Boxed example 4.3 contains implementation information for a conjoint analysis of the value of recreational fishing.

Although conjoint analysis has great potential for valuing environmental resources, there has not been much experience with it in this application. More research, particularly comparison studies with contingent valuation, needs to be done with this technique.

Benefit Transfer Approaches

The process of estimating values using revealed preference or stated preference approaches can be quite expensive. For example, a relatively simple but technically correct contingent valuation study can easily cost more than

Box 4.3 Use of Conjoint Analysis to Value Recreational Fishing Quality

In a study using conjoint analysis to value recreational fishing quality, recreational anglers would be presented with cards with different characteristics of recreational fishing trips printed on the cards. For example, they might be asked, "Which fishing trip would you prefer, trip A or trip B?"

Trip A, has the following characteristics:

1. The water in the river is sufficiently clear enough to see the bottom in water of 3 feet or less.
2. You see a pair of bald eagles during the trip.
3. Other anglers get in your way four times during the day.
4. You catch three largemouth bass of more than 3 pounds each and two of less than 2 pounds each.
5. You are required to pay an entrance fee of $11.

Trip B, has the following characteristics:

1. The water in the river is sufficiently clear enough to see the bottom in water of 1 foot or less.
2. Other anglers get in your way five times during the day.
3. You catch one largemouth bass of more than 3 pounds and six of less than 1 pound each.
4. You are required to pay an entrance fee of $5.

This type of question would be repeated several times for each angler in the sample, and one would obtain a sample of at least several hundred. The level of the characteristics (including price) would be changed to obtain the variation needed to statistically determine the relationship between each characteristic and preference. The final step is to estimate a preference function with the data. The estimated coefficients of the preference function can then be used to formulate an expression for consumer surplus. See Louviere (1988, 1996) for more details.

$100,000. Very often, these types of resources may not be available, a decision maker may not have the appropriate staff to conduct such a study, or there is not enough time to conduct the study before the decision needs to be made. An approach called benefit transfer has arisen to deal with these problems and to avoid the costly approach of conducting original valuation research where it is not necessary.

Benefit transfer refers to a process of taking values from studies that were previously completed in other areas and applying them to the area where the new decision must be made. For example, let's assume that a new mine is planned that threatens to negatively impact nearby streams with acid mine drainage. One of those impacts would be the effect on the trout in these streams and the associated losses in benefits to recreational anglers. In this case, the analyst need not undertake a new travel cost or contingent valuation study to compute the potential losses to recreational anglers. Instead, the analyst can look at studies that have looked at the value of recreational fishing in general, trout fishing in particular, and even focus on studies looking at the loss in recreational fishing value from acidification of trout streams due to acid rain.

Although benefit transfer is not a "scientific methodology" that is associated with hypothesis testing and formal statistical confidence intervals, there are a set of alternative methodologies that can be employed to maximize the quality of information available in the benefit transfer process. These methodologies generally focus on ensuring that the reference study (the previously implemented study whose results are being transferred) is congruous with the problem being studied. This congruity must take place in several dimensions, including the socioeconomic and ecological dimensions of the problem.

The importance of using a reference study that is congruous can be best illustrated by extending the example of the trout stream and potential acid mine drainage. Let's say that the stream that is being threatened by the potential mining activity is the Beaverkill River, an extremely high-quality trout stream within a 2 hours' drive from New York City. Let's say that the only reference studies available were from a high-quality trout stream in northern Canada and from a mediocre trout stream in New Jersey.

At first, one might think because both the Beaverkill River and the Canadian stream are both high-quality trout streams, the Canadian study would make the best reference study. One of the salient features of the Beaverkill River, however, is that it is available to the large New York City metropolitan area, making it extremely valuable. The Canadian river, in contrast, is in a remote area not easily accessible, so it would have a much lower value. This thinking might lead one to consider the New Jersey study as the appropriate reference study. Although that study would have a symmetric set of socioeconomic circumstances (including population density), the quality of that river is much lower than the Beaverkill River, so it would be inappropriate as well.

Neither of these reference studies can be used to provide an estimate of the expected value of the trout fishing on the Beaverkill River, but they could be used to provide a lower bound on the value of the Beaverkill River. In either case, one can make an argument that the value of the Beaverkill River would be higher than the reference studies. This process of developing lower bounds and upper bounds can be used to help understand the value of the environmental resource in question.

If many reference studies are available, then the process becomes much easier. The most appropriate reference study can be chosen or a weighted average of the value estimates of many studies can be employed, with the weights chosen according to the similarity between the reference study and the problem at hand. A way of formalizing this process is to use meta-analysis techniques.

Meta-analysis involves taking a large set of relevant studies and searching for statistical regularities in these studies. For example, if one were interested in measuring the benefit of reducing acid mine drainage to a recreational trout fishery, one could take the value measures from the hundreds of recreational fishing studies that have been completed and regress the value estimate on a set of variables describing the characteristics of the fishery and the characteristics of the population using the fishery. Then, the characteristics of the application (the Beaverkill River, in our example) could be substituted into the estimated equation to estimate the value of the trout fishery in the Beaverkill River.

Nonwillingness to Pay Value Measures: Avoidance Cost, Replacement, and Restoration Cost

In many instances, researchers do not focus on willingness to pay measures, but focus on cost-related measures as a source of value. Three cost-related techniques involve focusing on avoidance cost, focusing on replacement cost, and focusing on restoration cost. Policy analysts often focus on these types of cost measures because they are more direct and easier to measure than methods based on willingness to pay approaches such as the revealed preference and stated preference methods discussed earlier.

Avoidance cost refers to the costs that people incur to avoid the negative consequences of an environmental change. For example, if the drinking water becomes contaminated, then consumers may not suffer the consequences of increased probability of cancer and other diseases potentially caused by the contamination if they avoid the contaminated water by drinking bottled water or installing water purification systems in their home. To the extent that the avoidance measures eliminate the problem, they can be viewed to measure the social cost of the problem. Very often, however, the use of avoidance measures causes disutility to the person avoiding the avoidance measures, such as the inconveniences associated with carrying heavy bottles home from the store and not being able to use water directly from the tap.

Replacement cost focuses on the cost of re-creating what was lost to the environmental change. For example, if a proposed shopping center would destroy a set of wetlands, then the replacement cost would equal the cost of creating an equivalent set of wetlands that would provide the same array of ecological services. Restoration cost focuses on the cost of repairing the environmental damage, such as the cost of cleaning an oil spill that might have occurred in the wetlands and the cost of re-introducing plant or animal species that were exterminated by the oil spill.

The use of restoration and replacement cost as a measure of value has two major problems. First is the question of whether the restored or replaced environmental resource is equivalent to what existed before the damage. Equivalency has two dimensions in this case. First, does it provide an equivalent flow of ecological services? Second, is the value lower simply because it is no longer the ecosystem that evolved as a result of natural services? This issue of authenticity is very important, because the utility that people derive from interacting with a natural environment is often dependent on how "wild" they view the environmental system to be. Although city parks can be an enjoyable setting for a picnic, there is additional joy created by having a picnic in a forest that has a high degree of ecological integrity. A good example of the importance of authenticity can be gained by analogy with the art world. If a famous painting is discovered to be a forgery, its value falls immensely even though the quality of the brushstrokes, color, line, and so on has not declined.

Box 4.4 The Value of Nature

In a very controversial and highly debated article in *Nature*, Robert Costanza and his coauthors conducted an exercise to compute the total value of ecological services on the planet. This problem is obviously very difficult and, quite naturally, the authors had to make assumptions, use extrapolation techniques, and so on. These types of problems have led other authors to be somewhat skeptical about the ability to measure the total value of an ecosystem's services, let alone all the ecosystems on the planet. If these authors are so skeptical, how can Costanza and his coauthors claim to measure the value of global ecosystems?

The answer to this question has to do with intent. The intent of Costanza and colleagues is not to create a Rosetta stone for translating all ecological values into precise estimates that can be used to fine-tune environmental policy. Instead, their intent is to show that ecological services are important and that the value of the flow of ecological services is the same order of magnitude as world gross domestic product (GDP). They find that this value lies in the range of $16 trillion to $54 trillion per year, where world GDP is approximately $18 billion per year.

There are many criticisms of this work, including a criticism that it is impossible for value to exceed GDP because then willingness to pay exceeds income. Although many economists cite this as a fatal flaw in the work of Costanza, some reflection shows that this criticism is not appropriate. We can understand this argument by assuming that a middle-class person is facing the certain death of a loved one who has been kidnapped and is threatened with death if a 10 million ransom is not paid. Assume that there is a 100 percent chance of release (unharmed) if the ransom is paid and that the police are powerless to intervene. The middle-class person probably earns about $40,000–80,000 per year, could raise $100,000 through a second mortgage, and could maybe raise $500,000 more from close relatives and friends. Therefore, the ability to pay is limited to about $600,000 to

(continues)

Box 4.4 (continued)

keep the loved one alive, but certainly the person would be willing to pay more if he or she had it.

The typical economist might criticize this argument and say that the analogy is not appropriate because it involves what is essentially an infinite change, and willingness to pay measures are defined for marginal changes. There are two responses to this argument. First, this argument is definitional on the part of economists, and not natural law. Second, and more important, Costanza and colleagues never intended for their estimates to be used to value wetlands, forests, and ecosystems by the acre. They ask, if we have the certain death of all our ecosystems, what have we lost?

The answer to this question is not particularly helpful in many policy applications, especially at the local level, but the study is more designed to argue that we need global programs to halt massive desertification, deforestation, fisheries collapse, habitat loss, and other catastrophic change at the global level. Although others have attempted to use these total value estimates as a source of marginal value estimates, that was not the original intent of Costanza and colleagues, although some of the authors have attempted to do so postpublication, as have other observers. The reason the total values cannot be used for marginal values is further discussed in Chapter 5.

Summary

This chapter represents a basic introduction to the concept of value, with an emphasis on the economic perspective of value. Techniques for measuring economic value such as the revealed preference and state preference methods are introduced and procedures for their implementation are discussed. There are, however, many issues associated with proper implementation, and students who are considering engaging in this type of research are encouraged to do more reading.

Even though the economist's definition of value is not universally accepted, it can make a substantial contribution to the decision-making process. Revealed preference approaches such as hedonic pricing techniques and the travel cost method can help measure direct use values associated with environmental change. Stated preference valuation techniques such as the contingent valuation method and conjoint analysis can estimate indirect use values, although the measurement of indirect use values remains quite difficult, especially when considering the economic value of ecological services.

Although economic valuation cannot provide exact answers to all our resource allocation decisions, it can provide substantial insight to help us make informed decisions. Chapter 5 discusses techniques for organizing value information, such as cost-benefit analysis. Economic value should not be the only input to the decision-making process. Chapter 5 discusses other criteria, such as sustainability, equity, and the outcome of public participation processes, that should also help shape the final form of environmental policy.

Review Questions

1. Contrast the underlying premises of stated preference methods and revealed preference methods.
2. What is the underlying premise of hedonic price models?
3. List the potential biases associated with contingent valuation.
4. What are the primary differences between contingent valuation and conjoint analysis?
5. Assume that you have data that suggest that if
   a. travel cost is greater than or equal to $15, no trips are taken.
   b. travel costs are zero, 100 trips are taken.

   Draw a travel cost demand curve based on these data. Calculate ordinary consumer's surplus for the individual whose travel costs are equal to $5.
6. If construction workers are willing to accept a $1/2000$ annual risk of death if their income increases by $3000 per year, what is the collective willingness to be compensated to accept the loss of one life?

Questions for Further Study

1. What are the relative strengths and weaknesses of indirect and direct valuation techniques?
2. Can human life be valued?
3. What valuation techniques would you use to measure the value of improving water quality in a local lake or river? Why?
4. What valuation techniques would you use to measure the value of preserving tropical rain forests? Why?
5. Why is it possible to look at wages or housing prices and draw a conclusion about the value of environmental quality?
6. Why is it so difficult to measure the value of ecological services?

Suggested Paper Topics

1. Use the hedonic wage model to estimate willingness to pay for an environmental characteristic. The basic data set for estimating the hedonic wage model is the Public Use Micro-Data Set (PUMS) of the Census of Population. (Available at http://www.census.gov/main/www/pums.html.) This data set contains income and socioeconomic data on individual households. Because the data set also lists the city in which the household lives, all one needs to do is develop appropriate environmental variables (concentration of various air pollutants, drinking water quality, proximity of Superfund sites, toxic hot spots, and so forth). The Environmental Protection Agency, Department of Health, and Department of Energy collect and publish these types of data. See Epple (1987); Clark and Kahn (1989); Kask (1992); and Gegax, Gerking, and Schulze (1991) for references to this approach.
2. Conduct a contingent valuation study for a local environmental quality problem using students as your sample. Look to Mitchell and Carson (1989) and the NOAA blue-ribbon panel study (U.S. Department of Commerce, 1993) for guidance about how to structure the questions. Make sure to ask your professor if you need approval from your university's "Human Subjects Review Committee."
3. Conduct a contingent valuation study for a campus issue, such as adding a new fitness facility, building a new student parking lot, or making curricular changes. Look to Mitchell and Carson (1989) and the NOAA blue-ribbon panel study (U.S. Department of Commerce, 1993) for guidance about how to structure the questions. Make sure to ask your professor if you need approval from your university's 'Human Subjects Review Committee."
4. Write a critique of a valuation method, such as contingent valuation. Start with the most recent issues of the *Journal of Environmental Economics and Management*; *Land Economics*;

Environment and Resource Economics; Ecological Economics, and the *American Journal of Agricultural Economics.* (as well as the appropriate references at the end of this chapter) for critical discussion of the method you choose.

5. The *U.S. Fish and Wildlife Survey of Fishing, Hunting and Wildlife Associated Recreation* is available at http://fa.r9.fws.gov/surveys/surveys.html. If you have good computer skills, you might enjoy taking data from this survey and estimating a travel cost demand curve. Look at Brown et al. (1990) and Smith and Kaoru (1990a) as initial references.

Works Cited and Selected Readings

Adamowicz, W., J. J. Louviere, and M. Williams. Combining Revealed and Stated Methods for Valuing Environmental Amenities. *Journal of Environmental Economics and Management 26* (1994): 271–292.

Ajzen, I., and G. L. Peterson. Contingent Value Measurement: The Price of Everything and the Value of Nothing? 65–76 in *Amenity Resource Valuation: Integrating Economics with Other Disciplines*, edited by G. L. Peterson, B. L. Driver, and R. Gregory. State College, PA: Venture, 1988.

Balkan, E., and J. R. Kahn. The Value of Changes in Deer Hunting Quality: A Travel Cost Approach. *Applied Economics 20* (1988): 533–539.

Bell, F. W., and V. R. Leeworthy. *An Economic Analysis of the Importance of Saltwater Beaches in Florida*. Sea Grant Report 47, Florida State University–Tallahassee, 1986.

Bell, F. W., P. E. Sorenson, and V. R. Leeworthy. *The Economic Valuation of Saltwater Recreational Fisheries in Florida*. Sea Grant Report 47, Florida State University–Tallahassee, 1982.

Berger, M. C., G. C. Blomquist, D. Kenkel, and G. S. Tolley. Valuing Changes in Health Risks: A Comparison of Alternative Measures. *Southern Economic Journal 53*, no. 4 (April 1987): 967–984.

Bjornstad, D., and J. R. Kahn, eds. *The Contingent Valuation of Environmental Resources: Methodological Issues and Research Needs.* London: Edward Elgar, (1996).

Blomquist, G. C., M. C. Berger, and J. P. Hoehn. New Estimates of Quality of Life in Urban Areas. *American Economic Review 78* (1988): 89–107.

Bockstael, N. E., W. M. Hannemann, and I. Strand. Benefit Analysis Using Indirect or Imputed Methods. *Measuring the Benefits of Water Improvements Using Recreation Demand Models 2*. Washington, DC: Environmental Protection Agency, 1986.

Bockstael, N. E., K. McConnell, and I. E. Strand. *Benefits from Improvement in Chesapeake Bay Water Quality*, EPA Contract 811043-01, Washington, DC: Environmental Protection Agency, 1988.

Bockstael, N. E., I. Strand, and W. M. Hannemann. Time and the Recreation Demand Model. *American Journal of Agricultural Economics 69* (1987): 293–302.

Brookshire, D. S., M. A. Thayer, W. W. Schultze, and R. L. d'Arge. Valuing Public Goods: A Comparison of Survey and Hedonic Approaches. *American Economic Review 72* (1982): 165–177.

Brown, G., J. Callaway, R. Adams, et al. Methods for Valuing Acidic Deposition and Air Pollution Effects. *Acid Deposition: State of Science and Technology 27*: National Acid Precipitation Assessment Program. Washington, DC: U.S. Government Printing Office, 1990.

Brown, T. C. The Concept of Value in Resource Allocation. *Land Economics 6* (1984): 232–245.

Chambers, C., and J. Whitehead. A Contingent Valuation Estimate of the Benefits of Wolves in Minnesota. *Environmental and Resource Economics 26*, no. 2 (October 2003): 249–267.

Clark, D. E., and J. R. Kahn. The Two-Stage Hedonic Wage Approach: A Methodology for the Valuation of Environmental Amenities. *Journal of Environmental Economics and Management 16* (1989): 106–120.

Coursey, D. L., W. D. Schulze, and J. L. Hovis. The Disparity between Willingness to Accept and Willingness to Pay Measures of Value. *Quarterly Journal of Economics 102* (August 1987): 679–690.

Cummings, R. Relating Stated and Revealed Preferences: Challenges and Opportunities. 189–197. in *The Contingent Valuation of Environmental Resources: Methodological Issues and Research Needs*, edited by D. Bjornstad and J. R. Kahn. London, Edward Elgar, 1996.

Cummings, R. G., D. Brookshire, and W. D. Schultze, eds. *Valuing Public Goods: A State of the Arts Assessment of the Contingent Valuation Method*. Towato, NJ: Rowan and Allanheld, 1986.

Cummings, R. G., and G. W. Harrison. *Identifying and Measuring Nonuse Values for Natural and Environmental Resources: A Critical Review of the State of the Art*. Final Report. Washington, DC: U.S. Environmental Protection Agency, April 1992.

Cummings, R. G., and L. O. Taylor. Does Realism Matter in Contingent Valuation Surveys? *Land Economics 89*, no. 2, (May 1998): 203–215.

Cummings, R. G., and L. O. Taylor. Unbiased Value Estimates for Environmental Goods: A Cheap Talk Design for the Contingent Valuation Method. *American Economic Review 89*, no. 3, (June 1999): 649–665.

Desvousges, W. H., R. F. Johnson, and H. S. Banzhaf. Environmental Policy Analysis With Limited Information: Principles and Applications of the Transfer Method. Cheltenham, U.K. and Northampton, Mass.: Elgar, 1998.

Diamond, P. A., and J. A. Hauseman. Contingent Valuation: Is Some Number Better Than No Number? *Journal of Economic Perspectives 8* (1994):45–64.

Duffield, J. W., and D. A. Patterson. Field Testing Existence Values: An Instream Flow Trust Fund for Montana Rivers. Paper presented at Association of Environmental and Resource Economists meetings, New Orleans, January 1992.

Epple, D. Hedonic Prices and Implicit Markets: Estimating Demand and Supply Functions for Differentiated Products. *Journal of Political Economy 95* (1987): 59–80.

Fisher, A., L. G. Chestnut, and D. M. Violette, The Value of Reducing Risks to Death: A Note on New Evidence, *Journal of Policy Analysis and Management 8*, no. 1, (1989): 88–100.

Freeman, A. M., III. *The Benefits of Environmental Improvement: Theory and Practice*. Baltimore: Johns Hopkins University Press, 1979.

Gegax, D., S. Gerking, and W. Schulze. Perceived Risk and the Marginal Value of Safety. *Review of Economics and Statistics 73*, no. 4, (November 1991): 589–596.

Groothuis, P. A., and J. C. Whitehead. Does Don't Know Mean No? Analysis of 'Don't Know' Responses in Dichotomous Choice Contingent Valuation Questions. *Applied Economics 34*, no. 15, (October 2002): 1935–1940.

Gustafsson, A., A. Herrmann, and F. Huber, eds. *Conjoint measurement: Methods and Applications*. Second edition. Heidelberg and New York: Springer, 2001.

Haab, T. C., and K. E. McConnell. *Valuing Environmental and Natural Resources: The Econometrics of Non-Market Valuation*. Cheltenham, U.K. and Northampton, Mass.: Elgar, 2002.

Harrison, D., and D. L. Rubinfeld. Hedonic Housing Prices and the Demand for Clean Air. *Journal of Environmental Economics and Management 5* (1978): 81–102.

Hotelling, H. Letter to National Park Service. In *An Econometric Study of the Monetary Evaluation of Recreation in the National Parks*, dated 1947. Washington, DC: U.S. Department of Interior, NPS and Recreational Planning Division, 1949.

Huppert, D. D. Two Empirical Issues in Recreational Fishery Economics: Mail Survey Self-Selection Bias and Divergence Between WTP and WTA. In Fourth Annual Association of Environmental and Resource Economists Workshop: Marine and Sport Fisheries Economic Valuation and Management. Seattle, EPA230-08-88-034. Washington, DC: Environmental Protection Agency, June 1988.

ICF Inc. *Pollution Prevention Benefits Manual*. Washington, DC: Environmental Protection Agency, October 1989.

Johannesson, M., P.-O. Johansson, and R. M. O'Conor, The Value of Private Safety versus the Value of Public Safety, *Journal of Risk and Uncertainty 12* (1996): 263–275.

Johnson, L. E. *A Morally Deep World: An Essay on Moral Significance and Environmental Ethics*. Cambridge: Cambridge University Press, 1991.

Kahn, J. R. The Economic Value of Long Island Saltwater Recreational Fisheries. *New York Economic Review 21* (1991): 3–23.

Kask, S. B. Long-Term Health Risk Valuation: Pigeon River, North Carolina. 1–25 in *Benefits*

Transfer: Procedures, Problems and Research Needs. Proceedings of the 1992 Association of Environmental and Resource Economists Workshop, Snowbird, UT, June 1992. http://yosmite.epa.gov/ee/epa/eermfile.nsf/vwAN/EE-0078-03.pdf.

Kealy, M. J., M. Montgomery, and J. F. Dovido. Reliability and Predictive Validity of Contingent Valuation: Does the Nature of the Good Matter? *Journal of Environmental Economics and Management 19* (1990): 244–263.

Kealy, M. J., and M. Rockel. The Value of Nonconsumptive Recreation in the United States. Unpublished manuscript, 1990.

Krutilla, J. V. Conservation Reconsidered. *American Economic Review 47* (1967): 777–786.

Krutilla, J., and A. C. Fisher. *The Economics of Natural Environments*. Washington, DC: Resources for the Future, 1985.

Levin, I. P., J. J. Louviere, A. A. Schepanski, and K. L. Norman. External Validity Tests of Laboratory Studies of Information Integration. *Organizational Behavior and Human Performance 31* (1983): 173–193.

Louviere, J. Relating Stated Preference Methods and Models to Choices in Real Markets: Calibration of CV Responses. 167–188 In *The Contingent Valuation of Environmental Resources: Methodological Issues and Research Needs*, edited by D. Bjornstad and J. R. Kahn. London: Edward Elgar, (1996).

Louviere, J. J. Conjoint Analysis Modelling of Stated Preferences: A Review of Theory, Methods, Recent Developments, and External Validity. *Journal of Transport Economics and Policy 17* (1988): 93–119.

McConnell, K. E. Existence and Bequest Value. 74–104 In *Managing Air Quality and Scenic Resources at National Parks and Wilderness Areas*, edited by R. D. Rowe and L. G. Chestnut. Boulder, CO: Westview, 1983.

Milon, J. W. *Estimating Recreational Angler Participation and Economic Impact in the Gulf of Mexico Mackeral Fishery*. Prepared for Southeast Regional Office, NMFS, NA86wc-h-06616, RAS/CC31, 1988a.

Milon, J. W. Travel Cost Methods for Estimating the Recreational Use Benefits of Artificial Marine Habitat. *Southern Agricultural Economics 20* (1988b): 87–101.

Mitchell, R. C., and R. T. Carson. *Using Surveys to Value Public Goods: The Contingent Valuation Method*. Washington, DC: Resources for the Future, 1989.

Morey, E. R., and W. D. Shaw. An Economic Model to Assess the Impact of Acid Rain: A Characteristics Approach to Estimating the Demand for and Benefits from Recreational Fishing. 195–216 In *Advances in Applied Microeconomic Theory 8*. edited by V. K. Smith and A. D. Witte. Greenwich, CT: JAI Press, 1992.

Nash, R. F. *The Rights of Nature: A History of Environmental Ethics*. Madison: University of Wisconsin Press, 1989.

Neill, H. R., R. Cummings, P. Ganderton, G. Harrison, and T. McGuckin. Hypothetical surveys and real economic commitments. *Land Economics 70* (1994):145–154.

Nelson, J. Residential Choice, Hedonic Prices, and the Demand for Urban Air Quality. *Journal of Urban Economics 5* (1978): 357–369.

Plourde, C. Conservation of Extinguishable Species. *Natural Resources Journal 15* (1975): 791–797.

Portney, P. R. The Contingent Valuation Debate: Why Should Economists Care? *Journal of Economic Perspectives 8* (1994):1–18.

Ridker, R. G., and J. A. Henning. The Determination of Residential Property Values with a Special Reference to Air Pollution. *Review of Economics and Statistics* 49 (1967): 246–257.

Rosen, S. Wage-based Indexes of Urban Quality of Life. 74–104 In *Current Issues in Urban Economics,* edited by P. Mieskowski and M. Straszheim. Baltimore: Johns Hopkins University Press, 1979.

Schulze, W., G. McClelland, D. Waldman, D. Schenk, and J. Irwin. Valuing Visibility: A Field Test of the Contingent Valuation Method. Washington, DC: Environmental Protection Agency, Cooperative Agreement #CR-812054. 1990.

Schulze, W. D., and G. H. McClelland. Valuing Winter Visibility Improvement in the Grand Canyon. Unpublished paper presented at Allied Social Sciences Association meetings, New Orleans, January 1991.

Schulze, W. D., G. H. McClelland, and D. L. Coursey. Valuing Risk: A Comparison of Expected Utility with Models from Cognitive

Psychology. Unpublished manuscript, University of Colorado, Boulder, CO, 1986.

Seip, K., and J. Strand. Willingness to Pay for Environmental Goods in Norway: A Contingent Valuation Study with Real Payment. *Environmental and Resource Economics 2* (1992): 91–106.

Shrestha, R. K., A. F. Seidl, and A. S. Moraes. Value of Recreational Fishing in the Brazilian Pantanal: A Travel Cost Analysis Using Count Data Models. *Ecological Economics 42*, no. 1-2 (August 2002): 289–299.

Smith, V. K. Nonmarket Valuation of Environmental Resources: An Interpretive Appraisal. *Land Economics 69* (1993): 1–26.

Smith, V. K., and Y. Kaoru. Signals or Noise: Explaining the Variation in Recreation Benefit Measurement. *American Journal of Agricultural Economics 72* (1990a): 419–433.

Smith, V. K., and Y. Kaoru. What Have We Learned Since Hotelling's Letter? A Meta-Analysis. *Economic Letters 32* (1990b): 267–272.

Smith, V. K., and R. B. Palmquist. *The Value of Recreational Fishing on the Albemarle and Pamlico Estuaries*. Washington, DC: Environmental Protection Agency, 1988.

Smith V. K., V. Houtven, and S. K. Pattanayak. Benefit Transfer via Preference Calibration: "Prudential Algebra" for Policy. *Land Economics 78*, no. 1 (February 2002): 132–152.

Smith, V. K., and S. K. Pattanayak. Is Meta-Analysis a Noah's Ark for Non-market Valuation? *Environmental and Resource Economics 22*, no. 1-2 (June 2002): 271–296.

Spiegel, H. *The Growth of Economic Thought*. Durham, NC: Duke University Press, 1971.

Stoeckl, N. A 'Quick and Dirty' Travel Cost Model. *Tourism Economics 9*, no. 3 (September 2003): 325–335.

Thomas, M., and N. Stratis. Compensation Variation for Recreational Policy: A Random Utility Approach to Boating in Florida. *Marine Resource Economics 17*, no. 1 (2002): 23–33.

U.S. Department of Commerce. Natural Resource Damage Assessments Under the Oil Protection Act of 1990. 15 CFR Chapter IX, National Oceanic and Atmospheric Administration. *Federal Register 58* (10), January 15, 1993, Proposed Rules, 4601–4614.

U.S. National Acid Precipitation Assessment Program (NAPAP). *1990 Integrated Assessment Report*, Washington, DC, 1991.

Viscusi, W. K., The Value of Risks to Life and Health, *Journal of Economic Literature 31*, no. 4 (December 1993): 1912–1946.

Viscusi, W. K., W. Magat, and J. Huber. Pricing Environmental Health Risks: Survey Assessment of Risk-Risk and Risk-Dollar Trade-offs for Chronic Bronchitis. *Journal of Environmental Economics and Management 21*, no. 1 (July 1991): 32–51.

Whitehead, J. C., W. B. Clifford, and T. J. Hoban. Willingness to Pay for a Saltwater Recreational Fishing License: A Comparison of Angler Groups. *Marine Resource Economics 16*, no. 3 (2001): 177–194.

chapter 5

Environmental Decision Making: Criteria and Methods of Assessment

> *It should be quite clear, then, that there are no criteria to be laid down in general for distinguishing the real from the not real.*
>
> *John Langshaw Austin, Sense and Sensibilia, p. 76*

Introduction

Although it may be difficult to develop criteria that allow one to distinguish between the real and the imagined, it is essential to develop criteria to distinguish between alternative states of the real world. Without the aid of decision-making criteria, it would be difficult to make decisions about policies such as the limitation of emissions of greenhouse gases, whether a species should be allowed to become extinct, or whether we should drill for oil in the Arctic National Wildlife Refuge (ANWR).

Chapter 4 focused on the measurement of the economic value of environmental resources and damages to those resources. One question, however, remains: How do we use these values in making decisions concerning environmental policy? Cost-benefit analysis immediately comes to mind, but it is but one way to organize this type of information. More important, economic value is but one criterion that must be integrated with other criteria in the decision-making process.

This chapter shows how the economic value measures discussed in Chapter 4 can be used to test the "economic efficiency" of a potential decision or outcome. The chapter also focuses on additional criteria and discusses methods for simultaneously considering these diverse criteria.

Decision-Making Criteria

The development of a set of criteria on which to base public policy decisions is very much like selecting the soccer players for a country's World Cup competition. Everyone agrees on a few key players, but as one moves past the celebrated stars, there is considerable disagreement about who should fill the spots of the team. This analogy holds for decision-making criteria as well. For example, almost everyone agrees that economic efficiency is an important criterion, and some people think that it should be the only criterion, but what of ethical considerations, public participation, equity, sustainability and environmental stewardship?

Despite this potential for lack of consensus, this chapter suggests a set of criteria, with full knowledge that there will be disagreement and further discussion of the included criteria as well as of the omitted criteria. The demarcation developed in this chapter will help readers understand the need to consider a broad suite of decision-making criteria and think about alternative sets of criteria. The set of criteria given in Table 5.1 is suggested as a first partial list. The reader is encouraged to extend this list to other relevant criteria, which may vary with the context of the issue that is examined.

Table 5.1 Decision-Making Criteria

- Economic efficiency
- Equity
- Sustainability
- Environmental justice
- Ecological impact/environmental stewardship
- Ethics
- Public participation
- Advancement of knowledge

Economic Efficiency

The criterion of economic efficiency has to do with maximizing the difference between the social benefit and social cost of an economic activity, policy, or project. This evaluation method measures how close we come to the maximization of net social benefits. In theory, all social benefits and all social costs could be incorporated into the measure of economic efficiency, but in practice, only benefits and costs that are readily measured in monetary terms are incorporated into the measure. Thus, there is both a need to develop better valuation measures (as discussed in Chapter 4) and a need to develop additional criteria, because economic efficiency will often inadequately incorporate environmental impacts, equity, and other important societal consequences.

Economic efficiency is usually measured using one of two different concepts. The first is net economic benefit, which is generally measured as the total willingness to pay for a good or activity less the costs of providing the good or activity. This measure is the one most preferred by economists. The second is that of gross domestic product (GDP) (or net domestic product [NDP], a derivative of GDP), which is a measure of the value of market output. This measure is the one generally preferred by international development and lending agencies. These two measures are alternative measures of economic benefit and as such should not be added together.

Net Economic Benefit

Net economic benefit (Figure 5.1) can be measured as the area under a demand curve and above a supply curve for a particular good or service. The demand curve can be interpreted as a marginal willingness to pay function, so the area underneath it (CBQ0) can be interpreted as the total willingness to pay for the activity, or the total social benefit of the good or activity. The

Figure 5.1 **Net Economic Benefit**

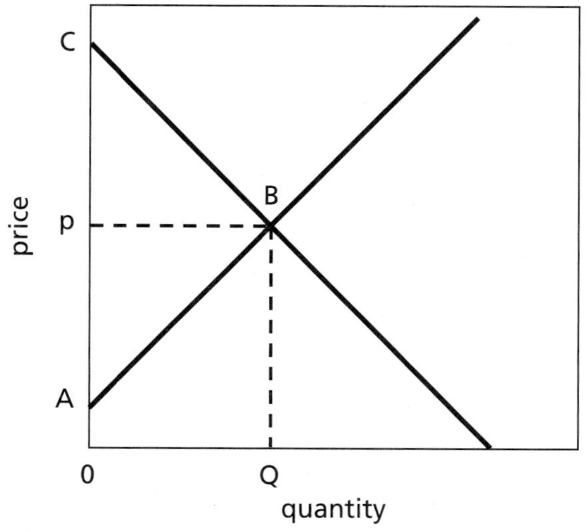

supply curve can be interpreted as the marginal opportunity cost of producing the good or service, so the area underneath it (ABQ0) can be interpreted as total social cost. Hence, the difference between the two, or area ABC in Figure 5.1, is the measure of net economic benefit. This concept is discussed more fully in Chapter 4. This measure does not include the cost of market failures associated with the good. The discussion of revealed preference and stated preference approaches in Chapter 4 presents alternative approaches to measure the changes in net economic benefits associated with market failure.

Gross Domestic Product

Gross domestic product is a measure of the total value of all goods and services produced in an economy. Because expenditures become income, GDP is also a measure of national income. Every single principles of economics textbook stresses that GDP is not a measure of social welfare (it is not even truly a measure of economic efficiency), yet many policy makers, especially those with international funding agencies, view it as such and use it as such.

It is very easy to understand GDP as a potential measure of economic efficiency by looking at Figure 5.1. The contribution of this particular good to GDP is simply its market value, or price multiplied by quantity, which is equal to the area of rectangle 0PBQ. As can be seen in this diagram, GDP is not based on an integrative concept, but merely multiplies equilibrium marginal benefit (price) and equilibrium quantity. Note that the opportunity costs of producing the product are not subtracted from the measure.

As mentioned, GDP is not a measure of social welfare because it does not measure other dimensions of the quality of life, such as health, environmental quality, social justice, freedom from crime, and access to education. Moreover, as GDP fails as a measure of social welfare, it also fails as a measure of economic efficiency. The failure of not taking costs into account has already been mentioned. The importance of this failure can be noted by an example. Increased presence of HIV/AIDS could increase GDP because so much money is being spent on health care. Net economic benefits, however, will not increase as a result of this expenditure. The other important failure as a measure of economic efficiency is that because GDP is based on market goods, it does not include production in the subsistence or informal sector. Thus, policy that is based on the performance of GDP can end up favoring formal economic activity over informal activity, leading to the displacement of small subsistence farms by commercial export-oriented agriculture. If that happens, it could lead to reductions in total output (GDP plus subsistence agriculture), even though the formal measure of GDP increases. The blind pursuit of growth in GDP can actually lead to the impoverishment of large segments of the rural population, as is discussed more fully in Chapter 18.

Although GDP is not an adequate measure of either economic efficiency or social welfare, it is often incorrectly used to measure both. GDP measures the income associated with output, and there is opportunity cost associated with producing this output. It does not measure the net benefit of the output. When the criterion of economic efficiency is used, it should be measured by the methodology described in Figure 5.1 and elaborated throughout Chapter 4.

Economic Efficiency and the Pareto Criterion

The examination of economic efficiency requires that benefits be compared with costs with the idea of improving society's well-being, but what criteria should be used for the comparison? Although many criteria have been suggested about what constitutes an improvement in economic efficiency, the criterion most employed by economists—the Hicks-Kaldor criterion, or the criterion of a potential Pareto improvement—is used here. A Pareto improvement is said to occur when resources are reallocated in a fashion that makes some people better off and no one worse off. In a complex real world, any reallocation is likely to hurt someone, so many economists have adopted the criterion of a potential Pareto improvement. A potential Pareto improvement is a reallocation whereby the gain of people who are helped is larger than the losses of those who are made worse off. It is called a potential Pareto improvement because if the gainers would compensate the losers for their losses, the gainers would still be better off. After compensation, the potential Pareto improvement becomes an actual Pareto improvement.

Many economists argue that public policies should be pursued provided that these policies improve economic efficiency, with the potential Pareto improvement viewed as the operational definition of improved social welfare. Note that no compensation need take place for the change to be deemed desirable, so some segments of society may be hurt by the change.

Also note that potential Pareto improvement could only function as a decision rule if economic efficiency were the only criterion on which policy should be based. Other criteria, such as equity and fairness, are also important. Cost-benefit analysis examines the magnitude of costs and benefits, but the question of who receives the costs and benefits, as well as the fairness of this allocation, is important as well. For example, most people would argue that a policy that benefited billionaires at the expense of minimum wage earners was not desirable even if it meets the criterion of being a potential Pareto improvement. Reiterating, the potential Pareto improvement does not consider equity issues, which are extremely important to the process of formulating policy.

Equity

As discussed, the level of net benefits is not the only criterion associated with benefits and costs. Another important aspect is the fashion in which the costs and benefits are distributed among the members of society. The equity criterion relates to these distributional criteria and is multidimensional. One has to be concerned about the distribution of costs and benefits across various components of contemporary society, including socioeconomic groups within a country, regions of a country, gender, and age. As the recent collapse of the Hague round of negotiations on the Kyoto Protocol suggests (see Chapter 7), an extremely important aspect of equity is the fairness of the distribution across countries. Of particular note is the effect of decisions on the distribution of costs and benefits between developing and developed countries. One additional dimension of equity, equity across generations, is an important impetus behind the development of an increasing concern with the sustainability of our actions.

Intracountry Equity

Both environmental degradation and environmental policy create consequences for reducing or increasing the differential in the quality of life that may exist across subgroups of a country's population. Initially, many economists argued that improving the quality of the environment would actually widen this social welfare gap. Environmental quality was perceived to be a luxury, with the improvement in environmental quality benefiting wealthier people more than the poor. Because stricter environmental policy may result in a loss of jobs in polluting industries and in higher product prices, it was often also argued that the poor bore a disproportionate share of the cost of improving environmental quality.

This view is not as widely held now, for several reasons. First, in many developing countries the poor are primarily agrarian, dependent on the environment and suffering the most from the effects of environmental degradation (soil erosion, deforestation, contaminated drinking water, and so on). Also, urban dwellers in these countries suffer from many environmental externalities, including contaminated drinking water, severe air pollution, and exposure to toxic waste. These concepts are discussed more fully in Chapter 18.

The same thing is true in developed countries such as the United States. Air quality tends to be the worst in the largest cities, especially in the inner-city areas where low-income people reside. Also, low-income and minority populations may face greater exposure to toxic waste and other environmental hazards (see this chapter's discussion of environmental justice and Chapter 17).

Equity across Countries

Equity across countries is extremely important to environmental policy. Some environmental problems, such as global warming, require international cooperation. There is also a demand in wealthy countries to preserve the environmental resources in the lower-income countries. In either case, the lower-income countries have to bear costs to generate benefits for higher-income countries. Obviously, many people, particularly those in developing countries, think that this burden is inherently unfair and that prosperous countries should compensate the lower-income countries for the costs they incur in improving the global environment. Another dimension of environmental equity that is often overlooked is the lower level of environmental quality in poorer countries, which inhibits their ability to improve their standard of living. These points are discussed in great detail in Chapter 18.

Equity across Generations and Sustainability

Equity across generations, or intergenerational equity, is an extremely important consideration in environmental policy. Because today's decisions may generate important environmental costs for future generations, and because future generations cannot participate in making current decisions, future generations may potentially pay the price for the actions of the current generation. For example, current emissions of greenhouse gases that cause global warming, current conversion of habitat that causes loss of biodiversity, and current generation of toxic and radioactive wastes all cause irreversible environmental change, which lowers the well-being of future generations.

Many people believe that the unfair treatment of future generations is made worse by the process of discounting, which makes future costs and benefits insignificant in comparison to current costs and benefits (see discussion of discounting later in this chapter). For this reason, they advocate a criterion of sustainability rather than efficiency (maximizing present values) for guiding policy.

The concept of sustainability is closely related to the concept of intergenerational equity. Sustainability is the desirable attempt to improve the condition of the current generation, but activities must be constrained so that this improvement does not compromise the ability of future generations to meet their needs and improve their quality of life. Actions that create benefits in the present but generate large environmental costs in the future could pass a cost-benefit test because of the impact of discounting when measuring the present value of future costs. Such actions, however, are unlikely to pass a sustainability test, which does not look at present values but, rather, examines barriers to future improvement in the quality of life that are created by today's actions. In other words, policies that benefit the current generation but diminish the prospects of future generations would not be allowed under this criterion. The criterion of sustainability is very important when examining environmental problems such as deforestation, global climate change, nuclear power, and biodiversity. The economic theory of sustainability is more fully discussed in Chapters 6 and 18.

Equity Indicators

Although income is only one component of the equity issue, decisions related to environmental policy often will have important effects on the distribution of income. The distribution of income has received much attention in the economics literature, and a set of measures has been developed to measure the inequality of the distribution of income, the primary measures for which are the Lorenz curve and the Gini coefficient.

Figure 5.2 contains an illustrative example of a Lorenz curve. The curve shows the percentage of income received by a given percentage of the society. In this example, the poorest 50 percent of the population receives only 20 percent of the nation's income. The diagonal line, where the two percentages are equal, represents a perfectly equitable distribution of income. The farther the Lorenz curve is skewed away from the diagonal line, the more inequitable the distribution of income. The curve can be transformed into a single variable called the Gini coefficient. The Gini coefficient is equal to 100*A/(A + B), where A is the area between the diagonal and the curve and B is the area underneath the curve. With a perfectly equitable distribution of income, A is equal to zero and the Gini coefficient is equal to zero. With a perfectly inequitable distribution of zero, B is equal to zero and the Gini coefficient is equal to 100. Gini coefficients can be used to describe the distribution of wealth as well. Table 5.2 contains Gini coefficients for selected countries. It also contains information on the percentage of population of the country that has income less than the international poverty level of an income of $2.00 per day.

Of course, as already indicated, income and wealth are not the only aspects of equity or fairness. Equal access to the law, education, opportunity, and health are among the many dimensions of the quality of life that are important. Of particular importance is equal access to environmental quality. This issue has become to be known as the environmental justice issue and forms one of the criteria that are suggested in this chapter as important to policy making.

Figure 5.2 **Equity and the Lorenz Curve**

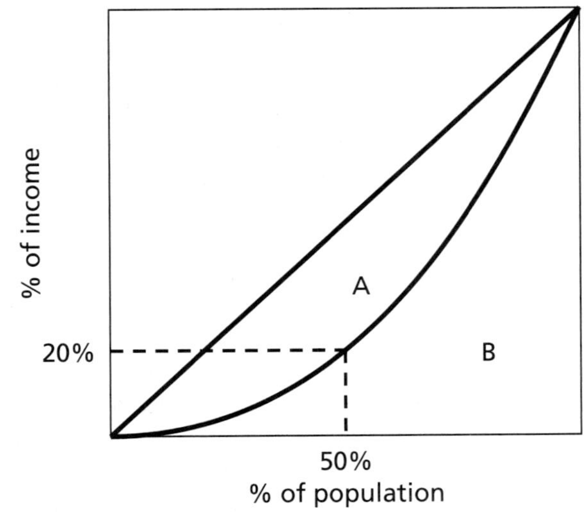

Table 5.2 **Gini Coefficients and Percentage of Population below the Poverty Level for Selected Countries**

Country and Year of Data	Percent Below $2.00 per day	Gini Coefficient
Bangladesh (1995–1996)	77.8	33.6
Brazil (1998)	26.5	60.7
Cameroon (1996)	64.4	47.7
Canada (1994)	Negligible	31.5
China (1999)	52.6	40.3
France	Negligible	32.7
Germany	Negligible	37.1
Honduras (1998)	45.1	56.3
India (1997)	86.2	37.8
Japan (1993)	Negligible	24.9
Kenya (1994)	62.3	44.9
Nicaragua (1998)	Not available	60.3
United States (1997)	Negligible	40.8
Turkey (1994)	18	41.5

Source: Data for this table taken from the World Bank, *World Development Report 2003*, New York: Oxford University Press, 2003. Similar information on all other countries can be found in this book.

Environmental Justice

The criterion of environmental justice has taken on increasing importance since the 1990s, as studies have suggested that certain segments of the population face disproportionate exposure to environmental risk, in both developed and developing countries. For example, in the United States, minorities, especially those of low income living in rural areas, face a disproportionate level of exposure to environmental hazards, particularly carcinogenic and mutagenic hazardous chemicals (Bullard 1990). Of course, those living in inner cities face disproportionate exposure to air pollution as well as hazards from intensely polluted urban streams, brownfields, and the lead paint in old buildings.

The same pattern holds in developing countries, with giant cities such as Mexico City, São Paulo, Beijing, Cairo, and Calcutta having levels of air pollution as well as exposure to toxic waste that surpass those of any city in the developed nations. In fact, whole cultures have developed in waste sites, where families actually live in the waste dump and generate income by recovering and selling useful material from the waste sites. Although this recycling activity may seem environmentally beneficial at one level, it generates incredibly high exposures to hazardous substances and abysmal living conditions for the participants, many of whom are children.

Environmental justice is an issue in rural areas of developing countries as well. Farm workers at industrial agricultural sites such as large banana plantations are exposed to high levels of pesticides, as are the villages downwind and downstream. Informal mining activity exposes workers and nearby populations to mercury, cyanide, and other toxic hazards. Global climate change threatens to increase the range of tropical diseases such as malaria and dengue fever. In addition, there is the issue of contaminated drinking water, perhaps the most significant environmental problem in the world.

Ecological Criteria

At the outset, it should be said that there is no consensus of how to develop measures of the quality or functionability of an ecosystem or ecosystems in aggregate. In fact, little progress has been made in terms of developing an indicator that can be used to guide policy. This section discusses several alternatives for assessing the status of ecosystems and their ability to contribute to social welfare.

The first question to be addressed is how to define a desirable state of an ecosystem. Two primary concepts have been advanced: ecosystem health and ecosystem integrity. Ecosystem health has to do with a system's ability to provide a flow of ecological services, and ecological integrity measures the closeness of that system to a hypothetical reference system that is completely unperturbed by human activity.

Ecosystem health is a controversial topic because it can be difficult to define the counterfactual, or what would constitute a healthy ecosystem in terms of the flow of ecological services. For example, you could get a set of services flowing from a southern pine or eucalyptus plantation, but not the full suite of ecological services that would be found in an Amazonian rain forest or Siberian boreal forest. This difficulty leads to questions of what level of ecological services is sufficient to conclude that an ecosystem is healthy.

Schrader-Frechette (1998) addresses this issue, arguing that ecosystem health can be measured with an extension of the traditional ecological risk assessment paradigm. She finds the original brand of risk assessment, focusing on animal risk assessment, an unproductive avenue to follow. This paradigm looks at toxicity research and incorporates this research into an assessment of risks of exposure from human activity. As Schrader-Frechette notes, this method is particularly inappropriate for most types of ecological risk, such as those that involve land use change and other environmental threats unrelated to toxic chemicals. It is not a promising road for developing an indicator of the effects of ecosystem impacts on social welfare.

Shrader-Frechette (1998) also discusses the "wholistic[sic] health approach" to ecosystem management and risk assessment. She notes that many proponents of the concept of ecosystem health believe it to be related to at least three ecosystem characteristics:

- An ecosystem's ability to maintain desirable vital signs
- An ecosystem's ability to handle stress
- An ecosystem's ability to recover after perturbations

She notes that the controversy about the use of this method is that there are no nonnormative value-free ways to operationalize this concept. In fact, she notes that in the human medical arena, we do not have a general holistic measure of human health related to the status of the entire being. In fact, it would be easier to find this measure for a human than for an ecosystem, because we know more about the relation between subsystems and the overall being for humans than we do for ecosystems. For example, if a person's arteries become clogged with plaque, we can make predictions about future heart attacks, longevity, and related outcomes. If a riverine ecosystem loses 20 of 45 species of freshwater mussels, however, what are the ramifications for ecosystem health?

Cairns (1995) cites several definitions of ecological integrity that he has previously developed and that have been developed by others. He advances that of Karr as particularly noteworthy, where biological integrity is defined as

> the capability of supporting and maintaining a balanced, integrated, adaptive biological system having the full range of elements (genes, species, assemblages) and processes (mutation, demography, biotic interactions, nutrient and energy dynamics and metapopulation processes) expected in a natural habitat of a region. (Cairns, 1995, p. 314)

Note the difficulty in any attempt to operationalize this concept because the definition has nine components, each of which is multidimensional. Although some attempts have been made to develop such an index, such as the Index of Biological Integrity, the concept has largely remained unimplemented.

For many urbanized, industrialized, or highly agricultural areas, the concept of ecological integrity might be inappropriate. A good case in point is the Tennessee River Valley, which has over 50 dams on the tributaries and main stem of the river. In a highly engineered system such as the Tennessee River system (or the Mississippi River, Columbia River, Colorado River, or almost any other major river system), the concept of ecological integrity may not be applicable, because much of the system is an engineered ecosystem rather than a naturally occurring ecosystem. Thus the concept of ecosystem health and looking at the flow of services from the human-made reservoirs (and the sections of river between the reservoirs) should be stressed, rather than making a comparison to the historic ecosystem which no longer exists, except possibly above the most upstream reservoirs. Box 5.1 contains a discussion of energy analysis, which is a very controversial method for measuring the direct value of ecosystems.

Any notion of a measure of ecosystem health or ecosystem integrity involves development of an aggregate measure by building up from measures of components or characteristics. Aggregation systems take on a life of their own and have distinct properties associated with the method of aggregation. Different methods for aggregation are discussed next.

At least four methods have been suggested or employed to develop operational indicators of environmental quality. They are the use of "representative" environmental variables, green GDP, the development of satellite accounts for the National Income and Product Accounts, and indices of sets of environmental variables.

Box 5.1 Energy Analysis

In many cases, natural scientists (see Odum and Odum, 1976) use an entirely different criterion, known as "energetics," "energy flows," or "energy," for evaluating potential projects or policy. This criterion uses an alternative theory of value based on the energy contained in a system or component of a system. It is neither purely biocentric nor purely anthropocentric. The approach is based on a theory that suggests that the one thing common to, necessary for, and scarce in both economic systems and ecological systems is energy. Thus, energy can be viewed as a "currency of exchange," and the value of any component of an economic system or ecological system is based on the energy embodied in that component. Economists reject this notion of value because it places too little emphasis on the scarcity of the component. Under this system, a barnyard goose could be viewed as more valuable than a whooping crane (an endangered species), and a large painting by the author of this textbook could be viewed as more valuable than a small painting by Picasso.

Although it is easy for economists to reject an energy theory of value, an energy criterion can still inform the decision-making process. The energy criterion will show if there is a negative flow of energy associated with a particular policy or project. This criterion should cause one to question the long-term sustainability of the project and even potentially its economic viability and is an argument for a more careful examination of these issues. Just as with any criterion, the energy criterion yields a particular type of information and should be used in conjunction with a full suite of criterion, such as those outlined in this chapter.

Representative Environmental Variables

Measures of individual types of pollution have been used in many studies, with the underlying assumption being that the trends associated with these individual pollutants are somehow representative of environmental quality. For example, sulfur dioxide pollution has been used as an indicator of overall environmental quality in the estimation of "environmental Kuznet's curves" (see Chapter 6), which purportedly show a U-shaped relationship between environmental quality and income (an inverse U-shaped relationship between income and concentrations of pollution). The use of a particular pollutant to proxy for environmental quality in general is conceptually similar to using output in the steel industry as a proxy for GDP or using incidence of lung cancer as a general indicator of the health of the population and has been criticized by Arrow et. al. (1995) and O'Neill et. al. (1996), among others. In particular, the measure is completely unrelated to both land use changes and water quality changes (with the exception of acidification of water bodies). In addition, sulfur dioxide is a fund or flow pollutant that does not accumulate over time, unlike carbon dioxide, chlorofluorocarbons, and heavy metals. This method could be applied to biodiversity by using indicator (canary in the coal mine) species as the representative environmental variables. For example, the spotted owl is suggested as an indicator species for the Pacific old-growth forests (United States and Canada), and the abundance and biodiversity of mussels in general has been suggested as a biodiversity indicator for some rivers in the Tennessee River Valley. In these two cases, it may be possible to define appropriate indicator species. What, though, would be the appropriate indicator species for an ecosystem as complex and diverse as the rain forests of the Amazon, the coral reefs of the South Pacific, or oceanic ecosystems?

Green GDP

One alternative is to subsume the ecological measure into the economic measure. For example, many economists, including Peskin (1976), Prince and Gordon (1994), Repetto et al. (1989), and Daly (1991), have argued that disastrous consequences can occur when macroeconomic policy is based on promoting the growth of GDP. They argue that not only does it ignore other aspects of the quality of life, but also that GDP has a serious flaw as a measure of economic progress.

This flaw is because measures of net domestic product (NDP) subtract the depreciation of human-made capital, but do not subtract the depreciation of natural capital. Thus, when a machine is worn out in the production of current income, the loss in income producing ability is subtracted from the measure of current income. The consumption of human-made capital is subtracted from GDP to give NDP, a more accurate measure of the current economic well-being of a nation. When a forest is clear-cut, however, soil is degraded; or stocks of minerals are depleted so as to produce current income, a similar debit is not made.

Although one can argue that this issue is just a definitional one and that all definitions are arbitrary in nature, there are serious implications when national economic policy is based on this flawed measure of NDP. If increasing current NDP is a primary policy goal, then natural capital and its ability to produce future income (or other services) may be expended even if doing so is detrimental to producing future social welfare. This problem is crucial in developed countries such as the United States, but it is perhaps even more important in developing countries where pressing needs to increase current income have caused catastrophic deforestation, pollution, soil erosion, and desertification.

As Repetto and colleagues indicate, this difference in the treatment of natural capital and human-made capital

> reinforces the false dichotomy between the economy and the "environment" that leads policy makers to ignore or destroy the latter in the name of economic development. It confuses the depletion of valuable assets with the generation of income. Thus, it promotes and seems to validate the idea that rapid rates of growth can be achieved and sustained by exploiting the resource base. The result can be illusory growth and permanent losses in wealth. (Repetto et al., 1989, p. 3)

Therefore, Repetto and others argue that the depreciation of natural capital should be factored into GDP in a fashion analogous to the depreciation of human-made capital. Repetto and colleagues recomputed Indonesia's national income and product accounts, making corrections for deforestation, soil erosion, and oil reserves. They found that the measured 7.1 percent annual growth rate of GDP is actually only 4 percent when these corrections are made. (Repetto et al., 1989, p. 4)

Although this type of analysis can aid in the formulation of macroenvironmental policy, it does not give complete information about the relationship between the health of the environment and social welfare. This measure only takes into account one pathway for the environment to affect social welfare, and most importantly, it ignores the direct effect of the health of the environment on social welfare. Although the value of these direct effects or nonpecuniary environmental services could be incorporated into national income and product accounts, that would be difficult if not impossible to do. It is much more difficult to monetize these other aspects of environmental quality than it is to monetize environmental effects such as oil depletion and soil erosion. Thus, the monetary conversion problem associated with willingness-to-pay measures (for example, the difficulty of measuring the value of ecological services and indirect use) is not eliminated with national income and product accounts; rather, it has simply been transferred to the national income and product accounts.

An additional problem with these macroeconomic approaches is the tendency to focus on environmental resources that are part of the economic production process and focus less on environmental resources that contribute more basic life support services or amenity benefits. More importantly, GDP and NDP are measures of the health of the economy, not the health of the environment. Separate measures of the health of the environment must be developed to better understand the relationship between environmental quality and social welfare. New approaches are particularly needed for measuring the value of ecological services such as biodiversity, because the path by which ecological services contribute to GDP is indirect. The contributions and potential contributions of ecosystem services to GDP would represent only a small subset of the impacts of ecosystem services on social welfare. These issues are discussed more fully in Chapter 6.

Satellite Accounts

In addition to the types of modifications of GDP already discussed, the United Nations Statistical Division recommends the development of a system of environmental satellite accounts to monitor environmental change. Satellite accounts are simply measures of environmental variables that are maintained side by side with the National Income and Product Accounts (the GDP accounting system). These environmental variables are measured in physical, not monetary, units and are not integrated into explicit or implicit measures of GDP.

As defined by Hamilton and Lutz:

> Satellite Accounts try to integrate environmental data sets with existing national accounts information, while maintaining System of National Accounts (SNA) concepts and principles as far as possible. Environmental costs, benefits and natural resource assets, as well as expenditures for environmental protection, are presented in flow accounts and balance sheets in a consistent manner. That way, the accounting identities of the SNA are maintained. One of the values of the System of Integrated Economic and Environmental Accounts (SEEA) framework compared to more partial approaches is that it permits balancing, so that rough monetary estimates can be made for residual categories (Hamilton and Lutz, 1995, p. 5).

Satellite accounts, however, represent (by intent) a disaggregation of measures of environmental change rather than an aggregation. They could serve as inputs for developing operational indicators of environmental change, but as an independent set of indicators they would suffer from the same problem as the indicators that the U.S. Environmental Protection Agency's Environmental Monitoring and Assessment Program (EMAP) collects. This problem revolves around the large number of measures that make the examination of trade-offs and overall trends more difficult. This is particularly true for biodiversity, as the number of individual species totals in the tens of millions. However, these satellite accounts could serve as a basis of an aggregate measure, in which the individual variables categorized in the satellite accounts are aggregate into a more general index.

Aggregate Indices

EMAP represents an effort to develop indicators of environmental quality. It attempts to develop overall indicators for individual ecosystems (such as forests, wetlands, or estuaries). In the case of estuaries, EMAP develops a series of over 20 indicators, but creates an aggregate index by summing the indicators based on water clarity, the benthic index (benthic refers to the community of species that live on and just below the floor of the water body), and the presence of trash (Schimmel et al., 1994). This process is indicative of a general procedure, often employed by natural scientists, to create aggregate indicators by summing all individual environmental indicators and dividing by the number of indicators to create an unweighted index. This unweighted index is virtually meaningless, because it implicitly and arbitrarily uses equal weights for each individual indicator. For instance, why should a 10 percent increase in the benthic index and a 10 percent increase in the presence of trash receive the same weight in the index? In addition, there is a potential problem of the level of the index being a function of the choice of the unit for measurement of each of the individual variables. For example, measuring one variable in parts per million and another in parts per billion will have very different impacts on the index. One way to get around this measurement problem is to normalize each variable by dividing by its maximum level, so that all the variables are then numbers between 0 and 1.

Although normalization solves the unit of measurement problem, it does not solve the problem associated with an arbitrary choice of equal weights for each variable. One way to develop more meaningful weights is to base them on expert opinion. One way to do so is through a Delphi process, whereby each expert states his or her opinion, and then experts discuss the different opinions until they arrive at a consensus. Of course, sometimes arriving at a consensus is not possible, so one could then proceed by averaging the weights that each expert has assigned. Although this method is certainly an improvement over the arbitrary choice of equal weights, Appendix 5.a outlines a more formal procedure for defining weights by examining individuals' or experts' willingness to make trade-offs.

Ethics

Ethical dimensions are particularly important to include when making decisions, but they are particularly difficult to quantify into indicators. In fact, each method used to develop indicators has ethical implications associated with it. Even the idea of using social welfare as the primary objective of decision making has ethical implications. For example, "deep ecologists" may argue that it is simply unethical to manage ecosystems for human benefit, because ecosystems have inherent rights that do not originate from human concession.

An individual, firm, or government agency may find itself confronted with certain ethical decisions regarding the environment. For example, if the opening of a mine were to threaten to cause the extinction of a species, but the species seems relatively unimportant to the stability of the ecosystem or to social welfare due to various types of redundancies (other species that provide the same type of ecological services), should the mining company go ahead and allow the species to become extinct? Although this decision is obviously going to be influenced by the provisions of national environmental codes involving endangered species, it represents the type of ethical choice that firms or agencies may face. This issue is very interesting; are there some cases in which it would be unethical to cause an environmental impact that in all other facets seems to improve social welfare? In other words, does the firm or agency have an ethical obligation for environmental stewardship independent of the impact of the environment on social welfare? Does an individual have the same responsibility? Obviously, this decision cannot be made by analysts but, rather, must be decided by society and the agency, firm, or individual.

One way to view the ethical concern is to look at behavior and determine what types of behavior can be considered ethical and what types are not. Another approach is to look at how value is determined and examine the ethical implications of the choice of value measures. This book has focused on an anthropogenic measure of value based on willingness to make tradeoffs (see Chapter 4), but that is certainly not the only approach. The economic approach to value and to the valuation of the environment is but one perspective for incorporating environmental values into social decision making. In contrast, several philosophical perspectives stress a biocentric perspective on value, rather than an anthropocentric approach.

In the Americas, the earliest of these perspectives was the Native American ethic, which existed prior to the arrival of settlers from the "Old World." Although there were many different tribes and cultures in both North and South America, and it is difficult to generalize across these cultures, some perspectives on the value of environmental resources were shared by many Native American cultures. First, Native Americans believed that although their actions affected the natural world, the human role was not to dominate or control nature. Native Americans typically believed that they were a component of the natural world and no more important than any other component. As a consequence, Native Americans viewed the land and all plant and animal species as intrinsically valuable, where value was not defined in terms of the satisfaction of human needs (Callicott, 1989; Suzuke and Knudtson, 1992). Box 5.2 contains an excerpt from a famous speech that eloquently describes the relationship of some Native American tribes to the environment.[1]

Biocentric approaches developed within the non–Native American culture as well. One of the most important developers of this approach was Aldo Leopold (Flader and Callicott, 1991), who developed an approach to value based on a land ethic. The basic thrust of his approach is that the components of nature are linked through the balance of the ecosystem; therefore, their value is based on ecological roles, and this value is independent of other sources of value.

---

[1]For years this speech had been attributed to Chief Seattle of the Duwamish tribe and delivered in 1854. The author has been identified as Ted Perry, who wrote it in 1972.

Box 5.2 Excerpts of a Speech Attributed to Chief Seattle, 1854

If we do not own the sparkle of the air and the sparkle of the water, how can you buy them?

Every part of this earth is sacred to my people. Every shining pine needle, every sandy shore, every mist in the dark woods, every clearing and humming insect is holy in the memory and experiences of my people. The sap which courses through the trees carries the memories of the red man. . . .

We know that the white man does not understand our ways. One portion of land to him is the same as the next, for he is a stranger who comes in the night, and takes from the land whatever he needs. The earth is not his friend but his enemy, and when he has conquered it, he moves on....

He kidnaps the earth from his children, and he does not care.... His appetite will devour the earth and leave behind a desert....

What is man without the beasts? If all the beasts were gone, man would die from a great loneliness of spirit. For whatever happens to the beasts, soon happens to man. All things are connected. . . .

Teach your children what we have taught our children, that the earth is our mother. Whatever befalls the earth, befalls the sons of the earth. If men spit upon the ground they spit upon themselves....

This we know: the earth does not belong to man, man belongs to the earth. This we know. All things are connected, like the blood which unites one family. All things are connected.

Whatever befalls the earth befalls the sons of the earth. Man did not weave the web of life, he is merely a strand in it. Whatever he does to the web, he does to himself....

The whites too shall pass: perhaps sooner than all the other tribes. Contaminate your bed, and you will suffocate in your own waste.

A more recent development is deep ecology (Devall, 1985), also a biocentric perspective. Deep ecology, developed by Norwegian Arne Ness, rejects a management approach toward the environment. Environmental resources are not viewed as existing for human benefit; in fact, it is unethical to use environmental resources to satisfy any human need except vital human needs. All components of the ecosystem, as well as the ecosystems themselves, have an intrinsic value and an inherent right to exist in unaltered form.

Ethical considerations are not conducive to the development of indicators or quantitative measures. Rather than developing indicators related to ethics, ethics can be treated as constraints to the decision-making process. Hence, a decision maker would consider other criteria such as equity, sustainability, and economic efficiency and try to make a decision that improves society along the lines of these criteria but that does not violate any ethical boundaries that society (and the decision makers) deem to be important.

Public Participation

Public participation is a very different type of decision-making criterion than the six criterion discussed above, because it relates more to process than outcome. It is not incongruous, however; experience has shown that some people are willing to accept an inferior outcome if they have been actively involved in the process of developing the outcome. In other words, the fairness and appropriateness of the process of arriving at the outcome is also considered to be important, and people do not focus exclusively on the desirability of the outcome. In general, environmental problems that are more local in nature (such as what to do about the toxic site near the elementary school or where to site the nuclear waste facility) generate a greater need for public participation. Many environmental decision processes legally require that public participation be a part of the decision-making process.

Public participation is more of an *ex ante* than *ex post* criterion. Before the decision-making process even begins, decision makers must make sure that they have appropriate levels of public participation. Of course, public participation is a ubiquitous concept, difficult to define and difficult to measure.

A good public participation process begins by identifying the stakeholders, or shareholders, in the decision. For example, if the environmental problem revolved around agricultural pollution of an estuary, stakeholders would include farmers, agrochemical suppliers, county extension agents, recreational anglers, commercial fishers, marina owners, boat owners, environmental groups, people living near the estuary, and other citizens who were concerned with the outcome. Productive processes seldom begin in a high school gymnasium full of shouting people. Rather, to create a group of workable size, representatives of the different positions must be selected. The next step is to develop a process by which the different stakeholders are able to express their concerns, and these concerns help define the decisions that are made. Skilled moderating is needed to help people understand that everyone has a stake in the outcome and that confrontation does not lead to resolution. All the results of a stakeholder process then must be communicated with the public at large.

In addition, one can move away from the stakeholder process, select citizens who are not charged with representing a particular group, and have them work together to develop recommendation. One way of doing so is role-playing, through which citizens step into the shoes of the various stakeholders and discuss the issues from each particular perspective, with the idea of everyone developing an understanding of all the different viewpoints. A slightly different alternative is to appoint a citizen jury, which weighs the evidence (cost, benefits, fairness, and so on) of alternative policies and makes a recommendation.

In the early days of the public participation process, government officials would often hold public hearings only after many of the important decisions had been made. Stakeholders commented on the plans already developed, but many stakeholders would have preferred to consider options that had been excluded from consideration. This old-style of public participation has been derogatorily referred to as DAD (decide-announce-defend). Stakeholders believed that they were being dictated to because they did not have a role in selecting among the many available alternatives to deal with the problem. Consequently, most environmental agencies now begin the public participation process early in the decision-making process.

Four major techniques incorporate public participation into the decision making process. These techniques

- Incorporate information about stakeholder preferences in the decision-making process
- Allow stakeholders to negotiate a solution among themselves
- Allow stakeholders to arrive at a solution through role-playing
- Empower a representative group of stakeholders to hear the evidence and make a decision, jury style

Serious ethical issues are associated with the last three methods, because the stakeholders must be chosen in some fashion and all citizens might not approve of the fashion in which stakeholders are fashioned, or they might not believe that these stakeholders are entitled to represent them. For this reason, the first method, incorporating information about stakeholder preferences, may be better. Of course, this information may be incorporated in a variety of ways, including survey research, focus groups, public meetings, and web-based interchanges.

Advancement of Knowledge

At first glance, it might seem strange to include the advancement of knowledge as a decision-making criterion, yet the advancement of knowledge contributes indirectly to social welfare by facilitating the development of future benefits and reduction of future costs. For example, research that contributes to the basic understanding of the properties of a material will result in future products and applications that contribute to social welfare both through increasing economic output and by improving environmental performance. Greater understanding of the process of nutrient cycling in tropical rainforests can lead to the development of more effective sustainable forestry management methods. An increased knowledge of the human genome will lead to future cures and treatments of disease.

These three examples have been chosen to show that this criterion of the advancement of knowledge is extremely diverse and has multiple attributes.

All the arguments that were made previously about how difficult it is to develop an indicator for ecological criteria are perhaps even more intense with respect to the advancement of knowledge. Nonetheless, the advancement of knowledge is an important criterion, and care must be taken to include it in the decision-making process. That is best done in a qualitative fashion, because experts in the field and related fields of knowledge qualitatively evaluate the importance of potential gains in knowledge associated with a project or decision.

A good example is pollution control. The cheapest and easiest way to meet an emissions standard might be to install an end-of-pipe pollution abatement treatment, which collects the pollution, where it can be disposed in a landfill or subjected to other treatment. Pollution policies that encourage this type of solution, however, may not be as good in the long run. The best long-run solution may be to change production processes to generate less waste. Policies should encourage the development of these technologies through economic incentives for pollution reduction and subsidization of research and development.

The Use of Multiple Criteria in Decision Making

The preceding sections focus on the development of decision-making criteria and the progress made in terms of actually implementing indicators of these criteria. As the discussion indicates, progress has occurred in some areas yet remains to be made in others.

The question now is how to take multiple decision-making criteria and jointly employ the criteria so as to inform the actual decision. In some ways, this problem is conceptually similar to the problem of including multiple attributes into a single indictor, but in other senses, it is much more difficult. If too much aggregation is done across criteria, then a lot of the information that is contained in the different criteria will be lost.

This section starts with a discussion of cost-benefit analysis, which has been frequently employed in the decision-making process and is even legally required of government agencies in many countries. Cost-benefit analysis focuses solely on economic efficiency. Even though cost-benefit analysis has this narrow focus, it is the first focus in the following analysis. One of the reasons this book focuses on cost-benefit analysis is that it is often implemented incorrectly. In this section, a set of guidelines and principles is developed. The discussion then moves to how to simultaneously employ a diverse set of decision-making criteria.

Cost-Benefit Analysis

Cost-benefit analysis has become an increasingly important tool in aiding decision making in environmental policy and other aspects of public policy, but it is often implemented incorrectly and interpreted inappropriately. The purpose of this section is not to make the reader an expert in cost-benefit analysis but, rather, to aid the reader in understanding what constitutes a well-implemented study and how that study can facilitate the decision-making process.

The most important concept to bear in mind when conducting cost-benefit analysis is that *cost-benefit analysis is not a decision-making tool; it is only an information-organizing tool.* It does not make the decision for the policy maker; it provides the policy maker with a certain type of information, information pertaining to economic efficiency. Although many government agencies and private firms mandate the use of cost-benefit analysis, the planner or decision maker should bear in mind that this tool only provides information on economic efficiency and does not provide information on any of the other decision-making criteria. Thus, cost-benefit analysis should be regarded as an information-organizing tool rather than a decision-making tool.

After realizing the proper role for cost-benefit analysis in decision making, one must be aware of the fundamental principle of cost-benefit analysis: *there is no single correct answer to a cost-benefit analysis exercise.* This issue is important because many policy makers are anxious to receive a single number upon which to base their decisions. Yet this type of thinking is fundamentally flawed. Because different assumptions about future states of the world or key analytical parameters (such as the discount rate or rate of growth of GDP) will have a big impact on the final outcome of the cost benefit analysis, the analysis should produce a suite of numbers reflecting the sensitivity of the cost-benefit analysis to alternative analytical assumptions.

A third important concept related to cost-benefit analysis is that it should be a dynamic analysis, investigating the cost and benefits of a decision far into the future. This requirement somewhat complicates the measurement process, because benefits and costs occur at different points in time, and benefits in different time periods must have different weights in the summation process.

The reason that benefits and costs in different periods must have different weights in the summation process is that people, both as individuals and as a society, prefer good things to happen sooner than later and bad things to happen later than sooner. Referred to in the economics literature as a positive rate of time preference it is why we are willing to borrow money at interest so as to increase current consumption (it is also why lenders need to be compensated with interest when they lend money). The discount rate is the rate of interest that measures time preference. For example, if you were willing to loan $100 for 1 year and receive $115 (but not less than $115) in return 1 year into the future, then your rate of time preference would be 15 percent, and 15 percent should be the discount rate that you use to convert future values, be they costs or benefits, into present values.

The process of discounting (a fuller discussion of discounting is found in the appendix to Chapter 2), or measuring present values, converts economic values in all time periods into economic values in the present period. The simplest version of a discounting formula is

$$PV = FV\left(\frac{1}{1+r}\right)^t \quad 5.1$$

where PV refers to the present value to be calculated, FV refers to the known future value, r represents the discount rate, and t represents the time period. This formula is based on discrete discounting, which assumes interest accrual in a periodic fashion. If interest accrues in a continuous fashion, then the continuous version of this formula should be used, where e represents the base of the natural logarithm:

$$PV = FV\left(e^{-rt}\right) \quad 5.2$$

Equations 5.1 and 5.2 represent the net present value of a single cost or benefit at a given point in time in the future. Most decisions, however, are more complicated than this one and involve benefits and costs at many points in time in the future. Thus, the present value of a decision represents the sum over time of discounted net benefits in each period:

$$PV = \sum_{t=0}^{\infty} \frac{B_t - C_t}{(1+r)^t} \quad 5.3$$

when discounting discretely, or

$$\int_{t=0}^{\infty} (B_t - C_t)e^{-rt}dt \quad 5.4$$

when discounting continuously.

The objective of cost-benefit analysis is to identify the alternative project, plan, or policy that has the greatest net present benefit, which will therefore maximize economic efficiency. As mentioned earlier, this process can sometimes be ambiguous because different analytical assumptions may identify different alternatives as having the highest net present value.

The Choice of the Discount Rate

A critical aspect of cost-benefit analysis is the choice of the discount rate by which to compute the present value of the net benefits of the decision. The first thing that usually comes to mind is the market rate of interest, but for several reasons, it should not be chosen.

First, the market rate of interest should not be chosen because there are many market rates of interest. Each market rate of interest is comprised of three components: a risk component, an inflation component, and a real, risk-free rate of interest. The inflation component should always be removed from the interest rate because all cost-benefit calculations should be conducted in real (inflation-adjusted terms).[2] The risk component reflects a compensation for the variations in the risk of default across different types of borrowers. For example, corporations such as General Electric or Intel borrow with a higher risk premium than does the U.S. government but with a lower rate than does the ordinary citizen. Because the risks of a public investment are shared by all the citizens of a society, and because society has a diverse portfolio of projects, many economists argue that in public decision making, if a market rate of interest is used, then it should be the real, risk-free rate. With few exceptions this rate has historically been in a range of 3 to 4 percent in the United States.

The choice of discount rate is critically important, because it speaks to the relative importance of the future. Table 5.3 shows the current value of $1 million of net benefits that occur at different points in time, with different discount rates. This table illustrates the role of the future, especially the distant future, when decisions are based entirely on cost-benefit analysis. For example, the cell at the lower-right-hand corner of this diagram shows that $1 million of net benefits that occur in 200 years only has a present value of less than one cent. Table 5.3 also shows how even small differences in the discount rate become very important the more we move into the future. After 10 years, the present value when calculated with a 3 percent discount rate is 90 percent of the present value when calculated with a 2 percent discount rate. After 200 years, however, the corresponding relationship is 13.5 percent. This acceler-

Table 5.3 **The Power of Discounting: The Present Value of $1 Million of Net Benefits Occurring at Different Points in the Future**

Discount rate	10 years	50 years	100 years	200 years
2%	$818,730	$367,879	$135,335	$18,315
3%	740,818	223,130	49,787	2,479
5%	606,530	82,084	6,737	45
8%	449,328	18,315	335	0.11
10%	367,879	6,737	45	0.0021

[2]Readers who are unfamiliar with the process of inflation adjustment should see the Consumer Price Index web site of the U.S. Bureau of Labor Statistics http://www.bls.gov/cpi as well as consulting a principles of economics textbook.

ating impact is due to the nonlinearity of the discounting process. With the discounting process, the distant future does not matter, and the higher the discount rate, the more quickly the future becomes unimportant. The reduction in the importance of the future that is generated by discounting is often called "the tyranny of discounting" and is a reason economic efficiency cannot be the only decision-making criterion. In fact, that is a primary reason people began to become concerned with the criterion of sustainability.

The market rate of interest is not the only interest rate that has been suggested as a discount rate. In fact, there is considerable controversy over what the appropriate rate should be.

Another theory is called the displacement theory. It is based on the viewpoint that because public investment tends to "crowd out" private investment; one should look towards the opportunity cost of the government investment as the means for discounting. With this logic, the opportunity cost of a government investment is rate of return on private investment, which in some ways can be likened to a market rate of interest. Another measure of the opportunity cost of a public investment is the interest rate that the government pays on public debt. With many developing nations having found themselves in unenviable and untenable debt positions, however, a tremendously high discount rate is implied. If developing nations used this choice as their discount rate, it would imply that the only investments that should be undertaken are those with an immediate payout and that future costs and benefits are completely unimportant. Of course, there is some truth to this argument, because compounding debt levels can seriously interfere with the future economic prospects of a country. This type of approach, however, can lead a nation into making decisions to obtain short-term gains with irreversible consequences that can seriously jeopardize its future well-being. The way that high levels of debt cause developing countries to make present-oriented decisions is a primary reason many people advocate a policy of debt relief or debt restructuring for developing countries.

As we entered the 1980s and progressed through the 1990s and people began to see more explicit evidence of the shortsightedness of projects and policies supported by cost-benefit analysis with high discount rates, economists began to develop insights into why a lower discount rate should be employed when providing guidance for long-term planning. One theory that suggests a lower discount rate is based on the mathematical fact that no individual investment can grow faster than GDP for long periods (hundreds of years) of time. This theory is based on the compound nature of growth. For example, if current GDP were $1 trillion and grew at a real rate of 2 percent per year, it would equal $54 trillion after 200 years. A relatively small investment of $1 million growing at 9 percent over that same period, however, would equal $66 trillion after 200 years, exceeding GDP. This example points out a logical argument against using high discount rates. Quite simply, it is not possible for an individual investment to grow faster than GDP for a long period of time, and the argument follows that the discount rate should be no greater than the long-term real rate of growth of GDP.

Of course, GDP is not a complete measure of economic efficiency (because it is only limited to market goods and services) and is even further off the mark as a measure of social welfare. For this reason and others having to do with a stewardship responsibility of the current generation, many economists argue that the discount rate should be even lower than real rate of growth of GDP. In a recent survey of environmental and policy economists, Martin Weitzmann (1998) found that the majority of those economists surveyed suggested a discount rate of 1 to 2 percent when evaluating long-term decision making.

Although this discussion is informative and can serve to prevent reliance on an unjustifiably high discount rate, in some senses it is superfluous. When a cost-benefit analysis is conducted with the aid of spreadsheet software, the present value calculations can be performed easily with a range of discount rates and the sensitivity of the present value measures to alternative choices can be easily seen. This sensitivity analysis can give a very clear picture as to which decisions favor the present and which favor the future. Even if a government agency has an official discount rate (mandated by legislative or executive authority) that must be employed, the sensitivity of the results to the choice of discount rates should be investigated and reported. One way of choosing the discount rates to employ in the analysis is to make sure that one of them is equal to zero, which gives equal weight to costs and benefits at every point in time. In addition, for developing countries a relatively high discount rate could be chosen to represent the urgency of the present situation. This rate could be equal to the rate that the developing country pays to service its external debt. In addition, a spectrum of rates in between, including a nonzero low rate (such as 1 to 2 percent) should be included. The analysis should be computed using four or five different rates. Then, by viewing the sensitivity of the present value of alternative projects to alternative assumptions about the magnitude of the discount rate, the decision makers can explicitly see the impacts of the choice of discount rate.

Determining Project or Policy Alternatives

The first step in implementing any cost-benefit analysis is to determine what should be evaluated. At first, the reader might think that the answer to this question is simple: just evaluate the project that is being proposed and see if it has benefits greater than costs. The problem with this approach is that the analyst and decision maker will never know if there is a better alternative than the proposed project.

For example, let's say that a proposal has been advanced to the Department of Energy for a project to develop a corn-based alcohol fuel as an alternative to gasoline. A cost-benefit analysis might reveal that this proposed project has net benefits. There might, though, be other projects involving different types of crops that could be converted into alcohol, different types of crops that could be used to produce vegetable oil, or completely unrelated energy technologies such as fuel cells, solar energy, wind energy, and many other potential clean energy projects. If the Department of Energy does not evaluate all the alternatives, it runs the risk of choosing a project that contributes less to society than potential alternatives.

The analyst must identify the credible alternatives to the proposed project and include them in the cost-benefit analysis. In defining the alternatives, the analyst must consider political feasibility, technical feasibility, and economic feasibility, among other characteristics.

An important example of the need to consider alternatives can be seen in the area of electricity generation. Let's say that the original question is whether or not to build a hydroelectric plant at a specific location to provide electric energy. Alternative projects that could also provide energy for the region could include

- Alternative locations for hydroelectric plants
- Conventional thermal plants (fossil fuels or nuclear)
- New technology plants (fuel cells, biomass fuels)
- Wind-driven electrical generation
- Solar generation (photovoltaic cells)

Unless all the alternatives are considered, the decision maker could wind up making a suboptimal decision.

Listing the Costs and Benefits

The next step in the process of cost-benefit analysis is to list the costs and benefits to make sure that everything that is relevant is considered. Let's continue with the example of the hydroelectric facility for this discussion, because there is a broad spectrum of costs and benefits associated with the construction and operation of a hydroelectric dam and generation facility. The potential costs associated with a hydroelectric facility include

- Planning costs
- Maintenance and operation costs
- Construction
- On-site environmental costs
- Off-site environmental costs
- Lost river recreation
- Land acquisition costs
- Displacement of people
- Indirect costs

The potential benefits of the hydroelectric facility include

- Electricity generation
- Reservoir recreation
- Flood control
- Creation of jobs (under some circumstances)
- Indirect benefits

The measurement of planning, maintenance, operation, and construction costs can be conducted in a straightforward fashion, based on the market prices of the labor, energy, materials, and other inputs into these processes. Care must be taken, however, to factor in the environmental costs of these actions. For example, soil erosion from the construction site could lead to increased turbidity in the adjacent river. Solvents used in maintenance processes could lead to pollution and environmental degradation.

The measurement of these and other environmental costs is a difficult process. On-site environmental costs refer to changes in environmental quality in the vicinity of the facility. Off-site costs include costs downstream of the facility as well as costs associated with the production of the inputs that are used in the maintenance, operation, and construction processes. The process of looking at environmental costs of all the inputs and outputs of an activity is called life-cycle analysis.

Different stated preference and revealed preference methods could be used in the process of measuring these environmental costs, but it is very difficult to measure the value of ecological services, as discussed in Chapter 4. For example, it is relatively easy to measure the loss in value in a recreational fishery for anadramous fish (such as salmon and trout) whose migration to spawning areas is blocked by the dam. Both the contingent valuation and travel cost approaches have been used in this type of application. Yet it is much more difficult to measure how the loss of the fish will cause additional changes in the ecosystem through their relationship with other species, and it is even more difficult to try to measure the willingness to pay to avoid these changes using contingent valuation or other techniques.

As indicated earlier, the loss in value associated with impacts on river recreation is more easily measured using either revealed preference or stated preference approaches. River recreation may include fishing, kayaking, canoeing, tubing, hunting, hiking, bird watching and wildlife observation, and more casual activities such as picnicking, swimming, and sunbathing. Because many studies have measured the value of these recreational activities in a wide variety of settings, benefit transfer (see Chapter 4) may be a good method of computing the value of these activities that would be lost from the construction of the reservoir.

The cost of the land acquisition required to build the dam and the reservoir is a little more complicated. In theory, this value is equal to the present value of the time stream of net benefits from the activities that take place on the land. In many cases, such as industrial farming, the value is equal to the market value of the land. For the family farmer, for whom the farming lifestyle is a significant component of his or her well-being and who has a significant emotional bond to the particular land holding, however, that will not be the case. It will also be true for families who have lived in their particular houses for a significant time. Also, if the land has significant cultural, religious, or historical significance, that value will not be captured in the market price of the land. One can attempt to measure the religious, cultural, and historical significance of the land through stated preference approaches or through benefit transfer from studies of these values at other locations, but it would be exceedingly difficult to measure the value that individual landowners place on their land, above its market value. This measurement difficulty exists because of the potential of two types of strategic behavior when landowners are responding to valuation surveys. First, if they want to remain on their land, then they have an incentive to overstate their willingness to be compensated so as to make the project fail the cost-benefit analysis. Second, if they are willing to vacate their land, then they still will have an incentive to overstate the value so as to try to increase the payment they would receive to sell their land to the government or electric utility company.

Related to the land acquisition cost is the cost of displacing people from their homes. This cost not only includes the cost of the actual relocation, but also the psychic or emotional cost that is incurred as relationships are broken and people leave the setting in which they are comfortable and in which they know how to function. This problem is not as significant in a highly mobile society such as the United States, but it can be quite traumatic in developing countries, especially when indigenous people are displaced. Of course, the second part of this dislocation cost is difficult to measure.

Indirect costs are costs brought about by an activity that exists because of the project but that is not part of the project. For example, if a new hydroelectric facility were built in a remote region of the Amazon, it would require the building of a new road to service the facility. Settlers are likely to follow the road, penetrate the rain forest, and cause deforestation with their farming activities. The social cost of this deforestation would be considered an indirect cost of building the hydroelectric facility.

In general, benefits are easier to measure than the costs, but the benefits are often measured incorrectly. For example, many people would view the benefit of the electricity that is generated as the quantity of electricity multiplied by its market price.[3] The benefit, however, is simply the difference between the cost of producing it in the proposed hydroelectric facility and the cost of producing it via the next best alternative, such as a fossil fuel plant. In many areas, the next best alternative may simply be to buy the electricity from another power plant on the grid. In areas such as California or Rio de Janeiro, where there is now insufficient capacity, however, the value must be determined more broadly, including the willingness to pay to avoid blackouts and other interruptions.

Flood control is also relatively easily measured. If hydrologists can predict the probabilities of different types of flood events with and without the dam, these probabilities can then be multiplied by the expected damages from property loss, and the difference between the two regimes can be calculated. Appendix 5.a explains the basic steps of expected value analysis.

---

[3]Note that q^*p is the contribution to GDP, which has already been shown to be an inferior measure of social welfare.

Reservoir recreation can be an important benefit associated with a new hydroelectric reservoir, but it is also often measured incorrectly. It could easily be measured through revealed preference methods such as travel costs, stated preference methods such as contingent valuation, or benefit transfer. It is in the benefits transfer process that errors often occur, because analysts often compute transfer value estimates that are inappropriate. An example is using the values for a reservoir in a populous area as estimates for the values of recreational fishing in an area that is likely to receive only little visitation because of difficult access, availability of substitutes, or other factors.

One category of benefits that is very misunderstood is the category of job creation. When ordinary citizens and politicians cite the benefits of a big project, such as the hydropower plant in the example here, they most frequently talk about the jobs that are being created, but is the creation of jobs a benefit?

The answer to this question is somewhat complicated. First, most of the jobs associated with the hydroelectric facility will be temporary construction jobs, filled by workers from outside the region, so the benefits are likely to be small and short-lived. Thus the question becomes whether the small amount of jobs in the operation and maintenance of the facility is a benefit. Another question would arise regarding the jobs created by firms that locate in the region to take advantage of the electricity.

The jobs created at the facility can be considered a social benefit if the country or region does not have full employment. Therefore, in a country such as the United States, these jobs cannot be considered benefits, unless they are better jobs (higher wages, better benefits, safer conditions) than the jobs the people will be leaving. In countries such as the United States, creating minimum-wage jobs does not generate any social benefits. Minimum wage jobs remain unfilled because there is not an adequate supply of labor to fill these jobs. In developing countries that typically experience high unemployment rates, these jobs can be considered social benefits, but again, if they are not above minimum wage, they may not create social benefits. In many developing countries, people can make more money in the informal sector (selling oranges on street corners, working as informal laborers, producing goods and services for informal markets, and so on) than they would in a minimum-wage job.

An important misunderstanding about the social benefits of jobs is associated with the jobs that are indirect impacts of the project, such as those in new factories that locate in the region due to the presence of the hydroelectricity. These jobs are seldom social benefits, because they are jobs that would have occurred elsewhere in the economy. For example, if a hydroelectric facility was built in one region of the country and an automobile factory then located in that area to take advantage of the cheaper electricity, one must be careful concerning counting the jobs in the automobile factory as social benefits. The reason is that if the facility were not built in the region of the hydro facility, the factory would have probably located elsewhere in the country. It is even entirely possible that the new automobile factory resulted in the closure of a factory elsewhere. In short, one must be careful in distinguishing between a transfer of benefits from another region and the creation of new benefits. This issue is important because in many countries significant amounts of federal tax dollars are spent by local governments in competition with other local governments to attract firms and jobs to locate in their regions.

The previous discussion illustrates how to estimate the benefits of a particular project. The same types of analysis must be repeated with the alternatives to the proposed project. Of course, there may be different benefit and cost categories associated with the alternative. For example, if the alternative is an oil-burning power plant, one must estimate the social costs of both air pollution and contributions to global warming.

Scenario Analysis

In the introductory remarks to the discussion of cost-benefit analysis, the importance of producing more than one number was emphasized. This subject is now discussed in further detail by following through on the hydroelectric facility example, and raising the rather obvious point that the benefits associated with the hydroelectric facility are likely to be a function of the price of oil. The higher the price of oil, the greater the cost savings associated with producing electricity by hydropower. Hydropower plants have long operating lives of 30 years of more. In computing the present value of the net benefits of the facility, what value of oil should be assumed for each year of the life of the project?

Many different things could happen in the future. Oil could become drastically scarcer or a carbon tax could be imposed, both of which would increase the future cost of oil. Alternatively, more oil discoveries could take place or technological innovation could occur in both oil production and in alternatives to oil, any of which would lower the price of oil.

Just as it is important to use different discount rates in conducting the cost analysis, one should use different future energy prices. One can then compute the sensitivity of the desirability of the project to changes in energy prices. One can also do the same thing for the choice among alternative projects.

In addition to the price of energy, the cost-benefit analysis will often be forced to make other assumptions or predictions about future states of the world. Among the variables that would be relevant for many cost-benefit analyses are the following:

- The rate of population growth
- The rate of growth of gross domestic product
- The level of global climate change
- The rate of technological innovation
- The strictness of environmental policy

It is recommended that scenario analysis be done with different discount rates and with a set of other variables such as the future price of energy and the future population growth. Using different values for these variables can greatly complicate an analysis, but it can also contribute to a better understanding of the net social benefits of alternative projects. For example, if one chose four different discount rates, three different paths for future energy prices, three different paths of population growth, and three different paths for the rate of growth of the economy, then there would be 108 different scenarios. Once the alternative values for each variable are chosen, the production of 108 scenarios will only take minutes in a spreadsheet calculation. The difficult part is comparing all these numbers and arriving at an understanding of the information contained in the scenario analysis.

For each scenario, each project can be rated as being the preferred project (or among a group that are similar, and preferred to, the rest), being in a group or projects that are good but not the best, being in a group of projects that are satisfactory, being in a group of projects that are unsatisfactory, or being in a group of projects that would be disastrous. A matrix can be made in which each row is a project and each column is a different scenario (permutation of the variables for which the sensitivity analysis is conducted). To create a visual comparison, the cells can be color-coded on a green-to-red spectrum, with bright green at the good end of the scale and bright red at the bad end of the scale, or the projects could be evaluated on a numerical scale of one to five (best = 5, good = 4, and so on). The pattern of desirability of each project across all the alternative scenarios can then be compared visually.

Although it may be difficult to compare all projects simultaneously in a quantitative sense, various decision rules can be made to allow qualitative comparison and determination of which projects are best from the point of view of economic efficiency. First, one can discard from consideration a project that is inferior to others in all scenarios. For example, in Table 5.4, in all scenarios project 4 has an equal or higher ranking than project 5, so project 5 need not be considered further. After completion of this elimination process, one can implement decision rules, where the decision rules each imply a different attitude towards risk. These decision rules could include some combination of the following rules:

- Choose the project that is in the top ranking in the most states of the world. This project is project 4 in Table 5.4.
- Choose the project that is in the top two categories in the most future states of the world. This project is project 3.
- Choose the project that is in the top three categories (satisfactory or better) in the most future states of the world. This project is project 2.
- Eliminate all projects from consideration that have some probability of disastrous results, no matter how unlikely. If rankings of 0 and 1 were considered disastrous, then that would leave only projects 2 and 3 under consideration. If only rankings of 0 were considered disastrous, then projects 2, 3, and 4 are left under consideration.
- Choose the project that performs best in the most likely future states of the world and do not worry about the least likely states. (This step cannot be evaluated in Table 5.4, because the example does not specify which scenarios are most likely.)

Table 5.4 **Evaluating Projects under Alternative Scenarios**

	Scenario 1	Scenario 2	Scenario 3	Scenario 4	Scenario 5	Scenario 6
Project 1	0	5	2	2	5	0
Project 2	3	3	3	3	3	3
Project 3	2	4	4	4	4	2
Project 4	1	1	5	5	5	1
Project 5	0	0	5	5	5	0

Many people argue that the type of qualitative analysis described in the bullets above is unnecessary and even counterproductive, as expected value analysis (see Appendix 5.b) can be used to provide a quantitative assessment of the desirability of each project across all possible future states of the world. This argument, though, implies risk neutrality for society as a whole, which may not be the case for important policy decisions. Moreover, the aggregation process causes information to be lost.

As can be seen from this discussion, once different future states of the world are considered, it becomes very difficult to develop quantitative decision rules and decision making becomes more of a qualitative process. This process is even further complicated when the decision-making process is extended to include multiple decision-making criteria in addition to economic efficiency. Decision making in this context is considered next, after the discussion of missing values.

How to Deal with Missing Values

One of the major problems facing cost-benefit analysts is how to deal with missing values. In particular, it may not be possible to estimate the value of certain types of environmental changes. These missing values should not enter the analysis as a zero value; just because they are difficult to measure, it does not mean that they do not exist. A variety of techniques exist to help evaluate the projects in the absence of information on all benefit and cost categories.

Because environmental costs are often the missing value, when evaluating a single project it is possible to do the cost/benefit analysis without the environmental costs. If the present value of the nonenvironmental costs is greater than the present value of the economic benefits, then the project can simply be rejected because the addition of environmental costs would only prejudice the analysis further in favor of the project being rejected.

If multiple projects are being compared, then this process is more difficult because the environmental cost estimates may be missing from all the alternatives. One way to construct the analysis, however, is to use the dominance method. The way this method works is that one constructs logical arguments about which projects have the greatest environmental costs and then tries to decide which project would be best. This method is the one that Krutilla and Fisher (1985) used in their analysis of the alternative choices of the pipelines with which to move Alaskan North Slope petroleum to the market. One alternative was the Trans-Alaskan Pipeline, which runs south from the North Slope to the ice-free port of Valdez, where the oil is loaded onto tankers. The other alternative was the Trans-Canadian Pipeline, whereby a pipeline would be built from the North Slope southeast to Winnipeg, Canada, where it would connect to the existing North American pipeline network. In their analysis, Krutilla and Fisher found that the Trans-Canadian Pipeline had greater economic benefits. They also argued that because the Trans-Alaskan Pipeline crossed an area of great seismic activity (and the Trans-Canadian Pipeline would not) and because the Trans-Alaskan plan involved the dangerous shipping through treacherous Alaskan waters, the Trans-Canadian Pipeline had lower environmental cost. Thus, in their analysis, the Trans-Canadian Pipeline dominated the Trans-Alaskan Pipeline both in terms of the measured present value of net economic benefits and the unmeasured environmental impacts. In this case, it is not necessary to estimate dollar measures of the environmental damages, because the ranking of the alternative projects is clear.[4]

A second method of comparing projects in the presence of missing values is to see how big the missing values must be to sway the balance toward one alternative or the other. Then, benefit transfer techniques and other types of information can be examined to determine if it is reasonable that the missing value exceeds these critical values. For example, incomplete analysis can also be useful if one looks at the difference between the measured benefits and the measured costs. If measured costs are greater than measured benefits, then there is generally no need to measure the environmental costs. If measured benefits are greater than measured costs, however, then one can still make a conclusion if a logical argument can be constructed about whether the unmeasured environmental costs are likely to affect the differential between costs and benefits.

For example, let's consider a potential dam project that results in the loss of river recreation, but the value of the river recreation has not been measured due to a lack of data. Let's assume that the present value of measured costs exceeds the present value of measured benefits by $1 million and that there are no benefits from the dam that remain unmeasured. Under these conditions, the dam would fail a cost-benefit test if the present value of river recreation exceeded $1 million. If, however, the present value of river recre-

---

[4]An interesting sidebar is that the Trans-Alaskan Pipeline was the one that was eventually built, and the environmental impacts were realized in the infamous *Exxon Valdez* oil spill.

ation was less than \$1 million and there were no other unmeasured costs (such as an indirect use value associated with the riverine ecosystem), then the dam would pass a cost-benefit test. Notice that it requires less information about unmeasured costs for the dam to fail the cost-benefit test than for the dam to pass the test. The present value of river recreation that exactly equates benefits and costs is \$1 million. What ability do we have to make a reasonable estimate of river recreation benefits when there are insufficient data (or insufficient time and money to obtain the data) to perform travel cost or contingent valuation studies?

The first step toward resolving this issue is to convert the present value of \$1 million into an equivalent stream of annual benefits. This conversion can be done according to equation 5.4, where X is the unknown annual benefits for which one solves the equation:[5]

$$\$1{,}000{,}000 = X + X\left(\frac{1}{1+r}\right)^1 + X\left(\frac{1}{1+r}\right)^2 + X\left(\frac{1}{1+r}\right)^3 + \ldots + X\left(\frac{1}{1+r}\right)^n \quad 5.5$$

If $R = 0.1$, then X will approximately equal \$90,000.

Now we have transformed the question from Is the present value of river recreation benefits likely to exceed \$1 million? to Are the annual river recreation benefits likely to exceed \$90,000? The two questions are mathematically identical, but the latter question is easier to conceptualize.

How can one estimate annual recreation benefits without a travel cost or contingent valuation procedure? One way is through the process of benefits transfer, discussed in Chapter 4. In this case, one would use the per trip value from studies of other recreational activity (such as river recreation in another region) and transfer those benefits to the problem at hand. One must be careful which studies one uses in such a transfer so that the activities, the recreational site, and the population of recreationists correspond between the study one is transferring from and the activity one is examining.

Other extrapolation methods can be used to develop a general impression of the unmeasured environmental benefits of preserving the river and then compare them to the cost differential between measured costs and measured benefits. These general impressions will often be much larger or much smaller than this differential, yet even though this general impression is imprecise, it can help make a determination whether total costs are greater than total benefits or vice versa. Other times, however, the general impression of unmeasured benefits will be roughly the same order of magnitude as the differential, and the imprecision becomes critically relevant. In these circumstances, it is

---

[5]The solution of this equation is based on an important geometric series, which takes the form $A = X + X*B + X*B^2 + X*B^3 + \ldots X*B^N$. If N approaches infinity and $0 < B < 1$, then $A = X[1/(1-b)]$.

The convergence of this geometric series has many important uses in economics. For example, it is used to derive the multiplier in macroeconomics, and it can show the extent to which recycling can extend the effective reserves of a mineral such as copper.

not possible to determine whether total benefits are greater than total costs or vice versa. Of course, the benefit transfer approach (see Chapter 4) may be applied if analogous studies have been completed.

Incorporating Multiple Criteria within a Public Participation Process

One way to incorporate multiple criteria within decision making is to use a public participation process. All the alternatives can be scored based on all the criteria, and then a public participation process can be used to choose an alternative. Although this process may at first seem to be very democratic, the problems discussed previously concerning who is chosen to participate in the process is a serious issue. More important, is that the democratic tradition in most countries is a representative democracy in which elected decision makers make decisions on behalf of their constituents. To completely turn this process over to selected groups of citizens represents a very different type of government.

That is not to say that the public participation process cannot facilitate the process of comparison of alternatives. In fact, the public participation process can provide information about how citizens attach importance to progress with respect to the various criteria.

Utilizing Weights for Multiple Decision-Making Criteria

If there is more than one decision-making criterion, then the decision makers must assign weights to the different criteria to make a decision. Assigning weights can be done implicitly and qualitatively, or explicitly and quantitatively. Before discussing methods for doing so, let's see how the decision set can be narrowed in an objective fashion.

For the sake of simplicity, this discussion will be kept in two-dimensional space, which is easier to visualize than *n*-dimensional space. The points in Figure 5.3 represent a set of different decisions; each one associated with a value of criterion 1 and a value of criterion 2.

A quick inspection of Figure 5.3 shows that points to the interior of the frontier are inferior to points on the frontier, because it is possible to move from an interior point to an exterior point and get more of both criteria. This process of identifying technically inferior decisions can be extended to more than two criteria. In addition, constraints associated with ethical behavior, environmental justice, or other criteria can rule out certain decisions that may be associated with a point along the exterior. Of course, the process described by this discussion and graph does not show which of the remaining frontier policies is best. To do that, weights must be given to the alternative criteria.

One way to assign weights is by informal discussion. Decision makers, experts, or stakeholders can discuss the merits of each of the exterior points and arrive at a consensus of which is best. Alternatively, formal weights can be assigned to each criterion. As mentioned in the discussion of ecological

Figure 5.3 **Ranking Alternative Decisions**

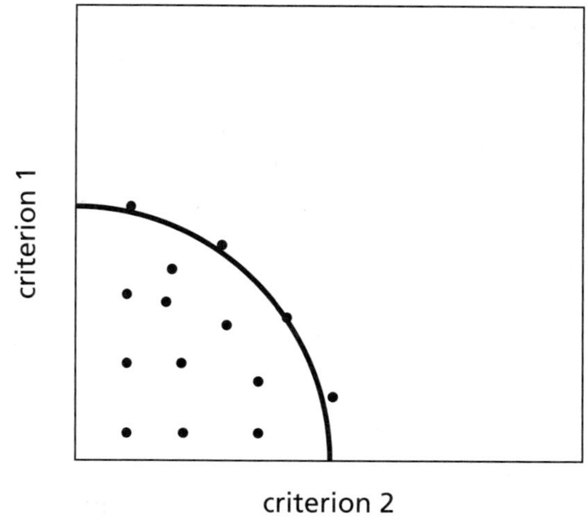

indexes, the decision to weight each criterion equally is a decision to assign weights. Again, in a formal process, weights could be assigned through a consensus among decision makers, experts, or stakeholders.

A more quantitative method for assigning weights is to use conjoint analysis. Instead of limiting the characteristics of the choice sets to environmental and economic variables, as described in the discussion of valuation, the characteristics could include variables or indicators related to the other criteria, such as sustainability, environmental justice, and equity. This method is further described in Appendix 5.b.

Marginal Analysis

Cost-benefit analysis is a good tool for measuring economic efficiency when one has to choose between a set of discrete alternatives such as whether or not to build a dam, or whether or not to build a toxic waste storage facility and where to place it if the decision is to build it. Sometimes in environmental policy, however, the choice must be made about which level to choose from a potentially infinite spectrum of levels. For example, to deal with the global climate change problem, policy makers must choose a level of carbon dioxide emissions for each year. Similarly, choices about how many hectares of wetlands to preserve, how much deforestation to allow, how large a fish harvest may be, and so on must also be made.[6]

---

[6]See Box 2.1 for a discussion of marginal analysis.

Marginal Damage Functions

Marginal damage functions were discussed in Chapter 3, where it was shown that the optimal level of pollution (E*) occurs at the level where marginal damages are equal to marginal costs. This optimal level is shown in Figure 5.4. Although one requires information on both abatement costs and damages to identify (or approximate) the optimal level of pollution, this discussion focuses on the process for identifying the damage functions. The major reason for this focusing is not because it is more useful than the abatement cost function in identifying the optimal level of pollution, but because a good understanding of the properties of marginal damage functions can help us better understand the impact of environmental change on social welfare.

As can be seen in Figure 5.4, a marginal damage function specifies a relationship between an incremental unit of emissions and the damages the emissions generate. As one might expect, the relationship between emissions and damages is actually a complex series of cause-and-effect relationships, diagramed in Figure 5.5.

The first set of relationships that must be considered shows how pollution emissions at a particular place generate concentrations of pollution in the environment. The pollution disperses over land, air, surface water, and groundwater. This dispersion is a complicated process to model, but with the availability of supercomputers, it is possible to do so. Other phenomena that affect the concentration of pollutants include the decay of the pollution and

Figure 5.4 **The Marginal Damage Function and the Optimal Level of Emissions**

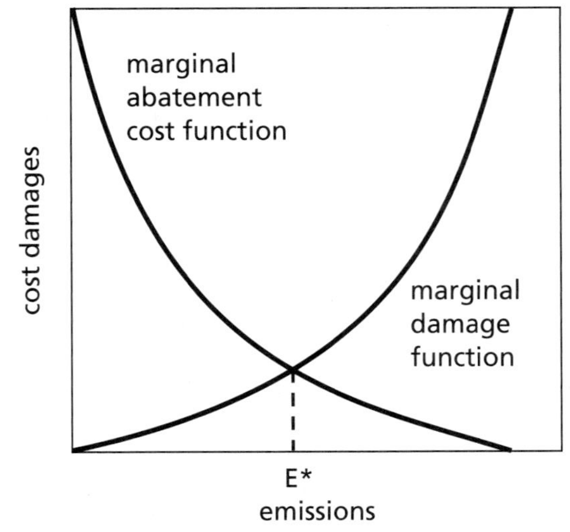

Figure 5.5 Component Relationships of the Marginal Damage Function

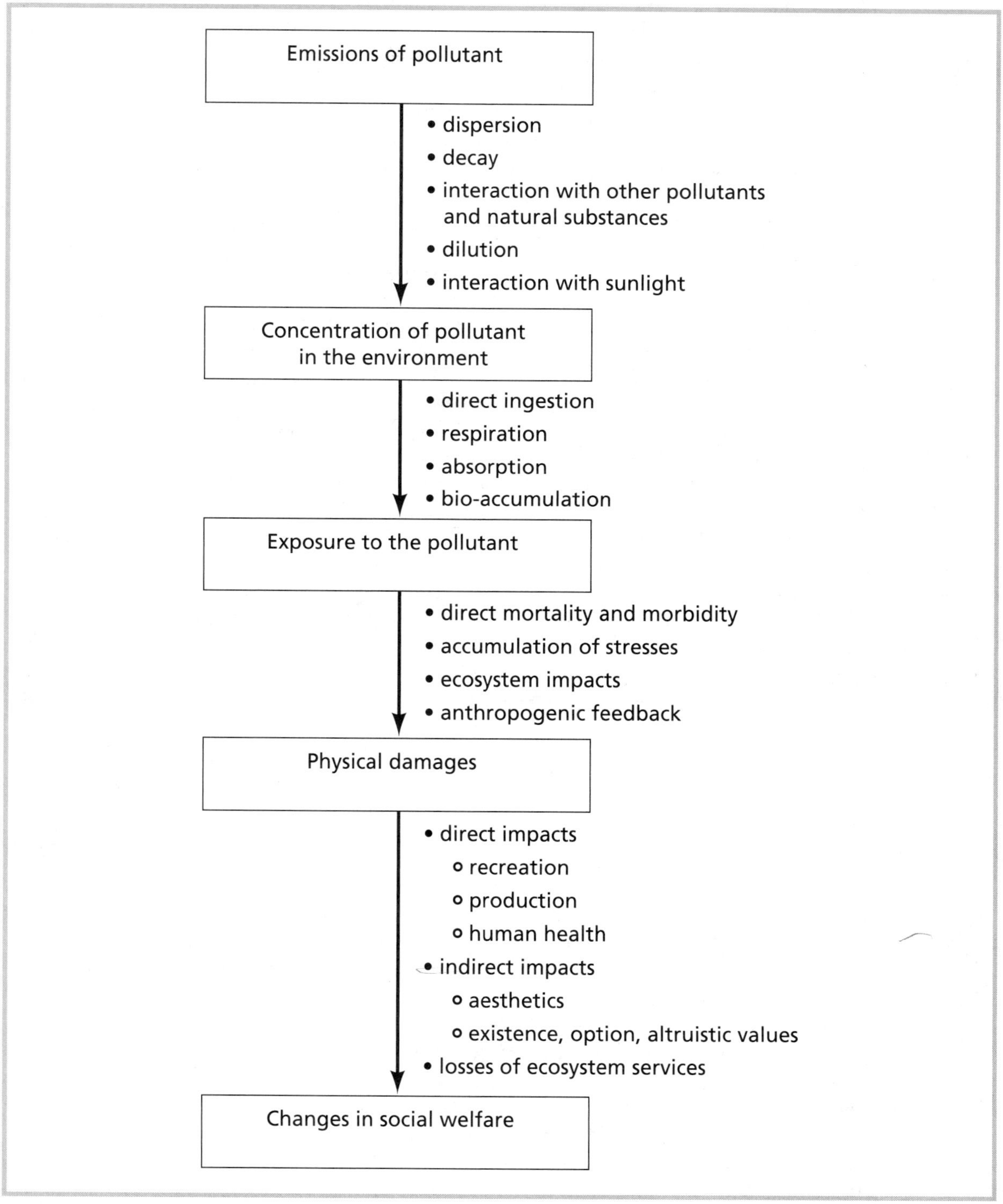

its interaction with sunlight, naturally occurring compounds, and other pollutants that may transform the pollutants into different substances, many of which are also harmful. For example, the emissions of sulfur dioxide are transformed in the atmosphere into sulfates, which lead to acid rain, smog, and tropospheric ozone (see Chapters 8 and 9).

The next set of relationships governs how individual organisms, ecological systems, and social systems are exposed to the concentrations of pollution. For example, one vector for exposure is bioaccumulation, where the concentration of a pollutant in an organism's biomass accumulates as the pollutant makes its way through the food web. For example, plankton in polluted water will absorb the pollutant, but the small fish that eat the plankton will develop a concentration of pollution in their tissue that is an order of magnitude higher than that of the plankton. The larger fish that eat the small fish will have a concentration an order of magnitude higher than the small fish, and the fish-eating birds that eat large fish will have a concentration an order of magnitude higher than the big fish. Such accumulation is one of the reasons that birds of prey such as eagles and ospreys are so vulnerable to DDT and other pollutants. Other ways in which organisms and ecosystems can be exposed are through absorption (through the skin or cell walls), direct ingestion, and respiration.

The next set of relationships relates exposure to physical damages. Obviously, there is direct mortality and morbidity, where the exposure to the pollutant either kills or sickens the organism. Included here are reproductive impacts, such as the impact of DDT on eagles' ability to produce viable eggs. Pollution-specific illnesses in humans are one of the major categories of preventable diseases and preventable death, in both developing and developed nations. Although the pathway of direct mortality and morbidity is relatively straightforward, other mechanisms by which exposure generates physical damages are more complex. They include

- Direct mortality and morbidity
- Accumulation of stresses
- Loss of habitat
- Ecosystem impacts
- Anthropogenic feedback effects

One of the most complex of these mechanisms is an accumulation of stresses. Individual ecosystems and organisms are subjected to multiple sources of stress. Increased stress from pollution can cause the organism to succumb or the ecosystem to degrade from these multiple stresses. Box 5.3 illustrates multiple stresses with an example.

Ecosystem impacts occur because of the connectedness of the components of an ecosystem. For example, if an invasive species such as kudzu fundamentally changes the forest edge by completely draping the forest trees and forest edge plants, there will be a negative impact on the plants that are covered (and eventually killed) by the kudzu. In addition, animals that depend on these plants for food or habitat will be negatively impacted, as will plants

Box 5.3 Multiple Stresses and Ridgetop Forests

An important ecological change has been taking place in the southern Appalachian Mountains. The ridgetop forests, boreal fir, and spruce forests that are typically found further north in Canada, Siberia, and northern New England, are declining in vitality and are actually experiencing die-offs. Scientists have identified three major culprits in their decline: acid rain, tropospheric ozone, and exotic insects.

All three factors weaken the trees, and the presence of one factor makes the other factors have greater impacts on the trees. For example, trees are less able to recover from infestations of sap-sucking or defoliating insects if their systems are already stressed. It is analogous to a human suffering from a severe illness such as cancer. The cancer-treating drugs make the patient more vulnerable to infections such as pneumonia, and the pneumonia further weakens the patient and reduces his or her ability to fight the cancer.

The joint impact of multiple stresses make it very difficult to estimate a marginal damage (MD) function for a particular type of stress. For example, assume that MD1 is the marginal damage associated with tropospheric ozone concentrations when no invasive insect pests are present. If the insects are present, however, then the damage caused by a particular level of ozone will increase with increasing the presence of insects pests, as shown in the figure, where the family of marginal damage represent the damages from ozone, given different levels of infestation. If one were to analyze a policy designed to reduce tropospheric ozone, what would be the benefits of reducing concentrations from c1 to c2? Obviously, the answer depends on the level of insect infestations.

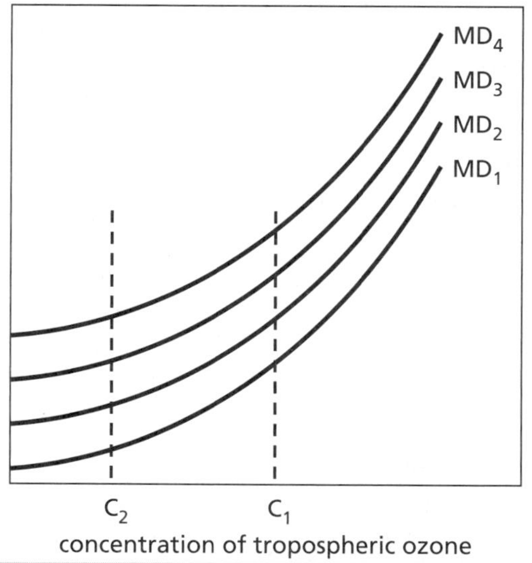

and animals that interact with them. Baskin (1997) contains a nice discussion of the connectedness of ecosystems, with many informative examples.

The Anthropogenic feedback effects refer to activities that humans undertake that exacerbate or mitigate the physical impact of pollution. They do not refer to direct remediation, but, rather, to changes in activities related to the environmental resource. For example, let's say that pollution negatively affects a fish population in an estuary. The reaction to the reduced fish population could be for people to fish more intensely, causing further reductions in the fish populations. Similarly, if the reaction were to fish less intensely, then the impact on fish populations would be lessened. Chapter 11 goes through the impact of pollution on fisheries, including these feedback effects.

Finally, the impact of the physical changes on social welfare must be determined. These functional relationships can often be estimated using the revealed preference and stated preference valuation techniques discussed in Chapter 4. The caveats expressed in these chapters concerning the difficulties of measuring indirect use values and the value of ecological services, however, are applicable in this case.

The Marginal Damage Function and Policy Analysis

It is quite unlikely that in many real-world situations it will be possible to completely identify the set of marginal abatement cost functions and marginal damage functions and solve for the optimal level of pollution. Even if it is not possible to identify the optimal level of pollution or even to have a narrowly bounded estimate of the marginal damage function, knowledge of the properties of a particular marginal damage function can help identify policy goals. Such knowledge can be found by identifying key points along the marginal damage function that signal different types of marginal damages associated with changes in the level of emissions.

For the illustrative pollutant in Figure 5.6, emissions levels that are in the region between zero and E_1 do not have great marginal damages. That may be because these initial levels are easily assimilated by the environment. As one increases the emissions levels into the range between E_1 and E_2, however, the assimilative capacity of the environment begins to become overtaxed and the damages associated with additional pollution increase. As pollution becomes even greater, the damages accelerate and may reach a point where they begin to cause systemwide collapse, as in the region to the right of E_3.

Even if it is not possible to estimate the marginal damage function, one can use knowledge that is developed about some of the relationships diagrammed in Figure 5.5. Using this knowledge, it is possible to make estimates about where the turning points of the marginal damage function may lie in Figure 5.6 (E_1, E_2, E_3). For example, it may make little sense to have a target level of pollution less than E_1 unless the marginal abatement cost is very low. Similarly, one would want to avoid the very steep portion of the marginal damage function (to the right of E_3). That leaves a broad range from E_1 to E_3 as containing the potential target level of pollution. If it is not possible to fur-

Figure 5.6 **The Marginal Damage Function and Policy**

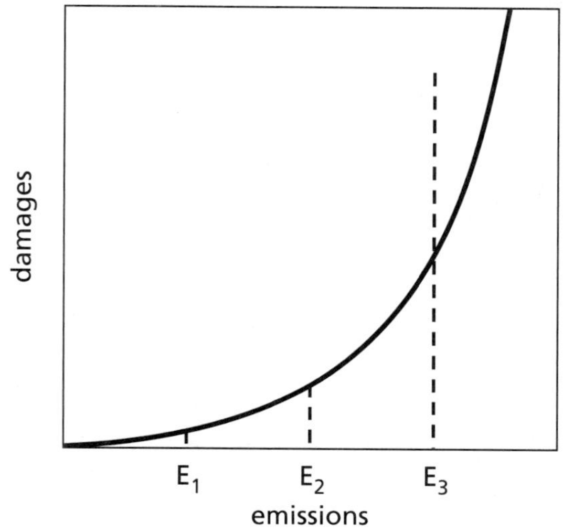

ther narrow the range based on knowledge of the relationships diagrammed in Figure 5.5, then the level must be determined through discussion in the decision-making process. The marginal damage function is a method of analysis that incorporates efficiency criteria and does not incorporate the other decision-making criteria discussed in this chapter. These decision-making criteria can also be used to further pinpoint a target level of emissions for environmental policy.

Summary

The science in support of environmental policy decisions has made important strides in recent years, but it is still not capable of converting every potential decision into a testable hypothesis. In fact, this level of precision may never be reached. Nonetheless, various research and analytical tools can help narrow the decision set and further guide the decision process.

Cost-benefit analysis has proven to be a useful tool in organizing information about economic efficiency, and indicators have been successfully developed for equity and some other criteria. In terms of making better decisions, however, the most important needs are to develop better indicators related to the nonefficiency related decision-making criteria. In addition, little progress has been made in terms of measuring the economic value of the full suite of ecosystem services, as discussed in Chapter 4. Finally, both quantitative and qualitative methods for evaluating alternative decisions across the full suite of decision-making criteria need to be developed.

appendix 5.a
A Trade-off–Based Indicator of Environmental Quality

There is a nonarbitrary way to develop an index of environmental quality that can incorporate a diverse set of indicators or criteria. Such an index can be set up either to construct an overall index of environmental quality or to assign weights to alternative decision-making criteria. This appendix focuses on an overall indicator of environmental quality, but the process is similar when developing weights for alternative decision-making criteria.

An overall indicator of environmental quality can be established by generating choice sets (see Chapter 4) that describe alternative states of the world in terms of their environmental characteristics. For example, characteristics in the choice sets could include variables related to the state of forests, estuaries, rivers, and wetlands; to atmospheric chemistry; to ambient air and water quality; and to the presence of toxic sites.[7]

A choice, or trade-off–based indicator can be developed by using discrete choice-based conjoint analysis (see Chapter 4) to present alternative states of the environment to the individual. The level of the physical environmental characteristics in the choice sets would be varied both within the choice sets presented to individuals and across individuals. This variation in the level of the characteristics of the alternative states of the environment would allow the estimation of a preference function. In this preference function, the probability of preference is estimated as a function of the levels of the physical characteristics. The derivatives (with respect to each physical characteristics) of the preference function can then be used as weights to aggregate the

[7]It is not the purpose of this appendix to define which characteristics should be included; that is a topic of further research. Rather, this appendix focuses on the development and justification of a method with which to develop an indicator of the health of the environment. Further information on this indicator of environmental quality can be found in Kahn (2003).

physical characteristics into a single index or set of indices. In other words, if the estimated preference function were of the form

$$\text{Prob} = \theta(C_1, C_2, C_3, \ldots C_n) \tag{5a.1}$$

where the C_i's refer to the levels of the environmental characteristics that define the alternative states of the world, then the index could be computed as

$$I = \sum_{i=1}^{n} \frac{\delta\theta}{\delta C_i} C_i \tag{5a.2}$$

Perhaps the most attractive aspect of this index is that the weights assigned to each characteristic are not arbitrarily chosen. Rather, they reflect peoples' relative evaluation of the importance of the characteristics, determined by their preference for one state of the world over another. In addition to the inherent desirability (at least from the point of view of an economist) of basing the indicators on willingness to make trade-offs, the trade-off–based foundation of the indicators would make the measures of the health of the environment analogous to the primary measure of the health of the economy (GDP), because GDP is a set of physical quantities that are weighted by people's willingness to make trade-offs, (which in the case of GDP are measured by prices). An indicator of the health of the environment that is based on "trade-off weighted" physical quantities would be completely analogous to GDP except that in this case, the trade-offs are measured through a survey process because market prices do not exist for the physical characteristics of the environment.

One of the major criticisms by noneconomists of willingness to pay measures and other methods based on individual choice is that they do not take into account expert knowledge of the consequences of environmental change. It is possible to incorporate expert knowledge into the trade-off–based indicator of environmental quality (or indicator of sustainability) by implementing a parallel choice process and separate index among a sample of experts.

An important policy consideration is the determination of how much importance to place on the expert index in comparison to the ordinary citizen index. This expert index could be kept separately and policies then could be evaluated with respect to both indices. Alternatively, the indices could be merged into one index. One way to do so is to include a statement in the survey to which citizens respond. This statement would indicate that experts are being asked to state preferences for alternative states of the environment in the same fashion. The citizens could then be asked (as part of the survey questionnaire) how much weight in the decision-making process expert opinion should be given relative to citizen opinion.

This appendix has illustrated that a trade-off weighted index of environmental quality has the potential to meet many needs in understanding the relationship between the health of the environment and social welfare. Outside of discussing conjoint analysis as a general framework in which the index could be estimated, however, the nuts and bolts of the estimation process have not been discussed here. A comprehensive discussion of all the estimation issues is beyond the scope of this appendix, but it is important to point out that the estimation process is quite complex. This trade-off weighted index does, however, have tremendous potential for solving the problem of developing meaningful indicators of environmental policy.

appendix 5.b

Expected Value Analysis

Expected value analysis is a way to compare alternatives, where each alternative has several possible outcomes, each of which occurs with a different probability. For example, let's say that you are deciding which of three games of chance to play, where the fee for playing is exactly \$1.00. The first game is a standard coin flip whereby if you get heads, you win \$2.00 and if you lose you get nothing. This expected value, or EV, can be diagrammed as in Figure 5b.1 and mathematically in the following way:

$$EV = -\$1.00 + 0.5(\$2.00) + 0.5(0) = 0 \quad \text{5b.1}$$

In general, if p_i is the probability of outcome of outcome i, and NB_i is the net benefits of outcome i, then the expected value of an alternative with m potential outcomes is

$$EV = \sum_{i=1}^{m} p_i(NB_i) \quad \text{5b.2}$$

Expected values can be very useful in cost-benefit analysis, because many outcomes will not be certain but will occur according to a probability distribution. One must be very careful, however, because expected value analysis is based on an assumption that the decision maker is risk neutral, meaning that the decision maker only cares about the expected value and not the risk. Certainly that would be the case for most students for the coin flip diagrammed in equation 5.b.1, where the expected value is zero. However, would most students regard the game in equation 5.b.1 as equivalent to the game in 5b.3? In this game, the expected value is still zero, but $10,000 is wagered instead of $1.00:

$$EV = -\$10{,}000.00 + 0.50(\$20{,}000.00) + 0.50(0) = 0 \qquad 5b.3$$

Most students would be risk adverse and not view the two games as identical, even though the expected values are the same. The reason is that if most students were to lose $10,000, it would seriously jeopardize the quality of their life, and the possibility of winning $10,000 does not compensate for the risk of disaster.

There are many reasons society or the public decision maker should be risk neutral. They include the following:

- Risks are spread over a large number of individuals, so even though the total loss may be high, the loss per person is not catastrophic.
- Risks are spread over a large number of public decisions or projects, so even if some projects fail, enough are successful to compensate for the projects that fail.

In some cases where the costs are likely to be extremely high and the consequences are likely to be irreversible, however, one can make a case that society should adopt a risk-adverse attitude toward these decisions. That is likely to be true with many environmental issues, such as protection of rain forests and other key ecosystems, global warming, the storage of nuclear wastes, and the use of heavy metals and other long-lived pollutants.

Review Questions

1. What is a potential Pareto improvement? What is its relevance to the decision-making process?
2. What is the real, risk-free rate of interest?
3. What is the difference between continuous and discrete discounting?
4. Given the data in the table at the top of the next page, conduct a sensitivity analysis for the following projects, using discount rates of 0, 1, 5, 8, and 10%. Assume that benefits and costs are only realized in the years listed in the table (do not extrapolate between years).
5. What are the non-economic criteria for decision making?
6. What is the Gini coefficient? How is it measured?
7. What reasons suggest that the social discount rate should be less than the real risk-free rate of interest?
8. Is the creation of jobs a societal benefit?

	Net Benefits in Year 1	Net Benefits in Year 10	Net Benefits in Year 30	Net Benefits in Year 50	Net Benefits in Year 100
Project A	1000	100	−10	−100	−10,000
Project B	100	100	100	100	100
Project C	−100	1000	1000	−100	−10,000
Project D	100	100	−1000	-10,000	−100,000
Project E	1000	1000	1000	−10,000	−100,000

Questions for Further Study

1. Is cost-benefit analysis objective?
2. What criteria should be used to develop global environmental policy, such as limiting greenhouse gas emissions?
3. What discount rate should a developing country use in cost-benefit analysis?
4. What decision-making criteria would you employ in developing a student alcohol policy for your university?
5. What decision-making criteria should be employed in developing an environmental management policy for your university?
6. How can one integrate multiple criteria in the making of a decision?
7. What decision-making criteria do you believe should have the highest weights in the decision-making process? Why?
8. Should developing countries and developed countries use different decision-making criteria and processes? Why or why not?
9. Which measure is better for measuring ecosystem impact, ecological health or ecological integrity?

Suggested Paper Topics

1. Choose a national or local environmental problem and outline the steps for conducting a cost-benefit analysis. Look at related studies in the literature (*Journal of Environmental Economics and Management, Land Economics, Ecological Economics, American Journal of Agricultural Economics*) for estimates of the value of closely related environmental resources.
2. Investigate the issue of environmental justice. Does the empirical evidence suggest that there is a problem? Make a hypothesis, survey the empirical evidence, and reach a conclusion about whether the evidence supports the hypothesis.
3. Using World Resources Institute, World Bank, and United Nations data for all countries, investigate if a statistical relationship exists between inequity in distribution of income (measured by the Gini coefficient) and inequity in access to environmental quality (measured by variables such as concentrations of air pollutants, access to clean drinking water, and so on).
4. Look at an alternative theory of value such as the energy theory of value and compare it with traditional measures of economic efficiency. Choose several types of environmental issues and show how you might come to different conclusions if you made the decisions based exclusively on each of these theories of value.
5. Students with a love for mathematics might want to investigate the literature in multiattribute decision analysis or multiattribute optimization and discuss how these mathematical models can be used to make decisions using a full suite of decision-making criteria.

6. Investigate the Native American perspective (or another indigenous perspective such as Australian aboriginal) on the environment and compare it with the Judeo-Christian tradition.

Works Cited and Selected Readings

Arrow, K., B. Bolin, R. Costanza, P. Dasgupta, C. Folke, C.S. Hollins, B. Jansson, S. Levin, K.B. Maler, C. Perrins, D. Pimentel, et al. Economic Growth, Carrying Capacity and the Environment. *Science 268* (1995): 520–521.

Austin, J. L. *Sense and Sensibilia*. New York: Oxford University Press, 1962.

Baskin, Y. *The Work of Nature: How the Diversity of Life Sustains Us.* Washington, DC: Island Press, 1997.

Bullard, R. *Dumping in Dixie: Race, Class and Environmental Quality*, Boulder Colorado: West View Press, 1990.

Cairns, J. Jr. Ecological Integrity of Aquatic Systems. *Regulated Rivers: Research and Management 11*, (1995): 313–323.

Callicott, J. B. *In Defense of the Land Ethic: Essays in Environmental Philosophy*. Albany: State University of New York Press, 1989.

Coase, R. H. The Problem of Social Cost. *Journal of Law and Economics 3* (1960): 1–44.

Commission for Racial Justice, United Church of Christ. *Toxic Wastes and Race in the United States*. New York: Public Data Access, 1987.

Daly, H. E. Towards an Environmental Macroeconomics. *Land Economics 67* (1991): 255–259.

Devall, B. *Deep Ecology*. Salt Lake City UT: Peregrine Smith Books, 1985.

Farmer, A., J. R. Kahn, J. A. McDonald, and R. O'Neill. Rethinking the Optimal Level of Environmental Quality: Justifications for Strict Environmental Policy, *Ecological Economics 36* (2001): 461–473.

Flader, S. L., and J. B. Callicott, eds. *Aldo Leopold: The River of the Mother of God and Other Essays*. Madison: University of Wisconsin Press, 1991.

Franceschi, D. and J. R. Kahn. Beyond Strong Sustainability. *International Journal of Sustainable Development* (forthcoming).

Gramlich, E. M. *A Guide to Benefit-Cost Analysis.* Englewood Cliffs, NJ: Prentice Hall, 1990.

Hamilton, K. and B. Luntz. Accounting for the Future, Environmental Department Working Paper, Washington: World Bank, 1995.

Hartwick, J. The Generalized R% Rule for Semi-durable Exhaustible Resources. *Resource and Energy Economics 15*, (1993): 147–152.

Jeffers, S. *Brother Eagle, Sister Sky: A Message from Chief Seattle.* New York: Dial Books for Young Readers, 1991.

Kahn, J. R. Trade-off Based Indicators of Environmental Quality, in *Does Environmental Policy Work: The Theory and Practice of Outcomes Assessment*, Ervin, D., J.R. Kahn and M. Livingston, eds. Cheltenham UK: Edward Elgar: 38–54.

Kahn, J. R., and R. O'Neill. Ecological Interaction as a Source of Economic Irreversibility. *Southern Economic Journal, 66*, no. 2 (1999): 381–402.

Krutilla, J., and A. C. Fisher. *The Economics of Natural Environments*. Washington, DC: Resources for the Future, 1985.

Nash, R. F. *The Rights of Nature: A History of Environmental Ethics*. Madison: University of Wisconsin Press, 1989.

Odum, H. T., and E. C. Odum. *Energy Basis for Man and Nature*. 3rd ed. York: McGraw-Hill, 1981.

O'Neill R.V., J. R. Kahn, J. R. Duncan, S. Elliot, R. Efroymson, M. Cardwell and D. Jones. Economic Growth and Sustainability: A New Challenge. *Ecological Applications 26*, no. 3 (1996): 23–24.

Pearce, D. W., and J. J. Warford. *World without End: Economics, Environment, and Sustainable Development*. New York: Oxford University Press, 1993.

Peskin, H. M. A National Accounting Framework for Environmental Assets. *Journal of Environmental Economics and Management 2*, (1976): 255–262.

Pezzey, J. Sustainability Constraints. *Land Economics 73*, no. 4 (1997): 448–466.

Porter, R. C. The New Approach to Wilderness Preservation through Benefit-Cost Analysis. *Journal of Environmental Economics and Management 9* (1982): 59–80.

Prince, R., and P. L. Gordon. Greening the National Accounts. *CBO Papers.*, Washington, DC: Congressional Budget Office, 1994.

Repetto, R., W. Magrath, M. Wells, C. Beer, F. Rossinni, et al. *Wasting Assets: Natural Resources in the National Income and Product Accounts*. Washington, DC: World Resources Institute, 1989.

Schimmel, S. C., et al. Statistical Summary: EMAP Estuaries, Virginia Province-1991. EPA/620/R-94/005, Washington, DC: Environmental Protection Agency, 1994.

Schrader-Frechette, K. S. What Risk Management Teaches Us about Ecosystem Management. *Landscape and Urban Planning 40* (1998): 141–150.

Suzuki, D., and P. Knudtson. *Wisdom of the Elders*. New York: Bantam, 1992.

Weitzman, M. Why the Far-Distant Future Should be Discounted at its Lowest Possible Rate, *Journal of Environmental Economics and Management 36* (1998): 201–208.

chapter 6
The Macroeconomics of the Environment

Thinking to get at once all the gold the goose could give, he killed it and opened it only to find—nothing.

Aesop, The Goose with the Golden Eggs, *c. 550 B.C.*

Introduction

In the debate over whether we need more environmental protection or less environmental protection, opponents of increasing environmental standards cite a detrimental impact of environmental regulation on the economy. In contrast, proponents of higher standards for environmental protection argue that the environment is the source of economic productivity and that lack of environmental protection will ultimately reduce the productivity of the economy, in a fashion somewhat analogous to killing the goose that laid the golden egg. Which hypothesis is correct? Can aspects of both hypotheses be correct?

Chapters 1 through 5 examined predominately microeconomic aspects of the environment and do not help us in developing answers to the above questions. Although developing an understanding of the microeconomic issues is critically important to understanding environmental economics, it is not sufficient. Microeconomic environmental issues involve choosing the optimal level of an environmental resource (this could be a quantity or a quality choice). Environmental resources are viewed as goods that provide services, and the optimal level of these services is found by equating marginal social benefits with marginal social costs in a manner that is identical to all other types of goods. Although economists tend to focus on these microeconomic rules for resource allocation, policy makers are very often concerned about macroeconomic impacts. For example, when George W. Bush announced that the United States would no longer be part of the Kyoto Protocol process for limiting greenhouse gas emissions, he cited as his reason the potential impacts on the macroeconomy of the United States.[1]

This chapter examines the relationship between the environment and the aggregate economy. Two major issues are associated with this relationship. The first involves the question of how environmental policy affects the economy as a whole. For example, what is the effect of environmental policy on international competitiveness? Does improving environmental quality or preserving existing environmental resources reduce the gross domestic product (GDP)[2] and decrease the number of jobs, or does it improve the economy? The second question focuses on how growth of the economy affects the environment. For example, does a growing economy imply that environmental quality must diminish?

These questions involving the relationship between environmental quality and the overall economy are becoming increasingly important for several reasons. As we begin to experience more systemwide environmental changes, such as the loss of biodiversity, acid precipitation, global warming, and ozone depletion, these relationships between the environment and the macroeconomy become more important. In addition, political discussions on future directions of environmental policy are increasingly focused on the effect of environmental improvement on jobs and GDP, as evidenced by the *recent actions* of the George W. Bush administration, such as global warming policy and the advocacy of producing oil in the Arctic National Wildlife Refuge (ANWR).

Although much of the current focus of environmental economics is on more microeconomic issues, the conceptual discussion of the interrelationship between the environment and the macroeconomy began early in the development of the field of environmental economics. Boulding (1966), who made the analogy of the earth to a spaceship, stressed that our activities were constrained by our endowment of resources and the ability of environmental systems to assimilate wastes. Rather than living in a "frontier" or "cowboy" society (where one can always expand the frontiers when currently utilized

---

[1]The costs of reducing greenhouse gas emissions are examined more closely in Chapter 7.

[2]Gross domestic product, or GDP, is a measure of national income. It is related to gross national product, or GNP, with which older readers may be more familiar. The primary difference between GDP and GNP is that GNP includes only the income of factors of production that are owned by citizens of the country, whereas GDP includes the income of all factors of productions that are employed in the country. For example, the income of a Japanese engineer or a Peruvian Major League Soccer player who works in the United States is considered part of GDP but not part of GNP. Because of the increased globalization of national economies, GDP has become the preferred measure of national income.

land areas are depleted, or resources are spoiled by waste), we live in a "spaceship" society where our inputs are finite, and we are trapped with our wastes. Although Boulding did not develop formal models of the relationship between the economy and the environment, his article was central in specifying the idea that the overall economy was constrained by the environment and that the economy impacts the environment and may change the nature of that constraint.

Conceptual Model of the Environment and the Economy

There are two different ways of conceptualizing the relationship between the economy and the environment. One way is looking at the relationship between the environment and individual economic actors, and computing how these individual effects aggregate up to effects on the total system. For example, air pollution affects the health of workers, which affects the productivity of industry, which affects the aggregate economy. Carbon taxes to address global warming could increase the cost of manufacturing and transportation for many types of activities, slowing economic growth. Another way of conceptualizing the relationship between the economy and the environment is to eschew a focus on individual impacts and their summation, and instead view the economy and environment as two interwoven systems, where the economic system is actually embedded in the larger earth system. For example, as the economy grows, urbanization displaces and fragments habitat. As global climate change proceeds, it places a variety of constraints on economic and social activity.

Which perspective is correct? The answer to this question depends on what issue we are looking at. If we are focusing on issues such as the impact of a cleaner environment on the productivity of the economy or the impact of environmental regulations, then the first perspective may be sufficient. If, however, we are looking at issues such as how much growth is possible and what steps are needed to assure sustainability, then the latter perspective is the one that should be taken.

An interesting conceptual model that combines both perspectives is contained in Figure 6.1, which diagrams how social welfare is affected by the health of the environment, the health of the economy, the health of the human population, and social justice. Other types of effects on social welfare could be included in the model, but Figure 6.1 focuses on only these four to keep the diagram a little simpler. It illustrates several ways in which interactions between the environment and the macroeconomy affect social welfare. In the conceptual model illustrated in Figure 6.1, the health of the environment, the health of the economy, the health of the (human) population, and social justice all affect social welfare, both independently and through their interaction with one another. Other areas of social policy, such as education

Figure 6.1 **Areas of Social Policy and Social Welfare**

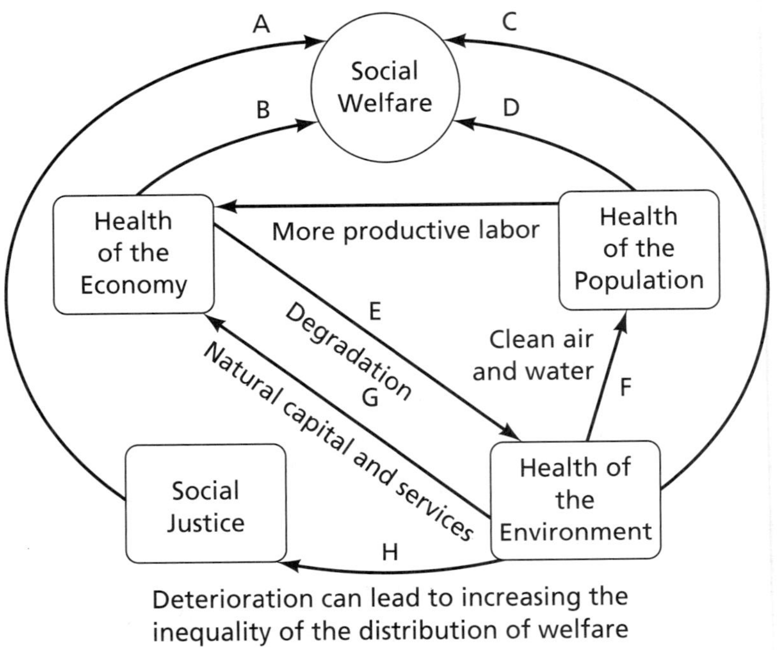

and culture, are important as well, but they have been excluded from the diagram in the interests of simplicity.

Environmental quality impacts social welfare in a variety of ways. People benefit from improved environmental quality if it beneficially affects their health (arrow F in Figure 6.1), if it improves social justice (H), if it improves the economy (G), or simply because they view their quality of life as higher if environmental quality is higher (C). Effects with an even more circuitous path of impacts can also be important. For example, improved environmental quality will increase the health of the population, which will increase the marginal productivity of labor, which in turn will increase the health of the economy.

Figure 6.1 is useful for illustrating some of the important paths by which the environment and the economy can affect one another and helps frame the discussion in this chapter. We are interested here not just in the arrows directly between the health of the economy and the health of the environment, but also in the more indirect paths by which they affect one another. Of course, our ultimate interests are the implications of the complicated functional relationships for social welfare.

The Impact of the Environment on Economic Productivity

As Figure 6.1 indicates, the relationships between the economy and the environment are quite complex, yet it is possible to highlight three basic mechanisms by which the environment and environmental policy affect economic productivity. The first has to do with the impact of environmental regulations on productivity (a negative impact), and the last two have to do with the impact of environmental quality on economic productivity (positive impacts).

The Negative Impact of Environmental Policy on Economic Productivity

Environmental policy forces firms to make decisions that are in the social interest, but not in their private interest. The process of "internalizing an externality" increases the expenditure of labor, capital, materials, and energy in order to reduce the level of the externality. These expenditures of additional inputs are likely to reduce the efficiency with which firms produce their economic outputs.[3] Reiterating, if firms devote resources to reducing emissions of pollutants, then the cost of producing their outputs increases. More importantly, these resources used to reduce pollution cannot be used to produce economic outputs. Thus, as we use resources to reduce pollution, the direct consequence will be a negative impact on gross domestic product. This impact will be worse if we rely on direct controls for environmental regulation rather than economic incentives, for all the reasons discussed in Chapter 3. As discussed there, direct controls limit options for pollution reduction and may force polluters to employ methods that cost more than others they might choose. In addition, direct controls do not allocate pollution reductions to the polluters who can reduce most cheaply. In other words, if we try to achieve our environmental goals through policies based predominately on direct controls, even more resources will be devoted to pollution control, leaving even less for production GDP.

The same arguments can be made with respect to land use. If land use is restricted so as to protect the environment, then the outputs produced in conjunction with that land would now require additional resources to produce the same level of outputs.

---

[3]It is possible that some types of expenditures on pollution control reduce cost by increasing energy efficiency or the need to deal with wastes. This possibility is discussed more fully in the discussion of the Porter hypothesis, later in this chapter.

The Positive Impacts of Environmental Quality on Economic Productivity

Although the use of resources to reduce emissions can have a negative impact on the economy, an increase in environmental quality also would be expected to have a positive impact on the economy. This positive impact occurs in two ways. First, environmental resources are an input to production processes. For example, clean water is needed to produce many products. The cleaner the water to begin with, the fewer resources are needed to further clean the water.

Second, environmental quality affects the productivity of other inputs. For example, the cleaner the environment, the healthier and more productive the labor force.[4] Another example of this type of impact is the positive impact of reduced air pollution (such as tropospheric ozone) on agricultural productivity. Reduced air pollution increases yield per acre of many crops, increasing the productivity of land and other agricultural impacts.

Important benefits to the economy can also be found through the impact on health and health care. The effect of improved environmental quality on the marginal productivity of labor was discussed earlier, but there is another very important one. Health care consumes a very large proportion of the national income in most countries, but particularly in the United States. If the population is healthier because it has cleaner water to drink, cleaner air to breathe, and less exposure to toxic substances, then fewer resources need be devoted to health care. This reason prompted China to act recently to reduce its air pollution; the horrible air quality in its big cities such as Beijing was creating such bad health impacts that it has become cheaper to improve air quality than to pay for the health care costs. This policy, of course, does not mean that air quality in China has become good (or even acceptable), but initial steps are being taken to reduce emissions.

Another important health benefit can occur if the health care industry is an industry characterized by increasing average cost,[5] then increasing environmental quality not only will reduce the resources necessary to treat environmentally related illness, but it could also reduce health costs generally by reducing the average cost of treatment. This effect is illustrated in Figure 6.2, where reducing the number of cases of treatment from N_1 to N_2 reduces the average cost of treatment from C_1 to C_2. This reduction in the average cost of general health care will occur only if the average cost of health care is increasing. Although there is some evidence to suggest this is true, this relationship is very difficult to measure due to the heterogeneous nature of disease and health care.

Throughout this book, the importance of ecological services is emphasized. Ecological services such as biodiversity, nutrient cycling, maintenance of hydrological cycles, maintenance of atmospheric chemistry and global cli-

---

[4]For example, children who are exposed to higher than background levels of lead suffer permanent neurological damages, including a permanent reduction in IQ.

[5]In this case, increasing average costs mean that for each additional case of illness, the cost of treating the illness is higher than for previous cases.

Figure 6.2 **Potential Reduction in Average Cost of Health Care from an Improvement in Environmental Quality**

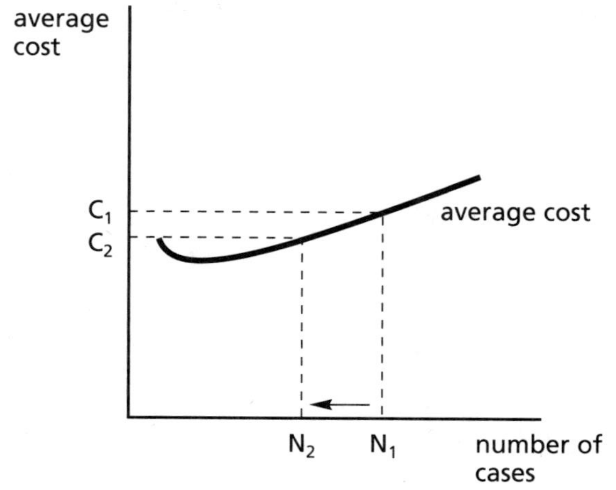

mate, flood control, soil formation, pollination, seed dispersal, and pest control have an important impact on the economy as well as the quality of life in general. Box example 6.1 contains an example of pest control provided by Mexican free-tail bats in the southwestern United States.

In summary, cleaner air, less exposure to toxic waste, cleaner water, more forests, more fish, greater levels of ecological services (such as biological diversity), and greater protection from ultraviolet radiation make the economy more productive. This impact on the productivity of the economy is in addition to the other beneficial aspects of environmental improvement, such as aesthetic, recreational, health, and ecological benefits.

Which Effect Dominates?

The previous sections describe both positive and negative economic impacts of improving environmental quality. This discussion leads immediately to the question of determining the net effect of these two opposing impacts. Unfortunately, this question is very difficult to answer. Theoretically, one would want to estimate an equation[6] of the following form:

$$GDP = f\,[\,L_1, K_1, EQ(GDP, L_2, K_2)] \qquad 6.1$$

[6]Students who are more familiar with economic and mathematical modeling will recognize this equation as a "reduced form," which is a single equation derived from a more complicated system of several equations. It should also be noted that in this equation, environmental quality is a function of GDP. The impact of GDP on environmental quality is discussed later in the chapter.

where L_1 is the amount of labor directly used to produce GDP, K_1 is the amount of capital directly used to produce GDP, EQ is the level of environmental quality, L_2 is the amount of labor used to reduce emissions, and K_2 is the amount of capital used to reduce emissions. This equation has the potential to show both the negative and positive impacts of environmental change

Box 6.1 Bats and Pest Control

When we think of bats, we think of eerie creatures, Halloween, and vampire movies. Maybe we appreciate their impact on mosquito populations. Unbeknownst to most people, bats make a vital contribution to the economy of the United States through their impact on agricultural pest populations. Professor Gary McCracken of the University of Tennessee has been researching this phenomenon, and he has reached some startling preliminary results.

In spring of each year, approximately 200 million Mexican free-tail bats migrate from Mexico to various locations in the southwestern United States. Once there, like an antiballistic missile defense system they rise at night to an altitude of up to 2 miles to feed on the billions of corn earworm moths (and other moths) that are also migrating north to the United States. The 20 million bats that summer in Bracken Cave in Texas eat approximately 250 tons of insects a night, and the total bat population consumes a startling 2.5 thousand tons of insects per night. To put this number in perspective, 2.5 thousand tons is equal to 5 million pounds, or about the same weight as 33,000 people (assuming an average of 150 pounds per person). This incredible amount of insects is eaten every night during the growing season by these bats, preventing one billion dollars of crop damage per year, according to McCracken's estimates.

If increased use of pesticides had a detrimental impact on bats or if increased urban sprawl, inappropriate outdoor recreational activity, or other environmental impacts threatened the sanctuary of their caves, bat populations could plummet. That would have a devastating impact on US agriculture, forcing much higher costs either through increased reliance on chemical pesticides or through reduced crop yields. The negative impact on agriculture would impact other industry (such as food processing and restaurants) that depend on agriculture, causing a negative multiplier impact on the overall economy that could exceed the impact on agriculture by a factor of two or more. Of course, increased pesticide use would have negative impacts on the ecosystem, which would also adversely impact ecosystem and human health and create further declines in economic productivity.

Source: University of Tennessee (1997).

on GDP. The negative impact would be seen as an increase in the amount of labor or capital devoted to abating emissions, which in turn reduces the amount of labor and capital that can be used to produce GDP. The equation also allows for the positive impact as an increase in environmental quality (EQ) can increase GDP for the reasons discussed earlier.

Unfortunately, none of the empirical studies really has attempted to estimate a relationship of the nature of equation 6.1. The primary reason, for all the reasons outlined in Chapter 5, is that it is very hard to determine how to measure environmental quality as a single variable (or even a set of variables). Air quality, water quality, the health of ecosystems (such as forests, wetlands, and aquatic ecosystems), toxic contamination, biodiversity, the density of the ozone layer, emissions of greenhouse gases, and many other measures of environmental quality could be defined. Which are most important, and how can they be combined into a single measure or a small set of measures? Although a process was suggested in Appendix 5.b, neither this methodology nor alternative methodologies with the same goal have yet been implemented to create an overall indicator of environmental quality. Even if a procedure for developing this variable could be implemented in the present or near future, it could be very difficult to develop it retrospectively into the past. This problem is of very serious concern because to estimate an equation of the nature of equation 6.1, it would be necessary to have an environmental measure not only for today but for the past 20 or 30 years so that one would have a sufficient number of data points to estimate the equation.

The lack of ability to include a comprehensive environmental quality measure in the analysis has substantially shaped the empirical studies of the relationship between the environment and the economy. It has caused people to focus on the negative impact (resources used to reduce emissions cannot be used to produce GDP) and has precluded them from measuring the positive impact (environmental quality is an input to producing GDP and makes other inputs more productive). For example, Jorgenson and Wilcoxen (1990) estimate that the impact of environmental regulation on the economy is to reduce GDP by 2.592 percent. Hazilla and Kopp (1990) find a cumulative impact through 1990 of a reduction of nearly 6 percent. An EPA Retrospective Study found a reduction in GDP of about 1 percent as a result of air pollution regulations between 1970 and 1990 (U.S. Environmental Protection Agency, 1997). However, the economic model (computable general equilibrium model[7]) that all these studies used only allowed them to

---

[7]A computable general equilibrium model is one of the entire economy that allows a direct impact to ripple through the economy and have indirect impacts on other sectors of the economy. For example, suppose that an environmental regulation caused electric utilities to increase abatement expenditures, thus raising the price of electricity. The higher price of electricity would increase costs in other industries, and the increased costs in these industries would have further effects on additional industries. A computable general equilibrium model captures the way that different markets are related and computes the indirect impacts as well as the direct impacts.

measure negative impact, and they did not attempt to measure the positive impact, presumably because of a lack of data.

Gillis et al. (1996) have attempted to rectify this problem by using the same type of computable general equilibrium (CGE) model, but they make a fundamental change by incorporating the impact of changes in environmental quality on economic activity. They do so by measuring the health benefits of the air quality regulations, including reduced medical costs, increased productivity, and impacts on agriculture and household soiling. Even though they only include a subset of the potential positive impacts, their estimation of the combined negative and positive impacts is that GDP is approximately 2 percent higher than it would be in the absence of air quality regulations.

Can Environmental Policy Make the Economy Stronger? The Porter Hypothesis

In the previous section on negative impacts of environmental policy on the economy, it was argued that stricter environmental policy will have a negative direct impact on the economy, because resources that could be used elsewhere in the economy are devoted to production. Some respected policy analysts, however, most notably Michael Porter (1990, 1991), argue that it is not clear that stricter environmental policy reduces overall resource availability and increases firms' costs. Because stricter environmental policy requires firms to cut wastes, increase the efficiency with which energy is used, and choose newer, more efficient production technologies, costs may be reduced. *World Resources 1992–93* cites several studies showing firms forced to reduce their release of pollution and wastes actually reduce their production costs (World Resource Institute, 1992). Porter (1990, 1991) further argues that the reduction in production costs associated with strict environmental policy not only directly stimulates the domestic economy, but also increases the competitiveness of the domestic economy relative to foreign economies, bolstering exports and reducing imports. This hypothesis that regulation can reduce production costs is essentially an argument that there are cost savings opportunities available that firms are not seizing. Many economists refer to these unseized opportunities as analogous to $5 bills lying on the sidewalk that no one bothers to pick up.

Are There $5 Bills on the Sidewalk?

Simpson (1993) points out that the most logical way to attempt to explain both the Porter hypothesis and the cases of cost reduction that have been observed is to differentiate between variable and fixed costs. Stricter environmental policy forces firms to change their production technologies, which increases their fixed costs in the short run as they install new equipment. Yet because the cleaner technologies reduce the firms' needs for inputs (such as energy) and produce less waste, which is expensive to treat or dispose, variable costs will be reduced after the new technology is installed. Advocates of the Porter hypothesis argue that the reduction in variable costs exceeds the increase in fixed costs, so total costs decline.

Many economists, though, do not believe that there are cost-reducing options available that firms do not voluntarily pursue. For government environmental policy to generate opportunities that would otherwise be unavailable to firms, there must be institutional barriers that prevent the firms from pursuing these cost-reducing opportunities.

Palmer and Simpson (1993) investigate the types of barriers that might prevent firms from pursuing these cost-reducing activities. These barriers include the inefficiency and shortsightedness of the firm and the difficulty of appropriating the benefits from research and development into cleaner technologies.

The explanation that firms may be stupid (or ignorant) and simply fail to take advantage of beneficial opportunities is not very satisfying. Although individual firms certainly have bypassed many golden opportunities, Palmer and Simpson (1993) suggest that it is difficult to imagine that this oversight would occur on a systematic basis, particularly since the free-market system encourages survival of the most efficient firms. Deviations from cost-minimizing behavior, however, could occur in industries in which there was little competition from either domestic or foreign producers (such as electric utilities). Also, if firms are shortsighted and inadequately consider the future benefits of current investments, then they might not undertake investments that lower costs in the long run. The free-market system, however, should also discourage this behavior. In the long run, firms that are farsighted should replace firms that are shortsighted, because Darwinian survival of the fittest will reward firms that engage in better planning.

Another reason firms may bypass cost-reducing opportunities is that the difficulty of appropriating the benefits from research and development prevents firms from engaging in the socially optimal level of research and development into technologies that are less polluting. If a potential technology is difficult to protect with patent laws (either because foreign competitors do not honor U.S. patents or because it is easy to modify the technology and get around the patent), then firms have little incentive to invest in such technologies. Yet it is then difficult to argue that government policies that encourage such research and development would increase competitiveness relative to foreign competitors (such as Porter, (1993), argues). If the technologies are easy to imitate, then it is not likely that their promotion will create a cost advantage for domestic producers, although it could produce a cost savings for all.

A further reason firms might not undertake these potentially beneficial investments is explored by Kahn and Farmer (1999) and related to the costs savings for all firms. Cost savings and increased profitability may be limited by strategic behavior of firms, generating an asymmetry in the nature of the potential rewards and penalties of adopting new technologies. Let's assume that there is an equal probability that a potential technology will either increase or reduce costs. Let's also assume that the technology is easy to copy. Under these circumstances, firms have no incentive to innovate. If they adopt the new technology and it proves to reduce costs, then the cost advantage will be short-lived because the technology will soon be copied by the firm's competitors. If the new technology proves to be a bust and increases costs, then the firm's competitors will not follow the innovating firm. Under these circumstances, it always pays to be a follower and not a leader, so research activities to find cost-reducing technologies might not be undertaken and firms might be unwilling to incur costs to implement existing, but cleaner, technologies. Under these circumstances, a stricter environmental policy *could* lead firms to develop and adopt technologies that are both more efficient and cleaner. These technologies may remain undeveloped and unimplemented without the policy, because firms strategically avoid becoming the leader in their pursuit.

The Impact of the Economy on the Environment

The impact of environmental policy and changes in environmental quality on the economy has already been discussed. The earlier discussion, though, covers only one set of interactions between the economy and the environment. The other set involves the impact of economic growth on the environment.

Herman Daly (1977, 1991) has written articulately about the impact of the scale of the economy on the environment. He argues that when we look at issues of internalizing the external environmental cost of an activity, we are missing the important point that we have to be concerned not just about the activities of individual economic actors, but also about the total impact of the total quantity of activities associated with the aggregate economy. *Ceteris paribus*, the more economic activity the more emissions and the more conversion of land from natural habitat into urban, industrial, suburban, and agricultural uses. Simply imposing a pollution tax will not protect the environment from destruction if the number of polluters keeps getting bigger because of the growth of the economy (and because of the growth of population). Consequently, Daly argues that policy makers need to consider limits to the amount of economic activity. He argues that growth of the economy should not be a direct policy goal.

A counterargument is that it is not the amount of economic activity that matters, but the nature of economic activity. If, as the economy grows, we adopt cleaner technologies, recycle more, switch to clean and renewable energy sources, and make similar changes in the environmental characteristics of economic activity, then the scale issue becomes less important. According to this argument, we need not be concerned about the scale of activity if we take steps to reduce the impact per unit of activity.

Of course, the total impact of economic activity depends on both the amount of activity and the impact per unit of activity. Policy could and should focus on both. We do not need to shut down economic growth, but, rather, make sure that growth is not pursued for the sake of growth and that we focus on sustainable patterns of development. As discussed in the next three chapters, a critical aspect of this subject is whether we will keep expanding our use of fossil fuels.

As might be expected, this issue is not one upon which economists have been silent. In fact, there has been much discussion of this issue in the environmental economics and economic development literature. One perspective argues that as the economy grows and as per capita income becomes greater, environmental quality will increase. The argument used to support this perspective says that as income increases, the demand for environmental quality will increase as well. This argument is patterned after a finding in the development economics literature that focuses on the relationship between the level of income and the equity of the distribution of income. The original Kuznet's curve finds a U-shaped relationship between the equality of distribution of income and the level of income. That is, low-income countries tend to have a balanced distribution of income, but as income per capita grows, the equality of its distribution becomes worse. There comes a point, however, where the further growth of income leads to improving equity, which continues as income becomes even higher.

An environmental Kuznet's curve (EKC) has been hypothesized, which argues that low-income countries have little detrimental impact on the environment because their level of economic activity is relatively low. Then, as the economy grows, fossil fuel use, waste, and water pollution tend to grow, reducing environmental quality. As income continues to grow, however, the demand for environmental quality also grows, and policies are put into place to reduce pollution and other sources of environmental degredation. The EKC hypothesis stipulates a U-shaped relationship between environmental quality and income (Figure 6.3) or an inverse U-shaped relationship between pollution emissions and income (Figure 6.4). Acceptance of this hypothesis can lead to a policy argument to focus entirely on the growth of income and not to worry about environmental protection, because eventually the growth of income will lead to action to improve the environment. Should we accept this hypothesis?

The World Bank (1992) and Shafik (1994) look at the data and find empirical evidence that supports this hypothesis with respect to some environmental problems but not others. These studies look at data across countries and charts environmental quality as a function of per capita income. These works show that an inverse U-shaped relationship exists for air pollution (see Figure 6.5) but not for other measures such as per capita municipal waste and carbon dioxide emissions. That is to say, as income initially increases, air pollution increases, but then it reaches a point where increases in per capita income cause a decline in air pollution. Although the World Bank does not find this proposition (that environmental quality will improve with increases in income) to be true in general, many people interpret the air pollution results to be true for environmental degradation in general. Based

Figure 6.3 **The Environmental Kuznet's Curve: The Relationship between Income and Environmental Quality**

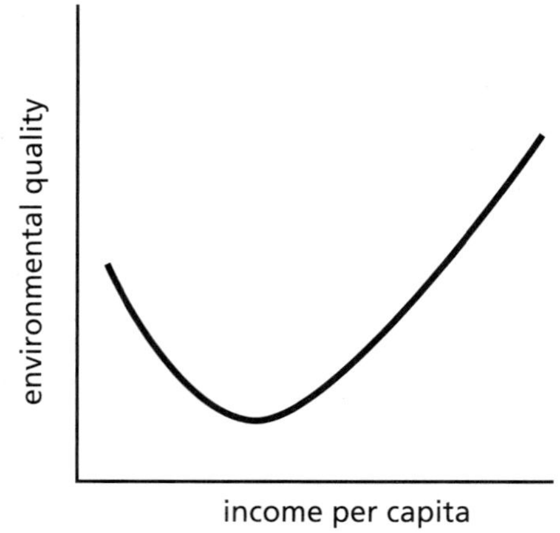

Figure 6.4 **The Environmental Kuznet's Curve: The Relationship between Income and Pollution Emissions**

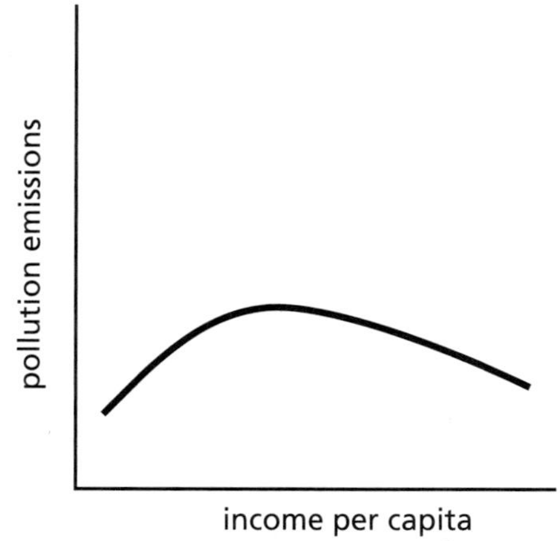

on this unwarranted generalization, it is often argued that an improvement in environmental quality is a natural outcome of increases in per capita income, leading to the type of policy prescription to focus on economic growth rather than either environmental protection or a combination of economic growth and environmental protection.

Figure 6.5 The Inverse U-Shaped Relationship between Pollution and Income Urban Concentrations of Sulfur Dioxide

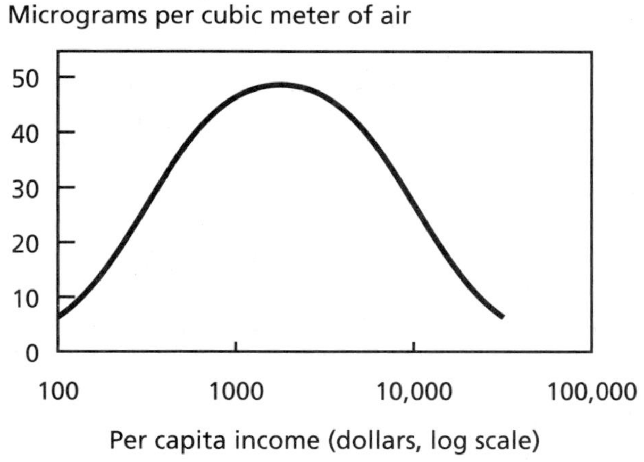

Source: Extracted from *World Development Report 1992: Development and the Environment*, New York: Oxford University Press, 1992.

In fact, the empirical research investigating the existence of an environmental Kuznet's curve does not really present convincing evidence that increasing income generates increasing environmental quality. One important problem is that the studies based on air pollution do not generalize well to total environmental quality, because emission of air pollution in itself is not a particularly good measure of general environmental quality. First, conventional air pollutants, such as sulfur dioxide, do not represent an environmental problem whose impacts accumulate over time. If impacts accumulate over time—even if the incremental environmental degradation becomes smaller as income increases—then the cumulative environmental impact will continue to grow larger. This effect is one reason most ecologists believe that land use issues and not emissions issues are the most pressing environmental problems. Related to this problem of using air pollution as a proxy for overall environmental change is that air pollution is not as damaging to ecological services as other types of environmental problems such as wetlands conversion, deforestation, and soil loss. In fact, if one looks at the poorest of nations, one sees that they suffer some of the worst environmental degradation in terms of contaminated drinking water, encroaching deserts, deforestation, soil loss, and so on. That is critically important because this type of environmental degradation reduces economic productivity in regions of already low productivity. The current environmental degradation may therefore prevent the future growth of income, blocking any potential positive impacts on the environment from increasing income. This point is discussed more fully in Chapter 18.

An additional potential obstacle to accepting the idea of the EKC hypothesis can be found in Rothman (1998), who argues that those studies that indicate the existence of an EKC have actually incorrectly measured the environmental impacts associated with higher-income countries. He argues that what should be measured is not the impact associated with the goods a country produces, but the goods a country consumes. His reason is that a lot of the pollution associated with the goods that a high-income country consumes is generated in low-income countries where those products are manufactured. For example, the majority of mining activity occurs in developing countries, but the majority of consumption of metal products occurs in developed countries.

A final problem with the argument that increasing income leads to environmental improvement is that the measures used for income may be flawed in that they do not measure the loss of environmental capital that is used to produce income. As discussed in Chapter 5, measures of income such as net domestic product do not subtract the depreciation of the income producing ability of natural and environmental capital, which can lead to an over estimate of the income that is used when estimating an environmental Kuznet's curve. In actuality, the income measure should be the type of "green" NDP discussed in Chapter 5.

The hypothesis that there is a U-shaped relationship between income and environmental quality remains controversial in the environmental economics literature. Its existence is accepted by some economists as an empirical finding, but there are important shortcomings associated with these studies and a lot of evidence to reject the EKC hypothesis.[8]

GDP, Sustainability, and Environmental Quality

One issue touched upon in the EKC debate is whether growth in current income depletes future income producing capability. This argument is central to those who advocate adjusting the measure of GDP to incorporate the loss of future income earning capacity, because some growth patterns are inherently unsustainable. For example, if the soil is made barren in pursuit of raising current income levels, then it is argued that these income levels are unsustainable and that future income levels must decline. In actuality, the question of the sustainability of economic growth and quality of life is much more complex and must be examined in further detail.

In pursuing this examination of sustainability, the focus is on sustainability of GDP, while recognizing that GDP is not a complete measure of social welfare or quality of life. This chapter focuses on the sustainability of the path of

[8]For those interested in digging deeper into this controversy, two scientific journals offer special issues addressing this topic: *Ecological Economics 25*, no. 2. (May 1998):143–229; and *Ecological Applications 26*, no. 3, (1996): 23–24. For the most up-to-date articles on this topic, search EconLit or individual journals such as *Ecological Economics* or *Journal of Environmental Economics and Management* using "Environment and Kuznets" as keywords.

GDP rather than on a multidimensional measure of development for several reasons. Quite simply, one reason is that the major purpose of this chapter is to examine the interaction between the macroeconomy and the environment. In Chapter 18, which examines the relation between the environment and development in developing nations, the focus is on the more multidimensional nature of sustainable development. Another reason to focus on the sustainability of a GDP path concerns the relationship between sustainable consumption and GDP. Because consumption must come out of what is produced, a focus on sustainable income will give insight about sustainable consumption.

Before taking a look at the sustainability of growth paths of GDP, it would be prudent to define what is meant by sustainable growth. Many people might view *sustainable growth* as an oxymoron. Figure 6.6 contains three growth paths that were originally defined by Pezzey (1989) and further discussed by Pearce and Warford (1993). These growth paths are defined by these authors to pertain to social welfare, but, with caution, one can view GDP in the same way.

Path A in Figure 6.6 is the type of growth path many people think of when they think of growth and sustainability as mutually exclusive. Initial levels of growth consume resources and degrade the environment, lowering future income-producing potential. Such a growth path could even fall below the minimum survivability level. Pearce and Warford (1993) point out that with conventional techniques of economic analysis that look at the present value of the path, this path could actually be viewed as optimal because it could maximize the net present value of social welfare (or income or consumption). Path B is a less severe version of path A. It also is associated with growth, then a peak, and then a decline, but it does stay above the minimum survivability level.

Path C is the growth path most people think of when they think of sustainable growth and sustainable development. Notice that this growth path is consistent with the definition of sustainable development provided by the U.N.'s Brundtland Commission Report. This definition is that sustainable development is a process that improves the well-being of the current generation without constraining the well-being of future generations. Notice that in this path of growth, GDP eventually achieves a plateau and does not necessarily continuously increase. Also note that if one were conducting an economic efficiency-based analysis, this growth pattern would not be optimal, because the present value of the path of GDP (or social welfare or consumption) is likely to be lower than paths where the values earlier in time are larger, such as paths A or B.

The important question becomes, How do we assure that we move onto a path such as path C and avoid the steps that will lead us to path A or path B? This question is critically important for developing countries, which currently may be perilously close to the minimum survivability level. It is vitally important that their income, consumption and social welfare increase to a comfortable level. On the other hand, these countries need to avoid pursuing current income at the expense of future income producing ability. As with

Figure 6.6 **Optimality, Survivability, and Sustainability of Consumption or Income Paths**

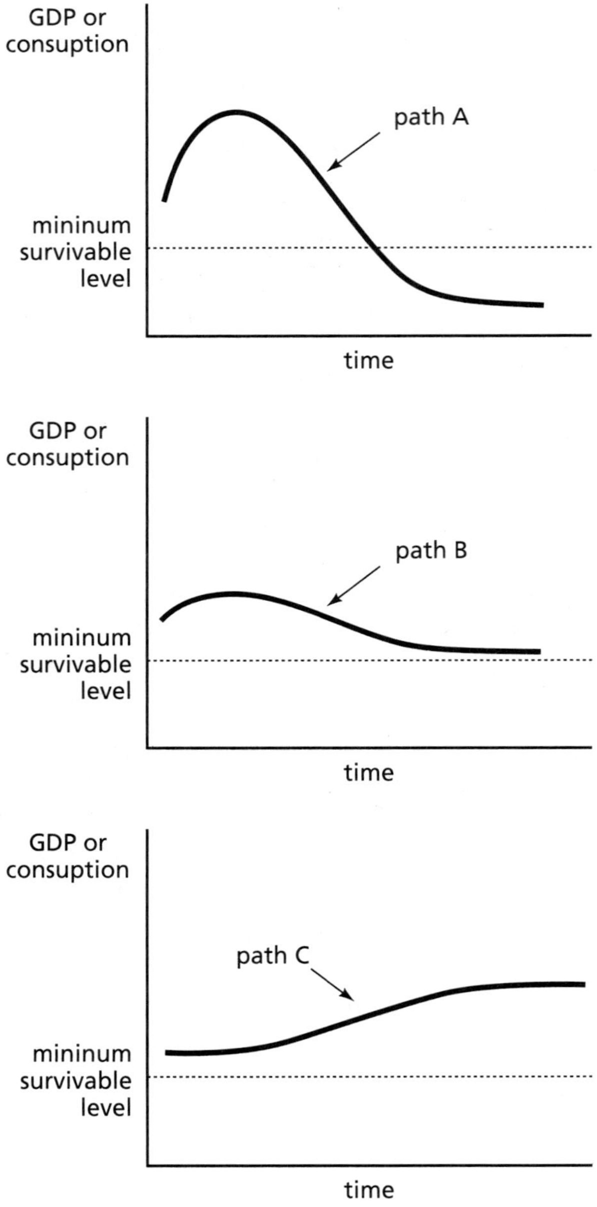

Source: Based on concepts developed by Pezzey (1989) and Pearce and Warford (1993).

most discussions of economic growth, capital accumulation has a critical role to play. The following discussion focuses on the relationship between capital accumulation and sustainable development.

The Role of Capital Accumulation in Sustainable Development

Economists' discussions of sustainability generally focus around the accumulation of capital. These early discussions focused primarily on artificial capital and natural capital. Artificial capital consists of human-made structures and goods that are used to produce other goods and are not consumed in the process. Artificial or human-made capital includes factories, the machines in factories, other buildings, highways, bridges, trucks, and computers. Natural capital consists of renewable and nonrenewable natural resources such as oil, wood, coal, minerals, and fish.

Economists' discussions of sustainability in the 1990s focused on whether sustainability could occur in the presence of a finite amount of natural resources (Hartwick 1993; Pezzey 1997). This development was quite natural in thought given the huge impact of Barnet and Morse's (1978) classic book, *Scarcity and Growth*. This book focused on the issue of whether we were running out of extractable resources. In fact, this type of examination goes back as far as the nineteenth century, when David Ricardo and Thomas Malthus looked at scarcity and its implications in the context of the availability of land.

Hartwick derived an axiom known as the Hartwick rule that suggests that sustainability is possible provided that the economic rents (the difference between revenue and the cost of extraction) are reinvested in artificial capital. The mathematical model used to derive the result is based on the assumption of substitutability between artificial capital and natural capital in the production of output. The Hartwick article has been frequently cited as an argument that we do not need to be concerned about sustainability, as if there is sufficient investment in artificial capital that will guarantee sustainability.

Unfortunately, the work by Hartwick, Pezzey, Barnett and Morse, and other neoclassical economists neglected two important types of capital, human capital (the quantity and quality of the labor force) and environmental capital. Environmental capital refers to renewable resource systems that provide a flow of ecological services. For the purposes of this discussion, environmental capital is the most important, because the importance of environmental capital implies that the Hartwick rule cannot be true in the real world (see Franceschi and Kahn, 2003). The reason is that the Hartwick rule (and other neoclassical economic treatments of sustainability and scarcity) is dependent on the assumption that the different types of capital are complete and perfect substitutes for one another. This assumption is appropriate only when looking at only human capital, artificial capital, and natural capital.

The assumption works well for human capital, artificial capital, and natural capital, because these types of substitutions are possible. If oil becomes increasingly scarce, then other types of capital such as developing more energy efficient cars and appliances, and developing alternative fuels can be substituted. On the other hand, it is not possible to make this assumption when talking about environmental capital, because it is not possible to produce ecological services on the same scale as provided by ecosystems.

The classic example is the provision of flood control services, which are often provided by ecosystems. Historically, the vast wetlands of the huge floodplain of the upper Mississippi River provided a tremendous amount of flood control services, but these wetlands were largely converted to farmland. Human capital was substituted for these ecological services in the form of levees and other flood control structures. The human capital, however, could not duplicate the complexity of the ecologically provided services; in particular, it did not remove the sediments to the river system, allowing the riverbed to grow to be above the surrounding land and necessitating even higher levees in a nonending cycle. The inadequacy of the human engineered system was demonstrated in 1993, when a "25-year" rain caused a "100-year" flood.[9]

Similarly, it would be absurd to think that human-engineered systems could sequester carbon at the scale of tropical rain forests, produce oxygen at the same scale as the phytoplankton layer and forests, create soil at the same scale as ecosystems, and maintain hydrological cycles at the same scale as forests and other natural ecosystems. Box 6.1 discusses the importance of the scale of ecological services with an example of pest protection provided by environmental resources.

Pearce and Warford (1993) and Franceschi and Kahn (2003) argue that it is inappropriate to assume that artificial capital, human capital, and natural capital can, in general, be good substitutes for environmental capital. If one drops the assumption of the substitutability of other types of capital for environmental capital that are found in the neoclassical models, then several important insights can be gained. First, as shown by Franceschi and Kahn, the Hartwick rule will no longer hold. Sustainable development then requires the maintenance of a certain stock of environmental capital plus growth in the stocks of other types of capital. In other words, sustainable growth of GDP (or consumption or social welfare) requires not only that the combined stocks of capital grow, but that environmental capital be preserved while the other types of capital stocks are increased. That is not to say that nothing can ever be done that has a negative impact on environmental capital. Rather, it implies that we must conserve environmental capital to provide an adequate flow of ecological services, both in the present and for the future.

---

[9]For more information on this flood, see Larson, (1996).

The discussion of sustainable development continues in Chapter 18, where it focuses on developing countries. In this chapter, there is more discussion of the multidimensional aspects of sustainable development as well as case studies from developing nations.

Environmental Taxation and Macroeconomic Benefits

Within the last decade, an energetic debate has developed surrounding the potential existence of macroeconomic benefits associated with environmental taxation. These macroeconomic benefits might arise if the revenue associated with an environmental tax was used to reduce the level of income tax (or property or sales tax).[10] This statement immediately raises the question of why tax dollars from one type of tax might be more beneficial than tax dollars from another source. The answer to this question is that environmental taxes (per unit pollution taxes) correct a market failure, whereas income taxes create a market failure by generating a level of labor that is less than socially optimal (the marginal social benefits of another unit of labor would be greater than the marginal social cost, so society would be better off with more labor).

In Chapters 2 and 3, it was shown how the existence of an unregulated environmental externality could generate an inefficiently high level of both the externality and the externality-generating activity (see Figures 2.2 and 3.5). The tax reduces these levels toward their socially optimal level. In contrast, a tax on income creates a market distortion by generating an inefficiently low level of labor. This contrast is illustrated in Figure 6.7, which depicts the marginal benefit and marginal cost functions for labor.[11] Here, L_1 is the amount of labor that market behavior would generate in the absence of a tax. If, however, an income tax is imposed, then the supply curve will shift up by an amount equal to the tax, because the individual's return to providing labor declines by the amount of the tax. The new level of labor will be L_2, which is associated with a reduction in consumers' and producers' surplus of the sum of the dark-shaded parallelogram and the light-shaded triangle. In this case, the cost to society is not equal to the loss in consumers' and producers' surplus because part of the loss to consumers and producers is not a loss to society. The tax payment is used to produce public services or make payments to other members of society, so it is not a loss to society. The total tax payment is equal to L_2 units of labor multiplied by the amount of the tax (equal to the area of the dark-shaded parallelogram). That leaves a net loss

[10]The following discussion takes place in the context of income taxes, but similar arguments could be constructed for sales and property taxes.

[11]In this discussion, it is assumed that there are no externalities or public good characteristics associated with labor.

Figure 6.7 **Labor Market Losses Associated with an Income Tax**

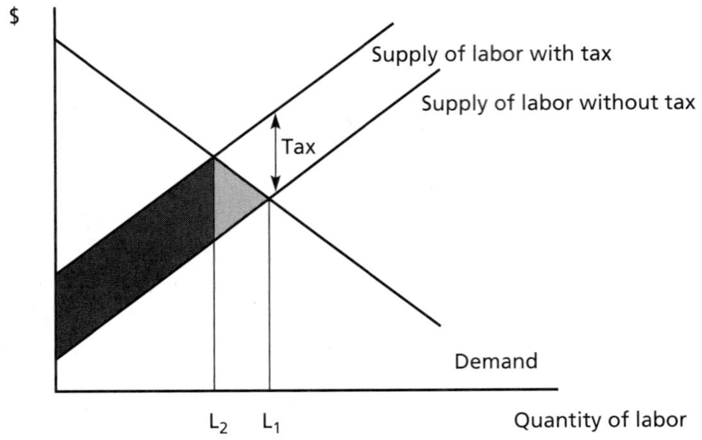

to society of the area of the light-shaded triangle. This loss of benefits arising from the tax is often called the deadweight loss of the tax.

In summary, if one were to substitute environmental taxes for income taxes, then there would be two benefits associated with the environmental taxes. The first benefit would be the correction of the market failure associated with the pollution externalities, which would lead to a higher level of social welfare.[12] The second benefit is the reduction of the market distortion in the labor market, which also will increase the level of social welfare. These two benefits are often called the "double dividend" associated with an environmental tax (see Pearce, 1991). A very intuitive explanation for the existence of the double dividend is that environmental taxes penalize something that is bad for society (pollution) whereas income taxes discourage something that is good for society (people working). If a government were to implement a pollution tax and use the revenue to reduce the income tax, it must increase the level of social welfare. The result is called the revenue recycling effect.

Although the arguments for the existence of an environmental taxation double dividend have intuitive appeal, there has been much controversy over its actual existence. Several noted economists (Bovenberg and de Mooij, 1994; Bovenberg and Goulder, 1996; Parry, 1995; Goulder, Parry and Burtraw, 1997) argue that an environmental tax can actually lead to greater distortion in the labor market, because the combination of an income tax

[12]Of course, if the environmental tax was too high, it could reduce the level of the externality below the level that was socially optimal. See Chapter 3 for a discussion of this point.

and higher prices for goods (the higher price is caused by the environmental tax) will lead to an even lower level of labor than with the income tax alone. This is called the tax interaction effect. These authors argue that the tax interaction effect exceeds the revenue recycling effect, leading to a greater distortion in the labor market.

The mathematics of these models are highly complex and will not be reproduced in this chapter, yet the models of the above-mentioned authors are based on conceptions of the economic production and abatement processes that may not adequately describe the choices facing individual firms. For example, in these models, pollution taxes are generally represented by a tax on the output of the firm, not a tax on the pollution. With a tax on the output the only way to reduce the tax burden is to reduce output rather than by reducing emissions per unit of output. More importantly, the models do not recognize environmental quality as having any positive impact on productivity. The presence of these positive impacts would mitigate the potential price increases associated with an environmental tax, and either of these two effects could lead to the revenue recycling effect being larger than the tax interaction effect.

As with many of the concepts in this chapter, the existence of a double dividend of environmental taxation is the subject of a controversial debate. Conceptual models of the problem can lead to conclusions on either side of the issue. A genuine understanding of the potential existence of a double dividend awaits the development of appropriate data to estimate the actual size of the revenue recycling and tax interaction effects.

The Environment and International Economic Issues

Several significant environmental issues are intertwined with international economic issues.[13] They include the global public good nature of many environmental resources, transfrontier pollution, the effect of globalization on environmental policy and international trade, and the effect of international trade policy on environmental quality.

Global Public Goods

Many environmental resources have global public good characteristics. That is to say, the environmental resources in one country generate public good benefits for people in other countries, or environmental resources span the

---

[13]Good sources of information on international environmental issues are the U.S. State Department's Oceans, Environment, and Science home page available at the United National Environment Programme at http://www.unep.org, Resources for the Future at http://www.rff.org, and the World Resources Institute at http://www.wri.org.

borders of several or all countries. Rain forests, wetlands, coral reefs, savannahs, and biodiversity are examples of environmental resources contained in one country that create public good benefits for citizens of other countries. Oceans, rivers, lakes, aquifers, and atmospheric processes are examples of resources that span international borders.

The difference between global public goods and local or national public goods is that with global public goods there will be international separation between those who benefit from the environmental resources and those who bear the costs of preserving the environmental resources. For example, the whole world benefits through the preservation of Brazil's rain forests, but Brazil bears the entire cost of preserving the rain forest. Thus, what is optimal from the global perspective is unlikely to be generated by the policies of a particular country, so global optimality cannot be generated without negotiating an international agreement. The difficulty of generating a negotiated agreement across countries is made more complex because it is often the lower-income countries that bear the cost of preserving the resources and the higher-income countries that receive the public good benefits from preserving them.

International policies that shift some of the benefits of preserving these environmental resources toward the countries that preserve them need to be developed. In other words, these potential Pareto improvements must be turned into actual Pareto improvements.[14] Policies for accomplishing this transformation vary across resources and are discussed in more detail in Chapters 13, 14, and 18.

Transfrontier Pollution

Transfrontier pollution is pollution generated in one political jurisdiction that creates damages in another political jurisdiction. The problems generated by transfrontier pollution become more complex when the boundaries the pollution crosses are international rather than state, provincial, or municipal boundaries. The country that generates the pollution does not consider all the social costs when devising environmental policy, because some of the social costs are borne by other countries. The result is an environmental policy that would generate a level of emissions higher than optimal from a global point of view.

For example, let's say that a number of countries border on a body of water, such as the Mediterranean Sea. A diverse set of European, Middle Eastern, and North African countries have coastlines on the Mediterranean Sea, and the rivers that flow into the Mediterranean Sea drain an even larger set of

---

[14]A potential Pareto improvement is a change where those who benefit gain more than the losses of those made worse off. If the winners compensated the losers then it would turn the situation into an actual Pareto improvement, where some people are made better off and no one is made worse off. See Chapter 5 for further discussion of this point.

countries. What are the incentives of an individual country with respect to its decisions to release pollution into the Mediterranean?

The individual country reduces its cost of production by using the Mediterranean as a disposal site for its waste. It receives 100 percent of this benefit. On the other hand, the environmental cost of the reduction in the quality of the Mediterranean is shared by all the countries with a coastline or that otherwise benefit from the ecological and economic services provided by the sea. Let's reformulate the discussion of private and social values introduced in Chapter 2 to look at the problem of transfrontier pollution. Let the private costs and private benefits of a transfrontier externality refer to the costs and benefits specific to the country that is generating the externality and the social costs and social benefits refer to the costs and benefits felt by the other countries that utilize the resources associated with the Mediterranean Sea. Just as in the discussion of the "invisible hand" in Chapter 2, the externality-generating country will choose a level of pollution that equates marginal private costs and marginal private benefits. Because the environmental costs felt by other countries do not figure into its decision, the level of pollution is much higher than optimal for the region as a whole. In addition, all individual countries act in this fashion, so transfrontier pollution can quickly become an environmental morass, with rapid deterioration of environmental resources and difficulty in acting because action requires countries to agree with one another about allowable levels of emissions.

To generate the appropriate level of emissions, international negotiation must be conducted. In Europe, this process tends to be easier, because the shared agencies of the European Union provide a structure within which the negotiations may take place. In North America, the process is more difficult, as the past controversy between Canada and the United States over acid rain attests (see Chapter 9). The North American Free Trade Agreement (NAFTA), passed in 1994, could provide a framework for resolving these issues. In the coming years, there is a high probability that NAFTA will merge with MERCUSOL, the South American free trade organization, resulting in a trade union covering all the Americas. If so, a mechanism for dealing with transfrontier pollution in the Americas could emerge.

Globalization, International Trade, and the Environment

In recent years, the movement toward more free trade and the "globalization" of economic activity has been under assault by critics. Protesters riot at economic summits, and the opposition articulates an argument that increased international trade, particularly trade conducted in a less restrictive trade environment, reduces social welfare. Protesters cite low wages, difficult working conditions, and child labor in developing countries as well as increased environmental degradation as results of free trade. Are the protesters right?

Because this book focuses on the environment, the environmental part of the question, which in itself is very complex, is examined. The reason is that increased trade has both positive and negative effects on the environment, and it is difficult to ascertain which effects will dominate. In addition, it is possible that future policies can increase the positive effects and reduce the negative effects, so we need to understand potential policy options and not just current policy choices to understand if increased trade will hurt or benefit the environment.

A good place to start in examining the net impacts of these effects is simply to list the potential impacts of increasing trade on the environment.

1. If increased trade increases economic activity, then, holding everything else constant, the increased activity will be associated with greater emissions of pollution.
2. Increased trade and increased income can give a country a greater ability to switch to cleaner technologies.
3. An increase in trade may change patterns of economic activity and change the mix of economic activity in a particular country. The new mix could either be cleaner or more polluting.
4. Elimination of trade barriers may sweep away important environmental regulations.

Each of these impacts is examined individually.

The first point is rather straightforward. Holding everything else constant, if you produce and consume more, you will pollute more. Because the whole purpose of international trade is to increase the level of economic activity of the trading partners, the result will be more pollution, more conversion of habitat to other land uses, and more environmental degradation in general. That is no different than the previous discussion of the potential impact of increased economic growth.

The second point is that the increased economic activity and income associated with trade may give the country an ability to have a cleaner environment. Some of that may be that the demand for environmental quality increases as income increases, as discussed in the earlier section on the environmental Kuznet's curve. Some of that may be because the increased income gives firms the ability to purchase newer technology. This newer technology is generally more efficient and cleaner than the technology it replaces. The final aspect may be that a country may have wanted a cleaner environment and even had the laws on the books for environmental protection, but, it may have lacked the resources to monitor environmental degradation and enforce the law. Increased economic activity associated with increased trade may give the country the opportunity to have stricter and more enforceable environmental policy.

The third point has to do with the emphasis of trade on a country's comparative advantages in the production process, so increased trade will change the mix of economic activities within a country. Although this point could have a positive or a negative impact on the environment, many people fear that the comparative advantage of low-income countries may be as a sink for pollution, creating pollution havens in developing countries. The fear is that because environmental protection may be more lenient in developing countries, firms may locate there to lower their costs. Moreover, some people believe that the terms of trade between developing and developed countries imply that the more beneficial economic activities take place in the developed country, leaving environmental degradation and other socially undesirable impacts to settle into the developing country.

Others argue that pollution havens are not likely to develop, because environmental compliance costs are very small in relationship to total cost and intercountry differences in the cost of environmental regulation tend to be correspondingly smaller. In fact, the most important factors in the location of industry are relative differences in the proximity to markets and sources of raw materials (lower transportation costs), labor costs, energy costs, legal costs, insurance costs, and the costs of dealing with alternative government bureaucracies.

Moreover, although the tendency is to think of dirty industries as the ones that migrate to developing countries to take advantage of lower labor costs, that is true for the cleaner, high-tech industries as well. Software, electronics, telephone reservation, and consumer service centers and similar clean industry are also moving to developing countries. This shift allows the generation of jobs and income with less impact on the environment.

It is very difficult to make a theoretical argument that increased trade is either unambiguously bad or unambiguously good for environmental protection and sustainable development. The first three points indicate that there are both positive and negative impacts of trade on the environment, and the balance could go either way. One important point, however, is that trade does not have a predetermined impact on a country's environment. Instead, trade may increase a country's choices. The country can choose a trade-assisted development path that is relatively green or one that is relatively dirty. To the extent a country makes choices that affect the global environment in a detrimental fashion, that is a concern for all nations. To the extent that a country pollutes its own resources, however, it can be argued that that is its own sovereign concern.

The fourth point listed also generates a lot of discussion. Many people argue that the international trade organizations and the rules for trade that are developed weaken countries' domestic environmental regulation. This hypothesis is examined in the following section.

The Effect of International Trade Policy on the Environment and Environmental Policy

International rules related to the openness of trade date to the General Agreement on Tariffs and Trade (GATT), which was implemented in 1947. A key provision of GATT is a feature designed to keep countries from developing artificial barriers to trade. An artificial barrier to trade is a prohibition on an imported product, based solely on the manner by which it is produced. For example, a country that is highly unionized cannot limit imports of products produced by nonunion labor. A country that is a large producer of rum (made from sugarcane) cannot limit imports of whiskey (made from grain).

Although many anti–free trade activists believe that GATT prohibits all discrimination on environmental grounds, that is not completely or necessarily the case. The part of the GATT agreement that potentially allows discrimination based on environmental grounds is Article XX. This article, according to Gaines (2002, p. 127).

> authorized deviation from any GATT doctrines for measures "necessary to protect human, animal or plant life or health" (XXb) or "relating to the conservation of exhaustible resources" (XXg).

The Article XX exceptions, however, are qualified by the condition that the measures not constitute an "arbitrary or unjustified discrimination" or "unjustified restriction on trade" (Gaines, 2000, p. 127). Gaines further elaborates that for a variety of reasons, Article XX has been very narrowly interpreted, making it difficult to implement any environmental measure not otherwise conforming to GATT provisions.

New international rules on trade have been codified in the World Trade Organization agreement, including a method for dispute resolution. The Appellate Body of the Dispute Resolution Understanding, however, has begun to develop a set of precedents related to trade-environment issues. Some of these precedents are discussed below.

In the early 1990s, with the NAFTA negotiations and the developing World Trade Organization (WTO)[15], significant attention was focused on the trade-environment relationship. This controversy was fueled by the famous tuna-dolphin case. This case arose because the United States had imposed an embargo on tuna imports from Mexico, asserting that Mexico was not taking sufficient steps to protect dolphins from drowning in fishing nets. The complaint by Mexico stipulated that this move was an unfair discrimination against Mexican-produced tuna and was upheld in the WTO dispute resolution process. The ruling elaborated a principal that countries should not take unilateral actions to deal with environmental problems outside the borders of the importing countries and that actions dealing with this type of problem should be based on international consensus, not on one country's position. In another case, the United States lost a dispute involving Venezuela and Brazil relating to clean air requirements for imported gasoline. The reason for the United States loss was because of differential treatment of U.S. and foreign refineries, but the WTO did recognize clean air as an exhaustible resource that could be protected under Article XX (Gaines, 2002, p. 124).

Many people interpreted these rulings as signifying that the World Trade Organization did not care about environmental protection and was willing to

[15]The World Trade Organization is the successor organization to GATT.

sacrifice the environment to promote freer trade. More recent rulings, however, have been more favorable to environmental protection. The shrimp-turtle case is a good example.

The harvesting of shrimp can lead to the death of sea turtles, because the towed dredge that scoops the shrimp from the water column can also capture sea turtles, where they are drowned in the mesh bag that collects the shrimp that are scooped by the dredge.[16] Turtles can be protected by placing a gate over the opening of the dredge with a mesh that is much bigger than the size of a shrimp but much smaller than the size of a turtle. Turtles that wind up in the path of the dredge simply bounce (unharmed) off the gate and are not captured. This gate has become known as a turtle excluder device, or TEDDIE and is required by U.S. law for shrimping operations in waters under U.S. jurisdiction. In an effort to protect sea turtles throughout their range, the United States placed an embargo on the importation of shrimp that were harvested in a fashion that led to sea turtle mortality.

Exporting countries such as Mexico called this embargo an unfair exclusion and filed a grievance with the WTO. Gaines (2002, p. 127) notes several important aspects of the adjudication of this case:

1. The Appellate Body recognized that the protection of sea turtles anywhere in the world represents a legitimate environmental concern.
2. International environmental law supports this position and can be used in defense of a national policy for the protection of the turtles.
3. The Appellate Body invited the testimony of scientific experts.

Despite these important steps forward in terms of making trade policy more environmentally protective, the ruling that followed was that the U.S. policy was applied in an unjustifiable and arbitrary fashion and thus constituted unfair discrimination. The U.S. response to this ruling, however, was to slightly modify the program to take care of the concerns about its arbitrary application, and the basic structure of the shrimp embargo was accepted as legitimate by the WTO. In other words, the United States was allowed to protect sea turtles in foreign waters by requiring that shrimp imports into the United States be produced in a fashion that did not cause the mortality of turtles.

NAFTA, Trade, and the North American Environment

The early 1990s saw an incredible discussion about trade and the environment, culminating in hyperbole, Ross Perot's "giant sucking sound," and positions that were more emotional than analytical. Although there was much discussion concerning the potential of NAFTA to reduce environmental quality in the United States and Mexico, the potential effect of NAFTA on environmental quality was probably misunderstood by most of the American

---

[16]See Chapter 10 for further discussion of the bycatch problem associated with shrimp and other fishing activities.

public. The primary fear was that NAFTA was going to lead to increased movement of U.S. industrial activity to Mexico, which would not only reduce the number of jobs in the United States but would also increase pollution in Mexico, because Mexico has more lax and less enforced environmental regulations than the United States. An additional fear was that this pollution would spill across the border as it moved through rivers, wind currents, and ocean currents and negatively affect environmental quality in the United States.

Obviously, if industrial activity increases in northern Mexico, this increase has the potential to adversely affect environmental quality in both Mexico and the United States. These points were discussed earlier in the general discussion of trade and the environment. Yet 10 years after the implementation of NAFTA, the worst fears have not come to pass. Part of the reason is due to the very fears themselves, the discussion they sparked, and the political momentum they developed, reflected in the negotiation and implementation of NAFTA in the last few years of George H. W. Bush's administration and the first few years of the Clinton administration. This process saw trade and the environment woven together in an integrated policy, with U.S. responsibility shared between the office of the U.S. Trade Representative and the EPA.

For the first time, an international trade agreement had put environment and trade on an equal footing and culminated with the establishment of the North American Agreement on Environmental Cooperation and several bilateral agreements between Mexico and the United States. In fact, NAFTA is being used as an example in ongoing WTO negotiations, illustrating how a trade agreement can simultaneously promote trade and environmental objectives (Gaines, 2002, p. 126).

Although NAFTA appears to be an agreement that has the potential to allow for the pursuit of environmental goals, the implementation of NAFTA has not prevented all reductions in environmental quality. In particular, on the Mexican side of the border with the United States, economic activity has increased significantly, with resulting migration that has created local declines in environmental quality. On the whole, however, NAFTA has been relatively benign in terms of environmental impact, although a final verdict awaits additional experience and more data.

Conclusions on Trade and the Environment

It is clear that trade can help the cause of sustainable development without sacrificing environmental protection. Although increasing economic activity can lead to increased environmental degradation, it can also provide the resources to implement environmental protection through policy and cleaner technologies. The potential for negative impacts, however, remains strong, requiring international cooperation to ensure that trade objectives do not dominate environmental objectives. On this front, there are reasons to be pessimistic as well as optimistic.

Summary

Both microeconomic and macroeconomic methodologies help guide the development of environmental policy. This chapter has focused on macroeconomic issues to complement the microeconomic methods discussed in Chapters 2 through 5.

The environment and environmental policy can have both a negative and positive impact on the economy. The negative impact occurs when resources that could be used elsewhere in the economy are devoted to reducing pollution. The positive impact occurs because environmental quality is an input to production processes and can positively impact the productivity of other inputs such as labor and agricultural land.

Many previous modeling attempts have concluded that increasing environmental quality will reduce the productivity of the economy, but these models did not allow for the existence of the positive impact. More recent conceptual developments and empirical studies, however, do not necessarily support that case. In fact, environmental regulations may increase economic productivity.

This chapter has just scratched the surface in highlighting some of the models that have been used to understand the effect of the environment on the macroeconomy. In the application chapters that follow, both microeconomic and macroeconomic theory are applied in an effort to understand the environmental issues that are the focus of the chapters. As an example, in this chapter the issue of whether environmental regulations and the pursuit of better environmental quality will lead to a loss of jobs has not been completely examined. Rather this issue is examined in the context of the focus of each chapter, where appropriate. For example, in the chapters on fossil fuels (Chapters 8 and 9), the macroeconomic impact of air quality regulations is addressed. Similarly, the employment impacts of alternative forestry policies are addressed in Chapter 12.

As a final note, it should be reemphasized that although macroeconomic implications are important, they should not be the sole determinant of environmental policy. Target levels of environmental quality should not be determined solely by the effect of environmental quality on GDP or NDP, but on the effect of environmental quality on social welfare, to which both GDP and environmental quality contribute.

Review Questions

1. What is the Porter hypothesis? Are there economic justifications for the effects Porter describes?
2. How does control of pollution affect GDP?
3. How does the WTO constrain environmental options?
4. Why should GDP be modified to include certain types of environmental degradation?
5. How do the environment and economy interact?
6. What is meant by the double dividend?

Questions for Further Study

1. What is the effect of environmental policy on international trade?
2. Is a Malthusian outcome sustainable?
3. What is the role of substitutability of capital in generating sustainable development?
4. What is the international significance of global public goods?
5. Can environmental policy increase international competitiveness?
6. How would you handle environmental issues in the latest reformulation of GATT?
7. Why is the macroeconomic analysis of environmental issues important?

Suggested Paper Topics

1. Look at the Porter hypothesis and determine whether stricter environmental policy can lead to more jobs. Start with the references by Oates, Palmer, and Portney (1993), Palmer and Simpson (1993), and Simpson (1993), and survey current journals for more recent papers.
2. Look at the impact of a WTO decision on the environment. Start with the book by Pearce and Warford (1993) and search bibliographic databases and the Internet on the WTO and the environment.
3. Choose an environmental problem such as global warming and examine the equity issues associated with it. Pay particular attention to intertemporal and North/South equity issues. Search bibliographic databases using the specific environmental problem and *equity* as keywords.

Works Cited and Selected Readings

Ayres, R. U., and A. V. Kneese. Production, Consumption, and Externalities. *American Economic Review 59* (1969): 282–297.

Baumol, W., and W. Oates. *The Theory of Environmental Policy*. Cambridge: Cambridge University Press, 1979.

Bimonte, S. Information Access, Income Distribution, and the Environmental Kuznets Curve. *Ecological Economics 41,* no. 1 (2002): 145–156.

Bovenberg, A. L., and Goulder, L. H. Optimal Environmental Taxation in the Presence of Other Taxes: A General Equilibrium Analysis. *American Economic Review* 86, no. 4 (1996): 985–1000.

Bovenberg, A. L., and R. A. de Mooij. Environmental Levies and Distortionary Taxation. *American Economic Review 84,* no. 4 (1994): 1085–1089.

Boulding, K. The Economics of the Coming Spaceship Earth. Pages 3–14 in *Environmental Quality in a Growing Economy*, edited by Henry Jarrett. Baltimore: Johns Hopkins University Press, 1966.

Bruyn, S. M. de, J. C. J. M. van den Bergh, and J. B. Opschoor. Economic Growth and Emissions: Reconsidering the Empirical Basis of Environmental Kuznets Curves. *Ecological Economics 25,* no. 2, (1998):143–229.

Daly, H. E. On Economics as a Life Science. *The Journal of Political Economy 76* (1969): 392–406.

Daly, H. E. *Steady-State Economics: The Economics of Biophysical Equilibrium and Moral Growth*. San Francisco: Freeman, 1977.

Daly, H. E. Towards an Environmental Macroeconomics. *Land Economics 67* (1991): 255–259.

Farmer, A., J. R. Kahn, J. A. McDonald, and R. O'Neill. Rethinking the Optimal Level of Environmental Quality: Justifications for Strict Environmental Policy *Ecological Economics 36* (2001): 461–473.

Franceschi, D., and J. R. Kahn. Beyond Strong Sustainability. *International Journal of Sustainable Development and World Ecology 10,* (2003): 24–220.

Gaines, S. E., International Trade. Pages 115–148 in *Stumbling Towards Sustainability*, edited by John C. Dernbach. Washington, DC: Environmental Law Institute, 2002.

Gillis,T., A. McGartland, D. Nestor, C. Pasurka, and L. Wiggins. *The Social Benefits of Air Quality Management Programs: A General Equilibrium Approach*. Washington, DC: Environmental Protection Agency 1996.

Goulder, L. H., I. Parry, and W. H. Burtraw. Dallas Revenue-Raising versus Other Approaches to Environmental Protection: The Critical Significance of Preexisting Tax Distortions. *RAND Journal of Economics 28,* no. 4 (1997): 708–731.

Hartwick J. Intergenerational Equity and the Investing of Rents from Exhaustible Resources. *American Economic Review 67* (1977): 972–984.

Hazilla, M., and R. J. Kopp. Social Cost of Environmental Quality Regulations: A General Equilibrium Analysis. *Journal of Political Economy 98,* no. 4 (1990): 853–873.

Jorgenson, D. W., and P. Wilcoxen. Intertemporal General Equilibrium Modeling of U.S. Environmental Regulation. *Journal of Policy Modeling 12*, no. 4, (1990): 715–744.

Kahn, J. R. Trade-off Based Indices of Environmental Quality—An Environmental Analogue to GDP. Pages 38–54 in *Does Environmental Policy Work? The Theory and Practice of Outcomes Assessment*, edited by Irvin, Livingston, and J. R. Kahn. London: Edward Elgar, 2003.

Kahn, J. R., and A. Farmer, The Double Dividend, Second-Best Worlds, and Real-World Environmental Policy. *Ecological Economics 30,* no. 3 (1999): 433–439.

Kaufmann, R. K., B. Davidsdottir, S. Garnham, and P. Pauly. The Determinants of Atmospheric SO_2 Concentrations: Reconsidering the Environmental Kuznets Curve. *Ecological Economics 25,* no. 2 (1998):143–229.

Knoester, A., and J. van Sinderan. Taxation and the Abuse of Environmental Policies. Pages 35–51 in *Environmental Economics*, edited by G. Boera and A. Silberston. New York: St. Martin's, 1995.

Larson, L. W. The Great USA Flood of 1993. Presented at IAHS Conference, Anaheim, CA, June 24–26, 1996. Online: http://www.nwrfc.noaa.gov/floods/papers/oh_2/great.htm.

Malthus, T. R. An Essay on the Principle of Population. Pages 15–129 in *An Essay on the Principle of Population, Text, Sources and Background, Criticism 2nd* ed., edited by P. Appleman. New York: W. W. Norton, 2003.

Oates, W., K. L. Palmer, and P. R. Portney. Environmental Regulation and Competitiveness: Thinking about the Porter Hypothesis. Discussion Paper 94-02. Washington, DC: Resources for the Future, 1993.

O'Neill R.V., J. R. Kahn, J. R. Duncan, S. Elliott, R. Efroymson, H. Cardwell, and D. W. Jones. Economic Growth and Sustainability: A New Challenge. *Ecological Applications 26,* no. 3, (1996): 23–24.

Palmer, K. L., and D. R. Simpson. Environmental Policy as Industrial Policy. *Resources 112* (1993): 17–21.

Parry, I. W. H. Pollution Taxes and Revenue Recycling. *Journal of Environmental Economics and Management 29,* no. 3 (1995): 564–577.

Pearce, D. The Role of Carbon Taxes in Adjusting to Global Warming. *Economic Journal 101* (July 1991): 938–948.

Pearce, D. W., and J. J. Warford. *World without End: Economics, Environment, and Sustainable Development*. Washington, DC: Oxford University Press, 1993.

Peskin, H. M. A National Accounting Framework for Environmental Assets. *Journal of Environmental Economics and Management 2* (1976): 255–262.

Pezzey, J. Economic Analysis of Sustainable Growth and Sustainable Development. Working Paper 15, World Bank, Environment Department. Washington, DC: World Bank 1989.

Pezzey, J. Sustainability Constraints versus "Optimality" versus Intertemporal Concern, and Axioms versus Data. *Land Economics 73* (1997): 448–466.

Porter, M. A. *The Competitive Advantage of Nations*. New York: Free Press, 1990.

Porter, M. A. America's Green Strategy. *Scientific American 264* (1991): 168.

Repetto, R., W. Magrath, M. Wells, C. Beer, and F. Rossini. *Wasting Assets: Natural Resources in the National Income and Product Accounts*. Washington, DC: World Resources Institute, 1989.

Rothman, D. S. Environmental Kuznets Curves—Real Progress or Passing the Buck? A Case for Consumption-Based Approaches. *Ecological Economics 25*, no. 2 (1998): 143–229.

Shafik, N. Economic Development and Environmental Quality: An Econometric Analysis. *Oxford Economic Papers 46* (1994): 757–773.

Simpson, D. R. Taxing Variable Cost: Environmental Regulation as Industrial Policy. Discussion Paper ENR 93–12. Washington, DC: Resources for the Future, 1993.

Tisdell, C. Globalisation and Sustainability: Environmental Kuznets Curve and the WTO. *Ecological*

Economics 39, no. 2, (November 2001): 185–196.

Torras, M. and J. K. Boyce. Income, Inequality, and Pollution: A Reassessment of the Environmental Kuznets Curve, *Ecological Economics 25*, no. 2 (1998): 143–229.

University of Tennessee. High Flying Research Reveals the Eating Habits of Bats. *Research Good News 3*, no 15 (1997): Online: http://research.utk.edu/ora/rag/goodnews/1997/08-13.html.

Unruh, G. C., and W. R. Moomaw. An Alternative Analysis of Apparent EKC-Type Transitions. *Ecological Economics 25*, no. 2 (1998): 143–229.

U.S. Environmental Protection Agency. The Benefits and Costs of the Clean Air Act, 1970 to 1990. Online: http://www.epa.gov/.oar/sect812/copy.html.0295?OpenDocument, 1997.

World Bank. *World Development Report 1992: Development and the Environment*. New York: Oxford University Press, 1992.

World Commission on Environment and Development. *Our Common Future (The Brundtland Report)*. New York: Oxford University Press, 1987.

World Resource Institute. *World Resources 1992–93*. New York: Oxford University Press, 1992.

exhaustible resources, pollution, and the environment

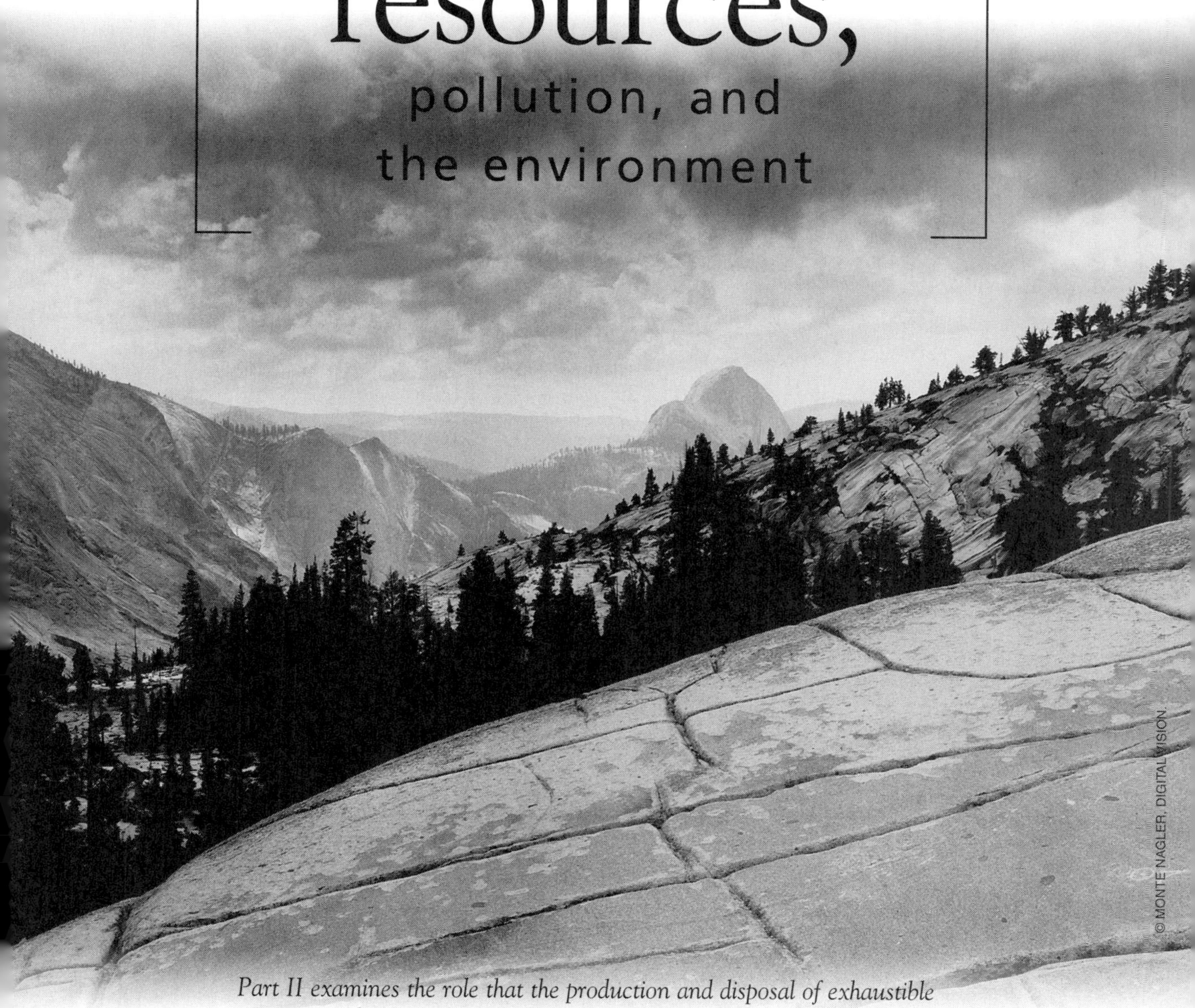

Part II examines the role that the production and disposal of exhaustible resources has on the economy and the environment. Energy figures prominently in this discussion because of its central role in economic processes and its role in the emission of greenhouse gases, other pollutants, and many other types of environmental problems.

chapter 7
Global Environmental Change: Ozone Depletion and Global Climate Change

The greenhouse effect itself is simple enough to understand and is not in any real dispute. What is in dispute is its magnitude over the coming century, its translation into changes in climates around the globe, and the impacts of those climate changes on human welfare and the natural environment.

Thomas C. Schelling, *Some Economics of Global Warming*

Introduction

When the first edition of this book was published in 1995, the problems of global climate change and ozone depletion were included together in the same chapter because their similarity made for interesting comparisons. Now, not that many years later, the two problems provide an interesting comparison because of their resounding differences.

Now, the ozone depletion problem, with the successful implementation of the Montreal Protocol, can largely be viewed as a problem that is moving toward solution. Although the chemicals emitted in the past that are now in the stratosphere will continue to have a depletion effect for several more decades, the release of ozone-depleting chemicals has declined to a small fraction of its former level, and the ozone layer is showing signs of recovery. The new chemicals that have been developed as a substitute for the ozone-depleting chemicals have an impact that is a small fraction of the previously used chemicals.

In contrast, a solution to the problem of global warming does not appear to be anywhere in sight. The concentration of greenhouse gases in the atmosphere is increasing at an alarming rate. The solution being discussed and agreed to by most nations, the Kyoto Protocol, does not require a meaningful reduction in emissions of the gases that are causing climate change. More alarmingly, because the issue has become highly politicized in many dimensions (see Box 7.1), a genuine solution to the problem of global climate change seems very far away. As is discussed later in the chapter, this issue could have profound, if not catastrophic, implications for both ecosystems and social welfare.

This chapter first focuses on the depletion of the ozone layer and the characteristics of this environmental problem that rendered it amenable to solution. A similar analysis is then conducted of the greenhouse gas problem, focusing on the characteristics of the problem that make it difficult to resolve. Before going into this discussion, the similarities between the two problems will be noted. These commonalities include the following:

1. Both problems are the result of pollutants modifying basic atmospheric chemistry, thereby altering atmospheric processes and functions.
2. Both problems are caused by stock pollutants that persist in the atmosphere for long periods (up to hundreds of years) after their emission into the atmosphere.
3. In both cases, the pollutants are global in the sense that their contributions to environmental problems are independent of the location of the emissions. It does not matter if the pollutants are emitted in New York, La Paz, Tokyo, or Nairobi, because the ultimate effect on atmospheric processes is identical.
4. In both cases, there is the potential for significant global environmental change and significant impacts on social, economic, and ecological systems.

Each of these commonalities is a characteristic that differentiates these types of pollutants from conventional pollutants, such as those that form smog. Consequently, these, atmosphere-altering global pollutants require a substantially different treatment in the development of policy.

That the basic effect of the pollutants is the alteration of the atmosphere (its chemistry, processes, and functions) is extremely important. It makes it much more difficult to estimate a damage function than it is to estimate one for conventional pollutants, such as those that form smog. For example, to test the relationship between smog and agricultural productivity, one can observe agricultural plots in high smog areas and low smog areas and (controlling for other influences) determine the effect of smog on agricultural yield. Similarly, one can measure how human respiratory ailments are influenced by smog levels. Because there are lots of agricultural plots and lots of people, it is possible to make enough observations to test whether smog affects people and plants. However, there is only one atmosphere, and it can-

Box 7.1 Science versus Politics: The Case of Global Warming

It is very interesting to hear students or citizens in general debate the issue of whether or not global climate change is a significant problem that needs to be addressed. Very often one might hear a statement that sounds somewhat like this one:

> "I am a Republican (or conservative), so I do not believe that global climate change is happening, and if it is happening, it is not a significant problem."

or

> "I am a Democrat (or liberal), so I believe that global climate change is real and a major environmental and social problem."

The acceptance or rejection of the hypothesis of the existence of global climate change, however, is not a question of ideology; it is a question of evidence and the objective analysis of the evidence. Similarly, the question of the social significance of global warming is a question of the analysis of scientific, economic, and social evidence.

Although rational and well-intended people may have different approaches to analysis and interpretation of evidence, it is not appropriate to bias interpretation of evidence to correspond to previously held beliefs. Students should be very careful in their reliance on Internet sites on global climate change, because many of them are created by groups (on both sides of the question) that deliberately paint a picture that corresponds directly to their ideological beliefs.

not be subdivided into smaller portions to increase the number of observations to provide a large enough sample to conduct statistical tests. The only way to make multiple observations is to look at the atmosphere, its characteristics, and the pollutants as they change over time. Because we have only recently begun collecting all of the appropriate data, it has been difficult to separate natural variation from pollution-induced variation, although substantial progress has been made in recent years. Much of this progress has been generated by developing data from ice cores and sediments that provide information going back thousands of years.

Both the pollutants that deplete ozone and the pollutants that are linked to global warming are stock pollutants, meaning that they have long lifetimes in the environment. Ozone-depleting chemicals may last up to 100 years in the stratosphere, and some of the greenhouse gases (gases that cause global warming) last even longer. A portion of the carbon dioxide released into the environment today may still be present 500 years into the future. The persistence of these pollutants is important, because when one assesses the damages associated with these pollutants (such as in estimating a marginal damage function), one needs to calculate the damages that current emissions will generate in the future. As the chapter-opening quotation from Schelling indicates, uncertainties involving the damages are the central scientific and policy questions. Since Professor Schelling published this article in 1992, many uncertainties, particularly on the scientific side, have been resolved. Significant uncertainties still remain, however, particularly on the impacts of global climate change.

The global nature of these pollutants makes them very different from other types of pollutants. For example, the emissions of nitrogen oxides and other pollutants in the southern California area increase the smog problem in that area. If the emissions are moved from southern California to New York, smog will increase in New York and decrease in California. The effects of the pollutants tend to be local and regional. In contrast, the effects of global pollutants are completely independent of the location of their emissions. This locational equivalence both complicates and simplifies the policy-making process. It simplifies the process because there is no need to account for geographic variability in the effects of emissions into taxes or marketable pollution permits (see Chapter 3 for a discussion of this need for geographic variability in pollution control instruments). It complicates the policy-making process because the problems cannot be dealt with by one country; the emissions of all countries matter. One country cannot unilaterally solve these problems. International cooperation is required to deal with these global externalities.

The Depletion of the Ozone Layer

Although the depletion of the ozone layer is one of our most widely discussed environmental problems, the causes of ozone depletion, its consequences, and the policy that has been implemented are not well understood.

Causes of the Depletion of the Ozone Layer

The basic problem leading to the depletion of the ozone layer is the emission of a set of chemicals that trigger a reaction in the atmosphere, causing ozone to be converted to oxygen. Although the transformation of ozone to oxygen may seem to be benign, or even beneficial, ozone blocks ultraviolet radiation from striking the earth, whereas oxygen does not.

The term *ozone layer* refers to the presence of ozone in the stratosphere. The stratosphere, the outer layer of the atmosphere, is separated from the troposphere (lower atmosphere) by the tropopause. An important characteristic of the atmosphere is that, throughout the troposphere, the air becomes colder the farther the distance from the earth's surface. This temperature gradient changes at the tropopause, where the lowest layer of the stratosphere is warmer than the highest level of the troposphere. The significance of this thermal relationship is that there is a layer of warm air sitting on top of a layer of cold air. Because hot air rises, there is little mixing of air across this temperature inversion. Also, once pollutants make their way into the strato-

Figure 7.1 **Troposphere, Tropopause, and Stratosphere**

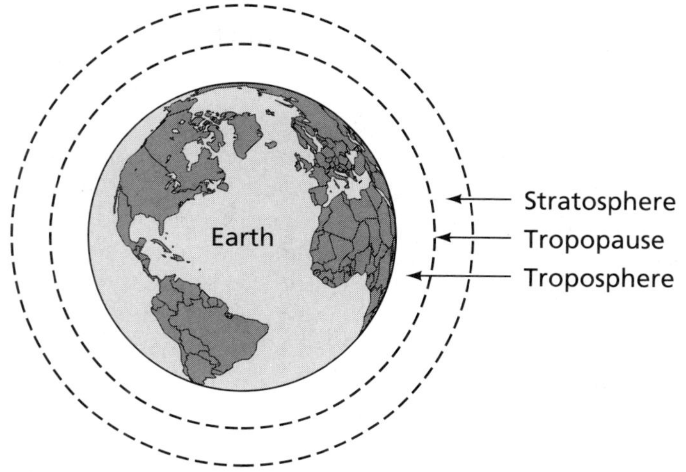

sphere, they tend to remain there, because they are above the rain and other mechanisms that can remove them from the atmosphere. Figure 7.1 contains a diagram of the atmosphere, which is not drawn to scale. If it were, then, the thickness of the atmosphere would be less than the thickness of the line used to depict the earth's surface.

The pollutants that most adversely affect the ozone layer are fluorocarbons, particularly those that contain chloride or bromide. Of these pollutants, those containing chloride (chlorofluorocarbons, or CFCs) are responsible for most of the depletion of the ozone layer.

These chemicals deplete the ozone layer by serving as a catalyst in a chemical reaction that converts ozone (0_3 and 0_1) to oxygen (0_2). This reaction is accelerated by the presence of ice crystals in the stratosphere, which is one of the explanations for the large loss in ozone over the Antarctic (50–60 percent loss) (World Resources Institute, 1992, p. 200). Because the CFCs act as a catalyst, they are not consumed in the reaction that converts ozone to oxygen, but remain in the stratosphere and continue the destruction of ozone for many decades.

Consequences of the Depletion of the Ozone Layer

As discussed in greater detail in Chapter 9, ozone in the lower atmosphere causes a variety of health, ecological, and agricultural damages. Based on that fact, one might wonder why there is so much excitement about the depletion of stratospheric ozone. Although ozone in the lower atmosphere (troposphere) causes damage, ozone in the upper atmosphere (stratosphere) does not come into contact with living organisms and fulfills a critical function:

blocking the penetration of ultraviolet light and limiting the amount of ultraviolet light that strikes the earth's surface.

Consequently, as the ozone layer becomes depleted, the amount of ultraviolet radiation striking the earth's surface increases. Because ultraviolet radiation causes living cells to mutate, this increase has profound consequences for human and ecological health. In October 1991, a panel of international scientists said that there has been a 3 percent reduction in stratospheric ozone. This 3 percent reduction in the protective layer of stratospheric ozone could lead to a 6 percent increase in the amount of ultraviolet radiation striking the earth's surface. This increase in radiation could lead to an additional 12 million cases of skin cancer in the United States over the next 50 years, with potentially bigger problems in the southern temperate areas (Australia, New Zealand, Argentina, Chile, and South Africa) where the ozone depletion is even greater than in the Northern Hemisphere (World Resources Institute, 1992, p. 200).

In addition to humans, other organisms also are adversely affected by increased ultraviolet radiation. Increased ultraviolet radiation damages most plants and could significantly reduce agricultural yields. In addition to altering agriculture, the increased ultraviolet radiation may have very important impacts on ecosystems, because the increased radiation may change competitive interactions among plant species in ecosystems (Caldwell et al. 1989). Perhaps the most important nonhuman effect is on the phytoplankton layer in the ocean. Phytoplankton form the foundation of the oceanic food web. In addition, the larval and juvenile stages of many fish live and feed in the phytoplankton layer. These organisms undergo metamorphosis several times before achieving adult form and are very vulnerable to the mutagenic effects of increased ultraviolet radiation.

In addition, increased ultraviolet radiation accelerates the deterioration of materials. Synthetic materials, such as plastics and nylon, are particularly susceptible to deterioration from ultraviolet radiation.

Uses of CFCs and Other Ozone Depleting Chemicals

CFCs and other ozone-depleting chemicals are valued in a variety of applications. They are used in refrigeration and air-conditioning systems, as propellants in spray cans, as propellants for manufacturing foam products, and as solvents to degrease and clean machine parts and electrical components. One property of these chemicals, called inertness, that makes them so useful is that they do not react with other chemicals. Unfortunately, this inertness also is what makes them persist so long in the environment, because their disaffinity for chemical reaction means that they do not readily break down into simpler and less harmful substances.

Policy toward Ozone Depletion

When the problem of ozone depletion was discovered in the 1970s, alternative solutions to the problem were proposed. Many economists favored traditional economic incentives. In particular, economist Peter Bohm constructed a powerful argument for the use of deposit-refund systems to recapture CFCs in refrigerator coils (see Box 7.2). Other economists argued that CFCs represented a perfect case for the use of marketable pollution permits or pollution taxes. Because CFCs are a global pollutant and the damages generated are independent of the location of the emissions, taxes or marketable pollution permits would not have to be modified to take into account the geographic

Box 7.2 Deposit-Refund Systems for CFCs

When the ozone-depletion problem was first recognized, Swedish economist Peter Bohm suggested that certain uses of CFCs would be well suited to a deposit-refund system. CFCs are contained in the coils behind refrigerators and freezers. As long as the coils remain intact, the CFCs remain isolated from the environment. When defunct refrigerators are disposed in landfills, however, the earth-moving equipment and shifting garbage break the coils (or they rust if not broken), and the CFCs are released into the atmosphere. If the CFCs could be removed from the coils before disposal, their release could be prevented.

Bohm (1988) suggested that a deposit-refund system would be appropriate for accomplishing this task. A fee paid when purchasing a refrigerator would only be refundable when the CFCs were removed from the coils at a licensed recycling center. As long as the fee or deposit was greater than the costs of transporting the refrigerator and removing the CFCs, appropriate incentives would exist to recycle the CFCs. Companies that sold new refrigerators would incorporate the deposit-refund systems into their prices. A price for a new refrigerator would be lower if there was a trade-in of an old refrigerator. The trade-in differential would be lower than the refund and higher than the company's cost of complying with the recycling. Both consumer and company would profit from recycling as long as the deposit/refund was greater than the cost of recycling.

An international treaty enacted in 1987 (the Montreal Protocol), however, incorporated the notion that CFCs are so destructive that their use should be banned. Consequently, because the substance is scheduled for a ban on production, the practical need for a deposit-refund system for CFCs has been eliminated. Chemical companies are developing substitutes for CFCs as their use is phased out. The substitutes for CFCs, however, also have an ozone-depleting impact (albeit a much smaller one), so deposit-refund systems, taxes, or marketable pollution permits might be necessary to generate the optimal level of use of these chemicals at the lowest social cost as well as to provide incentives to develop substitutes that do not deplete the ozone layer at all.

location of the emissions. The concept of a global pollutant warrants further discussion. As indicated earlier, with global pollutants, the location of the pollution emission is independent of the resultant environmental change. It doe not matter if a kilogram of CFCs are emitted in the United States or China or any other location. The impact on the ozone layer is the same. Moreover, the emissions of one country create damages that are shared by all the countries of the world.

The first policy the United States adopted toward ozone-depleting chemicals was not tied to an international agreement. It was a command and control type of policy, a 1977 ban on the use of CFCs as a propellant in spray cans of deodorants, hair sprays, and other consumer products. At first glance, one might think this move to be another case of abatement cost-minimizing economic incentives being rejected for more costly command and control techniques, a process that has happened repeatedly in the formulation of environmental policy and has led to a higher than necessary cost of attaining environmental policy.

In the case of these uses of CFCs, however, a ban is probably socially efficient. The reason is that very good substitutes exist for CFCs as propellants in spray cans. In other words, the cost of eliminating these emissions is low relative to the damages the emissions create. For example, substitutes for CFC-propelled deodorant spray include the use of more benign gases as propellants, mechanical (thumb) pumps, stick deodorants, roll-on deodorants, and more frequent showers. Figure 7.2 contains a graph of marginal abatement costs and marginal damages that relate positions of costs and benefits for CFC emissions from personal hygiene and other consumer spray products.

If the costs of abatement are low due to the availability of substitutes, then it is a case where the optimal level of emissions is at or near zero. Although an efficient level of emissions can be achieved with economic incentives, why incur the costs of such a program when a ban is so much cheaper in terms of administrative costs? (See Chapter 3 for a complete discussion of this point.)

In the 1970s and the 1980s, it was not apparent that the optimal level of CFC emissions from other sources (solvents, foam manufacture, refrigeration, and air conditioning) was equal to or almost equal to zero. One thing becoming increasingly clear, however, was that further ozone depletion policy could not be developed in the United States (or any other country) in isolation. Because ozone depletion is a global pollution problem, other countries' emissions of CFCs were just as important as U.S. emissions. Hence, effective policy must be developed in the context of an international agreement.

During the 1980s, the discovery of the hole in the ozone layer above the Antarctic, and the evidence of continued depletion at the midlatitudes, spurred the development of an international agreement on chemicals that deplete the ozone layer. This agreement is based on an internationally shared belief that the emissions of CFCs and other ozone-depleting chemicals generate damages far in excess of abatement cost, with the optimal level of emissions of CFCs equal to zero.

Figure 7.2 **Marginal Abatement Costs and Marginal Damages for CFC Emissions from Personal Hygiene Spray Cans**

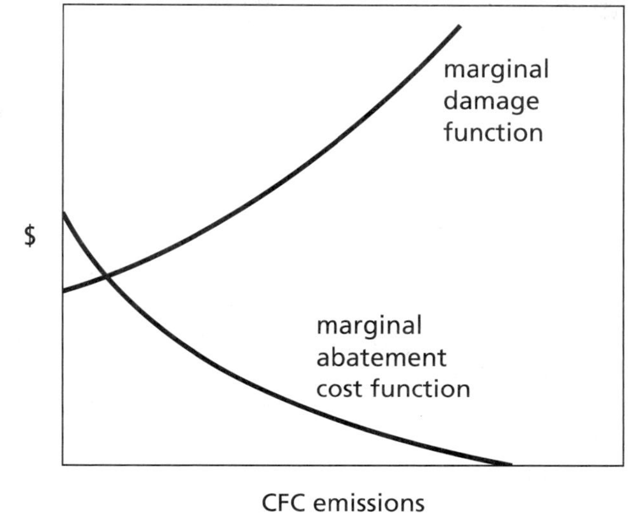

In 1987, the Montreal Protocol on Substances That Deplete the Ozone Layer was signed by most developed and developing countries. This international agreement was amended in 1990 to speed up the elimination of CFCs due to new evidence concerning ozone depletion to require the cessation of emissions of CFCs (and other ozone-depleting chemicals) by the year 2000 in developed countries and by the year 2010 in developing countries. More recent findings about the severity of the ozone-depletion problems generated support for renegotiating the Montreal Protocol to have earlier deadlines. In fact, the Dupont Company, the world's largest manufacturer of CFCs, unilaterally decided to end sales of CFCs to developed countries by 1996 (World Resources Institute, 1992, p. 200). The Montreal Protocol was amended again in 1992 to require total elimination of CFCs in developed countries by 1996 and by 2006 in developing countries.

An important remaining issue is how to treat replacements for CFCs, which also have an ozone-depleting effect (albeit a much smaller one). The importance of developing policies to deal with these substitutes has intensified as evidence has developed that suggests that hydrochlorfluorocarbons (HCFCs) and hydrofluorocarbons (HFCs) may be more ozone depleting than originally thought (Solomon and Albritton, 1992). One possibility is to place a tax on these substances, based on the ozone-depleting effect per kilogram of the substance. This tax would serve to decrease the use of all such substances, but discourage the most harmful substances the most. In addition, it would encourage technological development of less ozone-depleting chemicals or substitute chemicals that have no ozone-depleting effect whatsoever. As discussed in Chapter 3, the same result could be achieved with a marketable pollution permit system, provided that the permits took into account these differences among chemicals. In either case, more research must be conducted to understand the potential ozone depletion impact of each type of chemical better.

Why was the Montreal Protocol so successful? Why did most countries sign this accord and actually follow its provisions? The Montreal Protocol has been successful for a number of reasons, including a widespread acceptance of both the science of what causes ozone depletion and the magnitude of the resultant damages. The primary reason that the treaty was successful, however, was that the costs of compliance of the treaty were very low compared with the damages that would occur if emissions continued at past or accelerated rates. The underlying reason that the costs of compliance were low was that good substitutes were developed for CFCs. The same manufacturers that produced CFCs developed and produced the substitutes, so they did not oppose the Montreal Protocol on economic grounds. Similarly, consumers of CFCs could use the substitutes without large additional costs. Under these conditions, a consensus on a plan to limit emissions and the actual implementation of the plan were relatively easy to agree upon. Unfortunately, that has not been the case with global climate change.

Greenhouse Gases and Global Climate

Global warming is linked to the accumulation of a variety of gases in the atmosphere. These gases, which include carbon dioxide, methane, nitrous oxide, and water vapor, trap infrared radiation (heat) that would normally escape from the earth's atmosphere into space. The analogy to a greenhouse is made because the glass panels of a greenhouse allow light to enter (where it becomes converted to heat after striking the interior of the greenhouse), but block the escape of much of the heat. Actually, the analogy to a greenhouse is not an accurate depiction of what happens in the atmosphere, because the greenhouse gases absorb the heat rather than block its transfer. The presence of greenhouse gases in the earth's atmosphere and the absence of greenhouse gases in the moon's atmosphere explain the relative temperature differences between the earth and the moon, despite their approximately equal distances from the sun. The presence of very high concentrations of greenhouse gases on Venus and the absence of these gases on Mars also partially explain the temperature differentials between Venus, Earth, and Mars.

The earth's temperature (both on the surface and in the atmosphere) is always moving toward an equilibrium. If an equilibrium did not develop between the amount of heat entering the earth's atmosphere and the amount of heat leaving the atmosphere, then the earth would be either continually heating or continually cooling. The injection of more greenhouse gases into the earth's atmosphere upsets this equilibrium, because there are now more gas molecules to absorb heat. The temperature of the atmosphere and the temperature at the earth's surface increase until a new equilibrium is established. The amount of heat entering and leaving the atmosphere (in equilibrium) has not changed, but the stock of heat stored by the earth and its atmosphere has increased. The capacity to absorb heat is known as the radiative forcing of the gas. If the amount of greenhouse gases diminishes, then radiative forcing decreases, and a new equilibrium is established at a lower temperature. It may take hundreds of years for a new equilibrium to become established because of the existence of lagged effects. For example, the temperature of the oceans responds very slowly to changes in radiative forcing.

There is virtually no debate surrounding the proposition that the greater the level of greenhouse gases, the greater the equilibrium temperature of the earth. There is also little debate on whether anthropogenic emissions of greenhouse gases cause a significant increase in global temperature in comparison with current temperature levels and in comparison with natural fluctuations in the temperature levels. The debate centers on the magnitude and timing of the change, and its significance to human welfare.

Water vapor is the most important greenhouse gas in the earth's atmosphere, constituting about 1 percent of the total gases in the atmosphere. Carbon dioxide has an atmospheric concentration of approximately 0.04 percent (Solow, 1991). Other important greenhouse gases include methane, nitrous oxides, and CFCs (predominantly CFC-11 and CFC-12, although they will become increasingly less significant in the future due to the Montreal Protocol). There are significant anthropogenic emissions of all greenhouse gases except water vapor.

Sources of Greenhouse Gases

Anthropogenic emissions of greenhouse gases come from a variety of sources. To properly understand the emissions of carbon dioxide, which is the most important of the greenhouse gases, it is necessary to understand the "carbon cycle."

The carbon cycle refers to the movement of carbon from the atmosphere to the earth's surface. On the earth's surface, carbon is stored in the biomass of every organism. Carbon dioxide is also dissolved in surface water, with the oceans having the most significance in this regard. Carbon dioxide is removed from the atmosphere when a plant grows and is converted to carbon in the plant's tissues. For example, a tree is approximately 50 percent carbon by weight. When an animal eats a plant, the carbon is transferred from the biomass of the plant to the biomass of the animal. When a plant or animal dies, it decays and the carbon combines with oxygen to form carbon dioxide (CO_2), which is returned to the atmosphere. The CO_2 is reabsorbed when a new plant grows.

Anthropogenic activities, such as the burning of fossil fuels or deforestation, upset the equilibrium carbon cycle and cause an increase in atmospheric carbon dioxide. Fossil fuels, such as oil, coal, and natural gas, are the fossilized remains of prehistoric plants and animals. These fuels represent stored carbon, and their combustion causes increases in atmospheric concentrations of CO_2. Similarly, when forests are cut down, all the carbon except that which is preserved in wood products (construction materials, furniture, paper in books, and so on) eventually breaks down, and its carbon is released as carbon dioxide into the atmosphere. Because much less than 50 percent of the biomass of a tree is converted into lumber or wood products, deforestation can be a significant source of carbon dioxide emissions. Of course, when deforestation takes the form of "slash and burn" clearing (see Chapter 13) to create agricultural or cattle ranching areas, all the carbon is converted to CO_2 and the greenhouse effect is even more pronounced. When forests are replanted, carbon dioxide is drawn out of the atmosphere, thus implying a significant environmental advantage to using biomass fuels.[1] For example, if cars burn ethanol (which can be made from wood or crops such as corn) instead of gasoline, there would be a significant reduction of CO_2 emissions. Although the burning of any fuel releases carbon dioxide, burning gasoline represents the release of stored carbon, whereas burning ethanol from plants represents the cycling of carbon. As long as the crop from which the fuel is made is replanted, there would be no net increase in atmospheric CO_2 concentrations from the burning of biomass fuels. Because mature natural forests contain more biomass per acre than replanted forests, however, the conversion of mature natural forests to "energy plantations" would result in an increase in atmospheric CO_2. It would be better to plant these energy plantations in areas of previous deforestation. The same thing would be true for diesel fuel and heating oil, which can be made from vegetable oil.

Planting new forests would reduce atmospheric carbon dioxide concentrations. This process is known as sequestering carbon. The greatest opportunities for carbon sequestration exist in tropical areas, where growth rates are faster and where the amount of biomass per acre of forest is greatest. Carbon can also be sequestered by increasing the organic component of soil.

Methane (CH_4) comes from a variety of anthropogenic and natural sources. Natural sources include wetlands and other areas where anaerobic decay of organic matter takes place. Anthropogenic sources include emissions from ruminants (cud-chewing animals, such as cattle and sheep), wet rice cultivation, emissions from coal mines and oil and natural gas wells (natural gas is methane), and leakage from natural gas pipelines. Nitrous oxide (N_2O) originates from the burning of fossil fuels and biomass. Nitrous oxide also stems from agricultural fertilizers.

---

[1]This environmental advantage is relative to the generation of carbon dioxide emissions. There are other potential environmental problems associated with the large-scale production of biomass fuel crops. In particular, annual grain crops, such as corn or soybeans, which require annual plowing of the ground and large-scale use of agrichemicals, generate other environmental problems. If the biomass production resulted in the conversion of natural forests into energy plantations, then there would be very negative consequences in terms of ecological services. The full social costs of biomass fuels must be compared with the full social costs of fossil fuels in selecting the mix of fuels that maximize social welfare. More discussion of this issue is contained in Chapter 8.

Sources of CFCs and other ozone-depleting chemicals were discussed previously in the context of ozone depletion. Sources mentioned include refrigeration and air conditioning, propellants, foam manufacture, and solvents.

Atmospheric concentrations of CO_2 have increased from preindustrial levels of 280 parts per million (ppm) to 368 ppm. Methane (CH_4) has increased by an even greater percentage, from 700 parts per billion (ppb) to 1,750 ppb (IPCC, *Climate Change: Synthesis Report Summary for Policy Makers, 2001*, http://www.ipcc.ch.). These and other atmospheric changes are reported in Table 7.1.

Is Global Temperature Increasing?

The question of whether global climate is changing is a controversial question, because it has become a highly politicized issue. Although there was considerable scientific uncertainty about this issue when scientists began their studies in the 1980s, the uncertainty has been reduced by the research that has taken place over almost two decades. Virtually all the available evidence suggests very strongly that mean global temperature has increased as a result of anthropogenic greenhouse gas emissions and that it will continue to increase as continued emissions increase the concentration of these gases in the atmosphere. All the scientific evidence also suggests that there will be significant increases in sea level. Many uncertainties continue to exist about the nature of the regional distribution of global climate change, the impact of global warming on severe weather events, and the impacts of feedback events on global climate change. It is a misrepresentation of the evidence that has been developed, however, to suggest that there is substantial uncertainty in the relationship between anthropogenic emissions of greenhouse gases and global climate. Table 7.1 contains information on climate change that has already occurred, as well as impacts of this climate change. Figure 7.3 provides

Table 7.1 Twentieth-Century Changes in the Earth's Atmosphere, Climate, and Biophysical System[a]

Indicator	Observed Changes
Concentration indicators	
Atmospheric concentration of CO_2	280 ppm for the period 1000–1750 to 368 ppm in year 2000 (31 ± 4% increase).
Terrestrial biospheric CO_2 exchange	Cumulative source of about 30 Gt C between the years 1800 and 2000; but during the 1990s, a net sink of about 14 ± 7 Gt C.

(continues)

Table 7.1 (continued)

Indicator	Observed Changes
Atmospheric concentration of CH_4	700 ppb for the period 1000–1750 to 1750 ppb in year 2000 (151 ± 25% increase).
Atmospheric concentration of N_2O	270 ppb for the period 1000–1750 to 316 ppb in year 2000 (17 ± 5% increase).
Tropospheric concentration of O_3	Increased by 35 ± 15% from the years 1750 to 2000, varies with region.
Stratospheric concentration of O_3	Decreased over the years 1970 to 2000, varies with altitude and latitude.
Atmospheric concentrations of HFCs, PFCs, and SF6	Increased globally over the last 50 years.
Weather indicators	
Global mean surface temperature	Increased by 0.6 ± 0.2° C over the 20th century; land areas warmed more than the oceans (very likely).
Northern Hemisphere surface temperature	Increase over the 20th century greater than during any other century in the last 1000 years; 1990s warmest decade of the millennium (likely).
Diurnal surface temperature range	Decreased over the years 1950 to 2000 over land; nighttime minimum temperatures increased at twice the rate of daytime maximum temperatures (likely).
Hot days/heat index	Increased (likely).
Cold/frost days	Decreased for nearly all land areas during the 20th century (very likely).
Continental precipitation	Increased by 5–10% over the 20th century in the Northern Hemisphere (very likely), although decreased in some regions (e.g., North and West Africa and parts of the Mediterranean).
Heavy precipitation events; increased summer drying and associated incidence of drought in a few areas (likely).	Increased at mid- and high northern latitudes (likely).
Frequency and severity of drought	In some regions, such as parts of Asia and Africa, the frequency and intensity of droughts have been observed to increase in recent decades.

(continues)

Table 7.1 (continued)

Indicator	**Observed Changes**
Biological and physical indicators	
Global mean sea level	Increased at an average annual rate of 1 to 2 mm during the 20th century.
Duration of ice cover of rivers and lakes	Decreased by about 2 weeks over the 20th century in mid- and high latitudes of the Northern Hemisphere (very likely).
Arctic sea-ice extent and thickness	Thinned by 40% in recent decades in late summer to early autumn (likely), and decreased in extent by 10–15% since the 1950s in spring and summer.
Snow cover	Decreased in area by 10% since global observations became available from satellites in the 1960s (very likely).
Permafrost	Thawed, warmed, and degraded in parts of the polar, subpolar, and mountainous regions.
El Niño events	Became more frequent, persistent, and intense during the last 20 to 30 years compared with the previous 100 years.
Growing season	Lengthened by about 1 to 4 days per decade during the last 40 years in the Northern Hemisphere, especially at higher latitudes.
Plant and animal ranges	Shifted poleward and up in elevation for plants, insects, birds, and fish.
Breeding, flowering, and migration	Earlier plant flowering, earlier bird arrival, earlier dates of breeding season, and earlier emergence of insects in the Northern Hemisphere.
Coral reef bleaching	Increased frequency, especially during El Niño events.
Economic indicators	
Weather-related economic losses	Global inflation-adjusted losses rose an order of magnitude over the last 40 years. Part of the observed upward trend is linked to socioeconomic factors and part is linked to climatic factors.

[a] This table provides examples of key observed changes and is not an exhaustive list. It includes both changes attributable to anthropogenic climate change and those that may be caused by natural variations or anthropogenic climate change. Confidence levels are reported where they are explicitly assessed by the relevant Working Group.

Note: The IPCC scientists have assigned probabilities, when available. They are as follows: virtually certain = 0.99%; very likely = 90–99%; likely = 66–90%; medium likelihood = 33–66%; unlikely = 10–33%; very unlikely = 1–10%; exceptionally unlikely < 1%.

Source: Table SPM.2 of the IPCC report *Climate Change:Synthesis Report Summary for Policy Makers*. Online: http://www.ipcc.ch.2001.

an illustration of historical temperatures, going back more than 100 million years. Figure 7.4 gives an indication of how well the computer modeling efforts track actual temperature levels over the last 150 years. The solid line in Figure 7.4 indicates the observed mean global surface temperature, whereas the shaded band indicates the confidence interval of the predictions of the model.

Evidence comes from many sources. Scientists have taken ice-core samples of glaciers, allowing the comparison of carbon levels and temperatures going back hundreds of thousands of years. The pollen record (found in sediments in lakes) gives similar information going back thousands of years. Some human records go back many centuries, such as the record of the day that the cherry trees bloom at the imperial palace in Japan. The modern recording of temperature and rainfall on a systematic basis began in the mid nineteenth century. Scientists have used these data, as well as measurements of the heat-absorbing ability of the different gases to develop computer models of the relationship between the concentration of these gases and the global temperature. Scientists have been able to use these data and these computer models to distinguish between natural variation in temperature and variation in temperature due to increases in the concentration of these gases. There are various ways to test the validity of their work. For example, scientists can use data of some of the time span to develop the model and then see how well it predicts the actual temperature for the rest of the time span. A summary of some of the changes in global climate and the impacts of global climate that have already occurred is contained in Table 7.1.

This scientific evidence is not the result of individual scientists working in isolation. The Intergovernmental Panel on Climate Change (IPCC) is an

Figure 7.3 Historical Temperature Record

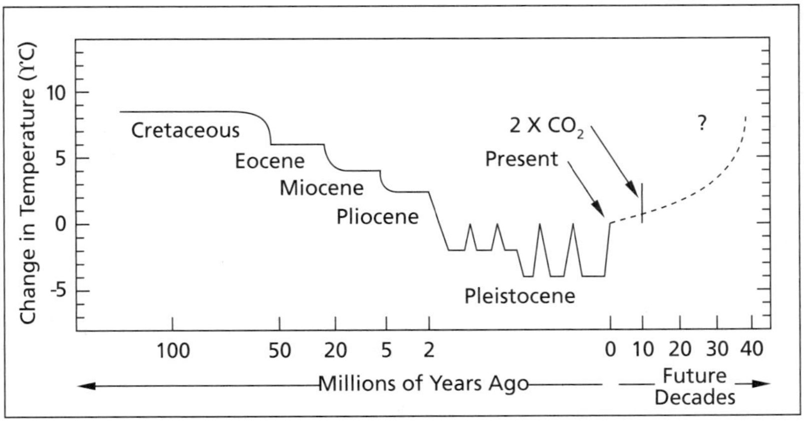

Source: Crowley (1996).

Figure 7.4 **Comparison between Modeled and Observations of Temperature Rise since 1860**

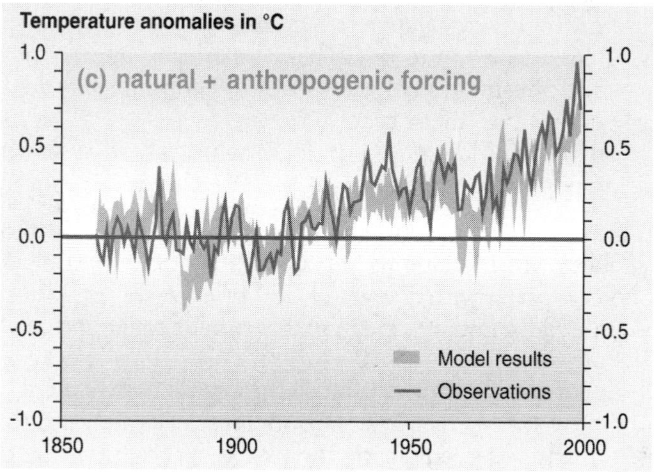

Source: IPCC (2001).

international scientific agency designed to share information and encourage cooperation of scientists throughout the world. In 2001, the panel completed its third assessment report on climate change (available at http://www.ipcc.ch). The best place to start an examination of the IPCC's information is with the *Synthesis Report for Policy Makers*. This report then leads to individual reports that contain in-depth discussion of the science and economics underlying global climate change.

What is the bottom line of predictions of global climate change? The answer to this question is actually very difficult to formulate, because it depends on the future path of emissions. The future path of emissions is the result of both individual decisions and the future policies of the governments of the various countries of the world. Because future emissions cannot be predicted, different scenarios of the emissions are used by the IPCC to calculate the extent of global climate change for each of these scenarios. Scenarios make explicit assumptions about economic growth, population growth, the diffusion of technology, and similar variables. Four classes of scenarios are used in the 2001 IPCC assessment, with six scenarios in total:

- A1: Based on assumptions of rapid economic growth, global population peaking in mid-twenty-first century, and reduction in regional differences in per capita income. Scenario A1F assumes strong reliance on fossil fuels, A1T assumes strong movement toward alternative technology, and A1B is a balance between A1F and A1T.

- A2: Is more of an "every country for itself" type of scenario, with a future characterized by strong and potentially growing differences across countries. Diffusion of technology is slow in this scenario. Population growth does not slow as in the A1 scenarios, nor is there a decrease in the income gap across countries.
- B1: Assumes a world of more global cooperation and a global movement away from smokestack industries to economies more dependent on services and information activities.
- B2: Describes a world focused on local solutions, with continuously increasing population as in A2.

Based on these scenarios, the IPCC reports that the concentration of CO_2 in the atmosphere will increase to between 540 to 970 ppm by 2100. These figures can be compared with a level of 280 ppm in the preindustrial period and 368 ppm in 2000. Similarly, mean global surface temperature will increase between 1.4° and 5.8° C (2.5° to 10.4° F) by 2100. Temperature will increase over this whole interval, with the projected increase between 0.4° and 1.1° C by 2025 and 0.8° to 2.6° C by 2050. This increase is in addition to the 0.4° to 0.8° increase already observed during the twentieth century. The temperature increases predicted in the 2001 assessment are substantially higher than those predicted in the 1995 assessment because of a better understanding of the cooling effect associated with other types of pollution, such as sulfur dioxide.

The estimates of sea-level rise are also higher than previous reports. The estimate for 1990 to 2100 is 0.09 to 0.88 meter, with 0.03 to 1.14 m by 2025 and 0.05 to 3.2 m occurring by 2050. Again, this increase is in addition to the twentieth-century rise of 0.01 to 0.2 m. Table 7.2 reports other physical changes that are likely to occur in the twenty-first century.

Table 7.2 Examples of Climate Variability and Extreme Climate Events and Examples of Their Impacts

Projected Changes during the 21st Century in Extreme Climate Phenomena and Their Likelihood	Representative Examples of Projected Impacts[a] (all high confidence of occurrence in some areas)
Higher maximum temperatures, more hot days and heat waves over nearly all land areas (very likely)	Increased incidence of death and serious illness in older age groups and urban poor.
	Increased heat stress in livestock and wildlife.
	Shift in tourist destinations.
	Increased risk of damage to a number of crops.
	Increased electric cooling demand and reduced energy supply reliability.

(continues)

Table 7.2 (continued)

Projected Changes during the 21st Century in Extreme Climate Phenomena and Their Likelihood	Representative Examples of Projected Impacts[a] (all high confidence of occurrence in some areas)
Higher (increasing) minimum temperatures, fewer cold days, frost days, and cold waves over nearly all land areas (very likely)	Decreased cold-related human morbidity and mortality.
	Decreased risk of damage to a number of crops, and increased risk to others.
	Extended range and activity of some pest and disease vectors.
	Reduced heating energy demand.
More intense precipitation events (very likely, over many areas)	Increased flood, landslide, avalanche, and mudslide damage.
	Increased soil erosion.
	Increased flood runoff could increase recharge of some floodplain aquifers.
	Increased pressure on government and private flood insurance systems and disaster relief.
Increased summer drying over most midlatitude continental interiors and associated risk of drought (likely)	Decreased crop yields.
	Increased damage to building foundations caused by ground shrinkage.
	Decreased water resource quantity and quality.
	Increased risk of forest fire.
Increase in tropical cyclone peak wind intensities, mean and peak precipitation intensities (likely, over some areas)[b]	Increased risks to human life, risk of infectious disease epidemics, and many other risks.
	Increased coastal erosion and damage to coastal buildings and infrastructure.
	Increased damage to coastal ecosystems such as coral reefs and mangroves.
Intensified droughts and floods associated with El Niño events in many different regions (likely)	Decreased agricultural and rangeland productivity in drought- and flood-prone regions.
	Decreased hydropower potential in drought-prone regions.

(continues)

Table 7.2 (continued)

Projected Changes during the 21st Century in Extreme Climate Phenomena and Their Likelihood	Representative Examples of Projected Impacts[a] (all high confidence of occurrence in some areas)
Increased Asian summer monsoon precipitation variability (likely)	Increase in flood and drought magnitude and damages in temperate and tropical Asia.
Increased intensity of midlatitude storms (little agreement between current models)[c]	Increased risks to human life and health. Increased property and infrastructure losses. Increased damage to coastal ecosystems.

[a] These impacts can be lessened by appropriate response measures.

[b] Information from WGI TAR Technical Summary (Section F.5).

[c] Changes in regional distribution of tropical cyclones are possible but have not been established.

Source: Table SPM.2 of the IPCC report *Climate Change: Synthesis Report Summary for Policy Makers* (2001). Online: http://www.ipcc.ch.

What Are the Consequences of Global Climate Change?

Tables 7.1 and 7.2 report many of the impacts associated with global climate change, but they really do not report the impact of global climate change on the quality of life. An examination of how these impacts affect social welfare is a very important exercise, especially because the impacts on social welfare are likely to be relatively high if the climate change that occurs is on the high side of the estimated range of likely change.

In the 1990s, much of the economics literature focused on the ability to mitigate the damages associated with climate change through adaptation. For example, if sea-level rise occurs slowly, then buildings in danger of inundation could be allowed to gradually depreciate and replacement buildings constructed farther inland. Particularly valuable areas such as Manhattan could be protected by seawalls. Similar adaptation could take place in agriculture and plantation forestry, with more heat-tolerant plant and animal species replacing less heat-tolerant species.

There are, however, limits on the ability of social and economic systems to adapt. Adaptation is much more difficult in developing countries that lack the resources and information infrastructure to implement change. For example, if corn production in Iowa is negatively affected by climate change, scientists in the land-grant universities, government agencies, and private industry will work to determine how to react. They would determine which of several strategies might be better, such as planting a different variety of corn, switching to an entirely different crop, or adjusting parameters such as the use of fertilizers, pesticides, and irrigation. After strategies are determined, agricultural extension agents would communicate this information to the farmers, with the process likely to move fairly smoothly. If farmers needed to take loans to implement the change, credit would be likely to be available, either through private institutions such as banks or through government sources. In contrast, small farmers in Africa who might be adversely affected by climate change (such as the southward movement of the Sahara Desert) do not have the information resources available to determine how to react to global climate change; even if they had the information, it is very probable that they would lack the financial resources to implement change, especially because credit markets are poorly developed in many rural areas of developing countries and so capital is not likely to be available to the farmers.

In addition, the ability to adapt to global climate change will depend on the magnitude of the change. If the higher range of the estimated range is actually realized, the change may be so great that the ability to adapt is limited (IPCC, 2001). This problem could arise in both developed and developing countries.

Several studies have attempted to directly quantify the effect of global warming on GDP or national income. For example, Nordhaus (1991) estimates the annual impact on the U.S. economy of a doubling of atmospheric CO_2. He finds that the mean estimate is approximately $12.63 billion (updated to 2004 dollars), which amounts to roughly 0.26 percent of national income. The sectoral breakdown of these impacts is listed in Table 7.3. Cline (1992) predicts a much greater impact of 2 percent of national income, but his results include a broader definition of damages, which include nonmarket impacts. If Nordhaus's estimates were adjusted to include nonmarket impacts, they would be roughly consistent with Cline's work. More recent studies of the economic impacts of global climate change tend to report damages on a per ton of carbon basis, allowing for a better comparison with the cost of reducing emissions. A group of these studies is summarized in Table 7.4. Damages from global warming may be even greater, because some types of impacts—in particular, the impacts on ecosystems and the resulting reduction in ecological services, the increased frequency and intensity of severe storms, the increased frequency and severity of El Niño episodes, the displacement of people in developing countries because of sea-level rise, and an increase in the incidence of tropical diseases such as malaria—are not factored into global warming.

One particular aspect of global warming that is likely to be quite costly is the effect of sea-level rise on low-lying Third World countries. Many island nations may be completely inundated under plausible sea-level rise scenarios, especially because at the same time sea level is rising, global climate change will increase the intensity and frequency of tropical storms. The combination of these factors implies that the storm surge (the movement of waves onto areas that are normally dry) will move much farther inland. Population in areas such as the river deltas of Bangladesh and Egypt (inhabited by tens of millions of people) is rapidly increasing. In the future, these areas may be lying entirely under water or at such a low elevation above sea level that they

Table 7.3 Impact Estimates for Different Sectors, for Doubling of CO_2

Sectors	Cost (updated to 2004 billions of dollars)
Severely impacted sectors	
Farms	21.6 to 19.76
Forestry, fisheries, other	small
Moderately impacted sectors	
Construction	negative
Water transportation	?
Energy and utilities	
electricity demand	3.36
nonelectric space heat	21.16
water and sanitary	positive?
Real estate	
Damage from sea level rise	
loss of land	43.1
protection of sheltered areas	1.83
protection of open coasts	5.7
Lodging, hotels, recreation	?
Total central estimate	
National income	12.63
Percent of national income	0.26

Source: E: William D. Nordhaus. *Global Warming: Economic Policy Responses*. (Cambridge, MA: MIT Press), 1991.

become even more vulnerable to storms. The costs to these people of losing their land and homes would be quite large, particularly because there is already a shortage of land in these countries. The developed countries have not been particularly hospitable in receiving refugees from Third World countries in the past several decades, which raises the issue of where the sea-level rise refugees could resettle. The suffering of these potential refugees, the

Table 7.4 IPCC Summary of the Social Costs of CO_2 Emissions in Different Decades (2004 \$/tC)

Study	Type	1991–2000	2001–2010	2011–2020	2021–2030
Nordhaus (1991)	MC		10.34 (0.43–93.4)		
Ayres and Walter (1991)	MC		42.51–49.59		
Nordhaus (1994)	CBA				
Best guess		7.51	9.64	12.19	14.7
Expected Value		17	25.51	37.55	NA
Cline (1992, 1993)	CBA	8.22–175.7	10.77–218	13.89–263.6	16.72–313.2
Peck and Tiesberg (1997)	CBA	14.17–17	17–19.8	19.8–25.5	25.5–31.7
Fankhauser (1994)	MC	28.76 (8.79–64.1)	32.31 (10.49–75)	35.85 (11.76–82.75)	39.4 (13.04–92.39)
Maddison (1995)	CBA/MC	8.36–8.64	11.48–11.9	15.7–16.3	20.83–21.54

MC = marginal cost study.

CBA = shadow value in a cost-benefit study.

Figures in parentheses denote 90% confidence interval.

Source: Table 6.1 in James P. Bruce, Hoesung Lee, and Erik F. Haites, Climate Change 1995: Economic and Social Dimensions of Climate Change: Summary for Policymakers, in *Climate Change 1995: Economic and Social Dimensions of Climate Change* (Cambridge: Cambridge University Press, 1996), p. 215.

political destabilizing effects on affected and neighboring countries, and the cost of relocating the refugees could be among the major potential costs associated with global warming.

Another area in which adaptation is not likely to have an important mitigative role is with natural systems. Although the pace of global climate change is relatively slow by human standards, it is extremely rapid by natural standards. For example, as global temperatures changed in North America (as glaciers advanced and retreated), forests changed. As the temperature increased, southern pine forests gradually moved north, and as the temperature decreased, northern hardwood forests gradually moved south. These changes could take place because temperatures changed at a pace that was relatively slow in comparison with the rate at which forests could expand. Animals would also migrate to their preferred climate zone and habitat.

The climate change associated with greenhouse warming, however, is taking place at a relatively rapid pace. Major effects are taking place within the lifetime of an individual tree. This pace is far too rapid for a forest to adjust by natural selection. In addition, the migration of plant and animal species is blocked by roads, farms, cities, and suburbs. Hence, species that are disadvantaged by the new climate regime may disappear as their ability to adjust is limited by barriers.

Ausabel (1991) argues that the most significant damages from global warming may lie in damages to natural systems, particularly those already stressed by interaction with human systems. Water resources are a prime example. Global warming may lead to a further drying of southern California from reduced precipitation and from reduced winter snowpack in the mountains because of higher temperatures (Gore, 1992). Water systems in southern California are already stressed from ongoing drought and overexploitation. Further stress could lead to their collapse, with profound implications for millions of people.

Finally, there is the very important impact of global climate change on the distribution of tropical diseases. Both the increased temperature and the increased moisture associated with global climate change may increase the geographic range of tropical diseases and make infection rates higher in areas in which the diseases already exist. Higher infection rates are likely for insect-borne illnesses, such as malaria, dengue fever, and leshmaniasis, which could become common in the southern United States and other currently temperate regions of the world as a result of global climate change.

The Importance of Surprises

One reason to be extremely cautious about the potential consequences of global climate change is the potential of unpredicted consequences. These surprises can come about as a result of the possible existence of threshold effects.

There are two types of thresholds with respect to the emissions of any type of pollutant. The first type is when increases in emissions generate no damages until a threshold is crossed. The second type is when marginal changes in emissions lead to marginal increases in damages until a threshold is crossed; then marginal changes in emissions lead to very large increases in damages. This latter type of threshold may be most relevant for global warming, although the former type may be important in some circumstances.

One example of this latter type of threshold is if global warming progresses to the point where the tundral permafrost begins to melt. If that were to occur, anaerobic decay of organic matter could lead to a massive release of methane, which would lead to an intensification of global warming.

A second possible threshold effect would occur if temperature change became severe enough to lead to even greater melting of polar ice caps. Not only would this event lead to an increase in sea-level rise, but the shrinking of the ice caps would reduce the amount of light reflected by the earth. Such a reduction in reflection would lead to an increase in heat absorption that would intensify global warming.

Both the melting of the permafrost and the shrinking of the polar ice caps can be classified as positive feedback effects. A positive feedback means that the indirect effects of a change intensify the direct effects of a change.

Another type of threshold effect would occur if climate changes lead to alterations in ocean currents. If the Gulf Stream stopped flowing, which would stop the movement of warm southern water to the colder northern regions, then much of Western Europe would experience the colder temperatures that are more typical of the northern latitudes. For example, the climate of Great Britain would more closely resemble that of Newfoundland, with the possibility of long periods of ice-locking of Atlantic, North Sea, and Norwegian Sea ports.

Threshold effects of the first type (no damages until a certain level is exceeded) may occur in some instances in a greenhouse environment. For example, global warming may raise summer temperatures in some areas by several degrees. This increase in itself may not have a harmful effect on trees and other plants. A small increase in average temperature, however, may be associated with a large increase in the length or frequency of severe hot spells, which could cause stress and lead to the demise of heat-sensitive plants. Global warming could also stress ecosystems in a way that made it easier for exotic plants and animals to invade the ecosystem, become established, and diminish the ecological services flowing from these ecosystems.

Global Warming Policy

Many characteristics of the global warming problem make it substantially different from other environmental problems. They include the following:

1. The necessity to deal with many different pollutants (all the greenhouse gases) simultaneously
2. The temporal separation between emissions and damages
3. The high degree of uncertainty underlying both the scientific understanding of physical impacts and the economic understanding of costs and benefits
4. The relative importance of equity issues, both across generations and across countries
5. The need to achieve international cooperation

The Necessity to Deal with Many Different Pollutants

Although carbon dioxide is the predominant anthropogenic greenhouse gas, global warming policy should not focus solely on carbon dioxide. For example, it may be cheaper to initially concentrate on reducing CFC emissions (particularly because of the ozone-depletion problem) or on methane emissions. At the margin, one wants to reduce global warming by reducing the greenhouse gas that is least costly to abate. Yet one cannot merely look at the cost of reducing a kilogram of carbon dioxide emissions and compare it with the cost of reducing a kilogram of N_2O or CFC-11 or CH_4. Each greenhouse gas has a different level of radiative forcing (heat-absorbing potential), and each greenhouse gas has a different atmospheric lifetime.

To measure the equivalency of the different greenhouse gases, the IPCC developed the concept of a global warming potential index (GWPI). The concept behind the GWPI is to compare the radiative forcing over the atmospheric lifetime of one particular gas with the radiative forcing over the atmospheric lifetime of 1 kilogram of carbon dioxide, which serves as the benchmark. This comparison is made as a ratio, with the lifetime radiative forcing of carbon dioxide as the base (denominator) of the index. By definition, the GWPI of carbon dioxide is equal to 1. The global warming potential of a greenhouse gas declines over time as the gas decays in the atmosphere. Figure 7.5 shows the time path of a hypothetical greenhouse gas. A hypothetical gas is depicted rather than an actual gas because the choice of a time path for an actual gas would involve a discussion of atmospheric chemistry issues beyond the scope of this chapter. The total global warming potential of a gas is the area under the time path (the integral of the time path). The GWPI of the hypothetical gas is equal to the integral of the time path for a particular gas divided by the integral of the time path for carbon dioxide.

The use of the integral-based indices is controversial, because it treats a unit of radiative forcing at one point in time as exactly identical to a unit of radiative forcing at another point in time. Different gases have differently

Figure 7.5 **Time Path of Radiative Forcing of a Hypothetical Greenhouse Gas**

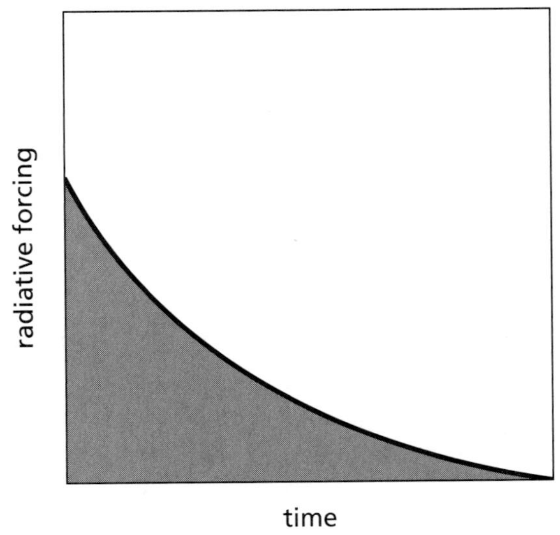

Note: The shaded area is the integral of the time path.

shaped time paths, so the time dimension is important. Even if one believes that the social discount rate is equal to zero (treat all costs and benefits the same, regardless of when they occur), the time dimension remains critically important.

For example, each kilogram of methane is associated with a much greater warming effect than carbon dioxide, but carbon dioxide lasts much longer in the atmosphere. Because the damages of global warming are a function of the ability to adjust to the changes, the more rapid the warming, the greater the damages that will occur. Although two gases may have the same total radiative forcing over time, they may have very different time paths. For example, in Figure 7.6, gas A represents a short-lived gas with a powerful warming effect, such as methane. Gas B represents a long-lived gas with a weaker warming effect. Although the total warming potential (the area under the time paths) is the same for these two gases, the warming associated with gas A occurs much earlier and will result in larger damages than the warming associated with gas B. Thus, global warming potential indices, as defined above, do not really measure the equivalence of different greenhouse gases because they do not measure equivalent damages, only equivalent total warming over time.

The proposition that damages associated with a given level of global warming are likely to be a function of both the time at which the warming

Figure 7.6 **Stylized Time Paths of Radiative Forcing of Two Gases with Approximately the Same Time Integral of Radiative Forcing**

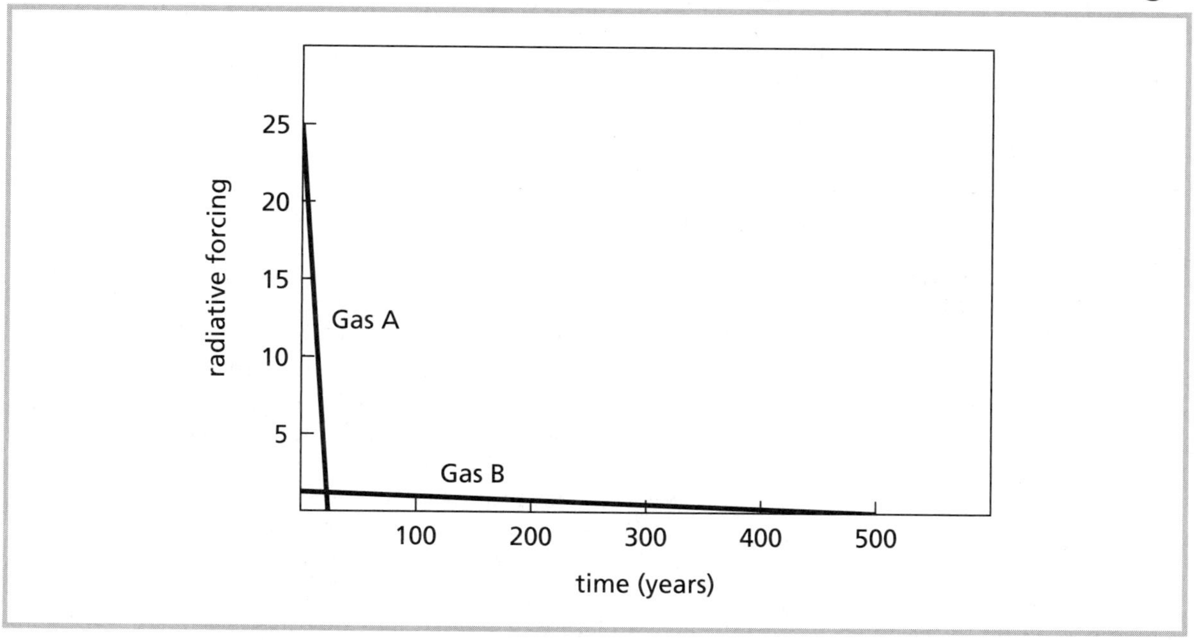

occurs and the rapidity of the warming merits further discussion. This time dependency of damages is due to a variety of factors. The state of the world changes as time progresses: population grows, technology improves, economies change and grow, and values and preferences change. A given level of global warming in one state of the world will be associated with a different level of damages than the same level of warming in a different state of the world. Also, damages will be a function of the speed at which global warming occurs, because the ability to adapt will be dependent on the speed at which warming occurs. Although global warming potential indices are designed to measure the relative effects of different greenhouse gases, they do not adequately deal with the time dimension, because they do not attempt to measure the social damages associated with the emissions. At best, they should be regarded as crude approximations of the relative greenhouse effects of different gases. At this time, they are not sufficiently robust to allow for the computation of an integrated system of taxes or marketable permits for the different greenhouse gases. However, because GWPIs do give a coarse indication of the relative importance of the different gases, they are presented in this chapter. Table 7.5 contains the 1992 IPCC estimates of the GWPIs for the major greenhouse gases.

Three different indices are presented in Table 7.5. They are for 50, 100, and 500 years, where the number of years is equal to the time period over which total radiative forcing is summed. For example, if one considers the total radiative forcing over 50 years, each kilogram of methane (CH_4) has 20 times the warming impact as a kilogram of carbon dioxide. If the impact is measured over 500 years, the corresponding index is equal to 4. Note the relatively high GWPIs associated with ozone-depleting gases (CFCs, HCFCs, HFCs, and CCL_4). Also, note that if the GWPI of a gas increases as the time increases, then that gas has a greater atmospheric lifetime than CO_2. If the GWPI falls with increases in the time interval, then the atmospheric lifetime of the gas is lower than CO_2.

The United Nations Framework Convention on Climate Change and the Kyoto Protocol

The efforts to forge a treaty to limit greenhouse gas emissions began in the late 1980s, but it did not result in any concrete accomplishments until the Rio Summit in 1992. There, the United Nations Framework Convention on Climate Change (UNFCCC: see http://unfccc.int) was created. As the name suggests, this was not an agreement on emissions limitations, but rather specifying it was a process for arriving at an agreement on emissions limitations. In addition to specifying a framework for negotiating a treaty to limit emissions, the UNFCCC stated two principles that are extremely important in terms of moving toward a treaty. The first principle is that the signatories to the Convention (which included the United States under the administration of President George H. W. Bush) accepted the proposition that anthropogenic activities lead to the accumulation of greenhouse gases in the atmos-

Table 7.5 **Global Warming Potential Indices (GWPI) for Various Greenhouse Gases for 50-, 100-, and 500-Year Time Intervals**

Time Interval	50 years	100 years	500 years
Gas			
CO2	1	1	1
CH4	20	11	4
N2O	280	270	170
CFC-11	4300	3400	1400
CFC-12	7600	6200	4100
HCFC-22	2700	1600	540
CFC-113	4900	4500	2500
CFC-114	6900	7000	5800
CFC-115	6400	7000	8500
HCFC-123	160	93	30
HCFC-124	810	460	150
HCFC-125	4600	3400	1200
HFC-134a	2000	1200	400
HCFC-141b	1100	610	210
HCFC-142b	2900	1800	630
HFC-143a	4600	3800	1600
HFC-152a	260	150	49
CCl4	1600	1300	480

Source: IPCC (1992)

phere, which in turn lead to global climate change. Second, the signatories to the treaty agreed that all nations had a common but differentiated responsibility to solve the problem of global climate change. Thus, it was agreed that all nations had a responsibility to take steps to diminish the problem of global climate change, but some nations (because of their higher income levels or greater levels of past and current emissions) have a greater responsibility to take steps to diminish the problem.

The Rio Summit was followed by a series of meetings to forge an agreement, eventually resulting in the Kyoto Protocol. The Kyoto Protocol goes into effect when two conditions are met. First, 55 percent of the nations of the world must sign and ratify the treaty. Second, the total 1990 emissions levels of the nations that have ratified the proposal must account for 55 percent of the 1990 emissions total. The first condition has been met easily. The second condition has not been met[2] and will not be met unless the United States or Russia signs and ratifies the treaty. The United States has already indicated that it will not do so (at least until there is a change in government), and Russia has made ambiguous sounds about whether or not it will sign the proposal. The UNFCCC web site has a "thermometer" web site that illustrates the gap in meeting the second condition.

The major provision of the Kyoto Protocol is to limit the emissions of "Annex I" countries to (more or less) 6 percent below 1990 levels by 2010. Annex I countries include high-income countries and the former Warsaw Pact countries (formerly communist Eastern and Central Europe). The qualification more or less is used because some countries will be required to limit emissions to a level a few percentage points below 6 percent of 1990 emissions levels, whereas other countries will be a few percentage points above this level. The UNFCCC web site contains the emissions limit for each Annex I country. Annex II countries, which include all countries not in Annex I (essentially the low- and middle-income countries of South America, Central America and Caribbean, Africa, Asia, and the Pacific Islands) are not required to limit their emissions at all.

An important aspect of the Kyoto Protocol is the specification of "flexibility provisions." These provisions are designed to allow countries that have a high marginal abatement cost to find cheaper opportunities to reduce emissions, essentially by trading emissions rights, although the treaty does not specify a formal mechanism for trading. Countries for which the cost of emissions reductions could be high include the high-income countries, because they already employ relatively energy efficient production technologies. Countries for which the cost of emissions abatement is likely to be relatively low include low- and middle-income countries that use old, energy-inefficient technology. Switching to newer, cleaner technology is a low-cost means of reducing emissions, one that is essentially unavailable to high-income countries that already employ these technologies.[3]

Three flexibility provisions are contained in the Kyoto Protocol: a bubble provision, joint implementation, and the clean development mechanism. The bubble provision treats a group of countries that are in a formal union as

---

[2]When this book went to press, the total emissions of the ratifying countries was 44.2 percent, according to the UNFCCC web site.

[3]A notable exception to this high-income country/energy-efficient and low-income country/energy-inefficient dichotomy is the passenger car, which could improve energy efficiency at relatively low cost in comparison with other facets of energy consumption in the United States and other high-income countries.

Box 7.3 Global Warming and Equity

Chapter 5 discussed three types of equity issues important to consider when examining environmental change and environmental policy: equity across groups in a country, equity across different countries, and equity across different generations. All three types of equity issues are significant when examining global climate change issues.

Intracountry equity has important implications for two reasons. First, there will be large regional differences in the impacts of global climate change. Some areas will become drier while some become wetter, some areas will become hotter while others become colder, and coastal areas have a whole set of impacts associated with sea-level rise and increased storm intensity. Second, different groups within a country will have different abilities to adapt to global climate change. For example, if a country has substantially increased summer hot spells, higher-income people who have access to air conditioning will suffer less than lower-income people who do not. High-income coastal cities will be able to construct seawalls for protection, but low-income or agricultural areas will remain vulnerable to erosion, inundation, and storm surge.

Equity considerations across countries are important both for the same reasons discussed with intracountry equity and for additional reasons. These additional factors concern the relative generation of greenhouse gas emissions across countries of different income levels. If high-income countries generate most of the greenhouse gas emissions, is it equitable to ask low-income countries to forgo potential economic growth by limiting greenhouse gas emissions?

Finally, intergenerational equity considerations are important because of the long period of time during which today's emissions will generate damages. Addressing the problem requires the current generation to incur costs, but if the problem remains unaddressed, future generations will suffer large damages from global climate change and sea-level rise. Because future generations are unrepresented in today's policy debates, it is critically important to consider the fairness of our decisions with regard to future generations.

if they were one country. The limitations of the individual countries are then summed to create a limitation for the whole group; reductions can take place in any country and count toward the group. The bubble analogy is used, because the provision can be viewed as an imaginary bubble of plastic above all the countries in the group, with only the virtual smokestack coming out of the bubble subject to limitations. The bubble provision is important for the European Union (EU), because some areas of the EU (such as former East Germany) and the former communist members of the EU still employ very inefficient technologies that can be replaced by more efficient technologies.

Moreover, the emissions for these former communist countries peaked around 1990, so they are actually producing fewer emissions than 1990, making it easier for the EU as a whole to meet its limits.

The joint implementation provisions allow an Annex I country to pay for some emissions reductions in another Annex I country. The paying country then gets credit for the reductions towards meeting its Kyoto restrictions, instead of the country that generates the emissions. This is somewhat similar to an emissions trading program, although formal permits would not necessarily be required. However, like an emissions trading program, joint implementation would help to ensure that emissions reductions take place at the lowest possible marginal abatement cost. Annex II countries are not allowed to participate in joint implementation, because they have no formal limits.

The clean development mechanism (detailed at http://cdm.unfccc.int) allows for limited trading opportunities between Annex I and Annex II countries, although it is even further from a true marketable permit system than joint implementation. The clean development mechanism allows an Annex I country (or a firm or nongovernmental organization within the country) to pay for a project that results in a reduction in an Annex II country that would not otherwise have occurred there. Because "would otherwise not have occurred" is somewhat subjective, the Kyoto Protocol has a formal procedure for determining if a particular project or investment would qualify.

What Is Wrong with the Kyoto Protocol?

Casual observation of the recent news media reveals two widely divergent positions among the public at large concerning the Kyoto Protocol. One group believes that the cost of implementing the Kyoto Protocol is extremely high, so the agreement should be abandoned. This position is the one held by the George W. Bush administration. The other group believes that the ratification and implementation of the Kyoto Protocol will save the world from global climate change. Both opinions are based on erroneous assumptions and are quite simply, very likely to be incorrect.

The cost of implementing the Kyoto Protocol (or some other variant of an emissions limitation agreement) will be considered in the following section. This section of the chapter deals with the inability of the Kyoto Protocol to have a significant impact on global climate change.

The Kyoto Protocol will be ineffective in slowing the onset of global climate change and reducing its magnitude for two reasons. First, the freezing of emissions at 1990 levels does not stabilize atmospheric concentrations of carbon dioxide, because carbon dioxide emissions remain in the atmosphere for centuries after their emissions. Atmospheric concentrations will continue to increase at a rapid pace before stabilizing at a level associated with dramatic climate change in the very distant future. Figure 7.7 illustrates different paths of accumulation and stabilization points for alternative emissions scenarios. To stabilize concentrations at a less damaging level, the current level of emissions must be frozen at a level substantially less than 1990 levels, and then

Figure 7.7 Emissions and Climate Stabilization

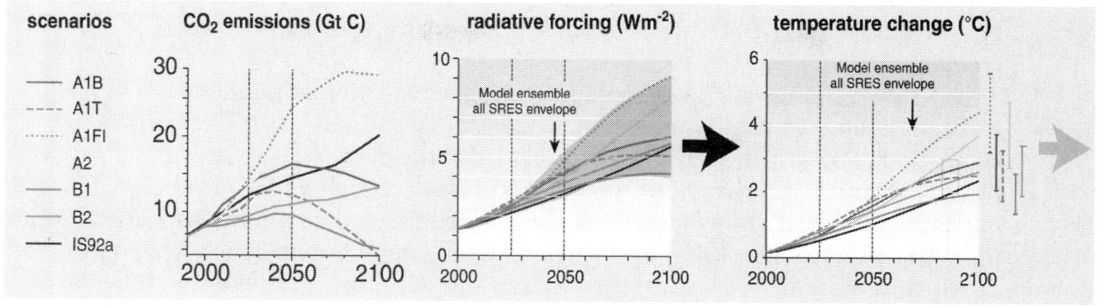

Source: IPCC (2001).

emissions must be continually reduced thereafter. Second, the Kyoto Protocol only requires a stabilization of emissions from Annex I countries. Annex II countries are not required to reduce emissions or even to have any future cap on emissions. There are no provisions to slow emissions from Annex II countries. This issue is particularly distressing, because Annex II countries include populous nations with rapidly industrializing economies, such as India, China, Brazil, and Mexico. These four countries have a combined population of about two and a half billion people. If these countries choose development paths that give them the same per capita emissions of carbon dioxide as currently seen in the United States, then the emissions from these four countries would exceed the current emissions levels of the entire world. Annex II countries need to stabilize their emissions levels, not necessarily at current levels but certainly below the levels currently seen in the industrialized West. If not, then mean global temperature could increase by even more than the 5.8° C that is the upper bound estimate of the IPCC.

In the opinion of the author of this book, the Kyoto Protocol will not substantially mitigate global climate change. One could think of the Kyoto Protocol as a Band-aid, as window dressing, or as the signatory nations taking credit for addressing global climate change when not much will be accomplished by the treaty. A new agreement needs to be negotiated and suggestions are provided later in this chapter.

What Is the Cost of Reducing Emissions?

The cost of achieving reductions in greenhouse gas emissions is an important aspect of the debate concerning global climate change policy. In fact, the cost of emissions reductions to the U.S. economy was the reason cited by President George W. Bush for pulling out of the Kyoto Protocol process.

Many studies have measured the cost of reducing greenhouse gas emissions to 1990 levels. They have been synthesized in two IPCC reports.[4] Studies of abatement cost generally fall into one of two categories, top-down studies or bottoms-up studies. Both types of studies are synthesized in the two IPCC reports.

Top-down studies are based on aggregate macroeconomic models such as the computable general equilibrium (CGE) models discussed in Chapter 6. CGE models look at how the various sectors of the economy are linked and how a potential disturbance to the economy (such as tighter environmental regulations) ripples its way through the interconnected economy, showing the ultimate impact on GDP. As mentioned in Chapter 6, two major types of problems are associated with these types of models. First, they do not show how an improvement in environmental quality can have a positive impact on GDP. This type of mechanism usually does not exist in these types of models. This omission is serious, because the reduction of CO_2 emissions will be partially achieved in a way that reduces the emissions of other types of pollution, such as volatile organic compounds, sulfur dioxide, nitrogen oxides, and carbon monoxide. For example, if reductions in CO_2 are achieved by utilizing more energy-efficient capital, all types of emissions will fall as less energy is used. This reduction in other types of pollution would have a positive impact on GDP, as discussed in Chapter 6. The other major problem is that these types of models impose the disturbance (such as restrictions on emissions or higher energy costs) on the economy, but do not allow the economy to adjust to the new conditions. They assume that economic activity will be conducted in the same way as in the past, without making adjustments.

According to the 1996 and 2003 IPCC reports, the impact of stabilizing greenhouse gas emissions at 1990 levels that is forecast by the top-down models is to reduce the GDP of OECD countries by 0.5 percent to 2 percent of the levels they would otherwise attain. If full emissions trading were allowed, the impact on GDP would be substantially lower (0.1 percent to 1.1 percent), according to these studies. Because of the problems listed, however, this forecast should be viewed as an upper bound estimate, with the actual cost likely to be below it.

The IPCC studies report that the bottoms-up studies show a much lower cost and that the 1990 levels could actually be attained at "negative cost," implying that production costs would actually be lowered through achieving the 1990 emissions levels. Bottoms-up models look at engineering cost estimates of implementing the type of technologies necessary to achieve the target emissions levels. Overall costs are low or negative. The initial capital costs of purchasing and installing more energy-efficient capital are more than offset by the energy savings that result. This benefit occurs without a drastic

---

[4]Intergovernmental Panel on Climate Change, Climate Change 2001: Synthesis Report (2003), and Intergovernmental Panel on Climate Change Summary for Policymakers: The Economic and Social Dimensions of Climate Change–IPCC Working Group III (1996). Both reports are available at http://www.ipcc.ch.

Box 7.4 Is Climate Change a Benefit-Cost Problem?

Although many economists believe that the development of global warming policy should be based on cost-benefit analysis, other scholars, such as Peter Brown of the School of Environmental Science at McGill University, argue otherwise. Brown's position is that the use of cost-benefit analysis has implications for centuries to come, so it is qualitatively different than the problems that cost-benefit analysis was designed to examine.

Brown (1991) argues that it is extremely difficult to measure costs and benefits associated with global warming. This opinion is shared by many economists. Brown references Epstein and Gupta (1990), who assert that the problem can be framed in principle in cost-benefit terms, but state that "for the moment, it is not feasible because of the profound uncertainties surrounding the MB [marginal benefits] and, for different reasons, the MC [marginal costs] curves (p. 33)." Brown argues that the problems of deciding what to measure, the possibility of surprises, the extremely long time horizons, and the difficulties of predicting technical change make the execution of a cost-benefit analysis virtually impossible. More serious than these problems in execution, Brown argues that problems of principle render cost-benefit techniques inappropriate. According to Brown, these problems revolve around discounting, differences in kind, distribution issues, the issue of rationality, and the scope of benefits.

Brown argues that there are three conceptual problems associated with discounting. First, he argues that some things cannot be discounted. Certain resources, such as cultural resources and national parks, we regard as our duty to preserve for posterity. The use of discounting would imply that it is acceptable and even desirable to eventually consume these resources. Second, even in applications where discounting may be important, there is a problem with determining the appropriate discount rate. Finally, Brown argues that discounting "imperils the future by undervaluing it."

Brown also suggests that there are substantial differences in kind among resources that are affected by global warming and typical market goods. Cost-benefit techniques require that everything be measured in a money metric and that

> it is foolish to think that literally everything under the sun should be subject to the measure of money. . . . The Congressional Medal of Honor cannot be bought, nor a chair in the Economics Department at the University of Chicago, at any price. New ivory cannot be legally purchased nor can a car without a seatbelt. (Brown, 1991, p. 36)

In addition, Brown points out that cost-benefit techniques do not adequately deal with distributive issues, including developed

(continues)

Box 7.4 (continued)

country/developing country and intergenerational issues, which are fundamental to the problem of global warming.

Brown also rejects the argument that rational decision making must be founded in the type of knowledge revealed by cost-benefit analysis. He argues that this assertion is based on a confusion about the meaning of rationality and suggests that rationality has two parts: an end (somehow specified) and a rational means to that end. Although cost-benefit analysis may be a rational means to the end of maximizing discounted present value, the rationality of that means does not imply that maximized present value is an appropriate end in the context of global warming.

Finally, Brown asserts that there is the question of the scope of the benefits. Cost-benefit analysis, founded in the principles of classical economics, looks at benefits and costs to humans. He argues that it is not clear that the analysis should only be concerned with humans and that global climate policy should be concerned with benefits and costs to other living organisms.

Brown argues that rather than viewing global climate change in a cost-benefit context, the global warming problem should be viewed in a "planetary trust" framework. Instead, he argues that we should adopt the framework of Edith Weiss (1984). As Brown describes the framework:

> . . . each generation has a responsibility to those who follow to preserve the earth's natural and human heritage at a level at which it is received. The responsibility to preserve certain definite things, for example, intact ecosystems and national monuments. Our obligations are not discharged simply by achieving the highest present value of consumption. (Brown, 1991, p. 38)

Is Brown correct? Is the global warming problem inherently unsuited to cost-benefit analysis? Obviously, people who reject the economic paradigm would answer yes to this question. Some people who accept the economic paradigm would also argue that cost-benefit analysis cannot answer every question and that issues such as discounting the distant future, other equity issues, measurement difficulties, and the rights of nonhuman organisms are not addressed by cost-benefit analysis. Many of these same economists, however, would also argue that even though cost-benefit analysis has limitations and should not be the only basis on which decisions are made, it still can contribute insight to the decision-making process. In short, cost-benefit analysis can add perspective to understanding the global warming problem, but it should not be the only perspective. See Chapter 5 for a discussion of additional and alternative criteria for evaluation.

movement away from fossil fuels. In addition are the benefits of reduced emissions of other types of pollution. Because these policies would result in an increase in social welfare, independent of the benefits of reduced global climate change, Nordhaus (1994, 1998) refers to these types of policies as "no regrets" policies. Thus, if we implemented these policies and it later turned out that the impacts of global change were far less than expected, then we would still think they are good policies.

If even the top-down models show a rather modest cost of attaining the 1990 emissions levels and if the bottom-down models show that it is likely to be a "no regrets" policy, why is there all this excitement about costs? There are three reasons. First, there is uncertainty about the costs, and some people may anticipate that the actual costs will turn out to be greater than anticipated. Second, the costs are felt very quickly as energy inefficient capital is replaced with more energy-efficient capital, necessitating substantial expenditures. The cost savings would then come in over the next several decades because less energy would need to be purchased. Finally, some sectors of the economy will be hurt more drastically than others. For example, the fossil fuel industry is a certain loser (unless it switches to the production of alternative fuels) if the reduction of emissions is required. Other sectors of the economy will benefit, but those that are likely to be hurt are certain to promote vigorously the idea that emissions limitations are too costly to implement.

Rethinking an International Treaty on Global Climate Change

It is clear that the Kyoto Protocol has problems, both in terms of what it does not do and the likelihood that the United States and Russia (maybe) will not participate in the accord. This section of the textbook[5] examines the obstacles to developing a better treaty and how the agreement could be structured to provide an effective program to reduce the problem of global climate change.

In previous sections of this chapter, four problems associated with the Kyoto Protocol were delineated:

- Ineffectiveness of initial levels of emissions reductions in preventing global climate change
- Lack of provisions to generate future reductions below the initial levels
- Lack of emissions reductions by developing nations, particularly large nations such as China, India, Brazil, and Mexico
- Potential high cost of emissions reductions, especially if the reduction is more ambitious than the Kyoto Protocol standard of 1990 emissions levels

[5]Much of this section is based on Kahn and Franceschi, "It is Broke, So Fix It: Suggestions for a Revised Treaty on Greenhouse Gas Emissions," 2004.

For a treaty to be effective, it must deal with all these issues. These four issues essentially reduce to one important point: An international treaty must result in greater reduction in emissions, yet not be too costly, either in total or for any particular country. If a treaty can generate effective reductions without objectionably high costs, then there is a good probability that the nations of the world would participate in the accord.

One point, that the initial levels of emissions reductions must be more ambitious than the Kyoto Protocol requires, is likely to cause problems in attaining an international consensus, especially because being aggressive in reducing emissions is likely to result in higher costs than those associated with the Kyoto Protocol (which could even be negative). Thus, it is critically important that the methods used to reduce emissions allow the maximum flexibility in choosing the lowest cost abatement strategies.

As discussed intensively in Chapter 3, both marketable pollution permits and pollution taxes can induce a reduction in emissions and minimize abatement costs by equating marginal abatement costs across polluters. In an international context, even with all countries participating in an accord, it would be somewhat more difficult to achieve. To minimize global abatement costs, we would either need a marketable carbon permit system that included all countries or we would need all countries to charge the same carbon tax.[6] Neither is very unlikely to occur, because the developing countries are not likely to agree to either a cap on their emissions or to charge a tax equal to the one that would be charged in developed countries.

Developing countries oppose such measures because they view the global warming problem as created by the industrialized countries; they believe that it is primarily the responsibility of the industrialized countries to make the sacrifices necessary to fix the problem. In particular, developing countries do not want to constrain their potential development as a result of meeting emissions limitations. Because their standard of living is already lower than that of the developed countries, the developing nations will not agree to immediate (and perhaps not future) limits on their emissions of greenhouse gases.

That developing countries will not accept a limit on emissions renders a global trading system unworkable. Although developed countries could implement such a system among the developed countries, it would have two major shortcomings. First, it would do nothing to limit the emissions of developing countries. Second, agreement on an initial cap does nothing to create the continuous reduction in emissions that will be needed into the future to stabilize atmospheric concentrations of greenhouse gases at levels that do not generate severe global climate change.

Cooper (1998) suggests an alternative treaty based on agreement on a tax level rather than on limits on emissions. Although he acknowledges that

---

[6] In this context, carbon refers to both carbon dioxide and the carbon dioxide equivalents of other greenhouse gases.

there may be difficulties administering such a tax in developing nations, he believes that it would be much more likely to achieve developing country participation under such a system. Kahn and Franceschi (2004) build on the proposal of Cooper and suggest a tax-based system that could be acceptable to both developed and developing nations.

The primary component of the proposed tax system is a set of differential taxes. Taxes have the important properties of always creating an incentive for technological innovation and always creating an incentive for reducing the level of emissions. This incentive is illustrated in Figure 7.8, which shows the marginal abatement cost function of a particular firm. If the marginal abatement cost function is equal to MAC_1 in Figure 7.8 and a tax is implemented equal to T_1, then the firm would immediately reduce its emissions to E_1. It would not stop there, however. By implementing technological innovation, the firm could reduce its marginal abatement cost to MAC_2. It would then have an incentive to reduce its emissions to E_2. It would cost the firm area acE_1E_2 in additional abatement costs to reduce from E_1 to E_2, but it would save area abE_1E_2 in taxes, for a net cost saving of area abc. As long as there is a tax, there is an incentive to look for technological innovation and reduce the level of emissions.

For the tax to be as effective as possible, it must, at a minimum, be inflation-proof. The tax should be indexed to inflation so that the real value of the tax does not decline over time. In addition, if aggressive reductions in

Figure 7.8 Carbon Tax and Reduction in Emissions

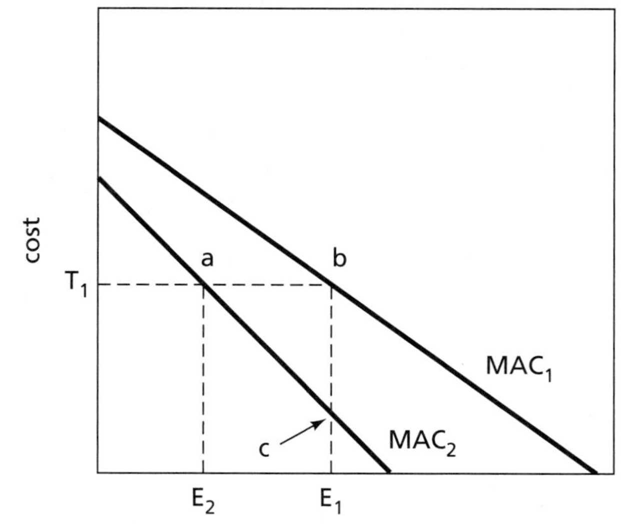

Source: IPCC (2001).

emissions are desired as we move into the future, the real value of the tax should be increasing over time. For example, the treaty could specify that the real value of the carbon tax should increase by 3 percent per year for the next 20 years, which would almost double the tax over these twenty years. In contrast, a system of marketable pollution permits would require an agreement on the level of permits every year. Either the permits must be short-lived in length, with the treaty specifying the decline in the number of permits each year, or the treaty must be periodically renegotiated, with a declining level of permits in each renegotiation.

A further advantage of a tax system is that it reduces uncertainty about costs of attaining emissions reductions. The cost can be no higher than the tax multiplied by the emissions levels, because if the abatement costs began to increase as emissions were reduced, the firms would pay the tax instead of further reducing emissions.

An important issue is why countries, particularly developing countries, might be willing to agree to participate in a tax system, especially given the political resistance to imposing taxes that is seen in many countries and is particularly important in the United States. An answer was developed in Chapter 6, when the double dividend of pollution taxes was discussed. The pollution tax could be used to reduce income tax, reduce corporate taxes, or invest in public investments such as education. Moreover, it would be possible to increase the likelihood of the participation of developing countries by devising a tax for developed countries where a portion of the taxes went into a fund that was distributed to developing countries for general development purposes. Developed countries that had higher per capita emissions could face a higher tax level. The per unit carbon tax in developing countries could be lower than that in developed countries, increasing the competitiveness of their industries. In addition, all the tax that was collected in a developing country would stay in that country, where it could be used for whatever purpose the country desired, such as lowering income taxes, investing in education, and research and development.

Over time, the emissions taxes that the various countries faced could be adjusted to try to equalize emissions per capita. The higher the emissions per capita, the higher could be the emissions taxes, giving these high emission countries an incentive to reduce even more. Although many details would need to be worked out to implement such an international system for controlling greenhouse gas emissions, the current Kyoto Protocol will not have a substantial impact on the atmospheric concentration of greenhouse gases and associated global climate change.

Summary

Global warming and the depletion of the ozone layer are important environmental problems that are quite different from conventional pollution problems. The long lags between emissions and damages, the long lifetimes of the pollutants, and the complexity of the scientific relationships make the development of policy a difficult question.

As a global society, we have moved more quickly on ozone-depleting chemicals than on greenhouse gases. International agreements call for bans on the most damaging of these chemicals, and policies are being developed to address all ozone-depleting chemicals.

In contrast, the movement toward resolution of the global climate change problem has been much more halting, and the Kyoto Protocol does not hold much promise for success. More innovative international agreements need to be implemented that will address the problems associated with the Kyoto Protocol. These problems include the following:

- Ineffectiveness of initial levels of emissions reductions in preventing global climate change
- Lack of provisions to generate future reductions below the initial levels
- Lack of emissions reductions by developing nations, particularly large nations such as China, India, Brazil, and Mexico
- Potential high cost of emissions reductions, especially if the reduction is more ambitious than the Kyoto Protocol standard of 1990 emissions levels

Review Questions

1. What are the major greenhouse gases, and what are their sources of emissions?
2. What is the evidence that average global warming is increasing?
3. What is the role of adaptability in mitigating the damages from global warming?
4. Why does the minimization of abatement costs require the development of policies to control all greenhouse gases and not just CO_2?
5. Assume that the time paths of the radiative forcing (RF) of a kilogram of two gases are given by the following linear equations:

   Gas A: RF = 70 – 0.25 (TIME)

   Gas B: RF

   Gas A: RF = 200 – 0.1 (TIME)

   What is the 50-year GWPI of gas A in terms of gas B? What is the corresponding 100-year GWPI?

Questions for Further Study

1. Why is international cooperation necessary for controlling greenhouse gas emissions?
2. What is the Montreal Protocol? Do its provisions make economic sense?
3. What does Nordhaus mean by "no regret" global warming policies? Can you think of any "no regret" polices in addition to those proposed by Nordhaus?
4. Can cost-benefit analysis be used to develop global warming policy?
5. What are the equity issues surrounding global warming policy?

Suggested Paper Topics

1. Look at the equity issues involving global warming policy. Pay particular attention to developed versus developing country issues.

Your best places to start are the web sites of the IPCC (http://www.unep.ch/) and the U.S. Global Climate Change Research Program (http://www.usgcrp.gov/). Also look at referenced works by Cline (1992), Dornbusch and Poterba (1991), Manne and Richels (1992), NAS (1991), Nordhaus (1994, 1998), and Weiss (1984).

2. Global warming and energy use are obviously intertwined. Look at alternative energy policies, particularly for developing countries, and see how energy policy can be used to reduce global warming. Make sure to talk about how policy can affect economic behavior; do not just concentrate on "technological fixes." Again, a good place to start is the web site of the IPCC. Also look at referenced works by Cline (1992), Dornbusch and Poterba (1991), Manne and Richels (1992), NAS (1991), and Weiss (1984), as well as current issues of *Energy Economist*.

3. Choose a particular sector of the economy (such as agriculture, transportation, electrical generation, or forestry) and look at how global warming will affect the industry and how the industry affects global warming. Suggest policies that can mitigate the impact of global warming on the industry. Suggest policies that can reduce the industry's impact on global warming at the least cost to the industry. Start by looking at works by Nordhaus and NAS.

4. Global warming requires international cooperation. Look at existing mechanisms for promoting international cooperation and discuss how institutions can be changed to increase cooperation. Pay particular attention to how new institutions can develop ways to increase a country's self-interest in reducing greenhouse emissions or sequestering carbon. Start by looking at referenced works by Böhringer, Finus and Vogt (2002), Cline (1992), Dornbusch and Poterba (1991), Kerr (2000), Manne and Richels (1992), NAS (1991), Swanson and Johnston (1999), and Weiss (1984), as well as current issues of *Energy Economist*.

5. Choose a particular country and analyze the impacts of global climate change on this country. Begin your search for resources with the IPCC reports.

Works Cited and Selected Readings

Adger, W. N. Social Capital, Collective Action and Adaptation to Climate Change. *Economic Geography 79* (2003): 387–404.

Ausabel, J. H. A Second Look at the Impacts of Climate Change. *American Scientist 79* (1991): 210–221.

Ayres, R. U., and J. Walter. The Greenhouse Effect: Damages, Costs and Abatement. *Environment and Resource Economics 1* (1991): 237–270.

Babiker, M., J. Reilly, and H. Jacob. The Kyoto Protocol and Developing Countries. *Energy Policy 28* (2000): 525–536.

Barker, T., J. Kohler, and M. Villena. Costs of Greenhouse Gas Abatement: Meta-analysis of Post-SRES Mitigation Scenarios. *Environmental Economics and Policy Studies 5*, no. 2 (2002): 135–166.

Bohm, P. Deposit-Refund Systems: Theory and Application to Environmental Conservation and Consumer Policy. Washington: Resources for the Future, 1988.

Böhringer, C., M. Finus, and C. Vogt, eds. *Controlling Global Warming: Perspectives from Economics, Game Theory and Public Choice*. Cheltenham UK: Edward Elgar, 2002.

Brown, P. G. Why Climate Change Is Not a Cost/Benefit Problem. Pages 33–34 in *Global Climate Change: The Economic Costs of Mitigation and Adaptation*, edited by J. C. White. New York: Elsevier, 1991.

Caldwell, M. M., A. H. Teramura, and M. Tevini. The Changing Solar Ultraviolet Climate and the Ecological Climate for Higher Plants. *Trends in Ecology and Evolution 4*, (1989): 363–367.

Carraro, C., B. Buchner, and I. Cersosimo. On the Consequences of the U.S. Withdrawal from the Kyoto/Bonn Protocol. Discussion Paper 2001/102, Fondazione Eni Enrico Mattei Note di Lavoro: 2001/102, 2001.

Cline, W. R. *Global Warming: The Economic Stakes*. Washington, DC: Institute for International Economics, 1992.

Cline, W. R. Give Greenhouse Abatement a Fair Chance. *Finance and Development 30* (1993): 3–5.

Cooper, R. Toward a Real Global Warming Treaty. *Foreign Affairs 77*, no. 2 (1998): 66–79.

Crowley, T. J. Remembrance of Things Past: Greenhouse Lessons from the Geologic Record. *Consequences 2*, no. 1, (1996): 2–13.

Dornbusch, R., and J. M. Poterba, eds. *Global Warming: Economic Policy Responses*. Cambridge MA: MIT Press, 1991.

Epstein, J. M., and R. Gupta. *Controlling the Greenhouse Effect: Five Regimes Compared*. Washington. DC: The Brookings Institute, 1990.

Funkhouser, S. The Economic Costs of Global Warming Damage: A Survey. University of Birmingham Economics Dept. Discussion Paper, March 1994.

Gore, A. *Earth in the Balance*. New York: Houghton-Mifflin, 1992.

Griffen, J. M., ed. *Global Climate Change: The Science, Economics and Politics*. Cheltenham UK: Edward Elgar, 2003.

Hall, D., and R. Howard. *The Long Term Economics of Climate Change*. Amsterdam: Elsevier, 2001.

Hourcade, J. C., and F. Ghersi. The Economics of a Lost Deal, Discussion Paper 01-48. Online: www.rff.org/rff/Documents/RFF-DP-01-48.pdf, December 2001.

Houghton, J. T., G. J. Jenkins, and J. J. Ephraums. *Climate Change: The IPCC Scientific Assessment*. Cambridge: Cambridge University Press, 1990.

Intergovernment Panel on Climate Change (IPCC). *1992 IPCC Supplement*. Cambridge: Cambridge University Press, 1992.

Intergovernment Panel on Climate Change (IPCC). *Climate Change 1995: The Science of Climate Change*. Cambridge: Cambridge University Press, 1996.

Intergovernment Panel on Climate Change (IPCC). Climate Change 2001: Synthesis Report. Online: http://www.pcc.ch/pub/un/sirens/spm.pdf.

Kahn, J. R., and D. Franceschi. It is Broke, So Fix It: Rethinking an International Treaty on Greenhouse Gas Emissions. Working Paper, Washington and Lee University, 2004.

Kolstad, C., and M. Toman. The Economics of Climate Policy, Resources for the Future. Discussion Paper 00-40REV. Online: www.rff.org/rff/Documents/RFF-DP-00-40.pdf, June 2001.

Krause, F., W. Bach, and J. Koomey. *Energy Policy in the Greenhouse*. London: Earthscan, 1990.

Lange, A., Expected Utility and MaxMin. *Environmental and Resource Economics 25* (2003): 417–434.

Leiby, P., and J. Rubin. Bankable Permits for the Control of Stock and Flow Pollutants. Optimal Intertemporal Greenhouse Gas Trading, unpublished paper, Oak Ridge National Laboratory, Oak Ridge, TN, 1997.

Lopez, T. M., A Look at Climate Change and the Evolution of the Kyoto Protocol. *Natural Resources Journal 43* (2003): 285–312.

Manne, A. S., and R. G. Richels. *Buying Greenhouse Insurance: The Economic Costs of CO_2* Emission Limits. Cambridge MA: MIT Press, 1992.

National Academy of Sciences (NAS). *Policy Implications of Global Warming*. Washington, DC: National Academy Press, 1991.

Nordhaus, W. D. Economic Approaches to Greenhouse Warming. Pages 33–67 in *Global Warming: Economic Policy Responses*, edited by R. Dornbusch and J. M. Poterba. Cambridge MA: MIT Press, 1991a.

Nordhaus, W. D. To Slow or Not to Slow: The Economics of the Greenhouse Effect. *Economic Journal 101* (1991b): 920–937.

Nordhaus, W. D. *Managing the Global Commons*. Cambridge, MA: MIT Press, 1994.

Nordhaus, W. D., ed. *Economics and Policy Issues in Climate Change*. Washington, DC: Resources for the Future, 1998.

Nordhaus, W. D., and J. Boyer. *Warming the World: Economic Models of Global Warming*. Cambridge, MA: MIT Press, 2000.

Peck, S. C., and J. J. Tiesbers, Global Warming Uncertainties and the Value of Information: An Analysis Using CETA. Pages 555–581 in *The Economics of Global Warming*, edited by T. Tietenberg, Cheltenham UK, 1997.

Pizer, W. A. Climate Change Catastrophes. Resources for the Future Discussion Paper 03-31. Online: www.rff.org/rff/Documents/RFF-DP-03-31.pdf, May 2003.

Quiggin, J., and J. Horowitz. Costs of Adjustment to Climate Change. *Australian Journal of Resource and Environmental Economics 47* (2003): 429–446.

Rubbelke, D. T. G. An Analysis of Differing Abatement Incentives. *Resource and Energy Economics 25*, no. 3 (August 2003): 269–294.

Schelling, T. C. Some Economics of Global Warming. *American Economic Review 82* (1992): 1–14.

Schneider, S. Climate Change Scenarios for Greenhouse Increases. Pages 17–48 in *Technologies for a Greenhouse Constrained Society*. Oak Ridge, TN: Oak Ridge National Laboratory, 1991.

Solomon, S., and D. L. Albritton. Time dependent ozone depletion potentials for short and long-term forecasts. *Nature 357* (1992): 33–37.

Solow, A. R. Is There a Global Warming Problem? Pages 7–28 in *Global Warming: Economic Policy Responses*, edited by R. Dornbusch and J. M. Poterba. Cambridge MA: MIT Press, 1991.

Toman, M., ed. *Climate Change Economics and Policy*. Washington, DC: Resources for the Future, 2001.

Weber, M., and G. Hauer. A Regional Analysis of Climate Change Impacts on Canadian Agriculture. *Canadian Public Policy 29*, no. 2 (June 2003): 163–180.

Weiss, E. B. The Planetary Trust: Conservation and Intergenerational Equity. *Ecology Law Quarterly 2* (1984): 445–581.

World Resources Institute. *World Resources 1992–93*. New York: Oxford University Press, 1992.

Yohe, G. W. The Cost of Not Holding Back the Sea: Economic Vulnerability. *Ocean and Shoreline Management 15* (1991): 223–255.

chapter 8

Energy Production and the Environment

> *Energy production and use are vital to the economies and environments of all countries. Furthermore, the mix of energy sources has profound consequences for environmental quality.*
>
> *World Resources 1992–93*

Introduction

The above quotation, which appears in the energy chapter of *World Resources 1992–93*, illustrates the central role of energy in both economic and environmental policy. The production and consumption of energy is not only crucial to the health of economies in both developed and developing countries, but it is responsible for a large portion of the environmental problems that these countries experience. In fact, the relationship between energy and the environment is so important that this book devotes three chapters to the subject. In Chapter 7, the problem of global climate change was discussed. As noted in that chapter, fossil fuel consumption is the primary source of the greenhouse gas emissions, which are responsible for global climate change. In Chapter 8, the focus is on the production of energy and how that impacts the environment. Of course other issues, such as the national security implications of energy imports are also discussed. Chapter 9 focuses on the use of energy and its implications for environmental quality.

The focus of this chapter—the relationship between energy production and the environment—is not what immediately comes to mind when people think about the relationship between energy and the environment. Problems such as global climate change, acid rain, and conventional air pollutants (sulfur dioxide, nitrogen oxides, particulates, carbon monoxide, volatile organic compounds, and so on) that are associated with the use of fossil fuels are what immediately come to mind. The production of energy, however, can degrade the environment in many different ways. For example, water quality is often adversely affected by energy production activities such as drilling for oil and gas, cooling energy facilities, coal mining, and the underground storage of oil and gasoline. In addition, oil spills (of both the infrequent but catastrophic and small but chronic nature) pollute oceans and inland waterways. The production of energy also destroys habitat. Strip-mining removes the whole surface of the land and leads to vast changes in the landscape and to acid drainage problems. Oil activities in the wetlands of Louisiana are contributing factors to the steady loss of wetlands. The controversy of whether oil should be produced in the Arctic National Wildlife Refuge (ANWR) focuses on its impacts on this fragile ecosystem and the animal and indigenous human populations that depend on this ecosystem. Other examples of impacts of energy production include the creation by coal mining of a large amount of solid waste, the impact of agriculture (biomass energy crops) on water quality, and aesthetic impacts of wind turbines for the generation of electricity.

Although many textbooks focus on the question of whether the market will ensure adequate supplies of energy in the future, this chapter focuses on the energy/environment interface. Questions of how the market supplies energy are also addressed, because the nature of the supply of energy has an important impact on its interaction with the environment. In addition, the chapter looks at the social cost of dependence on foreign oil.

The Historical Development of U.S. Energy Policy in the Post–World War II Era

The formulation of energy policy has been substantially influenced by concerns about supply and, in turn, it has influenced the way in which energy is supplied. Before examining the interactions between energy and the environment, an examination of past policy is useful, including an examination of those factors that motivated the policies and their effects on the supply of energy.

Intellectual Antecedents

Even though they did not focus directly on energy, two authors have had a very strong influence on the way the United States and other Western nations think about energy: Thomas Malthus (1798) and Harold Hotelling

Box 8.1 Oil Spills and the Optimal Level of Safety

In 1989, the *Exxon Valdez* ran aground in the Prince William Sound area off the coast of Alaska, causing a spill of millions of gallons of oil which killed fish, birds, marine mammals, and other organisms, and fouled the shore. This widely publicized event sparked a debate on whether we should ship oil in this area and continue the threat to the environment or halt the shipment of Alaskan oil in order to protect the environment. As with most highly emotional political debates, this one focused on two polar extremes and did not debate the critical issue.

The critical issue in this case is not to decide a thumbs up or thumbs down on Alaskan oil, but to determine the optimal level of safety in shipping Alaskan oil. There are many actions that can be undertaken to reduce the chances of a spill taking place, to reduce the magnitude of a spill if one does take place, and to reduce the damages associated with a spill of a given size. Actions that would lessen the chances of a spill taking place include placing computerized collision avoidance systems on oil tankers (and obstacles such as shoals and islands), requiring redundancy among key personnel (so that if the captain becomes incapacitated there is an equally skilled person in position to take over), and restricting other shipping when a tanker is in the shipping lanes. Actions that would lessen the amount of oil spilled if an accident did take place would include requiring double-hulled tankers and multiple oil compartments (like the cells of a car battery) in the tanker. These features reduce the amount of oil released if the hull is punctured. Actions that would lessen the damages of a spill that occurred would include requiring standby cleanup and containment equipment and crews that could be called into action the moment a spill occurs.

An important question for policy makers is how to ensure that appropriate safety measures are taken. Two options are available: economic incentives and command and control techniques. The system of economic incentives that would be most appropriate in this case is the development of liability rules. Liability rules would make oil transportation companies responsible to pay the damages for spills that they cause. Under CERCLA and the Oil Pollution ACT, the federal government, state governments, local governments, and Native American nations have the legal right to sue for damages to public resources from oil and chemical spills. In order for liability systems to be able to generate the optimal level of safety, court-awarded damages must be equal to the actual level of damages that are created by the spill. In addition, there must be a high degree of certainty that those who create the damage will be forced to pay for the damages, and that out-of-court settlements will not reduce the level of awarded damages to a level significantly below actual damages.

(1931). Malthus, whose work is discussed in more detail in Chapters 6, 18, and 19, argued that scarcity is inevitable because population grows to exhaust its resource endowment. Hotelling (whose work forms the conceptual basis for the discussion of dynamic efficiency in Chapter 2) argued that the invisible hand of the market would optimally allocate exhaustible resources and prevent shortages because the market price of a resource such as oil reflects both its current value and its future value. The debate about whether markets adequately address future supply continues to rage and is a motivating factor behind much of U.S. energy policy, particularly during the so-called energy crises of the 1970s.

Although the mechanics of dynamic market efficiency are discussed in Chapter 2 (with a numerical example in Appendix 2.b), it is worthwhile to summarize the intuition behind these mechanics, which are based on Hotelling's work. The fundamental proposition is that an oil producer (or producer of any other exhaustible resource) must be indifferent between selling a barrel of oil today and waiting for some future time to sell it. In other words, if the producer holds the oil, the producer will have higher income in the future if the price increases into the future. If the producer sells at the current time, he or she can take the revenue and invest it and earn income in the future.

If the producer expects prices to rise significantly in the future, he or she will plan to make more money by selling later, and the producer will wait. Other producers will behave similarly, reducing the amount of oil available in the present and increasing the anticipated amount of oil in the future. This behavior will increase price in the present and reduce expected price in the future. This type of price change will take place until all producers are indifferent between selling today and selling at some point in the future. As Hotelling demonstrates, today's price includes *user cost*, which is the opportunity cost of not having the oil available at other periods in the future. Because user cost is a component of market price, and because user cost is determined by the present demand, present supply, future demand, and future supply of oil, the market should efficiently allocate oil over the course of time, with user cost reflecting the scarcity value of the resource. As discussed in Chapter 2, dynamic efficiency requires that the price at any point in time be equal to marginal extraction cost plus marginal user cost. As detailed both in Chapter 2 and in the following paragraph, market forces ensure that this condition is met.

If future demand is perceived to be increasing or future supply is perceived to be decreasing, present user cost will increase. Current price will increase, which will reduce the quantity demanded, leaving more oil for the future. The higher current price will also encourage substitution of other fuels for oil as well as increased exploration for oil, investment in increased energy efficiency, and investment in technological improvements in oil extraction. In this depiction of market processes, completely running out of the resource (absolute scarcity) never occurs because increased price causes adjustments that mitigate scarcity. Scarcity is felt through increased price, which not only reduces the quantity demanded but also causes other adjustments that increase the supply of the resource and its substitutes.

This view of the way the market works implies that there is no need to have an energy policy, because the market works efficiently and will prevent a shortage of oil or other fuels. Of course, in his theoretical work, Hotelling assumed a market that met all the usual characteristics of a perfectly functioning market, including perfect information, no externalities, perfect competition, no public goods, and no monopoly or oligopoly power. Although some "free-market" advocates interpret him in this fashion, Hotelling never explicitly stated nor implied that consideration of these market failures was unnecessary.

In contrast, Malthus believed in the concept of absolute scarcity, which suggests that resources are used at an increasing rate until they are completely exhausted. Malthus argued that the population grows faster than the food supply, so the food supply not only acts as a constraint on growth but is always insufficient to allow the development of a surplus. People are always at the limit of the food supply and on the brink of starvation. Although Malthus's original arguments were couched solely in terms of land and food resources, his arguments have been extended by the "neo-Malthusians"[1] in terms of general resources and environmental quality. Neo-Malthusians argue that the growth of the economy and population will generate a dependence on resources that will eventually exceed capacity, so that both the economy and population face inevitable collapse. Although fewer people share this apocalyptic view of scarcity, many noneconomists believe in absolute scarcity and that one day we will simply run out of oil and other resources, with no effective substitutes available.

Although these two divergent views seemed to represent dominant paradigms of intellectual thought, U.S. energy policy did not follow either theory.[2] In the period before 1970, a state agency, the Texas Railroad Commission, controlled most of U.S. oil production through a set of Texas state regulations that defined drilling rights to underground pools that lay below lands owned by multiple owners. The regulations were ostensibly to protect against a common property externality, which is generated because the rate at which oil is removed from the pool determines how much can eventually be removed. The slower the retrieval rate, the greater the total output over time. Without regulations, multiple producers operating in a common oil field will race one another to remove the oil, which will lower the total amount that can be removed. Although this reason was the stated goal of regulation, the regulations also served to restrict present production and increase present price, creating short-term monopoly profits for oil producers.

The federal government also implemented several policies that operated mainly through favorable tax treatment. Intangible drilling expenses could be deducted as expenses, and an oil depletion allowance permitted oil deposits to be treated as depreciable assets. In addition, from 1959 to 1973, oil imports

---

[1]See Meadows et al. (1972), for example.

[2]The following discussion of the history of U.S. energy policy draws heavily on Alfred Marcus, *Controversial Issues in U.S. Energy Policy*, (Newbury Park, CA: Sage Publications, 1992).

were restricted, with the goal of promoting national security. This restriction also served to increase producer profits and reduce domestic oil reserves.

Natural gas policy was dictated by the Natural Gas Act of 1938, the purpose of which was to regulate natural gas transportation rates to keep them high enough to justify the large capital expenses of natural gas pipelines. Price regulation, however, was eventually extended past the transportation stage to regulate prices at the wellhead. This action seems to be part of an overall energy policy to keep prices low. As one might expect, however, this effort to keep prices low resulted in a reduction in production, a reduction in exploration activity, and a shortage of natural gas in the 1970s.

Government policy seemed to be oriented to keeping prices low and production and consumption high, probably because of a perceived link between cheap energy and economic growth. The shortsightedness of these policies, however, became apparent in the 1970s. This period saw declining U.S. oil production, an increase in oil imports, a shortage of natural gas, disruption of foreign oil supplies, and a drastic increase in energy prices. Policies designed to keep energy prices low combined with changing external factors to make prices rise through the 1970s rather than stay low. Marcus (1992, p. 46) lists three reasons price controls received popular support:

1. The existence of a widely held belief that high energy prices lead to inflation
2. Greater concern with equity than with efficiency
3. A perceived need to protect people from exploitation by oil companies that were believed to be earning windfall profits

This concern with oil company profits is understandable, because user cost is a component of the price of oil, and it creates a gap between marginal extraction costs and price. People who have not been exposed to the concept of user cost will perceive a disparity between price and marginal extraction cost as monopoly profits. Although monopoly profits could be present, user costs alone are capable of generating such a disparity. For example, people might read in the newspaper that in a particular oil field, oil is produced at a price of $8 per barrel and sold at the world price of $24 per barrel. They might conclude that the producer is making $16 of monopoly profit, which would represent a 200 percent markup over price. This $16, however, could reflect the scarcity value of not having the oil available in the future. Of course, the difference between price and marginal extraction cost could be a combination of monopoly profits and user cost. In any case, this difference is money that winds up in the pocket of the producer, fueling these equity concerns about exploitation of consumers by the oil-producing firms and oil-producing countries.

The Significance of OPEC

The Organization of Petroleum Exporting Countries (OPEC) is a cartel of oil-producing countries, formed in 1960 (by Iran, Iraq, Kuwait, and Saudi Arabia) as a way to counteract the economic power of the multinational oil companies. OPEC reached the zenith of its economic power in 1973 when oil prices quadrupled, and an OPEC oil embargo was imposed on the United States and other countries that supported Israel during the Yom Kippur War.

A cartel is an organization of producers that agree to act in concert as a monopolist and restrict output so as to raise prices and generate monopoly profits. All producers need not be members of the cartel; but the cartel must be large enough so that its quantity decisions affect market price. Noncartel producers will also benefit from the higher market price even though they are not part of the effort to restrict output.

There is little historical experience with cartels. Cartels of firms within a country are generally illegal under antitrust law (which is certainly the case in the United States). Cartels of countries that export raw materials (such as copper or cocoa) have been successful at times in raising the price of the raw material.

One factor that weighs heavily against the long-term viability of cartels is that cartel members have powerful incentives to cheat. Remember that the cartel raises prices by restricting output among its members. Each member lowers output, and that raises market price and makes all cartel members better off. If an individual member were to secretly raise its output, though, it could take advantage of the higher prices on a greater volume of output. Thus, each individual member has an incentive to cheat and produce more, but if too many cartel members do so, it will lower prices and eliminate monopoly profits. It is this incentive to cheat that has caused the collapse (and sometimes even prevented the establishment) of most cartels.

OPEC, however, was remarkably effective in raising prices in the 1970s. One reason is that there were other commonalities in addition to the goal of higher prices. Geographical proximity, a common religion, and a united front against Israel served to unite the Middle Eastern OPEC members. (In the early 1970s, Venezuela was the only non-Islamic, non-Middle Eastern member of OPEC.)

Although OPEC was remarkably effective in raising prices in the mid- and late 1970s, oil prices have generally declined through the 1980s and 1990s.[3] It is interesting that this decline was not foreseen in the 1970s, and policy was formulated as if energy prices would remain high and OPEC would continue to be an effective cartel.

OPEC lost effectiveness in maintaining high prices for several reasons. First, the cartel lost market power as non-OPEC sources of oil came on line in Mexico, the North Sea (Great Britain and Norway), and Alaska. To see how these new sources might affect oil prices, we can utilize an oligopoly model called the dominant firm model.

The dominant firm model is based on the idea that the dominant firm (in this case the oil cartel) views output of the rest of the world as beyond its control, so it attempts to set a price and then supplies the demand not met by the

---

[3]See the price data in Tables 8.1 and 8.2.

rest of the world. If the dominant firm is the low-cost producer (and it must be to be the dominant firm), then it can satisfy the unmet demand and earn some monopoly profits on its production. As the dominant firm sets price higher in an attempt to earn more profits, however, two market reactions serve to limit its ability to earn profits. First, as price increases, consumers will buy less oil, so that even though price is higher, less oil is being sold. Second, as price increases, the share of the output produced by the rest of the world (called the competitive fringe) increases, so the dominant firm will sell an even smaller amount of oil.[4]

The dominant firm model can be explained with the aid of the graph of Figure 8.1. In this graph, the supply curve of the competitive fringe is above the marginal cost (MC) curve of OPEC. The total demand curve for oil is represented by the demand curve D-D'. If, however, OPEC is taking the supply of the competitive fringe as given, then OPEC views itself as facing a demand curve that is lower than the total market demand curve. The demand curve that is relevant for OPEC is one that subtracts the quantity supplied by the competitive fringe from total demand, giving the residual demand left avail-

Figure 8.1 **The Dominant Firm Model**

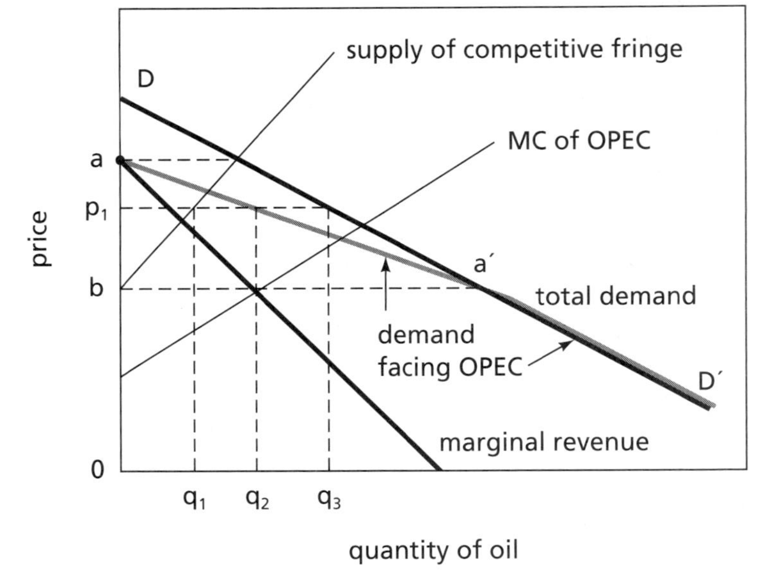

[4]A rather technical microeconomic note is that economists do not talk about supply curves for monopolists; they focus on the marginal cost curve instead. In Figure 8.1, the marginal cost curve of the monopolist is labeled "MC of OPEC."

able for OPEC (labeled "demand facing OPEC"). Notice that the vertical intercept of this residual demand curve is point a, because at prices greater than or equal to a, the competitive fringe is capable of supplying all the demand. As price creeps lower than a, however, not all the demand can be supplied by the competitive fringe, so there is a residual demand available to OPEC. At prices lower than b, the competitive fringe cannot supply any demand, so the total demand curve becomes OPEC's demand curve at point a'. Therefore, OPEC views itself as facing the kinked demand curve, a-a'-D'.

Given this demand curve, the marginal revenue function can be defined and the profit maximizing price of p_1 can be determined. The latter is the price corresponding to an OPEC output level (q_2) that equates MC and MR. Notice that at this price, total quantity demanded is q_3, with q_1 units produced by the competitive fringe and q_2 units produced by OPEC.

As can be seen in this figure, the greater the size of the competitive fringe (which would be reflected as a shift to the right of the competitive supply function), the lower will be the world price of oil. During the 1980s and 1990s, the competitive fringe (non-OPEC producers) has grown larger, as reflected in the downward pressure on prices. Tables 8.1 and 8.2 contain U.S. prices for crude oil and gasoline, which shows how energy prices fluctuated, with increasing prices in the 1970s, and a general downward trend since 1980.

Another reason prices may have fallen is because Saudi Arabia, the dominant producer within OPEC, has vastly different incentives from many other OPEC members. For a variety of reasons, Saudi Arabia would prefer to see lower prices than other OPEC countries would like.

The first reason has to do with relative size of reserves. Saudi Arabia has enough oil reserves to continue to pump at current rates for perhaps as long as 100 years. Other OPEC countries such as Libya, Venezuela, and Nigeria have a much lower ratio of reserves to current production levels. Consequently, Saudi Arabia has much more to lose from the development of alternative energy technologies, such as solar energy, which would reduce the future demand for oil and lower the future revenue that could be obtained by producing oil. Because higher current prices generate greater current motivation to invest in research and development of alternative energy technologies, Saudi Arabia would not necessarily advocate a price that maximized current monopoly profits. It would not, however, want to forgo all monopoly profits. Consequently, Saudi Arabia would advocate a price that is high enough to generate some monopoly profits but low enough to make it difficult for alternative technologies to become established. This type of oligopoly pricing strategy is called limit pricing, because the lower price limits the ability of alternatives to develop and become established.

Another reason, related to limit pricing, is that Saudi Arabia has less need for current revenue. Saudi Arabia is relatively sparsely populated, with a commensurately small economy. Under such circumstances, it is difficult for Saudi Arabia to invest all its oil revenues in its domestic economy because the economy is incapable of absorbing all the investment. Saudi Arabia can, and does, invest in other economies (such as in the United States). To a certain

Table 8.1 Crude Oil Refiner Acquisition Costs (price per barrel, inflation adjusted-updated to 2004 dollars)

Year	Domestic Oil	Imported Oil	Composite Oil
1968	14.41	13.02	14.22
1970	14.06	12.03	13.81
1972	13.61	11.95	13.28
1974	23.15	40.36	29.24
1976	24.67	37.62	30.38
1978	25.97	35.66	30.49
1980	50.14	70.36	58.09
1982	55.62	59.77	56.79
1984	47.14	47.72	47.31
1986	23.23	21.92	22.80
1988	21.70	21.42	21.59
1990	30.82	29.72	30.32
1992	23.95	23.39	23.69
1994	19.26	19.09	19.17
1996	24.52	24.36	23.81
1998	15.07	13.74	19.75
2000	32.11	30.55	31.16
2001	26.26	23.75	24.78

Note: Refiner acquisition costs are the costs that refiners pay for crude oil. The composite price is the weighted average of domestic purchases and imported purchases.

Source: U.S. Energy Information Administration: http://www.eia.doe.gov/emeu/aer/txt/ptb0519.html.

extent, however, it may wish to invest by protecting the future value of its oil reserves, rather than investing in foreign economies.

In contrast, countries such as Nigeria, Venezuela, and Indonesia have large populations and current pressing needs to develop their economies. They would advocate high prices now, especially because their reserves are expected to be exhausted much more quickly than those of Saudi Arabia.

Table 8.2 **Retail Gasoline Prices (price per gallon, inflation adjusted 2001 dollars)**

Year	Leaded Regular Gasoline	Unleaded Regular Gasoline	Average State and Federal Taxes	Pre-tax Retail Price*
1950	1.74	NA	0.489	1.25
1955	1.66	NA	0.503	1.16
1960	1.58	NA	0.604	0.98
1965	1.48	NA	0.585	0.90
1970	1.39	NA	0.503	0.89
1975	1.60	NA	0.403	1.20
1980	2.36	2.46	0.295	2.11
1985	1.70	1.84	0.36	1.41
1990	1.50	1.52	0.363	1.15
1995	NA	1.32	0.467	0.85
2000	NA	1.78	0.432	1.34

*In years where both leaded and unleaded gasoline was available, this price is the unweighted average of the pre-tax prices of both types of fuel.

Sources: Energy Information Administration, http://www.eia.doe.gov/emeu/aer/txt/ptb0522.html; Chevron Corporation home page, http://www.chevron.com/about/currentissues/gasoline/apiprice/gasoline_price_trends.shtm.

In summary, although OPEC has been successful in raising oil prices, it does not enjoy complete monopoly power. Although monopoly profits are still being earned, many factors have served to mitigate prices. Nonetheless, the existence of OPEC remains a focal point of U.S. energy policy.

OPEC and U.S. Energy Policy

In 1973, the fourth major war (the Yom Kippur War) erupted between Israel and the surrounding Arab countries. As a result of U.S. and other Western support for Israel, the Arab petroleum exporting countries imposed an oil embargo that resulted in a quadrupling of oil prices, causing a major disruption of the U.S. economy and prompting extreme fears of an economic future dominated by high energy prices, inflation, and a shortage of oil. At the same time, the price controls on natural gas were causing shortages of natural gas. The energy future of the United States looked bleak, and a series of laws were passed during the Nixon, Ford, and Carter administrations to deal with the perceived problems of a world oil market dominated by OPEC and the domestic shortage of natural gas. These legislative acts are summarized by Marcus (1992) and illustrated in Table 8.3.

The initial effort was to try to keep oil and energy prices at previous low levels. The Emergency Petroleum Allocation Act extended oil price controls, which had begun earlier as part of the wage and price controls that were undertaken by the Nixon administration to try to stem inflation. Of course, the attempt to keep domestic prices artificially low only served to stifle domestic production and increase U.S. dependence on oil imports. In fact, the price control efforts directly conflicted with the energy independence objectives of Project Independence. Before analyzing why so much attention was placed on keeping price at a low level, let's analyze the costs of energy dependence.

Dependence on foreign producers of oil is not necessarily bad. In fact, if the United States and other oil importing countries were dependent on a large number of countries for oil, foreign dependence would not be an issue. National security considerations would not be important, and prices would be lower because the large number of countries would not have monopoly power. In addition, a high proportion of the money that flowed out of the United States to purchase oil would probably flow back to the United States in the form of increased purchases of U.S. products by these countries. The United States and other oil importing countries, though, are dependent on a

Table 8.3 **The Evolution of Federal Energy Policy after the 1973 Arab Oil Embargo**

1973	The Emergency Petroleum Allocation Act
1974	Project Independence Federal Non-nuclear Research and Development Act Energy Supply and Coordination Act
1975	Energy Policy and Conservation Act
1977	Creation of Department of Energy (DOE) Federal Mine Safety and Health Amendment Acts Clean Air Act Amendments Surface Mining Control and Reclamation Act (SMCR)
1978	Power Plant and Industrial Fuel Use Act Natural Gas Policy Act (NGPA) Public Utilities Regulatory Policy Act (PURPA) Gas Guzzler Tax Building Energy Performance Standards
1980	Decontrol of Petroleum Prices

Source: Alfred A. Marcus, *Controversial Issues in Energy Policy*, 1992, p. 40, Reprinted by permission of Sage Publications, Inc.

relatively small number of organized countries in an area of the world that has been politically unstable and militarily vulnerable. Consequently, the question of foreign dependence dominates the political and public discussion of energy policy. See Tables 8.4 and 8.5 for data on U.S. dependence on imports of foreign oil.

Greene and Leiby (1993) analyze the question of the costs of foreign dependence in an interesting and insightful fashion by examining the cost of dependence on a foreign monopoly for oil supplies. It is the simultaneity of

Table 8.4 **Oil Imports by the US (1000s of barrels per day)**

Year	Persian Gulf	OPEC	Non-OPEC	Domestic U.S. Consumption
1960	NA	1314	500	NA
1965	345	1476	992	NA
1970	121	1343	2076	NA
1975	1155	3601	2454	NA
1980	1519	4300	2609	17056
1985	311	1830	3237	15726
1990	1966	4296	3721	16988
1995	1604	4002	8835	17725
2000	2487	5203	11459	19649

Source: U.S. Energy Information Administration, http://www.eia.doe.gov/emeu/aer/txt/ptb0504.html.

Table 8.5 **U.S. Imports as a Percentage of U.S. Consumption of Oil**

Year	Persian Gulf	OPEC	Non-OPEC	Total Imports
1980	9	25	15	40
1985	2	12	20	32
1990	12	25	22	47
1995	9	23	49	72
2000	13	26	58	84

Note: U.S. exports are not subtracted from imports to compute net imports. Total net imports as a percentage of U.S. domestic consumption would be less than the numbers reported in this table.

Source: Computed from data in Table 8.4.

the monopoly problem and the foreign dependence that generates the costs for U.S. society. Greene and Leiby separate the costs of dependence on a foreign monopoly into three broad components—the transfer of U.S. wealth to foreign producers, macroeconomic costs, and political and military costs—and measure them for the period 1972 to 1991. They argue that in the absence of an oil consumers' cartel, all the extra costs of oil imports are a loss to the U.S. economy. The reason is very simple. By raising prices through the restriction of output, the oil producers' cartel transfers consumers' surplus into monopoly profit. The monopoly profits are not seen as a loss from an efficiency perspective, but they are always a subject of concern from an equity perspective.

This loss is illustrated in Figure 8.2, where the marginal cost function is depicted horizontally for expositional simplicity. In this figure, p_1 represents the price associated with a competitive market structure for oil, and q_1 represents the competitive output. If the market structure is a monopoly, then p_2 is the price and q_2 is the corresponding output. In the competitive situation, consumers' surplus is equal to the total shaded area. In the monopoly situation, consumers' surplus is reduced to the area of triangle abp_2, with part of the loss a conversion to monopoly profits (rectangle p_2bdp_1) and with a deadweight loss equal to the area of triangle cbd.[5]

Figure 8.2 **Conversion of Consumer Surplus to Monopoly Profit**

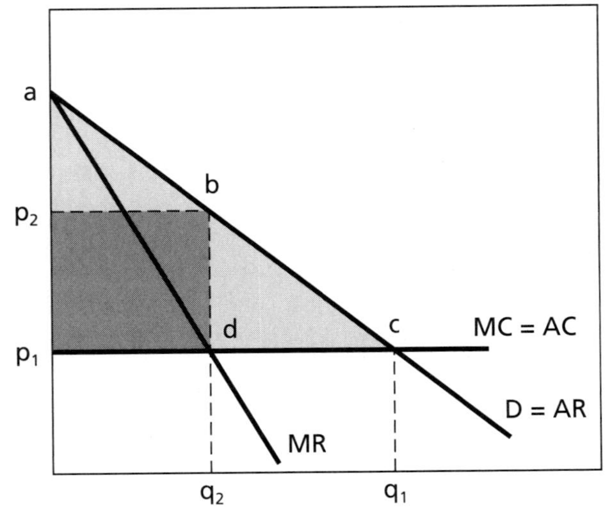

[5]Deadweight loss refers to the benefits of triangle cbd simply disappearing and not becoming someone else's gain.

In the typical analysis of a monopoly, only the deadweight loss is seen as a cost, because the monopoly profits represent a transfer from one segment of society to another. If one is defining society from a U.S. perspective, however, the transformation of U.S. consumers' surplus to profits for foreign producers represents a loss.

Macroeconomic losses occur when sudden price increases or shortages of oil (from an embargo, for example) shock the domestic economy and lead to inflation, losses in GDP, losses in employment, and other reductions in the health of the economy. These losses arise because a factor of production (oil) has become relatively more scarce as a result of the monopoly. With less of a factor of production, it is not possible for GDP to be as high as it was when the factor was more plentiful.

In addition to the costs of price shocks, there is a cost of mitigating price shocks. After the oil shocks of the 1970s, the United States developed the Strategic Petroleum Reserve, which buys oil and stores it for release during shortages. These releases are intended to make the shortage of oil less severe and therefore reduce the upward pressure on the price of oil. President George H. W. Bush released reserves from the Strategic Petroleum Reserve during the 1990 Gulf crisis to help prevent potential increases in the price of oil.

Finally, there are the military and political costs of depending on oil imports from a strategically sensitive and militarily vulnerable area of the world. In the Persian Gulf region, oil shipping lanes are very narrow and easy to disrupt. In addition, there is political instability in the area and there were concerns of possible Soviet expansion into the area in the 1970s and 1980s.

As Greene and Leiby (1993) point out, it is very difficult to ascribe military readiness costs and the actual costs of the Persian Gulf War to dependence on foreign oil. The reason is that military readiness costs are incurred to cover many possible problems, not just problems in the oil producing areas of the world. It is even more difficult to assign the costs of the Gulf War to U.S. dependence on foreign oil. Even if there was no U.S. dependence, the United States might have participated in this war to help oil-dependent allies or for other political reasons (such as to stop the proliferation of nuclear and chemical weapons). For this reason, Greene and Leiby assume that only one-third to one-half of the actual readiness and war costs can be attributed to oil dependence.

Table 8.6 shows several important patterns. First, the total social costs of dependence on a foreign monopoly for oil increase through the 1970s and decline through the 1980s. This pattern is consistent with the previous discussion that suggested a variety of market factors have weakened OPEC's monopoly power. Second, it should be observed that even though OPEC's market power has weakened, the costs of dependence on foreign oil are not trivial. The $93 billion of total costs in 1990 can be compared to GDP, which was $5513 billion in 1990.

Although this study focuses on the period ending with 1990, it has important implications for the present. It shows some of the costs associated with depending on foreign oil sources from a politically volatile region. Today,

Table 8.6 The Social Costs to the U.S. of Monopolization of the World Oil Market 1972–1991[a] (billions of dollars)

Year	Wealth Transfer to OPEC	Costs of Strategic Petroleum Reserve	Total GNP Loss	Military Costs[b]	Total Costs
1972	0	0	0	14.2	14.2
1973	3	0	17	14.2	34.2
1974	35	0	189	14.2	238.2
1975	35	0	177	14.2	226.2
1976	37	0.413	157	14.2	208.6
1977	46	0.589	167	14.2	227.8
1978	39	4.182	141	14.2	198.4
1979	60	3.954	219	14.2	297.2
1980	76	(2.63)	321	14.2	408.57
1981	64	4.382	301	14.2	383.5
1982	42	5.096	204	14.2	265.3
1983	33	3.046	147	14.2	197.3
1984	34	1.064	134	14.2	183.3
1985	27	3.299	103	14.2	147.5
1986	11	0.141	53	14.2	78.3
1987	18	0.194	61	14.2	93.4
1988	12	0.793	42	14.2	69.0
1989	19	0.546	49	14.2	82.7
1990	25	0.826	53	14.2	93.0
1991	15	NA	37	14.2	66.2[c]

Source: David L. Greene and Paul N. Leiby, *The Social Costs to the U.S. of Monopolization of the World Oil Market 1972–1991*, Oak Ridge National Laboratory Report Number 6744, Oak Ridge, TN, 1993.

[a] Greene and Leiby report many sets of results based on different assumptions about interest rates, rate of growth of the real price of oil, macroeconomic parameters, and so on to show the sensitivity of these costs to other economic variables. The results that are displayed in this table have been chosen to give the student an appreciation of the magnitude of the costs involved and should not be interpreted as Greene and Leiby's best estimate.

[b] Military costs are reported as a total for the 1980–1991 period. Average annual pre-1980 costs are assumed to equal the same value.

[c] This total does not include a 1991 estimate of SPR costs, as this was not available.

with international terrorism arising out of this volatile region, the conflicts in Afghanistan and Iraq, and the continued violence in the Middle East, the social cost of depending on oil from this region is likely to be much higher than that reported by Greene and Leiby during the 1970s and 1980s.

The Environmental Costs of Energy Production

Three main types of environmental problems arise from the production of energy. The first is emissions of pollutants that occur on a continuous basis from energy facilities. For example, oil refineries and electric power plants are important sources of emissions of air pollutants such as sulfur dioxide and volatile organic compounds. The second type of pollution is episodic releases of pollution such as spills of oil in transport. The third type of environmental impact is the alteration of natural ecosystems as a result of the production activities. For example, the development of oil production facilities in the Arctic National Wildlife Refuge would adversely affect the tundra, fragment the ecosystem, and interfere with the migration of the caribou. Strip-mining of coal results in the removal of mountaintops, filling of valleys, burying of streams, acidification of streams, and other environmental impacts. The development of oil and natural gas wells in the Louisiana bayous leads to the conversion of bayous to open water. Each of these types of environmental impact needs to be managed with different types of policies.

The conventional environmental policy instruments discussed in Chapter 3, such as marketable pollution permits and economic incentives, are very appropriate for the first type of pollution problem, continuous emissions emanating from energy facilities. Either type of incentive would lower the level of emissions in a fashion that minimized total abatement cost. For example, if sulfur dioxide emissions or volatile organic compounds are emitted by a refinery or a coal-burning power plant, these emissions can be controlled through the use of marketable pollution permits or direct controls. As discussed more thoroughly in Chapters 3 and 9, the United States has historically relied on direct controls to manage this type of pollution. Beginning with the Clean Air Act Amendments (CAAA) of 1990, however, the United States created a marketable pollution permit system for sulfur dioxide emissions. During the same time span, several European nations began instituting pollution taxes for sulfur dioxide, carbon dioxide, and other pollutants. These systems of economic incentives are further discussed in Chapter 9.

In contrast, the second type of environmental problem associated with energy production, episodic problems, cannot be adequately managed with economic incentives such as pollution taxes and marketable pollution permits. Here, not only the magnitude of the environmental problem needs to be controlled (for example, reducing the number of barrels of oil that are spilled per accidental spill) but also the probability of occurrence of spills need to be managed as well. Unfortunately, it is very difficult to construct a

Box 8.2 Oil versus Environment: The Case of the Arctic National Wildlife Refuge

One of the biggest political controversies involving energy and the environment is the controversy over whether we should allow oil exploration and production activity in the Arctic National Wildlife Refuge (ANWR). ANWR was created by the federal government shortly after Alaska became a state, with a goal of protecting the unique ecosystems and wilderness that exist in this part of Alaska.

Proponents of oil production feel that the positive impact of increased oil production on the U.S. economy and the reduction in dependence on foreign oil justify the risk to the ecosystems. Opponents of oil production argue that 95 percent of Alaska's North Slope is already available for oil production[6], and that the production activity would threaten the ecosystem, interfere with caribou migration and polar bear habitat, as well as destroy the culture of the Native Americans who live in the region. They also argue that the potential production levels of approximately 1 million barrels a day[7] will not have much of an impact on oil dependence, since this is less than 5 percent of U.S. daily consumption of oil. Furthermore, if we produced energy from other alternative sources such as biomass

The Artic National Wildlife Refuge

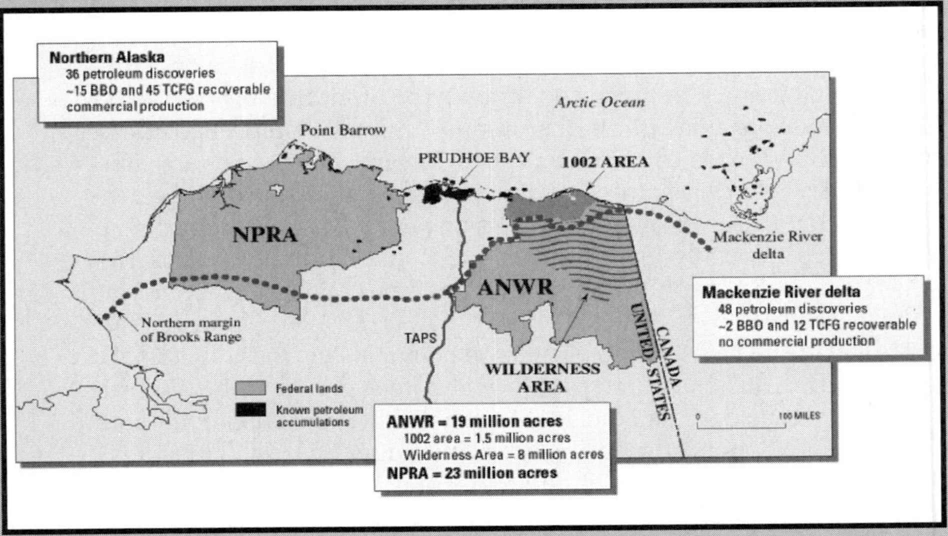

Source: U.S. Geological Survey, Arctic National Wildlife Refuge, 1002 Area, Petroleum Assessment, 1998, Including Economic Analysis. Online: http://pubs.usgs.gov/fs/fs-0028-01/fs-0028-01.htm.

(continues)

Box 8.2 (continued)

energy or co-polymerization, this would not only create jobs and other economic benefits in the same fashion (but different locations) as opening the oil reserve, but also reduce emissions of greenhouse gases.

In August of 2003, the U.S. House of Representatives authorized production activity to take place, but the U.S. Senate did not, effectively blocking the activity, because the existing laws require approval of both houses of the U.S. Congress before oil production activities can take place. Should we open the Reserve to maintain our domestic supply of oil, or should we preserve the unique resource for ourselves and future generations? Norman Change, an anthropology professor at the University of Connecticut has assembled an excellent and very balanced web site which contains a comprehensive set of links to arguments on both sides of the issue. This web site is available at http://arcticcircle.uconn.edu/ANWR/anwrpreface.html.

[6]Lazaroff, Cat, House Approves Arctic Refuge Drilling, Environmental News Service, August 2, 2003. http://207.126.116.12/culture/native_news/m14186.html.

[7]There is considerable uncertainty about both how much oil lies under the Arctic National Wildlife Refuge and how costly it would be to extract the oil. How much oil can be produced also depends on the world price of oil. See U.S. Geological Survey, Arctic National Wildlife Refuge, 1002 Area, Petroleum Assessment, 1998, including Economic Analysis, http://pubs.usgs.gov/fs/fs-0028-01/fs-0028-01.htm for more information about the probability distribution of the oil reserves under ANWR.

marketable pollution permit or tax on the level of risk of a spill, because that is much more difficult to measure than physical units of pollution, such as tons of sulfur dioxide emissions. One alternative is to use direct controls, and there is certainly a role for them. Basic safety and navigational codes are imposed on those who ship oil. Very strict safety regulations, technological requirements, operator training requirements, waste storage regulations, and other provisions are imposed on nuclear power. Another alternative that can be used separately or in combination with direct controls is an entirely different type of economic incentive liability system.

Liability systems establish liability for damages on the part of transporters of oil. If a spill occurs, the company can be taken to court and sued for damages. The Oil Pollution Act of 1990 (http://www.epa.gov/region5/defs/html/opa.htm) and the Comprehensive Environmental Response, Compensation, and Liability Act (http://www.epa.gov/region5/defs/html/cercla.htm) establish this liability, create mechanisms for measuring damages, and appoint local, state, and federal governments and Native American nations as the trustees for the public in the case of damage to publicly owned environmental resources. The idea is that if transporters of oil are responsible for damages that may result in spills, they will want to avoid this large cost and will take steps to reduce the likelihood of an accident and the magnitude of an accident. In addition, under this liability regime, they would also take steps to have rapid response programs to respond to an accident should one occur and limit the damages that might occur from a spill.

The third type of environmental impact, the impact of production activities on habitat and ecosystems, is also hard to manage through the use of environmental taxes or marketable pollution permits. Removal of the top layers of earth in strip-mining, dredging channels through the bayous for servicing oil wells, and the disruption of an ecosystem through the presence of a huge pipeline or other energy infrastructure are all types of activities that are difficult to manage in an incremental fashion using these types of economic incentives. As with accidents, direct controls can play a large part in managing such environmental impacts. For example, regulations can specify how service channels should be constructed in bayous, how pipelines should be constructed so that they do not interfere with animal migrations, how drilling muds should be handled, and so on in an effort to reduce the amount of environmental degradation associated with energy production activities. In addition, a type of economic incentive known as performance bonds can be employed.

Performance bonds require a firm to pay a large amount of money up front, before it begins its activities. This money is then placed in an escrow account, but is returned to the firm after completion of its economic activities, if it has met the appropriate environmental standards. For instance, coal companies engaged in strip-mining are required to post this type of performance bond to ensure that they restore the land after mining activities are completed. If they do not, then they forfeit the performance bond. The government then uses this money to pay a third party to restore the land to the appropriate condition. Obviously, the magnitude of the performance bond must be sufficient to give the firm an economic incentive to act in the social interest. Performance bonds are further discussed in Chapters 10 and 13.

Portfolio Theory and Energy Choices

The previous discussion suggests how the environmental costs associated with individual types of energy activities can be controlled. It does not, however, illuminate the question of whether the United States (and other countries) should have a proactive and encompassing energy policy to deal with the issues of assuring continued availability of energy and the environmental impacts of energy. As the discussion throughout this chapter suggests, countries such as the United States face a set of risks associated with the use of fossil fuels, especially when a large component of the fossil fuel use is oil imported from politically volatile areas. These risks include:

1. Potential economic impacts from price instability or from high prices associated with increasing scarcity
2. Social costs associated with the national defense and homeland security implications of dependence on oil from politically volatile areas
3. Potentially catastrophic global climate change and other severe environmental impacts associated with production and consumption of fossil fuels

An effective energy policy would seek to reduce these risks. Current U.S. energy policy is ineffective in reducing these risks, because it is based on the use of fossil fuels, especially in trying to increase domestic production of petroleum. First, a policy that has a cornerstone of increasing domestic petroleum supplies does nothing to reduce the third risk in this list, the risk of catastrophic environmental degradation (to say nothing of the costs of less than catastrophic environmental change). Second, the policy will not insulate the economy from price shocks associated with the oil market, because the price of oil is determined by the total demand and supply for oil in the world and U.S. production is only a small factor in the world supply of oil. Moreover, even if the United States could completely eliminate its reliance on foreign oil, the economic partners of the United States (all the countries that it trades with) will still be dependent on imported oil, so these countries would be susceptible to curtailments in supply associated with potential problems in the Persian Gulf region. If the economies of these countries were negatively affected by the price shocks or shortages, the economy of the United States would be as well, because the economies are all linked through international trade. Finally, because the stability of the global economic system is dependent on the oil from these volatile areas, the United States would need to protect the supply of oil through military and political action, regardless of its own independence from foreign oil.

The primary problem associated with current U.S. energy policy is that it is insufficiently diversified. Portfolio theory, which was developed to provide a better understanding of financial risk associated with investment strategies, indicates that the more diversified a portfolio of financial investments, the lower its risk. One can even lower the total risk of a portfolio by adding an investment that has a higher than average risk, provided that the risks associated with the additional investment are not correlated with the risks of the existing investments. For example, in a portfolio of financial investments, one cannot diversify away from risk by investing in 10 different telecommunications companies or 15 different steel companies. The problem is that if you only invest in telecommunications companies, the performance of the stocks are likely to move together. One reduces risk by investing in many different types of industries (or purchasing stock in a mutual fund that invests in a diverse portfolio of investments). Unfortunately, the economic, national security, and environmental risks for both foreign and domestically produced oil are highly correlated, so an energy portfolio consisting primarily of these two alternatives is not very diversified and is therefore associated with high levels of risks.

A more diverse portfolio that includes very different types of energy sources would be a much less risky portfolio. Before discussing how to choose among the alternatives, some background information on the various alternatives is provided.

Conventional Energy Alternatives

Conventional energy sources can be defined as those that are already employed at a significant level. If fossil fuels (coal, natural gas, oil and its derivatives such as gasoline, kerosene, and propane) are defined as the primary source of energy, then the alternative conventional substitutes for fossil fuels are nuclear power and hydropower. In both cases, these types of energy are used primarily to generate electrical energy.

Nuclear Power

Nuclear power has been the subject of considerable controversy since its emergence out of the World War II effort to develop nuclear weapons. Peaceful uses of nuclear power have been regulated heavily by the government because of the potential for disaster, because of national defense implications of the use of nuclear power, and because the fuel for a nuclear power plant could also be used to make a nuclear weapon.

Peaceful uses of nuclear power were promoted by the government to help spur technological innovation to help support nuclear-powered naval vessels. It was also believed that nuclear power had the potential for solving the nation's energy problems, even though it was apparent that the first generation of nuclear-powered electricity-generating plants would be more expensive than conventional ways of producing energy.

One of the biggest obstacles to establishing a nuclear power industry was the liability to which an electric utility would be exposed if there was a disaster at a nuclear power plant. Consequently, Congress enacted the Price-Anderson Act, which exempted individual utilities from having to pay damages as a result of an accident. Claims would be paid by a consortium of utilities (20 percent liability) and the federal government (80 percent liability). The amount of liability from any particular accident was also limited. Critics of nuclear power argue that this limitation of liability was an inappropriate government intervention into the marketplace. If the potential for liability was too great for nuclear power to be privately optimal, it was argued, then it cannot be socially optimal. In addition, critics argue that even if the liability limitation was necessary to allow nuclear power to develop in its initial phases, the industry is now a mature industry, so the subsidy implicit in the liability limitation should no longer be needed if nuclear power is truly competitive with the alternatives.

There are a variety of other sources of disparity between the private costs and social costs of nuclear power. Table 8.7 lists some of the costs of nuclear

Table 8.7 Components of the Social Cost of Nuclear Power

Cost	Extent of Incorporation into Price
Construction and operating costs	Electricity is priced on an average cost basis, so the higher costs of electricity that are generated by nuclear power are averaged across all units of electricity produced by all methods. Consequently, the price of electricity produced by nuclear power does not reflect the full private costs of producing the electricity
Expected damages from an accident	Limited by the Price-Anderson Act
Storage of spent fuel and waste	Charged to future electricity consumers, so not incorporated into current price
Decommissioning of retired nuclear power plants	Charged to future electricity consumers, so not incorporated into current price

power and the extent to which these costs are incorporated into price. When evaluating this table, note that other sources of energy are associated with externalities that make their social costs exceed price.

Nuclear power arose out of the wartime Manhattan Project, when physicists and engineers were the project managers. This scientific management continued into the peacetime nuclear program. Consequently, it was believed that risk could be managed by engineering systems to minimize the chances of an accident occurring.

Marcus (1992) points out that this focus on technical risk issues neglected the human factor. Undertrained, bored, intoxicated, or stressed workers could make mistakes as they monitored and adjusted systems. That was the case in the Three Mile Island incident, in which worker error compounded system failure. Marcus argues that it was not until very recently that the human factor received appropriate attention from regulators.

Although it was predicted that nuclear power would be more expensive than conventionally produced electricity, it was thought that costs would fall. That has not happened, primarily due to delays in obtaining permits and in construction. One possible reason is that the design of nuclear plants varies substantially from plant to plant, so there was little opportunity to learn by experience. In contrast, France uses a standard design in all plants, so it has been able to work many flaws out of its system as time progresses.

The construction of new power plants halted in the late 1980s and 1990s because of high costs and concerns over the possibility of accidents. Recent attention to global warming, however, has rekindled interest in nuclear power, which emits no carbon dioxide (or any of the criteria air pollutants). If new nuclear power plants are designed in the future, they will probably utilize what is referred to as "passive" safety systems. These systems rely on the laws of physics rather than on mechanical systems or human judgment to ensure that the reactor does not overheat or that the reaction does not accelerate to unsafe levels. The laws of physics, unlike mechanical systems (such as valves and pumps), do not fail. Also, with these systems there is less reliance on humans to make critical decisions.

An example of a passive system is a cooling system that moves the cooling water by relying on the property that hot water rises. Pumps can fail, valves can jam, people can make mistakes, but hot water always rises. Similarly, instead of relying on mechanical systems to lower graphite/boron rods into the reactor (to absorb neutrons and slow or stop the chain reaction if it is threatening to overheat or accelerate to the point where it could explode), passive systems have the rods held above the reactor by plastic. If the reactor begins to overheat, the plastic melts and the rods drop into the reactor. Again, there is no reliance on mechanical systems or human judgment.

Although better technology and better-trained operators can reduce the risk of an accident within a nuclear power plant, other risks associated with nuclear power are more difficult to ameliorate. These risks include the environmental risks associated with the storage of spent fuel and other radioactive wastes and the risks that uranium or plutonium that is used in power plants could wind up in the wrong hands, where it could be used to produce a nuclear weapon or "dirty bomb."[8]

The problem with nuclear waste is that it must be safely stored for an incredibly long period; it can remain dangerously radioactive for more than 100,000 years. The waste must be safely contained or it will contaminate groundwater and ecosystems and threaten human health. The existing and future nuclear waste from the current nuclear power plants is only a small part of our total nuclear waste problem, with the vast majority of nuclear waste coming from obsolete nuclear weapons. We must develop a way to safely store nuclear waste regardless of whether we expand the nuclear power program. There has, however, been a general opposition among the public to the construction of a nuclear waste storage facility. As the controversy over the Yucca Mountain storage facility attests, nobody welcomes such a facility in their region. This sentiment is often referred to as the NIMBY (not in my backyard) syndrome. These types of issues are more fully discussed in Chapter 16, which focuses on toxic waste.

The future of nuclear power has not yet been determined. No new plants have been started in the United States in recent years. Critics oppose nuclear power because of its high cost, the threat of an accident that would release radioactivity, and the problem of storage of nuclear waste. In addition, the potential interaction of nuclear power and terrorist activity is a reason to be cautious about the expansion of nuclear power. Proponents of nuclear power

[8]A dirty bomb does not produce a fission or fusion chain reaction; rather, a conventional explosion scatters radioactive material over a large area.

argue that safety can be improved by adoption of passive systems and by paying more attention to the role of people in safety. They also argue that nuclear power is environmentally preferable because it does not emit carbon dioxide or conventional air pollutants.

Hydropower

Hydropower is often associated with an image of cleanness, because the production of electricity using hydropower does require combustion and therefore does not create emissions of pollutants such as sulfur dioxide, nitrogen oxides, carbon monoxide, volatile organic compounds, particulates, or even greenhouse gases such as carbon dioxide. That is not to say, however, that hydropower is without environmental impacts. The primary environmental impacts of hydropower are associated with the dams and reservoir; they include inundation of terrestrial habitat, inundation of riverine habitat, sedimentation, reduction in aquatic dissolved oxygen levels, blockage of fish migrations, and conversion of free-flowing rivers into reservoirs.

A very interesting economic and environmental consideration is that because so many rivers have been converted into reservoir systems, free-flowing rivers and healthy riverine ecosystems have become increasingly scarce. This scarcity implies that the opportunity cost of constructing dams on free-flowing rivers is likely to be relatively high.

One of the primary impacts of hydropower activities has been its impact on Pacific salmon. A variety of species of Pacific salmon are endemic to the river systems from northern California north to Alaska and throughout the southern Alaskan coast, including the Aleutian Islands. In California, Oregon, Washington, and British Columbia, a series of dams block the major river systems, preventing the salmon from migrating from the open ocean to the headwaters of these rivers, where they spawn and where the fish remain as juveniles before returning to the ocean. Although fish ladders and elevators have been constructed to aid the fish in circumnavigating the dams, these tools are not terribly effective and have prevented many fish from reaching their spawning grounds. The impact of the dams, in combination with urban and agricultural water pollution and the uncontrolled harvest of salmon in the ocean (see Chapter 11), has led to a complete crash of salmon populations in California, Oregon, Washington and southern British Columbia.[9]

The environmental impacts of hydropower are typically managed by direct controls as part of the federal and state licensing process for the dams. As mentioned, free-flowing rivers have become relatively scarce, with a consequence that it is now very difficult to obtain approval for a new dam.

[9]See the web site of the Northwest Office of the National Marine Fisheries Service (http://www.nwr.noaa.gov) and the web site of the Gordon and Betty Moore Foundation (http://www.moore.org/program_areas/environment/initiatives/salmon/initiative_salmon.asp) for more information about the Pacific salmon problem.

Moreover, power companies that are going through the relicensing process for old dams are having trouble justifying the dams in light of their environmental impacts, and in some cases, dams are being ordered to be breached in an attempt to restore rivers and streams to their previous status.

In summary, it is quite unlikely that hydropower will offer a significant opportunity to reduce the need for the use of fossil fuels. As discussed, that is also likely to be the case for nuclear power as well. If the portfolio of energy sources is diversified, they will need to come from unconventional sources.

Alternative Energy Sources

Portfolio theory suggests that we should adopt a broad spectrum of energy sources. As indicated, however, the opportunity for hydropower and nuclear power to allow us to substitute away from fossil fuels in general and imported oil in particular seems to be relatively limited. Other alternative energy sources, which can be called unconventional alternatives, because their market penetration has not been as extensive as hydropower or nuclear power, are available. Wind, solar energy, biomass energy, thermal depolymerization, fuel cells, and geothermal are some of the energy alternatives that are important or that have the potential to have a large impact. In some ways, it is a misnomer to call them unconventional sources of energy, because energy sources such as wind and biomass fuels actually have been in use for centuries. Even though they have been utilized throughout history, their impact on the modern industrial economy has been relatively limited until very recently. Many of these types of unconventional alternative energy sources are discussed in turn.

Wind Energy

The wind is a very clean energy source that has the potential to supply a small but significant portion of our electric power needs. Large propeller blades are mounted on towers, and when the wind spins the blades, a turbine turns and generates power. With current technology, wind generation needs to be located in areas that have average wind speeds of at least 16 miles per hour. This requirement will become less stringent as technology improves. In locations that have such wind speeds, wind generation could supply as much as 20 percent of the power. In those areas, the cost of generating electricity with wind turbines is competitive with conventional types of power plants. The faster the wind blows, the cheaper the electricity. Another factor that determines cost is the distance that the electricity must be transmitted to the final customers. The greater the distance, the more that must be spent on transmission lines and the more electricity lost to resistance in the transmission process.[10]

[10]For more information, see National Renewable Energy Lab, U.S. Department of Energy, http://www.nrel.gov/wind/windfact.html.

The primary environmental cost associated with wind power is the aesthetic impact of the turbines. The towers are tall, and many towers are constructed in what are called "wind farms." Because the windiest areas are often along ridgetops, the impact on the view can be quite disturbing to many people. Many wind farms, however, can be located on cattle ranches and other areas where the aesthetic impact is likely to be minimal. In addition, there are some fears that the turbine blades can cause mortality to bird populations. The migratory patterns of birds are well known, however, and the areas that are important migration corridors can be avoided.

Solar Energy

The energy from the sun can also be used to produce electricity through the use of photovoltaic cells that convert the sun's light energy to electricity. Obviously, one disadvantage of solar energy is that it is only possible to produce energy when the sun is shining. This disadvantage is not a great one, however. Because the peak use of electricity occurs on hot summer days (mostly due to air-conditioning demand), solar energy can help reduce the need to construct expensive new-generation plants to cover peak demand. Solar energy would also eliminate the need to burn extra coal or oil during peak demand times.

Another big advantage of solar power is that it can be implemented at a small scale. In addition, it does not require the existence of high-capacity transmission lines or a grid of transmission lines to be effective. Each building could produce its own power from photovoltaic cells on its roof. This advantage makes solar energy a particularly ideal source of energy for rural areas in tropical countries, where the expense of connecting the village to the power grid can be enormous.

In areas that already are connected to the grid, the power can be transmitted into the grid when the user produces more electricity than he or she is using and the person with the solar cells paid for the power. If the power transmission companies are required to pay for this power supplied by people who have installed photovoltaic cells, then the adoption of solar power technology would be accelerated.

Biomass Fuels

Biomass fuels come from living sources. They are usually made from plants, but they can also be made from waste products. For example, human waste can be used to produce natural gas.

Liquid fuels are among the most important types of biomass fuels, because they can be used in existing cars, trucks, and boiler systems. Ethanol can be made from corn, sugarcane, and many other crops. Ethanol can be used either by itself or in a mixture with gasoline in normal automobile engines. Vegetable oil can be produced from almost any seed (soybean, palm, cotton, canola, corn, and so forth) and used as a substitute for diesel oil or boiler fuel.

There are two major environmental benefits to using biomass liquid fuels as an alternative to fossil fuels. First, the biomass fuels burn more cleanly because they are free of contaminants such as sulfur. Second, the biomass fuels do not contribute to the global warming problem because they create carbon cycles. The crops pull carbon out of the atmosphere; this carbon is then released to the atmosphere when the fuel is burned, but the carbon is pulled back out of the atmosphere with the growth of the crop in the following planting cycle.

Solid fuels are produced by pelletizing or shredding wood, dried grass, crop residues, or entire plants (such as industrial hemp or kelp) and burning this product in boiler applications to produce steam for the generation of electricity or for space heating. The solid fuels have the same type of environmental benefits as the liquid fuels in that they are free of contaminants such as sulfur and help with the global climate change problem.

Biomass fuels are not without their own environmental problems. First, many agricultural crops are grown with the aid of chemicals such as fertilizers, pesticides, and herbicides, which can pollute streams and have negative impacts on both aquatic and terrestrial life. The exposure of earth through plowing can also contribute to erosion and the presence of suspended sediments in water bodies. In addition, there is the possibility that forests, prairies, wetlands, and other important habitats could be converted into farmland to grow these energy crops. If we move to biomass fuels, it would be very important to implement environmental policies to protect the environment from these adverse impacts, with particular attention paid to creating incentives to avoid the loss of important habitat and ecological services.

Thermal Depolymerization[11]

Thermal depolymerization is a process that has been developed relatively recently that can convert any carbon-based substance (food waste, agricultural waste, human waste, plastic, medical waste, and so on) into oil. Although this process may seem to be a form of alchemy, preliminary success at pilot plants has been phenomenal, producing a high-quality light oil for approximately \$10 to \$12 per barrel.

The process works by taking a hydrated slurry of the waste and subjecting it to 600 pounds of pressure at 260° C for less than 30 minutes which causes the complex molecules to break down into less complicated molecules. The pressure is then vented off, which causes the water to flash off as steam. The heat from the escaping steam is captured and used in the process. After depressurization, the slurry is 90 percent free of water, and the slurry is allowed to settle to remove the minerals that have been liberated in this first stage of the process. The slurry is then sent into a second-stage reactor that is very sim-

[11] This section is based on Lemley (2003).

ilar to a conventional refinery. The slurry is heated to 480° C to further break down the molecules, and then it is sent through the refining process, resulting in the production of natural gas, light oils, heavy oils, and water. The process also produces powered carbon, which can be used for printer toners, tires, and other products. The oil can then be used to produce petroleum-based products such as gasoline and kerosene. The test plant has experimented with many different types of waste, and the first commercial-scale plant has been initiated at a large turkey-processing facility that packages 30,000 turkeys per day. The feathers, guts, feet, blood, heads, and other waste from the facility are converted into 10 tons of natural gas, 11 tons of minerals, 21,000 gallons of clean water, and 600 barrels of high-quality oil every day.

Obviously, the major advantage of this process is that it takes waste and converts it into a usable product. An interesting aspect of the process is that the high temperatures and pressures kill all pathogens, so animal waste, human waste, and even biomedical waste could be safely converted to oil. Such safety issues are becoming increasingly important, because a primary outlet for waste from meat-processing plants is disappearing. In the past, the unused parts of the animals were processed into powder, which was then used as a component of the feed that was fed to other animals. The use of animal organs in feed, however, has led to the rise of bovine spongiform encephalopathy (mad cow disease), and the use of animal parts in feed has been banned in many places.

Another important benefit of the process is that the minerals (including metals) that may be in the waste are captured as part of the cycle, so they are not released into the environment when the fuel is burned. Instead, they are used to manufacture new products.

Perhaps the most important benefit of the oil from waste is that it does not contribute to the global warming process, because it merely establishes another carbon cycle. For example, when soybeans grow, they pull the carbon from the atmosphere. When the soybeans are fed to turkeys, the carbon is transferred to the turkeys. When turkeys are eaten by people, the carbon is transferred to the people. When oil made from turkey guts, turkey excrement, or human excrement is burned, it is released into the atmosphere, but the next crop of soybeans pulls the carbon back out and the cycle starts anew. The important point is that we are not releasing stored carbon, as is the case with fossil fuels.

Does thermal depolymerization have the potential to be an effective substitute for petroleum? According to Lemley (2003), if all the agricultural waste in the United States were converted into oil and natural gas with this process, 4 billion barrels of oil per year would be produced. This 4 billion barrels per year is roughly equivalent to U.S. imports of oil in the year 2000 and is equal to 11 times the optimistic estimate of the production capability of the Arctic National Wildlife Refuge. In addition to agricultural waste, plastics, human waste, industrial waste, paper, and other carbon-based waste could easily be converted into oil and gas. Table 8.8 shows how different types of waste convert to oil, gas, and other products.

Table 8.8 Transformation of Waste into Economic Outputs Using Thermal Depolymerization

Waste Product (100 lbs)	Composition of Waste Product	Transformation of Waste Product via Thermal Depolymerization
Plastic bottles	Polyethylene terephithalate and polyethylene	70 lb of oil 16 lb of gas 6 lb of carbon solids 8 lb of water
Municipal liquid waste	75% sewage sludge, 25% grease-trap refuse	26 lb of oil 9 lb of gas 8 lb of carbon and mineral solids 57 lb of water
Tires	Including steel-belted	42 lb of oil 10 lb of gas 42 lb of carbon and metal solids 4 lb of water
Medical wastes	Transfusion bags, needles and razor blades, wet human waste	65 lb of oil 10 lb of gas 5 lb of carbon and metal solids 20 lb of water

Source: Unnumbered figure in Lemley (2003).

Fuel Cells

Fuel cells produce energy through a chemical process that converts hydrogen and oxygen into electricity and waste heat. It is not a combustion process, but a chemical process somewhat similar to a conventional battery. The oxygen can be injected into the fuel cell from the atmosphere. Although hydrogen is also available in the atmosphere, hydrogen is a very light (and explosive) gas and is difficult to store and distribute. A device called a reformer, however, can extract hydrogen from a hydrocarbon fuel such as alcohol, methanol, propane, or methane.[12]

Fuel cells are already in use in a number of pilot applications. One of the first applications in which they were used was city buses, because the first fuel cells were large and the city buses could handle the weight. Fuel cells could be used in cars and trucks or to produce electricity in a house or building. In fact, it would be possible to use a car that is currently parked in the garage to provide electricity to the house.

---

[12] See http://www.howstuffworks.com/fuel-cell.htm for more details.

Fuel cells produce significantly less emissions (less sulfur dioxide, carbon monoxide, volatile organic compounds), which makes their use cleaner than burning hydrocarbons. Fuel cells may or may not have a global warming impact. If the fuel cells operated solely with hydrogen, there would be no carbon dioxide created and no negative impact on global climate. If hydrogen is derived from a carbon-based fuel such as methanol or alcohol, however, the extraction process would emit carbon dioxide. For this reason, it is critically important that the fuel used to power the fuel cell be derived from a renewable source rather than from fossil fuels. A fuel derived from a renewable source would cycle carbon, whereas a fuel derived from a fossil fuel would release stored carbon.

How Do We Pick the Best Energy Alternative?

The previous section discussed several different types of alternative fuels, leading to the questions, Which type is best? Which type of alternative fuel should the United States and other governments support and develop as part of a national energy policy?

Actually, the answer to both is that we should not pick any particular fuel. First, it is difficult to know which one is best, because that involves forecasting future technological development. Second, portfolio theory suggests that it is important to have a mix of fuels.

The government could construct a national energy policy that encouraged the development of alternative fuels in several ways. One aspect of this policy could be price subsidies or tax breaks to innovative technologies. Such subsidies currently exist for ethanol. A more general approach would be to place a tax on fossil fuels, including petroleum and petroleum products. Such a tax would be appropriate due to the externalities associated with petroleum. The production and combustion of fossil fuels creates myriad environmental costs, including loss of habitat, air pollution, and global warming. In addition are the social costs associated with dependence on insecure foreign oil.

A modest tax on petroleum-based fuels (such as 10 to 20 percent of the price of a gallon of gasoline) would probably trigger large-scale development of alternative fuels such as oil made from thermal depolymerization and biomass-based fuels. The government does not need to pick which fuels to develop; rather, the market will choose those with the greatest promise. The market will have an incentive to move away from fossil fuels because of the incorporation of the additional social costs of fossil fuels into their price via the tax. Of course, environmental policy must be implemented to control potential environmental degradation associated with the alternative fuels.

Fuels such as biomass liquid fuels and oil from waste would probably have an economic advantage over fuel cells, because the current infrastructure (gas stations, refineries, pipelines, vehicles) could be used with these new fuels. Similarly, these fuels, as well as fuel cells, take advantage of the existing transportation infrastructure. In contrast, changing to an alternative transportation system (such as massive use of rail transit) would require a huge investment in infrastructure as well as a huge change in a culture that is based on mobility and individual car ownership. Investments of this sort and the required cultural changes would likely take much longer than the development of alternative fuels. This extra time would prolong the period that we are dependent on foreign oil, exacerbate global warming, and generate additional environmental degradation. A more viable plan would be to regard alternative fuels such as biomass and oil from thermal depolymerization as short-term solutions and implement more sweeping changes over the long run.

Summary

In the United States, energy policy is based on the continued availability of inexpensive fossil fuels, but this policy is not sustainable. The nonsustainability of current policy has less to do with the scarcity of fossil fuels than it has to do with the social costs associated with the use of fossil fuels.

Three sets of social costs associated with fossil fuels are particularly important. The first is the impact of the use of these fuels on greenhouse gas emissions and global climate change. The second is other types of environmental impacts, such as emissions of air pollutants, disruption of habitat, and oil spills. The third is the national security cost of being dependent on oil that is imported from regions of political volatility. Portfolio theory suggests that we can reduce the risks associated with energy use by diversifying our sources of energy.

One important way to bring about this diversification would be to place an externality tax on fossil fuels. Such a tax would encourage the development of alternatives such as biomass fuels, solar energy, fuel cells, and thermal depolymerization.

Review Questions

1. What important environmental problems are generated by the production of energy?
2. What market failures are associated with nuclear power?
3. What is a cartel and how does it function?
4. Why would Saudi Arabia advocate prices lower than those advocated by other OPEC nations?
5. How does user cost allocate an exhaustible resource over time?
6. What is the role of performance bonds in maintaining environmental quality in areas where energy is produced?
7. Is the price of energy too high or too low? Why?
8. What are the costs to the United States of depending on a foreign cartel for oil?

Questions for Further Study

1. Should solar energy be subsidized?
2. Should mass transit be subsidized?
3. Formulate an energy/environmental policy to carry the United States through the next 30 years.
4. What was wrong with the energy policies of the 1970s?

5. What was wrong with the energy policies of the 1980s?
6. What was wrong with the energy policies of the 1990s?
7. What is wrong with current energy policy?
8. Should we further develop nuclear power?
9. Why has the power of OPEC diminished?
10. Will a system of pollution controls or energy taxes adversely affect the U.S. economy?
11. How would pollution taxes affect the development of alternative clean sources of energy?
12. Why are energy price controls socially inefficient? Why would lawmakers enact an inefficient policy such as energy price controls?
13. Are biomass fuels a viable energy alternative? Why or why not?

Suggested Paper Topics

1. Develop an energy policy to take the United States through the next 30 years. Look at the National Energy Strategy (U.S. Department of Energy, 1991) and current issues of *Energy Economics* and *Energy Journal*. Also, look in general-interest journals, such as *Nature* and *Science*, as well as in the government documents section of the library.
2. Examine the economic barriers to the development of solar energy. Should the federal government seek to reduce these barriers? What actions could it take to reduce the barriers? Search bibliographic databases on solar energy and economics, solar energy and energy policy, and solar energy and technological innovation.
3. Look at the prospects of biomass fuels for reducing dependence on fossil fuels. Pick a particular fuel, or look at biomass in general. Be sure to look at the environmental costs associated with the biomass fuel.
4. Investigate the appropriateness of alternative energy technologies for developing countries.

Works Cited and Selected Readings

Akacem, M. OPEC Then and Now: Uncertainties in the Global World Oil Markets. *Pacific and Asian Journal of Energy 12*, no. 1 (June 2002): 23–36.

Bohi, D. R. *Energy Security in the 1980s: Economic and Political Perspectives*. Washington, DC: Brookings Institute, 1984.

Borgwardt, R. H. Platinum, Fuel Cells, and Future U.S. Road Transport. *Transportation Research: Part D: Transport and Environment 6*, no. 3 (May 2001): 199–207.

Dietl, G. Stability in the Gulf: Implications for Energy Security. *Pacific and Asian Journal of Energy 12*, no.1 (June 2002): 61–69.

Energy Statistics Sourcebook, 6th ed. Oil and Gas Journal Energy Database (1992). Tulsa: Pennwell Publishers.

Green, D. L., and P. N. Leiby. *The Social Costs to the U.S. of Monopolization of the World Oil Market 1972–1991*. Oak Ridge National Laboratory Report Number 6744, Oak Ridge, TN, 1993.

Griffen, J. M., and H. B. Steele. *Energy Economics and Policy*. New York: Academic Press, 1980.

Hotelling, H. The Economics of Exhaustible Resources. *Journal of Political Economy 39* (1931): 137–175.

International Energy Agency. Energy policies of IEA Countries: 2001 Review. Paris and Washington, DC: Organization for Economic Cooperation and Development, 2001.

Johansson, B. and M. Ahman. A Comparison of Technologies for Carbon-Neutral Passenger Transport. *Transportation Research: Part D: Transport and Environment 7*, no. 3 (May 2002): 175–96.

Malthus, T. R. An Essay on the Principle of Population 1798. In *An Essay on the Principle of Population: Text, Sources and Background Criticism*, edited by Phillip Appelman. Reprint New York: W. W. Norton 1975.

Marcus, A. *Controversial Issues in Energy Policy*. Newbury Park, CA: Sage Publications, 1992.

Meadows, D. H., D. L. Meadows, J. Randers and W. W. Behrens, III. *The Limits to Growth.* New York: Universe Books, 1972.

Mills, E. S., and L. J. White. Government Policies towards the Automobile Emissions Control. Pages 348–402 in *Approaches to Air Pollution Control*, edited by A. Frielaender. Cambridge, MA: MIT Press, 1978.

Mills, R. *Energy, Economics, and the Environment.* Englewood Cliffs, NJ: Prentice Hall, 1985.

Peirce, W. S. *Economics of the energy industries*, 2nd ed. Westport, CT: Greenwood 1996.

Salazar, J. G. Damming the Child of the Ocean: The Three Gorges Project. *Journal of Environment and Development 9*, no. 2 (June 2000): 160–74.

Tareen, I. Y., M. E. Wetzstein, and J. A. Duffield. Biodiesel as a Substitute for Petroleum Diesel in a Stochastic Environment. *Journal of Agricultural and Applied Economics 32*, no. 2 (August 2000): 373–81.

U.S. Department of Energy. *National Energy Strategy, 1991/1992*. Washington, DC: U.S. Government Printing Office, 1991.

U.S. Environmental Protection Agency. *Emission Levels for Six Pollutants by Source*. Nscc 91-600760. Washington, DC: U.S. Government Printing Office, 1990.

Webb, M., and M. J. Ricketts. *The Economics of Energy*. New York: Wiley 1980.

World Resources 1992–93. Washington, DC: World Resource Institute, 1993.

World Resources 1994–95. Washington, DC: World Resource Institute, 1995.

World Resources 1996–97. Washington, DC: World Resource Institute, 1997.

World Resources 1998–99. Washington, DC: World Resource Institute, 1999.

World Resources 2000–01. Washington, DC: World Resource Institute, 2001.

World Resources 2002–03. Washington, DC: World Resource Institute, 2003.

chapter 9
The Use of Energy and the Environment

The only certainty is uncertainty.

Pliny the Elder, Historia Naturalis

Introduction

Although the world is a complex place, with uncertainty surrounding many cause-and-effect relationships, one such relationship that has been well demonstrated has to do with energy and the environment. The way that we currently produce and consume energy has negative environmental impacts, although there is certainly uncertainty associated with the magnitude of many types of cause-and-effect relationships. Some of the negative environmental impacts of energy production and use have already been discussed in preceding chapters of the book. Chapter 7 focused on global warming and Chapter 8 on the environmental impacts of energy production. This chapter focuses on the impact of energy use on the environment, with a particular look at air pollution and acid rain.

Although all types of energy have some types of environmental impacts, fossil fuels are responsible for the majority of the negative impacts of energy use. The reason is both because of the large environmental impact per Btu[1]

[1]A British thermal unit (Btu) is a measure of the energy content of a fuel. It is the amount of energy necessary to raise a pound of water by 1° F.

of fossil fuel use and because of the magnitude of fossil fuel production and use. The alternatives to fossil fuels (such as biomass or fuel cells) also have negative environmental impacts, although not as large as those of fossil fuels. Any energy policy that shifts use into alternative fuels must contain environmental policies to manage their negative environmental impacts.

Perhaps the greatest negative interaction between energy and the environment occurs with air pollution, where the combustion of fossil fuels is the major source of the air pollutants that were initially regulated by the 1972 Clean Air Act, with amendments in 1977 and 1990. These pollutants, which include particulates, sulfur oxides (SO_x), nitrogen oxides (NO_x), carbon monoxide (CO), volatile organic compounds (VOCs), and lead (Pb), have strong effects on human health, either directly or through the formulation of tropospheric ozone and smog. Appendix 9.a presents data that show emission levels of these pollutants, by source, since 1940. Although one could study these data tables for weeks, a quick examination reveals two interesting relationships. The first is that, with the exception of lead and PM-10 (particulate matter less than 10 microns in diameter), energy use was the primary source of emissions. The second is that for most pollutants, emissions peaked in the past and are now declining. Carbon monoxide, volatile organic compounds, and lead all peaked in the 1970s and have been declining since. Sulfur dioxide emissions peaked a little later, in the 1980s. The declines in these emissions since they achieved their highest levels in the 1950s and 1960s makes sense, because the Clean Air Act was implemented in the 1970s. Two important criteria air pollutants, however, PM-10 and nitrogen oxides, have not followed this pattern. PM-10 has increased because of increasing emissions of "fugitive dust," which refers to dust from unpaved roads, paved roads, and other sources. Nitrogen oxides have increased because of increasing emissions from on-road vehicles (cars and trucks), off-road vehicles (bulldozers, cranes, railroad engines) and off-road engines (boat engines, lawn mowers, chain saws).[2] Diesel-burning trucks and off-road engines are particularly important sources of these emissions. In addition to its obvious role in fuel consumption, the use of energy is also responsible for virtually all the pollutants in the transportation sector and a good portion of the emissions in industrial processes (such as chemical manufacture). It is not an overstatement to conclude that the air pollution problem is primarily related to the use of energy. Appendix 9.a gives detailed information on the source of pollution emissions and their trend over time.

Figure 9.1 summarizes the changes in emissions levels from 1970 (before the Clean Air Act) to 2002. These graphs reinforce the trends just discussed. Note the progress made in reducing emissions of lead, one of the most dangerous pollutants. Also note the lack of progress in reducing nitrogen oxides.

[2]One hour of operation of a typical lawn mower creates as much emissions as 10 hours of operation of a typical car.

Figure 9.1 **Changes in Emission Levels for Criteria Pollutants**

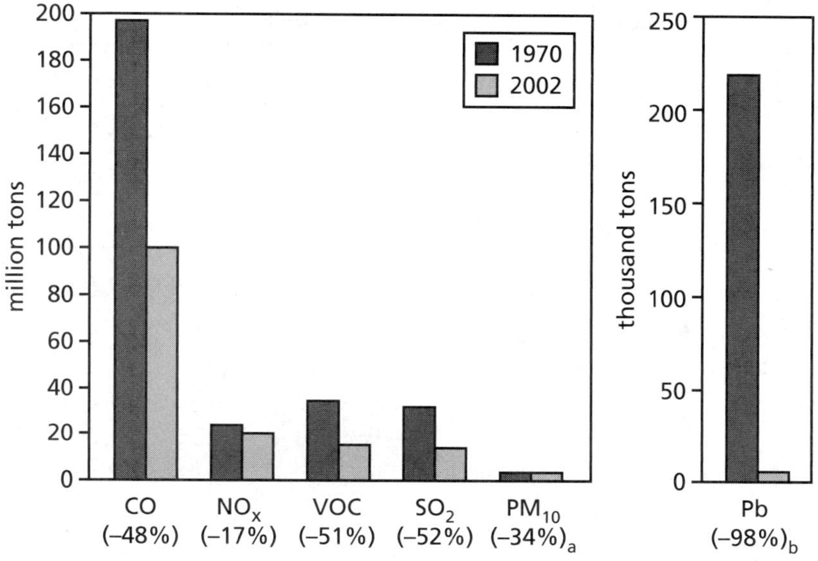

Source: USEPA, http://www.epa.gov/airtrends/highlights.html.

Despite the existence of progress in reducing pollution, the exposure of individuals to air pollution has not been satisfactorily reduced because the United States (as well as most other countries, including developing countries) has become decidedly more urban since 1970 and has not made as much progress in reducing exposure to air pollution in those urban areas. Despite the reduction in overall emission levels in the United States, approximately 98 million people (roughly one third of the U.S. population) live in "nonattainment areas." These areas are locations that persistently fail to meet national ambient air quality standards.[3]

Of course human health benefits are not the only benefits of reducing air pollution. Box 9.1 discusses the benefits and costs of the Clean Air Act.

Regulations on Stationary Sources of Pollution

Stationary sources of criteria air pollutants (smokestacks from factories and buildings) have been regulated under the Clean Air Act of 1972 and its

---

[3]For more information, see U.S. Environmental Protection Agency, http://www.epa.gov/oar/oaqps/greenkk.

Box 9.1 The Net Benefits of the Clean Air Act

In 1999, the U.S. Environmental Protection Agency completed a report to Congress, which represented a large study focusing on measuring the costs and benefits of the Clean Air Act (including the 1990 amendments) over the period 1990 to 2010. The methodology consisted of the following steps:

- Develop estimates of the emissions of the various pollutants over this time interval, with and without the Clean Air Act.
- Use these emissions estimates to model air quality, with and without the Clean Air Act.
- Estimate the cost of the emissions reductions that are required by the Clean Air Act.
- Develop quantitative estimates of the health and environmental impacts that are avoided by the emission reductions specified by the Clean Air Act.
- Develop estimates of the economic value of reducing these impacts.

The results of the study are rather striking. Even though the EPA could not measure the benefits of all the ecosystem changes, nor quantify the value of all the health effects, its central estimate indicates annual benefits of $71 billion (1990 dollars) in 2000 and $110 billion in 2010. This estimate can be compared with an annual cost estimate of $19 billion in 2000 and $27 billion in 2010. In other words, the EPA finds annual net benefits of the legislation to be $52 billion in 2000, and $83 billion in 2010. Thus, the ratio of benefits to

Emission Levels and the Need for Further Reductions

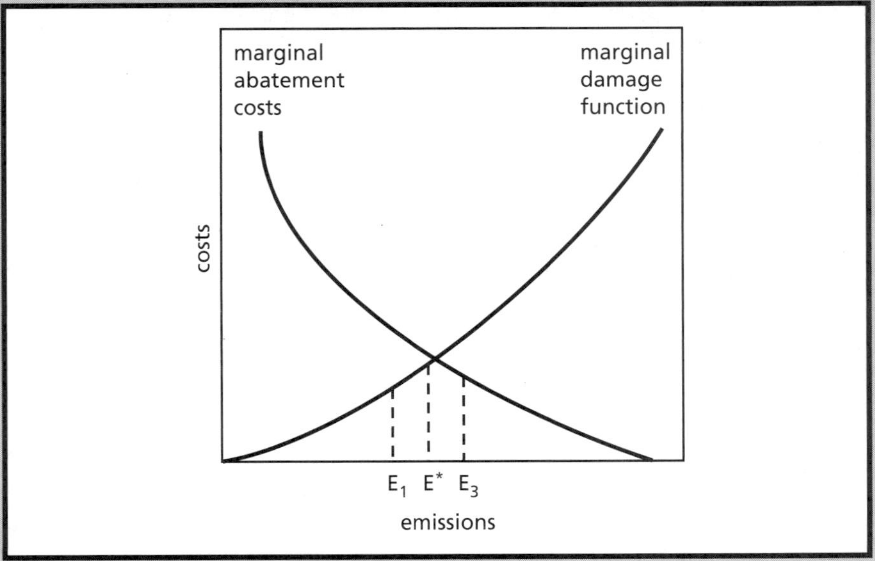

(continues)

Box 9.1 (continued)

costs is approximately 4 to 1, indicating that the Clean Air Act has been a relatively successful piece of regulation.

Do the benefit and cost numbers indicate that the United States should become stricter in terms of emissions standards? Unfortunately, this study cannot answer this question, because it provides point estimates of costs and benefits, not marginal damage and marginal abatement cost functions. For example, in the figure shown, emission levels of both E_1 and E_2 would have total benefits greater than total costs. If the current emissions levels were at E_2, we would want to become stricter and move to E*. The same thing would not be true if the current levels were at E_1. For the upper and lower bound estimates and for more details on this study, see U.S. Environmental Protection Agency (1999).

amendments (1977 and 1990). The basic thrust of these regulations has been command and control policies. The federal government established national ambient standards on the concentrations of each pollutant that would be allowed. States were then expected to develop implementation plans for meeting the ambient standards. Every state developed a set of plans based on command and control techniques, which unnecessarily increased the cost of meeting the ambient standards (see Chapter 3).

For example, the original regulations controlled air pollution in a smokestack-by-smokestack fashion. A firm that could reduce its abatement costs by switching production from one facility to another could not do so if the pollution emanating from one facility (or smokestack) increased, even if total pollution from the firm remained constant or decreased. In other words, these regulations did not allow firms to make cost-minimizing adjustments within their own facilities.[4] This point is particularly important because the regulations did not allow firms to meet environmental goals by reducing production activity at older, more polluting plants, and increasing production activity at more modern and less polluting plants. To rectify this situation, a modification to the regulations, called "pollution bubbles," was developed. In the bubble concept, each firm is treated as if a virtual bubble encased the entire firm's operations and all pollution from every smokestack within the bubble exited from a single imaginary smokestack. Only the imaginary bubble smokestack would be regulated, and firms could make any adjustments within the bubble as long as the pollution that left the bubble

[4]The minimization of abatement costs within a facility is generated by the same condition that ensures cost minimization in general. This condition is that the level of emissions from each source of pollution should be set so that the marginal abatement costs are equal across all sources of emissions.

conformed to emission limitations. These command and control techniques were not particularly effective in reducing pollution either, as evidenced by a large proportion of major urban areas that did not meet the ambient standards and still do not meet the ambient standards for one or more of the criteria pollutants.

The Southern California experience with command and control techniques is particularly enlightening. Southern California, primarily because of its heavy reliance on automobiles, could not meet the federal standards, despite requiring new sources of pollution to use the best available pollution control technology. Consequently, it was declared a nonattainment area, and no new sources of pollution would be allowed in the area. This regulation meant that there could be no growth in industry in the area, which implied a future of economic stagnation. To deal with this problem, a modification to the Clean Air Act was implemented that allowed new sources of pollution in nonattainment areas, provided that they induced existing polluters to reduce pollution by an amount equal to 150 percent of the pollution that would be generated by the new source. This "offset" system is very similar to a marketable pollution permit system. It is not as efficient as a true marketable pollution permit system, however, because it does not allow trades among existing polluters. This allowance is important because trades among all polluters could lower the cost of meeting environmental quality standards. As part of its efforts to meet ambient air quality standards, California currently has more stringent standards on emissions from automobiles than does the nation as a whole. In 2004, light trucks (pickup trucks, vans, and SUVs) will be required to meet the same emission standards as passenger cars in California. This requirement is a substantial departure from current federal policy, which does not regulate these vehicles as strictly as conventional passenger cars. Pollution from automobiles is more fully discussed later in the chapter.

Stationary Sources of Pollution and Acid Rain

Acid rain, or acid deposition, is an important type of environmental change that is generated by stationary sources of air pollution, particularly coal-burning electric power plants and other facilities where fossil fuels are used as a boiler fuel. Acid deposition refers to a process by which certain types of pollutants chemically transform into acidic substances in the atmosphere and then fall to the earth. The most widely discussed vehicle for the acidity to reach the ground is through acid rain, but other forms of precipitation (including acid snow and acid fog) and dry deposition are important mechanisms in the acidification problem. Acid deposition may cause a variety of harmful effects to ecosystems, agriculture, building materials, and possibly to human health. These impacts are discussed more fully in the next section.

Acid deposition has received considerable attention in the media and is generally regarded by the public as an important environmental problem, yet there is considerable uncertainty involving the actual damages generated by the emissions of acid deposition precursors.[5] This section of the chapter focuses on this uncertainty and how to develop environmental policy in the presence of this uncertainty.

The concern over the acid deposition problem began to accelerate in the 1970s, culminating in the Acid Precipitation Act of 1980, which established the U.S. National Acid Precipitation Assessment Program (NAPAP). This program is coordinated by an interagency task force and was established to provide information on the regions and resources affected by acidity, the extent to which acid deposition and related pollution are responsible for causing these impacts, the process by which pollutants are transformed into acids, the distribution of acid deposition, the magnitude of the effects, whether mitigation is required, and strategies to control acid deposition and related pollutants (U.S. National Acid Precipitation Assessment Program, 1991). NAPAP, originally established with a life of 10 years, was reauthorized by the 1990 Clean Air Act Amendments.

Acid rain belongs to a category of pollutants referred to as regional pollutants. Those pollutants have effects over more than just the vicinity of their emission. Their effects are felt in a broader geographic region, but they do not have global impacts in the manner of greenhouse gases or ozone-depleting chemicals. With carbon dioxide, the location of the emissions is relatively unimportant, because the gases mix completely in the atmosphere. With sulfur dioxide and nitrogen oxide emissions, however, the effects are felt primarily downwind of the emissions, so location is important.

Acid deposition problems often are manifest as transboundary (sometimes referred to as transfrontier) pollutants. Transboundary pollutants are emitted in one country and are transported across a national border to another country. For example, sulfur dioxide emissions in the United States affect environmental quality in Canada, and sulfur dioxide emissions in Canada affect environmental quality in the United States. U.S. emissions of sulfur are responsible for 50 to 75 percent of the sulfur deposition over most of eastern Canada, except those areas northeast of the metal smelter in Sudbury, Ontario. The contribution of Canadian emissions to U.S. sulfur deposition is less than 5 percent, except in areas of New York, New Hampshire, and Vermont and in most of Maine. In northeastern Maine, Canadian emissions are responsible for up to 25 percent of sulfur deposition (U.S. National Acid Precipitation Assessment Program, 1991). Acid deposition is also a transboundary pollution problem in Europe, where pollution generated in Great Britain and Germany causes acid deposition in Scandinavia.[6]

---

[5]Precursor pollutants are those pollutants that are chemically transformed to generate the substances that actually cause the environmental damage, in this case, the acid deposition.

[6]Because countries in Europe tend to be much smaller than North American countries, many pollution problems that are confined within national borders in North America constitute transboundary pollution problems in Europe. The smog problem is a good example.

What Causes Acid Deposition?

The most important precursor pollutants in the acid deposition problem are sulfur dioxide (SO_2) and nitrogen oxides (NO_x). Sulfur dioxide is the most important pollutant in this regard. Both types of pollutants are associated with the burning of fossil fuels. Sulfur dioxide is associated with the burning of coal and oil as a boiler fuel, such as in an electric power plant. Nitrogen oxides are also associated with boiler fuels, but automobiles and trucks are also an important source of NO_x.

Acid rain and other forms of acid deposition are caused when sulfur dioxide and nitrogen oxides form sulfate and nitrate in the atmosphere, which then combine with hydrogen ions to form acids. The sulfate and nitrate molecules are formed when sulfur dioxide and nitrogen oxides combine with oxidants in the atmosphere. An important oxidant in this process is tropospheric[7] ozone (O_3), which is formed when two pollutants (NO_x and VOCs) chemically interact in the presence of sunlight. Although VOCs are not directly responsible for acid deposition, their presence in the atmosphere leads to greater proportions of SO_2 being converted to sulfate and to greater proportions of NO_x being converted to nitrate. Appendix 9.a lists various anthropogenic sources of sulfur dioxide, nitrogen oxides, and VOCs emissions.

The chemical relationships among pollutants previously discussed illustrate the importance of dealing with different pollutants in a coordinated fashion. Reducing NO_x not only directly reduces acid rain, but it has an indirect effect by reducing ozone, which lessens the conversion of SO_2 to sulfate. Similarly, reducing VOCs has a direct impact of reducing tropospheric ozone and an indirect effect on acid rain, because less ozone implies that less SO_2 will be converted to sulfate. The same thing holds true for the conversion of NO_x to nitrate.

The interactions among these pollutants make the identification of the optimal level of pollution an extremely difficult problem. Because both increased NO_x and increased VOCs accelerate the conversion of SO_2 to sulfate, the marginal damages of SO_2 depend on the level of NO_x and VOCs. This relationship is illustrated in Figure 9.2, where the marginal damage function for SO_2 shifts upward as the level of NO_x and VOCs increases. Even if the marginal abatement cost function were known, one could not determine the optimal level of SO_2 emissions without also knowing the costs of reducing NO_x and VOCs, which results in shifting the marginal damage function for SO_2 downward from MD_4 to MD_3 to MD_2 and so on in Figure 9.2. To know the costs of shifting this damage function, one must know the marginal

[7]The troposphere is the lower level of the atmosphere. Ozone in the lower atmosphere causes numerous detrimental impacts. Ozone in the stratosphere (upper atmosphere) shields the earth from ultraviolet radiation. See Chapter 7 for a more detailed discussion of the relationship between the troposphere and the stratosphere.

Figure 9.2 **Marginal Damages of SO_2 as a Function of the Levels of Other Pollutants**

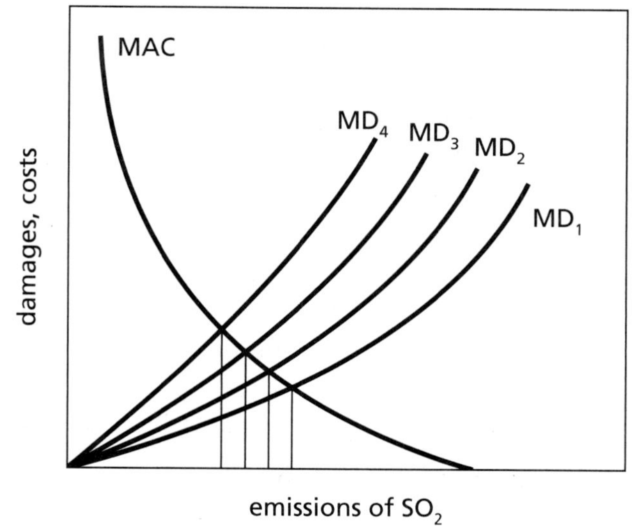

abatement costs for VOCs and NO_x. The problem of identifying the optimal level of SO_2 (or NO_x or VOCs) is actually even more complex than shown because the marginal abatement costs of one pollutant may be a function of the level of abatement of other pollutants. For example, changes to production processes that increase energy efficiency (increase the amount of work accomplished per unit of energy) will reduce all pollutants simultaneously.

"End of the pipe" abatement devices, such as "scrubbers" (used in electric utilities) or catalytic combusters (used in automobiles), however, may reduce the emissions of one pollutant but increase the emissions of other pollutants. Figure 9.3 illustrates the case where both the marginal damage function and the marginal abatement cost functions for SO_2 are a function of the levels of emissions of the other pollutants.

The optimal level of each of the three pollutants cannot be determined independently of one another. Independence of social impacts of pollution was an assumption that underlay the method in Chapter 3 for determining the optimal level of pollution. In case of acid precipitation, to achieve optimality the level of emissions of each pollutant must be chosen to minimize the sum of the total abatement costs (TAC) and total damages (TD) associated with all three pollutants. Equation 9.1 contains the total abatement costs, which are a function of the level of emissions of all three pollutants (E_1, E_2, and E_3). Similarly, total damages are a function of all three pollutants, as modeled in equation 9.2. Thus,

$$TAC = TAC(E_1, E_2, E_3) \qquad 9.1$$

$$TD = TD(E_1, E_2, E_3) \qquad 9.2$$

The minimization of the sum of total abatement costs and total damages requires that the marginal damages of each pollutant are equal to the marginal abatement costs of each pollutant. These conditions are contained in equations 9.3 through 9.5. Because the marginal abatement costs and marginal damages of each pollutant are a function of all the other pollutants, these three equations must be solved simultaneously to determine the optimal level of each pollutant. So,

$$MAC_1(E_1, E_2, E_3) = MD_1(E_1, E_2, E_3) \qquad 9.3$$

$$MAC_2(E_1, E_2, E_3) = MD_2(E_1, E_2, E_3) \qquad 9.4$$

$$MAC_3(E_1, E_2, E_3) = MD_3(E_1, E_2, E_3) \qquad 9.5$$

As this discussion of the acid deposition problem continues, it will be seen that little progress has been made in identifying the optimal level of each precursor pollutant. The interactions among the pollutants that have been discussed in this section represent an important component of this problem. Yet

Figure 9.3 **Abatement Costs and Damages as a Function of the Levels of Other Pollutants**

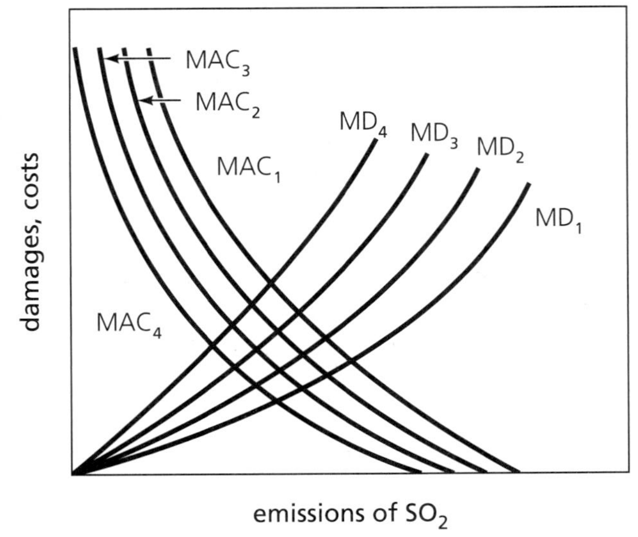

even though it has been difficult to identify the optimal level of pollution with any degree of certainty, that has not paralyzed the policy process because there was a general consensus that a lower level of acid precipitation was desirable. The information that was developed to specify target levels of each type of acid rain precursor was used in the development of 1990 Clean Air Act Amendments.

The Impacts of Acid Deposition

Acid deposition and related pollutants have many significant impacts on natural systems and human systems. Acidification of surface waters such as lakes and streams has detrimental effects on aquatic systems. Acid deposition is suspected of having detrimental effects on forests, particularly high-elevation coniferous forests. Sulfur dioxide, sulfate particles, and acid aerosols are all suspected of having detrimental effects on human health. Ozone, caused by the emission of nitrogen oxides, has harmful effects on both vegetation (natural forests and agriculture) and humans. The particles that generate acid deposition also serve to scatter light, creating a "pollution haze" and reducing visibility. Finally, acid deposition leads to the premature weathering and degradation of materials used in buildings, monuments, fences, and other structures, particularly paints, metals, and stone. Table 9.1 describes the effects associated with acid precipitation as presented in the *1990 Integrated Assessment Report* of NAPAP, which summarizes the information that supported the 1990 modifications to the Clean Air Act. Market effects indicate impacts that are felt by producers or consumers of goods that are bought and sold in markets. For example, tropospheric ozone has effects on agriculture, and acid deposition has effects on building materials. It is interesting that the very limited measurement of economic damages occurred during the first 10 years of NAPAP, as reflected in the *1990 Integrated Assessment Report.* Without this quantification of damages, it is extremely difficult to be confident that the target levels of reductions in NO_2, SO_2, and VOCs are the right level. Perhaps we should strive for more reductions or perhaps we have reduced emissions by too much. More recent studies have generated additional information on costs and damages. This evidence suggests that the optimal level of pollution is lower than the levels defined by the targets of the 1990 amendments to the Clean Air Act.

Acid Deposition Policy

As the previous discussion indicates, there is very little quantitative information concerning people's willingness to pay to prevent the impacts associated with acid deposition. Given the decade of study associated with the initial NAPAP program—and the hundreds of millions of dollars spent on research—one might wonder why.

This difficult question revolves around the purpose of science. The scientists who studied the acid deposition relationships in the 1980s were interested

Table 9.1 1990 Integrated Assessment Description of Economic Effects Categories for Regional Air Pollution

Effects Categories	Market Effect	Nonmarket Effect: Use	Nonmarket Effect: Indirect Use
Terrestrial Systems			
Agriculture	Q	+	+
Forests	Q	+	+
Other ecosystem	NA	+	+
Aquatic Ecosystems			
Commercial fishing	+	NA	NA
Recreational fishing	NA	Q	NA
Other water-based recreation	+	+	+
Other ecosystem	NA	+	+
Materials			
Building materials	+	NA	NA
Cultural materials	+	+	+
Visibility	NA	+	+
Health	NA	+	+

Source: U.S. National Acid Precipitation Assessment Program, 1991, Table 2.7-1, 152.

Note: A plus sign indicates that there is some potential for the economic valuation in a specific effect area to be influenced by changes in acid deposition and ozone. NA indicates that valuation is not applicable. Q indicates that NAPAP has targeted this area for valuation in quantitative terms in some part of the integrated assessment. Limited quantitative information from other studies is presented for visibility.

in testing hypotheses involving cause and effect in impacts. One of the best ways of testing these hypotheses was to focus on small geographic areas, such as individual lakes and ponds that were becoming acidified. Although the research developed important insights into cause-and-effect relationships, the knowledge gained was often specific to the location studied, and it was not easily generalizable to larger regions.

This lack of generability does not imply that the NAPAP research program did not contribute to the understanding of how to make acid deposition policy. That program, which spanned the 1980s, resolved many scientific questions concerning the dispersion of pollutants, the chemistry of its transformation into acid deposition, and many of the ecological effects of the acid deposition. Yet many of the physical impacts of acid deposition, such as effects on forests and human health, remain incompletely understood. In addition, very little research money was spent looking at the willingness to pay (or other measures of the societal significance) to prevent identified impacts from occurring. The feeling was that with so much uncertainty involving the scientific relationships, it would be meaningless to try to estimate economic relationships based on the scientific relationships.

Uncertainty, however, will always be present in measuring the benefits or damages associated with environmental change. We have already seen the importance of uncertainty in examining the question of global warming, which leads to an important policy question: How do policy makers develop a set of efficient policies to deal with acid deposition when the benefits of reducing acid deposition remain largely unquantified?[8]

Pre-1990 Acid Deposition Policy

The Reagan administration chose to deal with uncertainty in costs and benefits by requiring that more information be developed before implementing any reductions in the emissions of SO_2 or NO_x. In the early 1980s, most scientists who studied the problem believed that emissions of SO_2 and NO_x led to the problem of increased acid deposition. At that time there, however, was insufficient scientific evidence to prove a cause-and-effect relationship between SO_2 and NO_x emissions and acid deposition. Citing a lack of evidence of the existence of a problem, the Reagan administration did not propose any new policies for reducing acid deposition precursors (SO_2 and NO_x) which may be the reason that research funded by NAPAP tended to focus on establishing cause-and-effect relationships between emissions of pollution and regional acid deposition.

The lack of specific acid deposition policy should not be taken to imply that SO_2 and NO_x emissions remained uncontrolled. In fact, SO_2 and NO_x are "criteria pollutants" that were regulated under the 1972 Clean Air Act and the 1977 Clean Air Act Amendments. These regulations (enacted during the Nixon and Carter administrations), however, focused on the local effects of emissions of SO_2 and NO_x. Unfortunately, this local focus may have exacerbated the acid deposition problem.

One way in which a local polluter can minimize the effect of pollution emissions on local air quality is to build a tall smokestack and emit the pollutants hundreds of meters above the ground. If the emissions are released at high altitude, they will be transported outside the vicinity before they reach the ground, where they are monitored. By the time they reach the ground, they will be in another state and no longer be the concern of the jurisdiction in which they were emitted. The cost of reducing monitored emissions is much lower by using tall smokestacks than by using processes that remove the pollutants from the exhaust gases or processes that burn the fuel more cleanly.

These tall smokestacks were, to a large extent, responsible for the sulfur component of the acid deposition problem. Because the smokestacks injected the pollutants into the more powerful wind currents of higher altitudes, they

---

[8]See Chapters 3 and 5 for a discussion of marginal damage functions, marginal abatement cost functions, cost-benefit analysis, and other information requirements for developing policy.

transported the pollutants great distances (for example, from the Midwest to New England and Quebec).

Acid Deposition Policy and the 1990 Clean Air Act Amendments

Another important policy question that slowed the development of acid deposition policy concerned who should pay for the environmental improvements. Although this question is always important when formulating environmental policy, it is particularly important given the regional nature of the acid deposition problem. For example, a large portion of SO_2 emissions are generated by electric utilities in the Midwest, and a significant portion of the damages may be associated with forest and aquatic ecosystems in the Northeast and the Southeast. Electricity consumers in the Midwest might argue that electricity is a necessity that ecological benefits such as healthy forests and trout fishing are a luxury, so why should their electric bills increase so that New Englanders can enjoy better recreational fishing?

This argument may at first seem to be appealing, but the appropriate comparison is not total recreation with total electricity consumption. If the price of electricity goes up, consumers will eliminate the least important uses of electricity first (for example, by turning lights off in unoccupied rooms, adjusting the thermostat a bit, or skipping reruns of *Gilligan's Island*). These marginal uses of electricity are not inherently more valuable than the improvements in recreation. One must compare the changes in consumers' and producers' surplus associated with the two activities (see Chapter 4). These relative values are actually an empirical issue that must be resolved through measurement and not conceptual debate.

Although one cannot justify an argument that electric consumers should have preference over recreational anglers, important political problems are associated with developing legislation that benefits one region at the expense of another. Despite the overall benefits to the nation, legislative representatives will have trouble supporting a law that reduces their constituents' standard of living.

One way of dealing with this problem is to package several environmental policies into the same piece of legislation so that the benefits and costs of the entire package of environmental changes are not as unequally distributed. For example, the 1990 Clean Air Act Amendments (CAAA), which occurred during the first Bush administration, address not only acid rain, but also local air quality problems associated with ozone and carbon monoxide, pollution from cars and trucks (VOCs and N_2O), air toxics (heavy metals and other carcinogens, mutagens, and reproductive toxins), and stratospheric ozone and global climate protection.

Acid deposition is addressed by Title IV of the 1990 CAAA, which specifies a 10-million-ton reduction in annual sulfur dioxide emissions. These reductions were specified to be achieved by the year 2000, with electric utilities shouldering the primary burden of reduction.

An interesting aspect of Title IV of the 1990 CAAA is that it represents the first attempt by the federal government to implement a system of marketable pollution permits. Utilities that reduce pollution below the allowed levels may sell allowances to other utilities. Each allowance represents the right to emit 1 ton of SO_2. The purpose of the trading of allowances is to allow the reductions to take place among the firms that face the lowest costs of reducing pollution.[9]

Although many economists regard the incorporation of marketable pollution permits into the 1990 CAAA as an important step in improving the efficiency of environmental regulations, the system that was adopted does not have all the properties that economists believe are desirable in a pollution trading system. The primary criticism is that there is no attempt to make geographic distinctions associated with the location of emissions of SO_2, because SO_2 is traded across locations on a one-for-one basis. Even though the acid deposition effects of sulfur dioxide emissions may be relatively independent of location, sulfur dioxide also has local pollution effects that are quite sensitive to location.

To better understand this aspect, let's look at the first trade that occurred, when a Wisconsin utility sold allowances (permits) to the Tennessee Valley Authority (TVA; a federally owned and authorized regional electric utility) in Tennessee and five other southern Appalachian states. The sale of allowances from Wisconsin to the Tennessee Valley region requires the Wisconsin utility to pollute less and allows the TVA to pollute more. The costs of both the Wisconsin utility and the TVA must fall as a result of this trade; otherwise, both parties would not have agreed to the trade. The costs of reducing pollution by the amount of the traded allowances must be less than the price of the allowances, or the Wisconsin utility would not have agreed to the sale. Similarly, the electricity production costs of the TVA must fall, because the TVA would not have entered into the trade unless their savings in abatement costs was more than the price of the allowances. Both utilities save money, so the costs of producing electricity in both regions must fall. If the only effect of the sulfur dioxide pollution is its contribution to regional acid rain and if this contribution is independent of location (within the eastern United States), then there is no change in environmental quality (positive or negative), and the trade merely reduces costs and makes everybody better off. This benefit is, in fact, the rationale behind marketable pollution permits, discussed more fully in Chapter 3.

If, however, local pollution effects exist (the SO_2 affects local environmental quality as well as contributing to regional acid rain), then the trade will reduce local environmental quality in the Tennessee Valley and improve local environmental quality in Wisconsin. If the citizens of the Tennessee

[9]Chapter 3 discusses the cost minimizing properties of marketable pollution permits.

Valley value the reduction in electric costs more than the reduction in environmental quality, then the trade is still unambiguously a good idea. Both people in Wisconsin and people in the Tennessee Valley are made better off as a result of the trade. The social desirability of the trade becomes more ambiguous, however, if the citizens of Tennessee value the reduction in environmental quality by more than the reduction in the costs of generating electricity. Then the people of the Tennessee Valley become worse off. The trade may still be a potential Pareto improvement if the citizens of Wisconsin gain by more than the citizens of Tennessee lose. In addition to efficiency implications, there may be important regional equity considerations. Because of the potential problems that may be generated by local pollution effects, many critics of this system argue that local pollution effects need to be taken into account in the trading system. See Chapter 3 for a discussion of ways to incorporate geographic variability in the damages from pollution into a system of marketable pollution permits.

Other potential problems with the acid rain provisions of the 1990 CAAA is that not all emitters of SO_2 are incorporated into the system and that NO_x is not part of any trading system. Small polluters and mobile sources are not covered by these provisions. It may be that obtaining greater reductions from small emitters and mobile sources is cheaper at the margin.

The 1990 amendments did, however, take positive steps to reduce the acid rain problem. Research showed that the acid rain was primarily due to coal-burning power plants in the midwestern United States, so the 1990 CAA developed a plan to deal with this problem. The goal was to cut sulfur dioxide emissions by roughly 50 percent, or 10 million tons per year. Phase 1 of the program, which began in 1995, developed a cap on the emissions of the most polluting power plants. In January of 2000, all existing power plants over 25 megawatts and all new power plants (no matter what their generating capacity) were included in the program. Power plants participating in the program were entitled to trade emissions allowances with any other plant participating in the program. The fundamental assumption underlying the program is that the ability to trade allowances will reduce the costs (relative to a command and control system) associated with the large reduction in sulfur dioxide emissions that is the goal of the 1990 amendments.

A great fear of opponents of the sulfur trading program was that local air quality would decline precipitously in areas where utilities bought allowances. The idea was to allow trading over the whole region, because the particular location of the emissions was not important to the generation of acid rain. Because sulfur dioxide also has local impacts, however, people were afraid that unrestricted trading could lead to a large increase in pollution in certain areas of the country. Of particular concern were areas where most of the electric power generation was from older plants, where abatement was more expensive. In these areas, utilities would be likely to buy permits and increase their emissions of sulfur dioxide.

Although the system has lead to some patterns of trading that increase emissions in certain areas, it does not appear that it has caused any areas to violate the federal standards. Also, it does not appear as if there has been a noticeable increase in pollution in these areas as a result of the trading. Pollution in some areas, such as the eastern portion of Tennessee has been increasing, however, but it is difficult to determine how much of this change is a result of increased emissions on the part of power plants and increased emissions from industry, diesel trucks, and other sources of pollution.

The sulfur trading program has been relatively successful, although there has been less trading than anticipated. Many factors have contributed to the smaller than expected number of trades including uncertainty about the future, obstacles to trading created by state-level regulatory agencies, and a desire to bank emissions reductions for the future rather than selling them today. This lower volume of trades, though, has not interfered with the cost savings associated with the program. Burtraw (1996) estimates the long-term annual costs of complying with the emissions reductions with a command and control system as $1.82 billion, but finds that the trading system is likely to reduce this cost by approximately 45 percent, or $780 million dollars.

An interesting aspect of the program is that the price of allowances has been much lower than anticipated, implying that the program has lead to marginal abatement costs that are lower than predicted. It is not clear if this disparity was the result of poor forecasts, of innovations in abatement technology, or both. To give an example of how large the disparity between predicted and actual allowance price, the U.S. Environmental Protection Agency originally predicted an allowance price of $1500 per ton, but revised this projection downward to about $500 in 1990 as the amendments were being acted upon. In actuality, prices started out around $250–300 per ton in 1992, falling to $110–140 in 1995, and bottoming out around $70 per ton in 1996. In 1997, the price had risen slightly to $70 per ton (Bohi and Burtraw). The 2003 auction had a market clearing price of approximately $170 per ton.[10]

Although both positive and negative aspects are associated with the structure of the emissions trading system that the EPA has chosen, it is difficult to make a theoretical argument about the overall social benefits of the system. Such a verdict awaits more experience with the program, which was not fully implemented until 2000.

Table 9.2 contains a summary of the acid rain provisions (Title IV) of the 1990 Clean Air Act, and Figures 9.4 and 9.5 show the anticipated levels of emissions as a result of this legislation. When evaluating Title IV, it should be emphasized that the 10-million-ton reduction specified by the act was not chosen based on an indication that 10 million tons was the optimal reduction. Rather, it was chosen as a reduction level that was somewhat supported by the scientific research conducted on the relationship between emissions and impacts, and it was a reduction level that was acceptable to most members of Congress. As indicated earlier in this chapter, however, very little

---

[10]For more information, see U.S. Environmental Protection Agency, http://yosemite.epa.gov/aa/programs.nsf/0/06a411fee3006e238525651c00506e16?OpenDocument.

Table 9.2 U.S. EPA Summary of Title IV of 1990 Clean Air Act Amendments

SO_2 Reduction

A 10-million-ton reduction from 1980 levels, primarily from utility sources. Caps annual SO_2 emissions at approximately 8.9 million tons by 2000.

Allowance

SO_2 reductions are met through an innovative market-based system. Affected sources are allocated allowances based on required emission reductions and past energy use. An allowance is worth one ton of SO_2 and it is fully marketable. Sources must hold allowances equal to their level of emissions or face a $2000 excess ton penalty and a requirement to offset excess tons in future years. EPA will also hold special sales and auctions of allowances.

Phase I:

SO_2 emission reductions are achieved in two phases. Phase I allowances are allocated to large units of 100 MW[a] or greater that emit more than 2.5 lb/mmBtu[b] in an amount equal to 2.5 mmBtu multiplied by their 1985–87 energy usage (baseline). Phase I must be met by 1995, but units that install certain control technologies may postpone compliance until 1997 and may be eligible for bonus allowances. Units in Illinois, Indiana, or Ohio are allotted a pro rata share of an additional 200,000 allowances annually during Phase I.

Phase II:

Phase II begins in 2000. All utility units greater than 25 MW that emit at a rate above 1.2 lb/mmBtu will be allocated allowances at that rate multiplied by their baseline consumption. Fifty thousand bonus allowances are allocated to plants in midwestern states that make reductions in Phase I.

NO_x:

Utility NO_x reductions will help to achieve a 2-million-ton reduction from 1980 levels. Reductions will be accomplished through required EPA standards for certain existing boilers in Phase I and others in Phase II. EPA will develop a revised NO_x New Source Performance Standard for utility boilers.

Repowering:

Units repowering with qualifying Clean Coal Technologies receive a 4-year extension for Phase II compliance. Such units may be exempt from new source review requirements and New Source Performance Standards.

Energy Conservation and Renewable Energy:

These projects may be allocated a portion of up to 300,000 incentive allowances.

Monitoring:

Requires continuous emission monitors or an equivalent for SO_2 and NO_x and also requires opacity and flow monitors.

Source: The summary is taken directly from U.S. Environmental Protection Agency, 1990.

[a] A megawatt is a measure of the electricity-producing capacity of an electric power plant.

[b] Million British thermal units is a measure of the heat potential of a fuel. A Btu is the amount of heat necessary to raise 1 lb of water 1° F.

Figure 9.4 **Annual Emissions of Sulfur Dioxide in the United States**

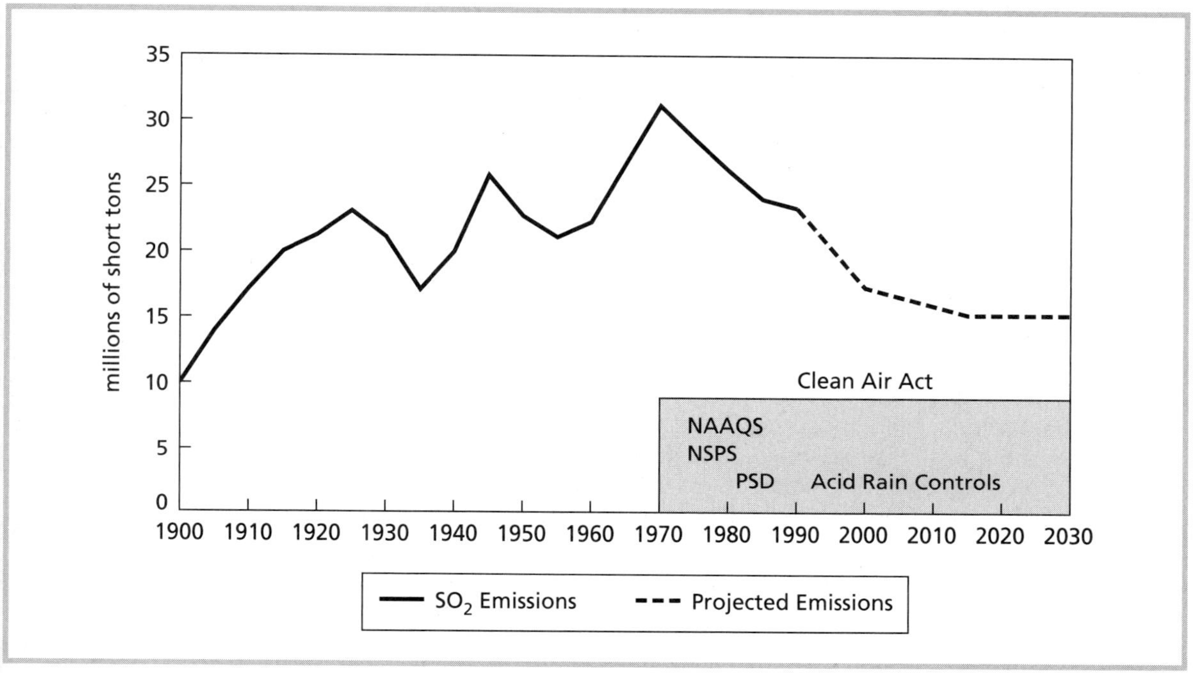

Figure 9.5 **Annual Emissions of Nitrogen Oxides in the United States**

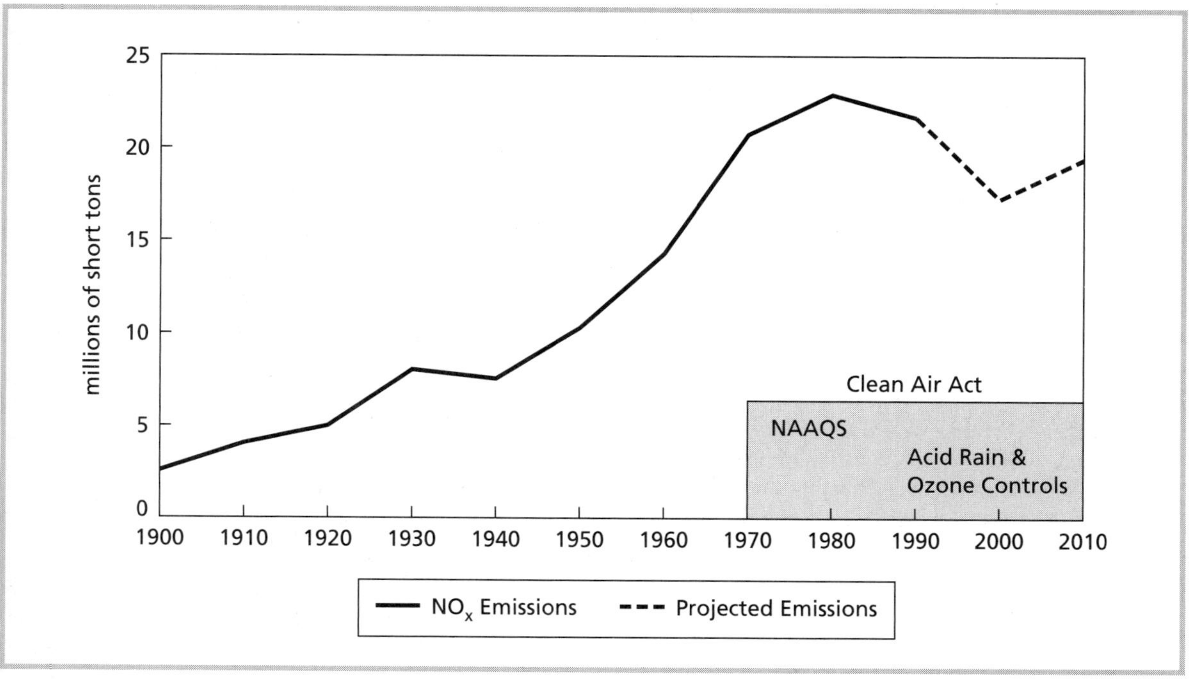

information has been developed on the value that people place on reducing these impacts.

The 1990 CAAA required NAPAP to conduct an assessment of the costs and benefits associated with this reduction by 1996. This report, NAPAP Biennial Report to Congress: An Integrated Assessment, is available online at http://www.oar.noaa.gov/organization/napap.html.

Title IV relies primarily on command and control provisions. As can be seen in Table 9.2, virtually every provision is a type of command and control regulation. The only exception is the trading of allowances. Although this exception is significant, the SO_2 trading system stops far short of being a true marketable pollution permit system. Only certain classes of polluters (utilities) are required to participate in the system, and NO_x is not included in any system of market incentives.

Finally, as the Clean Air Act was being prepared, an international agreement was being negotiated between the United States and Canada. Because there was considerable disagreement between the United States and Canada on acid deposition policy in the 1980s (the United States wanted to study the situation, Canada wanted immediate action), this cooperation marked an important step. The cooperation is reflected in the Clean Air Act, whose provisions reflect the negotiated agreements between the United States and Canada. The two countries entered into a "Bilateral Agreement on Air Quality" in 1991 to deal with acid deposition precursor pollutants and other types of air pollution.

Regulations on Mobile Sources of Pollution

Mobile sources of pollution (vehicles) have also been regulated in a command and control fashion. The primary instrument used is that of specifying abatement control devices for vehicles. The regulations specify a single national standard for automobile emissions, although California is allowed to employ stricter standards.

All automobiles are required to employ catalytic converters. The platinum in the converter serves as a catalyst that lowers the ignition temperature of many of the unburned hydrocarbons and other pollutants in gasoline. In other words, the converter facilitates the more complete burning of the gasoline. Although this method may seem to be an effective way of dealing with pollution, there are many problems associated with it. First, it controls all areas of the country in the same fashion, so that the same device is used in Barlow Point, Alaska, as in New York City. Obviously, an additional unit of emission has a much more severe impact in New York City than in Alaska. If Alaska and New York are treated uniformly, then New York is being undercontrolled, Alaska is being overcontrolled, or both.

Another problem associated with this technology-based approach to pollution control is that it does not give additional incentives to reduce pollution. It does not give people an incentive to drive less, to maintain their cars (a properly tuned and maintained car pollutes less), to drive their cars in a less-polluting fashion (avoiding rapid acceleration, stop-and-go driving, and cold-engine driving), to take mass transit, or to purchase a car that exceeds the standards. If people have no incentive to purchase cars that pollute less, then manufacturers have no incentive to design and manufacture cars that pollute less.

Air pollution from automobiles is also indirectly controlled by Corporate Automobile Fuel Efficiency (CAFE) standards, which specify the average miles per gallon that must be achieved by each automobile manufacturer. CAFE standards require that the average fuel efficiency across all cars produced by a manufacturer achieve a minimum level, which increases over time. Higher miles per gallon means that less gasoline is burned per mile driven, which means that there is less pollution per mile. CAFE standards, however, do nothing to reduce the miles that are driven and may even increase the total number of miles driven, because more efficient cars are cheaper to drive. For example, Green et al. (1999) find that only 80 percent of the energy savings that might be predicted from an improvement in miles per gallon are actually achieved. The 20 percent is lost because drivers increase the miles driven because of the impact of better gas mileage on the cost of driving.

Mills and White (1978) suggest a system that would give more of the appropriate incentives. Cars would be taxed based on the total amount of pollution that they generate each year. This amount would be computed by an annual diagnostic test in which the tailpipe emissions are measured to compute the pollution per mile, which is then multiplied by the total amount of miles (read from the odometer)[11] driven. There could be a base federal tax, and then local jurisdictions would be free to establish additional taxes based on their need to further reduce pollution.

Under such a system, drivers would have the choice of buying cars that emit different levels of pollution. Drivers who drive many miles per year or live in high-pollution (and high-tax) areas would have an incentive to pay more money to buy a less-polluting car. Drivers who drive only occasionally or live in low-pollution areas (low-tax areas) would minimize their costs by purchasing less expensive but higher-polluting cars. People would have an incentive to maintain their cars, because that would reduce their pollution per mile and their pollution tax. Automobile manufacturers would have an incentive to develop less-polluting cars because, under the tax system, consumers would be willing to pay more to purchase these less-polluting cars. Finally, the additional cost associated with driving would encourage people to live closer to work, to carpool, to use mass transit, and to make other pollution-reducing adjustments. The one adjustment for which incentives would not be generated is an incentive for people to drive in a less-polluting fashion (avoiding excessive acceleration, stop-and-go driving, and cold-engine driving).

[11]Obviously, it would be necessary to develop odometers that were more tamper resistant and create additional penalties for tampering with odometers.

Energy Policy and the Environment

Since the passage of the Clean Air Act in 1973, each presidential administration has integrated environmental policy and energy policies in various ways. In general, there have been two major thrusts of these policies when taken together, although different administrations have placed different emphasis on them.[12]

- Increase domestic supplies of energy and reduce dependence on foreign oil
- Promote a cleaner environment by requiring energy users to utilize cleaner technologies

In the 30 years since the passage of the Clean Air Act (and since the Yom Kippur War oil boycotts signaled the United States' heavy dependence on Middle Eastern oil), however, there has been a mixed record of success. Although air quality in general is better, the environmental impact of energy use is growing, especially when habitat destruction and global warming are considered. Although some progress has been made on the environmental front, the United States regressed on the issue of dependence on foreign oil. In fact, imports of oil from OPEC countries have increased by 387 percent between 1970 and 2000, and imports from the politically unstable areas of the Persian Gulf have increased by 2000 percent over the same period (see Table 8.4).

Despite the best intentions of many intelligent and conscientious decision makers, the United States has failed to develop a workable energy/environmental policy. Although it is never easy to trace a problem to a single source, the dominant factor in the failure of U.S. energy/environmental policy is a failure to allow the cost of energy, particularly imported petroleum, to reflect its true social cost. This social cost has two major components: the social cost of dependence on insecure imports of petroleum and the environmental cost of energy use, particularly with respect to fossil fuels.

Quite simply, the United States has a policy that has been designed to keep energy costs low, and economic efficiency requires that the price of energy should reflect its true social cost. Hence, the nation will never have a workable energy/environmental policy until the government and the voters develop the political will to raise the cost of energy and eliminate the disparity between the marginal private cost of energy use and the marginal social cost of energy use. Elimination of this gap will result in the following consequences:

- The higher cost will encourage the development of alternatives to fossil fuels.
- The higher cost will result in a reduction in the amount of pollution per unit energy used.

[12]It is beyond the scope of this book to provide a comparative analysis of the different policies of the various administrations.

- The higher cost will result in a reduction of energy use per unit of output.
- The higher cost will encourage the development and utilization of new technology that is both more energy efficient and less polluting.
- The higher cost will discourage the importation of foreign oil and encourage the development of alternative energy sources.

This disparity between price and marginal social cost can be eliminated in a variety of fashions. As the theory developed in Chapter 3 indicates, the least costly way to do so, in most cases, would be through a comprehensive series of marketable pollution permits or through a system of per-unit pollution taxes. The taxes would need to reflect all the social costs, including the costs of foreign dependence, air pollution, global climate change, and other environmental impacts. A combination of taxes and permits might be the best system, with a permit system used for large stationary sources of pollution (such as electric utilities, large manufacturing facilities, and refineries), and taxes used for mobile sources of pollution (cars and trucks) and small stationary sources of pollution (furnaces that heat homes and small commercial establishments). Taxes are suggested for small polluters because the transaction costs resulting from requiring each small polluter to participate in the permit market would be extremely high. As Chapter 7 suggests, a carbon tax is a promising method for internalizing the external cost of global climate change.

Sweden has developed an interesting set of environmental taxes. Box 9.2 contains a discussion of the Swedish system.

Taxes would also be a good way to incorporate the social cost of dependence on insecure foreign oil, because it would be extremely difficult to configure a permit system to limit dependence on foreign oil. Such a permit system would also probably be seen as an illegal barrier to free trade by the World Trade Organization, as would a tax that is placed only on oil imported from insecure areas or placed on imported oil in general. The tax would have to be placed on both domestically produced and imported oil to avoid being viewed as an illegal tariff.

Because externalities are also present in the production of energy, they would also need to be addressed. Liability and bonding systems would be effective in ensuring that spills, acid mine drainage, and alteration of the landscape and habitat were reduced to appropriate levels. Such systems are discussed in Chapter 8 in relation to energy production and are further analyzed in Chapter 10 in relation to mining.

Energy Use and Environmental Taxes

To adequately implement a marketable pollution permit system or emissions tax system, it must be possible to monitor emissions. As discussed in Chapter 3, it is important to place the tax directly on the emissions, rather than on inputs or economic outputs. It is often difficult, however, to monitor emissions in this fashion.

Box 9.2 Pollution Taxes in Sweden

The pollution tax system in Sweden, which has focused primarily on the industrial and electrical production sectors, has been very successful for two major reasons. First, fees per ton of emissions have been high enough in relationship to marginal abatement cost to provide a significant incentive to reduce emissions. Second, the method used to return the tax revenues to the firms increases, rather than decreases, a firm's incentive to reduce its pollution.

Sweden's carbon tax emanated from a reform of the entire tax system in Sweden. This reform reduced income taxes and energy taxes, but established the carbon tax (as well as the taxes on sulfur dioxide and nitrogen oxides). A carbon tax can be viewed as either an input tax or an emissions tax, because the carbon content of the fuel and the carbon emissions associated with burning the fuel are essentially one and the same. In contrast, the tax on sulfur dioxide that has been implemented in Sweden can be viewed as an input tax, because the tax is on the sulfur content of the fuel, not on the sulfur dioxide emissions of the firm. Therefore, firms have an incentive to use fuels that have a lower sulfur content, but they have no incentive to reduce the sulfur dioxide emissions associated with burning a given type of fuel. Of course, emissions are also controlled by the command and control system that is in place, but the sulfur tax should not be viewed as representative of a true pollution tax.

In contrast, the tax imposed on nitrogen oxides is a true emission tax and is a marvelous example of how to construct a pollution tax that gives both direct and indirect incentives. The nitrogen oxides tax was imposed in 1992 and applied to emissions from electricity- and heat-generating plants. A central feature of the program was the continuous emission monitoring (CEM) of plants. CEM is necessary because small changes in the operating characteristics of a fossil fuel–burning plant can drastically alter the level of emissions of nitrogen oxides. Hence, emissions cannot be computed with a mathematical formula based on type of technology and types of fuels. Although CEM is necessary to measure the emission levels and compute the tax liability effectively, it is relatively expensive; it has been estimated as $39,000 per plant per year, or roughly $520 per ton of nitrogen oxides emitted (Blackman and Harrington, 1999).

Although expensive from an absolute perspective, the cost is small from a relative perspective because the emission tax was set at $5200 per ton of nitrogen oxides, more than 10 times the cost of CEM. The high cost of monitoring, however, has meant that only large emitters such as electric power plants have been included in the tax program; smaller polluters are regulated by command and control only. Obviously, the government would not want to spend $39,000 to measure the nitrogen oxide emissions of a facility that was only emitting several tons per year.

(continues)

Box 9.2 (continued)

The best parts of the Swedish nitrogen oxides program are the incentives established by the method chosen to return the tax payments. The government made the decision that the tax program should have a neutral impact on the profitability of the electricity-generation industry as a whole. Therefore, a mechanism was constructed to return the tax to the firms. This return of the tax payments to the firms, however, is completely independent of the amount of pollution generated by the firm. Therefore, the return does not reduce the incentives of the tax system to reduce the level of pollution. In fact, the system increases incentives to reduce pollution by relating the return of the tax payments to the level of electricity that each firm produces. In otherwords, if a firm produces 5 percent of the total production of electricity, then it receives a payment equal to 5 percent of the total amount of pollution taxes collected.

Under this system, an electric power producer can improve its profitability in two ways. The first is to reduce its levels of nitrogen oxides production to reduce its liability. The second is to increase its production of electricity relative to the rest of the industry (and also relative to its production of nitrogen oxides). Therefore, a firm can always increase its profitability by being more efficient (producing more electricity and less nitrogen oxide) than other producers of electricity. This incentive is continuous because no matter how efficient a producer is, it can collect a greater amount of refund by being more efficient. The nitrogen oxide system has been extremely successful. Total emissions from monitored plants decreased by 40 percent in the first two years of the program (Blackman and Harrington, 1999).

If it is not politically or administratively feasible to develop a system of pollution taxes or permits, a second-best solution is to add a tax to the price of fuel based on the average amount of pollution of the fuel. For example, natural gas generates less pollution per unit of heat than oil, and generates less pollution per unit of heat than coal. Consequently, the per British thermal unit tax associated with coal would be higher than that associated with oil, and the tax for oil would be higher than the tax for natural gas. This type of fuel tax would not be quite as desirable as pollution taxes or permits, because the fuel tax would not provide as wide a range of incentives as either system. Both the fuel tax and the pollution tax/marketable permit systems would give people an incentive to use less energy in any activity and to develop new technologies for conserving energy and using energy more efficiently (more heat produced, miles driven, or electricity generated per unit of fuel combusted). Yet even though fuel taxes create incentives to burn less fuel and be more energy efficient, they do not give energy users an incentive to reduce emissions per unit of fuel that is burned.

The type of tax discussed would be very different than the Btu tax proposed (but never implemented) by the Clinton administration, which was a uniform Btu tax. This proposed tax was based entirely on the heat content (Btu content) of the fuel and was not designed as an environmental tax. Fuels with a lot of heat content per kilogram of fuel were taxed at a higher level than lower fuels. In other words, natural gas would face a higher tax than coal, which is the opposite relationship to the external costs of the fuel. It is crucial that the tax be based on the average environmental impact of a Btu of each type of fuel. In addition to a tax based on the impacts of conventional pollutants, the fuels should be taxed based on their contribution to accumulation of carbon dioxide in the atmosphere.

Carbon taxes that would be incorporated into fuel taxes could actually be as efficient a policy as taxing the carbon emissions themselves. The reason is that the carbon that is in the fuel is released as either carbon dioxide or as other pollutants.[13] Therefore, taxing the carbon content of the fuel is equivalent to taxing the pollution outputs.

Many people object to more taxes on both philosophical and practical grounds. Philosophical objections center on the argument that government is too big and too intrusive. Practical objections center on the idea that government spending tends to be wasteful, so the money is better left in private hands. People who advance these arguments about taxes and the role of government, however, would not necessarily argue against an energy tax. The tax makes sense from an efficiency point of view, and problems with increased tax revenue and increased role of government could be handled by balancing the increased revenue collections from a fuel tax with reduced income taxes so that total government tax revenue remained constant.[14] Alternatively, if society so desired, the additional revenue could be spent on education, other public goods, or simply reducing the national debt.

The importance of increasing the price of fuel (either through systems of pollution taxes and marketable pollution permits or through the use of fuel taxes) can be seen both in the pollution problems arising from energy and in the lack of progress that has been made in developing and promoting the use of alternative sources of energy. Alternative sources of energy include solar power, geothermal power, wind power, liquid fuels from renewable sources, dry fuels from renewable sources, energy from waste, and hydrogen fuel cells. Liquid fuels from renewable sources include ethanol and methanol from a variety of plant sources, including corn, sugarcane grasses, wood, and oil from a variety of vegetable sources (cottonseed, canola, soybean, palm oil, and so on). These fuels can be used as substitutes for gasoline in internal combustion engines or as boiler fuels. Dry fuels are primarily from wood and grasses and are used as boiler fuels.

---

[13]Incomplete combustion will result in emission of VOCs and carbon monoxide in addition to carbon dioxide. A relatively small amount of the carbon, however, is converted into these pollutants.

[14]See the discussion in Chapter 6 on the "double dividend" of environmental taxes.

These alternative sources of energy are generally less polluting than fossil fuels. For example, if wood is burned to generate steam and produce electricity, the pollution from the wood is small in comparison to the oil or coal that it would displace. Wood can be burned very efficiently, so that the combustion of the wood is very complete, leaving few unburned hydrocarbons in the emissions. Also, wood has virtually no sulfur content, so sulfur dioxide emissions would be greatly reduced. Finally, if the wood (or corn or other biomass fuel) is replanted after harvesting, then the burning of the biomass fuel does not increase global warming. Although the burning of the fuel releases carbon dioxide, if the feedstock is replanted, the growth of the new plants will pull carbon dioxide from the atmosphere. Thus, the burning of biomass fuels cycles carbon, rather than releasing stored carbon (see Chapter 7). Although biomass could fill a portion of the nation's energy needs, it would be very difficult to grow enough energy crops to replace a large portion of fossil fuel use in the short run. Thermal depolymerization processes (for making oil out of waste; see Chapter 8) and hydrogen fuel cells, however, have the potential for completely displacing fossil fuels. Liquid biomass fuels, oil from waste, and fuel cells are important alternative technologies that would not require the United States to replace its transportation infrastructure, in which trillions of dollars have been invested. Because this cost is avoided, it is more likely that a conversion away from fossil fuels would be politically feasible. It also does not require a change in American culture, which is based on the personal mobility that is generated by privately owned passenger cars.

Despite government-sponsored programs of research and development into alternative energy technologies, these technologies have been slow to develop. Quite simply, alternative energy technologies are more expensive for energy users than oil or coal, so they have not become established as important sources of energy. Although fossil fuels have a lower cost to the user, they have a higher cost to society.

Alternative fuels and energy technologies would be significantly advanced if the price of fossil fuels rose to incorporate the full social cost of these fuels. This effect is illustrated in Figure 9.6. In this example, it is assumed that the private cost and the social cost of the alternative fuels (biomass fuels, solar energy, and so on) are equal; that is, that there is no pollution associated with the use of these fuels. This assumption is obviously not true, but the full social costs of fossil fuels may frequently exceed the full social costs of alternatives. In this example, the alternative fuels and oil (which represent all fossil fuels) are measured in common units, such as Btus.

The marginal private cost curve for all fuels is constructed by horizontally summing the MPC curve for alternative fuels and the MPC curve for oil. If D_1 represents the total demand for fuels, then the market equilibrium quantity is t_1, where the total fuel MPC curve intersects the demand function. Notice, however, that the social optimum occurs where the total MSC curve intersects the demand function, with a smaller equilibrium quantity of t_2. If the private cost of oil was increased through an externalities tax, marketable pollution permit system, or fuel tax, then the MPC curve for oil could

Figure 9.6 **Effect of Pollution Taxes on Alternative Fuels**

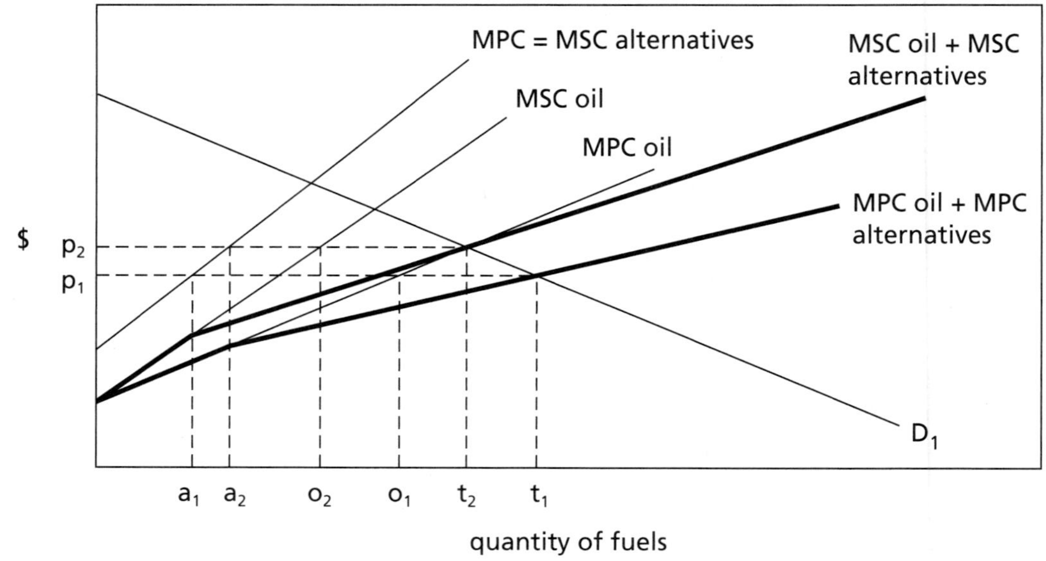

increase to be equal to the MSC curve of oil and would generate a market equilibrium equal to t_2. At this solution, which is associated with a higher price (p_2) for energy, oil usage declines from o_1 to o_2 and alternative fuel usage increases from a_1 to a_2. Notice that because oil usage declines, dependence on foreign oil will decline as well.

The increasing of the price of oil through the imposition of fuel taxes, marketable pollution permits, or pollution taxes has several desirable results. It reduces pollution, because alternative sources are generally cleaner. It also reduces reliance on oil, which will reduce dependence on foreign oil. At first glance, it might seem like a win-win solution, and the question might be posed, Why haven't we raised the price of oil through pollution taxes or fuel taxes? The answer is that there is a belief in the United States that economic success requires low prices for energy.

The Macroeconomic Impact of Fuel Taxes

Let's examine the proposition that low energy prices are a requirement for U.S. economic success. This question can be answered at several levels, including looking at production processes and examining other countries.

It is clear that other economies with higher energy prices have strong and growing economies. Table 9.3 lists gasoline prices in U.S. dollars per gallon for selected developed countries. Although this data is a little old, it does

Table 9.3 World Gasoline Prices (Average Price/Gallon for January 2003)

Country	Price
Belgium	3.92
Canada	1.86
France	4.19
Germany	4.46
Italy	4.29
Japan	3.35
Netherlands	4.75
Spain	3.33
United Kingdom	4.87
United States	1.45

Source: Energy Information Administration, http://www.eia.doe.gov/emeu/internationalpetroleu.htm

illustrate an important point that U.S. gasoline prices (as well as those of Canada) *are* extremely low compared with other countries. In many of these countries, the price of gasoline *is* over three times higher than the price in the United States, and in virtually every country (except Canada), the price is at least twice as high as in the United States. Much of this price differential is due to different levels of taxes.

It might seem odd to argue here that the price of oil and other fossil fuels should be higher, when in Chapter 8 it is argued that two major costs of dependence on foreign oil were the loss of wealth and the macroeconomic effects associated with high prices. Clearly, the loss of wealth does not matter in the case of pollution taxes or fuel taxes because the tax component of the price stays within the United States and does not wind up in the treasuries of foreign producers. U.S. consumers lose consumers' surplus, but the money is transferred to the U.S. treasury rather than foreign treasuries.[15]

One of the reasons that the price increases of the 1970s created undesirable macroeconomic effects is that they came so suddenly. Firms were unable to adjust quickly to the higher energy prices, so they used more energy and

[15]Of course, if the tax revenues are used unwisely, this statement will not be true. If they are used productively or to reduce income taxes, it will be true.

less labor and capital than cost minimization would dictate. The problem associated with rapid price increases, however, can be eliminated by gradually increasing the tax over a long period. For example, if a consumer knew that the tax on gasoline was going to increase by 20 cents per gallon per year for the next 10 years, the consumer would take the future high price into account when he or she decided what model of car to purchase today. Business managers would engage in the same type of advance planning, taking into account the future cost of energy when they made current decisions about production technologies, plant, and equipment.

One more potential source of macroeconomic cost associated with higher prices remains. When previously analyzing higher prices in the context of OPEC and foreign dependence, it was stated that higher prices make energy more scarce to energy users. Because energy is one factor of production, this scarcity must reduce total output or GDP. The same thing, however, cannot be said to be true as a result of higher prices caused by higher taxes because if taxes are efficiently utilized, they reduce the scarcity of other factors of production. For instance, the tax on energy can be used to finance government activities in lieu of a portion of income taxes. The lower income tax makes labor a cheaper factor of production, which can partially offset the effects of the increase in the price of energy. Similarly, if the energy tax money is used to invest in factors of production, such as improving education or infrastructure, the economy will become more productive, partially offsetting the decline in productivity generated by the increase in the price of energy.

In summary, pollution taxes, a system of marketable pollution permits, or fuel taxes will cause less of a negative impact on the macroeconomy than a corresponding increase in prices from OPEC monopoly power. The tax can create partially offsetting increases in productivity. In addition, the tax will serve to reduce pollution emissions, which will reduce global warming, acid deposition, smog, and many other pollutants. This increase in environmental quality will also serve to increase GDP to partially mitigate the negative impacts of the tax. If the relationship between environmental quality and economic output is strong enough, then the energy taxes will actually serve to enhance the performance of the macroeconomy, although the strength of this relationship has not been empirically estimated.

Transition and Future Fuels

Many people who study energy believe that sometime in the future (20 or 50 or 100 years from now) there will be radically different sources of energy. Technological innovation in solar energy or hot fusion could lead to cheap and environmentally friendly sources of energy. The question that remains is, How do we get from the present time to the time when these innovations in energy are available; in other words, what should be our transition fuel?

Before examining policies that try to steer the market in favor of a particular transition fuel, it would be useful to discuss how the forces of supply and demand would result in the switch from one fuel to another. This change is illustrated in Figure 9.7, where it is assumed that there are three possible fuels: oil, coal, and solar energy. In this example, both oil and coal have increasing marginal extraction costs, with the initial units of extraction of oil cheaper than coal. Assume that solar energy is available in unlimited quantities at a high constant marginal cost. If so, then oil is used first, with price determined by total marginal cost, which in this example is equal to total marginal extraction cost plus user cost (externalities are not incorporated into price). As the marginal extraction cost of oil increases relative to the marginal extraction cost of coal, the opportunity cost of the oil (user cost) decreases toward zero. Eventually, the total marginal cost (and price) of oil is equal to the total marginal cost (and price) of coal, and the market switches from oil to coal at time T_{oc}. A similar switch from coal to solar energy occurs at time T_{cs}.

Although increasing price will serve to generate a transition from one fuel to another, policy makers have been concerned with managing these transitions. One source of concern is that the market will not adequately spur research and development into new energy technologies (particularly radically different technologies, such as biomass and solar energy) especially because such research and development may be particularly risky for the investor. Another source of concern is the continual policy concern with abundant, cheap energy at a low price.

A more recent concern with energy transitions is the environmental effect of transitions. If environmental externalities are not incorporated into market

Figure 9.7 **Fuel Transitions**

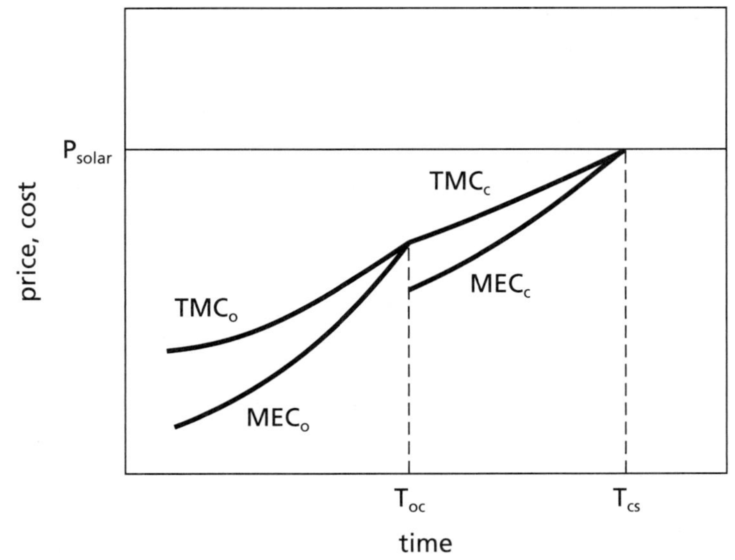

price, then the transition to cleaner fuels such as solar energy will take place later than socially optimal. Also, the market may choose relatively dirty fuels (such as coal) as the transition fuel, rather than cleaner ones (such as natural gas).

The Carter administration adopted a set of policies that defined coal as the transition fuel because the United States has abundant supplies of coal. This position has been largely abandoned due to high levels of pollution associated with the burning of coal. Of course, technological innovation in developing ways to burn coal cleanly could change this stance, and much progress has already been made in developing cleaner and more efficient coal-burning technologies. Nonetheless, the use of coal will increase atmospheric concentrations of carbon dioxide.

Another possibility is what is referred to as deep natural gas, which is thousands of feet deeper and more expensive to produce than conventional natural gas. Deep natural gas is advocated by its proponents because natural gas is the cleanest of the fossil fuels. One of the problems with both "clean coal" and deep natural gas, however, is that burning these fuels releases stored carbon, exacerbating the global climate change problem rather than mitigating the problem.

The debate over which fuel should constitute the transition fuel, however, is really an unnecessary debate. If all fuels included all social costs in their prices, then the market would pick the fuel with the lowest social cost as the transition fuel, and the movement toward the future fuels would be speeded by the higher current price of energy.

Energy and the Third World

Although U.S. citizens and citizens of other developed nations speak of an energy crisis in their respective countries, the real energy crisis is occurring in Third World nations. These nations, with less sophisticated economies, were much less capable of adjusting to the price shocks associated with the oil price increases of the 1970s. In addition to the types of macroeconomic effects that developed nations faced, Third World nations faced additional problems with their foreign reserve balances (holdings of internationally desirable currencies, such as U.S. dollars, German marks, and Japanese yen). The need to use more foreign reserves to purchase oil stretched their already thin foreign reserves. Many nations then borrowed foreign currencies for development projects and for imports of oil and other goods that began the big debt problems of the late 1970s and the 1980s (see Chapter 18 for a discussion of Third World issues).

The increase in the price of fossil fuels also forced even greater reliance on fuel wood, which is the primary source of energy in developing countries. The increased reliance on fuel wood was an important factor in the increase in deforestation in many areas of the world. The increased deforestation has led to myriad environmental and economic problems described in Chapters 13 and 18.

Environmental externalities from energy use are also responsible for the dreadful environmental quality of Eastern and Central Europe. The reliance on low-quality coal and the absence of any effort to abate pollution has led to air quality that is so bad that it is one of the leading causes of sickness and death in countries such as Poland, (the former) Czechoslovakia, and Romania. Similarly, very bad levels of air quality are found in the big industrial cities of the developing world, such as São Paulo, Santiago, Beijing, and Mexico City. These problems are also discussed further in Chapter 18.

Major environmental problems also occur in developing countries that produce energy for export. Many developing countries have less restrictive environmental laws or lack effective enforcement mechanisms than do developed countries which leads to environmental abuses by the foreign or domestic firms that produce the energy. For example, environmental (and social) conditions in petroleum-producing areas of Nigeria have deteriorated quite noticeably.

Summary

This chapter concludes a three-chapter focus on energy and the environment. These chapters have documented a strong environmental impact of energy use, including global climate change, acid rain, air pollution, water pollution, and habitat loss.

Although the Clean Air Act and other legislation in the United States (and similar legislation in other countries) has had some impact in reducing the negative consequences of energy use, much progress needs to be made. The dual problems of the social costs from environmental impacts from energy use and social costs of reliance on imported oil from insecure sources should be internalized through emissions permits or taxes, or addressed by incorporation into the price of energy. Internalizing the external cost of emissions and national security externalites through permits and taxes will generate a series of reactions that will lead to higher social welfare in the future.

appendix 9.a
Air Pollution Trends 1940–1998

Table 9a.1 **Total National Emissions of Carbon Monoxide, 1940 through 1998 (thousand short tons)**

Source Category	1940	1950	1960	1970	1980	1990	1996	1998
FUEL COMB. ELEC UTIL	4	110	110	237	322	363	391	417
FUEL COMB. INDUSTRIAL	435	549	661	770	750	879	1155	1115
FUEL COMB. OTHER	14,890	10,656	6250	3625	6230	4269	4603	3843
Residential Wood	11,279	7716	4743	2932	5992	3781	4200	3452
CHEMICAL AND ALLIED PRODUCT MFG	4190	5844	3982	3397	2151	1183	1100	1129
Other Chemical Mfg	4139	5760	3775	2866	1417	854	870	893
carbon black mfg	4139	5760	3775	2866	1417	798	841	863
METALS PROCESSING	2750	2910	2866	3644	2246	2640	1429	1495
Nonferrous Metals Processing	36	118	326	652	842	436	442	446
Ferrous Metals Processing	2714	2792	2540	2991	1404	2163	944	1006
basic oxygen furnace	NA	NA	23	440	80	594	117	126
PETROLEUM AND RELATED INDUSTRIES	221	2651	3086	2179	1723	333	356	368
Oil and Gas Production	NA	NA	NA	NA	NA	38	26	27
Petroleum Refineries & Publishing Products	221	2651	3086	2168	1723	291	322	334
fcc units	210	2528	2810	1820	1680	284	311	322
OTHER INDUSTRIAL PROCESSES	114	231	342	620	830	537	600	632
Wood, Pulp, Paper, and Publishing Products	221	220	331	610	798	473	391	416
sulfate pulping: rec. furnace/evaporator	NA	NA	NA	NA	NA	370	305	325
SOLVENT UTILIZATION	NA	NA	NA	NA	NA	5	2	2
STORAGE AND TRANSPORT	NA	NA	NA	NA	NA	76	78	80
WASTE DISPOSAL AND RECYCLING	3630	4717	5597	7059	2300	1079	1127	1154
Incineration	2202	2711	2703	2979	1246	372	404	413
residential	716	824	972	1107	945	294	330	336
Open Burning	1428	2006	2894	4080	1054	706	717	735
residential	NA	NA	NA	NA	NA	509	515	524

Source Category	1940	1950	1960	1970	1980	1990	1996	1998
ON-ROAD VEHICLES	30,121	45,196	64,266	88,034	78,049	57,848	53,262	50,386
Light-Duty Gas Vehicles and Motorcycles	22,237	31,493	47,679	64,031	53,561	37,407	28,732	27,039
light-duty gas vehicles	22,232	31,472	47,655	63,846	53,342	37,198	28,543	26,848
Light-Duty Gas Trucks	3752	6110	7791	16,570	16,137	13,816	19,271	18,726
light-duty gas trucks 1	2694	4396	5591	10,102	10,395	8415	11,060	10,826
light-duty gas trucks 2	1058	1714	2200	6468	5742	5402	8211	7900
Heavy-Duty Gas Vehicles	4132	7537	8557	6712	7189	5360	3766	3067
Diesels	NA	54	239	721	1161	1265	1493	1554
heavy-duty diesel vehicles	NA	54	239	721	1139	1229	1453	1514
NON-ROAD ENGINES AND VEHICLES	8051	11,610	11,575	11,970	14,489	18,191	20,232	19,914
Non-Road Gasoline	3777	7331	8753	10,946	12,760	15,394	17,074	16,812
industrial	780	1558	1379	535	709	723	592	563
lawn and garden	NA	NA	NA	5899	6764	8237	9305	9024
light commercial	NA	NA	NA	1905	2095	2877	3514	3566
recreational marine vessels	60	120	518	1763	1990	2117	2142	2156
Non-Road Diesel	32	53	65	430	829	1098	1282	1180
construction	20	43	40	254	479	662	794	728
farm	12	10	17	16	174	166	176	163
Aircraft	4	934	1764	506	743	904	949	955
Railroads	4083	3076	332	65	96	121	112	115
MISCELLANEOUS	29,210	18,135	11,010	7909	8344	11,122	11,144	8920
Other Combustion	29,210	18,135	11,010	7909	8344	11,122	11,144	8919
TOTAL ALL SOURCES	**93,616**	**102,609**	**109,745**	**129,444**	**117,434**	**98,523**	**95,480**	**89,455**

Note(s): NA = not available. For several source categories, emissions either prior to or beginning with 1985 are not available at the more detailed level but are contained in the more aggregate estimate.
"Other" categories may contain emissions that could not be accurately allocated to specific source categories.
To convert emissions to gigagrams (thousand metric tons), multiply the above values by 0.9072.

Source: U.S. Environmental Protection Agency, *National Air Pollution Emission Trends, 1900–1998*, EPA-454-R-00-002, March 2000. Online: http://www.epa.gov/ttn/chief/trends/trends98/.

Table 9a.2 **Total National Emissions of Nitrogen Oxides, 1940 through 1998**

Source Category	**1940**	**1950**	**1960**	**1970**	**1980**	**1990**	**1996**	**1998**
FUEL COMB. ELEC. UTIL.	660	1316	2536	4900	7024	6663	6057	6103
Coal	467	1118	2038	3888	6123	5642	5542	5395
bituminous	255	584	1154	2112	3439	4532	3748	3622
Oil	193	198	498	1012	901	221	103	208
residual	6	23	8	40	39	207	101	206
distillate	187	175	490	972	862	14	2	2
Gas	NA	NA	NA	NA	NA	565	265	344
natural	NA	NA	NA	NA	NA	565	264	342
FUEL COMB. INDUSTRIAL	2543	3192	4075	4325	3555	3035	3072	2969
Coal	2012	1076	782	771	444	585	567	548
Oil	122	237	239	332	286	265	231	216
Gas	365	1756	2954	3060	2619	1182	1184	1154
natural	337	1692	2846	3053	2469	967	978	943
Internal Combustion	NA	NA	NA	NA	NA	874	967	932
FUEL COMB. OTHER	529	647	760	836	741	1196	1224	1117
Commercial/Institutional Gas	7	18	55	120	131	200	238	234
Residential Other	177	227	362	439	356	780	783	700
natural gas	20	50	148	242	238	449	481	410
CHEMICAL & ALLIED PRODUCT MFG	6	63	110	271	213	168	146	152
METALS PROCESSING	4	110	110	77	65	97	83	88
PETROLEUM & RELATED INDUSTRIES	105	110	220	240	72	153	134	138
OTHER INDUSTRIAL PROCESSES	107	93	131	187	205	378	386	408
Mineral Products	105	89	123	169	181	270	286	303
cement mfg	32	55	78	97	98	151	172	182
SOLVENT UTILIZATION	NA	NA	NA	NA	NA	1	2	2

Source Category	1940	1950	1960	1970	1980	1990	1996	1998
STORAGE & TRANSPORT	NA	NA	NA	NA	NA	3	7	7
WASTE DISPOSAL & RECYCLING	110	215	331	440	111	91	95	97
ON-ROAD VEHICLES	1330	2143	3982	7390	8621	7089	7848	7765
Light-Duty Gas Vehicles & Motorcycles	970	1415	2607	4158	4421	3220	2979	2849
light-duty gas vehicles	970	1415	2606	4156	4416	3208	2967	2837
Light-Duty Gas Trucks	204	339	525	1278	1408	1256	1950	1917
light-duty gas trucks 1	132	219	339	725	864	784	1156	1132
light-duty gas trucks 2	73	120	186	553	544	472	794	785
Heavy-Duty Gas Vehicles	155	296	363	278	300	326	329	323
Diesels	NA	93	487	1676	2493	2287	2591	2676
heavy-duty diesel vehicles	NA	93	487	1676	2463	2240	2544	2630
NON-ROAD ENGINES AND VEHICLES	991	1538	1443	1931	3529	4804	5167	5280
Non-Road Gasoline	122	249	312	85	101	120	132	159
Non-Road Diesel	103	187	247	1109	2125	2513	2786	2809
construction	70	158	157	436	843	1102	1218	1230
farm	33	29	50	350	926	898	1001	999
Aircraft	NA	2	4	72	106	158	167	168
Marine Vessels	109	108	108	171	467	943	985	1008
Railroads	657	992	772	495	731	929	922	947
MISCELLANEOUS	990	665	441	330	248	369	452	328
TOTAL ALL SOURCES	**7374**	**10,093**	**14,140**	**20,928**	**24,384**	**24,049**	**24,676**	**24,454**

Note(s): NA = not available. For several source categories, emissions either prior to or beginning with 1985 are not available at the more detailed level but are contained in the more aggregate estimate.
"Other" categories may contain emissions that could not be accurately allocated to specific source categories.
In order to convert emissions to gigagrams (thousand metric tons), multiply the above values by 0.9072.

Source: U.S. Environmental Protection Agency, *National Air Pollution Emission Trends, 1900–1998*, EPA-454-R-00-002, March 2000. Online: http://www.epa.gov/ttn/chief/trends/trends98/.

Table 9a.3 **Total National Emissions of Volatile Organic Compounds, 1940 through 1998 (thousand short tons)**

Source Category	1940	1950	1960	1970	1980	1990	1996	1998
FUEL COMB. ELEC. UTIL.	2	9	9	30	45	47	49	54
FUEL COMB. INDUSTRIAL	108	98	106	150	157	182	166	161
FUEL COMB. OTHER	1867	1336	768	541	848	776	821	678
Residential Wood	1410	970	563	460	809	718	759	620
CHEMICAL & ALLIED PRODUCT MFG	884	1324	991	1341	1595	634	388	396
METALS PROCESSING	325	442	342	394	273	122	72	75
PETROLEUM & RELATED INDUSTRIES	571	548	1034	1194	1440	612	488	496
OTHER INDUSTRIAL PROCESSES	130	184	202	270	237	401	428	450
SOLVENT UTILIZATION	1971	3679	4403	7174	6584	5750	5506	5278
Degreasing	168	592	438	707	513	744	606	457
Graphic Arts	114	310	199	319	373	274	296	311
Dry Cleaning	42	153	126	263	320	215	157	169
petroleum solvent	NA	NA	NA	NA	NA	104	92	99
Surface Coating	1058	2187	2128	3570	3685	2523	2389	2224
industrial adhesives	14	41	29	52	55	390	356	160
architectural	284	NA	412	442	477	495	484	491
Nonindustrial	490	NA	1189	1674	1002	1900	1957	2012
cutback asphalt	328	NA	789	1045	323	199	135	144
pesticide application	73	NA	193	241	241	258	386	405
adhesives	NA	NA	NA	NA	NA	361	307	313
consumer solvents	NA	NA	NA	NA	NA	1083	1081	1099
STORAGE & TRANSPORT	639	1218	1762	1954	1975	1495	1286	1324
Bulk Terminals & Plants	185	361	528	599	517	359	211	217
area source: gasoline	158	307	449	509	440	282	163	167
Petroleum & Petroleum Product Storage	148	218	304	300	306	157	172	178

Source Category	1940	1950	1960	1970	1980	1990	1996	1998
STORAGE & TRANSPORT								
Petroleum & Petroleum Product Transport	57	100	115	92	61	151	118	122
Service Stations: Stage I	117	251	365	416	461	300	312	320
Service Stations: Stage II	130	283	437	521	583	433	397	409
WASTE DISPOSAL & RECYCLING	990	1104	1546	1984	758	986	423	433
ON-ROAD VEHICLES	4817	7251	10,506	12,972	8979	6313	5490	5325
Light-Duty Gas Vehicles & Motorcycles	3647	5220	8058	9193	5907	3947	2875	2832
light-duty gas vehicles	3646	5214	8050	9133	5843	3885	2839	2793
Light-Duty Gas Trucks	672	1101	1433	2770	2059	1622	2060	2015
Heavy-Duty Gas Vehicles	498	908	926	743	611	432	293	257
Diesels	NA	22	89	266	402	312	263	222
NON-ROAD ENGINES AND VEHICLES	778	1213	1215	1878	2312	2545	2664	2461
Non-Road Gasoline	208	423	526	1564	1787	1889	1982	1794
lawn & garden	NA	NA	NA	511	583	700	771	638
recreational marine vessels	16	32	124	736	830	784	777	780
Non-Road Diesel	12	20	23	187	327	390	422	405
construction	6	15	13	94	135	181	206	199
farm	6	5	8	39	138	126	120	111
Aircraft	3	110	220	97	146	180	177	177
NATURAL SOURCES	NA	NA	NA	NA	NA	14	14	14
MISCELLANEOUS	4079	2530	1573	1101	1134	1059	940	772
Other Combustion	4079	2530	1573	1101	1134	1049	891	721
TOTAL ALL SOURCES	**17,161**	**20,936**	**24,459**	**30,982**	**26,336**	**20,936**	**18,736**	**17,917**

Note(s): NA = not available. For several source categories, emissions either prior to or beginning with 1985 are not available at the more detailed level but are contained in the more aggregate estimate.
"Other" categories may contain emissions that could not be accurately allocated to specific source categories.
In order to convert emissions to gigagrams (thousand metric tons), multiply the above values by 0.9072.

Source: U.S. Environmental Protection Agency, *National Air Pollution Emission Trends, 1900–1998*, EPA-454-R-00-002, March 2000. Online: http://www.epa.gov/ttn/chief/trends/trends98/.

Table 9a.4 **Total National Emissions of Sulfur Dioxide, 1940 through 1998 (thousand short tons)**

Source Category	1940	1950	1960	1970	1980	1990	1996	1998
FUEL COMB. ELEC. UTIL.	2427	4515	9263	17,398	17,469	15,909	12,631	13,217
Coal	2276	4056	8,883	15,799	16,073	15,220	12,137	12,426
bituminous	1359	2427	5367	9574	NA	13,371	8931	9368
subbituminous	668	1196	2642	4716	NA	1415	2630	2440
anthracite & lignite	249	433	873	1509	NA	434	576	618
Oil	151	459	380	1598	1395	639	436	730
residual	146	453	375	1578	NA	629	430	726
FUEL COMB. INDUSTRIAL	6060	5725	3864	4568	2951	3550	3022	2895
Coal	5188	4423	2703	3129	1527	1914	1465	1415
bituminous	3473	2945	1858	2171	1058	1050	1031	1000
Oil	554	972	922	1229	1065	927	844	773
residual	397	721	663	956	851	687	637	568
distillate	9	49	42	98	85	198	187	184
Gas	145	180	189	140	299	543	556	558
FUEL COMB. OTHER	3642	3964	2319	1490	971	831	667	609
Commercial/Institutional Coal	695	1212	154	109	110	212	177	194
Commercial/Institutional Oil	407	658	905	883	637	425	338	275
Residential Other	2517	2079	1250	492	211	175	131	121
bituminous/subbituminous coal	2267	1758	868	260	43	30	17	18
CHEMICAL & ALLIED PRODUCT MFG	215	427	447	591	280	297	291	299
Inorganic Chemical Mfg	215	427	447	591	271	214	204	210
sulfur compounds	215	427	447	591	271	211	202	208
METALS PROCESSING	3309	3747	3986	4775	1842	726	429	444
Nonferrous Metals Processing	2760	3092	3322	4060	1279	517	283	288
copper	2292	2369	2772	3507	1080	323	114	119
lead	80	95	57	77	34	129	111	110
Ferrous Metals Processing	550	655	664	715	562	186	128	139

Source Category	1940	1950	1960	1970	1980	1990	1996	1998
PETROLEUM & RELATED INDUSTRIES	224	340	676	881	734	430	337	345
Oil & Gas Production	NA	14	114	111	157	122	95	96
natural gas	NA	14	114	111	157	120	95	95
Petroleum Refineries & Related Industries	224	326	562	770	577	304	234	241
fluid catalytic cracking units	220	242	383	480	330	183	153	158
OTHER INDUSTRIAL PROCESSES	334	596	671	846	918	399	350	370
Wood, Pulp & Paper, & Publishing Products	NA	43	114	169	223	116	102	108
Mineral Products	334	553	557	677	694	275	230	243
cement mfg	318	522	524	618	630	181	147	156
SOLVENT UTILIZATION	NA	NA	NA	NA	NA	0	1	1
STORAGE & TRANSPORT	NA	NA	NA	NA	NA	7	3	3
WASTE DISPOSAL & RECYCLING	3	3	10	8	33	42	41	42
ON-ROAD VEHICLES	3	103	114	411	521	542	316	326
Light-Duty Gas Vehicles & Motorcycles	NA	NA	NA	132	159	138	127	130
Diesels	NA	NA	NA	231	303	337	83	85
NON-ROAD ENGINES AND VEHICLES	3190	2392	321	83	175	916	1016	1084
Marine Vessels	215	215	105	43	117	251	237	261
Railroads	2975	2174	215	36	53	122	111	114
MISCELLANEOUS	545	545	554	110	11	12	17	12
Other Combustion	545	545	554	110	11	12	17	12
Fugitive Dust				NA	NA	0	0	0
TOTAL ALL SOURCES	19,952	22,357	22,227	31,161	25,905	23,660	19,121	19,647

Note(s): NA = not available. For several source categories, emissions either prior to or beginning with 1985 are not available at the more detailed level but are contained in the more aggregate estimate. Zero values represent less than 500 short tons/year.
"Other" categories may contain emissions that could not be accurately allocated to specific source categories.
The 1985 fuel combustion, electric utility category is based on the National Allowance Data Base Version 2.11, Acid Rain Division, U.S. EPA, released March 23, 1993. Allocations at the Tier 3 levels are approximations only and are based on the methodology described in section 6.0, paragraph 6.2.1.1.
In order to convert emissions to gigagrams (thousand metric tons), multiply the above values by 0.9072.

Source: U.S. Environmental Protection Agency, *National Air Pollution Emission Trends, 1900–1998*, EPA-454-R-00-002, March 2000. Online: http://www.epa.gov/ttn/chief/trends/trends98/.

Table 9a.5 Total National Emissions of Directly Emitted Particulate Matter (PM10), 1940 through 1998 (thousand short tons)

Source Category	1940	1950	1960	1970	1980	1990	1996	1998
FUEL COMB. ELEC. UTIL.	962	1467	2117	1775	879	295	287	302
Coal	954	1439	2092	1680	796	265	264	273
bituminous	573	865	1288	1041	483	188	195	200
FUEL COMB. INDUSTRIAL	708	604	331	641	679	270	255	245
Coal	549	365	146	83	18	84	77	74
Other	120	160	103	441	571	87	77	74
FUEL COMB. OTHER	2338	1674	1113	455	887	631	632	544
Residential Wood	1716	1128	850	384	818	501	503	411
CHEMICAL & ALLIED PRODUCT MFG	330	455	309	235	148	77	63	65
METALS PROCESSING	1208	1027	1026	1316	622	214	164	171
Nonferrous Metals Processing	588	346	375	593	130	50	35	37
copper	217	105	122	343	32	14	7	7
Ferrous Metals Processing	246	427	214	198	322	155	108	112
primary	86	98	51	31	271	128	86	91
PETROLEUM & RELATED INDUSTRIES	366	412	689	286	138	55	32	32
OTHER INDUSTRIAL PROCESSES	3996	6954	7211	5832	1846	583	327	339
Agriculture, Food, & Kindred Products	784	696	691	485	402	73	61	61
country elevators	299	307	343	257	258	9	6	6
terminal elevators	351	258	224	147	86	6	2	2
Wood, Pulp & Paper, & Publishing Products	511	798	958	727	183	105	78	82
sulfate (kraft) pulping	470	729	886	668	142	73	43	45
Mineral Products	2701	5460	5563	4620	1261	367	156	162
cement mfg	1363	1998	2014	1731	417	190	21	22
stone quarrying/processing	482	663	1039	957	421	54	24	24
SOLVENT UTILIZATION	NA	NA	NA	NA	NA	4	6	6
STORAGE & TRANSPORT	NA	NA	NA	NA	NA	102	90	94
Bulk Materials Storage	NA	NA	NA	NA	NA	100	87	91
WASTE DISPOSAL & RECYCLING	392	505	764	999	273	271	304	310
Open Burning	220	333	544	770	198	206	211	215
residential	220	333	544	770	198	195	194	197

Source Category	1940	1950	1960	1970	1980	1990	1996	1998
ON-ROAD VEHICLES	210	314	554	443	397	336	282	257
Diesels	NA	9	15	136	208	235	177	152
heavy-duty diesel vehicles	NA	9	15	136	194	224	168	144
NON-ROAD ENGINES AND VEHICLES	2480	1788	201	220	398	489	457	461
Non-Road Diesel	1	16	22	281	439	301	297	301
construction	0	12	12	102	148	149	147	150
farm	0	4	7	140	239	78	72	69
Railroads	2464	1742	110	25	37	53	27	27
NATURAL SOURCES	NA	NA	NA	NA	NA	2092	5307	5307
Geogenic - wind erosion*	NA	NA	NA	NA	NA	2092	5307	5307
MISCELLANEOUS	2968	1934	1244	839	852	24,542	24,836	26,609
Agriculture & Forestry	NA	NA	NA	NA	NA	5292	4905	4970
agricultural crops**	NA	NA	NA	NA	NA	4745	4328	4366
agricultural livestock**	NA	NA	NA	NA	NA	547	577	603
Other Combustion	2968	1934	1244	839	852	1181	1254	1018
Fugitive Dust	NA	NA	NA	NA	NA	18,069	18,675	20,619
unpaved roads**	NA	NA	NA	NA	NA	11,234	12,059	12,668
paved roads**	NA	NA	NA	NA	NA	2248	2390	2618
construction**				NA	NA	4249	3578	4545
TOTAL ALL SOURCES	**15,957**	**17,133**	**15,558**	**13,042**	**7119**	**29,962**	**33,041**	**34,741**

Note(s): NA = not available. For several source categories, emissions either prior to or beginning with 1985 are not available at the more detailed level but are contained in the more aggregate estimate. Zero values represent less than 500 short tons/year.
Categories displayed below Tier 1 do not sum to Tier 1 totals because they are intended to show major contributors.
In order to convert emissions to gigagrams (thousand metric tons), multiply the above values by 0.9072.

* Although geogenic wind erosion emissions are included in this summary table, it is very difficult to interpret annual estimates of PM emissions from this source category in a meaningful way, owing to the highly episodic nature of the events that contribute to these emissions.

** These are the main source categories of PM crustal material emissions. A report by the Desert Research Institute found that about 75% of these emissions are within 2 m of the ground at the point they are measured. Thus, most of them are likely to be removed or deposited within a few km of their release, depending on atmospheric turbulence, temperature, soil moisture, availability of horizontal and vertical surfaces for impaction, and initial suspension energy. This is consistent with the generally small amount of crustal materials found on speciated ambient samples. (See reference 6 in Chapter 2.)

Source: U.S. Environmental Protection Agency, *National Air Pollution Emission Trends, 1900–1998*, EPA-454-R-00-002, March 2000. Online: http://www.epa.gov/ttn/chief/trends/trends98/.

Table 9a.6 Total National Emissions of Lead, 1970 through 1998 (thousand short tons)

Source Category	1970	1975	1980	1985	1990	1996	1998
FUEL COMB. ELEC. UTIL.	327	230	129	64	64	61	68
Coal	300	189	95	51	46	53	54
bituminous	181	114	57	31	28	32	33
Oil	28	41	34	13	18	8	14
FUEL COMB. INDUSTRIAL	237	75	60	30	18	16	19
Coal	218	60	45	22	14	13	13
bituminous	146	40	31	15	10	9	9
Oil	19	16	14	8	3	3	5
FUEL COMB. OTHER	10,052	10,042	4,111	421	418	415	416
Misc. Fuel Comb. (Except Residential)	10,000	10,000	4,080	400	400	400	400
CHEMICAL & ALLIED PRODUCT MFG	103	120	104	118	136	167	175
Inorganic Chemical Mfg	103	120	104	118	136	167	175
lead oxide and pigments	103	120	104	118	136	167	175
METALS PROCESSING	24,224	9923	3026	2097	2170	2055	2098
Nonferrous Metals Processing	15,869	7192	1826	1376	1409	1333	1371
primary lead production	12,134	5640	1075	874	728	588	628
primary copper production	242	171	20	19	19	22	23
primary zinc production	1019	224	24	16	9	13	13
secondary lead production	1894	821	481	288	449	514	505
secondary copper production	374	200	116	70	75	76	83
lead battery manufacture	41	49	50	65	78	103	117
lead cable coating	127	55	37	43	50	16	1

Source Category	1970	1975	1980	1985	1990	1996	1998
Ferrous Metals Processing	7395	2196	911	577	576	529	542
coke manufacturing	11	8	6	3	4	0	0
ferroalloy production	219	104	13	7	18	8	4
iron production	266	93	38	21	18	18	19
steel production	3125	1082	481	209	138	160	173
gray iron production	3773	910	373	336	397	343	345
Metals Processing NEC	960	535	289	144	185	193	186
metal mining	353	268	207	141	184	192	186
OTHER INDUSTRIAL PROCESSES	2028	1337	808	316	169	51	54
Mineral Products	540	217	93	43	26	29	31
cement manufacturing	540	217	93	43	26	29	31
Miscellaneous Industrial Processes	1488	1120	715	273	143	22	23
WASTE DISPOSAL & RECYCLING	2200	1595	1210	871	804	609	620
Incineration	2200	1595	1210	871	804	609	620
municipal waste	581	396	161	79	67	76	75
other	1619	1199	1049	792	738	534	546
ON-ROAD VEHICLES	171,961	130,206	60,501	18,052	421	19	19
Light-Duty Gas Vehicles & Motorcycles	142,918	106,868	47,184	13,637	314	12	12
Light-Duty Gas Trucks	22,683	19,440	11,671	4061	100	7	7
Heavy-Duty Gas Vehicles	6361	3898	1646	354	7	0	0
NON-ROAD ENGINES AND VEHICLES	9737	6130	4205	921	776	505	503
Non-Road Gasoline	8340	5012	3320	229	158	0	0
Aircraft	1397	1118	885	692	619	505	503
TOTAL ALL SOURCES	220,869	159,659	74,153	22,890	4975	3899	3973

Note(s): NA = not available. For several source categories, emissions either prior to or beginning with 1985 are not available at the more detailed level but are contained in the more aggregate estimate. Zero values represent less than 500 short tons/year.

Categories displayed below Tier 1 do not sum to Tier 1 totals because they are intended to show major contributors.

In order to convert emissions to gigagrams (thousand metric tons), multiply the above values by 0.9072.

Review Questions

1. Assume that you are dealing with a very small country with one lake, one electric utility, and 1000 people who fish in the lake. Let the inverse demand for recreational fishing trips be

$$D_f = 200 - 10 \text{ trips} + 110 \text{ (catch per day)}$$

Let the inverse demand for megawatt hours (MWh) of electricty equal

$$D_e = 100 - 0.001 \text{ MWh}$$

Assume that emissions from the power plant affect the quality of the fishing and that a particular policy results in a reduction in emissions that increased catch per day from 5 to 10 while increasing the costs of producing electricity from \$7 per MWh to \$8 MWh. If each of the 1000 people who fish has a travel cost of \$10 to gain access to the lake, then does the policy increase or decrease net social benefits?

2. Look at pages 307–309, which discuss the SO_2 offset trading between a utility in Wisconsin and the TVA in Tennessee. Assume that the trade reduces Wisconsin electricity consumers' bills by a total of \$1 million and lowers Tennessee electricity consumers' bills by \$500,000. Also assume that the trade improves local environmental quality in Wisconsin by an amount that people value at \$2 million. If the local environmental quality in Tennessee declines as a result of this trade, then what is the most that Tennesseans would be willing to pay to avoid the environmental decline that would still make the trade a potential Pareto improvement?
3. What are the primary impacts of acid deposition? What valuation tools are available to measure the willingness to pay to avoid these impacts?
4. What distinguishes the acid rain problem from the global warming problem?
5. Why would a focus on local air pollution lead to increased regional transport of acid rain precursor pollutants?
6. What problems can be found in existing studies that attempt to measure the willingness to pay for increased visibility?
7. What important pollutants are generated by fossil fuel consumption?
8. What global and regional environmental problems are caused by fossil fuel consumption?
9. Describe an economic incentive for dealing with pollution from mobile sources.
10. Is the price of energy too high or too low? Why?
11. Under what circumstances would higher energy prices lead to economic dislocation in the United States?
12. What are the primary energy problems faced by developing nations?

Questions for Further Study

1. What is wrong with Title IV of the 1990 Clean Air Act Amendments? How would you change the amendments to make them more efficient?
2. How can the travel cost technique be used to measure the recreational fishing use values associated with reducing acid deposition?
3. Why is it easier to measure the impact of acid deposition on agriculture than on forests?
4. Should solar energy be subsidized?
5. Should mass transit be subsidized?
6. Formulate an energy/environmental policy to carry the United States through the next 30 years.
7. What was wrong with the energy policies of the 1970s?
8. What was wrong with the energy policies of the 1980s?
9. What was wrong with the energy policies of the 1990s?
10. What is wrong with current energy policy?
11. Will a system of pollution controls or energy taxes adversely affect the U.S. economy?
12. How would pollution taxes affect the development of alternative clean sources of energy?

Suggested Paper Topics

1. Survey the literature on measuring the recreational fishing impacts of acid rain. If you start with Brown et al. (1990) and with NAPAP's *1990 Integrated Assessment Report*, you will find references to most of the earlier work. Ask your government documents reference librarian how to locate these reports. Also, peruse current issues of the *Journal of*

Environmental Economics and Management, Land Economics, Journal of Agricultural Economics, and *Journal of Economic Literature* for additional references.

2. Write a paper looking at policy issues involving transfrontier pollutants. Look in recent issues of the *Journal of Environmental Economics and Management, Land Economics*, and *Environmental and Resource Economics* for references in this area.
3. Write a paper examining the current trading system for sulfur dioxide emissions. What are the nature of the trades that have taken place? What are the faults with the trading system? How would you modify the system to make it more efficient?
4. Choose a country that has implemented economic incentives to control air pollution, and analyze its system. Diagram the strengths and weaknesses of that approach and suggest ways to strengthen the system.
5. Develop an energy policy to take the United States through the next 30 years. Look at the *National Energy Strategy* (U.S. Department of Energy, 1991) and current issues of *Energy Economics* and *Energy Journal*. Also look in general-interest journals, such as *Nature* and *Science*, as well as Internet sites of the U.S. Department of Energy and U.S. Environmental Protection Agency. Look at the EPA web site, http://www.epa.gov, with particular attention to the new Clear Skies initiative.
6. Examine the economic barriers to the development of solar energy. Should the government seek to reduce these barriers? What actions could it take to reduce them? Search bibliographic databases on solar energy and economics, solar energy and energy policy, and solar energy and technological innovation.
7. Demand-side management is a policy that many electric utilities are undertaking to reduce the need to develop additional electricity-generating capacity. Examine this policy, how it affects utility profits, and how it affects social welfare.
8. Develop a transportation policy for U.S. urban areas. What are the objectives of your policy? (What market failures are you trying to correct?) What economic incentives would you employ? What command and control techniques would you employ? Why?
9. Investigate the relationship between per capita energy use and per capita income. What is the cause-and-effect relationship between the two? Data for an empirical investigation may be obtained from *World Resources*. Does your work show causation or correlation?

Works Cited and Selected Readings

Adamson, S., R. Bates, R. Laslett, and A. Potoschnig. Energy Use, Air Pollution, and Environmental Policy in Krakow: Can Economic Incentives Really Help? Technical Paper 308, Energy Series. Washington, DC: The World Bank, 1996.

Anderson, R., and A. Lohof. *The United States Experience with Economic Incentives in Environmental Pollution Control Policy*. Washington, DC: Environmental Protection Agency, 1997.

Bailey, E. M. *Allowance Activity and Regulatory Rulings: Evidence from the U.S. Acid Rain Program*. MIT-CEEPR 96-002WP. Cambridge, MA: Massachusetts Institute of Technology, 1996.

Baumol, W.J., and W. E. Oates. *Theory of Environmental Policy*. Cambridge: Cambridge University Press, 1988.

Blackman, A., and W. Harrington. The Use of Economic Incentives in Developing Countries: Lessons from International Experience with Industrial Air Pollution. Discussion Paper 99-39. Washington, DC: Resources for the Future, 1999.

Bloyd, C., J. Camp, G. Gonzelmann, J. Formento, J. Molburg, J. Shannon, M. Henrion, R. Sonnenblick, K. Soo Hoo, J. Kalagnanam, et al. *Tracking and Analysis Framework (TAF) Model Documentation and User's Guide*. ANL/DIS/TM-36. Argonne, IL: Argonne National Laboratory, 1996.

Bohi, D. R. *Energy Security in the 1980s: Economic and Political Perspectives*. Washington, DC: Brookings Institute, 1984.

Bohi, D. R. Utilities and State Regulators Are Failing to Take Advantage of Emissions Allowance Trading. *Electricity Journal 7*, no. 2 (1994): 20–27.

Bohi, D., and D. Burtraw. SO_2 Allowance Trading: How Do Expectations and Experience Measure Up? *Electricity Journal 10*, no. 7 (1997): 67–75.

Bohlin, F. The Swedish Carbon Dioxide Tax: Effects of Biofuel Use and Carbon Dioxide Emissions. *Biomass and Energy 15* (1998): 213–291.

Brookshire, D. S., R. C. D'Arge, W. D. Schulze, M. A. Thayer. *Methods Development for Assessing Air Pollution Control Benefits. Vol. 2: Experiments in Valuing Non-Market Goods: A Case Study of Alternative Benefit Measures of Air Pollution in the South Coast Air Basin of Southern California*. Washington, DC: Environmental Protection Agency, 1979.

Brown, G. M., et al. *Methods for Valuing Acidic Deposition and Air Pollution Effects*. NAPAP SOS Report 27. Washington, DC: National Acid Precipitation Assessment Program, 1990.

Burtraw, D. SO_2 Emissions Trading Program: Cost Savings Without Allowance Trades. *Contemporary Economic Policy 14* (1996):79–94.

Burtraw, D., A. J. Krupnick, E. Mansur, D. H. Austin and D. Farrell. The Costs and Benefits of Reducing Air Pollutants Related to Acid Rain. *Contemporary Economic Policy 16*, (1998): 379–400.

Burtraw, D., and E. Mansur. The Effects of Trading and Banking in the SO_2 Allowance Market. Discussion Paper 99-25. Washington, DC: Resources for the Future, 1999.

Carlson, C., Cropper, M., and Palmer K. *Sulfur Dioxide Control by Electric Utilities: What Are the Gains from Trade?* Discussion Paper 98-44. Washington, DC: Resources for the Future, 1998.

Center for Clean Air Policy (CCAP). *Growth Baselines: Reducing Emissions and Increasing Investment in Developing Countries*. Washington DC: CCAP, 1998.

Costanza, R., and C. Perrings. A Flexible Assurance Bonding System for Improved Environmental Management, *Ecological Economics 2* (1990): 57–75.

Darmstadter, J. The Economic and Policy Setting of Renewable Energy: Where do Things Stand. RFF Discussion Paper 03-64. Washington 2003. Online: http://www.rff.org/rff/Documents/RFF-DP-03-64.pdf.

Ellerman, A. D., and J. P. Montero. Why Are Allowance Prices So Low? An Analysis of SO_2 Emissions Trading Program. *Journal of Environmental Economics and Management 36*, no. 1 (1998): 26–45.

Energy Statistics Sourcebook, 6th ed. Oil and Gas Journal Energy Database. Tulsa: Pennwell Publishers, 1992.

Fischer, C., Who Pays for Energy Efficiency Standards. Resources for the Future, Discussion Paper 04-11. Washington, 2004. Online: http://www.rff.org/rff/Documents/RFF-DP-04-11.pdf.

Florig, K., W. O. Spofford, X. Ma, and Z. Ma. China Strives to Make the Polluter Pay: Are China's Market-Based Incentives for Improved Environmental Compliance Working? *Environmental Science and Technology 29* (1995): 268–273.

Foster, V., and R. Hahn. Designing More Efficient Markets: Lessons from Los Angeles Smog Control. *Journal of Law and Economics 38* (1995):19–48.

Freeman, A. M., III. *The Measurement of Environmental and Resource Values*. Washington, DC: Resources for the Future, 1993.

Greene, D., J. R. Kahn, and R. Gibson. Estimating the Rebound Effect For Household Vehicles in the U.S., *Energy Journal 20*, no. 3 (1999): 1–31.

Greene, D. L., and P. N. Leiby. *The Social Costs to the U.S. of Monopolization of the World Oil Market 1972–1991*. Oak Ridge National Laboratory Report Number 6744, Oak Ridge, TN, 1993.

Griffen, J. M., and H. B. Steele. *Energy Economics and Policy.* New York: Academic Press, 1980.

Grubb, M., and D. Ulph. Energy, the Environment and Innovation. *Oxford Review of Economic Policy 18* (2002): 91–106.

Hahn, R. W. and G. Hester. Marketable Permits: Lessons for Theory and Practice. *Ecology Law Quarterly 3* (1989): 361–406.

Hotelling, H. The Economics of Exhaustible Resources. *Journal of Political Economy 39* (1931): 137–175.

Kruger, J., and M. Dean. Looking Back on SO_2 Trading: What's Good for the Environment is Good for the Market. *Public Utilities Fortnightly 135* (August 1997): 30–37.

Loehman, E. D., Boldt, D., and Charkin, K. *Measuring the Benefits of Air Quality Improvements in the San Francisco Bay Area*. Menlo Park, CA: SRI International, 1981.

Marcus, A. *Controversial Issues in Energy Policy.* Newbury Park, CA: Sage Publications, 1992.

Mills, E. S., and L. J. White. Government Policies towards the Automobile Emissions Control. Pages 348–402 in *Approaches to Air Pollution Control,* edited by Anne Frielaender. Cambridge, MA: MIT Press, 1978.

Mills, R. *Energy, Economics, and the Environment.* Englewood Cliffs, NJ: Prentice Hall, 1985.

Oates, W. E., P. R. Portney, and A. M. McGartland. The Net Benefits of Incentive-Based Regulation: A Case Study of Environmental Standard

Setting. *American Economic Review 79*, no. 5 (1989): 1233–1242.

Organization for Economic Cooperation and Development (OECD). *Economic Instruments for Environmental Management in Developing Countries*. Paris: OECD, 1993.

Organization for Economic Cooperation and Development (OECD). *Implementation Strategies for Environmental Taxes*. Paris: OECD, 1996.

Organization for Economic Cooperation and Development (OECD). *Evaluating Economic Instruments for Environmental Policy*. Paris: OECD, 1997.

Portney, P., I. W. H. Parry, H. K. Gruenspecht, and W. Harrington. The Economics of Fuel Efficiency Standards. RFF Discussion Paper 03-44. Washington. Online: http://www.rff.org/rff/Documents/Rff-DP-03-44.pdf, 2003.

Rae, D. A. *Benefits of Visual Air Quality in Cincinnati—Results of a Contingent Ranking Survey*. RP–1742. Final report prepared by Charles River Associates for EPRI, Palo Alto, CA, 1984.

Rose, K. Implementing an Emissions Trading Program in an Economically Regulated Industry: Lessons from the SO_2 Trading Program. Pages 101–136 in *Market-Based Approaches to Environmental Policy: Regulatory Innovations to the Fore*. Edited by Richard F. Kosobud and Jennifer M. Simmerman. New York: Van Nostrand Reinhold, 1997.

Tietenberg, T., M. Grubb, A. Michaelowa, B. Swift, and Z. X. Zhang. Greenhouse Gas Emission Trading: Defining the Principles, Modalities, Rules, and Guidelines for Verification, Reporting, and Accountability. United Nations Commission on Trade and Development, August 1998. Online: http://rO.unctad.org/ghg/publications,intl_rules.pdf.

Tolley, G. A., A. Randall, G. Blomquist, R. Fabian, G. Fishelson, A. Frankel, J. P. Hoehn, R. Krum, E. Mensah, and V. K. Smith. *Establishing and Valuing the Effects of Improved Visibility in Eastern United States*. Report Grant #807768-01-0. Washington, DC: Environmental Protection Agency, 1986.

Toman, M., and B. Jemelkova. Energy and Economic Development: An Assessment of the State of the Knowledge. RFF Discussion Paper 03-13. Online: http://www.rff.org/rff/Documents/RFF-DP-03-13.pdf, 2003.

Tonn, B. E. *The Urban Perspectives of Acid Rain: Workshop Summary*. Oak Ridge, TN: Oak Ridge National Laboratory, 1993.

U.S. Department of Energy. *National Energy Strategy*, 1st ed., 1991/1992. Washington, DC: U.S. Government Printing Office, 1991.

U.S. Environmental Protection Agency. *The Clean Air Act Amendments of 1990: Summary Materials*. Washington, DC: U.S. Government Printing Office, 1990a.

U.S. Environmental Protection Agency. *Emission Levels for Six Pollutants by Source*, 91-600760. Washington, DC: U.S. Government Printing Office, 1990b.

U.S. Environmental Protection Agency. Benefits and Costs of the Clean Air Act, 1990 to 2010: EPA Report to Congress. EPA-410-R-99-001, November 1999. Online: http://www.epa.gov/oar/sect812/.

U.S. National Acid Precipitation Assessment Program (NAPAP). *1990 Integrated Assessment Report*, Washington, DC: National Acid Precipitation Assessment Program, 1991.

Wang, J., L. Zhang, and J. Wu. Environmental Funds in China: Experiment and Reform. Pages 15–30 in OECD, *Applying Market-Based Instruments to Environmental Policies in China and OECD Countries*. Paris: OECD, 1997.

Webb, M., and M. J. Ricketts. *The Economics of Energy*. New York: Wiley, 1980.

World Resources 1992–93. Washington, DC: World Resource Institute, 1993.

World Resources 1994–95. Washington, DC: World Resource Institute, 1995.

World Resources 1996–97. Washington, DC: World Resource Institute, 1997.

World Resources 1998–99. Washington, DC: World Resource Institute, 1999.

World Resources 2000–01. Washington, DC: World Resource Institute, 2001.

World Resources 2002–03. Washington, DC: World Resource Institute, 2003.

Yang, J., D. Cao, and D. Want. The Air Pollution Charge System in China: Practices and Reform. Pages 67–86 in OECD, *Applying Market-Based Instruments to Environmental Policies in China and OECD Countries*. Paris: OECD, 1997.

Yun, P. The Pollution Charge System in China: An Economic Incentive? Working paper, Renmin University, Beijing, 1997.

chapter 10

Material Policy: Minerals, Materials, and Solid Waste

"For you are dust, and to dust you shall return."

(*Genesis 3:17–19*)

Introduction

This above passage from the Bible illustrates the cyclical nature of human life. Although it is often unrecognized by consumers, producers, and our economic system in general, economic goods also have a cyclical life. They come from environmental resources, their form is changed, and they are returned to the environment when they leave the economic system.

In the past, we have not viewed the economic process in this circular fashion. Rather, we have viewed the process as producing goods with inputs and then consuming the goods, where the consumption of the goods completely eliminated the goods. In other words, consumption plus production was viewed to be equal to zero. Although it has always been true, it has now become increasingly apparent that the economic process does not eliminate matter, it generates wastes. As the law of mass balance implies, the mass of matter that goes into an activity must equal the mass of matter that comes out of an activity. If the mass of the good that is produced is less than the mass of the inputs used in production, then the differential has been converted into waste. After a good is consumed, all the mass of the good becomes waste.

The circular nature of human's use of materials provides a powerful argument for simultaneously examining both the input and the output side of the question of how to efficiently utilize material resources. This circular nature is diagramed in Figure 10.1, an illustration that forms the conceptual basis of a materials balance equation, which mathematically tracks the flow of materials through a system.

Let's begin our analysis of the circular flow of materials with the environment, because that is where raw materials originate and where wastes are disposed. Resources such as minerals are present in the environment, but must be extracted from whatever form and structure they take in the environment. For example, very few rocks contain nothing but copper. The copper is generally mixed with other substances in rocks that may be buried hundreds of feet below the ground. Because the soil and other rocks must be removed before the copper-containing ore can be removed, the extraction process creates wastes. The ore is then processed (refined) to remove the elements or compounds that are of value. Most ores contain only a small amount of the desired substance (often a fraction of a percent), thus, a large amount of waste is generated in this process. Because both mechanical and chemical processes are used in refining the ore, the waste can be hazardous to plants and animals and can contaminate groundwater and surface water.

The next step is to convert the mineral that is extracted from the ore into a material from which products can be made. For example, iron ore is converted to steel. There are two major categories of waste associated with this process. First, because these activities tend to be energy intensive, all the air pollutants associated with the combustion of fossil fuels (see Chapters 7, 8, and 9) are also present. Second, when the steel is made, various impurities that have no economic use are removed from the iron and must be disposed of.

Figure 10.1 **The Circular Nature of Materials Use**

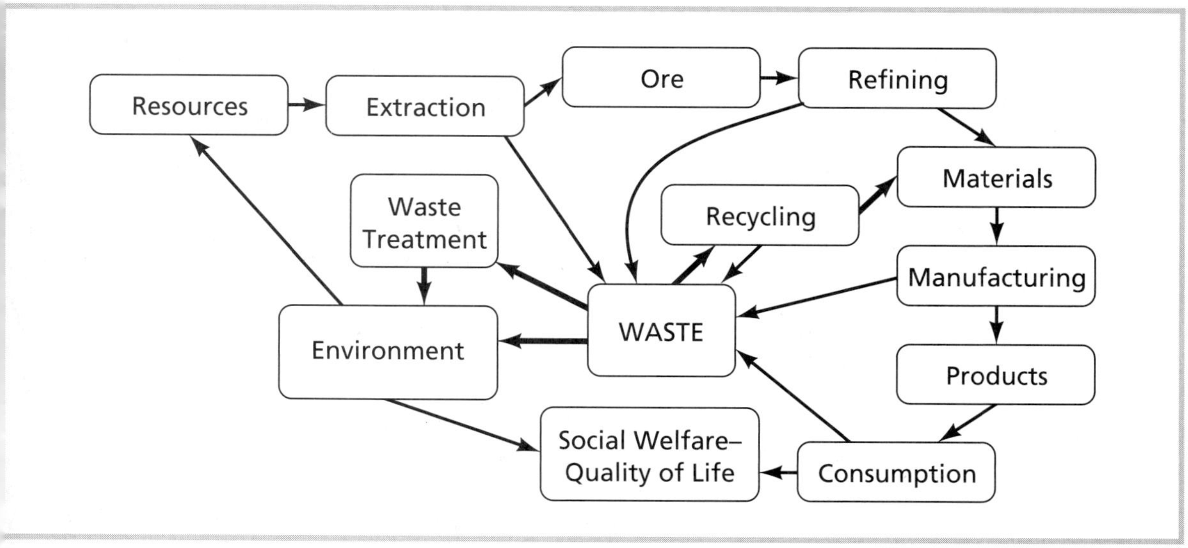

The material is then used to make a product. For example, the steel can be used to make the body of a car. Again, there are wastes associated with the use of energy and with portions of the materials that do not wind up as part of the product that is manufactured.

Finally, the product is consumed, either as a final good or as an intermediate product. Both the use and the final disposal of the product will generate waste.

As we look at the outer ring of the chain of economic activities in Figure 10.1, we focus on activities that have been examined within the conventional realm of economics. The theory of the firm, the theory of the consumer, and the theory of exhaustible resources have been taught in college economics courses since World War II. There are, however, market failures present in this chain of activities that have not been adequately studied. Inappropriate government interventions, imperfect competition, and externalities are present throughout this chain. In particular, we will focus on the flows within the interior of Figure 10.1 and discuss the market forces and the market failures that influence the flow of wastes.

This inner ring shows that all the activities generate wastes, which may be recycled, treated, and released into the environment, or released directly into the environment without any prior treatment. Do we have the socially efficient level of total waste? Do we have the socially efficient level of recycling, and do we have the socially efficient level of treatment? If not, how do we develop policies to reduce inefficiencies in this area?

This chapter focuses on these questions. Although the flow of materials is also based on fossil fuels and activities based on renewable resources, such as agriculture and forestry, the chapter focuses on the role of minerals in this cycle. Separate chapters are devoted to energy (Chapters 8 and 9), forestry (Chapters 12 and 13), and agriculture (Chapter 17).

The Economics of Mineral Extraction

The fashion in which the invisible hand of the market allocates mineral resources is virtually identical to the way in which it allocates fossil fuels such as oil. This correlation should not be surprising, because both fossil fuels and mineral resources are exhaustible resources. The major difference between fossil fuels and mineral resources is that the use of fossil fuels tends to dissipate the resource.[1] In contrast, the use of mineral resources tends to concentrate the resource.[2] The implication is that it is possible to recycle minerals but not fuels.

As discussed in the analysis of Chapters 2 and 8, for the market to allocate the resource in a socially efficient fashion the market price of an exhaustible

[1]The concentrated oil or coal is combusted and transformed into gases that go up a smokestack or out a tailpipe.

[2]The mineral is contained in a heterogeneous ore (such as iron ore) and concentrated into a homogeneous material (such as steel).

resource must be equal to the sum of marginal extraction cost and marginal user cost.[3] The greater the future value of the mineral, the greater the current opportunity cost, marginal user cost, and market price.

Although the potential for recycling exists with many minerals, recycling cannot eliminate the scarcity problem. The entropy law,[4] which is one of the laws of thermodynamics, says that matter (and the entire universe) is continually moving toward a less-well-ordered state. Thus, there is a constant loss of the well-ordered material. For example, moving parts wear, and the material that wears away is completely disordered. Some of the material may become contaminated with toxic substances or radioactivity so that it is not safe to recycle. Some materials become mixed with other materials during the production process, rendering recycling extremely difficult. The point is that if a fraction of the material is lost every time a material is used and recycled, the material will eventually become exhausted.

As illustrated in Chapters 2 and 8, the invisible hand will correctly allocate the mineral resource over time, provided that no market failures are present. As previously pointed out, however, market failures are present at every point along the circular flow of materials. An example of this type of market failure is found in Box 10.1, which examines the impact of coal mining on aquatic ecosystems.

Market Failures in the Extraction of Mineral Resources

There are many important externalities in the extraction of mineral resources. They involve environmental externalities, inappropriate government interventions, imperfect competition, and national security externalities.

Environmental Externalities

Environmental externalities are the result of the waste that is generated and the disruption of the landscape that occurs as a result of mining and refining activity. Because water is often used to help separate the usable mineral from the ore, mining tends to generate important water-quality problems. Also, the disruption of the surface of the land and the exposure of impurities in the rock lead to problems from pollutants that are carried to surface waters and groundwaters through the runoff of rainwater. Acid drainage from mines is a particulary important problem.

---

[3]This equation assumes that there are no externalities in the production or use of mineral resources. Obviously, the market will not be efficient in the presence of externalites, and efficiency would require some sort of intervention (taxes, marketable pollution permits, and so on) to reduce the level of the externality to the optimal level.

[4]See Chapter 19 for a detailed discussion of the entropy law and its implications for economic growth.

Box 10.1 Coal Dust and Mussel Biodiversity

Although tropical forests and coral reefs are among the most biodiverse ecosystems on the planet, the southern Appalachian Mountains are also a hotbed of biodiversity. These forested mountains contain numerous species of salamanders, and the rivers have large numbers of species of fish, crustaceans, and mussels. The upper Clinch River and its tributaries represent one of the longest free-flowing stretches of river in the eastern United States and constitute perhaps the most biodiverse river system in temperate North America. These free-flowing waters are home to one of the most diverse assemblages of freshwater mussel and fish species of any river in North America. Unfortunately, many of the watershed's mussel and fish species are on the decline. The U.S. Fish and Wildlife Service lists 22 mussels and 7 fish species as endangered or threatened. Moreover, the watershed has many species that are found nowhere else.

Several types of anthropogenic activities are causing the decline in species abundance. They include water pollution from sewage treatment plants and runoff from urban surfaces, agricultural fields, and pastures; and direct mortality cause by cattle walking in the river and crushing the mussels. In addition, coal particles that are in the effluent of coal-washing operations find their way into rivers and are ingested by the mussels, poisoning them.

Agricultural pollutants are relatively easy to reduce (see Chapter 17 for more details), because buffer strips of forest and other vegetation can be planted along the river to reduce runoff and the entrance of harmful substances. Similarly, the river area can be protected from cattle, with alternative sources of water provided to the cattle so that they do not need to walk into the river to drink.

Unfortunately, the problems associated with coal-washing operations are harder to ameliorate because of the economics of the coal industry in this particular region. The drainage of the upper Clinch River contains parts of the coal-mining areas of southwest Virginia, east Kentucky, and east Tennessee. The coal-mining industry is in a depression, with a constant loss of jobs in a geographic area in which jobs are not as plentiful as in other regions of the United States. The cost of mining Appalachian coal relative to western coal, the diminishing stocks of coal, and the global warming impacts of coal imply that the coal industry in the southern Appalachians will continue to decline in economic vitality. The coal-mining industry and its supporters argue that more environmental restrictions will lead to even greater economic problems for the coal industry and cause even greater losses of jobs.

This situation leads to an interesting policy question: Should increased burdens be placed on an industry that is in trouble, perhaps accelerating its demise, or should the process of developing alternatives to the dying industry be accelerated, providing protection to the natural environment and speeding the transition to a new economic environment?

A major component of the refining of many materials is a process known as smelting, in which intensely hot furnaces are used to melt the ore and separate the mineral from the waste material. Not only does smelting release pollutants as a result of the use of the energy in the furnace, but the ores often have impurities such as sulfur that are converted to gas and released in the smelting process. Both the large copper smelter operation at Copper Basin, Tennessee, and the large nickel smelting operation in Sudbury, Ontario, are associated with significant acid rain problems. In Tennessee, the smelting was done in the late nineteenth and early twentieth centuries in pits in the mining area, and the acid rain problem was extremely local, killing all vegetation for over 145 square kilometers (Raven, et al., 1993, p. 331). In the Sudbury area, the acid rain problem is more regional and is a major contributor to acid deposition in Canada and parts of the United States (see Chapter 7).

These problems of air pollution and water pollution are covered in substantial detail in Chapters 8 and 15. Consequently, these externalities are not discussed in great detail here except to note that they are important and that they create a disparity between the private cost of the mineral and the social cost. Many types of mining production technologies exist that do minimize these pollution problems, however. The policy difficulty is that these cleaner technologies may be more expensive than traditional techniques and therefore are not often employed, particularly in small-scale mining. In addition, an important externality is associated with mining that has not yet been discussed in as much detail, and that is that the creation of a mine often completely destroys the natural environment in its vicinity. Table 10.1 lists selected environmental impacts of mining projects, including both pollution and elimination of natural environments. The inclusion of a mining project on this list is not an indication that this mining should not take place, but, rather, a notation of the types of environmental costs associated with mining projects in general.

Because most of the convenient opportunities for mining have already been exhausted, many potential new mines are located in wilderness areas or other areas that have unique environmental properties. The opportunity cost of losing these environmental resources is usually not factored into the market price of the mineral. Moreover, because the benefits of preserving the environmental resource are primarily public good benefits (see Chapter 2 for a discussion of public goods), it is difficult for the landowner to capture these benefits. Consequently, the benefits of preserving the area are seldom included in the landowner's decision making.

John Krutilla (1967)[5] was the first to argue that the focus of conservation should be less concentrated on the resources that are extracted and more

---

[5]Krutilla's 1967 article in the *American Economic Review* is a landmark article, which the author of this textbook regards as one of several articles that began the field of environmental economics. It is an extremely readable article (not a lot of graphs and equations), and any student who is serious about environmental economics, environmental policy, or environmental studies in general should read it.

Table 10.1 Selected Examples of Mineral Extraction and Processing

Location/Mineral	Observation
Ilo-Locumba area, Peru, copper mining and smelting	The Ilo smelter emits 600,000 tons of sulfur compounds each year. Nearly 40 million meters per yer of tailings containing copper, zinc, lead, aluminum, and traces of cyanides are dumped into the sea each year, affecting marine life in a 20,000-hectare area. Nearly 800,000 tons of slag are also dumped each year.
Nauru, South Pacific, phosphate mining	When mining is completed—in 5–15 years—four-fifths of the 2100-hectare South Pacific island will be uninhabitable.
Para State, Brazil, Carajas iron ore project	The project's wood requirements (for smelting of iron ore) will require the cutting of enough native wood to deforest 50,000 hectares of tropical forest each year during the mine's 250-year life.
Russia, Severonikel smelters	Two nickel smelters in the extreme northwest corner of the republic, near the Norwegian and Finnish borders, pump 300,000 tons of sulfur dioxide into the atmosphere each year, along with lesser amounts of heavy metals. Over 200,000 hectares of local forests are dying, and the emissions appear to be affecting the health of residents.
Sabah Province, Malaysia, Mamut copper mine	Local rivers are contaminated with high levels of chromium, copper, iron, lead, manganese, and nickel. Samples of local fish have been found unfit for human consumption, and rice grown in the area Is contaminated.
Amazon Basin, Brazil, gold mining	Hundreds of thousands of miners have flooded the area in search of gold, clogging rivers with sediment, and releasing 100 tons of mercury into the ecosystem each year. Fish in some rivers contain high levels of mercury.

Source: Young, 1992, p. 106.

directed to the unique environmental resources that the mining (and other development activities) destroys. He emphasized the public good nature of the unique natural environments and the inability of the landowner to capture the benefits of preserving the natural environment. These benefits include preserving the area for recreation, habitat, biodiversity, scientific enquiry, and watershed protection, and the indirect use benefits that people derive from the existence of the area.[6]

Another important point about the destruction of unique natural environments as a consequence of mining is that these actions are irreversible. If we decide to carve up a wilderness because we believe that the minerals are more valuable to society and later we discover a substitute for the minerals, it is not possible to re-create the wilderness. A good example of this type of irre-

[6]See Chapter 4 for a discussion of indirect use values.

versibility is a recently developed coal-mining practice known as mountaintop removal. This technology represents a type of strip-mining, in which the tops and sides of mountains are carved away by gigantic earthmoving equipment to expose the narrow seams of coal in the mountain. There is an extremely high ratio of "overburden" removal, even relative to conventional strip-mining. There is no place to put the tremendous amount of rock and dirt removed from the mountain except in the neighboring valleys, where forests, streams, and former communities are buried beneath millions of tons of mining waste. As can be readily imagined, there is no possibility of returning the environment to its former status once mountain top removal takes place.[7]

The existence of potential irreversible damages suggests a responsibility to be cautious in embarking on a course of development. One major reason to be cautious is that the benefits of preserving the natural environment will tend to increase over time, whereas the benefits of developing the environment (such as mining) will tend to decrease over time. The benefits of preservation increase over time because the demand for outdoor recreation is increasing and because the number of substitute environments is declining as more and more areas become developed. The benefits of development tend to decline over time as mines become exhausted, as the capital equipment depreciates, as technology improves, and as substitutes are developed.

The significance of the decay of the benefits of development and the growth of the benefits of preservation is that development projects, for which the benefits of development are greater than the benefits of preservation in the current year, may be associated with the benefits of preservation being greater than the benefits of development in future years. Depending on the disparity between future benefits of preservation and future benefits of development, the present value of preservation may be greater than the present value of development even if current benefits and costs have a different relationship. Of course, the choice of discount rates will have an important effect on the outcome. Higher discount rates tend to minimize the impact of future values. Krutilla and Fisher (1985) and Porter (1982) discuss this issue in great detail.

Because the decision to mine or not mine a specific site is an either-or decision and not a marginal decision, it does not lend itself well to solutions such as incorporating marketable permits or taxes. A cost-benefit analysis (see Chapter 5) should be performed before the project is undertaken to determine if the social benefits of the mine exceed the social costs (which would include the forgone preservation benefits). Other decision-making criteria (discussed in Chapter 5), such as equity, sustainability, environmental justice and ecological risk, should be examined as well. Because mines require federal permitting, they are subject to the National Environmental Policy Act requirements for an environmental impact statement (EIS), which assesses the environmental impacts of the mine. Unfortunately, many environmental

[7]See the web site of the non-governmental organization Appalachian Voices (http://www.appvoices.org/mtr/default.asp) for more information on mountaintop removal.

impact statements only identify the ecological and human health risks that are associated with the project and do not discuss the societal consequences of these changes. Cost-benefit analysis, where the ecological costs are monetized and incorporated into the analysis, is generally not performed in an EIS. Other criteria such as equity and sustainability are frequently ignored as well.

So far, two types of environmental externalities associated with mining have been identified: the pollution associated with the mining activity and the destruction of habitat and unique environmental areas. In addition to these two environmentally oriented market failures are important nonenvironmental market failures that tend to make mining activity greater than the socially optimal level. These market failures are created by both inappropriate government interventions and imperfect competition, and they serve (as do the environmental market failures) to make the marginal private costs of minerals lower than the marginal social costs.

Inappropriate Government Interventions

The most important inappropriate government intervention is a depletion allowance. The depletion allowance is a provision in the tax code that allows firms to depreciate their mineral deposits the same way a manufacturing firm is allowed to depreciate its capital equipment. As the mining firms remove minerals from their mines, they can use the reduction in value of the mine as an expense that can be subtracted from total revenue to reduce taxable income. This deduction has the effect of reducing the private cost of production, because the taxpayers share in the cost of producing the mineral. This situation is shown in Figure 10.2, where MPC_1 represents the marginal private cost curve with no depletion allowance and MPC_2 represents the marginal private cost curve with the depletion allowance. Notice that the marginal private cost is below the marginal social cost (MSC) curve due to the environmental externalities that create a disparity between marginal private cost and marginal social cost. Note that the depletion allowance exacerbates this disparity. Further, because it increases the market level of output (from q_1 to q_2, which is even further from the optimal level, q^*), it increases the magnitude of the environmental costs.

Imperfect Competition

One additional market failure associated with mining is imperfect competition. Monopolistic or oligopolistic market structure in mining industries can lead to a loss in social welfare, because the monopoly or oligopoly restricts output below the optimal level so as to generate monopoly profits. (See Chapter 2 for a discussion of the social losses associated with monopoly.)

From the end of the nineteenth century through World War II, oligopolistic market structure was an important factor in steel and many other mineral markets. As the economy of the United States (and other nations) became more open to international trade, however, foreign producers of min-

Figure 10.2 **The Impact of Depletion Allowances**

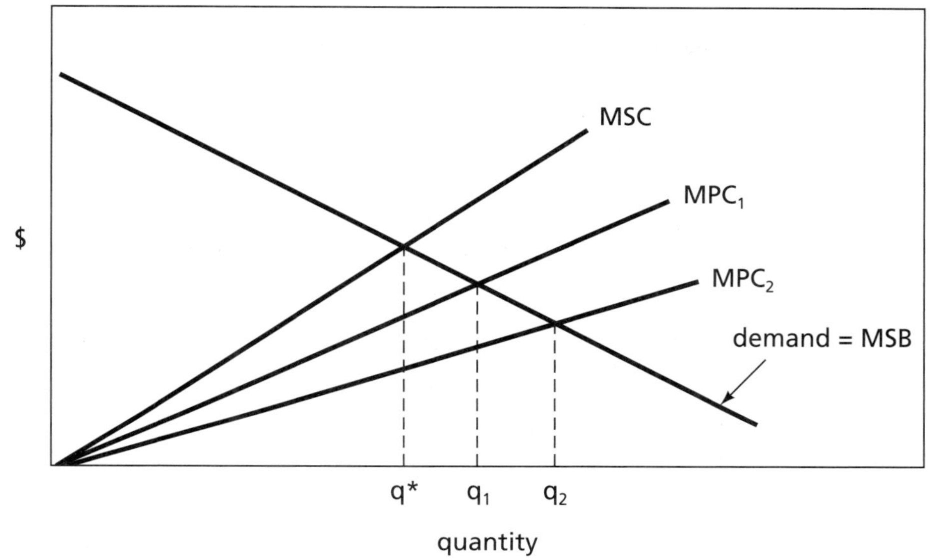

erals provided competition for U.S. producers. This aspect was particularly true for steel, where competition from German, Japanese, Korean, and Brazilian producers not only eliminated the monopoly profits of U.S. producers, but took a large portion of the market as well.

National Security Externalities

For the most part, monopoly does not represent a significant problem in mineral production. The one exception is when the minerals have strategic values. Strategic minerals are those that are important to aerospace and military applications, relatively rare, and generally found in countries of unpredictable political stability or potential hostility toward the United States and its military allies. They are generally rare metals that are mixed with common metals, such as steel or aluminum, to create alloys that have properties that the common metals do not have. These properties include the ability to remain stable and not become brittle at high temperatures, greater elasticity, and greater strength per unit weight.

Several policy options are available to mitigate the potential problems associated with potential politically generated shortages of strategic minerals. One option is to subsidize the development of domestic mines for these minerals, even though the extraction cost is much higher than the price on world markets (Table 10.2). In addition, these mines will generate environmental dam-

Table 10.2 **U.S. Net Import Reliance for Selected Strategic Minerals**

Mineral	Percentage Imported in 1990	Major Foreign Sources 1986–1989
Graphite	100	Mexico, China, Brazil, Madagascar
Manganese	100	South Africa, France, Gabon
Platinum-group metals	88	South Africa, U.K., [former] USSR
Cobalt	85	Zaire, Zambia, Canada, Norway
Nickel	83	Canada, Norway, Australia, Dominican Republic
Chromium	79	South Africa, Turkey, Zimbabwe, [former] Yugoslavia
Tungsten	73	China, Bolivia, Germany, Peru

Primary Source: U.S. Bureau of Mines.

Secondary Source: J.D. Morgan, 1993.

age, as illustrated in the potential molybdenum mine discussed in Box 10.2. Another option, which is probably associated with lower social costs, is to buy extra quantities of the minerals on world markets and stockpile the mineral against the possibility of future supply interruptions. A final option is to develop substitutes for the strategic materials. For example, ceramic materials are being substituted for metal alloys in many aerospace applications.

Environmental Legacies of Mining

One of the most vexing environmental problems associated with mining is that mines continue to create environmental problems long after the mining activity has ceased. Many old mines create serious environmental problems, including contamination of surface water and groundwater, underground fires, and exposure of humans and ecosystems to toxic substances. Environmental problems created by past activities are called environmental legacies,[8] because the mining process did not conclude with a proper "closure" or configuration on the mining area to minimize the likelihood of future problems.

Policy makers face two major problems when dealing with mine closure and the environmental legacy of mines. The first has to do with mines that

[8]Other types of environmental legacies such as toxic waste dumps, old and abandoned industrial sites, federal government weapons manufacturing and storage facilities, and leaking underground gasoline, oil, and chemical tanks are discussed in Chapter 16.

Box 10.2 Mining or Wilderness Recreation?

In *The Economics of Natural Environments* (1985), John Krutilla and Anthony Fisher outline a process for cost-benefit analysis and apply this process to five case studies in which a development project threatens to destroy a unique natural environment. One project is a potential molybdenum (a strategic mineral used in metal alloys) mine in the White Cloud Peaks Mountains in Idaho.

Krutilla and Fisher discuss three potential land uses for the White Cloud Peaks: recreation, grazing, and mining. All three activities tend to be mutually exclusive. Krutilla and Fisher examine the benefits of recreation in a fashion that shows the sensitivity of recreational benefits to user congestion. They use standard techniques for valuing the benefits of range grazing. The benefits of mining are shown to be small because there is an abundant supply of molybdenum, with prices projected to remain constant for several decades following the scheduled opening of the mine.

Although no official cost-benefit analysis was ever conducted of the conflicting uses of the White Cloud Peaks Mountains, Krutilla and Fisher's analysis shows that the decision to include this area in the Sawtooth National Recreation Area reflects sound economic judgment. Their analysis also shows that for these mountains, the benefits of wilderness recreation outweigh the benefits of alternative uses.

One potential use of the land that was not specifically examined by Krutilla and Fisher was a more intensive recreational use of the land, such as designating it as a national park. Because this option was not proposed at the time of the study and because the current use of wilderness recreation does not preclude the future development as a national park (mining or grazing would preclude that), however, there is an even more powerful argument to make the initial decision to allocate the area to wilderness recreation.

are already creating problems, where the owners of the mining site may have gone out of business or otherwise disappeared, leaving the mind abandoned with no one responsible for containing future damage. The second problem occurs with trying to develop policy to give current mine owners an incentive to close their mines properly.

The second problem is made serious by what Kahn et al. (2001) refer to as *temporal separation*. Temporal separation implies that there is a long period of time between when the economic activity (the extraction of the ore) is conducted and when abatement and prevention technologies are implemented to prevent problems far into the future after the mining activity ceases. There is also a temporal separation between the application of abatement and prevention technologies and environmental damages that occur far into the future.

Although it is possible to try to accomplish the goal of safe mine closure through direct controls, economic incentives might be better. In particular, economic incentives give the mine owner a current incentive to prevent future damages. One way of doing so is through the creation of a performance bonding system. Before beginning the mining project, the mine owner could be required to put money into an account, which would only be returned after succesful completion of the mine closure. In addition, the mine owner could be required to leave money in a fund to pay for periodic maintenance of the mining area to prevent problems from developing in the future. Another possibility is to require mine owners to buy insurance against future environmental problems associated with the mine. To qualify for the purchase of insurance, insurance companies would require the mine owners to institute a proper mine closure and make provisions for the future maintenance of the safety of the mine site. Box 10.3 discusses environmental problems associated with mining in the informal sector. As might be expected, there is even less accountability in this case.

Box 10.3 Mercury Pollution and Gold Mining in the Brazilian Amazon

Beginning in the early 1970s and continuing through the present, there has been a surge of gold mining in the Amazon region, especially the Brazilian Amazon. In contrast to other types of mining in Brazil and other countries, this gold mining is not conducted by large corporations but by small-scale entrepreneurs. Currently, there are well over 500,000 small-scale miners (known as *garimpeiros*) operating in the Brazilian Amazon. (The actual number depends on the price of gold. The higher the price, the more illegal miners.) Although these miners are unlicensed and unregulated and have operated in an illegal fashion, the mining activity is an important source of jobs and has an important regional economic impact. Unfortunately, this unregulated mining has lead to important environmental impacts, the most important of which is mercury pollution.

Mercury is added to the gold ore, where it bonds with the gold, creating an amalgam that is easily separated from the ore. The amalgam is then heated, and the mercury boils out of the amalgam. Because mercury is a liquid at ambient temperatures, however, it quickly condenses and falls back to earth, contaminating ecosystems and threatening human health (mercury has severe impacts on the central nervous system and can also lead to birth defects). Although the use of mercury in gold mining is illegal, the shear number of goldminers and their existence in the "underground" economy has made enforcement of the laws extremely difficult.

(continues)

Box 10.3 (continued)

Although a technology existed to reduce the mercury pollution, it was not adopted by the *garimpeiros*. This technology was a retort, a container in which the mercury/gold amalgam is heated but which condenses the fumes as they exit the container, capturing the mercury. This technology is similar in concept to the way a "moonshiner" distills alcohol. The advantage of this technology over existing technology is that the same mercury can be used again and again to extract the gold, lowering costs for the *garimpeiros* and at the same time reducing emissions of mercury into the environment.

Different people had different ideas about how to induce the *garimpeiros* to adopt the new technology. Some people argued for direct control, requiring the retort to be implemented, and others argued that a deposit-refund system should be placed on the mercury, which would give the *garimpeiros* even greater incentive to use the retort. Both solutions, however, require extensive monitoring and enforcement among over half a million small-scale miners operating on the fringe of legality.

This problem was studied by the Centro Tecnologia Mineral, a mining research institute of the federal government of Brazil. The conclusion was to control the problem in a way that required less reliance on monitoring and enforcement. Consequently, an extensive public information program demonstrating the proper use of the retort was implemented, emphasizing the cost savings associated with it (miners do not need to continually buy mercury if they recycle it), and educating the miners about the health (to the miners and general public) and environmental consequences of mercury emissions. Adoption of the retort technology has been impressively rapid. In the meantime, research is being conducted on developing mercury-free methods for extracting the gold from the ore.

Solid Waste and Waste Disposal

For most of recorded history, civilization has not been concerned with the solid waste that has been generated as a result of production and consumption activities. Even as we became aware of the environmental problems, such as water and air pollution, less attention was placed on the wastes that we disposed of on land.

In the late 1970s, however, many areas of the United States began to experience a shortage of areas that were suitable for landfills (areas where solid wastes are buried). As sites in the vicinity of cities became filled, urban areas sought to locate landfills at great distances from the cities. The problem of shortages of waste disposal alternatives was dramatically illustrated by the garbage barge from Islip, New York, whose unsuccessful voyages to Mexico and Caribbean countries seeking a garbage disposal site were chronicled nightly on television news shows and late-night talk shows.

Although the problem of where to put garbage is the question that receives the most public discussion, it is not the only or even the most significant problem. Developing new landfill sites and technical solutions to garbage disposal (such as incineration) do not really treat the solid waste problem; they treat the symptom of the problem. The real solid waste problem is that we are generating an inefficiently high level of waste. Solutions that do not address the problem of waste reduction are not likely to succeed because they treat the symptom of the problem, rather than the problem itself.

Why Do We Generate Too Much Waste?

The answer to the question of why we generate too much waste is extraordinarily simple, yet its implementation is quite complex. The simple answer is that people do not pay the full social costs of waste disposal at every level of the production process and in the consumption of the good.

This market failure is illustrated in Figure 10.3, which looks at the market for carbonated beverages. Carbonated beverages are a useful commodity to examine, because there is a one-to-one correspondence between the eco-

Figure 10.3 **Socially Efficient Level of Containers**

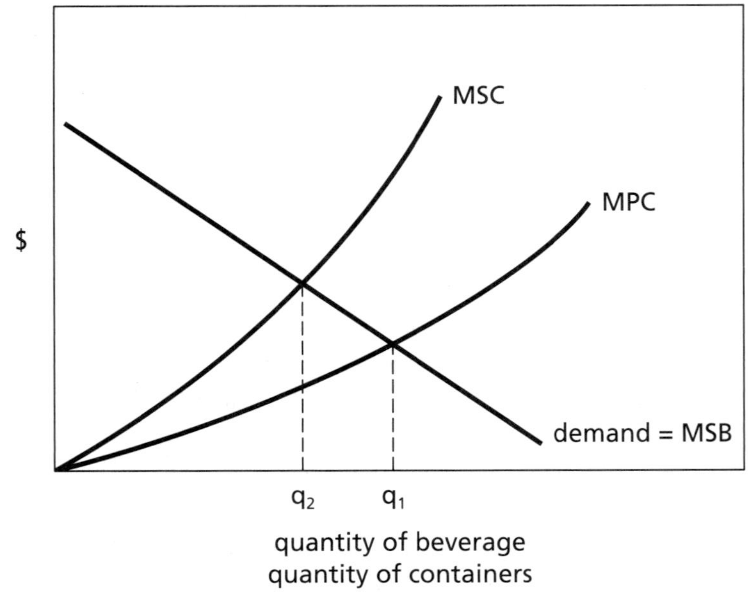

nomic output (the beverage) and the waste output (the container).[9] The advantage of looking at a product with this type of one-to-one correspondence is that the horizontal axis can represent both the economic output and the waste output. In Figure 10.3, the marginal social cost (MSC) function is depicted as being higher than the marginal private cost (MPC) function, due to the social costs from the waste associated with the product. An alternative way of expressing this relationship is to depict the marginal social benefit function below the marginal private benefit function. This market failure can be expressed in either fashion, because one could regard the costs of the post-consumption waste as either an addition to the private costs of production or a reduction of the social benefits of consumption. As can be seen in Figure 10.3, the market level of containers (q_1) is greater than the socially efficient level of containers (q_2).

If the analysis is extended to include the amount of waste as a variable input, then one must look at the demand and marginal cost of the material input. The marginal private cost of a material input (such as the packaging of a product) does not include the full cost of disposal or the costs of the externalities associated with the disposal.

This problem is slightly more complicated than the standard externalities that have been studied, because not only must one determine the socially optimal amount of waste, but one must also determine the socially efficient disposition of the waste. This situation is very different from sulfur dioxide waste, for example, where one must only determine how much of the waste to emit at any location.

This problem of also determining how to dispose of the waste can be illustrated by assuming that there are two options for disposal, a proper option (such as disposal in a landfill) and an improper option (such as unrestricted dumping).[10] In Figure 10.4, the total amount of waste is represented by the horizontal distance between the two vertical axes. The amount of waste properly disposed of is represented by the distance from the left vertical axis, and the amount improperly disposed of is represented by the distance from the right vertical axis. The sum of the properly disposed of waste and the improperly disposed of waste must equal total waste, which is the horizontal distance between the two axes. In this example, total waste is equal to 25 units. For example, if 15 units are properly disposed of, then 10 units are improperly disposed of. Both vertical axes measure costs.

Both improper disposal and proper disposal are associated with external costs. One would expect that the external costs associated with improper disposal are greater than those associated with proper disposal, or else the

[9]This example is an oversimplification, because waste is generated in the production of the beverage and the production of the container. It is also an oversimplification because there are multiple sizes of containers, which would vary the ratio between the economic output and the waste output.

[10]In this discussion, "proper" and "improper" refer to the relative environmental damages and do not imply anything about illegality or optimality.

Figure 10.4 Allocation of Waste between Proper and Improper Disposal

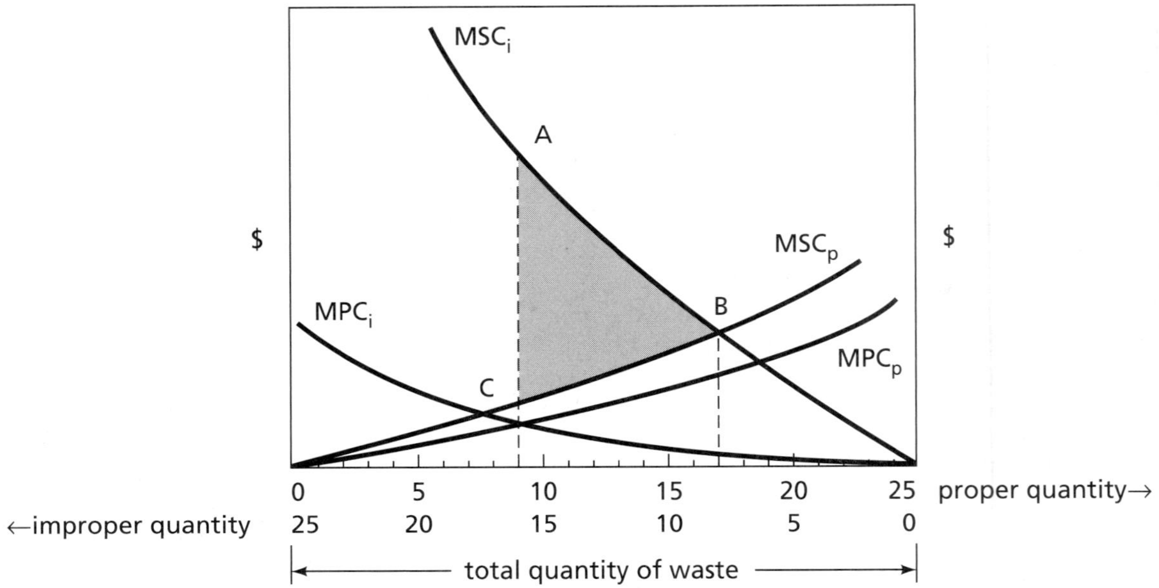

improper disposal would not be called "improper." These external cost differentials are reflected in Figure 10.4, where there is a greater disparity between the marginal private cost and marginal social cost curves for improperly disposed of waste (MPC_i and MSC_i) than between the marginal private cost and marginal social cost curves for properly disposed of waste (MPC_p and MSC_p).

The market allocation of waste disposal between these two alternatives will be determined by people comparing the marginal private costs of one option with the marginal private costs of the other option. In Figure 10.4, this equating of costs occurs when 9 units are properly disposed of and 16 units are improperly disposed of. The optimal allocation is 17 units properly disposed and 8 units improperly disposed, which occurs where the marginal social costs of both options are equal. The excess social cost associated with being at the market equilibrium instead of the optimal solution is equal to the area of triangle ABC.

For the purposes of expositional simplicity, the determination of the optimal amount of waste and the determination of the allocation of wastes across disposal options have been presented separately. In actuality, these decisions are mutually dependent and should be made concurrently rather than sequentially. Also, instead of the two options for waste disposal that are presented in Figure 10.4, there may be many options, each associated with different social costs.

Why the Private Cost of Solid Waste Does Not Equal Its Social Cost

Both properly and improperly disposed of solid waste generate environmental externalities. This section focuses on waste that is legally disposed of and leaves the issue of illegal dumping for later discussion.

Even waste that is stored in a landfill generates external costs. The landfill itself reduces the aesthetic value of the surrounding land because odors, vermin, and unsightliness reduce the benefits that people can derive from using the surrounding land. In addition, landfills can generate environmental harm, especially to groundwater and surface water. Even if the landfill is lined with impermeable clay or plastic, which keeps water from moving downward through the waste into the groundwater, water that has been contaminated by the waste can move back upward through the garbage (this process is called leachate) and be carried by rainwater runoff into surface water or groundwater under adjacent land. This leachate can carry a variety of pollutants from the mixed waste that is present in landfills. Although solid waste disposal sites are not intended to store toxic wastes, toxic wastes inevitably make their way into them. Many household and commercial products, including batteries, pesticide containers, cleaners, paint, solvents, and automotive oil, contain toxic substances.

In addition to the environmental externalities, a variety of market failures are caused by inappropriate government actions. Because trash disposal is often a government-provided or government-regulated activity, it is incumbent upon the government to charge a price (or set a regulated price) equal to marginal social cost. The price of trash disposal is generally not equal to marginal social cost for three reasons. First, the environmental costs associated with waste disposal are not incorporated into price. Second, the scarcity value of landfill space is not incorporated into market price. Finally, price is often based on average cost rather than marginal cost.

The lack of incorporation of environmental cost into market price has already been discussed in this book in other applications (air pollution, for example). The other two sources of the disparity between price and marginal social cost require more discussion, however.

Municipalities that operate landfill services generally charge a fee per ton of dumped garbage (called a tipping fee), which is designed to recover the costs of operating the landfill. Because landfill sites are a scarce and exhaustible resource,[11] however, there is an opportunity cost or scarcity value

---

[11]Very few sites are physically suited for a landfill. A necessary requirement is that there be a water-impermeable barrier between the area that will contain the trash and the underlying area. Of course, even if a site has the appropriate physical characteristics, it is not necessarily an acceptable landfill site. People who own land in the vicinity of a potential landfill will generally object to its nearby location. This objection, known as the NIMBY (not in my back yard) syndrome, makes it even more difficult to establish new landfill areas. Box 10.4 discusses the NIMBY syndrome.

Box 10.4 Economic Incentives and the NIMBY Syndrome

The NIMBY (not in my back yard) syndrome refers to the political difficulty associated with finding acceptable locations for waste disposal sites. Even though everyone recognizes the need for such sites, no one wants them to be located in their own community. Although the waste disposal site will create net benefits for society as a whole, the social benefits of the site are spread out among all members of society, whereas the social costs of the waste disposal site are borne primarily by the people living in the vicinity of the site. Everyone wants the sites to be established, only "someplace else." Of course, if every community takes this attitude, it will be very difficult to ever find a place to put the waste disposal site.

In Chapter 4, the concept of a *potential Pareto improvement* was introduced. A potential Pareto improvement occurs when an action creates more benefits for those that benefit than costs for those who are hurt by the action. The idea is that if the losers are compensated for their losses, the potential Pareto improvement could become an actual Pareto improvement whereby some people are made better off but no one is made worse off.

Clearly, the establishment of a needed waste disposal site would constitute a potential Pareto improvement but not an actual Pareto improvement, unless the community in which the site is located is compensated for environmental costs generated by the waste disposal site. Economists have suggested a plan by which the potential Pareto improvement can be turned into an actual Pareto improvement. The plan would involve the following steps:

1. Sites with the requisite physical and geographic characteristics would be identified.
2. The communities in which the eligible sites are located would be given an opportunity to bid on the minimum payment they would require from the waste disposal site operators to allow the site in the community. This payment could take the form of property tax rebates for current residents, increased funding of school systems, or the provision of other public goods. Communities could make the bid as high or as low as they wanted.
3. The site would be located in the community that required the lowest payment to accept the waste disposal facility.

Many economists think this plan is desirable. It creates an incentive for communities to accept the facilities and at the same time makes the recipient community better off, because it will not accept the facility unless the compensation is greater than the social costs imposed by the plant. This plan, however, is often criticized by noneconomists, who argue that some communities have less

(continues)

Box 10.4 (continued)

economic and political power at the beginning of the bargaining process, so the poor and less powerful communities will always wind up with lower environmental quality. Advocates of this system argue that poor communities should have the opportunity to accept the environmental costs in exchange for a more than offsetting increase in the quality of life, such as better schools. What do you think?

associated with burying a ton of waste today. This opportunity cost has seldom been incorporated into the tipping fee at a landfill. As municipalities see their future trash disposal options becoming increasingly limited, they have attempted to incorporate this scarcity value or opportunity cost into tipping fees to reduce the volume of garbage and to encourage the development of alternative waste disposal options. This adjustment, however, often requires raising tipping fees from the vicinity of \$5 to \$10 per ton to more than \$40 or \$50 per ton. Needless to say, voters would not react well to such a dramatic increase in the city's price for trash disposal, which makes politicians hesitant to fully incorporate the scarcity value of landfill sites into the price the city or county charges.

The final problem associated with the pricing of waste disposal services is that the pricing of the services is often based on average rather than marginal cost. With average cost pricing, the total cost of providing services is calculated and then averaged across customers. Customers receive a monthly bill that is independent of the level of waste they generate. Consequently, consumers do not have an incentive to conserve on the amount of waste that they purchase and dispose of into the waste stream.

Waste and Recycling

Recycling has received prominent attention as a possible solution to the solid waste problem, as well as contributing to the solution of the problems of mineral depletion and excessive use of energy. An increase in recycling would mean that we would use fewer minerals, have less mining to disturb the environment, use less energy (it takes less energy to recycle a material than to make new material from mineral resources), and have less waste to dispose of in landfills.

Why do many people believe that too little recycling occurs? The answer to this question has two major components. First, the market failures that prevent the social cost of waste from being reflected in either the market price of a product or the market price of waste disposal make it less profitable to recycle. Second, inertia that is built into our economic system makes it difficult for recycling to become established.

The effect of failure to incorporate social costs of materials and waste disposal into market price is shown in Figure 10.5. In this graph, it is assumed that recycled materials and virgin materials (made from extracted resources) are viewed by the consumer as identical. Therefore, one can refer to the demand for materials in total and develop a marginal private cost curve for materials by horizontally summing the marginal private cost curves for recycled materials and for virgin materials. Similarly, one can also derive a marginal social cost curve for materials in general by summing the marginal social cost curves for recycled materials and for virgin materials. In Figure 10.5, it has been assumed that there is a disparity between the marginal social cost curve and the marginal private cost curve for virgin materials, but that the marginal social cost curve for recycled material is equal to the marginal private cost curve for recycled material. Although there are externalities associated with recycled materials, they are not as severe as those associated with virgin materials. Consequently, even though it is not strictly true, the marginal private costs for recycled materials are assumed to be identical to the marginal social costs, allowing us to include one less curve in an already crowded graph.

The aggregate (both recycled and marginal) private cost curve intersects the inverse demand curve at q_1 units of materials, with r_1 representing the

Figure 10.5 **The Market for Materials and Recycling**

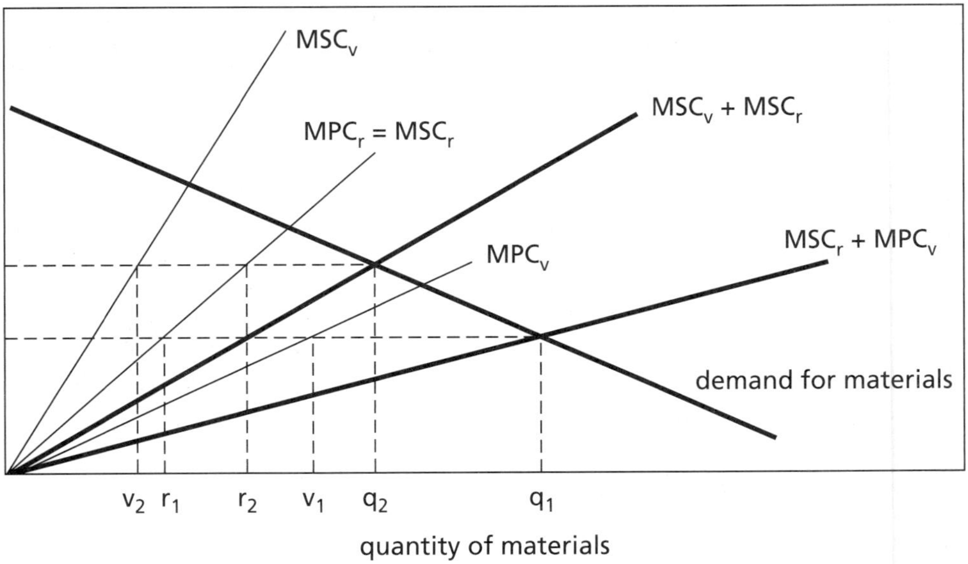

amount of recycled material and v_1 representing the amount of virgin material. (Note that $q_1 = r_1 + v_1$.) This set of quantities represents the total amount of material (q_1) and the allocation between recycled (r_1) and virgin materials (v_1) that market forces would generate. The optimal level would occur at q_2, where marginal social costs of materials are equal to marginal social benefits. Note that the optimal allocation of material between recycled and virgin is r_2 and v_2, and that $r_2 > r_1$ and $v_2 < v_1$. This allocation indicates that the market failures that generate the disparity between the MPC and MSC of virgin materials cause us to use too much virgin material and to engage in too little recycling. This problem is exacerbated because energy inputs do not reflect their true social costs (see Chapters 8 and 9). Because the production of virgin materials is more energy intensive than the production of recycled materials, the relative disparity between private cost and social costs is increased.

Another reason we may have less recycling than socially optimal is because of the "chicken and egg" problem. For there to be an extensive amount of recycling of materials, the cost of recycling must be relatively low. For the cost of recycling to be relatively low, however, an extensive amount of recycling must take place to achieve economies of scale in recycling. In other words, a lot of recycling must take place to lower costs, but a lot of recycling will not take place unless the cost is low.

This process is illustrated in Figure 10.6. When the amount of recycling is low, the short-run marginal cost curve is relatively high, such as smc_1 in Figure 10.6. For example, to recycle paper, paper must be collected where it is used (urban areas) and taken to the places where it is made (rural forested

Figure 10.6 **Long-Run Average Cost and Short-Run Average Cost**

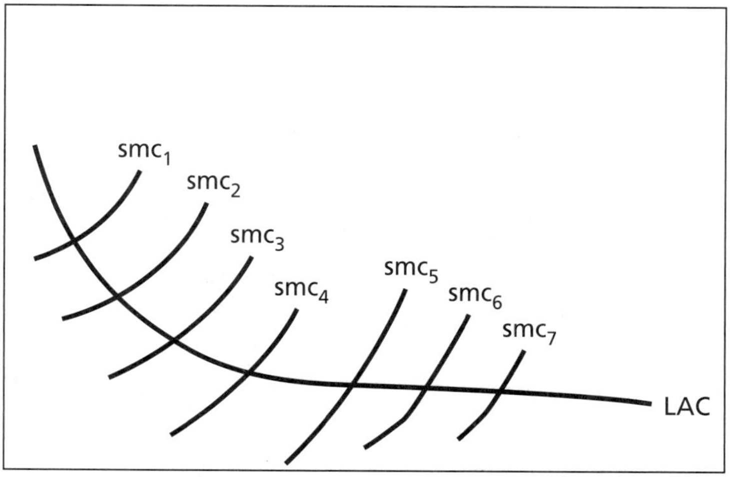

areas). As more and more paper is recycled, the infrastructure for recycling is expanded. For example, new paper factories will locate close to urban areas rather than in forested areas. Factories that recycle plastic beverage bottles into construction materials will be constructed near large urban areas. Trash collection companies will develop sorting mechanisms and storage areas for recycled materials, and local government and other institutions will develop "drop-off" areas for recycled materials. All these changes will lower the short-run marginal cost curve and cause a movement down the long-run average cost curve, where economies of scale will be realized.

This potential to achieve economies of scale is used as an argument for government intervention in the conduct of international trade. If a particular industry is not established in the home country, then the home country might provide protection from foreign competition to allow the industry to become established in the home country and to expand to the point where it achieves the low point or the flat region of the long-run average cost curve. Then the protection can be removed, because the industry will have achieved the low costs associated with economies of scale and can compete with the foreign competition without the need to continue protectionist policies.[12]

In a similar vein, one might argue the need for government intervention to allow the recycled materials industry to achieve the lower costs associated with economies of scale and to compete with the virgin material industry. In addition to incorporating the social costs of virgin materials into the price of virgin materials, the government could take other steps to help encourage recycling. It could do this in its role as a consumer rather than its role as a regulator.

Because the government is such a large consumer of materials (particularly paper to fuel the bureaucracy), it could require a certain percentage of recycled materials in the products that it purchases. This step in itself would move the recycling industry a substantial distance down its long-run average cost curve. The government could also introduce labeling requirements in which manufacturers were required to specify the amount of recycled material in their products so that consumers with a preference for recycled materials could exercise those preferences.

A Comprehensive Materials Policy

The first step in developing a comprehensive materials policy is to price both materials and waste disposal services correctly. A variety of options are available to do so, at both the federal and local levels.

[12]The potential of reducing long-term average costs is also used as an argument for government support of research and development.

Federal Materials Policy

Although many people tend to think of materials policy as a local problem, there are many dimensions in which federal policy can reduce inefficiency. These areas include mining and minerals policy as well as solid waste policy.

The federal government can adopt direct controls or economic incentives to help reduce the environmental externalities associated with mining. Of particular importance are policies pertaining to the safe closure of mines. Of course, many of these environmental externalities are already regulated by the Clean Air Act, the Clean Water Act, and a variety of mining laws and rules governing the use of federal lands. Much environmental degradation, however, takes place as a result of both abandoned mines and actively worked mines. In the United States, strip-mining and mountaintop removal are particularly bad in terms of their environmental impacts. Policies used to control environmental impacts of mining tend to be based primarily on direct controls, although liability and bonding systems are often used to ensure the restoration of mined lands. In addition, the government would need to maintain stockpiles of strategic materials so as to reduce the vulnerability associated with potential disruptions in supply.

An area in which the federal government could utilize economic incentives to increase social welfare is in helping reduce the quantity of solid waste that is produced. A packaging tax, which is based on the volume (or weight) of the packaging of a product, could be imposed at any governmental level. Similarly, a tax on the total amount of material in a product could be instituted at any governmental level. If this tax was sporadically instituted by only a few local or state governments, however, it may not have much of an effect on solid waste, even in these jurisdictions. The reason is that manufacturers might regard these few areas with the tax as being markets that are too small to warrant the development of special product lines or manufacturing processes. If the tax was instituted at the federal level, however, the entire market would be affected and manufacturers would have an incentive to reduce material inputs because the cost of the inputs has increased. Differential taxes could be implemented, with lower taxes levied on materials that are more easily recycled. Throughout the production process, manufacturers would have an incentive to reduce their use of material inputs and switch to materials that were more easily recycled. Similarly, consumers would have an incentive to buy products that would be associated with less waste.

For example, many products are sold with a large amount of packaging to call attention to the product and to discourage shoplifting. If the packaging became more expensive for manufacturers and retailers, they would substitute other attention-grabbing or antishoplifting measures.[13]

---

[13]Music CDs and audiotapes were formerly packaged in large plastic containers to deter shoplifting. Primarily as a result of consumer demand for less waste, the CDs and audio tapes were encased by removable (by store personnel) and reusable plastic cases. More recently, magnetic tags and electronic surveillance are also used as a substitute for both the large plastic packaging and the removable plastic cases.

Although a packaging tax could reduce the quantity of waste generated and the associated environmental effects, it is clearly a second-best policy. In the best of all worlds, both materials and waste would be priced according to marginal social cost. If institutional barriers or political inertia interfere with the ability to set prices correctly, however, a packaging tax may serve to increase social welfare.

In addition to reducing the quantity of waste, it is important to have an impact on the quality of waste. Policy instruments are necessary to remove some of the more hazardous wastes from the waste stream so that these wastes are not buried in landfills or incinerated in garbage-burning plants. For example, flashlight batteries contain nickel, cadmium, lithium, and other heavy metals that lead to adverse effects on human health and the health of ecosystems. A deposit-refund system could be placed on batteries so that they would be removed from the waste stream and handled separately and so that the heavy metals can be recycled into new batteries. Similarly, the unused contents of home pesticide containers, paints, solvents, drain cleaners, and other household chemicals can be extremely hazardous. A deposit-refund system on these containers (which would be allowed to be returned partially filled) could help remove these toxic chemicals from the waste stream. Of course, the chemical container deposit-refund system would be more difficult to implement than a deposit-refund system for flashlight batteries, because flashlight batteries could be safely handled by the retail stores at which the batteries were purchased. It probably would not be a good idea to bring partially used containers of pesticides and other household chemicals into the retail stores in which they were purchased as part of the deposit-refund system. A better idea is to have a central toxic waste handling facility with appropriate facilities and trained personnel to reduce the hazards of handling and properly disposing of these wastes.

Many European countries are experimenting with producer liability for waste. In these systems, the producer is responsible for taking back the product after its useful life is over and for paying the costs of disposal. In many ways, this liability system internalizes the cost of the externality associated with waste disposal. For example, a car manufacturer would then have an incentive to make the car in a fashion that enhances its recyclability. Although this option provides many useful incentives and can reduce the volume of waste, it does not necessarily result in the minimum cost of waste reduction, as would the correct pricing of waste. The producer liability approach, however, may be a good one when correctly pricing waste is difficult, or if consumers do not perceive the price of disposal as being incorporated into the price of the product.

State and Local Solid Waste Policies

Because many of our waste problems are location specific, their solution must be developed by state and local governments. The single most important action would be to develop a system for financing the collection and disposal of solid waste that incorporated the full social cost of waste into the price of collection and disposal. Homeowners, commercial establishments, and industrial establishments must be required to pay a price for trash removal that is based on the amount of trash that has been removed.

Two obstacles can keep this marginal cost pricing from taking place. First, as mentioned earlier, incorporating the scarcity value of landfill space into the market price of trash removal will result in a drastic increase in garbage removal fees, which will generate voter dissatisfaction. Second, there is a perception that marginal cost pricing will be difficult to monitor or expensive to implement.

Little can be done about the first problem except educating people about the extent of the solid waste problem, the difficulty of developing options for the disposal of waste, and the importance of correctly pricing waste disposal so as to create disincentives to the generation of waste. In addition, the political opposition to increasing fees may be blunted if the scarcity value of landfill space is gradually incorporated into tipping fees and garbage collection fees.

The perception that it is expensive or administratively unfeasible to move to a marginal cost pricing system for waste removal is probably a misperception. Although weighing each bag or can of trash and then charging the customer on this basis would truly be unwieldy, a variety of options could be implemented to move toward marginal cost pricing. Some of these options have been adopted in several communities (see Box 10.5). One example of a marginal cost pricing system is an "official bag" system. Garbage may only be accepted for collection if it is contained in an "official bag" that is printed with a logo or some other identifying feature. The price of the bag is set to include the full cost of waste disposal, including the scarcity value of landfill space. Alternatively, one could adopt a sticker system, whereby every bag or can of trash must have an "official sticker" attached to it. The garbage collection personnel would remove the sticker from the can after it has been emptied, and a new sticker is required for the next collection. The price of the sticker should be equal to the full social cost of the disposal of the waste.

Recycling programs must also be local in nature, because the cost of sorting garbage (separating the recyclable items from the nonrecyclable items) is lower when the recycling is done at the household or establishment level, where the trash is generated. If the garbage is collected into large truckloads and removed to a central facility before sorting, then the sorting process becomes more complicated and more expensive. Many communities have adopted mandatory or voluntary recycling programs and have attempted to reduce homeowner inconvenience by allowing the homeowner to place all recyclable items in one bin. The garbage collection personnel then sort the recyclable items as they remove them and place them in a truck or trailer that has a separate compartment for each class of recyclable good. The most common types of materials included in these recycling programs are aluminum cans, ferrous cans, glass, some types of plastics, newspapers, and corrugated cardboard.

In addition, many communities no longer allow yard waste (leaves, lawn clippings, branches, and so on) to be mixed with garbage. These communi-

Box 10.5 Experience with Marginal Cost Pricing of Garbage Disposal

Many economists are strong advocates of marginal cost pricing of garbage disposal. Rather than charging a monthly fee, economists argue that it is important to charge a price based on each unit of garbage generated. As this chapter emphasizes, economic theory argues that marginal cost pricing of garbage disposal will give both producers and consumers an incentive to reduce the amount of garbage that is generated.

Often, however, practical issues are involved in implementing economic solutions such as marginal cost pricing of trash. Will the system that looks good on paper work when implemented in the real world?

Morris and Byrd (1990) examined this question by analyzing the impact of marginal cost pricing (which they called unit pricing) on three U.S. communities that had switched to this form of pricing. Their results are presented in the table.

Estimated Daily Waste Per Resident (pounds per person per day)

	Perkasie, PA		Ilion, NY		Seattle, WA	
	Before Unit Pricing	After Unit Pricing	Before Unit Pricing	After Unit Pricing	Before Unit Pricing	After Unit Pricing
Waste generate	2.5	1.9	2.6	1.9	2.8	2.9
Waste recycled	0.2	0.7	0.1	0.3	0.5	0.5
Mixed waste collected	2.2	1.2	2.5	1.6	2.3	2.3

Source: Morris and Byrd, 1990, Table 3, p. 13.

ties generally have separate pickup for these yard wastes and then compost them into mulch, rather than having them take up space in the landfill. The mulch is available for gardening and landscaping at a nominal delivery charge. This program turns a waste product into an economic product.

Either marginal cost pricing system (the official bag and official sticker systems) would make the homeowner perceive a cost associated with each piece of garbage that he or she throws away. This type of pricing system can drastically improve the response to a voluntary recycling program, because the homeowner will save money by placing recyclable items in the recycle bin, saving the need to purchase as many official bags or official stickers. Similarly, the homeowner would have an incentive to separate yard waste from the collected trash, by composting the waste in a backyard compost pile, by self-delivery to the municipal compost site, or by having it collected for delivery to the municipal compost site.

Problems with Illegal Disposal

There is a potential problem with both increasing the cost of legal waste disposal and with moving to marginal cost pricing of waste. This problem arises because such policies increase the incentives for illegal disposal, because people try to avoid the increased costs of legal disposal. The private cost of proper disposal has increased, so we would expect to see more dumping. That will increase environmental damages, because the waste is released into the environment in general, rather than at a waste disposal facility.

To avoid an increase in the level of illegal dumping, policies must be developed to increase the expected penalty for illegal dumping. Because the private cost of proper disposal has increased, more illegal dumping will occur unless there is an increase in the fine for illegal dumping, an increase in the probability of being caught, or both. Increasing fines is relatively easy to do, but increasing the probability of being caught requires increasing the amount of resources devoted to monitoring and enforcement. Because these monitoring and enforcement costs are part of the costs of waste disposal, they should be incorporated into the price that people pay to dispose of their wastes.

Summary

Although the historic focus of material policy has been on the conservation of resources, the externalities and other market failures associated with our use of materials may be of much greater concern. These market failures occur throughout the cycle of use, from the mining of minerals to the disposal of economic products when their useful life is over. Various policies are necessary to reduce the economic inefficiency associated with these market failures.

Mining is associated with the destruction of natural environments as well as with pollution that affects air and water quality. A variety of direct controls and economic incentives can be utilized to mitigate these externalities.

In addition to the environmental externalities, market failures associated with imperfect competition and inappropriate government intervention affect the market for minerals. A very important federal policy is the depletion allowance, which reduces the private cost of mining and leads to an inefficiently high level of mining.

Many market failures are also associated with waste disposal. The environmental externalities associated with waste disposal are made more severe by policies that reduce the private cost of waste disposal below the market price. Chief among them are prices based on the average cost of waste disposal rather than on the marginal cost.

The solid waste problem will continue as long as these market failures remain uncorrected. The creation of more landfill sites or incinerators to process our increased volume of waste merely treats the symptom of the problem rather than addressing the cause of the problem. Stated quite simply, the problem is that waste disposal is underpriced, and as a consequence we generate too much waste.

Review Questions

1. What are the market failures associated with mineral extraction?
2. Assume that a particular community generates 10 million beverage containers per year. For beverage containers that are disposed in a landfill, let

   $$MSC_L = 0.05 + 0.01Q_L$$

   where Q_L is the quantity of containers disposed in the landfill, measured in millions of cans. Let the marginal social cost of recycled cans be

   $$MSC_R = 0.03 + 0.02Q_R$$

   where Q_R is the quantity of containers that are recycled, also measured in millions of cans. Calculate the social cost minimizing allocation of cans between landfill disposal and recycling.
3. Why might the market generate a less than socially optimal amount of recycling?
4. What is the impact of a depletion allowance on the cost of exhaustible resources?
5. What is the effect of average cost pricing of trash disposal services?

Questions for Further Study

1. What, if anything, should be done to encourage more recycling?
2. What are the advantages and disadvantages of a packaging tax?
3. What is the role for deposit-refund systems in material policy?
4. Is there a role for marketable permits in material policy?
5. How should policy deal with national security problems surrounding strategic materials?

Suggested Paper Topics

1. Investigate the success of policies to encourage recycling. Begin with papers by Hopper and Nielson (1991); Hong et al. (1993); Tiller, Jakus, and Vark (1997); Aadland and Caplan (2003); Eichner and Pethig (2003). Search recent issues of the *Journal of Environmental Management, Journal of Economic Literature, Forum, Nature*, and *Science*. Also check for stories in major newspapers such as the *Wall Street Journal, New York Times,* and *Chicago Tribune* as well as your local newspaper. Search the Internet for some recent case studies. Use your understanding of environmental economics to suggest policy refinements that could increase the amount of recycling.
2. Look at the impact of the mining industry on the environment and policies that have been developed to regulate this impact. How does current policy create appropriate incentives? Can policies be changed to be more efficient? Search bibliographic databases using mining and environmental policy, mining and environmental impact, and mining and environmental regulation as keywords. Check government documents of the Department of Interior (Bureau of Mines) and the EPA.
3. Investigate the development of new technology that makes useful products from recycled materials. What technologies seem the most interesting? What barriers exist to the devel-

opment of these technologies? How can economic incentives and other policies be used to speed the development and diffusion of these technologies.

Works Cited and Selected Readings

Addland, D., and A. Caplan. Willingness to Pay for Curbside Recycling with Detection and Mitigation of Hypothetical Bias. *American Journal of Agricultural Economics 85* (2003): 492–502.

Anders, G., W. Gramm, M. Charlse, C. Smithson. *The Economics of Mineral Extraction*. New York: Praeger, 1980.

Ayres, R. U. The Second Law, the Fourth Law, Recycling, and Limits to Growth. *Ecological Economics 29*, no. 3 (June 1999): 473–483.

Clausen, S., and M. L. McAllister. An Integrated Approach to Mineral Policy. *Journal of Environmental Planning and Management 44*, no. 2 (March 2001): 227–244.

Eichner, T., and R. Pethig. Corrective Taxing for Curbing Pollution and Promoting Green Product Design and Recycling. *Environmental and Resource Economics 25* (2003): 477–500.

Fullerton, D., and T. C. Kinnaman. Household Responses to Pricing Garbage by the Bag. *American Economic Review 86*, No. 4 (September 1996): 971–984.

Fullerton, D., and T. C. Kinnaman, eds. *The Economics of Household Garbage and Recycling Behavior*. Cheltenham, UK: Elgar Publishing, 2002.

Fullerton, D., and A. Wolverton. Two Generalizations of a Deposit-Refund System.

Working Paper: 7505, National Bureau of Economic Research, 2000.

Gielen, D. J., and Y. Moriguchi. Materials Policy Design. *Environmental Economics and Policy Studies 5*, no. 1 (2002): 17–37.

Gocht, W. R., H. Zantop, and R. R. Eggert. *International Mineral Economics*. New York: Springer-Verlag, 1988.

Hilson, G. Small-Scale Mining in Africa: Tackling Pressing Environmental Problems with Improved Strategy. *Journal of Environment and Development 11*, no. 2 (June 2002): 149–174.

Hilson, G., and B. Murck, Sustainable Development in the Mining Industry: Clarifying the Corporate Perspective. *Resources Policy 26*, no. 4 (December 2000): 227–238.

Hong, S., R. M. Adams, and H. A. Love. An Economic Analysis of Household Recycling of Solid Wastes. *Journal of Environmental Economics and Management 25* (1993): 136–146.

Hopper, J. R., and J. M. Nielson. Recycling as Altruistic Behavior: Normative and Behavioral Strategies to Expand Participation in a Community Recycling Program. *Environment and Behavior 23* (1991): 195–220.

Jakus, P. M., K. H. Tiller, and W. M. Park. Explaining Rural Household Participation in Recycling. *Journal of Agricultural and Applied Economics 29*, no. 1 (July 1997): 141–148.

Jenkins, R. R., S. A. Martinez, K. Palmer and M. J. Podolsky. The Determinants of Household Recycling: A Material-Specific Analysis of Recycling Program Features and Unit Pricing. *Journal of Environmental Economics and Management 45*, no. 2 (March 2003): 294–318.

Jordan, A. A., and R. A. Kilmarx. *Strategic Mineral Dependence: The Stockpile Dilemma*. Beverly Hills, CA: Sage Publications, 1979.

Kahn, J. R., D. Franceschi, A. Curi, and E. Vale. Economic and Financial Aspects of Mine Closure. *Natural Resources Forum 25* (2001): 265–274.

Keeler, A. G., and M. Renkow. Public vs. Private Garbage Disposal: The Economics of Solid Waste Flow Controls. *Growth and Change 30*, no. 3 (Summer 1999): 430–444.

Krutilla, J. Conservation Reconsidered. *American Economic Review 57*, (1967): 777–786.

Krutilla, J., and A. C. Fisher. *The Economics of Natural Environments.* Washington, DC: Resources for the Future, 1985.

Macauley, M. K., and M. A. Walls. Solid Waste Reduction and Resource Conservation: Assessing the Goals of Government Policy, Washington: Resources for the Future. Discussion Paper 95/32. 1995.

Mining, Minerals, and Sustainable Development Project. *Breaking New Ground: Mining, Minerals, and Sustainable Development. The Report of the MMSD Project*. London and Sterling, Va.: Earthscan; distributed by Stylus, Sterling, VA., 2002.

Morgan, J. D. Stockpiling in the USA. *Concise Encyclopedia of Material Economics, Policy, and Management*, edited by M. Bever. Oxford: Pergamen Press, 1993.

Morris, G., and D. Byrd. Unit Pricing for Solid Waste Collection. *Popular Government 56* (1990).

Palmer, K. F. Mineral Taxation Policies in Developing Countries: An Application of Resource Rent Tax. In P. Stevens, ed. *The Economics of Energy*, Volume 2, Cheltenham, UK: Elgar, 2000: 132–157.

Porter, R. C. Michigan's Experience with Mandatory Deposits on Beverage Containers. *Land Economics 59* (1983): 177–194.

Porter, R. C. The New Approach to Wilderness Preservation through Benefit-Cost Analysis. *Journal of Environmental Economics and Management 9* (1982): 59–80.

Raven, P. H., L. Berg, and G. B. Johnson. *Environment*. New York: Saunders, 1993.

Rudawsky, O. *Mineral Economics: Development and Management of Natural Resources*. New York: Elsevier, 1986.

Stevens, P. Resource Impact: Curse or Blessing? A Literature Survey. *Journal of Energy Literature 9*, no. 1 (June 2003): 3–42.

Tiller, K. H., P. M. Jakus, and W. M. Park. Household Willingness to Pay for Dropoff Recycling. *Journal of Agricultural and Resource Economics 22* (1997): 310–320.

Tilton, J. E. *Mineral Wealth and Economic Development*. Washington, DC: Resources for the Future, 1992.

Yates, A. J. The Equal Marginal Value Principle: A Graphical Analysis with Environmental Applications. *Journal of Economic Education 29*, no. 1 (Winter 1998): 23–31.

Young, J. E. Mining the Earth. Pages 102–121 in *State of the World 1992*, edited by Lester Brown. New York: W. W. Norton, 1992.

PART III

renewable resources

and the environment

© MONTE NAGLER, DIGITAL VISION.

Part III examines renewable resources and their interactions with the economy and the environment. Renewable resources are analyzed both as harvestable outputs and as components of ecological systems.

chapter 11

Fisheries

And they spoke politely about the current and the depths they had drifted their lines at and the steady good weather of what they had seen.

Ernest Hemingway, The Old Man and the Sea

Introduction

The ocean currents and depths have not changed from the period of which Hemingway wrote, but his old fisherman would be very surprised by the way fisheries have changed. Modern fishing technology, coupled with increased demand and open-access exploitation of fisheries, has driven many fish stocks to such low levels that they are threatened with extinction. For example, the Gulf Stream marlin, swordfish, and tuna that Hemingway's old fisherman pursued have declined precipitously in the last several decades. The problem is not limited to the Florida area; many of the world's important fisheries have collapsed. For example, the North Atlantic cod fishery is a mere shadow of its former self, causing economic hardship for fishing communities in both North America and Europe. Overfishing is not the only problem. Florida Bay and virtually every estuary and embayment in the world have become threatened by externalities from human economic and social activity. As rivers carry pollution into the estuaries, oil and chemical spills exact their ecological toll, and upstream water withdrawals increase the salinity of these delicate but vital ecosystems. In addition, many freshwater fisheries that are important subsistence fisheries, such as the Amazon River system, Lake Victoria, Lake Titicaca, and the Mekong River, are threatened by competition from commercial fisheries.

Although fish may not be the first environmental resource to come to mind when one thinks of environmental resources that deserve attention, the world's fishery resources are important for several reasons. Fish are a major source of protein for a large portion of the world's population. Even though fish are a renewable resource, they are destructible. Overexploitation and environmental change, such as pollution and loss of wetlands, threaten this important resource. Populations of many important species declined markedly in the late twentieth century, causing hardships for fishing communities, reducing nutritional sources for many rural communities in developing countries, and lowering the quality of life of people who take pleasure from recreational fishing. In addition, because the fish stocks interact with the other components of the ecosystem, a diminution in fish stocks will cause indirect effects to ripple through the ecosystem, reducing its overall stability, resilience, and ability to provide ecological services.

The decline in global, regional, and local fishery stocks has led to increased conflict among user groups. Fishing nations compete for limited stocks on the waters outside each country's 200-mile exclusion zone. Commercial fishermen and recreational anglers clash over who has access to limited nearshore stocks of steelhead, striped bass, and salmon as they swim up the rivers to spawn. In developing nations, commercial fisheries are in conflict with those who fish solely to feed their families, and as fish stocks decline, the ability to feed their families is seriously compromised. These conflicts make the development of fisheries policy even more difficult.[1]

In the United States, most commercially harvested species are harvested in saltwater, with the notable exception of crawfish. Some other freshwater species (catfish and trout) are important commercially, but they are mostly reared in tanks and artificial ponds and not caught in the wild. Most states in the United States have laws banning the commercial harvesting of freshwater species, although Native Americans have special fishing rights under various federal treaties.

Fish populations are declining throughout the world, as shown in Table 11.1, which presents the global fisheries picture. The maximum sustainable yield (explained more fully later) is the maximum amount that could be harvested year after year in a sustainable fashion. Exploitation beyond this level leads to declining populations. As can be seen in Table 11.1, the proportion of global stocks of fish that are in a state of decline rose from 10 percent in 1975 to almost 30 percent in 2002, with the figures much higher in some locations. Although 30 percent may not seem to be a high number, when the number of fisheries that are "fully exploited" (more fishing effort will lead to population declines) is considered, 30 percent rep-

---

[1]An excellent discussion of these issues is contained in Sloan (2003).

Table 11.1 **State of the World's Fisheries—Percentage [%] of Fish Stocks Exploited Beyond Maximum Sustainable Yield**

AREA	1975	1985	1995	2002
North Atlantic	13	17	23	23
Tropical Atlantic	10	28	33	35
North Pacific	22	25	22	32
Tropical Pacific	2	27	34	35
Antarctic Ocean	No data	No data	55	35
World	10	20	28	28

Source: Data in this table extrapolated from Figures 40, 41, and 42 in *The State of World Fisheries*, Food and Agricultural Organization of the United Nations, 2000. Online: http://www.fao.org/DOCREP/003/X8002e/X8002e06.htm.

resents almost all of the world's most important fisheries[2]). This overexploitation problem will continue to grow as the fishing fleets focus on fisheries that have not yet seen much exploitation, as fishing fleets compete for dwindling resources, and as world population grows.

Recreational fishing is also very important in the United States and other countries. According to the U.S. Fish and Wildlife Services[3] approximately 34 million adult Americans (over age 16) participated in recreational fishing in 2001, representing 16 percent of the U.S. population over age 16. These anglers engaged in well over one-half billion days of fishing and spent approximately $35 billion on fishing-related expenses.

Fisheries Biology

Fish are like any other animal in that they require food and oxygen in an appropriate habitat. Fish reproductive strategy is generally based on the principle of large numbers. Each reproducing female generates large numbers of eggs, in some cases numbering in the millions per female. Very few of these eggs, however, grow and survive to reproductive maturity.

The reproductive potential of a fish population is a function of both the size of the fish population and the characteristics of its habitat. To understand

[2]According to the Pew Commission on Oceans, 67 percent of the world's stocks of fish are declining. See http://www.pewoceans.org/articles/2002/10/25/pr_29891.asp.

[3]See http://fa.r9.fws.gov/ssurveys/surveys.html#surv_2001.

the relationship between growth and the size of the population better, let's initially assume that the characteristics of the habitat are held constant.

Both the growth of the population and the population itself are measured in biomass (weight) units, not by the number of individual organisms. Thus, growth can occur through the production of new organisms or through growth in the mass of existing organisms.

Figure 11.1 depicts a logistic growth function.[4] As shown in this graph, there is no growth when the population is zero. This point is fairly obvious, but it warrants some discussion. If there are no fish to reproduce or get larger, then there can be no growth. As population increases, the amount of growth increases. For example, at a population level of X_1, the annual growth will be G_1 and the rate of change of growth will be the slope of the growth function at X_1. The maximum growth rate is often referred to as the intrinsic growth rate.

Although the amount of growth will initially increase, the rate of change of growth is constantly declining. Eventually, the rate of change of growth becomes zero at X_2 and the amount of growth is at a maximum (G_2). For a population level greater than X_2, the rate of change of growth is negative and

Figure 11.1 **Logistic Growth Function**

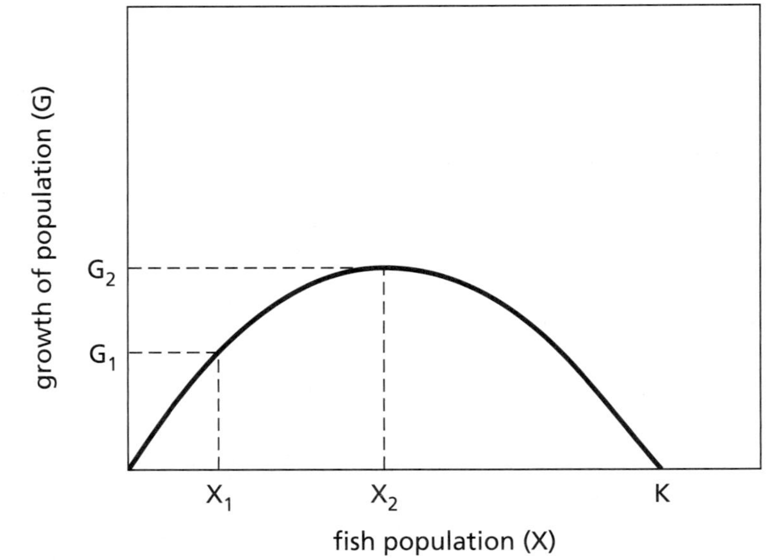

[4]Mathematically, the logistic growth function can be represented as $G = rX(1 - X/K)$, where r represents the limit of the growth rate as X approaches zero, K is the carrying capacity, and G represents growth as a function of a variable population (X).

declining. Eventually, the amount of growth falls to zero, which occurs at the maximum population at K (population cannot get bigger if growth is zero).

Biological factors generate the constantly declining growth rate and the eventual decline in the level of growth toward zero. For example, when population is low, the resources of the ecosystem are large relative to the needs of the population, enabling rapid growth. As the population grows, however, the surplus is eliminated, and there is competition for resources, such as food, spawning areas, and nursery areas (areas where juvenile fish can hide and escape predation). Also, as the population grows, the incidence of disease and parasites will grow, and cannibalism may also increase.

All these biological factors tend to slow growth as population increases. At K, the environment cannot support additional growth, so population remains constant. The point represented by K is often referred to as the carrying capacity of the environment and is a biological equilibrium. By a biological equilibrium, it means that once the population reaches K, it will remain at K unless disturbed by an outside shock such as a drastic change in water temperature or large chemical spill. For obvious reasons, zero population is also a biological equilibrium. Any level of population between zero and K is not in equilibrium, because positive growth will move the population toward K.

The growth function of Figure 11.1 represents a particular type, where the growth rate is always declining. The technical term for this type of growth function is a compensated growth function.

Figure 11.2 contains a depensated[5] growth function, where the growth rate initially increases and then decreases. Figure 11.3 contains a critically depensated growth function. In this function, X_0 represents the minimum viable population. If population falls below this level, growth becomes negative and population becomes irreversibly headed toward zero. The existence of a point of minimum viable population is critically important for management of exploited populations of animals. If managers make a mistake and allow too much harvest, they may doom the population to extinction even if they try to correct policy before the extinction actually occurs. The existence of a critically depensated growth function means that policy managers need to build an additional safety margin into their decision making to make sure that the population never falls below the minimum viable level.

The Optimal Harvest

So far, the behavior of fish populations independent of their interaction with humans have been examined. The interaction is important because the ability to harvest fish is influenced by the level of the fish population

[5]The opposite of a compensated growth function is a depensated growth function. Although the term *depensate* is not in collegiate dictionaries, it is commonly used in fishery population dynamics to distinguish this particular type of growth function from the logistic or compensated growth function.

Figure 11.2 **Depensated Growth Function**

Figure 11.3 **Growth Function with Critical Depensation**

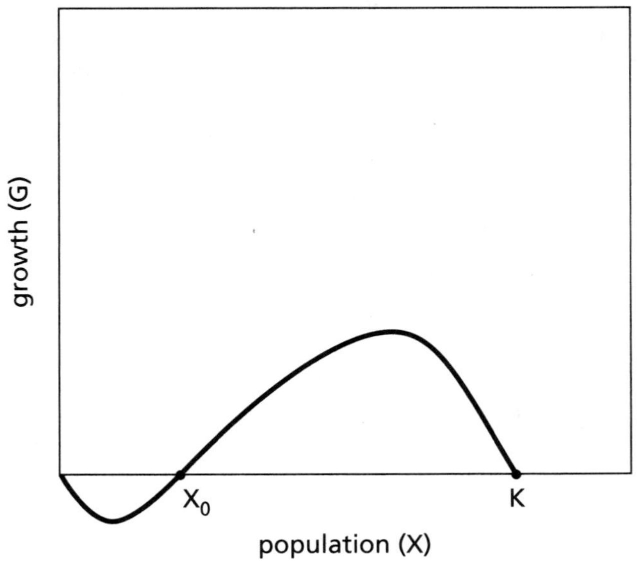

(also called the stock of fish, or fish stock), which is influenced by the level of the harvests.

To determine how harvesting affects a fish population, let's examine a growth function in Figure 11.4 and add a harvest equal to C_1. Note that because both growth and harvest are measured in biomass units, they can both be expressed on the vertical axis of the graph.

Let's assume that the fishery is initially unexploited, so in Figure 11.4 the population is K. Then, a harvest of C_1 units per year is removed from the fishery. Under these circumstances, the fish population declines, because there is no natural growth, and harvesting is removing a portion of the population. Population will fall toward X_2. At X_2, the population will continue to fall, because the harvest (C_1) is greater than the growth that a fish stock of X_2 can support. Simply stated, the amount of fish that humans are taking out (C_1) is greater than the amount that nature is putting back in (G_2). Therefore, the population must continue to shrink and will continue to shrink until the natural growth is equal to the harvest. For a harvest of C_1, this equality of harvest and natural growth occurs at X_1.

In Figure 11.5, it is shown that every harvest level but C_{msy} (maximum sustainable yield harvest) has two equilibrium populations associated with it. For example, a harvest level of C_1 is associated with equilibrium populations of X_1' and X_1''. Thus growth is exactly equal to the harvest level of C_1, and the population will remain unchanged at either of these levels. For example, if the population is equal to X_1', the harvest can equal C_1 year after year and

Figure 11.4 **Equilibrium Catch**

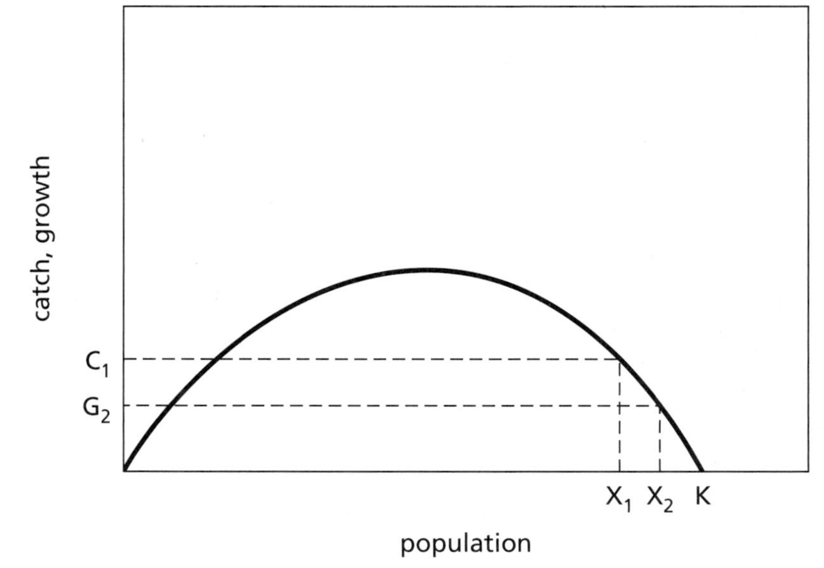

Figure 11.5 Maximum Sustainable Yield and the Equilibrium Catch Function

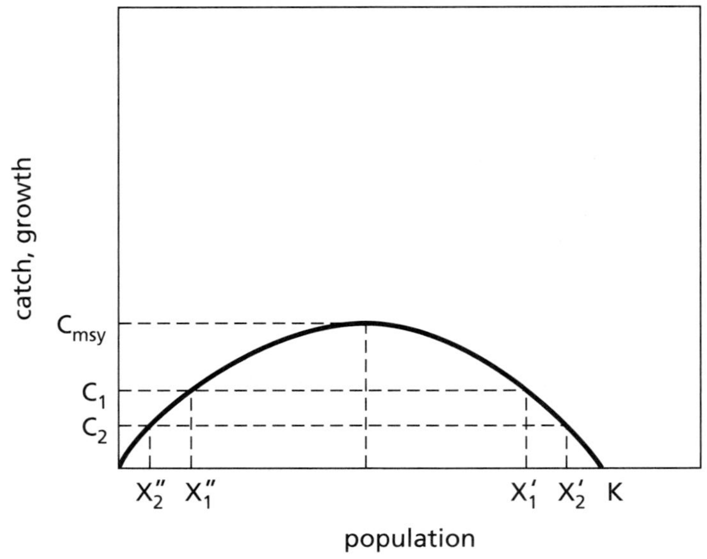

leave population unchanged at X_1". For this reason, C_1 is known as the sustainable or equilibrium catch associated with the population level X_1". The natural growth function can also be interpreted as an equilibrium catch or sustainable catch function. In the jargon of fishery management, it is known as a sustainable yield function.

C_{msy} is the maximum sustainable yield, as no level of the fish population can produce growth above this level. In the early discussions of fishery management, the achievement of maximum sustainable yield was the theoretical goal of management policies. More recent management policy in the United States, however, is to view maximum sustainable yield as a limit to be avoided, rather than a goal (Craig, 2000, p. 248). The reasoning is that if maximum sustainable yield is the target, then an increase in effort will lead to a decline in fish stocks. This decline can be relatively rapid if the growth function is depensated and lead to extinction if the growth function is critically depensated. For this reason, the goal of a precautionary approach would be to have population between the carrying capacity of the fishery and the level associated with maximum sustainable yield. In addition to the margin of safety, this level should be chosen to try to maximize social welfare, subject to the precautionary constraint. Several models that focus on maximizing net benefits are presented in the following sections, although they focus only on the economic benefits arising from the fishery and do not include social benefits such as the benefits of ecological services.

The Gordon Model and Its Evolution

An important general finding in economics is that the maximization of a physical quantity will not necessarily maximize the economic benefits of the activity for society. H. Scott Gordon made this point in a 1955 article in which he points out that uncontrolled access to fishery resources will result in a greater than optimal level of fishing effort. Gordon begins his analysis by deriving a catch function that represents a "bionomic" equilibrium, which he does by looking at fishing effort and the relationship of fishing effort, catch, and fish population.

Gordon's analysis begins by assuming that, holding effort constant, catch is proportional to the fish population. For example, if effort is held constant at E_1, then the catch that would result from that effort is given by the yield function Y_{E1} in Figure 11.6. If effort is increased to E_2, then the yield function shifts up to Y_{E2}.

Of course, not every point on each yield function is a sustainable yield. The sustainable yields can be found by superimposing the equilibrium catch function on the yield functions of Figure 11.6, as shown in Figure 11.7. As can be seen, only one point on each yield function is a sustainable yield (which is not necessarily true for a depensated growth function). In Figure 11.8, the one point of sustainable catch associated with each level of effort is graphed with the corresponding level of effort, rather than the fish population, on the horizontal axis. This graph is known as the sustainable yield function, because it shows the sustainable catch associated with each

Figure 11.6 **Yield Functions**

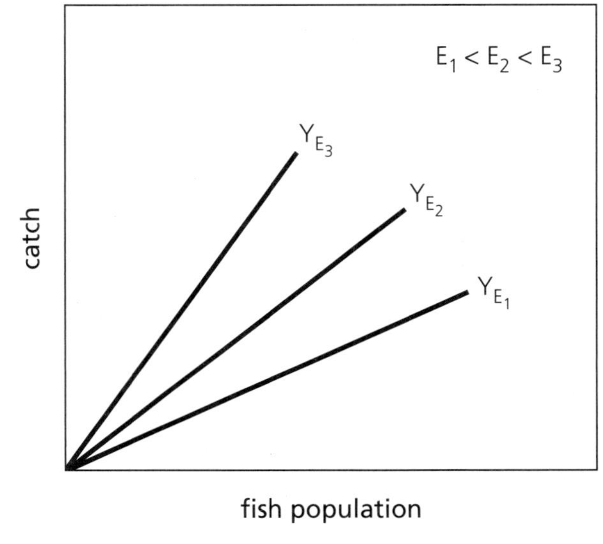

Figure 11.7 The Equilibrium Catch Function and Yield-Effort Functions

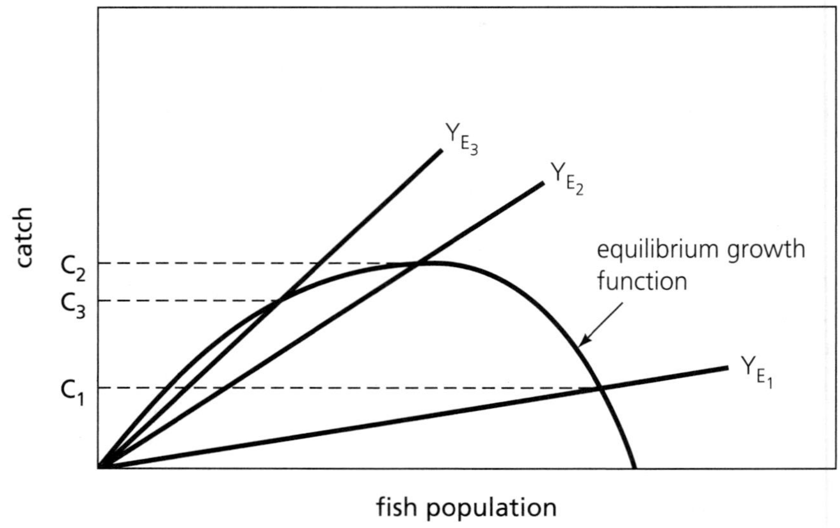

Figure 11.8 Sustainable Yield as a Function of Effort

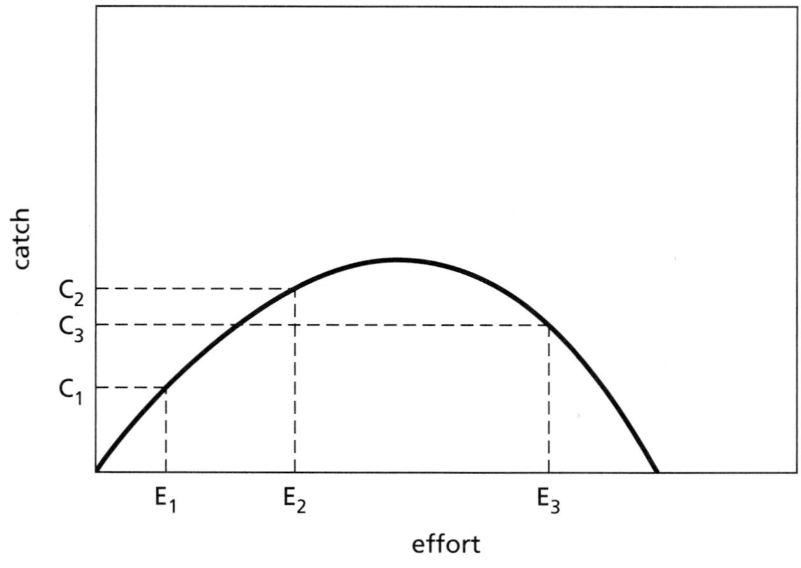

level of effort. Notice that as effort increases, sustainable yield increases and then decreases.

A sustainable total revenue function can be derived from a sustainable yield function. To simplify matters, Gordon (1955) assumes that the price of catch is constant. For this assumption to hold, the particular fish population and the catch from that population must be small in relation to the total market for that fish. For example, this assumption would be appropriate for the analysis of weakfish (sea trout) in a particular embayment, such as the Pamlico-Albemarle Sound in North Carolina. Because the price of weakfish is determined by the catch of weakfish (and substitute species) from the entire Atlantic and Gulf coasts, the catch in Pamlico-Albemarle Sound will be too small relative to total catch to affect price.

Given the assumption that price is constant, a sustainable total revenue function can be derived by simply rescaling Figure 11.8, as presented in the upper panel Figure 11.9, which also contains a total cost of effort function. Gordon (1955) assumes that the marginal cost of effort is constant, so total cost is a linear function. He suggests that net economic yield, shown as TR-TC, be maximized so as to maximize social benefits. Net economic yield is more often referred to as economic rent in modern fishery economics literature. Note that although TR-TC looks like a monopoly profit, it is very different. A monopoly profit is generated by restricting output to gain an increase in price.

Price, however, is constant in the model shown in Figure 11.9, so there can be no monopoly profit. The economic rent originates in the productivity of the fish stock, because the greater the fish stock, the more fish that can be caught with a given amount of effort. The optimal amount of effort occurs at E_2, which maximizes economic rent. Note that at this level of effort, the slopes of the TR and TC functions are equal, or MR = MC.

An optimal level such as E_2 is seldom realized in an actual fishery, due to the open-access nature of fisheries in general. Open access implies that anyone can participate in the fishery. At E_2, economic rents are being earned in the fishery. In general, economic rents are not available elsewhere in the economy, so effort (labor) will enter the fishery in pursuit of these rents. Although the entrance of more effort will cause rents to fall, effort will continue to enter until opportunities in the fishery are equivalent to opportunities elsewhere in the economy, which occurs when there are no rents in the fishery. This point occurs at E_1, where total cost is equal to total revenue. If effort were to exceed E_1, then TR would be less than TC and net losses would occur. Labor would then leave the fishery until the level of effort reached E_1 and there was no further incentive to leave.

Notice in Figure 11.9 that at E_1, AR = MC (also AR = AC, because MC is constant). A market equilibrium being determined by AR = MC rather than MR = MC may initially be confusing, but this equation is a result of the open-access externality and is based on an interaction among fishers. This interaction can best be illustrated with the aid of Table 11.2, which lists the total, marginal, and average catch associated with effort in a hypothetical fishery.

Figure 11.9 **Maximizing TR-TC**

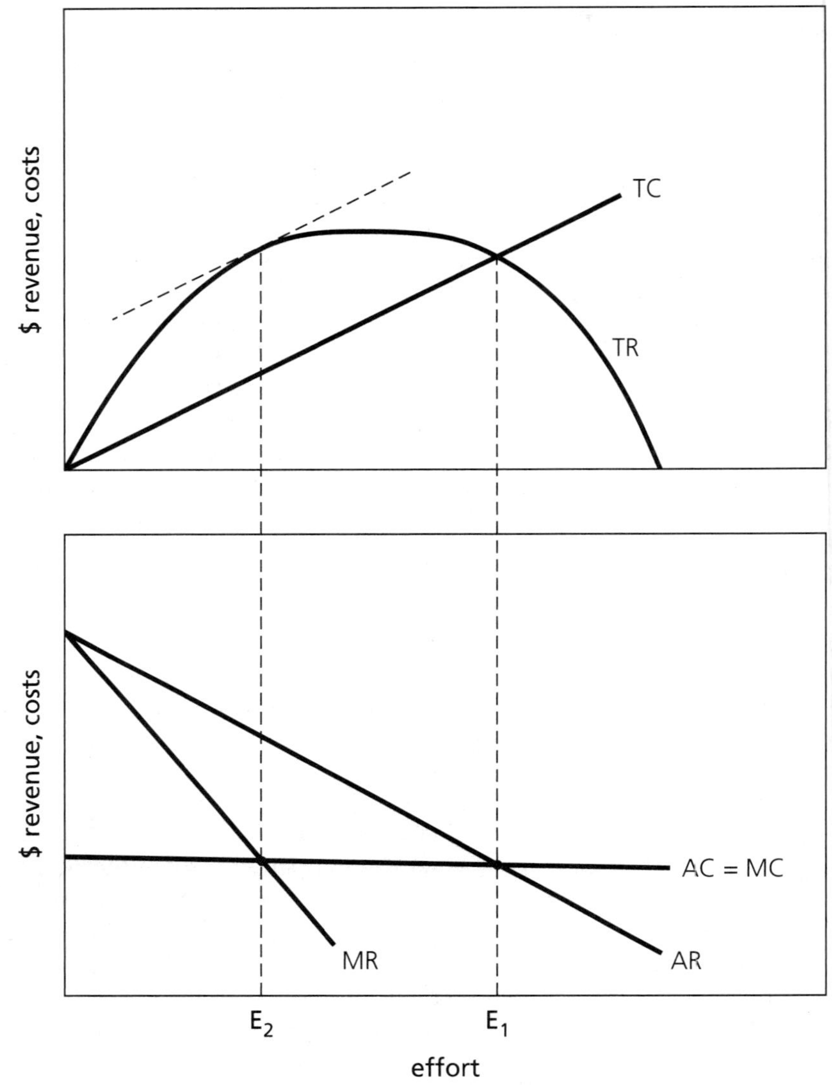

Initially, total catch, marginal catch, and average catch increase, then marginal catch (and average catch with it) begins to fall, but total catch continues to increase because marginal catch is still positive. Eventually, marginal catch becomes negative and total catch begins to fall. So far, nothing is different from total, marginal, and average product functions for conventional goods.

Table 11.2 The Relationship between Marginal Catch and Average Catch (measured in dollars, price held constant)

Level of Effort (No. of fishers)	Total Catch	Marginal Catch	Average Catch
0	0	0	0
1	70	70	70
2	150	80	75
3	240	90	80
4	320	80	80
5	390	70	78
6	450	60	75
7	500	50	71
8	540	40	68
9	570	30	63
10	590	20	59
11	600	10	55
12	600	0	50
13	590	–10	45
14	570	–20	41
15	540	–30	36

Yet there is a big difference in the allocation of total product across units of inputs (labor or effort). For example, examine the fifth fisher in the fishery. He or she adds $70 of catch to total catch. The fifth fisher, however, actually catches $78 of catch. The reason is that if all fishers have the same skill levels, then they each catch the same amount of fish (of course there will be random differences across fishers). In other words, the fifth fisher catches $78 worth of fish. Of that amount, $70 represents a new addition to total catch, but $8 of the catch would have been caught by existing fishers. When the fifth fisher decides to enter the fishery, he or she compares $78 to his or her opportunity cost, not to the $70 of new catch.

This point is very important because social efficiency requires marginal cost to be equal to marginal product. Let's assume that the opportunity cost

Box 11.1 Blue Crabs and the Loss of Salt Marshes

Wetlands are under constant assault from pollution and development. People like to have waterfront homes, and much of the remaining undeveloped waterfront is covered by wetlands, which leads to an interesting question. Should wetlands be converted into marinas or vacation condominiums?

To answer this question, information must be developed on the value of wetlands. Gary Lynne, Patricia Conroy, and Frederick Prochaska (1981) conducted a study to measure the value of salt marshes in terms of their beneficial effect on fisheries. They used a catch per unit effort fishery model to determine the value of Florida Gulf Coast salt marshes in producing blue crabs. Shellfish such as crabs and lobsters are well suited to examination with a catch per unit effort model; it is generally easier to define effort for this type of shellfish than for finfish because an unambiguous effort variable can be defined as the total number of traps used to commercially harvest the crabs.

Lynne and colleagues postulated that catch is related to the carrying capacity and to effort. The carrying capacity was posited to be related to the acreage of salt marshes. In their empirical model, they assumed that the carrying capacity was proportional to the natural logarithm of the total acreage of salt marshes, which implies a relationship that is increasing at a decreasing rate as in the graph below. They also used a regression with data on the total number of traps, dockside value of crab landings, and acreage of marshes. This function can be interpreted as a total product function, and the value of the marginal product of marshes can be determined.

The study found a relatively low marginal product for marshes of $0.25 to $0.30 in 1974 dollars per acre ($0.95 to $1.14 in 2004 dollars). One must be careful, however, in saying that the current value of marsh is about $1 per acre. First, this estimate is a marginal product and not an average product, so it can only be used to measure the value of small changes in total acreage of salt marshes. Given the flatness of the logarithmic function in the graph, one would expect the value of a marginal acre to be lower than the value of an average acre. Second, contribution to the viability of the blue crab fishery is only one of the many services that salt marshes provide. Nonetheless, this study represents an excellent example of how the catch per unit effort model can be used to help understand the value of environmental resources.

Studies such as this one, that focus on only one service of an ecosystem, do not estimate the value of the ecosystem, however. Rather, they provide an estimate of a lower bound on the value of the ecosystem. In other words, if a researcher can do a good job in estimating the value of a wetlands system in producing crabs, then policy makers will know that the value of the ecosystem is at least as high as the estimated value, but in actuality will be greater.

of a unit of effort (unit of labor) is $50 per day. In other words, if a worker is employed somewhere outside the fishery, then the worker would be creating $50 worth of social product. If, however, the opportunity wage is $50, then workers will continue to enter the fishery as long as average product is greater than $50. There is no further incentive to enter once average catch becomes equal to the opportunity wage of $50, which occurs at a level of effort of twelve fishers. At this point, the marginal catch of the twelfth fisher is actually zero. The optimal level of effort occurs at seven fishers, where marginal catch (marginal product in the fishery) and opportunity wage (marginal product in the alternative application) are equal. The optimal number of fishers and the open-access number of fishers are shown in Figure 11.10.

Although this model is very complicated, it is important to understand it because of its dominant impact on the way economists look at fisheries. The model is designed to focus on the inefficiency associated with open access and the loss in welfare associated with too much effort being employed in the fishery, but little else. Gordon makes the simple (but often unimplementable) suggestion of monopoly ownership at the solution to the problem. Although the solution of monopoly ownership has not made its way into policy, the focus of the Gordon model has. Policy focuses on controlling the level effort and con-

Figure 11.10 **Optimal and Open-Access Effort in a Hypothetical Fishery (based on Table 11.2)**

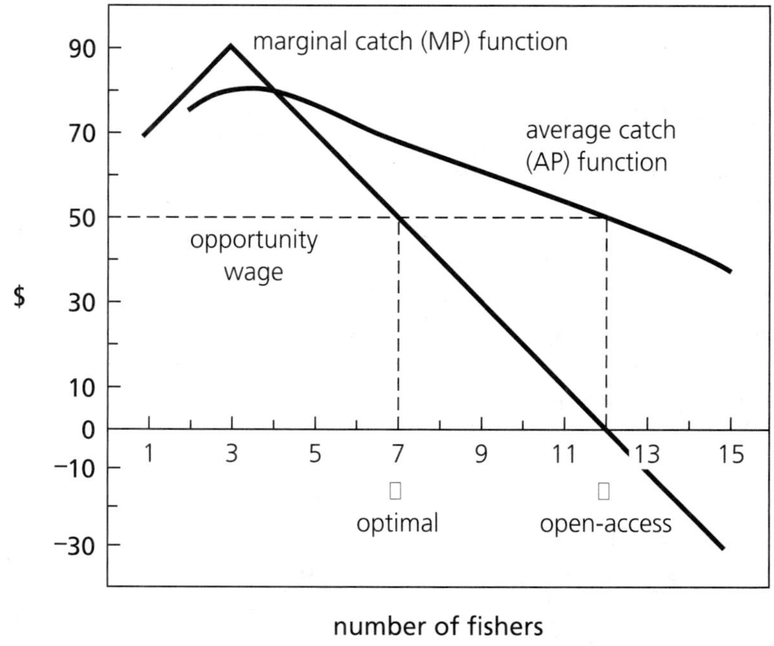

trolling the impacts of effort, but little else. As shown later, these policies have been ineffective, and world fisheries are on the brink of collapse.

The Gordon model, as with many fisheries models in the past and continuing into the present, looks at fisheries stocks as if they are independent of the environment in which they exist. As emphasized throughout this book, components of ecosystems are tied together by complex relationships, and changes in the population of a fish species can have effects that reverberate through the ecosystem. In addition, fishing techniques can directly and indirectly affect other organisms, modifying the habitat and having far-reaching consequences for the ecosystem. In the section that immediately follows, these type of ecosystem impacts are not included in the modeling; rather a more narrow focus on the economic dimensions of the problem is sought. A more interdisciplinary approach is incorporated into the discussion when these issues are examined in the policy analysis later in the chapter.

Shortcomings of the Gordon Model

Although the Gordon model is an excellent model for highlighting the problems associated with open access and too much effort, it has several shortcomings. The foremost is that the model is static (one period), whereas a dynamic model would be more appropriate. The Gordon model is dynamic in the sense that all equilibrium catch levels are sustainable, but it is static in the sense that it does not consider future costs and benefits. If $1 of future costs or benefits is viewed to be identical to $1 of present costs or benefits, then the dynamically optimal level of effort will be the same as the statically optimal level (E_2 in Figure 11.9). Future values have the same importance as present values when the discount rate is equal to zero. Clark (1985) shows that as the discount rate gets very large, the dynamically optimal level of catch approaches the open-access level of catch. As Anderson (1986) points out, this change in levels is because future income has no value with an infinite discount rate. Consequently, an owner of a fishery would use effort as long as the cost of effort is covered. In the long run, this cost will approximate the open-access level of effort. Discount rates between zero and infinity will imply a dynamically optimal level of effort between the statically optimal level (E_2) and the open-access level (E_1).

As Anderson (1986) points out, many other factors affect the optimal level of effort in a real-world fishery. In particular, pulse fishing (catching a large fraction of the population and then not fishing for several years to let the population recover) may be the best approach for certain fisheries.

Incorporating Consumers' and Producers' Surplus into Fishery Models

Another shortcoming of the Gordon model is that it does not consider consumers' and producers' surplus, which may exist and be important in many fisheries. The lack of consideration of consumers' and producers' surplus may be a particularly important emission for highly valued but threatened fish such as various species of salmon, Alaskan king crab, and redfish. Turvey (1964) was the first to highlight the possible importance of producers' and consumers' surplus. However, his model is relatively complicated and difficult to implement empirically. Rather than follow Turvey's approach, conventional demand and supply curves will be integrated into a fishery model. These types of models are developed and presented in Anderson (1986), Clark (1985), Kahn (1987), and Kahn and Kemp (1985). The models discussed in this chapter will most closely parallel those of Kahn (1987).

When switching from catch and effort models to demand and supply models, the horizontal axis is no longer measured in units of effort but, rather, in units of catch (catch is what is demanded and supplied). Although models based on effort are good for illustrating the open-access problem of inefficiently high levels of effort, they are difficult to implement empirically. One reason for this difficulty is that it is not clear how effort should be defined. Should it be measured solely in labor units (that is, person-hours)? This scheme is not good because different people may have different levels of capital available (that is, bigger and more powerful boats, larger nets, and so on). Effort is really an amalgam of labor, capital, and energy, and there are no clear guidelines on how to combine these separate inputs into one aggregate input. When the estimation of supply functions is discussed later, it will be seen that the definition of effort is less of an issue when catch, rather than effort, is the quantity variable. (See Appendix 11.a for a discussion of techniques for empirical estimation of fishery models.)

Let's begin the discussion by drawing conventional demand and supply curves for catch, as in Figure 11.11. A single demand and supply curve is insufficient to describe all the important changes, because changes in catch will change the level of the fish stock, and the level of the fish stock is not measured on either axis.

As is often the case when a third variable needs to be presented in a two-dimensional framework, it can be done through a family of functions. Because greater fish populations imply that more fish can be caught with the same amount of effort or inputs, a family of supply curves can be drawn, each defined for a different level of the fish stock, as illustrated in Figure 11.12. The greater the fish population, the closer the supply curve to the horizontal axis. Each level of the fish population has a unique supply curve associated with it. In Figure 11.12, there are a multiplicity of potential economic equilibria. It must be recognized, however, that these levels of catch, which represent economic equilibria, are not necessarily sustainable levels of catch. As mentioned earlier, there is only one equilibrium (sustainable) catch associated with each level of population. For the six population levels depicted in Figure 11.12, the equilibrium catches are depicted in Figure 11.13.

These equilibrium catch levels are then mapped onto the family of supply curves in Figure 11.14. For example, the equilibrium catch associated with a population of F_1 (the maximum population) is zero, and point A is the only

Figure 11.11 Demand and Supply Curves

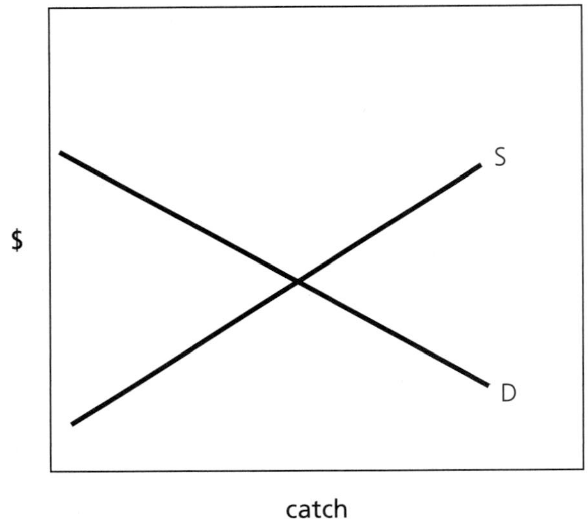

Figure 11.12 A Family of Supply Curves for Commercial Fishing

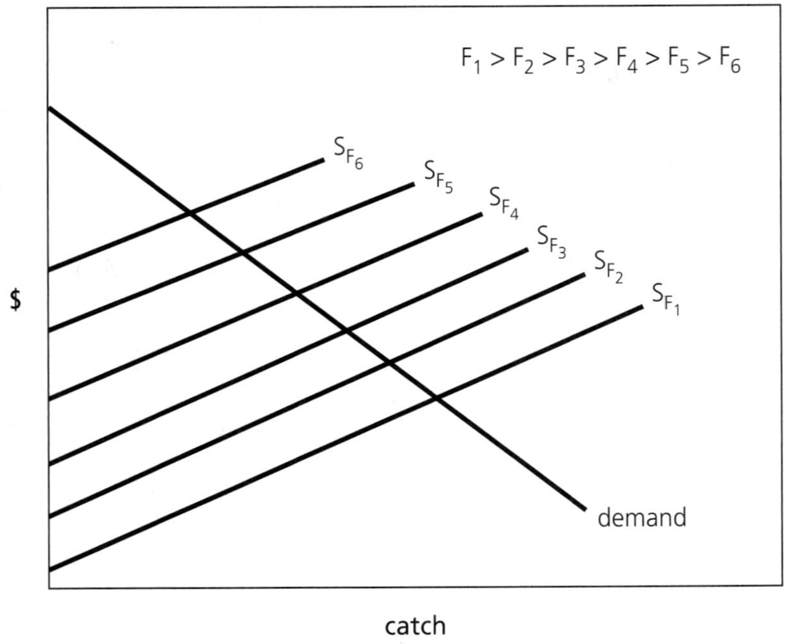

Figure 11.13 **Equilibrium Catch Function**

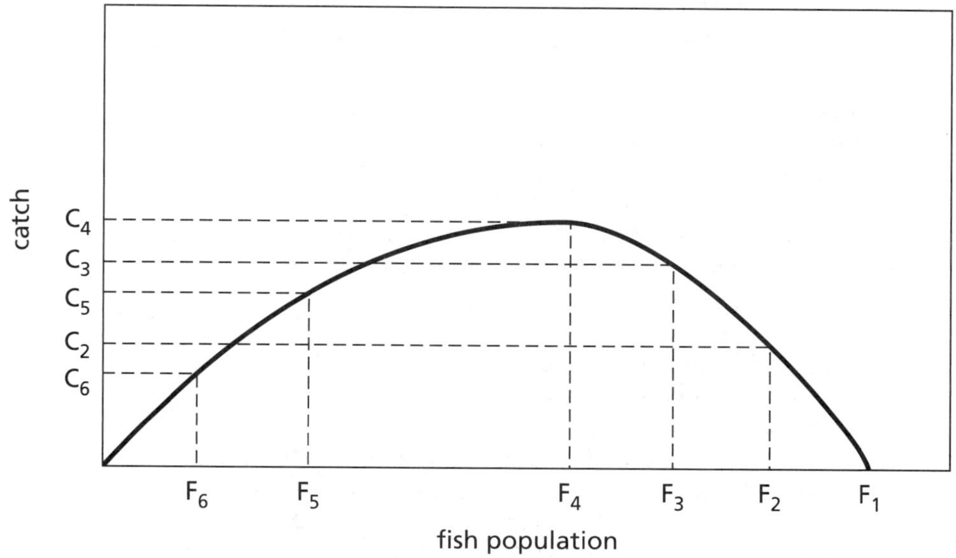

Figure 11.14 **Supply Function and Sustainable Catch Levels**

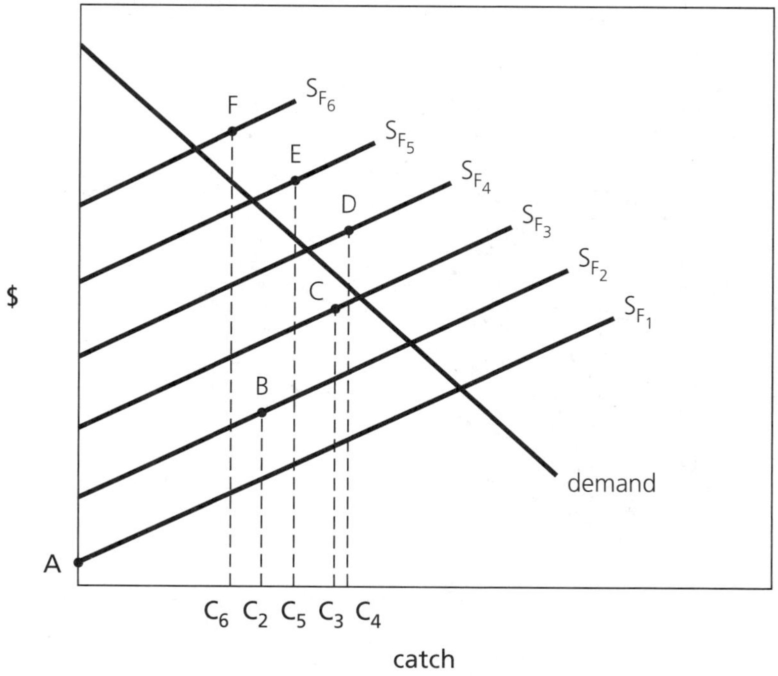

point of biological equilibrium on supply function S_{F1}. Similarly, C_2 is the equilibrium catch associated with a fish stock of F_2, so point B is the only point of biological equilibrium on supply curve S_{F2}. This process can be repeated for each level of the fish stock, and a locus of biological equilibria can be found. This locus is presented in Figure 11.15.

Notice that a market equilibrium could occur at point E, where S_{F6} and the demand function intersect the locus of biological equilibria. Also, notice that the sole owner of a fishery could find a better point than E. Point F in Figure 11.15 is also a point of biological equilibrium, but it is on a lower supply curve because the fish stock has been maintained at a higher level. The net economic benefits are shown in Figure 11.15. At point E, there would not be rent, but if the catch was produced at point F on supply curve S_{F3}, then the net economic benefits would include rent (area PEFB), consumers' surplus (area PDE), and producers' surplus (area BFA). The goal of fisheries management would be to choose a point along the locus of biological equilibria that maximizes the sum of these three sources of benefits. Although it is easy to find this point mathematically, there is no tangency or intersection to point to in the graph to reveal the optimal point of catch and population.

In addition to using this model to maximize the economic benefits derived from a fishery, it is possible to use it to examine other types of fishery management problems. For example, pollution is thought to be a major factor in

Figure 11.15 **Bioeconomic Equilibrium**

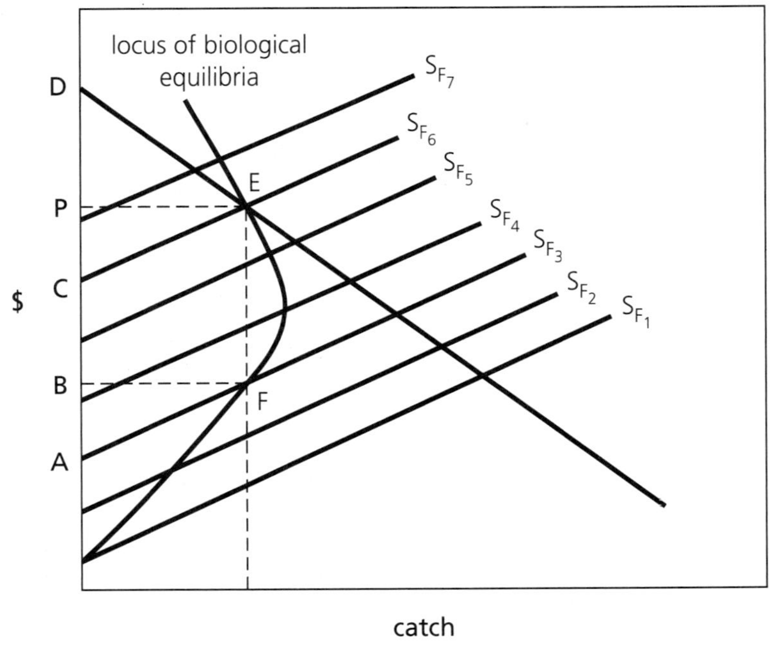

the decline of fish in estuaries, bays, and inland seas throughout the world (e.g., San Francisco Bay, Chesapeake Bay, Long Island Sound, Guanabara Bay, Aral Sea, Black Sea, Caspian Sea, Gulf of Mexico, Mediterranean Sea, Persian Gulf, Red Sea). It is possible to use this model to compute the fishery-related damages from pollution.

Let's assume that pollution does not affect the edibility of the fish (that is, through toxic or bacterial contamination) but does stress the ecosystem in which the fish resides. For example, lower dissolved oxygen levels could adversely affect many organisms and diminish the productivity of the food web. The effect of pollution of this nature would be to shift the natural growth function (which is also the equilibrium catch function) downward, as in Figure 11.16. Note that the pollution has lowered the carrying capacity of the environment (leftward shift of the right-hand endpoint of the curve), as well as the growth (height of the curve) that can be supported by a particular level of the fish stock.

The downward shift of the equilibrium growth function implies an inward shift of the locus of biological equilibria from B_1 to B_2 (Figure 11.17), with a reduction in catch, an increase in costs, and a reduction in social welfare. Most U.S. fisheries are open access, which complicates the measurement of changes in social benefits. Appendix 11.b discusses the measurement of consumers' and producers' surplus in the context of an open-access fishery; it also illustrates how to measure the change in consumers' and producers' surplus associated with a change in environmental quality.

Figure 11.16 **Downward Shift in Equilibrium Catch Function from Increased Pollution**

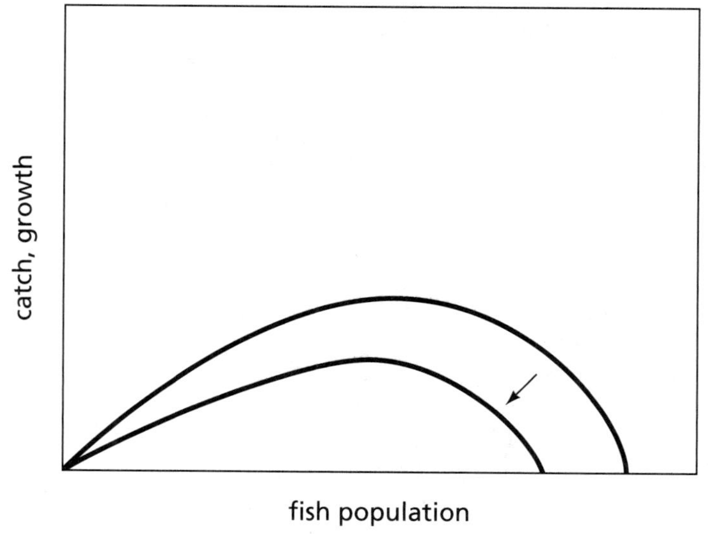

Figure 11.17 **Inward Shift of Locus of Biological Equilibria from Increased Pollution**

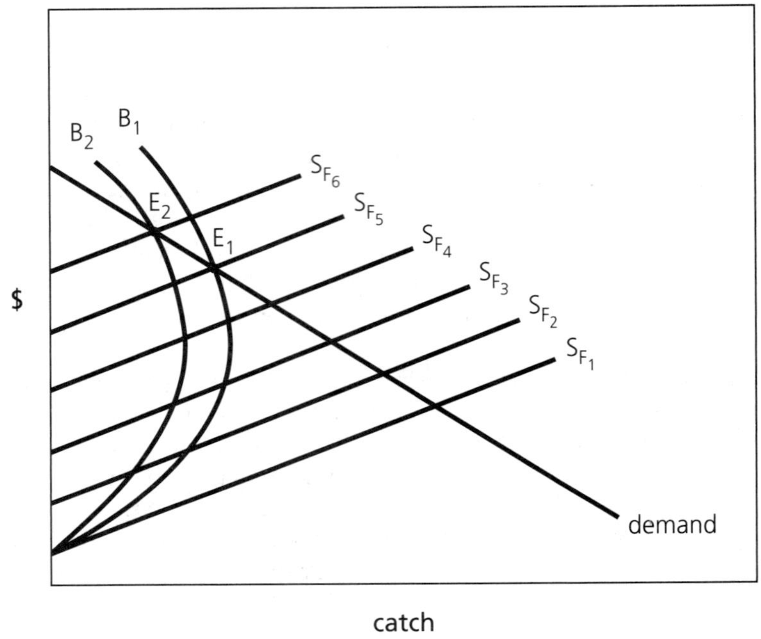

Current Fishery Policy

Past fishery policy focused on biological regulation, designed to protect the stock from overexploitation and potential collapse. In the past, little attention was paid to the problem of the inefficiencies generated by open access. Anderson (1986) calls those polices that can actually address the problem of entry as "limited-entry" techniques. He calls all other regulations or policies that do not explicitly address the problem of entry "open-access" techniques. These types of policies are discussed next.

Open-Access Regulations

Open-access regulations modify fishing behavior of those participants in the fishery without directly affecting participation in the fishery. Because open-access regulations typically raise the cost of fishing, however, they may indirectly affect participation in the fishery by causing the marginal fisher to become unprofitable and leave the fishery.

These open-access regulations are designed to maintain fish stocks at some target level. The fish stocks consistent with maximum sustainable yield were often the theoretical target of fishery management, although often management schemes were not put into place until stocks had shrunk well below the level consistent with maximum sustainable yield. Open-access regulations generally take the form of restrictions on how fish may be caught, which fish may be caught, when fish may be caught, where fish may be caught, and how many fish may be caught.

How Fish May Be Caught. Modern fishing technology can give a fishing fleet tremendous fishing power relative to the size of the fish populations. Sonar and spotter planes are used to locate fish. Satellite-based Global Positioning Systems, or GPS, can allow fishing boats to store ocean locations in their computer memory and return to the exact same spot. The length of nets and fishing lines are measured in kilometers, not meters. Although the use of this technology could generate tremendous cost savings in a properly managed fishery, its use in an open-access situation can be disastrous for a fishery.

In open-access fisheries, it is possible to protect the fish stock by forcing inefficiency on the fishers. For example, in Maryland's portion of the Chesapeake Bay, it is illegal to dredge for oysters under motorized power. Consequently, dredging must be done under sail power, which means that a boat must pull a smaller dredge and cover less bottom in a given time period than could be done by motorized boats.

Which Fish May Be Caught. The regulation of which fish may be caught generally revolves around restrictions on the minimum size of fish that are legal to harvest. The reasoning behind these regulations is to leave a portion of the fish stock in the water to provide a sufficient breeding stock to ensure future populations. Fishers generally implement this restriction by choosing a mesh size for their nets that allows the small, illegal fish to pass through the net, but retains the larger, legal fish.

In actuality, these regulations do not entirely conform to the biology of the situation, because it is the middle-aged fish that represent (pound for pound) the most prolific breeders in the fish stock. It would be impossible, however, to design regulations that correspond to this biology, because one cannot construct a net that allows the medium-sized fish to pass through but that captures the largest and smallest fish.

When Fish May Be Caught. Regulations concerning when fish may be caught are designed to control harvests by restricting the times during which fishing is legal. Sometimes these regulations take the form of restricting certain periods on a daily basis, but more often the fishing season is closed for a certain period on an annual basis. Many times the closed season occurs during the spawning season, for two reasons. First, the fishing activity may disrupt the spawning process. Second, some species become so extremely congregated during spawning that fishing effort could capture virtually the entire population.

The congregation associated with spawning, however, actually forms the basis of the fishery of some species, particularly anadromous species such as salmon.[6] In addition, for some species (for example, sturgeon, paddlefish, shad, and herring), the eggs (caviar) are the most valuable component of the fish.

Where Fish May Be Caught. Regulations on where fish may be caught are designed to protect fish stocks when they are congregated. For example, certain types of commercial fishing are banned in many embayments along the Atlantic coast, because the populations are so congregated that they are vulnerable to overharvesting. These types of regulation are also designed to protect vulnerable fishing habitats from being destroyed by the fishing process. The dragging of bottom-scooping nets and dredges through shallow areas may destroy important plant and animal communities on the floor of these areas.

How Many Fish May Be Caught. Often, open-access regulations take the form of limits on how many fish (sometimes measured in weight, sometimes in volume, and sometimes in number of fish) may be captured in a given time period. For example, the number of giant bluefin tuna off the Atlantic coast of the United States has declined precipitously in recent years. These fish, which usually weigh more than 500 pounds and often may weigh more than 1000 pounds, are highly sought for sushi for the Japanese market. In 1986, the dockside price for giant bluefin tuna was as high as $18 per pound (approximately $31 in 2002 dollars). Of course, by the time the fish gets to the market in Japan, the price is much higher. In 2001, a Pacific Bluefin tuna sold in the Tsukiji Central Fish Market for $391 per pound. (Ellis, p. 28). With such profitability, other forms of open-access regulation may not be effective in preventing the population from collapsing, so a limit of one fish per boat per day was established to limit exploitation. Even with this limit, the population of giant bluefin tuna is dangerously declining. This problem is discussed later in the section on the failure of fisheries management.

Economic Analysis of Open-Access Regulations

As mentioned previously, the primary effect of open-access regulations is to raise the cost of catching fish. If individual fishers are already operating in the most cost-effective manner (minimizing the private cost of catching fish), any restrictions on their activity must raise the cost of catching fish. On the other hand, because these regulations generally increase the size of the fish populations, the greater fish populations tend to lower costs. Analysis of the effects of open-access regulations must be careful to separate these two effects so that the effects of the regulations can be clearly understood.

These increases in cost generated by such regulations have the impact of eliminating the rent in the fishery at a lower level of fishing effort than would occur without the restriction. In other words, the increase in cost created by

[6]Anadromous fish are those that live their adult lives in saltwater and spawn in freshwater.

Box 11.2 Gulf Coast Redfish

Historically, redfish or red drum (*Sciaenops ocellata*) was pursued along the Gulf Coast only by recreational fishers and small-scale commercial fishers who responded to local demand. In the early 1980s, however, "Cajun cuisine" became a national fad, and many restaurants added a traditional Cajun dish, "blackened redfish," to their menus. This increase in demand raised the price of redfish and led to increased entry into the fishery and a drastic decline in redfish populations throughout the Gulf Coast states. It also led to a highly charged political fight between recreational and commercial anglers over how the fish stocks should be allocated through regulation. This conflict in the Gulf Coast redfish fishery is a prime example of the conflict between recreational and commercial fishers that occurs in many coastal fisheries.

Trellis Green a professor of Economics at the University of Southern Mississippi, conducted a study for the National Marine Fishery Service (NMFS) to determine the value of redfish in recreational fishing (Green, 1989). He used a travel cost model with the expected success of the angler as an explanatory variable. The model was estimated using data collected by the NMFS in intercept surveys, which are surveys that are executed at randomly chosen fishing sites.

Green found that increasing expected catch by 10 percent would increase net benefits (consumers' surplus) by between $5 and $14 per trip. In 1986, the typical redfish angler took approximately 30 trips per year and caught approximately 1.75 redfish per year. Extending this per-angler measure to the entire Gulf Coast redfish fishery means that a 10 percent increase in recreational catch (which is equal to 670,000 pounds of redfish) increases social benefits by between $10 and $17 million per year.

Although Green does not report value estimates for commercial fishing, he states that evidence from other studies suggests that "the marginal welfare loss incurred by the commercial fishery from red drum reallocation is not nearly so great as the gains to the recreational sector, at least in today's market" (1989, p. 54). He also suggests that the "Cajun cuisine" demand for redfish could be met by the development of redfish aquaculture. Years after the study was completed, the situation with redfish remains precarious, and the conflict among user groups continues.

these restrictions makes it less profitable to be involved in fishing, because the restrictions increase the amount of resources required to catch a given amount of fish. At the same time, the increase in fish populations associated with the regulations and reduced level of effort serve to reduce the cost of catching a given amount of fish. The net effect of the regulations, however,

Table 11.3 **Impact of Open-Access Regulations on Key Fishery Variables**

Variable	Impact
Costs to fishers	Increase
Resources used in fishing	Increase
Population of fish	Increase
Catch of fish	Increase or decrease
Consumers' and producers' surplus	Increase or decrease

will be to increase costs of fishing. Finally, the impact of the regulations on the catch of fish must be examined. If the current fish population is greater than the population associated with maximum sustainable yield, then the restrictions will serve to reduce catch. If, however, the fishery is highly exploited and the current fish population is lower than the level associated with maximum sustainable yield, then the restrictions will increase catch. Finally, in the process of raising costs to protect the stock of fish, open-access regulations actually exacerbate the problem of too many resources being devoted to the fishery by imposing additional inefficiency on the industry. Table 11.3 summarizes the impact of the open-access regulations on key variables in the fishery.

Aquaculture

Policies that promote aquaculture have interesting potential for protecting wild fishery resources. Aquaculture (sometimes called fishing farming or mariculture) is a process of raising fish in artificial or controlled environments and then harvesting these fish. Aquaculture is actually an ancient activity, going back thousands of years in China and Asia, where fish were cultivated in rice paddies and then harvested to provide a source of protein. Today, there is a reemergence of aquaculture. Well-established aquacultural activities include the following:

- Shrimp culture in artificial ponds in Asia and in Central and northern South America
- Salmon culture in floating pens in the ocean off the Chilean Pacific Coast and in Scandinavian fjords
- Oyster and mussel culture on artificial structures off the coasts of the North Atlantic and the temperate areas of South America
- Trout, catfish, crawfish, and tilapia farming in the United States

New activities currently being developed that could be viewed as still in the experimental stage include the following:

- Tuna culture in floating pens off the coasts of Japan and southern Florida
- Culture of a diversity of Amazonian river fish in enclosures in the Amazon River and tributaries
- Culture of red drum on the Gulf Coast of the United States

In addition, culture of reptilian species such as alligator, crocodile, cayman, iguana, and turtle is in various stages of development in various locations around the world.

Because fish produced through aquaculture are a substitute for fish produced by harvesting wild stocks, increasing aquaculture production can reduce the demand for wild stocks, thereby reducing pressure on natural stocks (see Caviglia-Harris, Kahn and Green, 2003). The increased size of fish stocks not only benefits fishers (by reducing costs of harvest) but also provides ecosystem benefits through the connectivity of the various components of the ecosystem, benefits to recreational fishers, and indirect-use benefits (see Chapter 4) to society as a whole.

Aquaculture, however, is not a magic bullet and is subject to several important problems. One problem is that the people who benefit directly from aquaculture are often not the same people who participate in commercial fishing. Therefore, policies that promote aquaculture will not necessarily result in economic development for communities whose economies are depressed because of fisheries collapse. Along the same vein, public policies to enhance aquaculture will not be supported by the multinational corporations that are major participants in many of the primary oceanic fisheries. In other words, communities and industries that are based on wild fisheries could suffer economic setbacks from the decline in demand for wild fish that aquaculture production may cause.[7]

The biggest problem with aquaculture is the potential for environmental externalities. For example, shrimp aquaculture on the coasts of Central and northern South America is often conducted in such a way that the environment is severely damaged. Mangrove forests are cut to create space for the artificial ponds where the shrimp are raised, and the massive amounts of shrimp in the ponds can generate excessive nutrient loadings into the estuary, severely reducing dissolved oxygen in the bordering estuaries. Other problems with aquaculture include modification of the genetic makeup of wild fish through crossbreeding with escaped hybridized fish, environmental damage from introduction of exotic species, and destruction of habitat.

[7]Just as in farming, much fishing has shifted from the family, community-based format to large industrial enterprises. Most offshore fishing is conducted by large boats that are owned by large corporations, not by independently owned vessels.

Aquaculture need not be damaging to the environment. As the case with any type of economic activity, to appropriately protect the environment externalities need to be internalized by public policy.

Limited-Entry Techniques

Limited-entry techniques also raise costs fors fishers, but they raise private costs in a way that lowers, rather than increases social costs. Taxes and other types of incentives may raise the cost to fishers, but they do so in a fashion in which the extra costs represent a transfer within society, rather than a loss of resources. Actually, by raising private costs in this fashion, social welfare can be increased.

A parallel argument was presented in Chapter 3 in the discussion of pollution regulations. In fact, open-access regulations can be viewed as analogous to direct controls (command and control techniques), and limited-entry techniques can be viewed as analogous to economic incentives for pollution control.

If limited-entry techniques are truly analogous to economic incentives for pollution control, then one would expect to be able to construct both price policies (similar to pollution taxes) and quantity policies (similar to marketable pollution permits). Actually, slightly more options exist for limited-entry techniques than for pollution, because either effort or catch can be taxed and because marketable permits can be established for either effort or catch.

The fishery economics literature tends to focus on permit-based systems, and when limited-entry techniques have actually been used in managing fisheries (New Zealand is a leader in this regard) they have also focused on permit-based systems. The name adopted for these systems is the individual transferable quota (ITQ).

ITQs are completely analogous to marketable pollution permits. A limit is placed on total catch, and each fisher in the fishery is allocated a portion of this total catch. This initial allocation can be done by auction, by lottery, or in proportion to past catch. This initial allocation then becomes the fisher's ITQ, and he or she can sell all or part of the quota. The level of effort is limited because the cost of effort increases, because people must now buy ITQs to fish. Note that this increase in cost has occurred without increasing the amount of resources needed to catch the fish. This cost increase serves to eliminate the disparity between the social and private cost of fishing associated with the open-access externality.

Limited-entry techniques can also be structured relative to effort instead of catch. For example, the fishery management agency could decide that only a fixed number of boats (say N) would be allowed in the fishery. These N permits could be also allocated by auction or lottery, or based on historical participation or some other mechanism. The issues associated with the initial allocation of ITQs (either catch- or permit-based) are completely analogous to those discussed for marketable pollution permits in Chapter 3.

The disadvantage of using effort-based techniques is that they only indirectly influence catch. For example, a boat that has a permit could catch fish with differing levels of intensity. In particular, if people respond by fishing longer hours or using more powerful fishing technologies, the limitation on effort may not have its full intended impact. The advantage of using effort-based techniques is that they are easier and less costly to enforce than catch-based techniques. All catch-based techniques require the measurement of catch, which is costly. A marketable effort quota could be enforced by requiring boats to display a poster-sized certificate, which could easily be checked with binoculars from a patrolling boat of the fishing authority. A more high-tech approach is to use cellular telephone technology whereby boats with a permit would broadcast a signal that reveals their location and that they have a permit. No measurement or weighing need take place. Alternatively, one could use this technology with a catch-based system and the boat could be electronically followed to port, where it would report its catch to authorities.

Catch-based ITQs are also subject to several potential problems. First, people might cheat on the quota, selling their catch to foreign fishing vessels outside the 200-mile limit or surreptitiously selling the catch on shore. Another potential problem is called high-grading, which arises because different-size fish of the same species have different market values. For example, a 10-kilogram salmon may be more than twice as valuable as a 5-kilogram salmon. If that is the case, once the quota is reached, as the boat catches more fish, fishers will throw less valuable fish that have been previously caught (and are now dead) overboard to make room within the quota for the more valuable fish. This practice is especially true for shrimp, for which very large shrimp have a premium value. The same phenomenon would occur if the limit is on a broad class of fish such as Pacific salmon and different if species (chinook, coho, king, and so on) have different market values. In addition, catch-based ITQs do not address other fishery management issues, such as the accidental capture of other species, a problem that is discussed later in the chapter.

In a recent article, Weitzman (2002) shows that in the presence of uncertainty about the growth that will occur in the fish stock, taxes on catch may be preferable to ITQs. The reason is that the important variable from a social point of view is the impact on the level of the stock of fish (the growth that occurs, or the escapement level in Weitzman's terminology), or the level of catch. With ITQs, if the stock and escapement level is lower than known, fishing boats will expand their effort to keep catch at the quota level. Although rent per kilogram of fish falls, rent is still earned, so effort will continue to be forthcoming. Thus, catch will remain constant at a time when the fish stock needs additional protection from harvest. A tax per kilogram of fish indirectly taxes effort, however, so the incentive to put forth more effort at this time will be diminished by the tax, easing the pressure on the fish stock.

The main differences in the effects on the fishery between open-access and limited-entry regulations can be seen by comparing Table 11.3 and

Table 11.4 **Impact of Limited Entry Regulations on Key Fishery Variables**

Variable	Impact
Costs to fishers	Increase
Resources used in fishing	Decrease
Population of fish	Increase
Catch of fish	Increase or decrease
Consumers' and producers' surplus	Increase or decrease

Table 11.4. They prove to be symmetrical, except for the effect on the amount of resources used in fishing, which increases under open-access regulations but decreases under limited-entry regulations.

Although most fishery regulation relies on open-access techniques, some management authorities have used limited-entry techniques. One important example is the Virginia oyster fishery, where oyster beds are treated as private property rather than as open-access resources. Not only does the creation of private property ownership of the oyster beds eliminate open-access exploitation, but it gives oyster bed owners an incentive to invest in their property (by seeding with larval oysters and by creating more structure upon which the oysters may attach).

In addition, the 200-mile economic exclusion zone, which the United States (and all other coastal countries) established under the authority of the United Nations Convention of the Law of the Sea in 1982, functions as a partial limited-entry technique. A coastal country is allowed to manage the ocean and the ocean bottom within 200 miles of its coastline for its own economic benefit. Most countries, the United States included, exclude foreign fishers from operating within the 200-mile economic zone. Such exclusions diminish (but do not eliminate) the open-access problem by limiting the number of fishers (excluding all foreign fishers from access to the fishery). This system does not work well in many developing countries, where cash-starved governments sell fishing rights to foreign fleets and the foreign fleets overexploit the fishery. Even when fishing rights are not sold, many developing countries lack enforcement resources, such as a naval force, to keep foreign fishing boats outside the 200-mile economic exclusion zone.

Why We Do Not See More Limits to Entry

The question often arises why more fisheries do not have limited access, given that it is so beneficial. There are two answers to this question. First, there is more limited access than is immediately apparent, because many limits to access are informal. Second, in most fisheries the problem of completely open access remains a serious problem, and it is probably caused by political barriers to limited entry that are generated by the fishers. It may seem strange that fishers would block limited entry, because they are the ones who would benefit most by it. This seeming paradox is examined after the issue of informal limits to entry is addressed.

Informal Limits to Entry. Many U.S. fisheries are contained in relatively small communities where many generations of families have participated in the fishery. Many fishing families believe that their historic participation in the fishery grants them property rights to fishing areas (either individually or jointly with other families). Newcomers to the fishery are likely to have their fishing efforts or fishing equipment sabotaged by existing fishers. For example, if a person tried to place lobster pots in an area that was not historically lobstered by his or her family, the lobster pots would quickly disappear. The 1985 movie *Alamo Bay* provides an excellent depiction of the tensions and conflicts between historic fishing and shrimping families from the Gulf Coast of Texas and an immigrant group of fishers from Vietnam.

Profit Maximization and Limited Entry. It seems clear that pure profit maximizers would favor limited entry. Pure profit maximizers would see the potential economic rents associated with limited entry, and most would probably support limits to entry so as to obtain these potential rents. Conversely, fishers who are not profit maximizers may not see the same gains associated with limits to entry.

A possible explanation for the opposition to limited entry among current fishers is that these fishers may be utility maximizers rather than profit maximizers. This situation may be particularly true for fishers from communities and families that have been fishing for many generations. Also, the less capital intensive the fishery, the more likely it is to be populated by utility-maximizing fishers. Inshore fisheries that require smaller boats and less equipment are more likely to be utility maximizing than offshore fisheries that require large ships with onboard fish-processing factories.

If a fisher is a utility maximizer, income will have an important positive effect on utility, but not the only effect. In particular, the ability of traditional participants (and their children) to have access to the fishery is likely to be critically important. Some of the people whose access to the fishery is limited by proposed regulation will be from these traditional groups. In small isolated fisheries, all those who are forced from the fishery will be from these close-knit communities. Consequently, to protect the participation of themselves, their children, and their friends and neighbors, they lobby against the imposition of limited-entry access techniques. Of course, they often oppose many types of open-access techniques because, as explained earlier, they raise the cost of fishing.

Although this discussion presents a reasonable argument that utility-maximizing fishers might oppose limited-entry policies, no formal evidence has yet been provided that would indicate that some fishers might be utility maximizers and not profit maximizers. This discussion suggests that some fishers have been in fishing families for many generations and may derive pleasure from their choice of lifestyle. They work outdoors, on the water, enjoying considerable independence as their own bosses. Although these factors may be job characteristics that many people desire, what evidence exists to suggest that utility motives and not profit motives dominate their decision making?

One piece of evidence that would support the utility-maximizing hypothesis would be if fishers turned down more profitable employment so as to participate in the fisheries. This type of evidence is not likely to be found in geographically and economically isolated fishing areas, where fishing may be the only source of employment.[8] In contrast, such evidence can be found in traditional fisheries that are located on the periphery of expanding metropolitan areas, such as eastern Long Island (New York metropolitan area), the Chesapeake Bay (Baltimore, Washington, D.C., and Norfolk metropolitan areas), South Florida, and in most Pacific port cities of the United States. In these areas, fishers could use some of the skills they have developed in fishing (welding, carpentry, and engine mechanics) to take jobs in construction, manufacturing, or other areas. These fishers, however, have chosen to remain in the lower-paying occupation of fishing, indicating that the utility they derive from their lifestyle is an important factor in their economic decision making.

Another factor that may be critically important in the opposition to limited entry has to do with the time path of income. To move to a better regime in the future with a greater fish stock, greater catch, and greater income, it is necessary to reduce catch today. If fishing firms are worried about going out of business or if fishing families are worried about supporting the family in the short term, then they might oppose policies such as limited entry (or any limitations on catch) that reduced income in the short term. Such opposition would be particularly true if these fishing enterprises had difficulty in gaining access to loans. In fact, with the ongoing collapse of fish stocks throughout the world, these enterprises would very likely have difficulty obtaining the loans from banks. Sloan suggests the use of fishery recovery bonds in this case. Taxes on fish products would be used to create a fund, the income from which would be used to pay fishers to cease fishing until the collapsing fish stock recovers.

A final factor generating opposition to limited-entry techniques may be uncertainty (in the minds of the fishing firms and fishing families) about whether these policies will actually succeed and prevent a complete collapse of the fish stock in the future. The greater the uncertainty about the future, the more likely the fishing firms and families are to oppose policies that would reduce their income in the present for uncertain benefits in the future.

---

[8]Of course, when fishing is the only source of employment, fishers may be even more concerned about limited-entry policies forcing some of the community out of the fishery.

The Failure of Fisheries Management

Failure is a very strong word to use in an academic textbook such as this, yet it is appropriate to use it when describing the situation in our global fisheries. The reason as mentioned in the introduction to the chapter, is that the major fisheries are characterized by complete and utter collapse. After reading the previous sections on policy instruments, this situation may seem somewhat paradoxical. If there exists a suite of policy and management tools to protect our fisheries, then why have they reached such a desperate state?

The answer to this question is both simple and complex. The simple version is that we have not really solved the open-access problem for oceanic and migratory species. If a species passes out of a nation's Exclusive Economic Zone (EEZ) as part of its migratory behavior, fishing boats from other nations have the opportunity to harvest the fish. If this is the case, the country will over-harvest the fish when in its EEZ, because it knows the stock will be depleted by other countries. Of course fish that are outside the EEZ on the high seas are truly an open-access fishery.

Although Nations have entered into international agreements to regulate harvests of migratory species such as tuna, there are two problems associated with these treaties. First, harvest quotas may be unrealistically high because of domestic political pressures and over-estimates of the population of the target species. Second, countries may tolerate cheating on the part of their nation's fishing boats because of domestic political pressure and because they might believe that other countries are cheating. Sloan (2003) discusses these issues and other reasons underlying the collapse of global fisheries.

Other Issues in Fishery Management

Although most of the literature in fishery economics focuses on the issue of the optimal level of effort and catch, many other issues in fishery management need attention.[9] These issues include problems associated with the following:

1. Incidental catch (unintended catch) of other fish species and of marine mammals and turtles
2. Destruction of fishery habitat through fishing activities
3. Destruction of wetlands and related terrestrial habitat through non-fishing activities
4. Pollution of fishery habitat
5. Management of recreational fishery resources

---

[9]Important Internet sites that discuss fishery management issues include the U.S. National Marine Fisheries Service (http://king~fish.ssp.nmfs.gov), the Canadian Department of Fisheries and Oceans (http://www.ncr.dfo.ca), the Congressional Research Service (http://www.cnie.org/nle/leg-11.html), the Pew Commission on the Oceans (http://www.pewoceans.org/articles/2002/10/25/pr_29891.asp), and the American Fisheries Society (http://www.fisheries.org/html).

Incidental Catch

Many types of fishing gear do not discriminate among fish species, and both the desired species and a spectrum of untargeted species are caught by this gear. Among the most notorious of such gear is the gill net, which is pictured in Figure 11.18.

Gill nets, whose lengths are often measured in kilometers, are vertically suspended in the water, like underwater fences. The fish do not see these nets because they are generally made of clear nylon or black line. The fish attempt to swim through the net, but the mesh is of a size large enough to allow their heads to poke through, but too small to allow their bodies to pass through. When the fish attempt to back out, their gill covers become ensnared in the net, and they remain trapped and tangled in the net in a fashion that renders them unable to breathe, killing them in a relatively short period of time.

The problem is that because the net kills everything it captures, the fishers cannot release the fish for which there is no market. Also, dolphins, seals, and sea turtles often become entangled in these nets (as well as other types of fishing nets) and are unable to reach the surface of the water so that they can breathe (these animals all breathe with lungs, not gills). Unable to breath, these marine mammals and turtles drown.

Sometimes these nets or pieces of these nets break away (they are often cut by boat propellers) and drift off. Because these nets are generally made of nylon, they do not biodegrade but continue to "ghost fish" for decades.

Another indiscriminate fishing method is called long-lining. A longline consists of line with baited hooks every several meters that may be 10 kilometers long or longer. These lines are employed off the Atlantic coast and in other locations in pursuit of highly profitable swordfish, tuna, and sailfish, but for every swordfish caught, hundreds of nonmarketable fish—especially nonmarketable species of shark—are caught. This factor has been important in declining shark populations. The death of these sharks is especially serious because sharks take decades to reach reproductive maturity and are not prolific breeders. Although viewers of movies such as *Jaws* may view this decline as beneficial, shark attacks on humans are extremely rare.[10] As a top predator, sharks play a crucial role in the marine ecosystem. They are also very valuable in recreational fishing, a large portion of which is catch and release.

Attempts at dealing with the problem of incidental catch have been met with stiff resistance by commercial fishers, who argue that costs will increase if indiscriminate fishing methods are banned to protect the untargeted species.

---

[10]An interesting digression concerning shark attacks on swimmers and surfers is that many observers believe that shark attacks have been increasing in recent years and that an important factor in the attacks has been the collapse of offshore fisheries. Although these theories have not yet been formally published in scientific journals, many marine biologists believe that the decline in oceanic fish stocks has caused sharks to move closer to shore looking for food. If this theory is true, then the increased incidence of shark attacks could be viewed as an externality associated with commercial fishing and should be incorporated into policy when establishing open-access or limited-entry regulations.

Figure 11.18 **Gill Net**

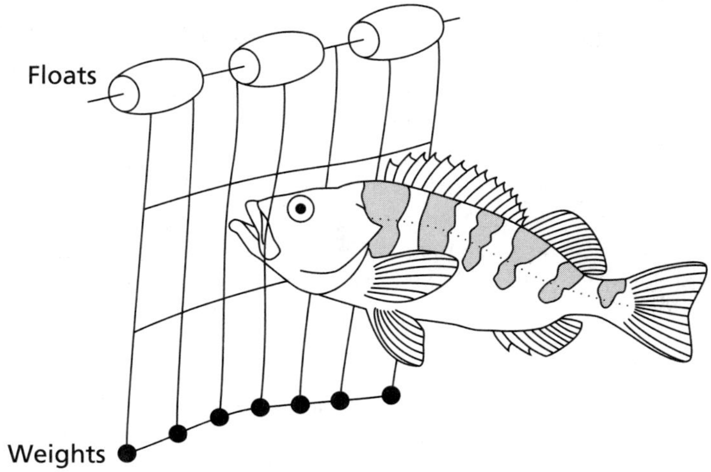

This situation is, of course, a classic externality problem. The fisher who uses indiscriminate fishing methods imposes costs on society through the killing and stock depletion of untargeted species. Economic theory suggests that social welfare would be increased if these costs were internalized, but that has proven to be difficult from both a political and practical perspective.

The question for policy makers is whether to enact policies to deal with the situation. Owing to the difficulties of monitoring, restrictions on fishing methods may be preferential to policies based on economic incentives. For example, rather than tax fishers for every sea turtle that gets caught in their shrimp nets, require them to install turtle excluder devices (TEDDIES) that allow the shrimp through the entrance to the net, but bump the sea turtles out of the net. The TEDDIES also keep large fish, which are generally discarded by the shrimpers if they wind up in the nets, out of the nets altogether. Another example of a restriction on fishing methods would be to ban gill nets and long-lining. Should policy makers go ahead and implement these restrictions? The economist would answer this question by asking whether the policies provide a potential Pareto improvement: Do the people who benefit from the policy benefit by more than the losers lose? This question needs to be answered on a case-by-case basis for each potential restriction, although most analysts believe that the elimination of the indiscriminate fishing methods generates a net benefit for society, because the impact on the nontargeted species is simply staggering.

Policies to restrict incidental catch may increase costs for commercial fishers, reducing their incomes, hurting their families, and perhaps driving some of them out of business. This possibility represents an interesting equity issue, because the benefits of protecting untargeted species are spread out over a large number of people but the costs are concentrated on very few. Should fishers be compensated for adopting more conserving fishing techniques? As in most cases, economic theory does not provide answers for these important equity issues. If, however, one were to adapt the "polluter pays principle" from pollution emissions to fisheries, it would indicate that compensation to the fishing industry should not take place. The polluter pays principle has been widely adopted by high-income countries and is an official policy of the Organization for Economic Cooperation and Development (OECD). This principle requires polluters to bear the economic cost of reducing their emissions to the level specified by environmental laws and policies.[11]

Destruction of Fishery Habitat

Another important impact of fishing is that the techniques used often create damage to the ecosystem in which the fish exist, diminishing the productivity of the fishery and ecological services in general. Damage can occur, for instance, when contact of fishing gear with the floor of the estuary or ocean uproots aquatic plants, breaks coral, dislodges shellfish, kills benthic organisms, and creates problems of turbidity.

One ecosystem most sensitive to destructive fishing techniques is the coral reef. Coral reef ecosystems are among the planet's most diverse ecosystems, comparable in diversity to rain forests. Several different types of activities, however, can damage the coral systems. First, contact of anchors, boat bottoms, and fishing gear with the coral can kill it. Second, and even more destructive, is that fishers in many developing countries in the South Pacific throw explosives into the water, killing or stunning the fish, which are then easily collected. Unfortunately, the explosions kill many other organisms, including the coral. Similarly, large reef fish such as grouper fetch incredibly high prices when sold live for restaurant consumption in Asian countries such as Taiwan and Japan. These prices often exceed $200 per kilogram. The fish are collected live by injecting cyanide into the holes in the coral in which they hide, stunning and disorienting the fish. The fish are easily collected and then put into tanks of clean water to recover and purge their systems of the cyanide. The same technique is used to collect fish that are sold in aquarium stores for display in home aquariums. Unfortunately, the coral is very sensitive to and is killed by contact with cyanide.[12]

---

[11]Some of these costs may be passed on to consumers in the form of higher prices for goods, but that is entirely consistent with the polluter pays principle.

[12]Most aquarium enthusiasts do not want to be responsible for the destruction of coral reefs, so the aquarium industry has developed a relatively credible system for certifying fish that are captured using techniques that do not harm the coral reef. See (http://www.aquariumcouncil.org) for more details.

Destruction of Wetlands and Related Terrestrial Habitats

As discussed throughout this book, ecosystems are mutually dependent, connected through a vast array of complex relationships. Other habitats, including Alaskan temperate rain forests, free-flowing rivers, upland and coastal wetlands, tropical rain forests, and even desert ecosystems, are critically important to fisheries, and there the destruction is often more devastating than overfishing.

For example, the temperate rain forests of the Pacific Northwest (northern California, Oregon, Washington, British Columbia, and Alaska) are critically important to maintaining riverine habitat, which is essential to the survival of anadromous fish such as salmon and steelhead. The forests modulate the flow of water (making the high flow and low flow less extreme), keep water temperatures cool in the summer, and protect the streams from sedimentation. This last point is critically important, because salmonids need gravel stream bottoms to reproduce. If the forests are destroyed, erosion causes sedimentation on the river bottom, which causes fish eggs to suffocate.

An additional problem facing fish in the Pacific Northwest, and elsewhere, are hydroelectric dams that form barriers to the upstream migration of anadromous fish, restricting their spawning grounds. In addition, water pollution and low water levels from water withdrawals for agricultural and municipal uses reduce the suitability of rivers for fish. Therefore, these salmon have five major problems that threaten not only their abundance, but their existence:

- Deforestation
- Hydroelectric dams
- Pollution
- Water withdrawals for agriculture and municipal use
- Overfishing

If public policy only addresses a subset of these problems without addressing the others, salmon populations are likely to continue to decline. It is necessary for policy to simultaneously address all the issues in a coordinated fashion. This task is often challenging, because different government agencies have responsibility for forests, oceanic fish, energy, water, and pollution. For this reason and because of entrenched political interests (such as farmers who want access to cheap water), many people are pessimistic about the future of Pacific salmon.

Pollution of Fishery Habitat

Overexploitation is not the only anthropogenic factor responsible for the decline of fisheries; pollution also has an important effect. In the United States, many fisheries are in decline because pollution has diminished habitat. Pollution and loss of habitat have affected virtually every freshwater species and many saltwater species as well. Saltwater species that reside in estuaries and other nearshore areas are vulnerable to pollution that is carried to the marine environment by rivers. Anadromous species, such as salmon, steelhead, shad, and striped bass, are particularly vulnerable to riverine pollution and other alterations of riverine areas, such as dams and reservoirs. Many species of fish are contaminated with toxic substances that make the fish unsafe to eat.

In the development of the model of demand and supply for fish presented in Appendix 11.b, it is shown how the damages associated with these types of pollution can be measured. Chapter 15 discusses water pollution in more detail and presents various policy instruments that can be used to move the level of pollution toward a more optimal level.

In developing countries, soil erosion from deforestation and intensive cultivation of hillside lands have had severe effects on fisheries. Soil erosion affects water quality not only in the rivers but in reservoirs, estuaries, lagoons, and coral reefs into which the rivers carry the soil. Often, high levels of fecal coliform bacteria and other infectious organisms associated with human wastes are found in these water bodies and contaminate the fish, particularly shellfish. Chapter 18 discusses the market failures that lead to soil erosion and environmental degradation in developing countries and the policies that can be developed to mitigate these problems.

Management of Recreational Fishery Resources

The economic analysis of recreational fishing resources is similar to commercial fishing in many ways. In most North American recreational fisheries, there is unrestricted access to the resource, leading to open-access exploitation. Policies such as creel limits (restrictions of how many fish may be kept), restricted seasons, and size limits may help protect the fish stock from destructive exploitation. The theoretical goal of recreational fishing management, however, should not be the limitation of effort, because it is the effort or act of fishing that is the source of social benefits. Effort is not considered a cost in this case but, rather, a source of benefits.

Each recreational fisher is receiving positive net benefits from participation in the fishery. These benefits include the utility derived from the process of fishing, from catching fish (which may be released or kept and eaten), and from a variety of other sources, such as being in the outdoors, enjoying the scenery, viewing wildlife, and being with (or, in some cases, being away from) family and friends. The goal of recreational fishing management, however, should not be to maximize participation, because each participant imposes costs on other participants by increasing congestion and reducing the fish stock. On the other hand, recreational fishery managers seldom take steps to limit participation (in the United States, recreational fishery management is generally done on a state-by-state basis, except for special management of national parks and forests), because their budgets are to a large extent determined by the sale of fishing licenses to participants.

Nonetheless, recreational fishing management does attempt to address some of the external costs associated with the open-access nature of this resource. These policies include the following:

1. *Stocking fish.* The enormous number of eggs produced by a single female fish makes the rearing of fish in hatcheries relatively inexpensive. In the controlled conditions of a hatchery (no predation, abundant food, and disease prevention), a very large number of eggs hatch into fish and grow to a size where they can be released into the wild with a high probability of survival until they are caught by recreational anglers. Obviously, this policy is designed to reduce the problem of open-access depletion of recreational fish stocks.
2. *Closed seasons.* Recreational fisheries often have closed seasons to protect the fish stocks. As with commercial fisheries, these closures often coincide with spawning periods to protect the vulnerable spawning adults and ensure that spawning activity is not disturbed.
3. *Access improvements.* The creation of additional access points, such as boat launching ramps, fishing piers, parking areas, and artificial reefs, tends to spread out recreational fishing activity, which reduces congestion and spreads the impact on the fish stocks over a wider area. These improvements may also reduce the cost of access to the individual angler and may improve the aesthetic quality of the trip. Of course, both the reduced cost and the increased quality may encourage the participation of more anglers, which would increase congestion somewhat.
4. *Catch and release.* Catch and release programs are based on the idea that a recreational angler does not have to kill his or her catch to produce utility from fishing. Catch and release means that after capture, a fish is released back into the water to grow larger, to reproduce, and to be caught and enjoyed by future anglers. Catch and release programs are based on both moral suasion and command and control. As a moral suasion policy, catch and release is promoted by fishery managers and recreational fishing organizations (such as Bass Anglers' Sportsman's Society and Trout Unlimited) as a general philosophy toward fishing and conservation. Catch and release programs can also be of the command and control variety. In these command and control programs, high-quality and sensitive fishing areas are declared as catch and release areas, and no fish may be kept from these areas. These areas also have special gear restrictions that are designed to maximize the chances of survival for a released fish. Live bait (which fish swallow more deeply than artificial lures) is generally prohibited in catch and release areas, as are multiple hooks. Hooks often are required to be barbless to minimize the damage from the hook.
5. *Size and creel limits.* Size limits place restrictions on the minimum (and sometimes maximum) size of fish that are legal to keep. Creel limits place restrictions on the maximum number of fish per day that

may be kept. Both restrictions are designed to protect the reproductive viability of the fish stocks by restricting the harvesting of reproductive fish.

All the aforementioned policies are focused on managing fishery resources relative to fishing activity. Of course, another area of policy is determining how to regulate activities when other activities impinge on recreational fishing activity. Both types of policies, but particularly the latter, require information on value on which to base cost-benefit analysis to use resources optimally.

To find the benefits associated with a particular recreational fishing activity, a valuation study must be done. Such studies generally take the form of contingent valuation or travel cost studies. (See Chapter 4 for a discussion of these valuation methodologies.) Table 4.2 presents a summary of a subset of valuation studies of recreational fishing.

Table 11.5 A Comparison of Alternative Estimates of the Benefits of Water Quality Improvements from Boatable to Fishable Conditions (updated to 2004 dollars)

Study	Original Estimate	2004 dollars
Vaughn-Russel	\$4.00 to \$8.00 per person per day was the range over the models used (1980 dollars)	\$9.10 to \$18.18
Loomis-Sorg	\$1.00 to \$3.00 per person per day over the regions considered based on increment to value of recreation day for coldwater fishing (1982 dollars)	\$1.94 to \$5.83
Smith, Desvouges, McGivney	\$0.98 to \$2.30 per trip using first-generation generalized travel cost model with Monongahela sites, boatable to fishable quality (1981 dollars)	\$2.02 to \$4.74
First Generation—Generalized Travel Cost Model	\$5.87 to \$54.20[a] per trip (\$2.24 to \$122.00 per visitor day[b])	\$12.10 to \$111.74 (\$4.62 to \$251.52)
Second Generation—Generalized Travel Cost Model	\$0.08 to \$5.43 per trip (\$0.04 to \$18.78 per visitor day) for Corps sites, change from boatable to fishable water quality (1977 dollars)	\$0.25 to \$16.79 (\$0.34 to \$56.19[c])

Source: Taken directly from Smith and Desvouges (1985) and converted to 2004 dollars.

[a] These estimates relate only to the Marshallian consumer surplus.

[b] The reason for the increase in the range of benefits per day is that some trips were reported as less than a day. The appropriate fractions were used in developing these estimates.

[c] The numbers in parentheses are the per-day consumer surplus, whereas those above are the per-trip estimates.

Freeman (1979) and many others note that one of the major benefits of improving water quality can be attributed to recreational uses of water resources, including boating, swimming, and recreational fishing. Smith and Desvouges (1985) conducted a travel cost study to estimate the benefits of improving water quality in Army Corps of Engineers reservoirs from a quality level that is suitable for boating but not fishing to a water-quality level that is suitable for fishing. They summarize their results and the results from similar studies, which is reproduced as Table 11.5. In a study based on hedonic wages (compensating wage differentials), Clark and Kahn (1989) show that the annual value in recreational fishing of 10 percent improvements in dissolved oxygen, pH, and total suspended sediments are \$2.67 billion, \$2.49 billion, and \$572 million in 2004 dollars, respectively.

Summary

Fishery resources are renewable but destructible. The destructibility problem is amplified by the open-access nature of many of the world's fishery resources, many of which are currently collapsing.

For commercial fishing, optimal management requires the limitation of effort to a level that maximizes the sum of consumers' surplus, producers' surplus, and fishery rent. Actual fishery management seldom achieves this goal and is based on developing restrictions on how, when, where, and how much fish can be caught. In addition to the problems associated with maximizing the value of a commercial fishery in isolation, there are other important policy questions. These questions revolve around the issue of resource utilization conflicts. Of particular importance are the incidental catch of untargeted species (fish, marine mammals, and sea turtles), conflicts between recreational and commercial fishing, conflicts between commercial fishing and subsistence fishing, the pollution of fishery habitat, and the destruction of both fishery habitat and related habitats such as wetlands.

appendix 11.a
Conducting an Empirical Analysis of a Fishery

For many fisheries, data on landings (catch) and value (from which price can be computed) have been collected since the 1950s or 1960s. This database generally gives enough observations to estimate market demand and supply curves for the catch of a particular species or for a group of species that together make up a single market.

The quantity demanded of any product is a function of the price of the good, the number of potential consumers, the income of these consumers, and the price of substitute goods. The key to identifying appropriately what values to use for these variables is to define the market appropriately. For example, if one were to examine the demand and supply of Alaskan king crab, the relevant market would be the entire United States. If, however, one were to focus on Chesapeake Bay blue crabs, it might be better to define the market as the mid-Atlantic section of the United States.

A good variable to use for a price of substitute goods is the consumer price index (CPI) for meat, poultry, and fish. This information, as well as data on population and per capita income, can be accessed at the web site of the Bureau of Labor Statistics (http://www.bls.gov). When looking at any monetary variable, values should be normalized with the general CPI to hold the effects of inflation constant.

Following this discussion, quantity demand can be estimated in the following form:

$$Qd_t = a_1 + a_2P_t + a_3PSUB_t + a_4POP_t + a_5PCI_t + \varepsilon_t \qquad 11a.1$$

where Qd is the quantity demanded of the fish, P is the price of the fish, PSUB is a price variable for substitutes, POP is the population of the market region, PCI is the average per capita income of the market region, and ε is the error term.

Quantity supplied will be a function of the price of the fish, the price of key inputs, the income from alternative opportunities for the fisher, and the abundance of fish. Both the price of labor and the price of energy can be used as prices for key inputs. Depending on the region in question, one could use the hourly wage in manufacturing, the hourly wage in services, or the hourly wage in agriculture as the price of labor. The wage in an alternative labor market also functions as a measure of the opportunity cost of alternative income-making opportunities for the fisher. It does not, however, adequately handle this issue, because in addition to working in an alternative job, a fisher could pursue an alternative species. Yet when looking at alternative species, one must be careful to distinguish between species that are jointly pursued with the target species (which would shift the supply curve to the right) and species that are pursued as alternatives to the target species (which would shift the supply curve to the left).

Finally, it is critically important to include a population variable. Although it is difficult to find an actual population variable (where the population is directly estimated), it is possible to find variables that indicate relative changes in population size, such as frequency surveys of adult populations or of juvenile populations. During these surveys, fish are collected according to netting procedures that do not vary from year to year. These variables can then be used to create an index of abundance. If using a juvenile abundance index, one can make the simplifying assumption that population equals an unknown constant multiplied by the index, or

$$F_t = \alpha_t \qquad \text{11a.2}$$

Then, the supply function can be specified as

$$Qs_t = b_0 + b_1P_t + b_2P_{energy_t} + b_3P_{labor_t} + b_4P_{S_{1t}} + \cdots + b_{n-1}P_{S_{mt}} + b_nI_t + \phi_t \qquad \text{11a.3}$$

where Qs is the quantity supplied of the fish, P is its price, P_{energy} is the price of energy, P_{labor} is the price of labor, P_S, through P_{SM} are the prices of the m alternative fish species, I is the index of abundance, and ϕ is the error term.

The final step is to estimate the equilibrium catch function. It would be convenient to use a logistic growth function, which would have the following form:

$$Q_{eq_t} = rF_t\left(1 - \frac{F_t}{K}\right) \qquad \text{11a.4}$$

where Q_{eq} is the equilibrium catch, r is the intrinsic growth rate, K is the carrying capacity, and F is the abundance of the fish. It is unlikely, however, that we are onserving equilibrium catch in any year, so this equation cannot be directly estimated. We can, though, specify an identity that indicates that

$$F_t = F_{t-1} - Q_{t-1} + rF_{t-1} - \left(\frac{r}{K}\right)F_{t-1}^2 \qquad \text{11a.5}$$

This equation merely indicates that abundance in year t (F_t) is equal to abundance in year t–1 (F_{t-1}) minus catch in year t–1 (Q_{t-1}) plus growth in year t–1 (rF_{t-1} + $(r/k)(F^2_{t-1})$).

The terms can be rearranged to yield

$$F_t = (1 + r)F_{t-1} - \left(\frac{r}{K}\right)F_{t-1}^2 \qquad \text{11a.6}$$

If F_t is available, then this equation can be directly estimated. If only an index of abundance is available, then making use of the assumption that $F_t = \alpha I_t$, the function can be rewritten as

$$\alpha I_t = \alpha(1+r)I_{t-1} - \alpha\left(\frac{r}{K}\right)(I_{t-1})^2 - Q_{t-1}$$

or

$$I_t = (1+r)I_{t-1} - \left(\frac{r}{K}\right)(I_{t-1})^2 - \left(\frac{1}{\alpha}\right)Q_{t-1} \qquad \text{11a.7}$$

or

$$I_t = \beta_0 I_{t-1} - \beta_1(I_{t-1})^2 - \beta_2 Q_{t-1}$$

In equilibrium, I_t must equal I_{t-1}, so the equilibrium catch equation may be determined by substituting I_t into equation 11a.7 for I_{t-1}, and rearranging terms, or

$$Q_t = \left(\frac{\beta_0 - 1}{\beta_2}\right)I_t - \left(\frac{\beta_1}{\beta_2}\right)I_t^2 \qquad \text{11a.8}$$

Therefore, one can estimate equation 11a.7 and from it derive an equilibrium catch equation equal to equation 11a.8. If you have data on important environmental variables such as water quality, then they may be included as right-hand side variables in equation 11a.8 because they are shifters of the equilibrium catch equation.

After the demand, supply, and equilibrium catch equation are estimated, one can solve all three equations for the bioeconomic equilibrium and compute equilibrium catch and the consumers' and producers' surplus associated with this level of catch. If environmental variables are included in the equilibrium catch equation, one can use the system of equations to compute the loss of social benefits associated with the pollution of a fishery, as conceptually discussed in Appendix 11.b.

One important caution in this process is that the equations estimated in this model contain endogenous right-hand side variables, so it is not possible to conduct these estimations with an ordinary least-squares regression. Rather, a two-stage least-squares regression must be employed. This method, discussed in an econometrics textbook, is relatively easy to implement.

Sources of data include the U.S. Bureau of Labor Statistics (http://www.bls.gov) for economic variables; the National Marine Fisheries Service (http://www.st.nmfs.gov/sti/commercial) for catch, value, and indices of abundance; variable state agencies such as departments of fisheries, environment, and natural resources for indices of abundance, catch, value, and environmental variables; and the U.S. Environmental Protection Agency (http://www.epa.gov) for data on water quality. In addition, one can consult the Sea Grant Institutes at coastal land grant universities. Data are available for Canada and other countries from analogous sources, but it is difficult to find fisheries data in most developing countries. Examples of empirical research can be found in *Marine Resource Economics*, *Journal of Environmental Economics and Management*, *American Journal of Agricultural Economics*, *Land Economics*, and *Environmental and Resources Economics*. Many authors make their data available on their web sites after their papers are published.

appendix 11.b
The Impact of Pollution on an Open-Access Fishery

This appendix further amplifies the discussion, beginning on page 395, that examines the impact of pollution on an open-access fishery. In the text, it was shown how one arrived at a new equilibrium associated with a new level of environmental quality. That discussion, however, did not present how to measure the damages associated with a negative change in environmental quality or the benefits associated with a positive change.

The first step is to compute the consumers' and producers' surplus associated with the prechange equilibrium (there will be no rent because it is an open-access fishery), which is a little complicated. In an open-access fishery, the market supply function is based on average cost, not marginal cost. Hence, consumers' and producers' surplus cannot be computed as the area between the demand and supply functions; rather, the marginal cost function must be derived from the average cost function, and then benefits can be measured as the area between the marginal cost and demand functions. This procedure is done for the marginal and average cost curves associated with E_1 (from Figure 11.17) in Figure 11b.1. The locus of biological equilibriums is left out of the figure so that the cost curves can be more clearly examined.

Although E_1 is the equilibrium level of catch, resources are wasted achieving it. In particular, the open-access leads to a catch level that is in excess of the level at which marginal cost equals marginal benefits (C*). Therefore, the net economic benefits must be computed as area ABE* minus area E^*DE_1. Not only is there a loss of all rent from being on the wrong point on the locus of biological equilibriums, but there is the social loss of area E^*DE_1, which must be subtracted from the positive benefits. A similar measure could be computed for the postpollution equilibrium of E_2 (from Figure 11.17), and the difference between the two would represent the losses that pollution generated to the producers and consumers of the striped bass fishery.

Figure 11b.1 **Consumers' and Producers' Surplus in the Open-Access Fishery**

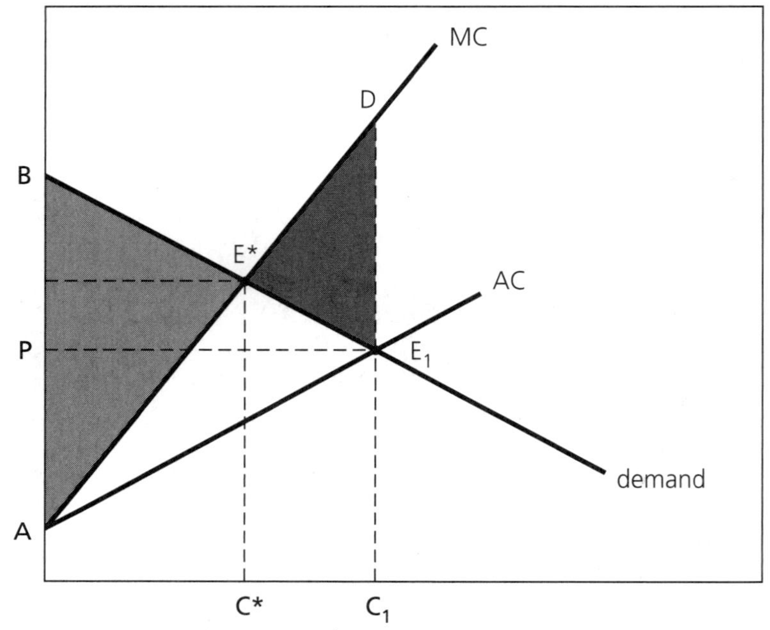

Review Questions

1. Under what conditions would the imposition of open-access regulations raise the level of average cost? Illustrate this rise with a graphical model of an open-access fishery.
2. Draw a graph that shows how the expansion of aquaculture can increase the population of the "wild" stocks of fish.
3. What is meant by *carrying capacity*?
4. Why is the maximum sustainable yield not necessarily the optimal sustainable yield?
5. What is the difference between open-access and limited-entry fishery management policies?
6. Why can it be dangerous to try to pursue maximum sustainable yield as a fishery policy?

Questions for Further Study

1. What is the relevance of a depensated growth function for fisheries management?
2. Would the sole owner of a fishery ever harvest the fishery to extinction?
3. What are the major unresolved management issues in marine fisheries?
4. How would you optimally regulate a purely recreational fishery?
5. Why, in an open-access fishery, is the inverse of the supply function the average cost function and not the marginal cost function?
6. What is the difference between the bionomic equilibrium of the Gordon model and the bioeconomic equilibrium of the supply and demand model presented in this book?

7. Compare ITQs with marketable pollution permits.
8. How would environmental change affect a logistic growth function?

Suggested Paper Topics

1. Estimate demand and supply functions for a regional open-access fishery of your choice. Check Appendix 11.a for guidance.
2. Investigate the issue of international conflict over fishery resources. Discuss the efficiency and equity implications of current attempts to deal with the conflict, such as the 200-mile economic zone and international agreements such as the Law of the Sea and the Convention on Biodiversity. What general international law principles (common concern, shared but differentiated responsibility) can be applied to the problem? How would you develop better policy for fishery resources that are shared by several nations? Begin with Anderson's *The Economics of Fishery Management* (1986) for discussion of this issue and also examine journals such as the *Journal of Environmental Economics Management, Marine Resource Economics, Resource Economics*, and *Fisheries Bulletin*. Search bibliographic databases using international fisheries policy, treaties and fisheries, and fisheries and international law as keywords. Also, search on specific species or types of fish, such as shrimp, salmon, tuna, and groundfish.
3. If you live in a coastal state (including the Great Lakes states), you might want to look at an issue of local concern. Talk to staff members at your state's Sea Grant Institute, which is housed in your state's land grant university, as well as your resource economics professors. Also, if your university has a marine resources department or fish and wildlife department, you might look to professors there for help in locating an interesting issue. Make sure your paper does more than just state the physical dimensions of the problem. Look at the market failure and policy attempts to deal with the market failure. What are the efficiency and equity implications of the policy? Can you develop any means to improve on the policies?
4. Investigate policies designed to ameliorate the decline of Pacific salmon in the United States and Canada. How effective are these policies? What must be done to restore salmon populations? Is there evidence that the benefits associated with these policies are greater than the cost? See the Gordon and Betty Moore Foundation initiative on wild salmon at http://moore.org/program_areas/environment/initiatives/salmon/initiative_salmon.asp.
5. Investigate the problem of incidental catch, either in general or in a specific fishery. What are the social costs associated with incidental catch? How can these external costs be internalized? Is it possible to use economic incentives, or must direct controls, or a combination of both, be employed?
6. Investigate conflicts between developed and developing countries with regard to the exploitation of oceanic fisheries.

Works Cited and Selected Readings

Alam, M. F, H. O. Ishak, and D. Squires. Sustainable Fisheries Development in the Tropics: Trawlers and License Limitation in Malaysia. *Applied Economics 34*, no. 3 (2002): 325–337.

Anderson, L. G. *The Economics of Fishery Management*. Baltimore: Johns Hopkins University Press, 1986.

Anderson, L. G. (ed.). *Fisheries Economics: Collected Essays.* 2 vols. International Library of Environmental Economics and Policy. Aldershot, UK, Burlington, VT, and Sydney: Ashgate, 2002.

Barbier, E. B., I. Strand, and S. Sathirathai. Do Open Access Conditions Affect the Valuation of an Externality? Estimating the Welfare Effects of Mangrove-Fishery Linkages in Thailand. *Environmental and Resource Economics 21*, no. 4 (2002): 343–367.

Boremann, J., B. Nakashima, J. Wilson, and R. Kendall (eds.). *Northwest Atlantic Groundfish: Perspectives on a Fishery Collapse.* Bethesda, MD: American Fisheries Society, 1997.

Buerger, R., and J. R. Kahn. The New York Value of Chesapeake Striped Bass. *Marine Resource Economics 6* (1989): 19–25.

Caviglia-Harris, J., J. R. Kahn, and T. Green. Demand Side Policies for Environmental Protection and Sustainability. *Ecological Economics 4* (2003): 119–132.

Cicin-Sain, B., and R. Knecht. *Integrated Coastal and Ocean Management: Concepts and Practices*. Washington, DC: Island Press, 1998.

Clark, C. W. *Bioeconomic Modelling and Fishery Management*. New York: Wiley, 1985.

Clark, D. E., and J. R. Kahn. The Two-Stage Hedonic Wage Approach: A Methodology for the Valuation of Environmental Amenities. *Journal of Environmental Economics and Management 16* (1989): 106–120.

Copes, P. The Individual Quota in Fisheries Management. *Land Economics 62* (August 1986): 278–291.

Craig, R. K., Oceans and Estuaries. Pages 227–256 in *Stumbling Towards Sustainability*, edited by J. C. Dernback. Washington, DC: Environmental Law Institute, 2002.

Dayton, P., S. Thrush, and F. Coleman. *Ecological Effects of Fishing in Marine Ecosystems in the United States*, 2003. Pew Oceans Commission. Online: http://www.pewoceans.org/oceanfacts/2002/10/25/fact_29889.asp.

Edwards, S., A. J. Bejda, and R. A. Richards. Sole Ownership of Living Marine Resources. NOAA Technical Memorandum NMFS-F/NEC-99. Woods Hole Fisheries Science Center, Woods Hole, MA, May 1993.

Edwards, S. F. Are Consumer Preferences for Seafood Strengthening? Tests and Some Implications. *Marine Resource Economics 7* (1992): 141–151.

Ellis, R., *The Empty Ocean: Plundering the World's Marine Life*. Washington, DC: Island Press, 2003.

Field, J. D. Atlantic Striped Bass Management: Where Did We Go Right? *Fisheries 22*, no. 7 (1997): 6–9.

Field, J. G., G. Hempel, and C. P. Summerhayes. *Oceans 2020: Science, Trends, and the Challenge of Sustainability*. Washington, DC: Island Press, 2002.

Fordham, S. V. *New England Groundfish: From Glory to Grief. A Portrait of America's Most Devastated Fishery*. Washington, DC: Center for Marine Conservation, 1996.

Freeman, A. M., III. *The Benefits of Environmental Improvement: Theory and Practice*. Baltimore: Johns Hopkins University Press, 1979.

Goodyear, C. P. Status of the Red Drum Stocks of the Gulf of Mexico. NOAA/NMFS SEFSC contributions MIA-95-96-47, 1996.

Gordon, H. The Economic Theory of the Common Property Resource: The Fishery. *Journal of Political Economy 62* (1954): 124–142.

Green, T. *The Economic Value and Policy Implications of Recreational Red Drum Success Rate in the Gulf of Mexico*. Report to the National Marine Fisheries Service, University of Southern Mississippi, 31 July 1989.

Helvarg, D. *Blue Frontier: Saving America's Living Seas*. New York: Freeman, 2001.

Kahn, J. R. Measuring the Economic Damages Associated with the Terrestrial Pollution of Marine Ecosystems. *Marine Resource Economics 4* (1987): 193–209.

Kahn, J. R., and W. M. Kemp. Economic Losses Associated with the Degradation of an Ecosystem: The Case of Submerged Aquatic Vegetation in Chesapeake Bay. *Journal of Environmental Economics and Management 12* (1985): 246–263.

Krishnan, M., and P. S. Birthal. Aquaculture Development in India: An Economic Overview with Special Reference to Coastal Aquaculture. *Aquaculture Economics and Management 6*, no. 1 (2002): 81–96.

Loomis, J., and C. Sorg. A Critical Summary of Empirical Estimates of the Values of Wildlife, Wilderness, and General Recreation Related to National Forest Regions. Unpublished paper, U.S. Forest Service, 1982.

Lynne, G. D., P. Conroy, and F. J. Prochaska. Economic Valuation of Marsh Areas for Marine Production Processes. *Journal of Environmental Economics and Management 8* (1981): 175–186.

National Marine Fisheries Service. *Our Living Oceans 1999: The Economic Status of Fisheries*. Online: http://www.st.nmfs.gov/st2/pdf.htm.

Pauly, D., and J. Maclean. *In a Perfect Ocean: The State of Fisheries and Ecosystems in the North Atlantic Ocean*. Washington, DC: Island Press, 2003.

Scott, A. The Fishery: The Objectives of Sole Ownership. *Journal of Political Economy 62* (1955): 112–124.

Sloan, S. *Ocean Bankruptcy: World Fisheries on the Brink of Disaster*. New York: Lyons Press, 2003.

Smith, M., and J. E. Wilen. The Marine Environment: Fencing the Last Frontier. *Review of Agricultural Economics 23*, no. 1 (2001): 31–42.

Smith, V. K., and W. H. Desvouges. The Generalized Travel Cost Model and Water Quality Benefits: A Reconsideration. *Southern Economic Journal 52* (1985): 371–381.

Smith, V. K., W. H. Desvouges, and M. P. McGivney. Estimating Water Quality Benefits: An Econometric Analysis. *Southern Economic Journal 50* (1983): 422–437.

Status of Fishery Resources Off the Northeastern United States for 1986. NOAA Technical Memorandum NMFS-F/NEC-43, 1986.

Thorpe, A., and E. Bennett. Globalisation and the Sustainability of World Fisheries: A View from Latin America. *Marine Resource Economics 16*, no. 2 (2001): 143–164.

Turvey, A. Optimization and Suboptimization in Fishery Regulation. *American Economic Review 54* (1964): 64–76.

U.S. Department of Commerce. *Current Fishery Statistics* (state landings data). Washington, DC: U.S. Government Printing Office, various years.

Vaughn, W. J., and C. S. Russell. Valuing a Fishing Day. *Land Economics 58* (1982): 450–463.

Weitzman, M. L. Landing Fees vs. Harvest Quotas with Uncertain Fish Stocks. *Journal of Environmental Economics and Management 43*, no. 2 (2002): 325–338.

Wieland, R., S. Iudicello, and M. Weber. *Fish, Markets, and Fishermen: The Economics of Overfishing*. London: Earthscan, 1999.

Wilder, R. J. Listening to the Sea: *The Politics of Improving Environmental Protection*. Pittsburgh, PA: University of Pittsburgh Press, 1998.

chapter 12

Temperate Forests

The bears don't write letters and the owls don't vote.

Lou Gold, forest advocate

Introduction

The historical emphasis of forest economics has been on how to maximize the wealth to be derived from the harvesting of the forest's wood. This emphasis is not surprising given that the first foresters were employed by large landowners who were concerned with maximizing the income to be derived from their land. This attitude toward forests was shared by many early conservationist thinkers (prior to 1900) whose primary concern was that the material wealth provided by forests not be squandered. In contrast, some of the later conservationists, such as John Muir (1838–1914), believed that the forest was a synergistic system and that the benefits derived from a forest were derived primarily through the preservation of the forest, although timbering of some forestland was certainly appropriate.

Today this debate still rages. Do we want spotted owls or lumberjacks? Should we allow roads in roadless areas? Is the primary purpose of the forest to provide economic benefits through harvesting the wood? Is the primary purpose of the forest the provision of ecological services? Should some forests be devoted to harvesting and some preserved for their ecological and recreational benefits? How do we make these decisions? The debate over these questions even reached the polling places in 1990s, as initiatives to prevent the harvesting of pristine (old-growth) forests were placed on the ballot (and defeated) in California, Oregon and Washington states, and it continues still, with plans for more ballot initiatives in 2004.

This chapter looks at the traditional problem of how to maximize the income derived from timbering as well as the more general problem of maximizing the total social benefits arising from the forest. These total social benefits include the benefits from timbering as well as the benefits from preservation. To understand the benefits that can be derived from the forest more fully, it is necessary to understand the basics of forest ecology. As the title suggests, this chapter focuses on temperate forests. Temperate forests are found north of the Tropic of Capricorn and south of the Tropic of Cancer and include the many different types of forest found in North America.

Forest Ecology

The major point associated with forest ecology is that a forest is more than a collection of trees. It is a system of plant, animal, bacterial, and fungal organisms that interact with the physical environment and with one another. Removing one type of organism from the forest may have far-reaching effects. An example of this interdependency is examined later in the chapter in the discussion of old-growth or "ancient" forests.

Another important point is that a forest is an example of the type of ecosystem known as a climax community. This community is an ecosystem that has arisen out of competition with other communities of organisms. For example, an area of land may be initially colonized by pioneer species such as grasses. Very soon, small woody plants (bushes and shrubs) become established, followed by fast-growing tree species such as poplar. Eventually, the dominant plant form becomes a slower-growing tree, such as oak, maple, spruce, or fir. These taller trees are most successful in competing for sunlight, water, and nutrients.

Although it may be apparent that the different organisms interact with one another, it is less obvious how the organisms interact with the physical environment. The process of soil formation and nutrient cycling is a good example of this type of interaction.

Nutrient cycling refers to the process by which the basic life nutrients (phosphorus, potassium, and nitrogen) are absorbed from the physical environment by the various organisms in the ecosystem, transferred from organism to organism, and eventually returned to the physical environment. In temperate forests, the soil plays a crucial role in this process because it is the place where nutrients accumulate and are slowly released to the other components of the ecosystem.

Figure 12.1 illustrates nutrient cycling in a typical temperate forest. The nutrients in the soil are absorbed by the roots of trees and other plants. When these trees and plants drop their leaves or die and decay, their nutrients are returned to the soil. In addition, nutrients are cycled through the ecosystem when animals eat the plants. When these animals eliminate their wastes, the nutrients are returned to the soil. Some animals are eaten by other animals, which further extends the food web based on the trees. Finally, dead animals are eaten by a host of organisms, which eventually return the nutrients to the soil.

Figure 12.1 **Nutrient Cycling in the Temperate Forest**

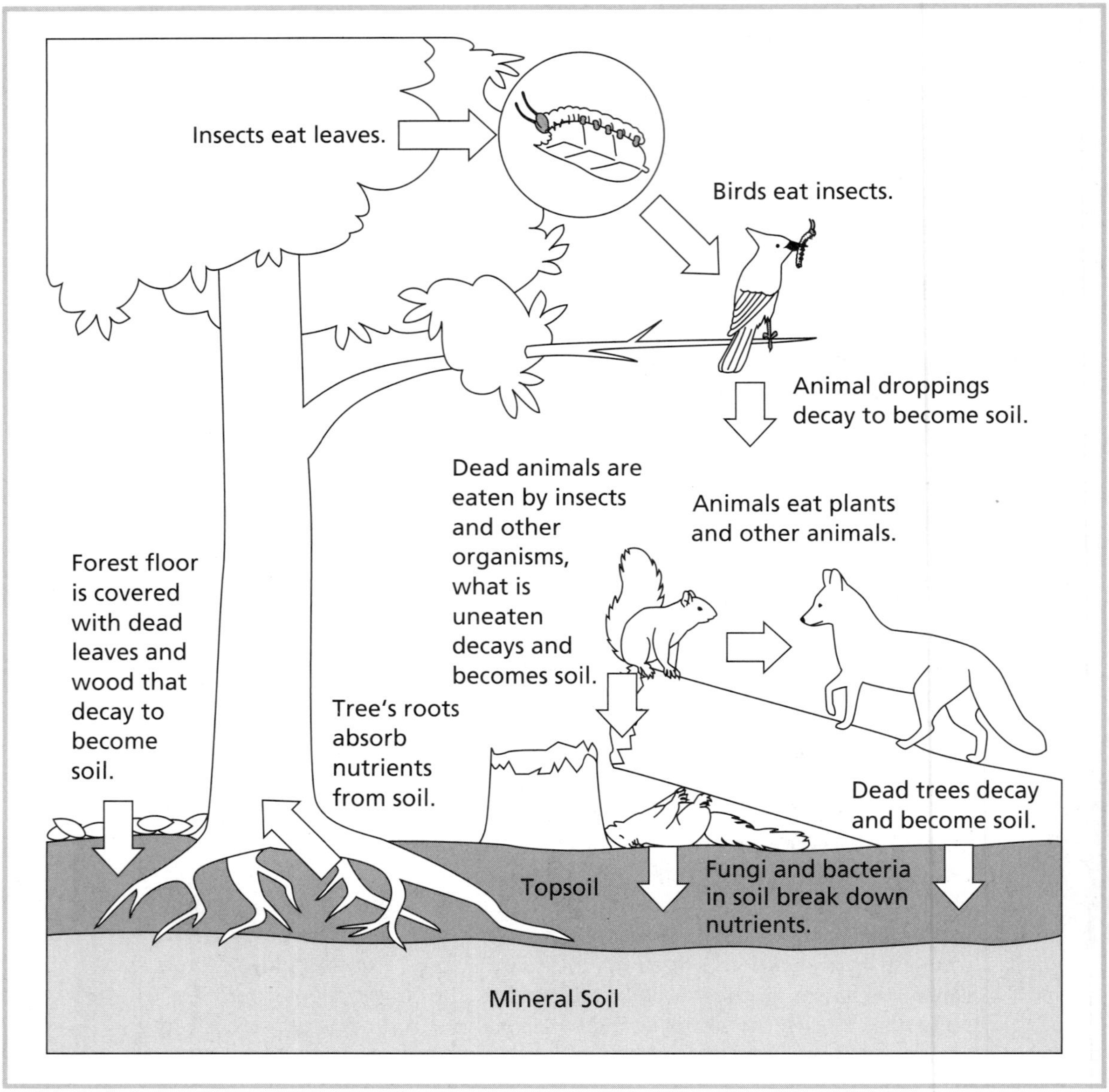

In addition to playing an essential role in nutrient cycling, forests play an essential role in carbon cycling. The process of photosynthesis converts carbon from the carbon dioxide in the atmosphere to carbon in sugar in a tree's leaf cells. This carbon, the basic building block of life on this earth, is then available to other organisms as it is transferred along the food chain. As discussed in Chapter 7, carbon dioxide buildup in the atmosphere is the leading contributor to potential global warming. Forests remove carbon dioxide from the atmosphere and sequester it in their woody tissue, which is approximately 50 percent carbon by weight.

Forests also play an important part in the hydrological cycle. Water rolls down the stem of the tree and follows the roots down into the soil. When rain falls on the leaves of trees, it slowly trickles off the leaves of the trees, slowing the velocity of the rain to the ground. The organic matter in the soil acts as a sponge and absorbs the water as the water slowly makes its way into the aquifers and surface waters. In the absence of forest cover, the rain impacts directly on the soil, which has less organic matter and less absorptive capability than forest-covered soil. Not only does the water immediately run off into surface waters (without as much reaching the underground aquifers), but the runoff leads to soil erosion that diminishes the productivity of the soil and to turbidity in surface waters. The reduction in the capacity to store water also means that forest plants will have less water to draw on and that the surface waters will have less flow and volume during the drier summer months. This result has important implications not only for the plant and animal communities, but also for the human communities that depend on the flow of water from the forests.

As is evidenced by the discussion of nutrient and hydrological cycles, the forest ecosystem is an important provider of ecological services. In addition to the importance of the forests' contribution to nutrient cycles, forests are extremely important in terms of flood protection, biodiversity, soil formation, erosion control, and gaseous exchange. Gaseous exchange refers to the process of releasing oxygen into the atmosphere and pulling carbon dioxide out of the atmosphere where it is stored in the living tissue of the trees and the organic component of the soil. This sequestration of carbon is important in mitigating both the accumulation of carbon dioxide in the atmosphere and the global climate change that accompanies this accumulation.

In addition to these ecological services, forests provide important aesthetic and recreational benefits. Also, many production activities can take place in the forest, including harvesting animals, mushrooms, and berries; mining; grazing of livestock; and of course, harvesting of wood.

Harvested wood is used for a variety of purposes, including construction material (both boards and manufactured products such as plywood and particleboard), furniture, paper, fiber (for disposable diapers and other products), and chemicals. Harvested wood is also used as a fuel for heating homes and as a boiler fuel, and it can be converted into methanol (wood alcohol) that can be used to fuel internal combustion engines in cars and other vehicles.

The Privately and Socially Optimal Management of Forests

Before discussing the privately and socially optimal management of forests, it is necessary to spend some time talking about the ownership of forests. Certainly, the privately optimal management of forests is going to depend on whether the forest owner is a utility maximizer or a profit maximizer. If the owner is a utility maximizer, preferences will play an important role in the outcome. Forest ownership can be divided into three primary categories.

The first ownership category is forests that are owned by households. Because households are utility maximizers rather than profit maximizers, it is difficult to talk about a single management strategy for the household forest owners. For example, some households may be concerned with maximizing the income they receive from the forest, whereas others may rather enjoy the aesthetic benefits of keeping their forests intact or believe that they have a stewardship responsibility to leave the forest intact. Another type of individual may engage in selective harvesting while still keeping the forest relatively intact to enjoy the nonpecuniary benefits of having forested property. Some households may be concerned with passing the forest on to their children, who can then choose how to maximize it.

The second major class of forest ownership is ownership by firms of the forest products industry. These firms are profit maximizers that seek to maximize the present value of earnings derived from the forest. These firms own a substantial amount of forestland and include well-known firms such as Boise-Cascade, Weyerhauser, and Georgia-Pacific as well as a host of smaller firms. In addition to harvesting timber from their own land, forest product firms lease harvesting rights from both household forest owners and from the third category of forest ownership, public ownership.

Publicly owned forests include national parks, national forests, parks and forests operated by state and local governments, and other publicly owned tracts of forests, wildlife refuges, game management areas, and nature preserves. Different types of public forests are operated with different goals in mind, but in general these forests are managed for multiple uses and not just the generation of a stream of income from timber harvesting.

Maximizing the Physical Quantities of Harvested Wood

An interesting footnote to renewable resource management is that, historically, resource managers were concerned with maximizing physical flows (such as cubic meters of wood or tons of fish) rather than maximizing the net private or net social benefits. For example, many forestry scientists advocated a management strategy designed to *maximize the physical amount of wood* to be derived from the forest. There are two basic methods for doing so. One option is to let the forest grow until it reaches its peak volume of wood and then cut it. The forest is replanted, and the process is allowed to repeat itself. The other method chooses the length of the harvest-replant-harvest cycle to maximize the total harvests of wood that can be achieved over time. This harvest-replant-harvest cycle is called the rotation of the forest. In this case, the length of the rotation is chosen to maximize the flow of wood from the forest. The length of time in the rotation for either of these strategies is critically dependent on the way in which the trees grow. In examining growth, one must keep in mind that generalizations are difficult to make because growth conditions depend on the density of trees, soil conditions, weather and rainfall conditions, and the incidence of disease and pests. It is important to look at the growth of a stand of trees, rather than an individual tree, because a tree in isolation grows more quickly than a tree that is competing with other trees for sunlight, nutrients, and water. After replanting, the trees initially grow at a rapid percentage rate, but because their size is small, the growth in the mass of wood is relatively small. As the trees grow larger, their capacity to grow increases as well. Eventually, the growth slows as the trees mature, and growth can become negative as the disease and death associated with aging have a greater impact than the production of new biomass. Table 12.1 and Figure 12.2 describe the growth of a 1-acre stand of a hypothetical tree species as a function of the age of the trees in the stand (all the trees in the stand are the same age). As can be seen in Figure 12.2, the volume of wood first increases at an increasing rate and then at a decreasing rate. The volume of wood can actually decline as the trees become very old, but this decline is not shown in either the graph or the table.

Table 12.1 Total Volume of Wood, Annual Increment, and Mean Annual Increment (cubic feet of wood) on a 1-Acre Stand of a Hypothetical Tree Species

Age	Total volume	Annual increment	Mean annual increment
10	0	0	0
20	75	7.5	3.75
30	200	12.5	6.66
40	750	55.0	18.75
50	1400	65.0	28.00
60	2100	70.0	32.50
70	2550	45.0	34.30
80	2900	35.0	36.25
90	3200	30.0	35.55
100	3450	25.0	34.50
110	3650	20.0	33.18
120	3800	15.0	31.67
130	3900	10.0	30.00
140	3950	5.0	28.20
150	3975	2.5	26.60
160	3975	0	24.84

Figure 12.2a Total Volume of Marketable Wood of a Hypothetical Tree Species, 1-Acre Stand

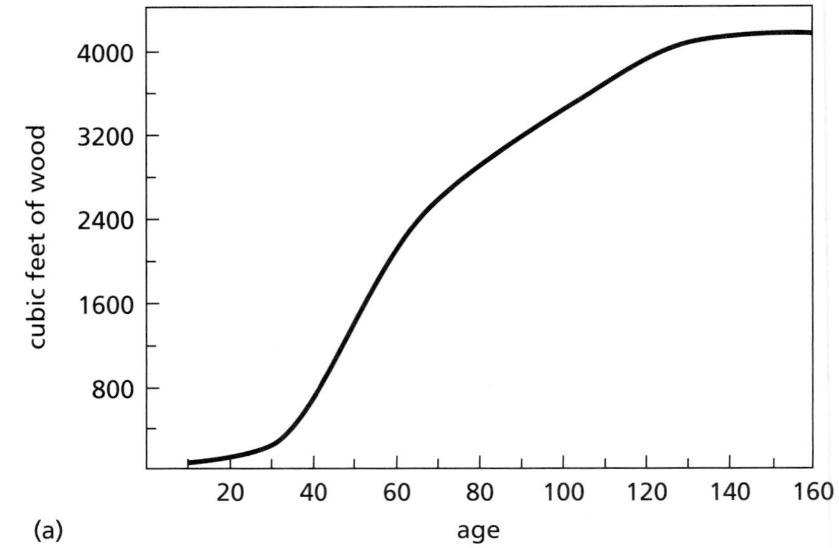

Figure 12.2b Annual Increment and Mean Annual Increment for a Hypothetical Tree Species, 1-Acre Stand

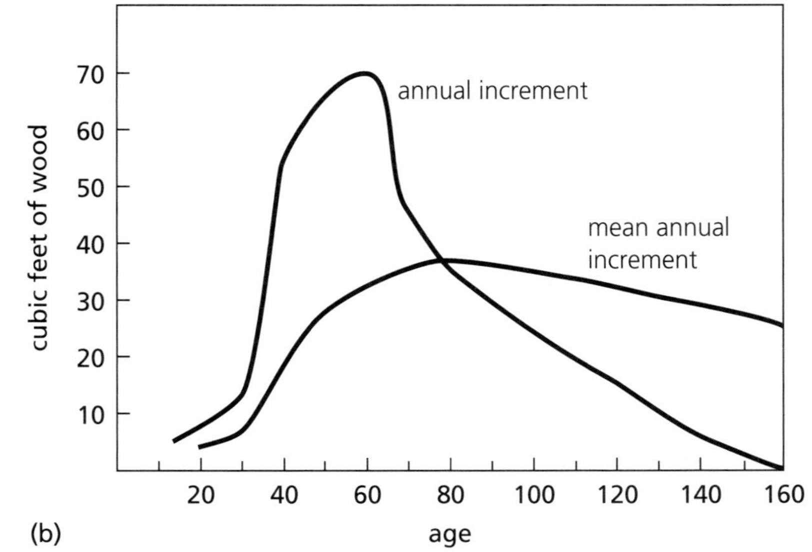

It is relatively easy to see when the forest grows to its peak size: it is when the growth (annual increment) declines to zero.[1] The peak size for this hypothetical forest can be seen from Table 12.1, Figure 12.2a, or Figure 12.2b to occur when the stand of trees is 160 years old.

It is not as easy to see when the total amount of wood that is harvested over time is maximized, although it is relatively easy to conceptualize the trade-offs that are involved. One way to increase the flow of wood is to harvest more frequently. The more frequently the forest is harvested and replanted, however, the younger and smaller the trees. The other way to increase the flow of wood is to harvest less frequently and have bigger harvests. The optimal compromise between these two conflicting strategies is to harvest at the forest age that maximizes the average growth of the tree over its lifetime. If average growth is maximized over a sequence of multiple rotations, then total growth (and the total flow of wood) will be maximized as well. The average growth rate, or mean annual increment, of the hypothetical tree species is contained in the fourth column of Table 12.1 and is also drawn in Figure 12.2b. Notice that the average growth rate is maximized when it is equal to the marginal growth rate (annual increment), which in Figure 12.2b occurs at approximately 80 years for this hypothetical tree species, a time that is substantially shorter than the rotation that maximizes individual harvest (160 years). Table 12.2 shows the sensitivity of the total wood harvest to the length of the rotation by showing the total amount of wood that can be harvested over a 500-year period, for different rotation lengths. One interesting insight that can be gained is that the penalties (in terms of lower than maximum volume of wood) for having too short a rotation are substantially higher than the penalties for too long a rotation. For example, a rotation that is approximately 40 years shorter than the flow maximizing level gives a 500-year harvest of 9375 cubic feet, which is approximately 52 percent of the maximum level (18,115 cubic feet). A rotation length that is approximately 40 years longer than the optimal level, however, yields a 500-year harvest of 15,835 cubic feet, which is 87 percent of the maximum level. The reason for this difference can be seen in the asymmetry of the growth functions in Figure 12.2b, which is due to the small amount of growth that takes place in the first several decades of a tree's life.

Although maximizing these physical quantities of wood has been used as a management strategy in the past and is still advocated by some natural scientists concerned with forestry management, it is an inefficient policy, even when managers are only concerned with the benefits arising from harvesting wood. The reason it is inefficient is the same reason that maximizing the sustainable yield of the fishery (see Chapter 11) is inefficient. In both cases, the costs and benefits associated with different quantity levels have not been incorporated into the management strategy. In the case of the forests, one

[1]Every field of study has its own technical jargon, and forestry management is no exception. Annual increment can be thought of as the annual growth, or the marginal product of the forest (marginal with respect to time). Mean annual increment can be thought of as the annual amount of growth, or the average product of the forest (the total product divided by the number of years of the rotation).

Table 12.2 **Length of Rotation, Number of Rotations per 500 Years, Total Harvest over 500 Years**

Length of rotation	Number of rotations per 500 years	Total volume of wood (cubic feet) harvested over 500 years
10	50.00	0
20	25.00	1875
30	16.66	3330
40	12.50	9375
50	10.00	14,000
60	8.33	16,250
70	7.14	17,150
80	6.25	18,115
90	5.55	17,775
100	5.00	17,250
110	4.54	16,590
120	4.16	15,838
130	3.84	15,000
140	3.57	14,100
150	3.33	13,250
160	3.13	12,420

must consider the costs and benefits associated with making the rotation longer or shorter.

Although Faustmann (1849) developed a method for including these costs and benefits, and a derivation of an optimal rotation in terms of these costs and benefits, Bowes and Krutilla (1989) indicate that his work was not widely known for approximately a century. Bowes and Krutilla credit Gaffney (1957) and Pearse (1967) with bringing Faustmann's work to the attention of American forestry researchers and forest managers.

The Optimal Rotation

The choice of the optimal length of rotation is a conceptually simple problem. The forest manager simply asks the question, Are the benefits of making the rotation a year longer (or a year shorter) greater than the costs? The complexity involves determination of the costs and benefits and evaluating them over an infinite or extremely long time horizon. A good way to examine the problem is to start with a forest stand of newly planted trees and then each year thereafter evaluate the costs and benefits of letting the trees continue to grow for another year.

Figure 12.3 contains a schematic drawing of the fashion in which benefits and costs accrue over time. First, there is the revenue from the initial harvest (or the costs of planting if the area is not currently forested), then the costs of planting, and then maintenance costs such as disease control, fire prevention, thinning, pruning and removal of dead wood, and pest control. Benefits come at a set of intervals, and costs come at a different set of intervals. The revenue from the harvest is often called the stumpage value and represents the proceeds from the sale of the wood, less the costs of harvesting.

The forest manager's job is to maximize the present value of this stream of costs and benefits (see Appendix 2.a for a review of present value and discounting) by deciding the optimal rotation length. As mentioned, the optimal rotation length is determined by comparing the costs and benefits of increasing or decreasing the rotation length.

The costs of letting the trees grow for another year (or a shorter period of time) include both out-of-pocket costs and opportunity costs. Out-of-pocket costs include expenses for disease prevention, thinning, pruning, and removal of dead wood, fire prevention, and control of pests. Opportunity costs are based on forgone income from two sources. The first is the income that could be derived from earning interest on the revenues that would have been obtained had the trees been harvested instead of allowed to grow for another year. The second is the rent that could have been obtained had the

Figure 12.3 Time Paths of Benefits and Costs from Timbering

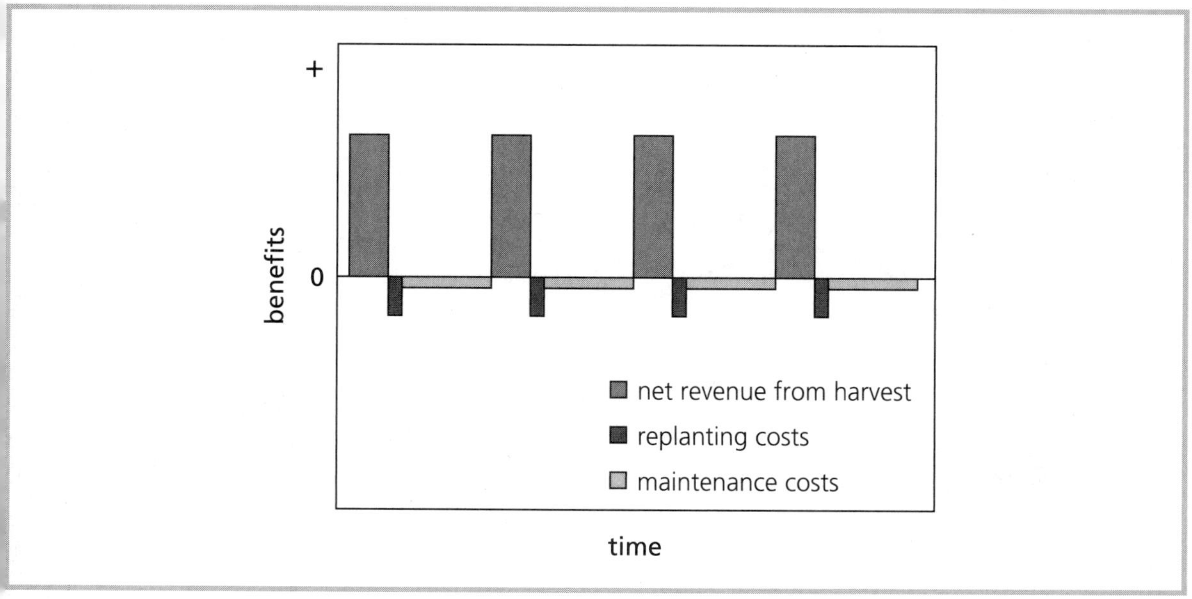

forest been cut and the land rented. In most forestry models, it is assumed that the only use of the land is forestry, so this opportunity cost would be the rent that would be obtained from leasing out a newly replanted forest stand.

To simplify the analysis, the out-of-pocket costs are usually assumed to be zero and only the two opportunity costs are considered when determining the optimal rotation. The reader can implicitly include these other costs by realizing that under most circumstances, the introduction of additional costs of waiting will shorten the rotation. An additional assumption made is that the real price of a cubic foot of wood does not change over time. If the price were to change, then there would be additional benefits (or costs) associated with increasing or decreasing the rotation.

The assumption that out-of-pocket costs are zero implies that a periodic cutting of the forest stand is efficient, unless the costs of harvesting are so high (that is, because the forest is remote or inaccessible) that stumpage value is negative for a rotation of any length. If, however, out-of-pocket costs are sufficiently high, then it is possible that the forest should never be cut, or cut once and abandoned.

Before determining the optimal rotation, a short discussion of the benefits of allowing the trees to grow is in order. The benefits of allowing the trees to grow are that if you wait, you have more wood to sell in the future. As one might expect, the benefits will be critically dependent on the shape of the marginal growth (annual increment) function. This additional revenue or change in stumpage value is represented by the function $\Delta V/\Delta t$ in Figure 12.4

Figure 12.4 **Determination of the Length of the Optimal Rotation (based on Howe, 1979)**

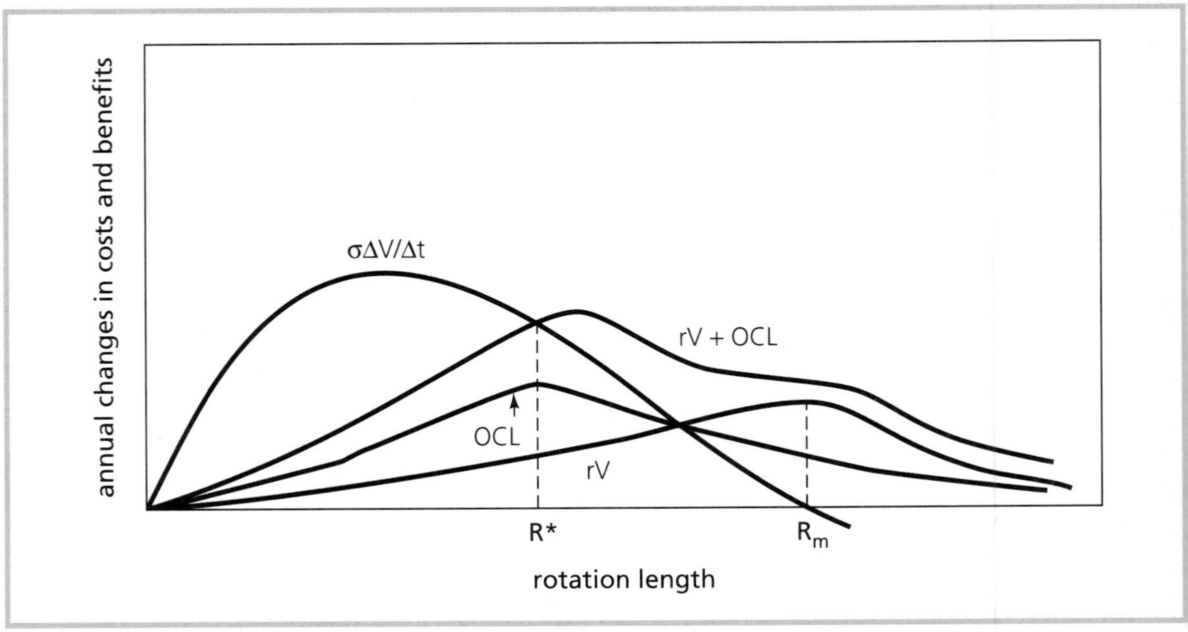

where $\Delta V/\Delta t$ is the rate of change of stumpage value [$V(t)$] and represents the change in stumpage value as rotation length is changed. The forgone interest opportunity cost is represented by $rV(t)$, where r is the interest rate and $V(t)$ is the stumpage value. This function will be based on the total growth function (see Figure 12.2a), and it reaches its maximum at the time when lengthening the rotation has no impact on stumpage value ($\Delta V/\Delta t = 0$). This point is labeled R_m in Figure 12.4.

The last cost to be considered is the opportunity cost of the land. Because we have limited (by assumption) the use of the land to forestry, it may at first seem as if there is no opportunity cost associated with letting the trees grow for an additional period of time. By letting the trees grow longer, however, not only is the interest income that could be realized from the sale of the harvest deferred, but the interest that could be earned on the proceeds to be derived from the sale of land is deferred as well. This opportunity cost also equals the annual rental value of the land, because equilibrium in land markets implies that the rent is equal to the product of the market value of the land and the rate of interest. Notice that the maximum of this opportunity cost of the land (OCL in Figure 12.4) will occur when the rotation is at its optimal length, because the forest will be most valuable (have the highest rent) when it is optimally managed.

Reiterating, the sum of the two opportunity costs is represented by the curve labeled rV + OCL. When these marginal opportunity costs are equal to the marginal benefits of changing rotation length ($\Delta V/\Delta t$), the present value of the whole future stream of harvests is maximized and the rotation can be said to be optimal. This optimal rotation length is equal to R^*.

The preceding discussion has attempted to present an intuitive and graphical analysis of the determination of the optimal rotation. Readers who are uncomfortable with this graphical analysis are referred to Appendix 12.a for a more intuitive verbal explanation. Readers who are comfortable with calculus and would like to see a more sophisticated derivation are referred to Pearse (1967) or Howe (1979). The Howe discussion is particularly useful in deriving the effect of external changes on the optimal rotation. For example, Howe discusses the effect of changes in timber prices, severance taxes, planting and management costs, and property taxes.

These external changes discussed by Howe can also be evaluated in terms of their effect on the cost and benefit functions in Figure 12.4. For example, any external change that shifts $\Delta V/\Delta t$ upward will, *ceteris paribus*, lengthen the optimal rotation. Any external change that shifts either rV or OCL upward will, *ceteris paribus*, shorten the optimal rotation. The problem in conducting a sensitivity analysis of this nature is that many external changes affect more than one function and can therefore lead to ambiguous results.

This ambiguity can be illustrated by looking at the changes generated by an increase in the price of timber. This change would shift $\Delta V/\Delta t$ upward, because the revenue to be gained by further growth will increase as the price of wood increases. In addition, both opportunity cost functions would shift upward as well. The forgone interest opportunity cost (rV) would shift upward, because an increase in the price of timber will increase stumpage value (V). The opportunity cost of the land (OCL) will shift upward, because the rental value (or the lost interest from the proceeds of the sale of land) will increase if the revenues to be derived from the land increase.

The effect of an increase in the price of timber on $\Delta V/\Delta t$ will be to lengthen the rotation. The effect of an increase in the price of timber on the two opportunity costs (rV and OCL) will be to shorten the rotation. Which effect will dominate? The answer depends on the rate of interest. The smaller the rate of interest, the smaller the effect on rV and OCL, so the lengthening effect will tend to dominate. In other words, with low rates of interest, an increase in the price of timber will tend to lengthen the optimal rotation, whereas with high rates of interest, an increase in the price of timber will tend to shorten the rotation.

One obvious shortcoming of the optimal rotation model is its assumption that the only benefits that arise from the forest are the benefits of harvesting it. In actuality, many benefits are associated with a standing forest, such as watershed protection, biodiversity, wildlife habitat, and recreation. Bowes and Krutilla (1989) point out that the relationship between the length of the rotation and the nonharvest benefits is likely to be irregular, owing to the many different types of nonharvest benefits, which will have differing functional relationships with the rotation length. For instance, some benefits might be an increasing function of rotation length, whereas others might be decreasing. Some could exhibit a U-shaped relationship (decreasing and then increasing), and some could have an inverted U-shape. When all these different relationships are aggregated, a function with multiple peaks and valleys is likely to result, as is the case in Figure 12.5. This function shows the relationship of the present value (PV) of the whole time stream of nonharvest benefits as a function of the rotation length. The function in Figure 12.5 has been drawn arbitrarily for the sake of illustration. The actual shape of this function would vary from forest to forest.

In Figure 12.6, the relationship between the length of the rotation and the timber benefits (harvested benefits) is shown. The length of the rotation that maximizes the benefits from the timber harvest can be seen to be R_t.

The total benefits of the forest are the sum of the harvested benefits and the nonharvested benefits. This sum is represented by the highest function in Figure 12.6. Notice that the maximum of this function is to the right of the maximum of the timber harvest function, implying that considering nonharvest benefits will lengthen the optimal rotation. This conclusion is clearly dependent on the shape of the nonharvested benefit function. Bowes and Krutilla (1989) point out that this optimal rotation will be somewhere between the rotation length that maximizes the harvested benefits and that which maximizes the nonharvested benefits. They point out that if the nonharvested benefits increase with rotation length and are large enough, it may be optimal to leave the stand unharvested forever. That is likely to be the case for our ancient growth forests.

One section of the scientific literature in forestry economics and forestry management tries to examine these nonharvest benefits in the context of a

Figure 12.5 **The Present Value of Nonharvest Benefits as a Function of Rotation Length**

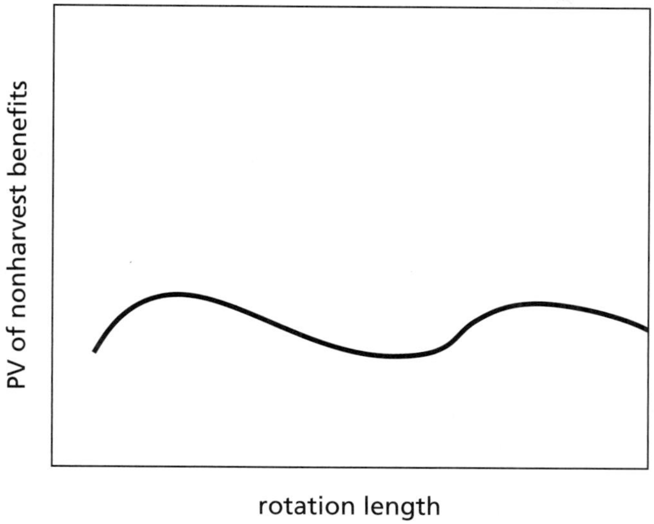

Figure 12.6 **Optimal Rotation When Nonharvested Benefits Are Considered**

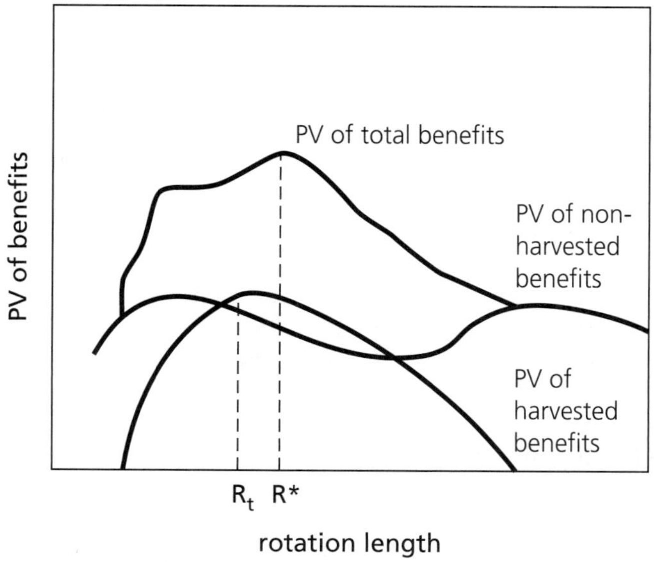

Faustmann-type model of optimal rotation. These models, however, may be inappropriate for examining management policy with respect to these nonharvest benefits. One of the most glaring problems associated with trying to incorporate these nonharvest benefits into a model based on the determination of an optimal rotation is that many of them may depend more on *how* the forest is harvested not *when* the forest is harvested. For example, clear-cutting and selective cutting have very different impacts on the ability of the forest to provide ecological services. The degree of forest fragmentation caused by the harvesting is extremely important to species habitat and biological diversity. In addition, the lack of disturbance of streams and rivers (through sedimentation or increased exposure to sunlight) is very important to the health of aquatic ecosystems.

Multiple Use Management

One shortcoming of the preceding discussion about harvested and nonharvested benefits is that it is looking at one forest stand in isolation. Both the harvested benefits and the nonharvested benefits from a particular stand of forest are dependent on the quantity and quality of other forest stands. For harvested benefits, the price of timber is an indication of the quantity and quality of other forest stands. A similar indicator does not exist for nonforested benefits. Compounding the problem is that harvesting a forest stand and eliminating its nonharvested benefits may actually reduce the nonharvested benefits from other nearby forest stands. For example, if a strategically located forest stand was clear-cut, this action could scar the whole landscape and reduce the aesthetic and recreational benefits to be derived from the surrounding forests. In addition, the clear-cut could adversely affect aquatic life in water courses that might be affected by runoff from the clear-cut. Although the Multiple Use Sustained Yield (MUSY) Act of 1960 specifically charges the U.S. Forest Service (USFS) with managing to promote benefits from both timber and nonharvested benefits, this task is not an easy one. One problem is that different outputs of the forest are not necessarily compatible. To understand this issue more thoroughly, a discussion of the different uses specified by the MUSY Act follows.

One set of uses generates revenue for the USFS. These uses include timber, grazing, mineral and energy mining, and fee recreation. Fee recreation is limited to special sites, where the fee is charged to recover the costs of special facilities. Most recreation use on national forestland does not have an entrance or user fee (Bowes and Krutilla, 1989, p. 20).

Readers may find it strange to see the grazing of livestock as a forest use, because forests and livestock are not generally associated. A forest, however, need not be completely covered by the canopies of trees. In fact, a forest is generally defined as an area in which at least 10 percent of the land area is covered by the canopy of trees. Thus in some areas that are defined as forests, up to 90 percent of the area can be exposed to sunlight and contain the grasses and other forage plants that livestock require. About 100 million acres of national forestland is currently available for leasing to ranchers, with about half of it viewed as suitable for grazing (Bowes and Krutilla, 1989, p. 18). Bowes and Krutilla indicate there is considerable evidence to suggest that the fee the USFS charges for this use is considerably below the fair market value of the forage. Another set of uses does not generate revenues; these uses are often called nonmarket uses, to differentiate them from the revenue generating or market uses. These nonmarket uses include open-access (unpriced) recreation, watershed maintenance, wilderness, and fish and wildlife.

Not surprisingly, the pursuit of market benefits often conflicts with the pursuit of nonmarket benefits. For example, a scarred clear-cut area filled with stumps and slash (the branches and other parts of the tree that are not suitable for lumber and that are left on the forest floor) is not suitable for recreation and has greatly diminished watershed attributes. It is not difficult to see how the pursuit of other market benefits, such as mining and grazing, conflict with nonmarket uses.

What is more surprising is that many nonmarket uses conflict with one another. For example, too many recreationists can lead to environmental degradation that could destroy the wilderness or reduce the vegetative cover and diminish the watershed attributes of the forest. Even different recreational uses can be incompatible with each other. A backpacker who is in the forest to enjoy its serenity is not going to appreciate a motorcyclist screaming past on a trail bike.

It is easy to say that national forests should be managed so that forestlands are allocated to the mix of competing uses that maximize the net benefits to society. The conflict among these uses and the difficulty of measuring many of the costs and benefits, however, makes this a difficult task. Although the MUSY Act of 1960 states that the multiple uses should be promoted, many critics of U.S. forest policy believe that the management is slanted toward timber production.

An interesting principle of economics that has tremendous implications for the management of public forests is the principle of comparative advantage. This principle was originally used to describe incentives for trade among nations, but it can be applied in a variety of contexts. It dictates that a resource should be used not in its absolutely best application, but in the application in which it is best in comparison to other resources that could be utilized.

The principle of comparative advantage is most easily understood when it is applied to labor markets. For example, if a person has a Ph.D. in economics from MIT but is also the world's best tire changer, that person should be an economics professor. Many people are adequately skilled in changing tires (and more can be generated with minimal training), but few people are skilled in teaching economics and conducting research. In other words, relative to the rest of the labor market, that person's comparative advantage is as an economics professor, not a tire changer, which the market will reflect by paying him or her a higher wage as an average economics professor than the person would receive as the world's best tire changer.

When applied to forests, the theory of comparative advantage argues that even though some of the best wood in the world can be produced from the old-growth redwood, spruce, fir, and sequoia forests in the Pacific Northwest, the comparative advantage of these forests is in the production of ecological services, aesthetic benefits, and recreational opportunities. This point may seem rather obvious for the truly unique spectacles of these redwood and sequoia forests, but it is generally true for primary forests in general.[2] It may also be true for many high-quality second-growth forests, such as the mixed hardwood forests that cover most of the Appalachian Mountains from Maine to Georgia.

The reason these second-growth forests may be more valuable is that they have been largely undisturbed for the last 100 to 150 years, so they are producing ecological services almost as a pristine forest. More important is that the wood from forest plantations (areas that are planted with trees with the purpose of future harvest) and the wood from low-quality second-growth forests are good substitutes for wood from a primary (or high-quality second-growth forest). Forest plantations, however, are a poor substitute for natural forests in terms of providing ecological services. By design, forest plantations are low in biodiversity of tree species, but they are also low in biodiversity of other plant species and animal species, primarily because the trees, being all the same age, have interlocking crowns and allow little sunlight to penetrate to the forest floor. The principle of comparative advantage is further discussed in the section on ancient forests.

Below-Cost Timber Sales

One of the primary pieces of evidence cited by critics of USFS policy is the existence of below-cost timber sales. In the late 1970s, the National Resources Defense Council focused on the existence of below-cost timber sales and the inefficiencies they create, including depressing the profitability of privately owned forests (Bowes and Krutilla, 1989, p. 293). Below-market timber sales are those sales of timbering rights on public land, in which the revenues generated by the harvest do not cover the timber-related forest management expenses. This comparison is usually made over an intermediate length of time, such as a 5-year period.

Although many complex issues surround the proper use of public forest-land, a general guideline is that a forest should be used for timbering if the present value of the net benefits (net of management costs) of all the multiple uses is greater than it would be without timbering. Because it is difficult to allocate particular costs to specific uses, this value comparison is difficult for a particular forest manager to evaluate. For example, roads must be built if an area is to be timbered, but the roads may also help recreationists gain access to the area.

---

[2]Primary forests are forests that have never been logged, so they have a natural process of development uninfluenced by large anthropogenic disturbances. Primary forest is a synonym for old-growth forest. Ancient forest refers to a forest in which the age of the majority of trees exceeds 300 years or more.

For this reason, roads are usually not included as timbering costs when the costs of timbering public forest are computed. This exclusion may lead to a flawed process for the following reasons:

1. The quantity of roads required for timbering a given forest is far in excess of the quantity of roads necessary for recreationists.
2. Roads that are unpaved or poorly designed may lead to erosion and other environmental damage.
3. Many types of recreational and other nonmarket benefits may be reduced by the presence of logging activity.
4. The existence of roads precludes the forest area from future designation as a wilderness area.

Timbering roads are generally built by the USFS when the forestland is opened for leasing to private timber concerns. The timbering concerns bid on the land (more than one company may bid on a site, but often the bids are uncontested). The USFS decides whether or not to accept a bid based on its forest management plans for the tract of forest, but the cost of the roads is usually not a factor in its decision to accept or reject the bids.[3] In fact, because the roads are often built before the bids are decided, they are treated as sunk costs. If the fees paid by the timbering companies do not cover all USFS timber management costs, including the roads, then there is potential for inefficiencies to arise. This process is not necessarily inefficient if the forest roads serve other uses. Then, one can argue that when the USFS builds these roads, it corrects a market failure by creating a public good. If these roads do not serve other uses, however, or if the benefits in the other uses are small relative to the costs, then the USFS may create inefficiencies by building them, as illustrated in Figure 12.7.

In Figure 12.7, MPC represents the costs to the timbering companies of harvesting the wood, exclusive of the cost of the roads and fees that the company pays to the USFS for harvesting rights. If neither of these costs is borne by the firm, then m_1 square miles of forest will be harvested, because that is the point at which the marginal private costs of harvesting another unit of forest is equal to the marginal private benefits (marginal revenue). The optimal level, however, is either at m_3 or m_4. The optimal amount of harvesting would be m_3 if the social costs of harvesting only included the private costs and the road costs, whereas the optimal level would be m_4 if social costs also included the benefits from recreation and other uses of the forest that might be reduced by harvesting as well as the benefits from the ecological services.

If the fees charged for harvesting rights are less than the costs that the USFS pays for road building or other services, then a greater than optimal amount of public forest will be harvested. The amount harvested will be equal to m_2, and the optimal level would be m_3 or m_4.

[3]For a complete discussion of past USFS policy and its planning systems, see Bowes and Krutilla (1989). For more recent information on National Forest Service policy, check the USFS web site at http://www.fs.fed.us.

Figure 12.7 Excessive Harvesting of Public Forests as a Result of Subsidized Road Building

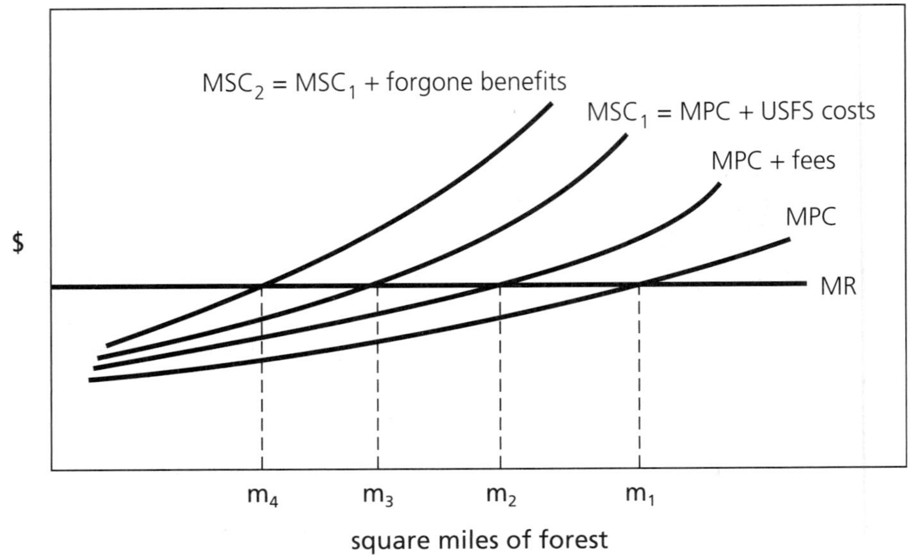

The optimal level will be m_3 if the social costs of harvesting consist of the sum of private costs and costs incurred by the USFS. If that occurs, then MSC_1 is the relevant marginal social cost curve, and the intersection with the marginal revenue (MR) curve occurs at m_3 in Figure 12.7. Several aspects of the marginal revenue curve are worthy of discussion. First, the curve is presented as horizontal, because any individual forest is small (and therefore its harvest will not have an effect on market price). Second, marginal revenue will be equal to marginal social benefit, unless the harvesting of the wood increased the benefits derived from other multiple uses. If this increase were to occur, then the marginal social benefit curve would be above the marginal revenue curve. For the purposes of this analysis, however, this situation will not be considered; it is a straightforward extension of the arguments being presented.

This market failure will be even more pronounced when the harvesting of the trees reduces benefits from other uses of the forest such as recreation, wildlife, wilderness, and watershed protection. If that were the case, then the relevant marginal social cost function will be MSC_2 and the optimal level of public forest to be leased for cutting will be m_4.

As just demonstrated, below-cost timber sales may lead to an inefficiently high level of forestland being timbered. A special case is when the optimal level of harvesting is zero, but the below-cost sales lead to positive levels of harvesting. This situation is illustrated in Figure 12.8. In Figure 12.8a, the marginal social harvesting cost function (MSC_1) lies entirely above the

Figure 12.8 **When the Optimal Area of Harvest Equals Zero**

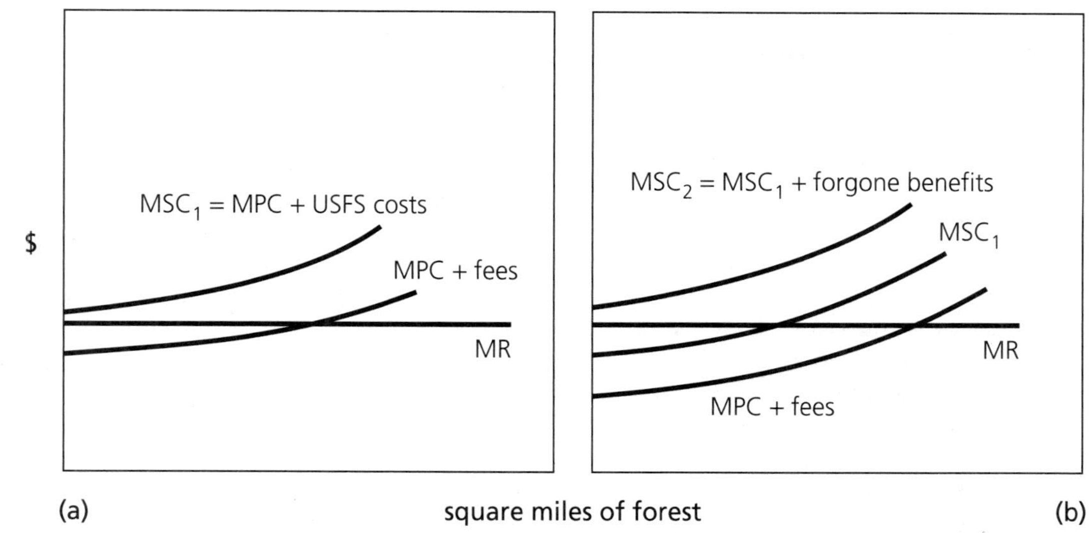

marginal revenue function. In Figure 12.8b, MSC_1 lies partially below the marginal revenue function, but if forgone benefits from other uses are considered, then the marginal social cost function (MSC_2 in this case) lies entirely above the marginal revenue function.

Note that there will also be a rent associated with the forest because the trees have value. Many people argue that the public sector should capture this rent by charging high enough fees for harvesting rights so that the harvesters only earn normal profits and do not capture any rent. They argue that because the forests are publicly owned, the public and not private firms should earn the rents associated with harvests. If this type of pricing was implemented, fees would be likely to increase substantially. Note, however, that this argument is an equity-based argument, centering on who should earn rents, not on how much forest should be cut. As long as property rights to the forests are adequately defined, the capture of the rents has no effect on the size of social benefits, only on who receives them. The preceding discussion of below-cost timber sales is an efficiency-oriented discussion, revealing the possibility of social losses as a result of pricing policy. The same arguments would apply to the leasing of grazing or mineral rights on public forestland.

Ancient Forests

At the beginning of the chapter, the question of the proper use of North American "old-growth" or "ancient" forests was raised and deferred until background information on forestry economics was developed. Old-growth or ancient forests are forests that have never been logged and therefore are in their original state. Old-growth forests are substantially different from forests that have been logged and replanted or logged and naturally reforested.

There are several reasons for the large differences between the ecosystems of old-growth and previously logged forests. These differences arise from the continuity of the ancient forests, the sheer size of the ancient trees (which may be 300 to 2000 years old, depending on the species), and the diversity of the age of the trees of old-growth forests (in comparison with previously logged forests, which tend to have trees of uniform age).

With the exception of central prairies, western deserts, and Alaskan tundra, the United States was once almost entirely forested. Virtually the entire area east of the Mississippi River was covered by forest. Although the amount of forestland is still large, the old-growth forests have dwindled to a small fraction of their original distribution. What is left is primarily in the temperate rain forests of the Pacific Northwest and Alaska and is shrinking rapidly due to clear-cutting of forests. The same situation prevails in Canada, where the pace of harvesting in British Columbia is alarmingly rapid. Europe is even in worse shape, with virtually no primary forest except some isolated mountain patches and larger areas in the Scandinavian countries.

The trees in the Pacific Northwest ancient forest are composed primarily of coniferous species, among which Douglas fir, coastal redwood, and sequoia are prominent. These trees will grow to hundreds of feet in height and 10 to 30 feet in diameter.

The huge old trees occasionally die, and their death shapes the ecosystem. Standing dead trees provide homes for many species of animals, but when they fall they provide their most significant services to the ecosystem.

When one of these huge trees falls, it knocks down everything in its path, creating a swath of sunlight that promotes the growth of plants on the forest floor. These plants provide food for a wide variety of animals. In contrast, in a previously logged forest, the trees tend to be of uniform age and height (especially if forests were artificially replanted), which allows little penetration of light to the forest floors. Because all the trees are roughly the same mass, falling trees tend to be supported by (or roll off of) their neighbors, rather than taking them down with them.

The fallen tree provides nutrients for new generations of trees. In fact, seeds of new trees germinate and become established in the rotting wood of the fallen trunk, and the new trees grow right out of the dead trunk. Because this trunk is elevated (by its own diameter) above the forest floor, the seedling trees do not face as vigorous competition from other plants as they would if they were growing on the forest floor.

In addition, fallen trees provide homes for voles, a mouselike species of mammal, which are critical to the old-growth ecosystem. Voles' primary food is a trufflelike fungus. In eating this fungus they ingest but do not digest another type of fungus, which they spread throughout the forest soil. This fungus attaches itself to the roots of coniferous trees and makes the soil nutrients more available to the trees, facilitating their tremendous growth and enabling them to deal more effectively with the summer dry season. (Although these forests receive a tremendous amount of rain over the year, summers tend to be very dry.)

The huge fallen trees provide a haven for voles during forest fires, because the trees are so large and moist that their interiors remain cool. The fires kill most of the floor plants and also the fungi that are in the top layers of soil. After the fire, the voles venture out of the logs and defecate, reestablishing this fungus in the soil. The large, ancient trees are protected from the fire by their thick bark, and the fire actually helps perpetuate the forest as the heat triggers (after some delay) the dropping of seeds from the cones of these trees onto a forest floor that has been cleared of competing plants by the fire.

Ecologically, these large forests are very different from logged and replanted forests.[4] One would think that the comparative advantage of ancient forests, particularly the spectacular coastal redwoods and sequoias, would be to leave them standing. The reason is that replanted forests are good substitutes for ancient forests as producers of timber but poor substitutes for ecosystems. The USFS continues to allow this harvesting (as do the corresponding state agencies on state forests and the provincial government of British Columbia), even subsidizing the process through road building and other management programs.

In the beginning of the chapter, it was mentioned that this controversy revolved around what is more important: spotted owls or timber-related jobs. The jobs issue is often used by the USFS and its advocates as a reason for subsidizing the harvesting of forests (Bowes and Krutilla, 1989). Because the forest is the only source of economic activity in many remote rural regions, many often believe that the forest must be harvested to provide jobs to support the region's population.

In actuality, this process involves a net loss for society as a whole, because it costs as much as $3 of government expenditure for every $1 timbering job wage that is created. In some cases, the timbering may eventually cost more jobs than it creates because of the ecological damages. For example, the cutting of the Tongass National Forest in southwestern Alaska may cost many salmon fishing-related jobs, because the soil erosion associated with clear-cutting makes the rivers inhospitable to salmon reproduction. In addition to these monetary costs, the subsidization of the harvest of old-growth forests lowers the market price of wood, adversely affecting employment in areas of the country where wood is primarily harvested from privately owned forests.

In addition to these direct monetary costs are the costs to society of the loss of the ancient forests. These costs are likely to be high, because the amount of ancient forests has shrunk so drastically in recent years. If there were abundant ancient forests, then the loss in value associated with cutting a particular ancient forest would be relatively small, because a great deal of forests would exist. This association is shown in Figure 12.9, where in the vicinity of x stands of ancient forests, the marginal willingness to pay to prevent the

[4]Not all types of forest are associated with such disparities between the ecological values associated with replanted forests and the ecological values associated with old-growth forests. A good example is the spruce and fir forests of northern Maine. These forests are primarily owned by the forest product industry and are often clear-cut. Areas that were clear-cut 60 years ago are now very similar in ecological and recreational values to the original forest.

Figure 12.9 **Loss in Value from Cutting Down a Stand of Ancient Forest**

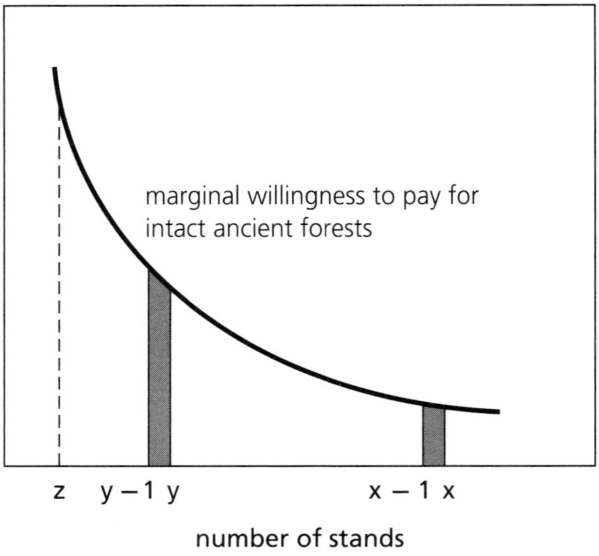

cutting of one stand is relatively low. As one moves along the demand curve to a point where ancient forests are less abundant, such as in the vicinity of y, the willingness to pay becomes much larger, however. Many forest advocates argue that the United States is currently to the left of a point like z, where the old-growth forests are so scarce that their value becomes asymptomatically large. Note that if replanted forests were good substitutes for ancient forests, the demand curve in Figure 12.9 would not have the very inelastic portion to the left of z. Instead, the intercept would be much lower, implying that the cost of cutting the last stand of ancient forests is low, because replanted forests would be good substitutes based on this assumption. It should be reiterated, however, that for many types of forests, replanted forests are not good substitutes from an ecological and recreational viewpoint, and the opportunity costs of cutting the remaining ancient forests are likely to be quite high.

Current policy toward old-growth forests is in a state of flux, with many new laws being introduced before Congress, the Endangered Species Act up for reauthorization, and many policy decisions actually being made in the federal courts. Of particular interest are policies toward roadless areas (should roads be built and harvesting allowed?) and fire suppression (see boxes 12.1 and 12.2).[5]

---

[5] For current information on the status of old-growth forests and forest policy in general, check the USFS web site (http://www.fs.fed.us). In addition, discussion of harvesting subsidies, roadless area policy, and fire suppression can be found at the National Environmental Library link to Congressional Research Service reports. Online: http://www.cnie.org/NLE/CRS.

Box 12.1 Measuring the Value of Spotted Owls

The bitter controversy over the use of ancient forests was conducted in the absence of any quantitative measures of the benefits of preservation until Jonathan Rubin, Gloria Helfand, and John Loomis (1991) conducted a study to measure the benefits of spotted owl preservation.

Rubin and his colleagues used a contingent valuation method (see Chapter 4) to measure people's willingness to pay to preserve the spotted owl. Their first step was to construct a survey that discussed the spotted owl, its habitat, and the competing (commercial) uses of its habitat. People were asked to select an amount (check-off values ranged from zero to $500) that they would be willing to pay to be completely sure that the spotted owl continued to exist in the future. This survey was conducted using randomly selected residents from the state of Washington (where a substantial amount of spotted owl habitat exists). The average willingness to pay was approximately $35.

The results were then extrapolated to the rest of the United States by using a formula from another study (Stoll and Johnson, 1984) that suggests that the willingness to pay for an environmental resource declines by about 10 percent for every 1000 miles distance between the resource and the residence.

Then, Rubin and his colleagues compared the preservation benefits that they calculated with the preservation costs (loss of timbering jobs and increase in the price of wood) that were estimated by the U.S. Department of Agriculture. They found that short-run preservation benefits are approximately $1.4881 billion, with short-run preservation costs equal to $1.335 billion. Long-run benefits are computed to equal $1.481 billion, compared with long-run costs of approximately $0.497 billion, for a net benefit of preservation of almost $1 billion. They suggest that this benefit represents such a large potential Pareto improvement that appropriate policy might be to compensate the people in the timber industry who lose from preservation.

Summary

Forests are a resource that provides many benefits to society. In addition to providing wood, they provide a habitat for wildlife, a reserve for biological diversity, sites for recreation, wilderness, watershed protection, and many other benefits.

If a forest is managed solely for the income to be derived from harvesting wood, which is how a profit-maximizing firm would manage forests that it owns, then the present value of the stream of harvests would be maximized. This maximization is accomplished when the trees are cut at an age at which the income gains to be derived from waiting an additional year before har-

Box 12.2 Fire Suppression and Forest Management

For more than 100 years, the U.S. Forest Service (and state agencies) have operated under the premise that all forest fires should be extinguished as quickly as possible. Fire suppression, as well as fire prevention, has been a central part of management policy. This perspective of forest fires as evil has been ingrained into American culture, with Smokey Bear's plaintive cry, "Remember, only you can prevent forest fires."

Forest fires in the western United States have been more frequent and more extensive recently, and have burned large tracts of forest and thousands of houses. In a natural ecosystem in the western United States, however, forest fires are actually good for the forests and are a natural and constructive force in the forest ecosystem. How can these two statements possibly be reconciled? The answer to this seeming paradox is that a century of fire suppression has drastically altered the nature of forest fires.

Forests in the West evolved in conjunction with periodic summer fires that are caused by lightning strikes, so the forest species adapted to fire. Some of this adaptation was already seen in the discussion of voles in the old-growth forests. Almost all western forests had adapted to fire in one fashion or another, however. In addition, Native Americans set fires to improve habitat for deer and other hunted species, so fire-tolerant species were further favored.

In general, small fires that burn the litter on the ground and understory plants do not burn the tall trees. In fact the cones from pine, fir, spruce and other coniferous trees open as a result of a fire's heat and release their seeds several weeks after. The fire has previously prepared the ground by eliminating competition from the plants on the forest floor, and the seeds of the trees have a head start over their potential competition. Because the fires are frequent, the amount of combustible material on the forest floor is limited, the fires are small, and large trees are not hurt by the fire.

Fire suppression has had many adverse affects on the forest, but the primary one is allowing the accumulation of large loads of combustible material on the forest floor, in terms of fallen limbs, plants, dead limbs low on the trunks of small trees, and many small trees. This large load of combustible material burns with much greater intensity than the fires in the time before fire suppression policy. Fires can reach into the crowns of the large trees, igniting them and creating a raging inferno that spreads from tree to tree with incredible speed, killing the mature forest. It is interesting to read accounts of the western forests from the early nineteenth century, such as those of explorers Meriwether Lewis and William Clark. In their journals they write of riding at full speed on horseback through western pine forests, a feat that would be impossible to accomplish today because of the increased density of small trees, understory plants, and fallen limbs and other forest floor litter. If the policy

(continues)

Box 12.2 (continued)

of fire suppression is not abandoned, with an eventual return to a more natural regime, then forest fires will continue to develop into massive conflagrations.

Returning to a policy that allows fires to burn and exert their influence on the forest ecosystem is both difficult and controversial. It is difficult because the current load of combustible material makes fires so much more intense than those in forests that have not experienced fire suppression policies. It is controversial because people have built houses in the forest, and even a low-intensity natural fire can threaten to burn houses in its path.

Reducing the load of combustible materials is a difficult task. Prescribed (intentional) low-level burns have been tried in an effort to reduce the stock of combustible material on the forest floor, but this practice has met with mixed success. Some of these fires have expanded beyond the original intent and have turned into some of the biggest wildfires in recent years, such as the 2000 fire that entered into the Los Alamos (nuclear) Research Laboratory. Other possibilities are to remove the fallen material on the forest floor and to thin the forest by selective harvesting of trees. When harvesting, care must be taken to remove the slash (limbs) of trees, because the slash is often a large part of the combustible load in many forests that are harvested. Selective harvesting is controversial; many environmentalists view it as an unwanted anthropogenic disturbance and believe that if some logging is allowed for these purposes, it will soon expand to more general and destructive logging. Environmentalists charge that the plans for thinning focus on large economically valuable trees rather than on smaller trees and brush that create the fire hazard. A program to remove the load of combustibles in western U.S. forests could improve the employment situation for people in the forest industry, providing jobs that do not destroy the old-growth forests and that improve the quality of forests in general.

The policy conflict is likely to persist because its origins are in two important conflicts involving benefits. First, there is a disparity between private and social benefits, because the fire suppression policy protects the private homes located in the area and the timber value of standing timber but fundamentally changes the forest. Although fire suppression provides protection in the short run, the accumulation of combustible materials implies greater intensity and more destructive fires in the future. Both the fire suppression policy and the more intense fires lead to a loss of ecological services in the future.

vest are exactly offset by the income losses generated by waiting. This time period is called the optimal rotation.

Public forests should be managed with more than profit maximizing in mind, because the Multiple Use Sustainable Yield Act of 1960 requires all the benefits of forests to be recognized in developing management strategies.

Although the USFS is genuinely concerned about promoting nonharvest benefits, many critics of USFS policy argue that there still exist some biases toward harvesting and away from activities associated with leaving forest stands intact. In particular, below-cost timber sales and subsidized road building are criticized as leading to overharvesting of the nation's public forests. This criticism may be particularly true for ancient forests for which previously logged and replanted forests are not a good substitute.

appendix 12.a
An Intuitive Approach to the Optimal Rotation

The determination of the optimal rotation (how long to let a forest grow before harvesting and replanting) is a type of economic problem known as a dynamic optimization problem. This class of problem examines a decision in which there are both costs and benefits of waiting to act, and then determines when the action should be taken.

The classic textbook example of this type of problem is when a person owns a bottle of investment wine (wine purchased to be resold, not purchased to be consumed). The older the bottle of wine, the higher the price for which it can be sold. Once the sale is made, however, the owner can put the money in the bank and earn interest (or otherwise invest the money). The solution to this problem is quite easy at the conceptual level, although the mathematical modeling can often be quite complex. The solution is that as long as the benefits of waiting another unit of time (higher sale price) are greater than the costs of waiting another unit of time (forgone interest income), the person should continue to wait and not sell. On the other hand, if the benefits of waiting are less than the costs, then the person has waited too long. The exact moment at which the person should sell the bottle of wine is when the benefits of waiting a unit of time are exactly equal to the costs, thereby maximizing the present value of his or her net income from selling the wine.

The exact same thing is true of the forest, except instead of waiting to sell a bottle of wine that is just sitting in the wine cellar, the forest owner is allowing the forest to grow until the point in time that the present value of net income will be maximized. The benefits of waiting another unit of time is that the trees in the forest grow bigger and there is more wood that can be sold. The costs of waiting another unit of time are the interest income that could be earned on the revenue gained by selling the wood and the rental value of the land if, instead of growing trees, the land was rented to someone else (of course, the person renting it could also grow trees). Note that in these examples, the price of wood is assumed to be constant over time. In the real world, the price could either go up or down as a result of the interplay between demand and supply.

Some insight into this decision can be gained by looking at the function in Figure 12.2a, which shows the total volume of wood as a function of the age of the forest. Note that between the ages of 0 and 30 years, the growth is slow but the volume of wood is also small, so there is not much point in selling. Between 40 and 60 years (more or less), the growth is very rapid and the volume of wood increases dramatically. After 70 years, growth begins to slow. As growth slows, the benefits of waiting become smaller in relation to the interest and rental income that could be earned. For many hardwood species (oak, maple, cherry), the optimal rotation is between 70 and 100 years. For softwood species (such as pine), the optimal rotation is much shorter, often between 30 and 60 years. If the softwood tree is being used for paper pulp, the optimal rotation is on the shorter side, because the diameter of the trunk is irrelevant to the production of paper.

Review Questions

1. Discuss the framework for maximizing the stream of income arising from timberland. What are the conditions that define the optimal rotation? What economic and biological factors influence these conditions?
2. Discuss the concept of multiple use/sustained yield management. What benefits should be considered when pursuing this type of management? How should these benefits be compared?
3. How does the inclusion of nonharvested benefits affect the optimal rotation?
4. Draw a growth function for a typical stand of trees. What factors determine its characteristic shape?
5. Use the data in Table 12.1 to calculate the optimal rotation of this hypothetical forest stand (to the nearest 10 years). Assume that the price of wood is $1.00 per cubic foot; that all harvesting, planting, and maintenance costs are equal to zero; and that the interest rate is 5 percent.
6. What are the implications of the theory of comparative advantage for forest management?

Questions for Further Study

1. Discuss the jobs/environment trade-off in managing old-growth forests. How would you resolve this issue? (Make sure to consider both efficiency and equity considerations.)
2. Should forest fires be prevented? Why or why not?
3. What does the principle of comparative advantage imply for the multiple use/sustained yield management of forests?
4. How would you measure the use and indirect use benefits associated with old-growth forests?
5. How would the following events affect the length of the optimal rotation of a forest?
   a. higher price of wood
   b. increased probability of fire or disease
   c. higher interest rates
   d. lower transportation costs
6. What ecological services are provided by the forest? How is each service affected by the length of the rotation?

Suggested Paper Topics

1. Use data from the most recent issue of *World Resources*, *FAO Yearbooks*, or the U.S. Department of Agriculture sources listed in the references and socioeconomic data from the *U.S. Statistical Abstract* or *Economic Report of the President* to estimate a demand curve for timber. Use forecasts of future economic growth in the United States and the rest of the world to forecast the future demand for timber.

2. Discuss the open-access externalities associated with rangeland and past and present federal policy to mitigate these externalities. Do you think that past policy was efficient? Do you think that present policy is efficient? How would you modify policy to maximize the social benefits of rangeland?
3. Examine the writings of an American conservationist such as John Muir. How do the values expressed in his writing correspond to concepts of value discussed in Chapter 4 of this book? What are the economic implications of the management concepts he discusses?
4. Compare the writings of John Muir and Gifford Pinchot. How do differences in their philosophies imply differences in emphasis on the benefits of alternative uses of the forests? How do their theories correspond to different philosophies that are articulated today?
5. Discuss the implications of acid precipitation for forest health. Are the damages associated with acid precipitation likely to be significant? How should these implications affect the development of air pollution and forest policy?
6. How has U.S. policy toward federal forests evolved over time? In what directions do you think it should move in the future? Why?
7. Discuss the relative positions of the Clinton and G. W. Bush administrations on preservation of roadless areas in U.S. national forests. What do these positions imply about which type of benefits are seen to be most important? See the reports of the Congressional Research Service (http://www.cnie.org/NLE/CRS) to get you started in the right direction.
8. Siberia contains the largest area of primary temperate forest in the world. How can what we have learned in the United States and Canada benefit the sustainable development (and preservation) of Siberian forests?

Works Cited and Selected Readings

Ballart, X., and C. Riba. Forest Fires: Evaluation of Government Measures. *Policy Sciences 35*, no.4 (2002): 361–377.

Bowes, M. D., and J. V. Krutilla. *Multiple Use Management: The Economics of Public Forest Land*. Washington, DC: Resources for the Future, 1989.

Brown, G., and C. C. Harris. The United States Forest Service: Changing of the Guard. *Natural Resources Journal 32*, no. 3 (Summer 1992): 449–466.

Clawson, M. *Forests for Whom and for What?* Washington, DC: Resources for the Future, 1975.

Daniels, T. Purchasing Development Rights to Protect Farmland, Forests, and Open Space. Pages 123–141 in *Property Rights, Economics, and the Environment*, edited by M. D. Kaplowitz. Stamford, CT: JAI Press, 2000.

Ellefson, P. V. *Forest Resource Economics and Policy Research: Strategic Directions of the Future*. Boulder, CO: Westview Press, 1989.

Faustmann, M. On the Determination of the Value Which Forest Land and Immature Stands Poses for Forestry. Pages 27–55 in *Martin Faustmann and the Evolution of Discounted Cash Flow*, edited by M. Gane. Institute Paper No. 42, Commonwealth Forestry Institute, University of Oxford, 1968. Reprinted from and originally published in German in *Allegemeine Forest und Jagd Zeitung*, vol. 25, 1849.

Gaffney, M. Concepts of Financial Maturity of Timber and Other Assets. *Agricultural Economics Information*, series 62. North Carolina State College, Raleigh, September 1957.

Harrison, S., J. Bennett, and C. Tisdell. The Role of Non-market Valuation in Forest Management and Recreation Policy. *Economic Analysis and Policy 32*, no. 2 (2002): 1–10.

Howe, C. *Natural Resource Economics*. New York: Wiley, 1979.

Nelson, R. H. Rethinking Scientific Management Resources for the Future Discussion Paper 99/07. Washington, DC: Resources for the Future. 1998.

Nelson, R. H. *Burning Issue: A Case for Abolishing the U.S. Forest Service*. Political Economy Forum series. Lanham, MD., and Oxford, UK: Rowman and Littlefield, 2000.

Organization for Economic Cooperation and Development (OECD). *Market and Government Failures in Environmental Management: Wetlands and Forests*. Paris: OECD, 1992.

Pearse, P. H. The Optimum Forest Rotation. *Forestry Chronicle 43* (1967): 2.

Plantinga, A. J., and J. Wu. Co-benefits from Carbon Sequestration in Forests: Evaluating

Reductions in Agricultural Externalities from an Afforestation Policy in Wisconsin. *Land Economics 79*, no. 1 (2003): 74–85.

Putz, F. E., Economics of Home Grown Forestry. *Ecological Economics 32*, no. 1 (2000): 9–14.

Rubin, J., G. Helfand, and J. Loomis. A Benefit-Cost Analysis of the Northern Spotted Owl. *Journal of Forestry Research 89* (1991): 25–30.

Sahajananthan, S., D. Haley, and J. Nelson. Planning for Sustainable Forests in British Columbia through Land Use Zoning. *Canadian Public Policy 24*, (1998): S73–S81.

Sedjo, R. *Government Interventions, Social Needs, and the Management of U.S. Forests*. Washington, DC: Resources for the Future, 1983.

Sedjo, R., Biodiversity: Forests, Property Rights, and Economic Value. Pages 106–122 in *Conserving Nature's Diversity: Insights from Biology, Ethics, and Economics*, edited by G. van Kooten et al. Aldershot, UK, Burlington, VT, and Sydney: Ashgate, 2000.

Stoll, J., and L. A. Johnson. Concepts of Value, Nonmarket Valuation, and the Case of the Whooping Crane. *Transactions of 49th North American Wildlife and Natural Resources Conference*. Washington, DC: Wildlife Management Institute, 1984.

U.S. Department of Agriculture, Forest Service. *An Analysis of the Timber Situation in the United States, 1952–2030*. Forest Report No. 23. Washington, DC: U.S. Government Printing Office, 1982.

U.S. Department of Agriculture, Forest Service. *An Assessment of the Forest and Range Land Situation in the United States.* FS-345, Washington, DC: U.S. Government Printing Office, 1980.

chapter 13

Tropical Forests

The unsolved mysteries of the rain forest are formless and seductive. They are like unnamed islands hidden in the blank spaces of old maps, like dark shapes glimpsed descending the far wall of a reef into the abyss. They draw us forward and stir strange apprehensions. The unknown and the prodigious are drugs to the scientific imagination, stirring insatiable hunger with a single taste. In our hearts, we hope we will never discover everything. We pray there will always be a world like this one at whose edge we sat in darkness. The rain forest in its richness is one of the last repositories on earth of that timeless dream.

Edward O. Wilson, The Diversity of Life

Introduction

Tropical deforestation is an area of environmental degradation that has captured media attention and is perceived as a metaphor for and indicator of the decline of the biosphere. Although tropical deforestation is not a new phenomenon (it has been taking place for hundreds of years), the pace of deforestation has accelerated, particularly since the late 1970s. This acceleration has raised global concern because the rain forests are important ecological resources, providing both regional and global ecological, social, and economic benefits.

What is the future for the tropical rain forests? Will they continue to disappear, following the paths of the old-growth forests in Europe and North America? In those places, with a few notable exceptions in the far north, old-growth forests have disappeared, replaced by farmland, urban areas, second-growth forests, and forest plantations. How should we proceed with policy to protect the tropical forests? How can the competing needs of economic development and preservation be balanced? This chapter examines the economic and ecological relationships that shape the answers to these questions.

Definition of a Tropical Forest

Tropical forests are defined by the Food and Agricultural Organization as areas located between the Tropic of Capricorn and the Tropic of Cancer, and where at least 10 percent of the area is covered by woody vegetation. Although one tends to think of rain forests when one thinks of tropical forests (in rain forests, virtually all the area is covered by the canopies of trees), there are also tropical dry forest areas where there is a mixture of grassland and forests. Many of these dry forest areas are semiarid, whereas tropical rain forests will receive over 100 inches of rain per year, with the wettest areas receiving well over three times that amount of rainfall. Figures 13.1 and

Figure 13.1 **Distribution of Tropical Forests**

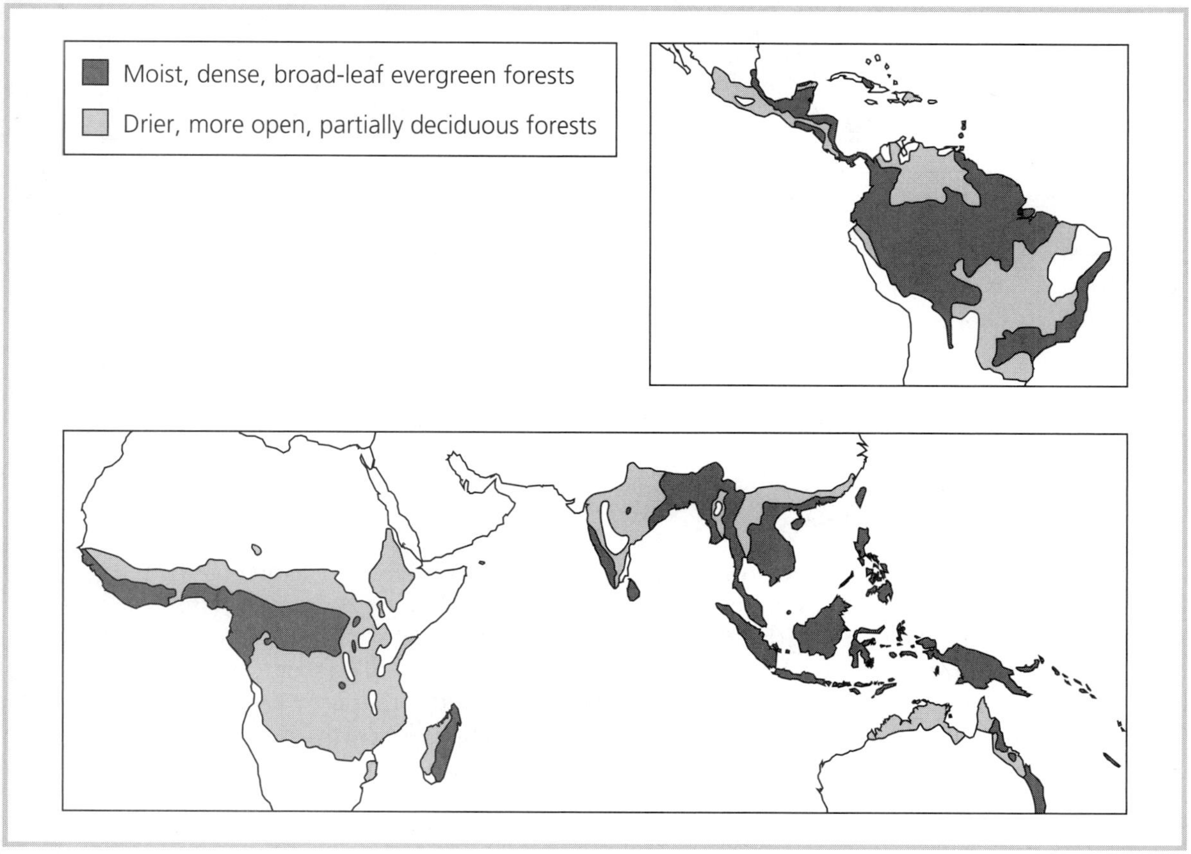

Source: Food and Agricultural Organization, 1987, pp. 2–3.

Figure 13.2 **Extent of Tropical Forests (in millions of hectares)**

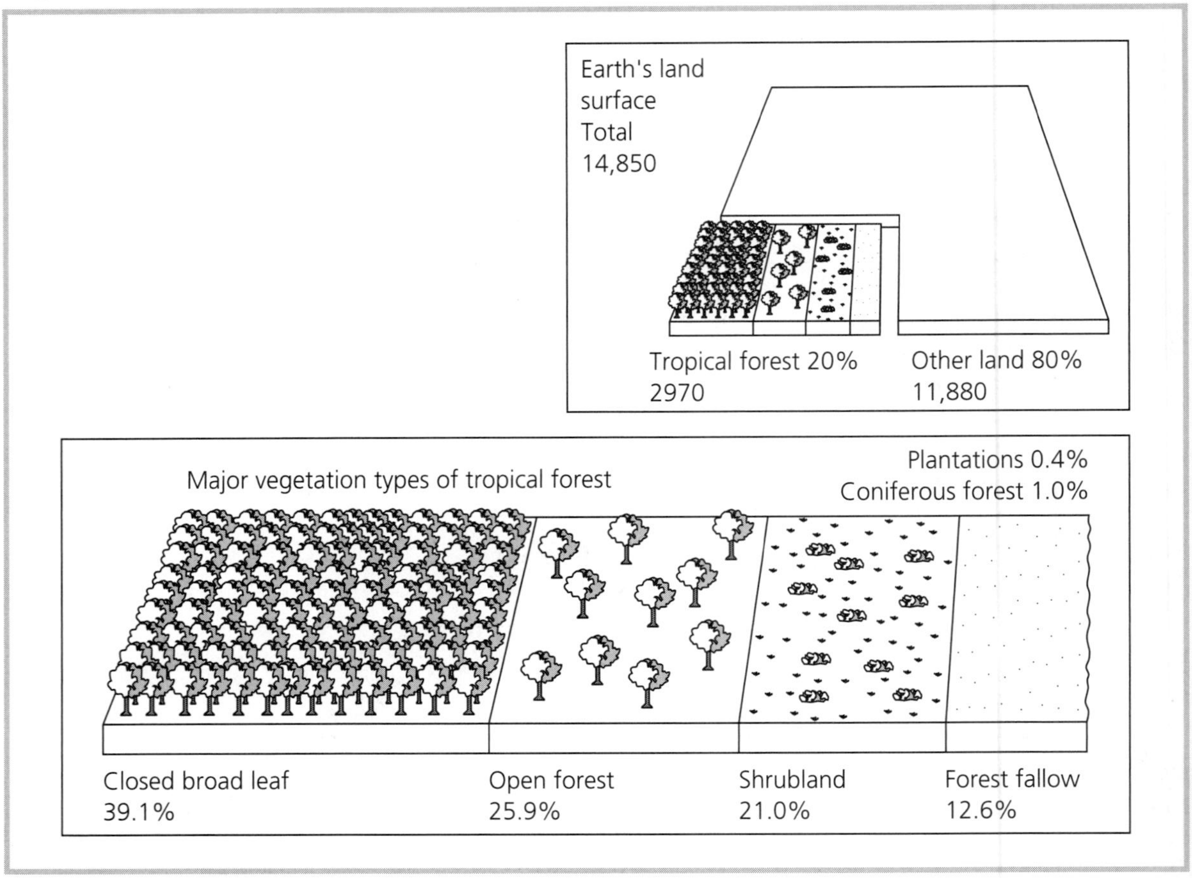

Source: Food and Agricultural Organization, 1987, pp. 2–3.

13.2 show the distribution of tropical wet and dry forests and the share of the earth's surface that they occupy.

Tropical Rain Forests

Tropical rain forests tend to be dominated by broad-leaved evergreens with completely interlocking canopies. In many rain forests, there are actually multiple canopies, with some giant trees rising above the first canopy. The trees that rise above the primary canopy are frequently called emergent trees. In many areas, these trees support the growth of vines that grow up the trees to try to reach the sunlight above the canopy. Epiphytes (such as orchids and bromeliads) take seed in dead organic matter (detritus) that has accumulated on the limbs of trees.

There is a constant struggle in the tropical rain forest for access to sunlight and nutrients. Below the canopy, there is an understory of shrublike plants and a series of nonwoody plants that occupy the forest floor. Typically, these understory and floor plants have less stringent requirements for sunlight. Many of the understory plants are stunted versions of the dominant trees that will experience accelerated growth when the death of giant trees allows light to penetrate to the forest floor. Figure 13.3 contains a line drawing of a cross section of the typical forest.

Little sunlight penetrates to the rain forest floor, generating an environment where most of the animal species are arboreal, because it is the leaves in the canopy that form the basis for the food web. These animals, which include a multitude of insects, spiders, scorpions, birds, lizards, snakes, frogs, and mammals, live in the trees and seldom venture to the forest floor. The arboreal environment provides an ecosystem that is extremely rich in species diversity, with up to 95 percent of the world's plant and animal species found in rain forest habitat (Perry, 1990). According to Perry, as many as 10 to 30 million yet to be discovered species live in the rain forest (science has currently identified a total of about 2 million species in the entire world). It can easily be seen that tropical rain forests support many times the number of species as temperate forests, with the differential measured in terms of many orders of magnitude. Rain forest rivers are correspondingly more diverse than

Figure 13.3 **The Multiple Layers of the Tropical Rain Forest**

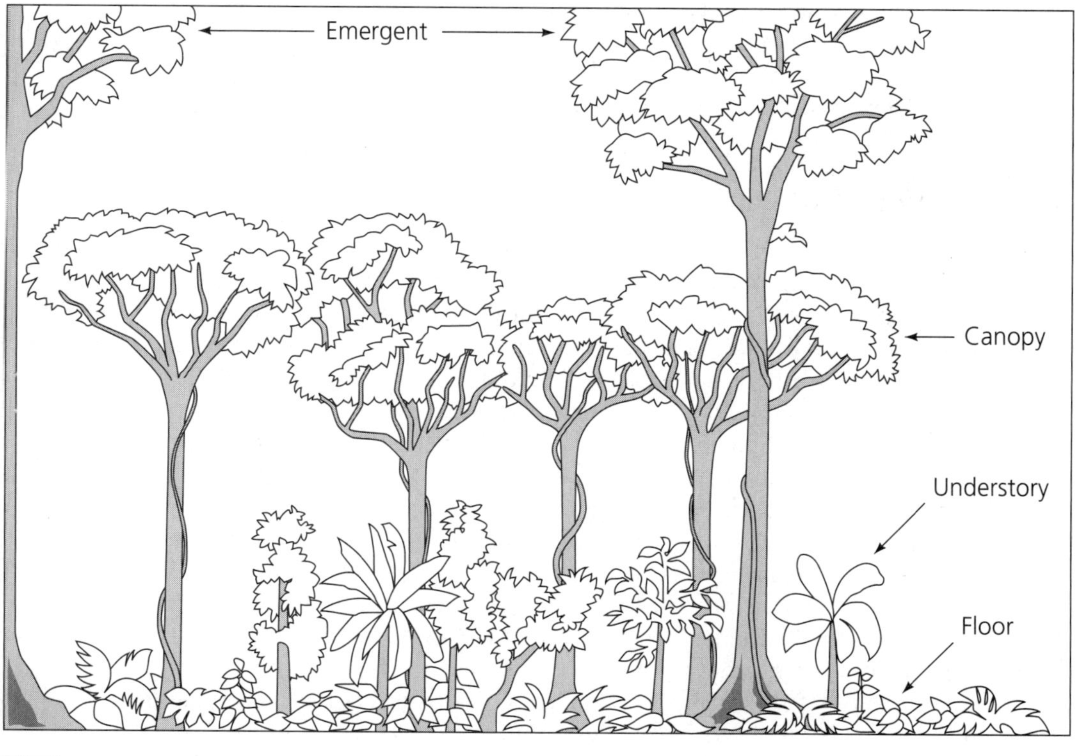

their temperate counterparts. (See Chapter 14 for more discussion of the importance of biodiversity.)

Tropical rain forests have a very different nutrient cycle in comparison with temperate forests. In temperate forests, the nutrients are stored in the soil. In contrast, the soil of the rain forest is relatively barren of organic matter because it decays so rapidly in the hot, moist environment of the rain forest. Consequently, the tropical soils are mostly mineral soils with little organic matter. This lack of organic matter within the soil does not mean the nutrients are lost, however; the top layer of soil contains a dense lattice of the roots of the trees, vines, and other forest vegetation that immediately absorb the nutrients as they percolate through the soil and become available to the roots. Thus, rather than being stored in the soil, the nutrients are stored in the biomass of the plants, particularly in the immense trees that can approach 200 feet in height, or more.

Tropical Dry Forests

In contrast, the tropical dry forest has decidedly less rainfall than the wet forest and, consequently, less biomass per hectare, less coverage by trees, and a greater ratio of nutrients in the soil versus nutrients in the biomass (although still a lower ratio than temperate forests). Animal life in the dry forest tends to be more terrestrial (and less arboreal) than in a wet forest, because the grass that covers the areas under the trees and between the trees also forms a significant basis for the food web. That is not to say that the leaves of the trees are unimportant, but that the grass is also important. The sparser the tree coverage, the greater the relative importance of the grass.

Benefits of Tropical Forests

The primary importance of tropical forests is as a source of ecological services, including the maintenance of hydrological cycles, sequestration of carbon, nutrient cycles, and the provision of habitat for a variety of species, including humans. An additional important benefit of tropical forests is that they provide a variety of goods that may be extracted from the rain forest, including wood and wood products to be used in construction, furniture, or the manufacture of paper and wood products such as plywood and hardboard. Many valuable tree species are native to the rain forests, including mahogany, zebrawood, rosewood, padauk, bubinga, cocobolo, and teak. In addition, tropical forests, particularly tropical dry forests, are harvested for fuelwood, which is the only source of energy for the majority of people who inhabit the tropics. It should be stressed that although extraction is important, it is not the major social benefit of tropical forests. Rather, that role lies in the ecological services that the forests can provide.

For example, one of the most important of these ecological services is the maintenance of hydrological cycles, providing storage, purification, and recycling mechanisms for the water contained in these systems. The canopies, understories, and floor plants of rain-forested areas soften the impact of the torrential rainfall and prevent it from eroding the mineral soils and generating runoff that would carry away the nutrients before they reached the roots. This protection is important even in tropical dry forests, where the annual rainfall may be low, but is often concentrated in a rainy season with torrential downpours. The lessening of the force of the rain allows it to percolate through the soil (rather than running off), where it can be absorbed by the roots of plants. What is not absorbed by the plants slowly makes its way through the soil to the rivers and streams. Because this movement is slow, it does not carry much soil into the streams and rivers. The water that is taken up by the plants is released through the leaves into the atmosphere. In large rain forests, such as the Amazon, the water that is transpired by the forest actually falls back on the forest. In other words, large rain forests affect the regional climate, including creation of their own rainfall.

Deforestation may lead to important soil erosion problems. Dams and hydroelectric facilities located downstream of deforested areas often have problems with siltation from erosion of soil. The siltation will partially or completely fill the reservoir. It also causes problems in bays, lagoons, and river mouths, where aquatic life is diminished as a result. In regions where fisheries are an important source of food and income, this impact on fisheries can have catastrophic effects on local communities.

Although tropical dry forests experience less rainfall, the role of forest vegetation is equally important to the hydrological cycle. Without the trees, shrubs, and grasses, the rainfall would roll off the ground and less would be absorbed. As a consequence, many rivers that have water throughout the year would shrink or disappear during the dry season. As discussed in the following section on deforestation, the removal of the trees very often causes semiarid dry forests to turn into desert.

Tropical forests also provide a habitat for many different life-forms. As mentioned previously, most of the species on earth reside in the rain forest. What is not often realized is that this reservoir of life-forms offers the key to treating many human medical problems. More than 25 percent of the new medicines originate in a tropical rain forest life-form. Although many argue that potential medical advances are the primary benefit of maintaining species diversity, others stress that the existence of the diversity and the plants and animals themselves are important benefits of the forest.

Although there is a much smaller number of species in tropical dry forest areas, these areas also represent an important plant and animal habitat. In particular, some of our largest (and most endangered) mammals live in tropical dry forest habitats. In addition to the animals and plants, the forest represents an eco/agro system that supports populations of indigenous peoples. The forests provide fruits, edible plants, animals, and materials for construction of dwellings, clothing, and other objects. Indigenous groups of people have developed agricultural systems that are compatible with the forest ecosystems (see Box 13.1). In addition to providing food for domestic use, the rain forest provides many outputs that can be exported, including coffee, fruit, nuts, honey, cocoa, and rubber.

Box 13.1 Agricultural Systems of Indigenous Amazonians

In a 1990 *New York Times* article, William K. Stevens reports the work of several anthropologists who found that the ancient inhabitants of the Amazonian rain forest and their present-day descendants have developed a system of agriculture that actually shaped the character of the rain forest so that it was capable of supporting a sophisticated civilization. This civilization, which may have lasted for several thousand years, consisted of a system of agricultural villages and chiefdoms that may have numbered into the millions of people. Some of the settlements are thought to have been inhabited by as many as 4000 people.

Stevens reports that Dr. Darrell Posey, who studied the Kayopo tribe, found that one important technique was to clear small, circular fields by felling large trees so that they fall outward from the center of the circle, which also knocks down the smaller trees. The leaves from the fallen trees provide nutrients for the most nutrient-demanding plants, which are planted along the perimeter of the circle. Tuber crops, such as yams, sweet potatoes, and manioc, are planted between the fallen trees. The tree trunks are then burned under carefully controlled conditions just before the first rains of the rainy season. The roots of the tuber plants keep the soil from washing away. The ashes from the trunks provide nutrients for the crops. Additional crops, including corn, beans, rice, pineapples, papaya, mangoes, and bananas, are planted. The shorter crops and tubers tend to be planted in the inner zones of the circle, and the taller crops, including fruit trees, tend to be planted in the outer zones of the circle. Eventually, the jungle encroaches on the circle and gradually moves toward the center. The encroachment of the jungle brings other species of fruit trees, which are harvested, as well as medicinal herbs. It takes about 12 years for the jungle to completely reclaim the patch of land.

Notice that this type of agriculture does not result in the permanent destruction of the forest, nor the destruction of the soil, as do some conventional agricultural techniques. Different villages traded food crops and tree species. This trade in plants may be partially responsible for the diversity of species in the rain forest.

Finally, tropical forests, particularly tropical rain forests, play an important role in maintaining the atmosphere's chemistry. The massive amount of plant material in the rain forest is roughly half carbon by weight. This carbon is derived from atmospheric carbon dioxide through photosynthesis. This process also results in oxygen being released into the atmosphere. Thus, as the rain forests shrink through deforestation, atmospheric carbon dioxide will increase. This increase in atmospheric carbon dioxide will exacerbate global warming (see Chapter 7). Also, the rain forest is the largest terrestrial source of oxygen.

One of the most remarkable aspects of the rain forest is that it is both remarkably robust and incredibly fragile. Although that statement may seem paradoxical, it is not, because the forest recovers rather quickly from small-scale disturbances, whereas it may take many decades (if not centuries) for it to recover from large-scale disturbances.

Natural disturbances occur when an emergent tree falls (see Figure 13.2), taking other trees with it, creating a disturbance from which the forest recovers quickly. There are several reasons why recovery is rapid. First, the nutrient cycle is uninterrupted because roots from the adjacent undisturbed area underlie the disturbed area. Leaves and other organic matter fall into the disturbed area, providing nutrients for plants that may be taking seed there. The small scale of the disturbance and shade from the neighboring trees protect the soil from baking in the tropical sun and from erosion by wind and rain.

Another important aspect of the scale of the disturbance is that small-scale disturbances do not drive pollinators and seed dispersers from the area. Therefore, trees and other vegetation can move back into the disturbed areas rapidly.

In contrast, with the exception of indigenous activities (see Box 13.1) human-generated disturbances tend to be larger than natural disturbances. Because they remove the vegetation from large areas, human-generated disturbances completely interrupt the nutrient cycle and seed dispersers and pollinators flee the areas. Because the area does not rapidly regenerate, it is subject to erosion, compaction, and baking. Very often, these deforested areas resemble lunar landscapes or a *Mad Max* movie set because they are so badly degraded. Because the natural mechanisms that allow recovery have been removed by the large size of the disturbance, recovery may never occur, or occur very slowly over many generations.

Deforestation

As seen in the previous discussion, tropical forests have public good benefits that can be threatened by economic activities that generate large-scale disturbances. These public good benefits accrue to people in both the country that contains the forest and all the other countries of the world, potentially leading to a two-tiered market failure problem. First, because there are public good benefits, private owners or open-access users of forests may cut them down at a rate that exceeds the rate that is socially optimal from the point of view of the country or region that contains the forest. Second, if the country seeks to develop policy to deal with this type of market failure, then it has no incentive to consider preservation benefits to the citizens of the rest of the world. In other words, even if countries choose internally efficient policies to address market failure, they may not be globally efficient. Of course, many observers of the situation would say that policies are not efficient even from a domestic perspective. A variety of market failures such as poorly defined or enforced property rights, imperfect information, and inappropriate government interventions may lead to these inefficiently high rates of deforestation.

Deforestation Estimates

Although there is considerable controversy concerning the amount of deforestation of tropical forests that is taking place, there is a consensus among those examining the problem that deforestation is occurring at a rapid pace. The most comprehensive source of data concerning the rate of deforestation for the period before 1990 is FAO (1993). The FAO data are summarized by Brown and Pearce (1994) and are listed in Table 13.1. As can be seen in this table, the annual rate of change in forested area over the period 1981–1990

Table 13.1 Estimates of Forest Cover Area and Deforestation by Geographic Subregions

Geographic regions and subregions	Number of countries surveyed	Total land area (10^6 ha)	Forest area (10^6 ha) 1980	Forest area (10^6 ha) 1990	Annually Deforested Area (10^6 ha)	Rate of change 1981–1990 (% per annum)
Africa	**40**	**2236.1**	**586.6**	**527.6**	**4.1**	**–0.7**
West Sahelian Africa	9	528.0	43.7	40.8	0.3	–0.7
East Sahelian Africa	6	489.7	71.4	65.3	0.6	–0.8
West Africa	8	203.8	61.5	55.6	0.6	–0.8
Central Africa	6	398.3	215.5	204.1	1.1	–0.5
Tropical Southern Africa	10	558.1	159.3	145.9	1.3	–0.8
Insular Africa	1	58.2	17.1	15.8	0.1	–0.8
Asia	**17**	**892.1**	**349.6**	**310.6**	**3.9**	**–1.1**
South Asia	6	412.2	69.4	63.9	0.6	–0.8
Continental Southeast Asia	5	190.2	88.4	75.2	1.3	–1.5
Insular Southeast Asia	5	244.4	154.7	135.4	1.9	–1.2
Pacific Islands	1	45.3	37.1	36.0	0.1	–0.3
Latin America	**33**	**1650.1**	**992.2**	**918.1**	**7.4**	**–0.7**
Central America/Mexico	7	239.6	79.2	68.1	1.1	–1.4
Caribbean	19	69.0	48.3	47.1	0.1	–0.3
Tropical South America	7	1341.6	864.6	802.9	6.2	–0.7
Total Tropics	**90**	**4778.3**	**1910.4**	**1756.3**	**15.4**	**–0.8**

Source: Food and Agriculture Organization of the United Nations. *Forest Resource Assessment 1990: Tropical Countries. Plan*, FAO Forestry Paper 112. Rome: FAO, 1993.

HA = hectares. 100 hectares equals 1 square kilometer or 0.386 square mile.

averaged a little less than 1 percent per year (0.8 percent), with the highest rate of deforestation in Asia and Central America/Mexico and the greatest amount of deforestation taking place in tropical South America. The average amount of deforestation taking place in the tropics is 15.4 million hectares per year, or approximately 59,444 square miles per year. This annual amount of deforestation is a little larger than the area of Florida or the United Kingdom.

These estimates were based largely on self-reported data from the countries that contained the data (with some satellite verification). Data for more recent years are based almost exclusively on satellite imagery. Although imagery can be interpreted in various ways, it is more reliable than the data in Table 13.1, which is largely self-reported data. Table 13.2 contains the more recent data that is based on satellite imagery. Although the data in this table are not reported in a way that is completely symmetric to Table 13.1, it is notable that despite global concerns, deforestation remained a significant and sometimes growing problem in the 1990s. Although deforestation rates of 0.2 percent or 0.4 percent may seem relatively small and innocuous, they actually can be insidious, because the forest loss associated with these seemingly slow rates accumulates quite rapidly. Such accumulation is demonstrated in Table 13.3, which shows cumulative forest loss at different deforestation rates. Even at the relatively slow rate of 0.2 percent, only 82 percent of today's forests would remain after 100 years. For a deforestation rate of 0.4 percent, the corresponding figure is 70 percent, and for 1.0 percent, it is 36 percent. Of course, any rate would be on top of the deforestation that had occurred up to the present time. In places such as the west coast of Africa, many Caribbean islands, and some Central American countries, most of the forest has already been lost.

Table 13.2 Forested Area and Deforestation Rates during the 1990s

Region	Land area in 2000 (1000s HA)	Forested area in 2000 (1000s HA)	Percentage of land area in forest in 2000	Forest change 1990–2000 (1000s HA)	Annual rate of change 1990–2000
Africa	2,987,394	649,866	21.8	–5262	–0.8%
Asia	3,084,746	547,793	17.8	–364	–0.1%
North and Central America	2,136,966	549,304	25.7	–570	–0.1%
Oceania	549,096	197,623	23.3	–385	–0.2
South America	1,175,741	885,618	50.5	–3711	–0.4

Deforestation rates for selected countries (1990–2000)

Venezuela –0.4 Columbia –0.4 Brazil –0.4 Cote D'Ivoire –3.1 Tanzania –3.4 Indonesia –1.2

Source: FAO 2004 data compiled by Mongabay Rainforest web site: http://www.mongabay.com/defor_index.htm.

Table 13.3 **Remaining Amount of Forest at Selected Deforestation Rates over Different Time Periods**

	Deforestation Rates			
	0.2%	**0.4%**	**1%**	**2%**
20 years	98%	92%	82%	67%
40 years	96%	85%	67%	45%
60 years	92%	79%	55%	30%
80 years	85%	73%	45%	20%
100 years	82%	70%	36%	13%

Activities That Lead to Deforestation

The three activities that are primarily responsible for tropical deforestation are cutting trees for timber, cutting trees for fuelwood, and conversion of land to cropland or rangeland. All three activities are important in all regions of the tropics. In addition, mining and urbanization are sources of deforestation, but not to the same extent as the other three activities.

A very important caveat is that although activities such as timbering, agriculture, and fuelwood production have led to global problems with deforestation, these activities do not have to generate the massive levels of deforestation seen in the past. In fact, it is possible to engage in these activities in a way that mimics natural disturbances so that the forest eliminates the disturbances quickly, the forest recovers quickly, and the flow of ecological services is never interrupted. In the following sections, timbering, agriculture, and fuelwood are examined, market failures that cause them to generate excessive deforestation are looked at, methods for sustainable production are discussed, and policies to create incentives for better methods are analyzed.

Timbering Activity

Timbering is a major source of deforestation. Although sustainable forestry is feasible, much of the harvesting activity results in severe deforestation.

Sustainable Harvesting. The most important relationship to understand concerning timbering activity and deforestation is that timbering activity does not have to lead to deforestation. Even though harvesting disturbs the forest, it is possible to engage in harvesting activity in which the disturbances caused by harvesting are similar to natural disturbances. Two basic methods are possible: the strip method of harvesting and the selective method of harvesting.

The strip method defines small, fingerlike areas and cuts all the trees within this area. The total cutting represents less than 6 to 10 percent of the volume of wood in the general area where the harvesting activity takes place. For example, in an area of 1000 hectares, the area from which trees are actually removed would be less than 60 to 100 hectares, with these areas scattered through the 1000 hectares in small, fingerlike plots of less than one-half hectare.

After this harvesting activity takes place, the entire 1000-hectare section of the forest is left unharvested and undisturbed while the forest moves back into the small clearings. To guarantee a recovery back to the approximately original state of the forest, the area would not see harvesting activity again for a minimum of 30 years.

The selective harvesting method would see the harvest of individual trees, not of a small clearing. These individual trees would be scattered through the whole 1000-hectare area, with the total amount of trees that are harvested representing less than 6 to 10 percent of the volume of wood in the 1000-hectare area. After 6 to 10 percent of the wood was harvested, the area would be left alone for a minimum of 30 years, after which the harvesting could begin again. Of course, while removing the trees, care must be taken to avoid collateral damage to the ecosystem, such as damage to nonharvested trees, spillage of oil or transmission fluids, compaction of the soil, reduction in tree-species diversity, or other types of environmental harm. See Box 13.2 for a description of a project in Brazil that uses the selective method of harvesting.

Box 13.2 Combining Sustainable Forestry and Sustainable Agriculture

In the western part of the Brazilian state of Amazonas, on the Rio Juruá near the town of Carauaria, a very promising sustainable agroforestry project was initiated as a social investment of a Brazilian pension fund. The project, known as APLUB Agroforestal, is remarkable in the way it combines a set of activities to generate a higher rate of sustainability than would be possible for each of the activities individually.

The headquarters and the sawmill of the project are located on a site that experienced degredation in the past (an abandoned natural gas terminal and failed rubber plantation), so the establishment of these operations has not lead to any new deforestation. The project has a 900,000-hectare concession of pristine forest from the federal government, and the forest should stay remarkably intact given the operating plan.

The initial plan has earmarked 30,000 hectares of land on which sustainable forestry will take place. The 30,000 hectares has been divided into 30 tracts of 1000 hectares, with

(continues)

Box 13.2 (continued)

timbering activity taking place on only one tract each year. After the year's harvesting activity, the tract is to be left alone for the next 30 years. Not only does the project leave plenty of time for recovery, but it harvests in a very gentle fashion. Much of the area is in várzea, a type of flooded forest ecosystem where the intense rains of the rainy season cause the river to rise 15 meters and flow deep into the forest. APLUB takes advantage of this natural cycle by felling trees during the low-water season and then floating them out of the forest and down the river to the sawmills during the high-water season. This keeps bulldozers, skidders, and other heavy equipment off the soil, preventing its compaction, eliminating erosion problems, and protecting other trees from damage by the heavy equipment. APLUB selectively removes no more than 6 percent of the volume of wood from each 1000-hectare tract, making sure to harvest a variety of species and minimize the intrusion into the forest and the disturbance caused by the harvesting activity. In summary, the harvesting activity is consistent with the type of disturbances from which the forest rapidly recovers. Although the project was only in its third year in 2003, the management plan looks to be genuinely sustainable from an ecological perspective.

Forest recovery is not enough, however, to make an operation sustainable. It must also be economically sustainable. APLUB is using the previously degraded land (the failed rubber plantation that was converted by previous owners to pasture) for agricultural activities. Swine and chickens are raised in pens and coops, turtles and fish are raised in small artificial impoundments, and cattle are raised in the pastures. APLUB combines the sawdust from the sawmills with the manure from the livestock operations and allows the combination to compost. The compost is then used to rehabilitate the degraded soil, and fruit trees are planted in the restored area. The feature of this operation that increases the sustainability of the entire project is that the wastes of one part of the project are used as inputs to another part of the operation. In addition, the income from the sale of meat, fish, eggs, and fruit makes the operation more profitable. The other important features of the project are that it hires people from the local communities, pays good wages, and promotes safe working conditions. Although APLUB Agroforestal is still in its early phases (harvesting began in 2001), it appears as they have generated a good model for sustainable economic activity in the rain forest.

Why Is Most Timbering Activity Destructive of the Rain Forest? Even though it is technically possible to harvest wood in a rain forest in a manner that keeps the forest intact, there are relatively few examples of this type of activity today. In the past, virtually all commercial harvesting of rain forests

Figure 13.4 **Time Paths of Income for Sustainable versus Nonsustainable Forestry**

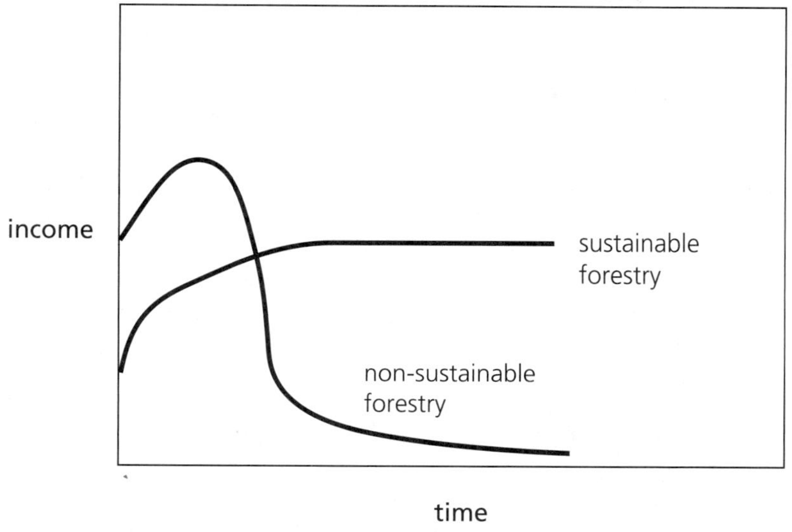

resulted in the destruction of the forest, for two basic reasons. First, it may be the privately optimal thing to do. Second, a series of market failures and poorly designed government policies give harvesting firms an incentive to be shortsighted and unconcerned about destruction of the forest.

It may be privately optimal to clear cut a forest, because that gives a burst of income in the present. Figure 13.4 compares the income paths of sustainable and nonsustainable forestry. Nonsustainable forestry gives an initial level of high income but low levels of income in the future because the forest is destroyed by the clear-cutting, the soil productivity is destroyed, and so on. In contrast, sustainable forestry gives lower levels of income, but these levels can be maintained forever. Unfortunately, if the firm's rate of time preference or discount rate is sufficiently high, then it will choose the unsustainable path over the sustainable path, because the present value of the unsustainable income stream is greater than the present value of the sustainable income stream.[1] To create an incentive for firms to adopt the sustainable approach, policies must be adopted that shift the unsustainable path downward, shift the sustainable path upward, or both.

[1]See Chapters 2 and 5 for more discussion of present value, discounting, and discount rates.

One of the major market failures has already been addressed: the rain forest has public good properties, creating social benefits that the landowners cannot capture. In other words, in many of these countries deforestation rates are likely to be inefficient from that particular society's point of view, even on publicly owned land. Moreover, in addition to this internal inefficiency, there will be global inefficiency as well. The global inefficiency exists because of the role of the forests as ecological treasures and storehouses of biodiversity and their importance in global carbon cycling make the forests valued by the rest of the countries of the world. As discussed earlier, these values are global public good benefits, and a forested country is not likely to be in a position to capture the benefits that other countries derive from the forest. The country will only consider the domestic costs and benefits of deforestation and not take into account the global benefits. For example, the forests in Madagascar create benefits for Europe in terms of the sequestration of carbon, providing storehouses of biodiversity, existence value, and so on. Madagascar, however, cannot charge a price to Europeans for these benefits they enjoy. In other words, the tropical forests constitute a global public good, so deforestation rates that are optimal from a forested country's point of view may not be optimal from a global point of view.

Therefore, the maximization of private net benefits often leads to the decision to cut down the rain forest, especially given the relative income paths depicted in Figure 13.4. Even when the rain forest is publicly owned, however, it is often harvested in a destructive fashion because of poorly designed concessionaire agreements by which governments lease the harvesting rights to publicly owned land.

One of the major reasons that destructive harvesting takes place is a market failure generated by the way many forested countries issue leases (concessionaire agreements) for harvesting rights. Very often, these leases are for too short a time period. This time frame generates two perverse incentives for the harvesting firms. First, they have the incentive to harvest as much as possible now, because they may not have access to the forest in the future. Second, they have no incentives to reduce environmental costs associated with the harvesting activity. As a consequence, many unharvested trees, particularly immature trees, are damaged or killed. Also, no attempts are made to leave the forest floor a suitable place for new trees and to configure the harvesting disturbances so that they are similar to natural disturbances, promoting rapid recovery of the forest to its approximate original state.

Many forestry economists have indicated that there is a rather simple solution to the problem: simply make the leases long-term, which will give the harvesting firms an economic incentive to think about the future. If that is done, then when the harvesting firms cut trees in the current period, they will have an incentive to make sure that they leave the forest in a position where they can cut trees in a future period. Although they may have an incentive to protect their future income potential, however, long-term leases do not give the firms an incentive to protect the flow of ecological services into the future. In fact, they may give the firms an economic incentive to convert a natural forest (which is very high in ecological services) to a plantation forest (which is very low in ecological services[2]). Therefore, it is difficult to protect the forest from environmental degradation simply by extending the life of the lease.

Economists have also suggested using the fee structure of the lease for protecting the forest. The fee structure is simply the way that the firm pays for its harvesting rights. For example, an area-based fee charges the firm per hectare in which it operates. This type of fee system gives the firm perverse incentives; because it pays by the unit of land area, it has an incentive to cut as much wood as possible from the specific area, given that the fee is independent of the volume of wood that is cut. In other words, the area-based fee gives the firm an economic incentive to cut every tree for which the price is greater than the cost of extraction. Area-based fees also lead to a process known as high-grading, whereby firms have an incentive to focus on those tree species that give the highest profit, such as mahogany and teak. The problem with high-grading is that it fundamentally changes the composition of the forest, which can have impacts on the stability of the forest ecosystem and the ability to produce ecological services. It also fundamentally changes the aesthetic character of the forest, leading to a loss of existence values.[3]

Another type of fee structure is known as the uniform revenue-based fee. With these fees a firm pays for its harvesting rights by paying a fixed percentage of total revenue. This type of system is better than the area-based system, because the payment the firm has to make increases as it cuts more trees. Although it gives an economic incentive against aggressive harvesting, it still retains an incentive for the firms to high-grade because they pay a fraction of their revenue, rather than a fraction of their profits. Hence, firms have an incentive to focus on cutting trees that have a high selling price relative to cost of extraction. Again, this practice may lead to focus on high-profile species such as mahogany and teak, and it also gives an incentive to focus harvesting in lower-cost areas (primarily where transportation is less costly) such as in the proximity of roads and rivers.

Another type of fee structure is known as the undifferentiated volume-based fee. This type of system charges firms per cubic meter of wood that they harvest. In the undifferentiated system, the fee is constant across all species of trees. Although this system removes the incentive for extremely aggressive harvesting that is associated with the area-based fee system, it also leads to problems with high-grading. Because the fee is constant across tree species, it makes sense for a harvesting firm to focus on the tree species that generate the most profit per cubic meter. In contrast, the differentiated volume-based sys-

---

[2]Plantation forests are typically monocultures of fast-growing trees such as pine or eucalyptus. Because the trees are planted at the same time, they are all the same size, the canopies completely interlock, and no sunlight penetrates to the forest floor. Therefore, it is very difficult for other plants to grow on the soil beneath the trees, which has implications for both the food web and the hydrological protection service of the forest. In addition, neither pine trees nor eucalyptus are good sources of food. In fact, animals that have not evolved in Australia generally cannot eat the eucalyptus trees because of the chemicals that they contain. The combination of these factors, and that only one tree species is planted, implies that the biodiversity of a plantation forest is usually extremely low.

[3]See Chapter 4 for a definition of existence values.

tem removes this incentive by charging a different fee for each type of tree species. Although this system removes the incentive to high-grade (if the fees are set properly!), it is more difficult to administer in terms of monitoring costs.

Clearly, the differentiated volume-based system is the best because it creates disincentives against aggressive harvesting and does not create incentives to high-grade. This conclusion leads to the question of whether the differentiated volume-based fee system is sufficient to ensure the rapid recovery of forests to their original state and ensure the continued flow of ecological services. To answer this question, it is necessary to look back to the properties of the types of disturbances from which the forest can recover. The forest will only recover from disturbances that mimic natural disturbances. The forest simply cannot recover from disturbances that are large in scale or that are not narrow in shape. The fee system can influence how many and what type of trees are harvested, but it cannot influence how the harvesting activity is conducted, which determines if the harvesting activity mimics natural disturbances. In addition, while harvesting it is important to avoid collateral damage, such as damaging other trees and plants, and compacting soils with machinery. In short, lease systems and fee structures can be used to manage how much is cut and what is cut, but they cannot provide incentives along the lines of how the forest is cut. To ensure that the rain forests are not destroyed by the process of harvesting, policy must be developed to control the fashion in which the forest is cut. In terms of developing policy to ensure that harvesting methods are consistent with the recoverability of the forest, governments have choices between the two broad categories of environmental policy: direct controls and economic incentives.

Direct controls specify the techniques that harvesters would be required to use and place other restraints on their activities to protect the rain forest. If they violated these regulations, then they would be subject to penalties. Economic incentives would make it more profitable to harvest in a sustainable fashion.

For environmental problems in general, direct controls are viewed to have lower monitoring and enforcement costs than economic incentives. Yet that is not true for the case of forestry, because it is possible for firms to engage in "hit-and-run" harvesting. Hit-and-run harvesting refers to a firm that acts as if it is conforming to environmental regulations, but then goes out into the forest and harvests intensively and destructively, only to disappear before penalties can be enforced. The firm will then reemerge under a new guise and repeat the process. Because the assets of the forestry firm (trucks, bulldozers, chain saws, sawmills mounted on truck beds, and so on) are highly mobile, it is difficult to actually locate the physical location of the firm after it abandons a harvesting site and impossible to seize assets as a penalty for violating the environmental regulations. Economic incentives can work better than direct controls, because they can be configured to provide an incentive that exists even before the cutting begins. The most useful economic incentive for environmental management of forests is the performance bond.

A performance bond works by collecting money from the firm before it begins its activities. The money is placed in an escrow account at a bank, awaiting compliance by the firm. If the firm complies with environmental regulations, then it receives its money back; if not, then the performance bond is forfeited. Most performance bonds in existence today focus on providing an incentive for remediating damages, such as with strip-mining of coal (see Chapter 10). With the forest, however, remediation of deforestation does not work, because clear-cutting eliminates the soil productivity and the ability of the forest to recover from the disturbance. In short, the damage cannot be remediated. Consequently, the focus of the performance bonds should be preventing large-scale disturbances. Box 13.3 shows how indicators can show the extent to which harvesting disturbances mimic natural disturbances.

Box 13.3 Incorporating Ecological Constraints into Economic Incentives

Since the mid 1970s, ecologists have been conducting intensive research on the characteristics of the forest that promote its sustainability. For example, ecologists have determined that when land is cleared in timbering or for conversion to agriculture, the forest has a better chance of regenerating if several conditions are met. First, there should be a large ratio of the amount of undisturbed area to the amount of cleared area. Second, the area that is cleared should have a high ratio of the edge of the cleared area to the surface area of the cleared area. In other words, because the forest regenerates from the edge, narrow fingers of cleared area have a better opportunity to regenerate than circular or rectangular areas. These narrow fingers of cleared areas mimic natural clearings (generated by huge emergent trees being toppled by the wind), so natural processes exist to reforest the cleared area. More importantly, they do not disturb the nutrient cycle. These alternative configurations of forested and cleared area are presented in the figure.

Given this knowledge of the ecology of the area, how can economic incentives (or other types of policies) be constructed to ensure that timbering activity conforms to these ecological requirements? One way to do so is to modify the performance bond systems discussed in the section of this chapter on timber leases. A firm that wanted to harvest timber would have to post a large bond (pay a large deposit), which would then be returned if it harvests in an ecologically sustainable fashion. The greater the ratio of the amount of undisturbed area to cleared area, the larger the proportion of the deposit that is returned. Similarly, the greater the ratio of the edge of the cleared area to the surface area of the cleared area, the greater the percentage of the deposit that is returned. This system would give harvesting firms an economic incentive to harvest in an ecologically sustainable fashion. Other important ecological variables could also be integrated into this system.

(continues)

Box 13.3 (continued)

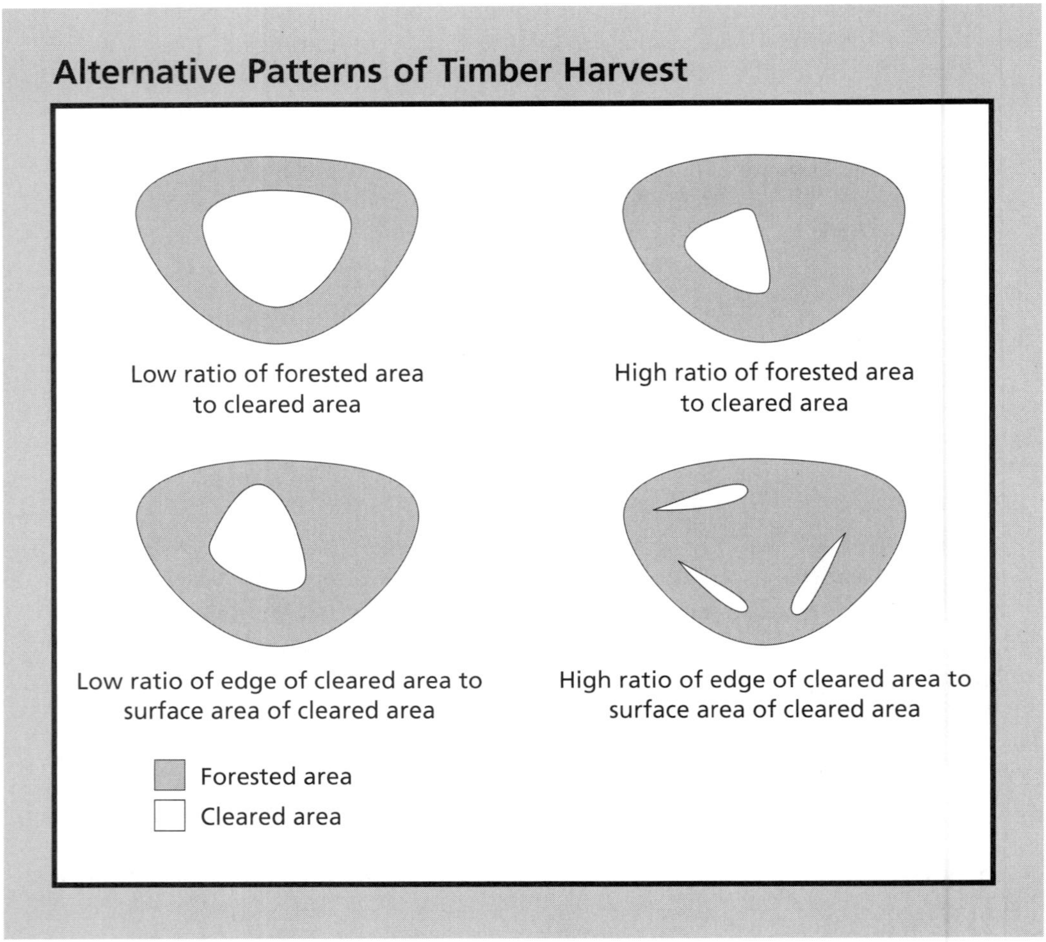

Leases can also be configured to give an incentive for environmental protection. The first step in the process is to make the leases long term and marketable, giving a private incentive to protect the forest as a source of timber income. As discussed earlier, however, this step is insufficient to protect the forest and the flow of ecological services. In a report to the Organization for Economic Cooperation and Development (OECD), Kahn (2002) outlines a process for creating incentives for environmental protection.

First is the development of a system of ecological zoning. Ecological zoning is a process that examines the forests in a country or region and assigns legal uses to the forest. Forests of unusually high biodiversity, great importance for watershed protection, critical spawning habitat, and other important features should be set aside as protected area. Indigenous reserves should be established. Some area could be set aside for agriculture and some forest area reserved for leasing to sustainable forestry operations.

Once the areas to be leased are established, they must be inventoried so that the government understands their value in sustainable forestry. The leases should then be auctioned, with the idea of creating a fee structure for the harvesting rights to allow a forestry firm to share some of the economic rents available from the timber. If the government shares these rents with the harvesting firm, then it makes participating in the harvesting activity more lucrative, which gives the firm an economic incentive to follow environmental regulations to maintain its access to this profitable activity.

The second step is to take the area that is leased to a harvesting firm and divide it into smaller sections. For example, a 30,000-hectare concession might be subdivided into 30 subunits of 1,000 hectares, with only one subunit to be worked each year.

The next step is to define the environmental regulations regarding harvesting activity. These definitions would include restrictions on how much is cut, what is cut, and how it is cut. A performance bond would be required. The magnitude of the performance bond should be sufficiently high to ensure that the environmental regulations are followed during the first year as the first subunit is being worked.

If the firm is found to be out of compliance with the environmental regulations as it worked this first unit in the first year, then the firm would be required to forfeit its performance bond and would also give up the rights to harvest the remaining 29 subunits. This policy should provide a powerful incentive to follow the environmental management plan. A firm that was compliant in the first year would move into the second work subunit in the second year, and the same type of restrictions and penalties would apply as in the first year and would apply in the following years as the firm began working successive subunits.

Of course, there are design, implementation, and monitoring issues that are too numerous to be discussed here. The reader is referred to Kahn (2002) for more details on these issues.

Fuelwood Harvesting

A second activity that may lead to excessive levels of deforestation is the cutting of forests for fuelwood. In dry tropical forest areas, and in mountainous tropical forest areas, this activity is an extremely important source of deforestation, because more people rely on fuelwood as a source of energy than on fossil fuels (Food and Agricultural Organization, 1987). The reliance on fuelwood increased as the foreign exchange problems associated with the energy crises of the 1970s, falling export prices, the debt crises of the 1980s, and the economic crises of the late 1990s forced countries to reduce their imports (or increase their exports and cut down on domestic consumption) of fossil fuels such as coal and oil.

Again, the question arises of why the forests cannot be managed properly for a sustained harvest of fuelwood. The answer is, again, that there are market failures. Unlike the case of the timbering, however, this failure is unrelated to firm actions and concessionaire agreements. Instead, the deforestation for fuelwood consumption is largely a result of individual household action, poorly defined property rights, lack of information, and lack of access to alternatives.

Because many forest areas are open-access resources, individual households have no incentive to manage the forests for either maximum sustained yield or maximum economic benefit. Rather, there is a race to harvest the wood before someone else harvests it. This problem, combined with conversion to agriculture and open access to livestock grazing, may lead to rapid degradation of the forest and an inability of the forest to regenerate itself. This situation is particularly true in areas where the livestock eat the leaves and bark from trees and shrubs as well as overgrazing the grass (goats are notoriously bad in this regard). In many areas of sub-Saharan Africa, deforestation leads to desertification.

In order to understand how to develop policies to deal with these market failures, it is necessary to examine why the forested areas lack a clear definition of property rights. In many cases, this lack of definition is due to the shift from a traditional economy to a national economy. For example, in many areas of sub-Saharan Africa, forested areas were communally owned by clans, villages, or tribes. Although these areas were common property within the clan, village, or tribe, they were not open access and there existed a clear set of rules on the utilization of land. When these areas were colonized by European countries, the commonly owned resources became owned by the central government, and the rules of use broke down. Box 13.4 discusses cultural traditions that provide mechanisms for protecting common property resources among Amazonian Indians. Very often, when the countries became independent, title to the land passed from the colonial government to the new independent national governments, rather than passing back to the clans, villages, or tribes. The national government could not enforce rules governing the use of the forested land the same way a smaller unit of society, such as a clan or tribe, could, largely because of the difficulty that a central government with little resources has in monitoring and enforcing the law and property rights in remote areas. Also, the process of creating nations out of these smaller social units would sometimes generate conflict as to which smaller unit had claims to the land.

One way to reduce the overexploitation caused by open-access public forests is to give property rights to tracts of the forest to smaller units, such as a village. The village can then develop social institutions to control open-access overexploitation. The village can also prevent outsiders from exploiting the forest and has an incentive to expend some resources (such as guards) to protect its resource base. Additional policies could consist of planting new forests that were managed specifically for fuelwood and reducing the demand for fuel.

Planting fuelwood forests has several important benefits associated with it. First, the availability of wood from the planted forests reduces the pressure on existing natural forests, lessening the loss of ecological services associated with deforestation. Second, the planting of new forests in previously degraded areas helps protect watersheds, renew the vitality of the soil, provide habitat, and create other ecological services. If the newly planted forests are subject to the same open-access pressures, however, then they will be quickly eliminated as

Box 13.4 Why Supernatural Eels Matter

Kenneth Taylor (1990) points out that, particularly in traditional societies, the social institutions that develop to prevent open-access exploitation need not take the form of laws or governmental bodies. He cites two examples in the Amazon that illustrate that religious or spiritual beliefs may be just as effective.

The Yanomami Indians set aside large tracts of forestlands that exist in the boundary regions between villages. These lands can only be hunted to supply infrequent intervillage festivals. The Yanomami do not think of these areas as game preserves, but rather as a means of commemorating the dead and honoring their visitors. Yet these beliefs provide a game preserve in which animals may breed in relative sanctuary, and the beliefs prevent intervillage competition for the animals living in these boundary areas.

The Kayopo believe that in certain portions of rain forest rivers there exist supernatural electric eels that could kill any person who fishes in those waters. Consequently, the Kayopo avoid these areas. It is probably not coincidental that these waters that are supposedly protected by the supernatural eels are also the primary breeding areas of the most important species of fish. The myth serves to prevent a type of destructive exploitation (harvesting fish when they are geographically concentrated and susceptible to overharvesting) by providing a social structure to govern the use of a common property.

well. To avoid rapid depletion, the new forests must be linked to community or cooperative ownership.

Another potential set of policies is to reduce the demand for fuelwood. There are two major ways of doing so. One is to develop and distribute woodstoves that are more efficient in heating and cooking than existing stoves and open fires. A number of simple but effective technologies exist, such as backdraft stoves, which provide more efficient burning and more usable heat per kilogram of firewood. Another alternative is to move toward technologies that do not require the use of wood. For example, solar cookers are feasible in many of the tropical areas of the world. In both cases, policies will not be successful if authorities simply focus on providing access to the new technology. Information to go along with it must be provided, including demonstration that the new technology can provide the same quality of cooking or heating at lower cost to the family.

Conversion to Agriculture

Conversion to agricultural uses is the third major cause of deforestation. In some areas of the world, this conversion is the result of population growth and migration of rural populations engaged in subsistence farming. In other areas, the conversion is the result of the activity of large agricultural business.

Subsistence Farming. In traditional forest societies, conversion of forestland occurred at a relatively small scale and was not permanent. Small patches of the forest were cut and burned for cultivation of crops in the cleared area. Becausee these patches were relatively small and surrounded by forest on all sides, the patches were quickly reclaimed by the forest and the traditional farmers would then clear a new patch (see Box 13.1). This type of "slash-and-burn" agriculture does not result in significant permanent deforestation. It can be practiced year after year, along with sustainable forestry and the harvesting of nontimber forest products such as rubber, nuts, fruit, honey, and meat from wild animals.

More recently, however, the speed at which the slash-and-burn agriculture takes place has accelerated, and such large patches are cleared that the forest does not regenerate. The impetus for this large-scale clearing comes from two sources. The first is the immigration of settlers from nonforest regions. The second is from industrial agriculture. This type of large-scale clearing to plant field crops such as corn, rice, or soybeans does not mimic natural disturbances and has very negative impacts on the forest and the soil. The agricultural productivity of the cleared land is not great, because tropical forest soils have little organic matter and nutrients. The ash from the cleared and burned trees temporarily provides nutrients for crops, but, typically, after several years the land is no longer fertile enough to support crops. The land is typically used for cattle ranching at this point, but it is not productive enough to support high densities of cattle. Eventually, the soil may become too acidic to support even pasture grasses. For small-scale farmers, in either the crop stage or the livestock stage of agriculture, the land has the potential to be more productive when using sustainable agroforestry practices than when it is completely cleared for field crops or cattle.

Although indigenous populations have long been able to produce abundant food without destroying the rain forest, recent immigrants to rain forest areas typically do not know the techniques associated with sustainable agroforestry. Either as participants in government resettlement programs or as refugees from poverty and other undesirable living conditions, they flock from the more populated areas of tropical countries and move into the lush green rain forest, hoping for an existence that is as abundant as the forest itself. Yet they cut the rain forest, using agricultural techniques with which they are familiar. In addition to the lack of information about the more sustainable techniques, they are pushed toward less sustainable techniques by pressing current needs. In Figure 13.5, which is very similar in nature to Figure 13.4, unsustainable methods give an initial burst of income as the burned forest provides a fertile area for cultivation for a few years. As the nutrients disappear, however, the productivity of the land collapses, causing the family to clear and farm a new piece of land. As long as there is additional uncleared forest to which the farmer has access (either legally or as a squatter), the short-run strategy is always to clear the forest and plant crops. In contrast, sustainable methods may have a plateau that

Figure 13.5 **Alternative Time Paths of Income from Sustainable and Conventional Agriculture**

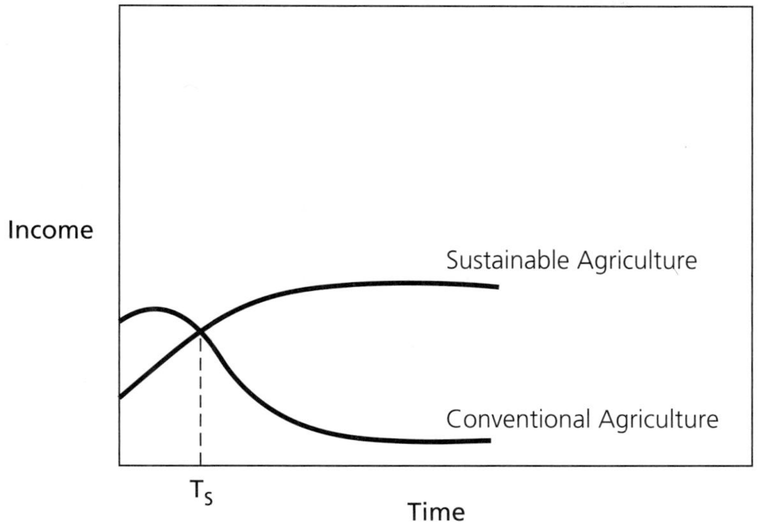

is higher than the peak of the unsustainable methods. Farmers, however, will not make the switch to invest in sustainable methods, because that may reduce their income in the short run. How can economic and environmental policy encourage farmers to make the switch? There are several important steps that policy makers can take, but before the policies are discussed, the techniques that allow for sustainable agriculture are presented.

As might be expected from the earlier discussion of sustainable forestry, the types of disturbances that allow agriculture to proceed in harmony with rain forest ecosystems are those in which disturbances mimic natural disturbances.[4] Small areas are cleared, lightly burned to avoid disturbances to the roots of nearby trees, and planted with a mixture of root crops (manioc, yams), annual crops (beans, corn, squash), and perennial crops (fruit trees, nut trees, coffee bushes, cacao trees). After several years, the forest begins to move back into the clearing and the annual crops can no longer be grown because of the lack of sunlight. The root crops can be productive for several more years, and the perennial crops for decades. Farmers can clear new patches and start the process again. In addition, farmers can collect fruits, nuts, honey, fish, fiber, meat (birds, mammals and reptiles), and medicinal

[4] This discussion takes place in the context of tropical rain forests. In tropical dry forests, sustainable agriculture is generated through a fallow process that allows the return of grassland and scrub, as well as interplanting with economically productive trees. For more discussion of sustainable agriculture in a tropical dry forest context, see Barbier (2004).

plants from the forest for their own consumption or for sale to markets. Caviglia (1999) shows that in the Amazonian state of Rondônia the potential income from these sustainable activities is significantly higher than from conventional production of some combination of annual crops (corn, beans, and so on) and cattle.

Farmers, however, do not choose these more profitable sustainable techniques because of market failures. Therefore, policy must be developed to counteract these market failures.

The first step is to make sure that the small farmers have secure property rights to their land. Secure property rights implies more than just ownership on paper; it also implies an ability to protect the property rights from those who might try to usurp them. Property rights are crucially important because if farmers do not have them, it makes no sense for farmers to invest in the long term. The greater the probability of being thrown off the land, the greater the incentive to use cultivating strategies that create benefits in the short run, despite being costly in the long run. In other words, if a farmer fears that he or she may be thrown off the land, then the farmer might as well clear the forest and plant crops and get high production now, not worrying about reducing soil productivity in the future. In fact, if the farmer's production techniques diminish the quality of the soil, the probability that someone with more money, political connections, or more guns will covet this land and force the farmer off the land is further reduced.

The second step is to provide information about how to produce in a sustainable fashion. Because many of the immigrants are arriving from unforested regions (or from urban areas), they do not understand the rain forest ecosystem and they do not have the knowledge required to farm in harmony with the forest. This information could be provided directly by the government, provided by nongovernmental organizations, or distributed through local farmers cooperatives.

The third requirement is for short-term financial assistance. If small farmers are going to invest in the future, they need funds or other assistance for the investment to take place. A very important aspect of this need is the provision of funding to purchase seedlings (or direct provision of the seedlings) for perennial plants such as fruit, nut, cacao, and coffee trees that can be "shade grown" under the forest canopy. The other important aspect of short-term assistance is to help provide sustenance for the farmer's family while the investment is coming to fruition. Many perennial plants such as fruit, coffee, and cacao trees take 3 or more years before they begin to produce. The family must be fed in the meantime. This assistance can take the form of loans, cash grants, or food aid.

The fourth type of policy that would help provide an incentive for farmers to switch to sustainable agricultural methods is policies that increase the profitability of the sustainably produced products, particularly nonforest timber products that are collected in the rain forest. One such program would shift the sustainable income path in Figure 13.5 upwards and shift the intersection between the two time paths to the left, which would reduce the severity of the short-run difference between the sustainable and conventional (nonsustainable, annual crop) agricultural methods. A demand enhancement program could increase awareness of nontimber forest products and the price people are willing to pay for them. For example, an Amazonian fruit called açai has the highest level of iron of any natural product. Not only is it enjoyed as a juice, in smoothies, and in products such as ice cream, but it provides enough iron to rectify iron deficiencies in most anemic people. Similarly, a fruit called camu-camu has 10 times the vitamin C of orange juice, a fruit called guaraná has 10 times the caffeine as coffee, and a Polynesian fruit called noni may be useful in treating high blood pressure. These examples are just a few of the products that can be sustainably produced by gathering fruits, leaves, nuts, fiber, and other renewable outputs of the rain forest.

An important part of any demand enhancement program is ecological certification. Such certification would allow consumers to vote for rain forest preservation with their consumer dollars by making purchases that support products that are produced without injuring the forest. It would also be important for sustainably produced timber.

Industrial Agriculture. In many areas of the tropical world, rain forests are being cleared to provide space for industrial agriculture. Such clearing manifests itself in different ways in different parts of the world, but industrial agriculture generally focuses on crops for export, such as coffee, cocoa, sugar, palm oil, soybeans, corn, and cotton, as well as cattle and other livestock. In addition, much forest is lost to crops that are transformed into drugs and illegally exported, such as opium poppies, coca, and marijuana. This section of the chapter focuses on legal crops and livestock; and impact of illegal crops on deforestation will not be further examined.[5]

Industrial agriculture is able to delay the onset of loss of soil fertility through the use of manufactured fertilizers, pesticides, and herbicides. Depending on the exact techniques that are used and the original quality of the soil, a deforested section of rain forest may remain productive in soybean or coffee production for as many as 15 to 20 years before succumbing to eventual degradation.

The conversion of rain forest to industrial agriculture may be suboptimal for several reasons. The first is the traditional externality story: farming firms do not take account of the external costs of their actions in terms of destroying rain forest and the ecological services and public good benefits that are provided by it. The second is that very often government policies provide further incentive to convert rain forest to export crop production. For example, fertilizer subsidies and tax credits are two ways that governments subsidize industrial agriculture.

Figure 13.6 illustrates these two sources of market failure for the case of a particular crop such as soybeans. The highest marginal cost curve (MSC)

---

[5] The interested reader will find much information available about the impacts of drugs on deforestation. A 2004 Google search of "deforestation and cocaine" yielded over 7000 hits. Similarly, "marijuana and deforestation" yielded 4500 hits, and "opium and deforestation" generated over 5000 hits.

Figure 13.6 **Impacts of Incentives on Agricultural Production**

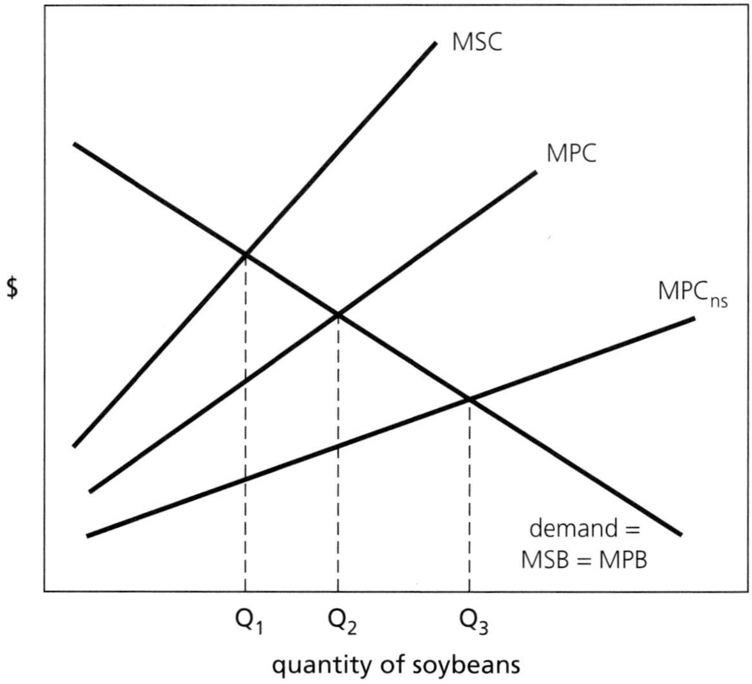

represents the true social cost of soybean production, including the costs of losing the benefits of the rain forest. If there is no difference between marginal private benefits and marginal social benefits of soybeans (and for simplicity we will assume that is true), then the optimal level of soybean production will be at Q_1. Absent an internalization of the external costs, however, market forces alone would yield a higher level of production at Q_2, where marginal private cost is equal to marginal private benefits. Obviously, the market is associated with a higher level of soybean production than the optimal level. When, however, the government provides additional incentives, as one might expect, the amount of soybean production would be even higher. In Figure 13.6, MPC_{ns} shows the marginal private cost curve, net of subsidies. Because the government provides economic benefits to producers through programs such as fertilizer subsidies or income tax credits, the cost of production is even lower than simple marginal private cost. This lower cost leads to an even greater production level (Q_3 in the example) and even greater levels of deforestation than the market alone would give. One of the most important types of policy to reduce incentives is simply to eliminate government programs that give an economic incentive to suboptimally high levels of deforestion.

Macroeconomic Reasons for Deforestation

In the previous sections, various microeconomic reasons for inefficient levels of deforestation were outlined. These reasons, which focus around market failures within the forested country, could be related to macroeconomic conditions in the country. The relationship between these macroeconomic conditions and microeconomic problems may be illustrated by asking the question, Why should a country establish a system of property rights or tax incentives that lead to inefficient use of the resource, when alternative systems exist?

There are three potential answers to this question:

1. The forested countries are not cognizant of the effects of these laws and policies.
2. The laws and policies are not designed with efficiency goals, but instead are a mechanism for transferring wealth from one segment of the economy to another (from indigenous forest dwellers to wealthy cattle ranchers, for example).
3. Economic conditions prevent the country from acting in its long-term interests.

The first explanation is not a particularly satisfactory one, because it means that the forested countries do not learn from experience. If outside observers are cognizant of the inefficiencies of these policies, then it would be reasonable to assume that internal policy makers must also be aware of them. Although one might see unexpected detrimental impacts from policy, it is unrealistic to assume that they would continue in the long run without some additional motivation for keeping the policies intact.

The second explanation may be important, but it is extremely difficult to address. The use of government policy for transferring wealth leads to inefficiencies in virtually every country on the earth. For example, in Chapter 12 there is discussion of how the U.S. Forest Service subsidized the cutting of old-growth Pacific forests to maintain the economic base of that region. If the inefficient policies leading to rapid deforestation are really a mechanism for transferring wealth, then one would not expect to see these policies reversed without substantial effort, because political and cultural traditions and barriers may sap the will of well-meaning policy makers to develop more efficient policies.

The third explanation, that economic conditions may prevent a country from acting in its long-term interests, is interesting because it is an explanation that can be addressed both by tropical countries and by European and North American countries interested in preserving tropical rain forests. Kahn and McDonald (1995) hypothesize that macroeconomic conditions, particularly high levels of external debt, may constrain countries and force them to take actions to meet short-term cash needs that are not in their long-term interest. For example, the best long-term strategies may be to use the forests as a sustainable resource, but the need to meet interest and debt obligations (among other short-run economic pressures) may force the countries to use the forests as an exhaustible resource. The importance of debt on the economic conditions of the countries cannot be overstated, because many countries spend as much as $1 of every $2 or $3 of gross domestic product to meet the interest obligations on their debt.

Kahn and McDonald (1995) conducted a regression analysis that looked for a relationship between debt and deforestation. Their study found the debt elasticity of deforestation to be between 0.17 and 0.31. In other words, for every 10 percent that debt is reduced, annual deforestation may be reduced by between 1.7 and 3.1 percent. Brown and Pearce (1994) examine many empirical studies of the causes of deforestation. These studies show that other macroeconomic factors may also contribute to this problem, including falling prices for the raw materials that tropical countries export, rising energy prices, increasing population, domestic hyperinflation, high urban unemployment, and increasing urban density. More research needs to be done on the relationship between macroeconomic conditions and environmental degradation, both in developing and developed countries.

Rain Forests as a Global Public Good and International Policy

Earlier in the chapter, the public good nature of rain forests was mentioned. Rain forests provide habitats for many species, are reservoirs of biological diversity, harbor many plant and animal species that may be of medicinal or agricultural importance, and are important in terms of global carbon cycles. Consequently, one expects the tropical rain forests to be valued by people who live throughout the globe, particularly in temperate countries.

If people outside a forested country value the forests, then it is likely that the rate of deforestation taking place in the forested country is greater than socially optimal. The reason is that the costs and benefits of outsiders do not become included in the cost-benefit analysis or other decision-making process of the forested country.

Many residents of developed countries have suggested that countries with tropical forests have an obligation to the world to preserve them because of their global public good. This argument has not been well received by the forested countries for two major reasons. First, the developed countries of Europe and North America already eliminated most of their original forests as these countries underwent economic development. The tropical countries argue that if Europe and North America fueled their industrial development with deforestation and other forms of environmental degradation, then why should currently developing countries be subjected to a different standard? Second, if preserving the rain forests benefits the wealthier developed countries, then why should the poorer developing countries bear the cost of this preservation?

Although both arguments have intuitive appeal, they merit careful examination. As suggested earlier, it is likely that the high rates of deforestation are not in a forested country's best interest, especially in the long run. Market failures and macroeconomic considerations may generate more deforestation (and other types of environmental degradation) than is in a country's self-interest. If these problems can be addressed and deforestation slowed, then the level of income should rise in these countries. One thing is clear, however: whatever level of deforestation is optimal from a forested country's perspective, a slower rate is optimal from a global perspective, owing to the global public good nature of the rain forests.

This difference in optimal deforestation rates implies that important issues surround the question of whether the poorer developing countries should be asked to bear the costs of the lower levels of deforestation. Lowering deforestation levels would make the world better off, but could make the forested countries worse off. Clearly, these lower levels of deforestation will not be achieved unless the forested countries are compensated for their losses.

Debt for Nature Swaps

One mechanism for accomplishing this compensation is the debt for nature swap, originally proposed by Thomas Lovejoy in 1984.[6] A debt for nature swap is an agreement between an organization (usually a nongovernmental organization, or NGO) and a forested country. The NGO buys and retires a portion of the forested country's external debt in exchange for a promise to preserve a forest tract. External debt is the money that a country owes to foreign banks, foreign governments, and international development agencies, which must be repaid in hard currency (for example, U.S. dollars, euros, Japanese yen).

As mentioned earlier, external debt is a tremendous drain on a developing country's economy, with many countries owing in the tens of billions of dollars. For some countries, as much as $1 of every $2 of its gross domestic product goes to paying its debt service. Because the banks who hold the debt view their prospects for full and timely repayment as problematic, the debt can be purchased by the NGO for a fraction of its face value. The debt can be discounted as low as $0.05 to $0.30 on the dollar.

One feature that is increasingly becoming a characteristic of debt for nature swaps is the establishment of a fund in the forested country's domestic currency that will be used to finance the preservation of the forest tract. For example, the money can be used to hire forest rangers to enforce prohibitions against damaging uses of the forest.

Several important questions have been raised concerning debt for nature swaps, however:

1. Will the countries renege on the agreements due to the lack of enforceability of the agreements? For example, if an NGO, such as The Nature Conservancy or the Sierra Club, retires part of the debt of the forested country in exchange for protecting a forest tract, and if several years later the country decides to convert the forest to pasture, there is little the NGO can do to prevent it from happening. Of course, such an action would damage the country's international

[6] See *Time Magazine* online article, "The Green Century," http://www.time.com/time/2002/greencentury/enwilderness.html.

reputation and would probably preclude future debt for nature swaps and other sorts of environmental cooperation, so the costs of reneging are high. Yet the possibility of such an action cannot be dismissed.
2. Will forested countries negotiate a debt for nature swap for a preservation action it would have taken anyway, meaning that there is no net preservation gain as a result of the swap?
3. Will countries use their reduced indebtedness to qualify for more loans so that the net debt reduction of the debt for nature swaps is small, if not zero?

The Tropical Forestry Action Plan

The Tropical Forestry Action Plan (TFAP) is a large-scale effort organized by the Food and Agricultural Organization (1987), World Resource Institute, World Bank, and United Nations Development Program to conserve and develop tropical forest resources on a long-term, sustainable basis. The TFAP is designed to reduce deforestation pressures by direct action to restore degraded areas and provide methods for meeting economic needs in a sustainable fashion. There are five operational goals of the TFAP, which it refers to as priority areas:

1. Integrate forestry and agriculture to conserve the resource base and make more rational use of the land.
2. Develop forest-based industry.
3. Restore fuelwood supplies and support national fuelwood and wood energy programs.
4. Conserve tropical forest ecosystems.
5. Remove institutional barriers to wise use of forests.

A sample of projects supported by the TFAP include the following:

1. Restoring degraded land in Ethiopian highlands by providing "food for work" for peasants to work on conservation projects, such as terracing deforested hillsides and planting trees
2. Planting grasses and multipurpose trees for fodder in Nepal by paying wages for tree planting for the first 2 years of the project
3. Developing forest plantations of fast growing trees in Pakistan to increase incomes of farmers
4. Encouraging farmers in Kenya to plant trees for fruit, shade, windbreaks, and fuelwood

The TFAP is important in two major ways. First, it provides a framework in which forested countries can recognize the importance of their forests and develop plans to protect them. Second, it provides direct interventions to reverse degradation and mitigate some of the economic pressures that lead to deforestation.

Although the TFAP serves as an important demonstration plan and does yield important results in terms of both improving rural standards of living and reducing deforestation, it is not a panacea. It cannot, by itself, deal with all the microeconomic and macroeconomic conditions leading to greater than optimal levels of deforestation. Similarly, it does not and cannot fully address the important population pressures that contribute to deforestation. Many national, state, and local governments, farmers cooperatives, NGOs, and other institutions, however, are working to develop projects in the spirit of the TFAP, looking for ways to increase income generated by sustainably produced forest products and increase environmental preservation and the quality of life of forest communities in the process.

Summary

Tropical forests are diverse ecosystems that provide many benefits, including both consumable and nonconsumable benefits. Consumable benefits include wood, meat, fruit, honey, nuts, fiber, rubber, and fodder. Nonconsumable benefits include a full suite of ecological services (habitat, biodiversity, watershed protection, carbon sequestering), cultural values, and existence values.

Tropical forests are disappearing at an alarming rate. Microeconomic conditions, such as poorly defined property rights, land tenure systems, tax incentives, and short-term concessionaire agreements, are important causes of deforestation. Macroeconomic conditions, such as the level of external debt, import and export prices, and the general standard of living, may also contribute to the rapid rate of deforestation. In addition, population growth generates additional demands for land and exacerbates the microeconomic and macroeconomic factors that lead to deforestation.

One important factor in reducing deforestation is improving the economic conditions that tend to promote it. These conditions include both market failures and macroeconomic conditions. Elimination or mitigation of these factors requires efforts at both the national and international levels. At the international level, the provision of debt relief in the form of debt for nature swaps and the provision of information are essential. In addition, the provision of information and environmental investment provided by programs such as the Tropical Forestry Action Plan provide much promise. More research into causes of deforestation and more research into the development of policy remedies are necessary if the irreversible loss of tropical forests is to be avoided, however. Of particular importance is the development of policies that provide economic incentives for sustainable alternatives to activities that are destructive of the rain forest.

Review Questions

1. What are the fundamental ecological differences between tropical rain forests and temperate forests?
2. Describe the economic activities that result in the deforestation of rain forests. What market failures are associated with each activity? Suggest policies to deal with these market failures.
3. What policies should developed countries pursue toward tropical deforestation?
4. Why do "supernatural eels" matter? What is the relevance of "supernatural eels" to policy?
5. Why do concessionaire agreements with timber companies tend to be short run in nature? What inefficiencies does that generate? How would you modify these agreements to eliminate these inefficiencies?

6. What are the strengths and weaknesses of debt for nature swaps as an international policy to slow deforestation?

Questions for Further Study

1. Do fast food hamburgers lead to deforestation?
2. What are the strengths and weaknesses of the Tropical Forestry Action Plan? How would you modify the plan to make it more effective?
3. What is the relevance of the worldwide energy crisis for tropical deforestation?
4. Can the development of increased tourism save the tropical rain forests?
5. Is it possible for the United States to unilaterally preserve tropical rain forests? Why or why not?
6. Explain the difference between local, national, and global public goods. What is the importance of this distinction for policy?

Suggested Paper Topics

1. The chapter mentions several social institutions that developed among indigenous Amazonian peoples to protect common property resources. Choose an indigenous group from another region (that is, North America, Australia, Africa) and discuss the role that community social institutions play in maintaining the integrity of renewable natural resources. Do literature searches on the region, indigenous people, and rain forests.
2. Discuss the current experience with debt for nature swaps. What factors are likely to affect their desirability from the forested country's perspective? What factors are likely to increase their desirability from the creditor countries' perspective? What recommendations can make these programs more effective? Search bibliographic databases for rain forests and debt, and debt and the environment.
3. Formulate a hypothesis about the relationship between economic variables and deforestation. Use data from the World Bank (http://www.worldbank.org/poverty/wdrpoverty/report/index.htm, 2001), the United Nations (http://hdr.undp.org/reports/global/2001/en), and World Resources Institute (http://earthtrends.wri.org/), to test your hypothesis. For example, what is the relationship between deforestation and population growth, gross domestic product, or debt? How does this relationship vary by region of the world? How does it differ between countries that contain primarily dry forests and countries that contain primarily rain forests?
4. Look at deforestation in a particular country and the activities that lead to deforestation. How do market failures affect these activities? What policies can you suggest to alleviate the market failures?
5. Development projects of the World Bank and other development agencies have been criticized as an important factor in the rapid deforestation of the 1980s. Discuss the evidence that either supports or refutes this position. If you find support for this position, what changes in policies can you suggest to reduce this type of pressure on forests? Search bibliographic databases for World Bank and the environment. Also, check World Bank reports for internal discussion on this issue.
6. What is the impact of illegal drug activity on deforestation. What policies can be used to ameliorate this problem?

Works Cited and Selected Readings

Andersen, L. E., C. W. J. Granger, E. J. Reis, D. Weinhold, and S. Wunder. *The Dynamics of Deforestation and Economic Growth in the Brazilian Amazon*. New York: Cambridge University Press, 2002.

Arnold, J. E. M., and M. R. Perez. Can Non-timber Forest Products Match Tropical Forest Conservation and Development Objectives? *Ecological Economics 39*, no.3 (December 2001): 437–447.

Barbier, E. B. Environmental Project Evaluation in Developing Countries, Valuing the Environment as an Input. Pages 55–82 in *Does Environmental Policy Work: The Theory and Practice of Outcomes Assessment*, edited by D. E. Ervin, J. R. Kahn, and M. L. Livingston. Cheltenham, UK: Edward Elgar, 2004.

Bird, G. Loan-Loss Provisions and Third-World Debt. *Essays in International Finance*, No. 176. Princeton, NJ: Princeton University, Economics Department, International Finance Section, 1989.

Bishop, R. C. Endangered Species and Uncertainty: The Economics of a Safe Minimum Standard. *American Journal of Agricultural Economics 60* (1978): 10–18.

Brown, K., and D. Pearce (eds.). *The Causes of Tropical Deforestation.* London: University College London Press, 1994.

Capistrano, A. D. Tropical Forest Depletion and the Changing Macroeconomy 1967–1985. Pages 68–95 in *The Causes of Tropical Deforestation,* edited by K. Brown and D. Pearce. London: University College London Press, 1994.

Caviglia-Harris, J. L., and J. R. Kahn. Diffusion of Sustainable Agriculture in the Brazilian Tropical Rainforest: A Discrete Choice Analysis. *Economics Development and Cultural Change 49* (2001): 311–334.

Caviglia, J. L. *Sustainable Agriculture in Brazil: Economic Development and Deforestation.* Cheltenham, UK: Edward Elgar, 1999.

Caviglia-Harris, J., and J. R. Kahn. Carbon Annuities as a Policy to Promote Sustainable Agroforestry and Slow Global Warming. *International Journal of Sustainable Development*, 2003.

Caviglia-Harris, J. L., J. R. Kahn, and T. Green. Demand-Side Policies for Environmental Protection and Sustainable Usage of Renewable Resources. *Ecological Economics 45*, no. 1 (April 2003): 119–132.

Centeno, J. C. *Forest Concession Policy in Venezuela.* Online: http://www.ciens.ula.ve/~jcenteno/concess.html. Washington, DC: World Resources Institute, 1995.

Dale, V.H., F. Southworth, R. V. O'Neill, A. Rose, and R. Frohn. Simulating Spatial Patterns of Land-Use in Rondonia, Brazil. Pages 29–56 in *Some Mathematical Questions in Biology*, edited by R. Gardner. Providence, RI: American Mathematical Society, 1993.

Dos Santos, A., M. Nuvunga, and E. Salati. *Workshop: Forest Policies and Sustainable Development in the Amazon.* United Nations Development Programme/Fundação Brasiliera para o Desenvolvemento Sustentavel, Rio de Janeiro: 1997.

Ehui, S. K., T. W. Hertel, and P.V. Preckel. Forest Resource Depletion, Soil Dynamics and Agricultural Productivity in the Tropics. *Journal of Environmental Economics and Management 18* (1990): 136–150.

Fearnside, P. M. Saving Tropical Forests as a Global Warming Countermeasure: An Issue That Divides the Environmental Movement. *Ecological Economics 39*, no. 2 (November 2001): 167–184.

Fisher, A. C., M. Hanemann, and W. Michael. Valuation of Tropical Forests, edited by P. Dasgupta, and K. S. Mailer. Pages 505–528 in *Environment and Emerging Development Issues* Vol. 2. New York: Oxford University Press, 1997.

Food and Agricultural Organization of the United Nations. *Forest Resource Assessment 1990: Tropical Countries.* FAO Forestry Paper 112. Rome: FAO, 1993.

Food and Agricultural Organization of the United Nations. *Tropical Forestry Action Plan.* Rome: FAO, 1987.

Food and Agricultural Organization of the United Nations. *Forest Resources of Tropical Africa.* UN32/6.1201-78-04 Technical Report No. 2. Rome: FAO, 1981a.

Food and Agricultural Organization of the United Nations. *Forest Resources of Tropical Asia.* UN32/6.1201-78-04 Technical Report No. 3. Rome: FAO, 1981b.

Food and Agricultural Organization of the United Nations. *Los Recurses Forestales de la America Tropical.* UN32/6.1201-78-04 Technical Report No. 1. Rome: FAO, 1981c.

Gillis, M. Indonesia: Public Policies, Resource Management, and the Tropical Forest. Pages 43–114 in *Public Policies and the Misuse of Forest Resources*, edited by R. Repetto, and M. Gillis. Washington, DC: World Resources Institute, 1998.

Gray, J. A. Tropical Forest Pricing Policies and Rent Collection in South East Asia. *Journal of the Asia Pacific Economy 1*, no. 2 (1996): 171–184.

Gray, J. A. Forest Concession Policies and Sustainable Management of Tropical Forests. *Workshop: Forest Policies and Sustainable Development in the Amazon*, edited by A. Dos Santos, M. Nuvunga, and E. Salati. Rio de Janeiro: United Nations Development Programme/Fundação Brasiliera para o Desenvolvemento Sustentavel, 1997.

Gray, J. A., and L. Hägerby. *Forest Concessions in Nicaragua: Policies and Pricing.* Managua, Nicaragua: Administracion Forestal Estal, Ministerio del Ambiente y Recursos Naturales, ADFOREST MARENA, 1997.

Head, S., and R. Heinzman. *Lessons of the Rainforest.* San Francisco: Sierra Club Books, 1990.

Hyde, W., and R. A. Sedjo. Managing Tropical Forests: Reflections on the Distribution of Rent. *Land Economics 68*, no. 3 (1992): 343–350.

Kahn, J. R. The Development of Markets and Market Incentives for Sustainable Forestry: Application to the Brazilian Amazon. Organization for Economic Cooperation and Development, Environment Directorate, 28 March 2002. Online: http://www.olis.oecd.org/olis/2001doc.nsf.

Kahn, J. R., and J. A. McDonald. Third World Debt and Tropical Deforestation. *Ecological Economics 12* (1995): 107–123.

Kahn, J. R., F. McCormick, and V. Nogueira. Integrating Ecological Complexity into Economic Incentives for Sustainable Use of Amazonian Rainforests. *Journal of Sustainable Forestry 12*, (2000): 99–122.

Kramer, R. A., N. Sharma, and M. Munasinghe. Tropical Forests and Sustainable Development: A Framework for Analysis. Environment Paper No. 13. Washington, DC: World Bank, 1995.

Lanky, J. P. *An Interim Report on the State of Tropical Forest Resources in the Developing Countries*. Rome: FAO, 1988.

Lefler, K. B., and R. R. Rucker. Transactions Costs and the Efficient Organization of Production: A study of Timber-Harvesting Contracts. *Journal of Political Economy 99*, no. 5 (1991): 1060–1087.

Lovejoy, T. Conservation Planning in a Checkerboard World: The Problem of the Size of Natural Areas. Pages 289–301 in *Land and Its Uses, Actual and Potential: An Environmental Appraisal*, edited by F. T. Last, M. C. B. Hotz, and B.G. Bell. New York: Plenum Press, 1986a.

Lovejoy, T., et al. Edge and Other Effects of Isolation on Amazon Forest Fragment. Pages 257–285 in *Conservation Biology: The Science of Scarcity and Diversity*, edited by M. E. Soulé. Sunderland, MA: Sinauer, 1986b.

Mendelsohn, R., Property Rights and Tropical Deforestation. *Oxford Economic Papers 46* (1994): 750–756.

Myers, N. *Deforestation Rates in Tropical Forests and Their Climatic Implications*. London: Friends of the Earth, 1989.

Panaiotov, T. *Not by Timber Alone: Economics and Ecology for Sustaining Tropical Forests*. Washington, DC: Island Press, 1992.

Perry, D. Tropical Biology. Pages 25–38 in *Lessons of the Rainforest*, edited by S. Head, and R. Heinzman. San Francisco: Sierra Club Books, 1990.

Repetto, R. *The Forest for the Trees? Government Policies and the Misuse of Forest Resources*. Washington, DC: World Resources Institute, 1988.

Repetto, R., and M. Gillis. *Public Policies and the Misuse of Forest Resources*. Washington, DC: World Resources Institute, 1989.

Shilling, J. D. Reflections on Debt and the Environment. *Finance and Development 29* (1992): 28–30.

Sizer, N., and R. Rice. *Backs to the Wall in Suriname: Forest Policy in a Country in Crisis*. Washington, DC: World Resources Institute, 1995.

Sizer, N. *Profit without Plunder: Reaping Revenue from Guyana's Tropical Forests without Destroying Them*. Washington, DC: World Resources Institute, 1996.

Sohngen, B., and R. Mendelsohn. An Optimal Control Model of Forest Carbon Sequestration. *American Journal of Agricultural Economics 85*, no. 2 (May 2003): 448–457.

Stevens, W. K. Research in 'Virgin' Amazon Uncovers Complex Farming. *New York Times*, 3 April 1990: C1.

Taylor, K. I. Why Supernatural Eels Matter. Pages 184–195 in *Lessons of the Rainforest*, edited by S. Head and R. Heinzman. San Francisco: Sierra Club Books, 1990.

United Nations Development Programme. *Human Development Report 1990*. Oxford: Oxford University Press, 1990.

Vincent, J. Rent Capture and the Feasibility of Tropical Forest Management. *Land Economics 66*, no. 2 (1992): 212–223.

Von Moltke, K. International Economic Issues in Tropical Deforestation. Paper presented at the Workshop on Climate Change and Tropical Forests, Sáo Paulo, 1990.

World Bank. *World Tables*. Baltimore: Johns Hopkins University Press, various years.

World Bank, *World Development Report*. New York: Oxford University Press, various years.

World Resources Institute. *World Resources 1992–93*. Washington, DC: World Resources Institute, 1993.

chapter 14

Biodiversity and Habitat Preservation

If Charles Darwin were writing today, his masterwork would probably be known as The Disappearance of Species.

Edmund Wolf, *Conserving Biological Diversity*

Introduction

This quotation by Edmund Wolf (1985, p. 124) is jestful, but it emphasizes an increasingly important environmental problem: the extinction of plant and animal species. Extinction is occurring at an unprecedented rate, and it results in a loss of biodiversity, which can be defined as the total variety of life on earth. Biodiversity is extremely important for ecosystem function with many direct benefits to humans.

Although the above definition of biodiversity is general, one can specifically define the process that leads to the loss of biodiversity, which is extinction. A species becomes extinct when the last individual organisms of the species die. Species may, however, decline to a point where even though they exist, the population has fallen below the minimum viable level and the species becomes doomed to eventual extinction. This subject is discussed more fully later in the chapter. There are many natural and anthropogenic sources of extinction, with each anthropogenic source exacerbated by market failure.

Natural extinctions occur when the environment changes, and some species find themselves at a competitive disadvantage and are displaced by other species that are better adapted to the new conditions. Natural extinctions may also occur when random changes in a species' population gives one species a competitive advantage over another. Over time, the species with the disadvantage may be completely displaced by the species with the advantage.

Table 14.1 Estimated Acceleration of Mammal Extinctions

Time period	Extinctions per century	Percent of present stock of species lost	Principle cause
Pleistocene (3.5 million years)	0.01	—	Natural extinction
Late Pleistocene (100,000 years)	0.08	0.002	Climate change, Neolithic hunters
A.D.1600–1980	17	0.4	European expansion, Hunting and commerce
A.D.1980–2000	145	3.5	Habitat disruption

Source: From *State of the World, 1985: A Worldwatch Institute Report on Progress Toward a Sustainable Society*, by Lester R. Brown et al, eds. Copyright © 1985 by Worldwatch Institute. Reprinted by permission of W. W. Norton & Company, Inc.

Natural extinctions are always occurring, usually at a relatively slow pace, although there are often rapid and massive extinctions. The disappearance of the dinosaurs is an example of a massive and rapid extinction, but it actually took place over a period of about 2 million years.[1] Table 14.1 lists extinctions of mammals over recent history and shows the extremely rapid rate of extinction that has occurred in modern times. This rapid loss of species cannot be attributed to the types of naturally occurring environmental changes that led to the extinction of the dinosaurs. Rather, these extinctions are primarily due to anthropogenic factors.

The concept of marginality is different in this chapter than in many of the other chapters of this book. In Chapter 11, for example, the marginal unit is a fish and the allocation question is how to choose the level of harvest that maximizes social welfare. In this chapter, the primary question revolves around providing the optimal level of biodiversity, and the marginal unit is not an organism but an entire species or an entire ecosystem.

Anthropogenic Causes of Species Extinction

There are several important anthropogenic causes of extinction. They include excessive loss of habitat, competition from nonnative species, and harvesting of the species. These causes are all exacerbated by market failures, where people make economic decisions that do not incorporate the full social costs of their actions. Table 14.2 lists observed declines in animal species and their

[1]See the Massive Extinction web site of the Natural History Magazine for more information on the rapid rate of extinction in the modern era: http://www.well.com/user/davidu/extinction.html.

Table 14.2 Observed Declines in Selected Animal Species, Early 1990s

Amphibians	Worldwide decline observed in recent years. Wetland drainage and invading species have extinguished nearly half of New Zealand's unique frog fauna. Biologists cite European demand for frog's legs as a cause of the rapid nationwide decline of India's two most common bullfrogs.
Birds	Three-fourths of the world's bird species are declining in population or threatened with extinction.
Fish	One-third of North America's freshwater fish stocks are rare, threatened, or endangered; one-third of U.S. coastal fish have declined in population since 1975. Introduction of the Nile perch has helped drive nearly half the 400 species of Lake Victoria, Africa's largest lake, to or near extinction.
Invertebrates	On the order of 100 species are lost to deforestation each day. Western Germany reports one-fourth of its 40,000 known invertebrates to be threatened. Roughly half the freshwater snails of the southeastern United States are extinct or nearly so.
Mammals	Almost half of Australia's surviving mammals are threatened with extinction. France, Western Germany, the Netherlands, and Portugal all report more than 40 percent of their mammals as threatened.
Carnivores	Virtually all species of wild cats and bears are seriously declining in numbers.
Primates	More than two-thirds of the world's 150 primate species are threatened with extinction.
Reptiles	Of the world's 270 turtle species, 42 percent are rare or threatened with extinction.

Source: From *State of the World 1992: A Worldwatch Institute Report on Progress Toward a Sustainable Society*, by Lester R. Brown et al. Copyright © 1992 by Worldwatch Institute. Reprinted by permission of W. W. Norton and Company, Inc.

anthropogenic causes. Table 14.3 lists the number of species in the United States and the rest of the world that are declining to the point that extinction is a possibility. Endangered species are those in danger of becoming extinct through all or a significant part of their natural range. Threatened species are those that are likely to become endangered in the foreseeable future. Table 14.4 lists the endangered mammalian species in the United States.[2]

Loss of Habitat

While open-access harvesting and competition from nonnative species have figured prominently in the decline and demise of many species, the loss of habitat is currently a more pressing problem. Many species are found only in a limited range of habitat, and if this habitat is destroyed by conversion into another land use or contaminated by pollution, the species will become extinct. This problem is particularly important in association with the massive deforestation

[2]Note that the number of endangered species changes very quickly. Go to the web sites listed in Tables 14.2 and 14.3 for up-to-the-minute information.

Table 14.3 Endangered Species in the United States and the Rest of the World: Summary of Listed Species and Recovery Plans as of September 2003

Group	Endangered		Threatened		Total species	U.S. Species with recovery plans*[a]
	U.S.	Foreign	U.S.	Foreign		
Mammals	65	251	9	17	342	54
Birds	78	175	14	6	273	77
Reptiles	14	64	22	15	115	32
Amphibians	12	8	9	1	30	14
Fishes	71	11	44	0	126	96
Clams	62	2	8	0	72	57
Snails	21	1	11	0	33	22
Insects	35	4	9	0	48	29
Arachnids	12	0	0	0	12	5
Crustaceans	18	0	3	0	21	13
Animal subtotal	**388**	**516**	**129**	**39**	**1072**	**399**
Flowering plants	571	1	144	0	716	574
Conifers and cycads	2	0	1	2	5	2
Ferns and allies	24	0	2	0	26	26
Lichens	2	0	0	0	2	2
Plant subtotal	**599**	**1**	**147**	**2**	**749**	**604**
Grand total	**987**	**517**	**276**	**41**	**1821**	**1003**

Total U.S. Endangered	**987**	**(388 animals, 599 plants)**
Total U.S. Threatened	**276**	**(129 animals, 147 plants)**
Total U.S. Species	**1263**	**(517 animals,[c] 746 plants)**

[a]There are 532 distinct approved recovery plans. Some recovery plans cover more than one species, and a few species have separate plans covering different parts of their ranges. This count includes only plans generated by the USFWS or jointly by the USFWS and NMFS, and includes only listed species that occur in the United States.

[c]Nine animal species have dual status in the United States.

Source: Taken directly from the U.S. Fish and Wildlife TESS web page at http://ecos.fws.gov/tess_public/TESSWebpage.

Table 14.4 Endangered and Threatened Mammals in the United States as of 2003

Status	Species name
E	Bat, gray (*Myotis grisescens*)
E	Bat, Hawaiian hoary (*Lasiurus cinereus semotus*)
E	Bat, Indiana (*Myotis sodalis*)
E	Bat, lesser long-nosed (*Leptonycteris curasoae yerbabuenae*)
E	Bat, little Mariana fruit (*Pteropus tokudae*)
E	Bat, Mariana fruit (= Mariana flying fox) (*Pteropus mariannus mariannus*)
E	Bat, Mexican long-nosed (*Leptonycteris nivalis*)
E	Bat, Ozark big-eared (*Corynorhinus (=Plecotus) townsendii ingens*)
E	Bat, Virginia big-eared (*Corynorhinus (=Plecotus) townsendii virginianus*)
T(S/A)	Bear, American black (*Ursus americanus*)
XN,T	Bear, grizzly (*Ursus arctos horribilis*)
T	Bear, Louisiana black (*Ursus americanus luteolus*)
E	Caribou, woodland (*Rangifer tarandus caribou*)
E	Deer, Columbian white-tailed (*Odocoileus virginianus leucurus*)
E	Deer, key (*Odocoileus virginianus clavium*)
E,XN	Ferret, black-footed (*Mustela nigripes*)
E	Fox, San Joaquin kit (*Vulpes macrotis mutica*)
E	Jaguar (*Panthera onca*)
E	Jaguarundi, Gulf Coast (*Herpailurus (=Felis) yagouaroundi cacomitli*)
E	Jaguarundi, Sinaloan (*Herpailurus (=Felis) yagouaroundi tolteca*)
E	Kangaroo rat, Fresno (*Dipodomys nitratoides exilis*)
E	Kangaroo rat, giant (*Dipodomys ingens*)
E	Kangaroo rat, Morro Bay (*Dipodomys heermanni morroensis*)
E	Kangaroo rat, San Bernardino Merriam's (*Dipodomys merriami parvus*)
E	Kangaroo rat, Stephens' (*Dipodomys stephensi (incl. D. cascus)*)
E	Kangaroo rat, Tipton (*Dipodomys nitratoides nitratoides*)
T	Lynx, Canada (*Lynx canadensis*)
E	Manatee, West Indian (*Trichechus manatus*)
E	Mountain beaver, Point Arena (*Aplodontia rufa nigra*)
E	Mouse, Alabama beach (*Peromyscus polionotus ammobates*)

(continues)

Table 14.4 (continued)

Status	Species name
E	Mouse, Anastasia Island beach (*Peromyscus polionotus phasma*)
E	Mouse, Choctawhatchee beach (*Peromyscus polionotus allophrys*)
E	Mouse, Key Largo cotton (*Peromyscus gossypinus allapaticola*)
E	Mouse, Pacific pocket (*Perognathus longimembris pacificus*)
E	Mouse, Perdido Key beach (*Peromyscus polionotus trissyllepsis*)
T	Mouse, Preble's meadow jumping (*Zapus hudsonius preblei*)
E	Mouse, salt marsh harvest (*Reithrodontomys raviventris*)
T	Mouse, southeastern beach (*Peromyscus polionotus niveiventris*)
E	Mouse, St. Andrew beach (*Peromyscus polionotus peninsularis*)
E	Ocelot (*Leopardus (= Felis) pardalis*)
XN,T	Otter, southern sea (*Enhydra lutris nereis*)
E	Panther, Florida (*Puma (= Felis) concolor coryi*)
T	Prairie dog, Utah (*Cynomys parvidens*)
E	Pronghorn, Sonoran (*Antilocapra americana sonoriensis*)
E	Puma (= cougar), eastern (*Puma (= Felis) concolor couguar*)
T(S/A)	Puma (= mountain lion) (*Puma (= Felis) concolor (all subsp. except coryi)*)
E	Rabbit, Lower Keys marsh (*Sylvilagus palustris hefneri*)
E	Rabbit, pygmy (*Brachylagus idahoensis*)
E	Rabbit, riparian brush (*Sylvilagus bachmani riparius*)
E	Rice rat (*Oryzomys palustris natator*)
E	Seal, Caribbean monk (*Monachus tropicalis*)
T	Seal, Guadalupe fur (*Arctocephalus townsendi*)
E	Seal, Hawaiian monk (*Monachus schauinslandi*)
E,T	Sea-lion, Steller (*Eumetopias jubatus*)
E	Sheep, bighorn (*Ovis canadensis*)
E	Sheep, bighorn (*Ovis canadensis californiana*)
E	Shrew, Buena Vista Lake ornate (*Sorex ornatus relictus*)
E	Squirrel, Carolina northern flying (*Glaucomys sabrinus coloratus*)
E,XN	Squirrel, Delmarva Peninsula fox (*Sciurus niger cinereus*)
E	Squirrel, Mount Graham red (*Tamiasciurus hudsonicus grahamensis*)

(continues)

Table 14.4 (continued)

Status	Species name
T	Squirrel, northern Idaho ground (*Spermophilus brunneus brunneus*)
E	Squirrel, Virginia northern flying (*Glaucomys sabrinus fuscus*)
E	Vole, Amargosa (*Microtus californicus scirpensis*)
E	Vole, Florida salt marsh (*Microtus pennsylvanicus dukecampbelli*)
E	Vole, Hualapai Mexican (*Microtus mexicanus hualpaiensis*)
E	Whale, blue (*Balaenoptera musculus*)
E	Whale, bowhead (*Balaena mysticetus*)
E	Whale, finback (*Balaenoptera physalus*)
E	Whale, humpback (*Megaptera novaeangliae*)
E	Whale, right (*Balaena glacialis (incl. australis)*)
E	Whale, Sei (*Balaenoptera borealis*)
E	Whale, sperm (*Physeter catodon (=macrocephalus)*)
E,XN,T	Wolf, gray (*Canis lupus*)
E,XN	Wolf, red (*Canis rufus*)
E	Woodrat, Key Largo (*Neotoma floridana smalli*)
E	Woodrat, riparian (= San Joaquin Valley) (*Neotoma fuscipes riparia*)

KEY:
E: Endangered **XN**: Experimental Population, Non-Essential
T: Threatened **T(S/A)**: Similarity of Appearance to a Threatened Taxon

Source: U.S. Fish and Wildlife Service web page, http://ecos.fws.gov/tess_public/TESSWebpageVipListed.

that has occurred in tropical rain forests, because those forests contain as much as three-quarters of all the earth's species (see Chapter 13). Other important losses of habitat are associated with the loss of temperate forests, destruction of coral reefs, loss of wetlands, and pollution of numerous aquatic environments.

The loss of habitat may be associated with either open-access or private property resources. For example, coral reefs tend to be open access and are destroyed both by pollution that is carried to the coral lagoons by rivers and by fishing activity. Upstream polluters make their decisions concerning waste disposal without considering the social costs associated with the negative effects on coral reefs. Similarly, fishers make use of fishing techniques that lower their costs but are destructive of the reefs, such as fishing with explosives or posions. Also, recreationists (particularly in Florida and the Caribbean) damage coral reefs by anchoring their boats on the reef, by removing coral from the reefs, and by harvesting shellfish that are predators to animals such as starfish (which, in turn, are predators of the animals that create the coral reefs). Global warming also has a negative impact on coral reefs.

On the other hand, privately owned habitat is also lost. Although the destructive interactions associated with open-access resources are not present with privately owned resources, market failures still occur. For example, an owner of wetlands who is contemplating converting the wetlands to condominiums does not consider the social value of leaving the wetlands intact. Thus, the owner makes decisions based on equating marginal private costs and private benefits, and the ecological services of the wetlands are ignored. The wetland owner makes his or her decision concerning conversion of wetlands by comparing the private net benefits of conversion with the private net benefits of preservation. The social net benefits are generally excluded from consideration. In other words, there are negative externalities associated with the conversion of habitat to other uses. In many countries, including the United States, there are laws that regulate and sometimes prohibit the destruction of wetlands. Wetlands, however, are still being lost at a rapid rate.

Competition from Nonnative Species

Competition from nonnative species is the second-leading cause of loss of biodiversity and can also be viewed as an externalities problem. A person introduces an exotic species (a species from another area) because he or she expects to realize benefits from this species. The exotic species, however, is often associated with large ecological and social costs, because the exotic species will outcompete or prey upon native species. Nonnative species also arrive as hitchhikers with the importation of other species, with the importation of goods, and in the luggage and on the person of international travelers. The externality that occurs here is that people engaged in transportation or travel activities devote insufficient resources toward reducing the probability that their activities will result in the harmful introduction of a nonnative species. A good example is the fish from Eastern Europe and Asian waters that have been introduced into the U.S. Great Lakes in the ballast water of tanker ships. These fish compete with native fish for food and habitat, as well as eat the eggs of native fish.

Nonnative species have their impact on native species by direct predation, competition of ecological resources, or destruction of habitat. An example of direct predation can be found in island ecosystems. For example, many ground-nesting birds evolved in island ecosystems, because the islands lacked predators that would interfere with the nesting process. The intentional introduction of pigs and the accidental introduction of rats, however, have led to the loss of many island bird species, including the dodo bird of Mauritius and Reunion (islands off the southeast coast of Africa). Alternatively, introduced species outcompete native species. For example, well-meaning fishery managers introduced European brown trout into eastern U.S. streams to provide more angling opportunities for recreational fishers. In many areas, however, the more aggressive brown trout has completely displaced the native brook trout. Similarly, the European house sparrow outcompetes the eastern bluebird for nesting sites and has displaced this bird from a large part of its natural range. Introduced insects are an important cause of the loss of ridgetop forests in the United States, because gypsy moth caterpillars and other nonnative insects (such as the wooly adelgid) decimate forests and render them more vulnerable to other stresses such as acid rain and tropospheric ozone (see Chapter 9).

Open-Access Harvesting

Excessive harvesting is often thought to be the main cause of extinction. Although that is not the case, excessive harvesting is associated with some of the most notorious extinctions in North America and some of the most visible current problems in Africa and Asia.

In North America, the near extinction of the American bison (more commonly referred to as buffalo) was caused by excessive hunting.[3] Although the buffalo had been hunted for thousands of years by Native Americans, herds were plentiful, numbering in the millions. With the westward expansion of Americans of European and African descent, however, hunting quickly decimated the herds. Why could buffalo herds sustain hunting by Native Americans but perish under hunting by non–Native Americans?

The answer to this question is that under Native American control, buffalo herds were common property (not owned by a particular person) but not open-access resources. This crucially important distinction is often confused in the literature. Common property resources often have restrictions on their use, whereas open-access resources do not. In the case of the Native American and the bison, cultural traditions dictated the method and magnitude of hunting, and these traditions tended to conserve the resource. Hunters who killed more than could be effectively used violated these cultural norms and received social sanctions. Also, intertribal competition for herds was prevented by the division of grazing areas into hunting areas specific to each tribe, although these boundaries were subject to fluctuation. If one tribe violated the hunting grounds of another, it could expect violent retribution. This combination of intertribal and intratribal social rules prevented the open-access exploitation and overharvesting of the buffalo herds.

In contrast, when the Native Americans lost control of their hunting grounds to non–Native Americans, the buffalo herds became open-access common property, with no restrictions on their use. Consequently, no individual hunter had an incentive to preserve the resource. Conservative hunting by one person was considered pointless, because the buffalo would be killed by someone else instead. Buffalo were killed for sport and profit, with the hides being the chief source of profit. Meat was seldom utilized, with the exception of the tongue; most of the meat was left on the carcass to rot. A destructive race began, with each buffalo hunter seeking to shoot as many buffalo as possible

[3]The American bison was hunted to the point that it was extinct in the wild. Today's increasing bison herds are descended from animals that were preserved in zoos.

Box 14.1 Elephants and the Ivory Trade

The population of African elephants has been in severe decline, caused by illegal hunting for their ivory tusks. A single tusk will bring a poacher (person engaged in illegal hunting) several hundred dollars, which is the approximate per capita gross domestic product in many African countries. Because of this relatively large potential income, many rural dwellers have a strong incentive to illegally hunt elephant.

There has been considerable controversy over how to deal with this problem. Several southern African countries had been relatively successful by giving property rights to elephants to neighboring villages. The local inhabitants then had an incentive to report nonlocal poachers to police authority. Also, federal governments compensated villages for crop damage by elephants. Under such a plan, villages would manage elephants as a renewable resource, harvesting some individuals for food or promoting lucrative sport hunting by foreigners, but leaving the herd intact to produce more elephants.

Other countries that have not adopted this approach have been less successful in protecting elephant herds. In countries such as Kenya, large herds have been decimated by those engaged in ivory trade. Although this difference may be construed as evidence that creating property rights and markets works in preventing the extinction of endangered species, there may be other differences between the southern African states and the central and eastern African states that have more trouble maintaining their herds. First, population pressures and associated loss of habitat may be greater, especially in eastern African countries such as Kenya. Second, owing to greater police and military power, borders may be more secure in southern African states (particularly South Africa). This security is critically important because, in countries such as Kenya, a large proportion of poachers cross borders to enter the country, particularly from Somalia and Sudan.

As a result of the decline in elephant herds, the Convention for International Trade in Endangered Species (CITES) banned the international trade in ivory in 1989. Although this ban may at first appear to be a completely positive move, some negative aspects may be associated with it. Countries that have maintained elephant herds by establishing property rights for local inhabitants lose the incentives by which local inhabitants manage and protect herds. If villagers cannot earn income from the legal sale of ivory, then they have less incentive to manage and protect elephant herds. Also, the national governments of African countries lose revenue that they could earn by gathering tusks from elephants that die of natural causes.

Nonetheless, it is believed that this ban might be the only way to prevent the disappearance of elephants from most central and eastern African countries. Because the ban is relatively recent and the reproductive cycle of

(continues)

Box 14.1 (continued)

elephants is relatively long, it is too soon to see if it will protect the herds or if additional steps are needed. Of interest is that the ivory ban may work well, because the primary use of ivory is for carving jewelry, sculptures, and knickknacks. There are many substitutes for ivory for this purpose, especially soft stones such as jade and soapstone, so economic theory would suggest that the ban has a chance to be successful. For up-to-date information on this problem search the bibliographic databases for elephants and CITES.

before the buffalo were shot by competing hunters. Under this type of open-access harvesting pressure, the buffalo quickly disappeared from the prairie.[4]

Modern examples of this type of open-access harvesting pressure include many of the large mammals of Africa and Asia, such as the elephant, rhinoceros, tiger, bear, and leopard. These animals are valued by hunters for body parts, such as the elephant's tusks, the rhino's horn, the bear's gallbladder, and the leopard's skin (see Boxes 14.1 and 14.2). Illegal hunting activity by poachers threatens these animals with extinction. In addition, there is a large impact associated with illegally harvesting live animals in the wild for the pet industry. Parrots, macaws, snakes, turtles, and tropical fish are examples of animals that are threatened by these activities. Although both types of these hunting activities are usually forbidden by law, it is extremely difficult to enforce these prohibitions because of the high profits associated with the illegal trade. These problems with enforcement are further discussed in a subsequent section.

Of course, fish are another example of species that face open-access harvesting. As discussed in Chapter 11, many species are being overharvested and are threatened by population collapse and potential extinction.

Costs of Losses in Biodiversity

Biodiversity is important for a variety of reasons. First, biodiversity promotes ecosystem stability.[5] The more diverse a system, the greater its ability to withstand shocks and stresses. If biodiversity promotes ecosystem health and function, then biodiversity promotes all the services derived from ecosystems,

---

[4]See Chapter 11 for formal economic models of open-access resources.

[5]The relationship between biodiversity and ecosystem stability is a relatively contentious area of scientific debate and depends on the definition of stability. If stability is defined as returning the ecosystem to the exact original state, then more diversity means less stability, because the greater the number of species in the system, the more difficult it is to repopulate species that have left the ecosystem because of the shock. If stability is defined as the ability to withstand a shock and continue to provide the same type and level of ecological services, however, then more biodiversity implies more stability.

Box 14.2 Viagra, Male Impotence, and Endangered Species

One of the greatest threats to wild animals has been the perceived effect of medicines made from certain animal body parts on male sexual performance. Powders and pills made from rhinoceros horn, elk antlers, and the penises of large predators (tigers, leopards, bears) are believed to cure male sexual impotence and increase overall performance in this area.

Although it is too early to measure the impact, medicines such as Viagra that are designed (and demonstrated in clinical tests, unlike the animal parts) to deal with these problems may reduce the pressure on these animals and help protect them from extinction. Consider the graph shown here. If D_1 represents the demand before the development of Viagra and its competitors MC_1 represents the marginal cost of supplying the parts, then Q_1 units of parts will be illegally harvested in the wild. The development of Viagra and its competitors creates a substitute for these animal parts, which will shift the demand for the animals parts to D_2.

The greater the perceived effect of Viagra and related drugs, and the lower the price of these drugs, the greater the downward shift in the demand for animal parts from these endangered species, which has some interesting implications for policy! In societies with high demand for the animal parts, information about Viagra and related drugs could be provided to appropriate segments of the population, and its use could even be subsidized.

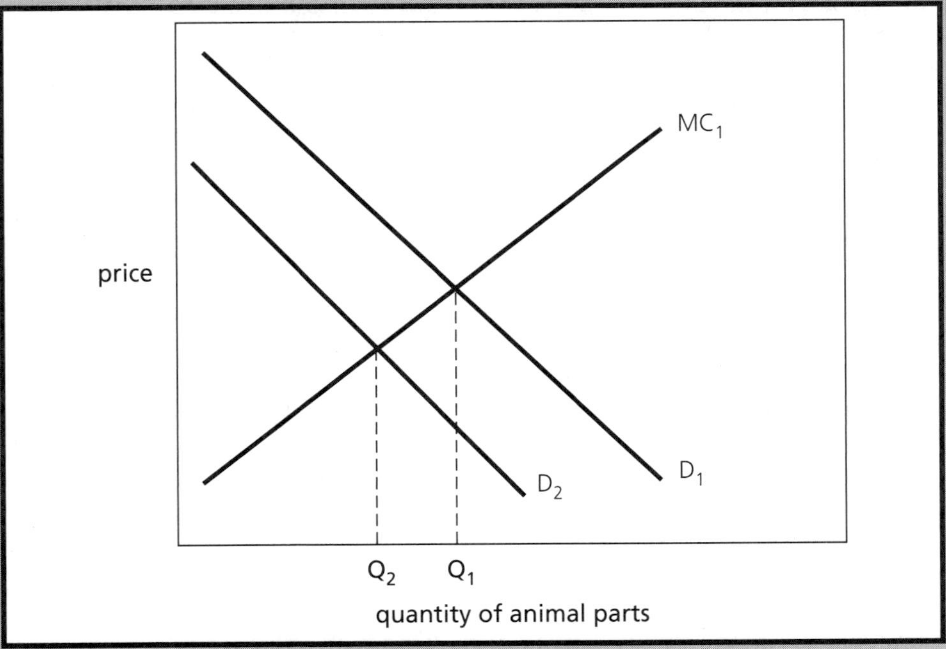

such as protection of freshwater supplies, production of oxygen, absorption of carbon dioxide, nutrient cycling, and provision of habitat. In addition, people view a healthy and biodiverse ecosystem as intrinsically more valuable than a degraded or less biodiverse system. Second, plants and animal species have a value because they may be used to produce economic goods. The species may provide goods directly, such as fruits or nuts that are consumed directly, or they may be a direct source of natural chemicals and compounds (Sedjo, 1992). Third, the organisms' genes may be a source of genetic information. Such information may be used in the development of new varieties of plants with different properties than existing varieties (for example, the development of new crops with higher yields through crossbreeding).

The information from existing species may also be used to create new plants or animals through genetic engineering. Genetic engineering may transfer properties across species that are widely different (such as from bacterium to a plant), whereas crossbreeding transfers properties across related species or varieties within a species.

Ecosystem health, preservation of genetic information, and potential use of genetic information in commerce are important, but it should be remembered that biodiversity may be important simply because people think that it is important. Although this statement may seem tautological, many people desire biodiversity, deriving greater utility from more diverse ecosystems than less diverse ecosystems. People may also feel that it is society's ethical responsibility to maintain biodiversity.

Costs of Losses of Habitat

Although one of the important reasons for preserving habitat is to preserve biodiversity, habitat provides many other important services. Obviously, habitat provides an environment in which plants and animals can exist. The other services can be crucially important to ecological and social systems. For example, tropical forests and the phytoplankton layer are the principal mechanisms for producing oxygen and removing carbon dioxide from the atmosphere. A description of the services of many habitats (that is, tropical forests, temperate forests, aquatic systems) are provided in the individual chapters of this book. To provide an example, however, let's discuss the costs of losing wetlands (a particularly stressed type of habitat).

Wetlands play a unique ecological role as a transition zone between aquatic ecosystems and terrestrial ecosystems. One critical aspect of this role is nutrient cycling. The wetlands serve as a vast store of nutrients from terrestrial sources that are gradually released into aquatic ecosystems. Wetlands also serve as the beginning of the food web for many aquatic systems. The nutrients flowing from the wetlands begin the food web in the aquatic systems, and many aquatic organisms feed directly in the wetlands. Many estuarine shellfish and finfish are critically dependent on the productivity of the wetlands. (Box 11.1 discusses the role of wetlands in blue crab production.) Each of the many different types of wetlands interacts with surrounding ecosystems in different ways. Different types of wetlands include forest wetlands, freshwater marshes, saltwater marshes, bogs, bayous, and mangroves.

One of the most important roles of wetlands is serving as a buffer against storms. Wetlands absorb storm water, preventing or lessening floods from high levels of rain. This reservoir function also reduces the impacts of droughts. Wetlands also provide a buffer to dampen storm surge and wave damage from coastal storms.

A very good example of the flood control services can be found in the wetlands that formerly existed in the upper Mississippi River system. These wetlands provided a tremendously important storage area for heavy rainfall, but they were drained to provide land for agriculture. Artificial means such as dams and levees were constructed in an attempt to substitute for the lack of natural flood control services, but these have not been very successful. For example, in 1993 a 25-year rainfall (a storm of a magnitude that one would expect to occur only once in 25 years) caused a 100-year flood. The reason the 25-year rainfall caused the 100-year flood was a loss of the flood control services of the wetlands.

Other important roles of wetlands include serving as a habitat for many species of animals and providing a spawning and nursery area for fish and other aquatic species. In addition, many people use wetlands as an area to recreate, including canoeing and other boating activities, fishing, and hunting. Wetlands also provide a livelihood for many people through their contributions to several industries, including recreation, tourism, commercial fishing, and fur trapping. Box 14.3 discusses the economic value of wetlands.

Policies for Maintaining Biodiversity and Protecting Habitat

Much of the discussion of the importance of biodiversity stems from the potential of organisms to provide medicines and other important chemicals. Some of the most promising cancer treatments are associated with chemicals that occur in plants. For example, an important treatment for childhood leukemia was found in the rosy periwinkle (tropical rain forests of Madagascar), and the Pacific yew (old-growth forests of the Pacific Northwest United States) contains a chemical that is used to shrink tumors. Animals also provide important potential treatments, although usually with less frequency than plants. For example, enzymes in the skin of an African frog may provide important treatments for burn victims.[6]

Many of today's new medicines come from rain forest and coral reef ecosystems. At first glance, that seems extremely logical; these ecosystems contain the most species, so one would expect the most medicines to come from

[6]Although it is difficult to extrapolate from a sample of only one or two observations, the author of this textbook has personal experience with two rain forest biodiversity products. The first is an ointment made from the fat of an electric eel, which is used to treat athletic injuries, arthritis, and similar inflammations. The second is the oil of the nut of the andiroba tree, which provides an extremely effective insect repellent, as well as a treatment for insect bites and small wounds.

Box 14.3 Economic Value of Wetlands

Robert Anderson and Mark Rockel (1991) of the American Petroleum Institute conducted a survey of various studies that have attempted to measure the value of wetlands. Some studies focused on individual functions of the wetlands, whereas others looked at multiple functions. They summarized the results of their survey in a table, reproduced here. The individual studies that are referenced in this table are listed in this chapter's references.

Although these values are subject to empirical debate, they have been included in this example to give the student an idea of what has been estimated in terms of the value of a habitat.

Anderson and Rockel Summary of Estimates of the Functional Values of Wetlands (updated to 2004 dollars)

Wetland function	Value ($/acre/year)	Capitalized value ($/acre at 5% discount rate)
Food conveyance	$345[1]	$6890
Erosion, wind, and wave barriers	$0.80[2]	$16
Flood storage	N.A.	N.A.
Sediment replenishment	N.A.	N.A.
Fish and shellfish habitat	$58[2], $119[3]	$1263–2380
Waterfowl habitat	$301[1]	$6024
Mammal and reptile habitat	$22[4]	$432
Recreation	$11[4], $44[5], $137[3], $126[5]	$126, $901, $2741, $2525
Water supply	N.A.	N.A.
Timber	N.A.	N.A.
Historic and archaeological use	$58[6]	$11,687
Educational and research use	$11	$126
Water quality improvement	N.A.	N.A.

Source: Anderson and Rockel, Discussion Paper #065, Washington, D.C.: American Petroleum Institute, 1991. Reprinted courtesy of the American Petroleum Institute.

[1]Gupta and Foster, 1975; [2]Farber, 1987; [3]Bell, 1989; [4]Farber and Costanza, 1987; [5]Thibodeau and Ostro, 1981; [6]combines recreation, nature, and cultural values, Gupta and Foster, 1975.

these ecosystems. The reasons for their importance to medical treatment are much more complex, however.

Because these ecosystems are so diverse, and because there are so many species competing for the same resources or preying upon each other, they have evolved with complex survival strategies. Many of these survival strategies involved the development of chemical defense systems to give the species a competitive edge. It is these active chemicals in the chemical defense systems, the result of natural selection in an intensely competitive environment, that provide the basis for medicines that can be active against diseases.

The discussion of the importance of biodiversity also revolves around the importance of maintaining a gene pool for agriculture. New properties, such as frost or disease resistance, can be transferred from wild plants to agricultural varieties by hybridization (sexual transfer) or through genetic engineering. Genetic engineering is particularly important because the crossbreeding and hybridization of important crops, such as corn and wheat, have sacrificed some of their disease resistant properties for greater yields. It is important to preserve wild species so that these traits (as well as new traits) can be brought back into agricultural crops.

Although both the medicinal potential and agricultural potential are important reasons to preserve biological resources, it is also important to remember that biodiversity is critically important to ecosystem health. We should not develop policies that are only oriented toward commercial applications and merely focus protection activities on plants and animals that are judged to have the greatest potential for medicines, other chemicals, and agriculture. We should also recognize the noncommodity benefits associated with this dimension of biodiversity and compare all the benefits and costs when developing policies that focus on preserving the many dimensions of biodiversity.

Because the future benefits of biodiversity are unknown, but could be quite large, this example is the type of environmental problem in which the precautionary principle should be applied. When that principle is applied, policy would be created that protected biodiversity as if the benefits were very large, even though we cannot completely prove that they would be large and we cannot fully measure them. The idea of the precautionary principle is that if we act in a cautious fashion and it turns out that we were overly cautious, the costs of this error are not likely to be too great. If we are not cautious and it turns out that caution was warranted, however, the costs are likely to be immensely large.

Another reason to invoke the precautionary principle in biodiversity protection has to do with the idea of a minimum viable population of a species. The concept of a critically depensated growth function was introduced in Chapter 11 and is reproduced in Figure 14.1.

As can be seen in Figure 14.1, at population levels lower than P', growth becomes negative and the population moves towards extinction. Even if population is somewhat above P', a shock could send population below P' and headed toward extinction. Therefore, prudent policy would set a minimum level of the species a safe distance above P', such as P*. This way, if a shock

Figure 14.1 **The Minimum Viable Population Level**

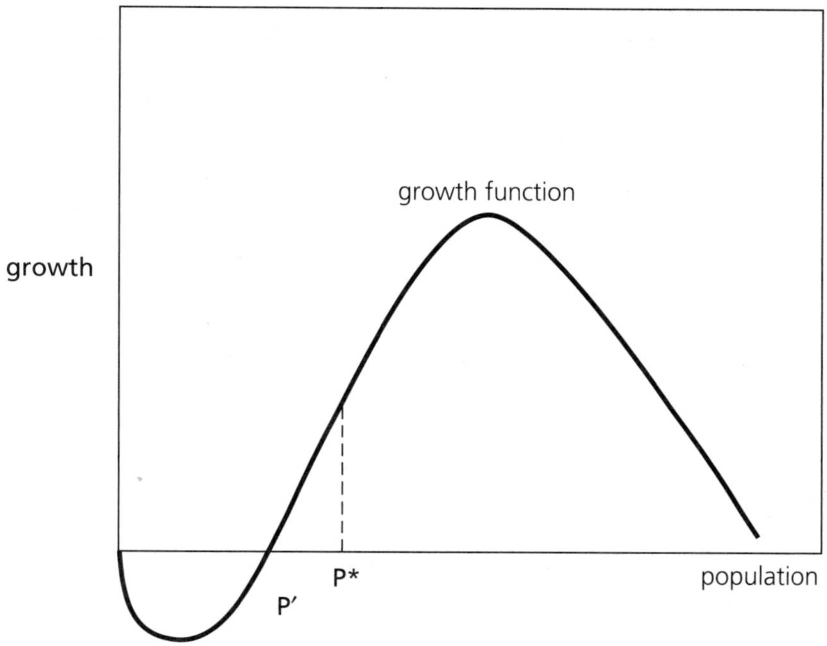

such as a drought, epidemic, or other event takes place, the population will still fall but will stay above the minimum viable level.[7]

Captive breeding programs are often implemented if the population in the wild falls below the minimum viable level. In captive breeding programs, all or a significant portion of the wild population is captured and bred in captivity. Breeding takes place under controlled conditions in captivity, and mortality of the young is greatly reduced. After a sufficient captive population is developed for breeding purposes, new offspring are released into the wild. High-profile captive breeding programs in the United States have included ones for the peregrine falcon, bald eagle, California condor, black-footed ferret, and red wolf.

Policies to Reduce Loss of Habitat

Loss of habitat occurs as human activity encroaches on natural ecosystems. It is an inevitable result of economic and population growth. The creation of farms, cities, roads, and so on results in a loss of habitat, as does pollution of ecosystems. Loss of habitat, however, often occurs at a rate in excess of what is socially optimal. This excessive loss of habitat results when people confront choices about

[7]See Bishop (1978) for a general discussion of the minimum safe standard.

Figure 14.2 **Market and Optimal Levels of Habitat Preservation**

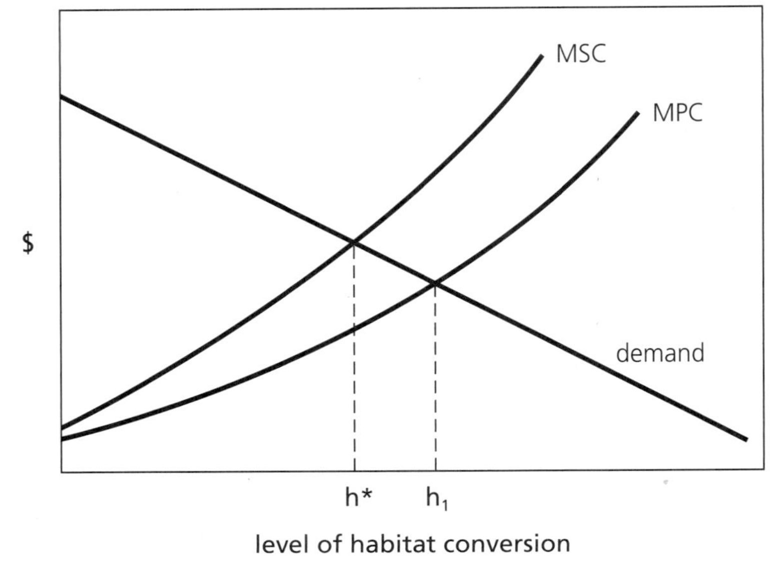

how to utilize habitat but do not have incentives to incorporate preservation values into their decision making. Consequently, the marginal private cost of converting habitat to development purposes is less than the marginal social cost. As can be seen in Figure 14.2, the market converts h_1 units of habitat, which is greater than the socially optimal level of habitat conversion, h*.

For any set of policies to address the problem of loss of habitat, it must attempt to rectify this disparity between the private cost and social cost of converting habitat for other uses. Alternatively, policies could attempt to make the private benefits of preservation equal to the social benefits. Closing the disparity between the private costs and social costs of conversion and closing the disparity between the private benefits and social benefits of preservation are extremely difficult tasks. The reason is that the benefits of habitat preservation have public good characteristics (nonrivalry and nonexcludability in consumption).

Sedjo (1992) suggests a novel approach for reducing the disparity between the private benefits and social benefits of preserving tropical rain forests. As property rights are currently structured, the forested country does not generally benefit from the discovery of medicinal plants in its country. After the plant is discovered, the crucial chemical in the plant is usually identified, isolated, and then produced through chemical means or genetic engineering in pharmaceutical laboratories outside of the forested country. Consequently, the forested country does not earn much economic return from the discovery of a medicine that is based on plants within its borders. Sedjo suggests redefining property rights so that the forested country retains rights to share in the royalties associated with a medicine that is derived from a plant found within its borders, even if the medicinal chemical is eventually produced commercially outside the country with artificial means or through genetic engineering (if the plant's range spanned several countries, they would share in the rights). This type of plan would require an international treaty to be implemented. Language similar to Sedjo's is contained in the Convention on Biodiversity, which was proposed during the 1992 environmental summit in Rio de Janeiro. This convention, however, has not been signed and ratified by all countries, including countries with large pharmaceutical industries such as the United States.

Sedjo's plan would help internalize the costs of habitat loss with respect to the commodity value of plants and animals, but it would not deal with some of the other public good benefits of habitat preservation. For instance, it would not incorporate the carbon sequestration benefits of preserving forests. These benefits, however, could be internalized by a system of marketable carbon permits or carbon annuities, in which countries received positive benefits from preserving their forests.[8]

Other values of habitat preservation may prove more difficult to incorporate into private benefits or private costs. For this reason, public policy incorporates command and control methods. Prohibitions on certain types of habitat destruction have been enacted in the United States. For example, several federal and state statutes restrict the destruction of wetlands. In addition, the creation of national parks and wildlife sanctuaries protects some of the most critical habitats. Private nongovernmental organizations, such as The Nature Conservancy, purchase important habitats and either privately manage the habitats or donate the habitats to state governments or the federal government to turn into public sanctuaries.

The first questions that must be answered in the development of policies to protect habitat are how much should be protected and what level of protection should be afforded. Because there are many different types of habitat that are facing different types of threat of loss and degradation, it is very difficult to devise an "optimal" solution. More practically, one can develop a prioritization scheme to identify which habitat areas should be protected first. Criteria that might be part of a prioritization system include

- Uniqueness of the habitat
- Biodiversity contained in the habitat
- The importance of the habitat for the provision of ecological services (for example, watershed protection of a town's only source of drinking water)

---

[8]The same thing could be accomplished by a marketable carbon permit system that required forested countries to purchase carbon permits for every unit of forest converted to nonforest uses. It is unlikely, however, that the forested countries would agree to a system that penalized them for deforestation. They would obviously prefer a system that required the wealthier countries to partially compensate them for preserving rain forests. See Chapters 12 and 17 for more discussion of the role of wealthier countries in preserving environmental quality in developing countries and Chapter 7 for a discussion of trading greenhouse gas emission permits.

- The existence values associated with the habitat
- The cost of protecting the habitat

The Endangered Species Act of 1973 is a particularly important and controversial piece of legislation, designed to protect the habitat of endangered species. Part of the controversy is that the only criterion of importance to the act is the impact of habitat protection on the prospects of an endangered species. Under this act, it is illegal to use any federal funds in a fashion that might further threaten an endangered species. Because federal funds are utilized in all sorts of infrastructure (roads, sewers, and so on), this legislation applies to a surprisingly large proportion of development projects. The Endangered Species Act also applies to projects requiring federal permits.

A major criticism of the Endangered Species Act is that it is oriented toward protecting species that are already in trouble but does nothing to directly protect other species from becoming endangered or threatened. Critics of the act argue that direct protection of habitat (both domestically and internationally) is a critical component of policy directed toward preserving biodiversity. The act required reauthorization by Congress in the 1990s, but that has not yet occurred. Even though it has not been reauthorized, the act remains in effect as long as Congress appropriates funds for its implementation. For current information on the status of the Endangered Species Act, check the web sites of U.S. agencies such as the National Forest Service, the Fish and Wildlife Service, and the Environmental Protection Agency. Box 14.4 discusses the Endangered Species Act and its relation to the Tellico Dam and the snail darter controversy.

Two basic types of policies are available for protecting and preserving habitat in general. The first is to create protected areas, such as national parks and nature preserves. The second is to restrict uses of privately owned lands. For example, there are federal and state laws that restrict the destruction of wetlands.

A recent source of controversy is how one defines a wetland. Federal legislation originally defined wetlands relative to the soil type and vegetation in the area. In 1991, however, the Bush administration proposed a new manual that also stipulated a condition that the area in question must be inundated for 15 consecutive days during the growing season or saturated for 21 consecutive days during the growing season. Ecologists and environmentalists were upset with this definition because the determination of whether an area was a wetland would then be sensitive to the time at which an assessment was conducted. They also objected to these criteria because the soil and vegetation type of the area in question are direct evidence of saturation and inundation. The new definition would have eliminated some important wetland areas from legal protection and protected areas that ecologists did not consider to be wetlands. The net result of the redefinition would have been to drastically reduce the amount of protected wetlands. Landowners who object to federal restrictions on conversion of wetlands generally favored these new definitions, and environmentalists opposed them. In the end, these new definitions were not actually put into place, partially because many state governments objected to them.

Box 14.4 Endangered Species Act and the Snail Darter

The Endangered Species Act was the subject of considerable controversy shortly after enactment, when it was invoked by environmentalists to stop the construction of Tellico Dam on the Little Tennessee River near Knoxville. (See Gramlich, 1990, for an insightful discussion of the Tellico Project, its costs and benefits, and the Endangered Species Act.) The project had originally been proposed before World War II to provide industrial development to this depressed corner of Appalachia, but by the time the project was reproposed by the Tennessee Valley Authority (TVA) in the mid-1960s, over 20 reservoirs had been constructed within 100 miles of the Tellico site. In addition, Knoxville, Tennessee, had developed a thriving economy based on manufacturing, the activities of the Oak Ridge National Laboratory, and the provision of services to the East Tennessee region.

Because the Knoxville area was not one of abnormal structural unemployment, and because job programs rarely create new jobs but merely transfer their regional location, the creation of jobs in this area would not generate a net social benefit from a national perspective (see Chapter 4 for a discussion of this issue). Gramlich (1990) shows that, under careful analysis, the total costs of the project would exceed the benefits.

The TVA, however, produced other estimates of the benefits, which included the creation of jobs. These estimates indicated that the net benefits from the dam were positive. In the meantime, a species of fish called the snail darter, and believed to exist only in this portion of the Little Tennessee River, was discovered. Opponents of the project seized upon this opportunity to invoke the Endangered Species Act to block the completion of the dam. Congress, however, created the Endangered Species Committee, which had the authority to allow a project to cause the extinction of a species. This committee, nicknamed the God Squad because it decided on the potential extinction of species, actually ruled against the dam, but Congress still allowed the completion of the dam. The snail darter was transplanted to another stream in the region and has not become extinct.

The final results of this political process were that a dam was constructed that had more costs than benefits and that the Endangered Species Act was substantially weakened by the creation of the Endangered Species Committee. In this case, the invocation of the Endangered Species Act caused attention to be shifted from the costs and benefits of the dam and focus entirely on the snail darter.

The development of wildlife refuges or nature preserves is normally thought of as a government activity; but this type of public good is increasingly provided privately. Although it is difficult for an individual citizen to protect habitat and promote biodiversity when acting alone, nongovernmental organizations (NGOs), such as The Nature Conservancy, can act as individual citizen's agents. These NGOs collect money from individual citizens and then use the funds to buy critical habitat from private landowners. The land is then usually donated to a local, state, or federal government agency that maintains and protects the biodiversity preserve.

The private provision of public goods runs counter to a particular economic theory that suggests that public goods, such as nature preserves, will seldom be privately provided. This theory offers two reasons to support this hypothesis. First, because it is not possible to exclude consumers from enjoying the benefits of a public good, it is not possible for the private landowner to extract a price and capture the public good benefits of protecting habitat and biodiversity. Second, the free rider problem will prevent a group of individuals from collectively paying for the public good. The free rider problem suggests that because people cannot be excluded from enjoying the benefit of the public good, they will not agree to pay for its provision, in the hopes that other people will pay for it and then the nonpayers can enjoy the benefits. Of course, if a large number of people have this attitude, then the public good will not be provided.

The private provision of this type of public good can take place because of the role of some NGOs, such as The Nature Conservancy. First, these groups serve to reduce the free rider problem by providing an organization through which individual citizens can commit (and seek the commitment of others) to protect the habitat. Second, they reduce the transaction costs to the individual citizen. The individual citizen is relieved of the burden of trying to decide which habitat is most important, of negotiating with landowners, and of negotiating with government agencies. The importance of these NGOs in reducing the transactions cost of habitat preservation (and other types of environmental improvement) cannot be overstated. Without these organizations, it is not likely that much private preservation activity would take place.

In addition, government agencies at the federal, state, and local levels provide economic incentives for landowners to preserve habitat on their land. A common type of economic incentive is to allow tax benefits for placing land into a conservation easement, a designation that prevents its future development, even if the land is sold. The Conservation Reserve Program (CRP) of the U.S. Department of Agriculture is a good example of a program that provides economic incentives for habitat protection. The CRP is discussed more fully in Chapter 17.

Policies to Reduce Problems with Nonnative Species

Policy for prevention of introduction of nonnative species is difficult to develop, because monitoring is difficult to implement. The United States has a policy of prohibiting importation of plants and animals where there is believed to be a risk to native species (or to nonnative but economically important crops). This process is called blacklisting, because it is a policy of identifying species that should be prohibited based on evidence of risk. In contrast, an alternative policy is "white listing,"[9] whereby people would have to prove that the imported species is safe (rather than the government having to prove it is dangerous) before it could be imported. In addition, a set of policies exist to prevent accidental importation in luggage, cargo, and vehicles. This set of direct controls makes it illegal to have undeclared plants and animals in possession when crossing borders. Random inspections and fines are the basis of the implementation of the direct controls.

It is difficult to adapt economic incentives to this type of environmental problem because of the problems associated with measuring risk levels and monitoring activities. The most promising economic incentive to adapt to this situation would be liability systems, which could make importers liable for future damages associated with plants and animals that they import. Although such a liability system is in place for toxic waste (see Chapter 16), it might be more difficult to trace the chain of cause-and-effect relationships and responsibility for invasive species than for toxic waste.

Policies to Reduce Open-Access Exploitation

Because open-access exploitation problems are caused by poorly defined property rights, it would seem that a logical solution would be to better define property rights. For example, property rights to elephants could be assigned to neighboring villages (see Box 14.1). This proposal has the potential to work when the market for the animal products is primarily in the vicinity of the animal's habitat, such as when the animal is hunted for subsistence. Properly defined property rights can eliminate a destructive competition among villages. It can also give the villages an incentive not to kill wild animals as a nuisance or because they destroy crops. In fact, if villages sell hunting rights to foreign hunters, they can earn large amounts of money. Not only does it give the villages an economic incentive to reduce their own harvest of these animals, it gives them an economic incentive to protect the animals from illegal harvest by others. If each village is assigned a management area, then each village has an incentive to manage its herd as a long-term asset. Hunting to extinction would eliminate a long-run source of food. Of course, the management area has to be large enough to correspond to the entire range of the herd. If animals migrate from one management area to another, then people might feel pressure to kill them when they are in their area, because once they move to another area they might be killed by someone else.

Many times it is not practical or politically feasible to assign property rights. For example, in the United States there is a tradition of public access to wild fish and game resources. Attempts to assign private property rights would be viewed as unfair and would be political suicide for any legislator who might propose it. The resources, however, are protected from overexploitation by rules governing their use. There are season limits, limits on the

[9]For more information on policy and other aspects of invasive species, see the web site of the National Invasive Species Council (http://www.invasivespecies.gov).

number of animals harvested, and restrictions on how and where the animals may be harvested. Certain animals that are rare, endangered, or threatened are not allowed to be hunted at all. Although these rules are occasionally ignored, they are obeyed on the whole within the United States and have served fairly well in protecting animal populations from overexploitation.[10]

Both the definition of private property rights and the development of restrictions with penalties for noncompliance are ineffectual when the profits from illegal harvesting are high relative to the opportunity wage (what the hunter could earn in an alternative occupation). As the United States has found with the illegal drug trade, if the profits are high enough, people will engage in the illegal activity. This rationale is also true with illegal trade in animal products, which can create drug trade–like profits for participants. Under these circumstances, policies aimed at the supply side alone cannot be effective, because high demand will always mean high profits. Policies aimed at the demand side, however, can be very effective when combined with policies aimed at the supply side. A combination of prohibitions on all sales of the animal product and publicity campaigns that make it socially unacceptable to use animal products (wear furs, ivory jewelry, and so on) can eliminate the profitability of the illegal trade.

Such was the rationale behind the ban on ivory by the Convention for International Trade in Endangered Species (CITES) (see Box 14.1). As long as there was some legal trade in ivory, there would be opportunities for profitable illegal trade. To dramatize the importance of banning all sales of ivory, President Daniel Arap Moi of Kenya in 1992 ordered the burning of government stockpiles of ivory. Although some people criticized this action because the government ivory could have been legally sold for several million dollars, Moi wanted to demonstrate the importance of stopping all trade in ivory. In the United States, the Fish and Wildlife Service of the Department of the Interior has the responsibility for enforcing laws that prohibit the sale of endangered species.

Summary

Biodiversity, or the total variety of life on earth, is important for a multitude of reasons. It is important to ecosystem stability and contributes both directly and indirectly to social welfare. Among the most important reasons to preserve biodiversity is the preservation of genetic information that can be a source of medicines, industrial products, and agricultural crops.

There are three primary anthropogenic sources of loss of biodiversity: overharvesting, competition from nonnative species, and loss of habitat. All these sources of loss of biodiversity stem from market failures, whereby the

[10]Commercial fishing in marine areas is a notable exception, where the rules have not been effective in protecting the population of many species, such as tuna, swordfish, Atlantic salmon, and striped bass. See Chapter 11 for more discussion on commercial fishing.

benefits of preserving (or opportunity costs of destroying) biodiversity are not incorporated into private decision making. The loss of habitat is the most important contemporary source of loss of biodiversity.

Both command and control and economic incentives can be used to reduce the socially inefficient loss of habitat. Economic incentives include a variety of mechanisms to allow landowners to capture the benefits of preserving habitat. For example, countries that have tropical rain forests can be given the right to share the profits associated with medicines developed from rain forest plants. Command and control techniques include a variety of prohibitions on land use, including prohibitions on the direct destruction of the habitat (such as the draining of wetlands) or restrictions on pollution and other activities that may damage the habitat.

Review Questions

1. What are the economic forces that lead to extinction?
2. What is the difference between an open-access resource and a common property resource?
3. What are the economic benefits of preserving biodiversity?
4. What policies are available to deal with open-access exploitation?
5. What policies are available to deal with loss of habitat?
6. What policies are available to reduce problems associated with competition from nonnative species?

Questions for Further Study

1. How can the definition of property rights protect biodiversity on both a domestic and an international basis?
2. The Pacific yew tree has a chemical that can be used to treat cancer, but there are a limited number of trees and the tree must grow for many decades before it produces the chemical. How would you allocate the trees between current cancer patients, future cancer patients, and leaving the trees in their natural state?
3. What are the flaws of the Endangered Species Act? How would you improve it?
4. What types of costs and benefits of preserving biodiversity can be measured with current valuation techniques? (See Chapter 4 for discussion of techniques.) What types of costs and benefits are difficult or impossible to measure?
5. Should a private landholder's options on how to use his or her land be limited by legislation to protect biodiversity?
6. Wetlands tend to have more protection than other types of habitat. Is there justification for this practice?
7. Define the elements of a national policy to protect biodiversity.
8. Define the important elements of an international treaty that would protect biodiversity.

Suggested Paper Topics

1. The measurement of biodiversity is a critical issue that spans both natural science and economics. How should one measure biodiversity in a way that is both scientifically credible and useful for policy? Start with articles by Solow et al. (1993) and Weitzman (1992). Also look at biodiversity related articles in *Nature, Science,* and the environmental economics journals (*Journal of Environmental Economics and Management, Land Economics, Environmental and Resource Economics*, and so on).
2. Look at the measurement of the value of biodiversity. Look at both articles related to the measurement of the value of biodiversity and existence values in general. Start with the article by Brown and Goldstein (1984). Search bibliographic databases on biodiversity and value, biodiversity and society, biodiversity and economics, and biodiversity and benefits. Also look at articles on contingent valuation and

other nonmarket valuation techniques. (See Chapter 4 for references.)

3. Look at the cost-benefit analyses surrounding Tellico Dam and the snail darter. Were these analyses conducted correctly? What improvements can you suggest? Develop a protocol for valuing the preservation of endangered species. Start with the reference by Gramlich (1990) and also search bibliographic databases on snail darter and economics, snail darter and environmental policy, and snail darter and cost-benefit analysis.
4. Examine the Convention on Biodiversity. What are its strong points? How would you modify the treaty to make it more effective?

Works Cited and Selected Readings

Asafu-Adjaye, J. Biodiversity Loss and Economic Growth: A Cross-Country Analysis. *Contemporary Economic Policy 21*, no. 2 (April 2003): 173–185.

Anderson, R., and M. Rockel. Economic Valuation of Wetlands. Discussion Paper 065. Washington, DC: American Petroleum Institute, 1991.

Barbier, E. B., and C. E. Schulz. Wildlife, Biodiversity, and Trade. Pages 159–181 in *The Economics of International Trade and the Environment.* Edited by A. A. Batabyal, and H. Beladi. Boca Raton, FL, and London: CRC Press, 2001.

Batabyal, A. A. A Theoretical Analysis of Habitat Conversion and Biodiversity Conservation over Time and under Uncertainty. *Keio Economic Studies 39*, no. 2 (2002): 33–44.

Begossi, A. Scale, Ecological Economics, and the Conservation of Biodiversity. Pages 30–43 in *The Environment, Sustainable Development, and Public Policies: Building Sustainability in Brazil* edited by C. Cavalcanti. Cheltenham, UK and Northampton, MA: Edward Elgar, 2000.

Bell, F. *Application of Wetland Valuation Theory to Florida Fisheries*. Sea Grant Publication SGR-95, Florida State University, 1989.

Bishop, R. C. Endangered Species and Uncertainty: The Economics of a Safe Minimum Standard. *American Journal of Agricultural Economics 60*, (1978): 10–18.

Brown, G. M., and J. H. Goldstein. A Model for Valuing Endangered Species. *Journal of Environmental Economics and Management 11*, (1984): 303–309.

Daily, G. C., and K. Ellison, *The New Economy of Nature: The Quest to Make Conservation Profitable*. Washington, DC: Island Press, 2002.

Eisworth, M. E., and J. C. Haney. Allocating Conservation Expenditures across Habitats: Accounting for Inter-Species Distinctness. *Ecological Economics 5* (1992): 235–250.

Evenson, R., and B. Wright. The Value of Plant Biodiversity for Agriculture. Pages 187–210 in *Agricultural Science Policy: Changing Global Agendas*, edited by M. Julian, P. G. Pardey, and M. J. Taylor. Baltimore and London: Johns Hopkins University Press for the International Food Policy Research Institute, 2001.

Farber, S. The Value of Coastal Wetlands for Protection Against Hurricane Damage. *Journal of Environmental Economics and Management 14* (1987): 143–151.

Farber S., and R. Constanza. The Economic Value of Wetland Systems. *Journal of Environmental Management 24*, (1987): 41–51.

Ferraro, P. J., and R. D. Simpson. The Cost-Effectiveness of Conservation Payments. Resources for the Future Discussion Paper 00/31, 2000.

Gramlich, E. M. *A Guide to Benefit-Cost Analysis.* Englewood Cliffs, NJ: Prentice Hall, 1990.

Gupta, T. R., and J. H. Foster. Economic Criteria for Freshwater Wetland Policy in Massachusetts. *American Journal of Agricultural Economics 57* (1975): 40–45.

Krcmar-Nozic, E., G. C. van Kooten, and B. Wilson, Threat to Biodiversity: The Invasion of Exotic Species. Pages 68–87 in *Conserving Nature's Diversity: Insights from Biology, Ethics, and Economics*, edited by C. van Kooten, E. H. Bulte, and A. R. E Sinclair. Aldershot, UK, Burlington, VT and Sydney: Ashgate, 2000.

Lynne, G. D., P. Conroy, and F. Pochasta. Economic Valuation of Marsh Areas for Marine Production Processes. *Journal of Environmental Economics and Management 8* (1981): 175–186.

MacDonald, D., Bartering Biodiversity: What Are the Options? Pages 142–171 in *Environmental Policy: Objectives, Instruments, and Implementation*, edited by D. Heim. Oxford and New York: Oxford University Press, 2000.

McNeely, J. A. *Economics and Biological Diversity: Developing and Using Economic Incentives to Conserve Biological Resources.* Gland, Switzerland: IUCN, 1988.

Morrisette, P. M. Conservation Easement and the Public Good: Preserving the Environment on Private Lands. *Natural Resources Journal 41*, no. 2 (Spring 2001): 373–426.

Nunes, P. A. L. D., J. C. J. M. van den Bergh, and P. Nijkamp. *The Ecological Economics of Biodiversity: Methods and Policy Applications*. Cheltenham, UK, and Northampton, MA: Edward Elgar, 2003.

Organization for Economic Cooperation and Development. *Harnessing Markets for Biodiversity: Towards Conservation and Sustainable Use*. Paris: OECD, 2003.

Pearce, D., D. Moran, and D. Biller. *Handbook of Biodiversity Valuation: A Guide for Policy Makers*. Paris: OECD, 2002.

Polasky, S., ed. *The Economics of Biodiversity Conservation*. Aldershot, UK, Burlington, VT, and Sydney: Ashgate, 2002.

Ryan, J. C. Conserving Biological Diversity. Pages 9–26 in *State of the World*, edited by L. Brown. New York: W. W. Norton, 1992.

Scudder, G. G. E. Biodiversity: Concerns and Values. Pages 16–29 in *Conserving Nature's Diversity: Insights from Biology, Ethics, and Economics*, edited by C. van Kooten, E. H. Bulte, and A. R. E Sinclair. Aldershot, U.K., Burlington, VT, and Sydney: Ashgate, 2000.

Sedjo, R. A. Property Rights, Genetic Resources, and Biotechnological Change. *Journal of Law and Economics 35* (1992): 213.

Sedjo, R. A. Biodiversity: Forests, Property Rights and Economic Value. Pages 106–122 in *Conserving Nature's Diversity: Insights from Biology, Ethics, and Economics* edited by C. van Kooten, E. H. Bulte, and A. R. E Sinclair. Aldershot, UK, Burlington, VT, and Sydney: Ashgate, 2000.

Shogren, J. F., and J. Tschirhart (eds.). *Protecting Endangered Species in the United States: Biological Needs, Political Realities, Economic Choices*. Cambridge, New York, and Melbourne: Cambridge University Press, 2001.

Simpson, R. D. Economic Perspectives on Preservation of Biodiversity. Pages 88–105 in *Conserving Nature's Diversity: Insights from Biology, Ethics, and Economics* edited by C. van Kooten, E. H. Bulte, and A. R. E Sinclair. Aldershot, UK, Burlington, VT, and Sydney: Ashgate, 2000.

Sinclair, A. R. E. The Loss of Biodiversity: The Sixth Great Extinction. Pages 173–185 in *Conserving Nature's Diversity: Insights from Biology, Ethics, and Economics*, edited by C. van Kooten, E. H. Bulte, and A. R. E Sinclair. Aldershot, UK, Burlington, VT, and Sydney: Ashgate, 2000.

Solow, A., S. Polasky, and J. Broadus. On the Measurement of Biological Diversity. *Journal of Environmental Economics and Management 24* (1993): 60–68.

Thibodeau, F. R., and B. D. Ostro. An Economic Analysis of Wetland Protection. *Journal of Environmental Management 12* (1981): 19–30.

Tisdell, C. *The Economics of Conserving Wildlife and Natural Areas*. Cheltenham, UK, and Northampton, MA: Edward Elgar; distributed by American International Distribution Corporation, Williston, VT, 2002.

U.S. Statistical Abstract. Washington, DC: U.S. Government Printing Office, various dates.

Weikard, H. P. Diversity Functions and the Value of Biodiversity. *Land Economics 78*, no. 1 (February 2002): 20–27

Weitzman, M. L. On Diversity. *Quarterly Journal of Economics 107* (1992): 363–406.

Wolf, E. C. Conserving Biological Diversity. Pages 124–146 in *State of the World*, edited by Lester Brown. New York: W. W. Norton, 1985.

chapter 15

Water Resources

We never know the worth of water until the well runs dry.

English Proverb

Introduction

In the history of the United States, water has played a central role, but water has always been regarded as abundantly available. Water supplies were abundant in the East, and as the eastern population expanded and moved westward, there was sufficient land with available water to support the populations that were moving westward. Although much of the West was (and is) semiarid and the availability of water influenced choice of location, the overall availability of water did not appear likely to place constraints on the growth of population or the economy. In fact, there are tremendously large populations in areas with little rainfall, such as southern California and Arizona.

Because water was not viewed as a scarce resource, it was not managed to prevent or mitigate increasing scarcity. As we moved through the later half of the twentieth century, important water problems arose because the use of water has lessened its availability and, in many parts of the United States, the well is running dry. Water scarcity is an even greater problem in other parts of the world, particularly in semiarid areas where population growth is far exceeding the availability of water.

Four distinct problems affect the availability of water. First, in many areas of the country the use of water exceeds the rate at which it is being replenished. Second, many activities use water as an input, and when the water is returned to surface waters or groundwaters, its quality is diminished. Third, many activities use surface or groundwaters as a means to dispose of waste, or waste inadvertently escapes into these waters. Finally, degradation of ecosystems weakens their ability to store water and modulate the drought/flood cycle. An important manifestation of this problem is that the elimination of forest ecosystems has led to regional climate change in many areas of the world and actually reduced the amount of rainfall in these regions. As these four types of problems indicate, water problems have both quantity and quality dimensions.

Of course, these quantity and quality problems also exist outside the United States, often on a more serious scale. Lack of clean drinking water is probably the most pressing environmental problem that the world faces. In many developing countries, intestinal disorders from contaminated drinking water are the primary cause of death of children under 5 years of age. The World Health Organization (WHO) has estimated that more than 1 billion people do not have access to uncontaminated drinking water. (Raven et al., 1993, p. 281).

Dimensions of Water Resources and Water Issues

The solutions to water resources problems are not straightforward because of the complexity of water resources and the activities that affect their availability and quality. This section discusses the characteristics of water resources and human activity that impact our ability to develop policy.

Hydrological Cycles

An understanding of hydrological cycles is essential to understanding water resource problems. The hydrological cycle refers to the movement of water from the atmosphere to the ground and then its evaporation and return to the atmosphere.

Water vapor in the atmosphere condenses and falls to the ground as some type of precipitation (rain, snow, sleet, and so on). Some of the precipitation lands directly in surface water (not surprising, because three-fourths of the earth's surface is covered by water). Some of the precipitation falls on land, where most of it evaporates before it can be available for use. Water that falls on land may also move downhill along the surface of the ground until it reaches surface water (river, lake, and so on). Some water penetrates the surface of the ground and becomes groundwater. Some groundwater remains underground in aquifers, and some groundwater flows into surface waters. In the United States, 66 percent of the precipitation returns to the atmosphere directly by evaporation; 31 percent runs off to rivers, streams, and lakes; and 3 percent seeps underground. These percentages are averages and vary across the country as topography, soil type, ground cover, and land use vary.

Forests and other terrestrial ecosystems play a very important role in the hydrological cycle. The leaves and stems of trees break the impact of the rain, slowing its descent and allowing more of the moisture to be absorbed into the ground. In addition, the water follows the branches to the trunk, flows down the trunk, and enters small spaces between the trunk and the ground, continuing to follow these gaps along the roots deep below the ground. The organic matter on the forest flood acts as a sponge, soaking up water, where it gradually flows downward into the soil.

The net effect of the forest is to allow more of the rainwater to become groundwater and less to immediately enter streams and rivers. The groundwater later makes its way to the surface through springs and feeds the streams and rivers. The existence of healthy forests means that there is less water in streams directly after a rain and more water in streams during dryer periods.

As discussed in Chapter 14, wetlands play a similar role in modulating the drought/flood cycle. The elimination of wetlands reduces the ecosystem's ability to store water, causing heavy rainfall to move immediately into streams and rivers and generating higher levels of flooding. Similarly, with no wetlands to store water and gradually release it into rivers, river volumes are much lower during droughts and other periods of low rainfall.

Nutrient Cycling

Another important cycle that is relevant for water issues is the nutrient cycle. The nutrient cycle refers to how the basic nutrients (nitrogen, potassium, and phosphorus) move through the ecosystem. For example, nutrients are contained in the tissues of living and dead organisms. When the organisms die and decay, the nutrients are released in the soil or water and become available to plants, which absorb them. The plants are then eaten by other organisms that absorb the nutrients, and the cycle continues. This cycle is part of a healthy ecosystem, be it aquatic or terrestrial. Problems arise when additional organic wastes from human activity are introduced into the ecosystem. These wastes cause special problems in aquatic ecosystems as the processes that break the wastes down into basic nutrients remove dissolved oxygen from the water. Dissolved oxygen is essential for aquatic life. Furthermore, the nutrients can contribute to algae blooms (massive growths of algae) that block light from penetrating the water. The algae also have short life spans, and when they die and decay they further remove oxygen from the water. If all the oxygen is depleted, then the decay process shifts from bacteria that operate in the presence of oxygen to bacteria that operate in the absence of oxygen. This anoxic decay leads to the "rotten eggs" smell associated with polluted waters. Agricultural runoff, suburban runoff, paper plants, food processing, stockyards, and discharge from sewage treatment plants are among the most significant anthropogenic sources of nutrients.

Water Consumption

In Chapter 1, a resource taxonomy was developed that defined renewable resources as those in which the stock regenerates itself, resource flows as never-ending flows that come from a nondepleting stock, and exhaustible resources as those that have no regenerative capacity. Different water resources meet each of these definitions, and some are actually a combination of categories.

Water, in general, meets the definition of a renewable resource. The evaporation from the oceans and other water sources creates the precipitation that replenishes the oceans. Smaller water bodies, however, do not generally replenish themselves. The evaporation from a river does not provide the water source for the river. An important exception is a large forest system such as the Amazon rain forest, where water vapor from evaporation from surface waters and transpiration by trees generates rain, much of which falls to the earth in the confines of the rain forest. Reducing the size of the rain forest could thus reduce the amount of rain that falls in the region and is an important consequence of deforestation.

Water in riverine systems can be viewed as a resource flow. The water that arrives at any particular point along the river is independent of the amount of water that is taken out at that point. More important, a decision to remove water today will not affect the amount of water that can be taken out tomorrow. One can, however, view river water as exhaustible in the sense that an upstream user's decision to remove water reduces the amount of water available to downstream users.

Groundwater resources can be viewed both as an exhaustible resource and a resource flow, depending on the nature of the resource. If the removal rate is high relative to recharge rate, then the aquifer should be viewed as an exhaustible resource. This exhaustibility is especially true for what is often called "fossil water," which is water that accumulated slowly in underground aquifers over millions of years. Although these aquifers may contain very large amounts of water, they are being recharged at a very slow pace. For all practical purposes, the rate of recharge can be viewed as negligible. Thus, the resource can be viewed as exhaustible: once removed, it will never be replaced. A good example of this type of water resource is the Ogallala Aquifer, which underlies eight western and midwestern states (Montana, Wyoming, Nebraska, Colorado, New Mexico, Texas, Oklahoma, and Kansas).

All three classifications of water resources may be adversely affected by degrading uses of water that add contaminants of some nature to the water. Uses of water that do not adversely affect quality are called benign uses.

Water as an Input to Production and Consumption Activities

Water is essential to all life processes and most economic processes. As demonstrated later, however, water is not always used in a socially optimal fashion. Let's examine water as both a resource flow and as an exhaustible resource and then discuss how market failures inhibit the optimal use of water in both cases.

Water as a Resource Flow

Imagine a river flowing down from the mountains, through farms, to a city. The rain and snow in the mountains ensure that there will be a continual flow of water in the river, year after year. If the flow of the river is much larger than the withdrawals of water to meet consumptive and productive needs and if the uses of the water are benign, then there will be no resource allocation problem. Even if the water is available at zero cost and zero price, all the needs for water will be satisfied and there will be no market failure.

Now let's change the scenario so that the flow of the river is not capable of meeting all the needs at any point in time. Even though there is a continual supply of water at any point in time, there will be a shortage of water at each point. At a price that is equal to zero, more water will be demanded than is available. As price is increased above zero (but the actual cost of obtaining water remains zero), the least valuable needs will be left unsatisfied and the more valuable needs will be met. As long as the value of a gallon of water is greater than the price, people will purchase that gallon. If price is continually raised, then eventually the quantity demanded will exactly equal the amount of water that is available. At this point, the willingness to pay for water will be equal to its price.

An alternative way of looking at this problem that illustrates how essential scarcity is in determining price is contained in Figure 15.1. In this figure, g_o represents the daily volume of water that may be removed from the river, the cost of extraction is equal to zero, and demand is represented by D_1. Under these circumstances, all the demand that exists at zero price will be satisfied. If, however, demand shifts upward to D_2, then all the demand that exists at zero price cannot be satisfied. Because there is unsatisfied demand at zero price, there will be upward pressure on price, which will increase to p_2. Notice that in this case, the price is solely determined by the opportunity cost of the

Figure 15.1 **Scarcity and the Price of Water**

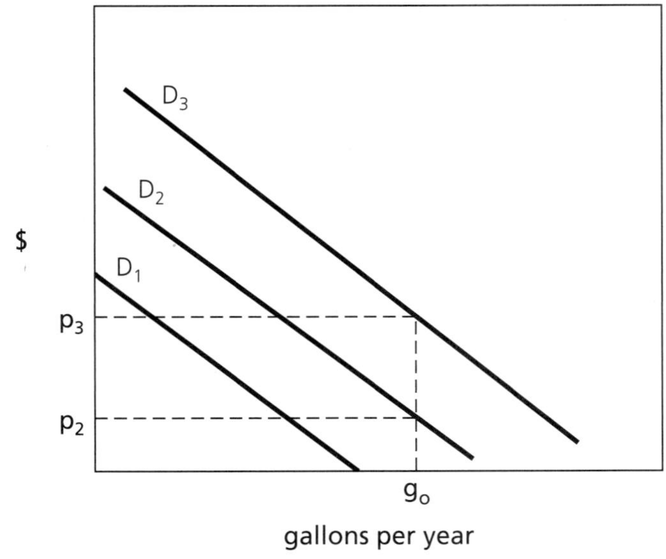

water, because the cost of producing water has been assumed to be zero. As demand increases, the opportunity cost of consuming the fixed flow of water increases, which is reflected in an increased price. For example, if demand shifts further outward to D_3, then price will increase to p_3. Notice that the difference between price and the cost of production is a type of user cost, generated by the scarcity of the water in the present period.

The reflection of scarcity in the price of water will ensure that water is used in its most valuable applications, because only applications whose value equals or exceeds opportunity cost will be willing to pay the price that reflects the opportunity cost. For a market and a price to exist, property rights to the water must be well defined. Of course, if there is a cost of producing the water (purification, transportation, and so on), then the marginal costs of production will also be reflected in price.

Even though this type of water resource is being continually replenished, it does not mean that there will be no shortage of water. If property rights are not defined appropriately or if some other market failure keeps price from incorporating the scarcity value of water, then price will be too low. The quantity demanded will exceed the quantity supplied, and a shortage will exist. This shortage is depicted in Figure 15.2, where it is again assumed that there are no costs associated with producing a fixed supply of water of g_o. Here, the price at which the quantity demanded would equal the fixed quantity supplied is p_0. If, however, some mechanism caused price to be at a lower level, such as p_1, then the quantity demanded would be g_1 and the shortage of water would be $g_1 - g_o$ (Box 15-1).

Figure 15.2 **Water Shortage Caused by Low Price**

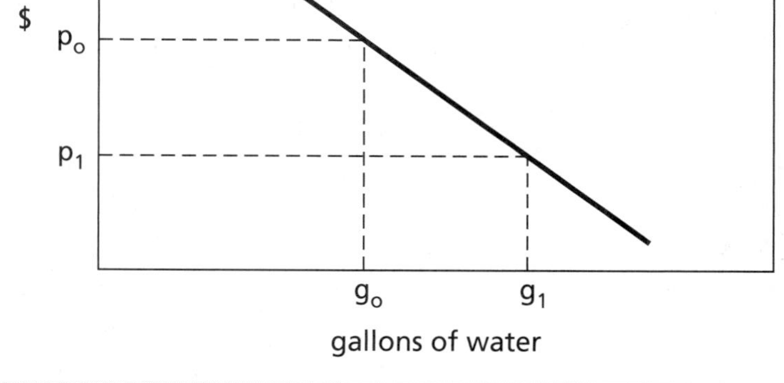

Box 15.1 Water Shortages and Water Conflicts in New York City

New York City obtains its water from reservoirs in the Catskill Mountains and other areas in upstate New York. This system of reservoirs and distribution pipelines began in the nineteenth century. Despite the elaborate system, New York City has chronic problems with shortages of water, especially during summer periods of less than normal rainfall in upstate New York. During the 1970s and 1980s, the shortage of water forced New York City to adopt emergency water regulations, in which many uses of water become prohibited.

New York City proposed a series of technical responses to this problem, including taking more water from currently exploited river systems, exploiting new river systems (mostly in the Adirondack region), and repairing the antiquated delivery systems so that less water leaks from the system. Upstate residents object to additional water withdrawals from upstate river systems, because the withdrawals created low flows in the river, increasing their temperatures and reducing dissolved oxygen. These effects reduce the ecological productivity of their rivers, particularly as a trout habitat.

The technical solutions that were proposed could not provide long-term relief from shortages; as they only addressed the symptoms of the water problem and not the cause. The cause was that many users did not pay for the water they consumed. Water use was almost completely unmetered in New York City. People had no incentives to conserve water because they did not pay any price for water. The price should include both the opportunity cost of not having the water available for another use and the recreational and ecological opportunity cost of removing the water from the rivers. New York City's water problems and the misallocation of upstate water resources would be present as long as the scarcity value of water was not reflected in the price people paid.

New York City found itself in an interesting dilemma because it was impossible to price water correctly; installing water meters for every single use in New York City would be prohibitively costly. In the absence of an ability to charge consumers the appropriate marginal price for water, what is the next best solution to this problem of excess demand for water?

New York City has embarked on a multifaceted program to reduce the demand for water. First, water is metered wherever practical. In particular, water is metered as it comes into big apartment buildings (although not in the individual residential units of the building), so apartment owners have a financial incentive to repair leaking pipes and faucets and install water-saving appliances. Second, water-efficient appliances (shower heads, toilets, and so on) are required in new construction and when old appliances are replaced. Third, and perhaps most important, New York City has embarked on an innovative set of public education and public participation programs to reduce the general demand for water and to eliminate leaks and other wasteful uses of water.

In eastern and Great Lake states, water resources can be viewed primarily as resource flows. Most cities and agricultural areas in this region depend on surface water or groundwater that is generally replenished by normal rainfall. Where chronic water shortages exist, however, it is almost always a result of the price being too low. Of course, any area can have water problems caused by a prolonged or episodic drought.

One mechanism that often leads to urban water problems is the process by which water is priced and distributed to customers. In virtually every urban area, this distribution is done by either a regulated water utility or a municipal water company. In both cases, political or regulatory forces can push the price of water below its opportunity cost.

Let's first examine the case in which water is provided to consumers by a regulated monopoly. A city would award the exclusive right to distribute water to a private company. The general practice for determination of the price that a regulated monopoly is allowed to charge is rate of return regulation (see a regulatory economics or industrial organization textbook for a more detailed explanation of rate of return regulation). Regulated utilities are allowed to charge a price that yields them a reasonable rate of return (after expenses) on their capital investment. Notice that such a price does nothing to incorporate the scarcity value of water; it only incorporates the scarcity value of the other inputs used in purifying and distributing the water.

If the price is below opportunity cost, then more water will be demanded than is available. Then some other mechanism must be used to allocate water, and there is no guarantee that this mechanism will allocate water efficiently. For example, new uses of water may be prohibited, even though they may be more highly valued than some existing uses.

Alternatively, the city may elect to provide the distribution of water as a city service. In this case, there will be political pressures from the electorate to keep the price of water low. Again, there will be no mechanism to ensure that price includes opportunity cost.

Another potential problem exists when users are not forced to pay the marginal costs of water but instead pay only average cost. This system is used for apartment buildings, where the building as a whole is metered but individual apartment dwellings are not metered. Although the total cost of water will be incorporated into all tenants' rent, tenants pay no extra cost for extra water use. Their monthly costs are independent of how much water they use. Therefore, they have limited incentives to conserve their use of water.

Even if water is priced according to the marginal willingness to pay, there still may be market failure. The reason is that adequate flows of water in a river are necessary to support the riverine ecosystem, but aquatic organisms obviously cannot participate in water markets. If the ecological cost of water withdrawals is not incorporated into market price, a greater than optimal level of water withdrawals will occur. There are two basic ways in which the price can be set to reflect the ecological opportunity cost of water withdrawals. First, the government can put a tax on water use to discourage its use. Second, nongovernmental organizations can enter water markets and buy water rights, but leave the water in the stream.

Water as an Exhaustible Resource

When the rate of use of a stock of water is much greater than the rate of recharge of the stock, the resources can be regarded as an exhaustible resource. This state describes the reality of water resources in many western states, particularly those overlying the Ogallala Aquifer and other slowly recharging aquifers. The economic analysis of water as an exhaustible resource is very similar to the analysis of water as a resource flow, only there is an additional opportunity cost to consider.

First, there is the same opportunity cost of not having the water available for another current use, which can be called the contemporaneous opportunity cost. Second, because current use depletes the stock and makes it unavailable for future use, there is the opportunity cost of not having the water available for future use. This opportunity cost may be called the intertemporal opportunity cost. Both the contemporaneous and the intertemporal opportunity costs are components of user cost and must be incorporated into price if water is to be efficiently allocated among all its alternative uses, both present and future.

Water and Property Rights

In the previous discussion of urban uses of water, it was assumed that the municipality had the right to withdraw water from the river and aquifer, and distribute it to consumers (or to grant this right to a regulated utility). The only allocation question that remained was if the municipality or utility would price the water appropriately so that water would be allocated to its most valuable uses.

In the real world, the problem is more complicated, because nontransferable property rights, which prevent the flow of water to its most beneficial uses, exist. The critical factor is that these rights to use water, unlike most property rights, cannot be transferred, and it is the lack of transferability that prevents the water from being sold to its most beneficial uses.

Property rights to water are a big issue in the western United States, where the natural dryness of the region exacerbates conflict over water. Because the definition of property rights varies substantially across western states, it is very difficult to generalize about property right structures for water. Perhaps the most important type of property rights to water are appropriation-based water rights.

Appropriation-based water rights make water available for use by anyone who can apply it to beneficial purposes. Priority goes to the user who established his or her appropriation-based rights first. Initially in many states, these rights tended to be nontransferable, which meant that water rights could not be transferred to other uses, even if the new uses had higher values. The increasing demand for water associated with growing urban areas, however, has led many of the western states to make appropriation-based water rights transferable. Some states even allow the state or private parties to buy appropriation-based rights to leave the water in the river for beneficial ecological purposes, an important way to generate environmental improvement as a win-win situation. People who contribute money to buy water rights for ecological protection are better off, because they value the ecological improvement by an amount equal to or greater than their contribution. Farmers and other current users of water are better off, for if they voluntarily agree to sell a portion of their water rights, they must value these rights less than the revenue they receive from selling their rights. Unfortunately, the opportunities for this type of market-based environmental improvement are limited, because some western states do not define in-stream uses such as recreation or ecological protection to be legally "beneficial uses," and thus they are ineligible for transfer. Consequently, in these states people cannot use the water rights system to generate ecological improvement (Box 15-2).

Degrading Uses of Water

So far, the only opportunity cost of water use discussed is that one use of water makes it unavailable for other uses (either current or future). Uses may have an additional cost, however, if the use of water renders it unfit for other uses. A particular use of water may have an adverse effect on water quality, leading to negative impacts on other water uses.

There are three types of water uses that degrade water quality. The first type is when removal of water from surface water bodies or groundwater aquifers generates ecological damage. For example, heavy withdrawal of water in coastal areas, such as southern Florida, has led to saltwater intrusion into the aquifer. The second is when a direct consumer of water uses it and then returns it to the hydrological cycle with wastes or contaminants. For example, residential use of water adds human waste and other contaminants. Even after treatment in a sewage treatment plant, the water that is returned to the river or lake will be augmented by nutrients and other contaminants that can generate ecological damage and reduce the usefulness of the water for other purposes. The third type is represented by activities that generate wastes that are either directly deposited into or make their way through natural mechanisms (such as the runoff of rainfall) into water bodies. For example, rainfall runoff carries agrichemicals (pesticides, herbicides, and fertilizers) from agricultural fields into surface water and groundwater. Table 15.1 summarizes the sources and impacts of pollutants that adversely affect water quality.

U.S. Policy Toward Water Pollution

U.S. policy toward water pollution has historically focused on large point sources of pollution. Point sources of pollution are specific points where the pollution enters the water body, such as the end of an effluent discharge pipe. Attempts to control pollution have met with mixed success. Organic pollutants from large sources have been reduced. However, nonpoint sources of pollution and inorganic toxic pollutants continue to represent a major problem.

Table 15.1 Sources and Impacts of Selected Pollutants

Pollutant	Sources	Impact on aquatic organisms	Impact on health and welfare
Sediment	Agricultural fields, pastures, and livestock feed lots; logged hillsides; degraded streambanks; road construction	Reduced plant growth and diversity; reduced prey for predators; clogging of gills and filters; reduced survival of eggs and young; smothering of habitats	Increased water treatment costs; transport of toxics and nutrients; reduced availability of fish, shellfish, and associated species; shortened life span of lakes, streams, and artificial reservoirs and harbors
Nutrients	Agricultural fields, pastures, and livestock raw and treated sewage discharges; industrial discharges	Algal blooms resulting in depressed oxygen levels and reduced diversity and growth of large plants; release of toxins from sediments; reduced diversity in vertebrate and invertebrate communities; kills fish	Increased water treatment costs; risk of reduced oxygen carrying capacity in infant blood; possible generation of carcinogenic nitrosamines; reduced availability of fish, shellfish, and associated species; impairment of recreational uses
Organic materials	Agricultural fields and pastures; landscaped urban areas; combined sewers; logged areas; chemical manufacturing and other industrial processes	Reduced dissolved oxygen in affected waters; kills fish; reduced abundance and diversity of aquatic life	Increased water treatment costs; transport of toxics and nutrients; reduced availability of fish, shellfish, and associated species
Disease-causing agents	Raw and partially treated sewage; animal wastes; dams that reduce water flows	Reduced survival and production in fish, shellfish, and associated species	Increased costs of water treatment; river blindness; elephantiasis, schistosomiasis, cholera, typhoid, dysentery, reduced availability and contamination of fish, shellfish, and associated species
Heavy metals	Atmospheric deposition; road runoff; industrial discharges; sludges and discharges from sewage treatment plants; creation of reservoirs; acidic mine effluent	Declines in fish populations due to failed reproduction; lethal effects on invertebrates, leading to reduced prey for fish	Increased costs of water treatment; lead poisioning, itai-itai and minimata diseases; kidney dysfunction; reduced availability and healthfulness of fish, shellfish, and associated species
Toxic chemicals	Urban and agricultural runoff; municipal and industrial discharges; leachate from landfills	Reduced growth and survivability of fish eggs and young; fish diseases	Increased costs of water treatment; increased risk of rectal, bladder, and colon cancer; reduced availability and healthfulness of fish, shellfish, and associated species

(continues)

Table 15.1 (continued)

Pollutant	Sources	Impact on aquatic organisms	Impact on health and welfare
Acids	Atmospheric deposition; mine effluent; degrading plant materials	Elimination of sensitive aquatic organisms; release of trace metals from soils, rocks, and metal surfaces, such as lead pipes	Reduced availability of fish, shellfish, and associated species
Chlorides	Roads treated for removal of ice and snow; irrigation runoff; brine produced in oil extraction; mining	At high levels, toxic to freshwater life	Reduced availability of drinking water supplies; reduced availability of fish, shellfish, and associated species
Elevated temperatures	Urban landscapes; unshaded streams, impounded waters; reduced discharges from dams; discharges from power plants and industrial facilities	Elimination of cold water species of fish and shellfish; reduced dissolved oxygen due to increased plant growth; increased vulnerability of some fishes to toxic wastes, parasites, and diseases	Reduced availability of fish, shellfish, and associate species

Source: From *World Resources, 1992–1993*, by World Resources Institute. Copyright © 1993 by World Resources Institute. Used by permission of Oxford University Press, Inc.

Note: See source for references on specific events.

One of the major thrusts of attempts to reduce water pollution were programs to reduce the impact of the discharge of municipal sewage. Before the implementation of the 1972 Clean Water Act, many small and medium-sized cities had no sewage treatment facilities, and untreated waste was often discharged directly into rivers and lakes. In large cities (which often had treatment plants), treatment was inadequate. This inadequate sewage treatment led to very severe degradation of water quality in virtually every river that flowed through metropolitan areas.

Lake Erie, which borders on Ohio, Pennsylvania, New York, and Ontario, was particularly hard hit. Pollution from municipal and industrial discharge was so extensive that many parts of the lake became completely anoxic and incapable of supporting aquatic life. Thriving recreational and commercial fisheries were decimated.

The 1977 amendments to the Clean Water Act, however, required all municipalities to develop and upgrade their sewage treatment facilities. Both primary treatment (removal of suspended particles) and secondary treatment (breakdown of organic wastes) were required, and eventual goals were

Box 15.2 Water Shortage and Conflict in Southern California

Southern California has been plagued by water shortages that were exacerbated by prolonged drought through the late 1980s, early 1990s, and the first few years of the 2000s. Although one expects water problems when a metropolis of millions of people develops in a desert, the problem has also been exacerbated by the way water rights are defined for the water that flows down from the mountains (which usually receive plentiful rain and snowfall).

Farmers in southern California have appropriation rights to much of the available water, paying a fraction of what the water's value would be in alternative uses (residential, commercial, and industrial uses). Farmers use this water to irrigate crops that can be cheaply grown elsewhere in the country (such as soybeans and rice). Their rights to inexpensive water, however, make it profitable to plant these crops in southern California. In effect, the farmers are subsidized by the availability of water at a fraction of its true value.

This definition of water rights and the resulting price of water, which is below opportunity cost, will continue to stress the water resources of southern California and reduce the amount of water available for residential uses. There is simply not enough water in southern California for both agriculture and population to continue to grow. In addition, the removal of much of the water from the rivers has led to severe ecological damage in many river systems.

established to minimize the release of all nutrients. The federal government would pay 75 percent of the costs of the facility, and local governments would be responsible for the remainder of the construction costs and for operating costs.

The primary reason for the federal government to subsidize wastewater treatment plants has to do with the difference between the local social benefits of treatment and the regional or national benefits of treatment. The benefits of wastewater treatment are felt by all the people who live downstream of a particular community, not just the people residing in the community. Therefore, the social benefits to the nation of treating a particular community's wastewater are greater than the social benefits to the community. Consequently, the level of treatment provided by individual communities would be lower than socially optimal, necessitating federal government intervention to correct this market failure. Of course, the federal government could require the treatment without the associated subsidies, but this action would not be politically expedient. In addition, many communities simply would not have the tax base to improve their sewage treatment plants.

One interesting aspect of these subsidy programs is that they do not cover the costs of operating the plants, only of building the plants. Because local governments have to pay the operating costs, they have an incentive to choose plant designs that rely more on capital equipment (which the federal government subsidizes) than on variable inputs (labor and energy) that are unsubsidized. Thus, the subsidy system leads to a nonoptimal mix of inputs in the production of sewage treatment, and, in extreme cases, local governments have not had the funds to properly maintain the capital equipment.

The construction of many of these plants was completed during the 1970s, with a rapid effect on water quality. Aquatic systems are capable of processing and assimilating organic wastes such as sewage, but the problem was that the assimilative capacity of the environment had been exceeded by the massive releases from municipal sewer systems. As the inputs of organic waste were reduced, water quality improved. Drastic changes in water quality occurred in areas such as Lake Erie, that now support thriving walleye, trout, and bass populations. The Potomac River, whose recovery was speeded by several tropical storms that helped flush existing wastes from river bottom sediments, is another example of an urban water body that has rapidly recovered and now supports fish populations that require clean water. Bass fishing guides now take clients on fishing trips in Washington, D.C. A favorite fishing spot is along the river wall at the famous Watergate building.

These subsidized improvements in municipal sewage treatment plants were required by the Water Pollution Control Act of 1972, the Clean Water Act (CWA) of 1977, and the 1977 and 1987 amendments to the CWA. In addition to focusing on sewage treatment, these acts also focused on other large point sources of pollution, such as paper plants, food processing facilities, and other industries. These acts were based on command and control techniques. All discharges were illegal unless authorized by the National Pollution Discharge Elimination System. Dischargers were required to meet two technology-based standards. Polluters were required to use best practical technology (BPT) for conventional pollutants and the best available technology (BAT) for toxic pollutants. The difference between BPT and BAT is that BPT allows for the consideration of the cost of the technology, whereas BAT does not.

Economic incentives have not been employed to deal with water quality problems. Although a marketable pollution permit system was established for paper plants on the Fox River in Wisconsin, so many restrictions have been placed on the ability to make trades that few trades have been made.

In some senses, it would be easier to develop a functioning system of marketable pollution permits (or taxes) to control water pollution because of the greater ease in measuring the dispersion of emissions (pollutants move with water and wind currents). The development of such a system, however, would require more interstate cooperation, because all the major river systems span several states. For example, rivers that bring nutrients into the Chesapeake Bay flow through Maryland, Virginia, Delaware, West Virginia, Washington, D.C., Pennsylvania, and New York. Similarly, some U.S. watersheds span international borders with Mexico and Canada. Of course, this problem is even bigger in Europe, where countries tend to be geographically smaller.

As might be expected, the system of command and control policies led to the problems associated with command and control technologies that were discussed in Chapter 3. Firms were not free to choose the cheapest way to reduce pollution, which led to much higher than normal costs. Industries had to employ the same types of control mechanisms, regardless of the effect of their emissions on environmental quality. For instance, a polluter in a region where emissions were lower than the capacity of the environment to break down and assimilate the pollutants had to install the same control devices as in an area where the environment's capacity is exceeded.

Unfortunately, the Clean Water Act and associated amendments have not been as successful as possible in meeting the goals of the legislation. The overall goal is to restore and maintain the chemical, physical, and biological integrity of the nation's waters. Operational goals included water bodies that were clean enough to support both fishing and swimming by 1983 and the elimination of all discharges by 1985.

Of course, anyone who understands the laws of mass balance knows that the elimination of all discharges is impossible to obtain. Although it is possible to recycle, to reuse, to change the form of waste, and to change the media into which it is disposed, it is impossible to eliminate the waste. The law of mass balance states that the mass of the inputs going into an activity must equal the mass of the outputs coming out of the activity. The law of mass balance cannot be repealed.

There has been mixed success in meeting the other goals. Reduction in organic wastes from point source polluters and municipal waste treatment plants has improved water quality in some water bodies to the point that it sustains healthy fish populations. In regions where nonpoint sources of pollution are important, however, water quality remains poor. Combined sewer outflow is an important problem in many urban areas. Box 15.3 discusses this problem in greater detail.

The Clean Water Act has not been amended since 1987. A major component of the 1987 amendments was to require states to develop total maximum daily loads (TMDL) which specified the concentration of pollutants which would be sufficiently low to allow impaired water bodies to recover. TMDL standards have not yet been developed for many watersheds and nonpoint source pollution remains a major obstacle to the restoration of water quality in the United States.

The major sources of nonpoint source pollution are agricultural, urban, and suburban runoff. In particular, nutrients from agricultural pollutants adversely affect water quality in areas like Chesapeake Bay (and its tributaries) and San Francisco Bay (and its tributaries). In recent years, more attention has been paid to nonpoint source pollution, with new regulations requiring farmers to institute "best farming practices" to control nutrient runoff and soil erosion. It is clear that in many areas of the United States, agriculture remains the biggest contaminator of water resources. That is true in other countries as well, particularly in developing countries. The impact of agriculture on water quality and related policy options are further discussed in Chapter 17.

Even though some progress has been made in controlling organic pollutants, the problem of toxic pollutants has not been similarly reduced (it may even be increasing), and many areas that have healthy fish populations (such as the trout and salmon fisheries of the Great Lakes) have advisories and prohibitions against eating the fish because of contamination with PCBs, mirex, dioxin, heavy metals, and other toxic substances.

Box 15.3 Combined Sewer Outflow

One of the most serious threats to water quality in the United States comes from combined sewer outflow. Combined sewer outflow refers to storm sewers connected to the sewage treatment system. In most urban areas, storm sewers carry the runoff from rainfall that falls on paved urban areas and consequently does not sink into the ground. The problem is that because sewage treatment plants are generally operating at near capacity in treating the water that is returned in the sanitary sewer system, the storm runoff from heavy rainfalls overloads the sewage treatment system and causes the treatment system to be bypassed. Not only storm water but also untreated sewage bypasses the treatment system. As a consequence, rivers and lakes in most urban areas (not just the largest cities) receive periodic doses of untreated sewage, which can substantially reduce water quality and make recreation unhealthy in the water body in the period following the heavy rainfall. The bypass of the system also allows the roadside trash that is swept into storm sewers to bypass the sewage treatment systems, and the trash is released into rivers and other water bodies. Combined sewage outflow is suspected to be one of the important causes of the beach debris problem that has been experienced on the Atlantic coast, especially in the area between New Jersey and Massachusetts.

Although this problem is well understood, its solution is not easy to develop. The solution calls for rerouting the storm sewers, increasing the capacity of the sewage treatment plants, or both, all of which are extremely expensive, especially in an era when local governments have little budget flexibility. For example, it has been estimated that solving the combined sewage outflow problem in New York City would cost tens of billions of dollars.

Many cities are looking at innovative methods for dealing with sewage treatment needs. New development projects (subdivisions, malls, industrial parks, and so on) are generally required to construct holding ponds to store storm runoff and allow it to be absorbed into the ground or released more slowly (after sediments drop out) into surface waters. Some municipalities are also exploring the possibility of constructing large wetlands to cleanse sewage by natural processes.

Arcata, California, has developed a 63-hectare wetlands on a former garbage dump to deal with a portion of the city's sewage. The purified water that flows out of the wetlands is used to irrigate other wetlands and used to support an oyster aquaculture operation in the adjacent bay. Processed wastewater is also used to support aquaculture in many other countries particularly in Southeast Asia (World Resources Institute, *World Resources 1992–93*, p. 169).

There has been some discussion in the environmental economics literature about the feasibility of economic incentives to control pollution in water resources. The discussion focuses both on pollution taxes and marketable pollution permits. In general, there has been even less movement toward economic incentives to control water pollution than exists for air pollution. The reference section at the end of this chapter lists some books and articles that discuss economic incentives in water pollution policy.

International Water Issues

As mentioned in the introduction to this chapter, water problems in other countries (particularly developing countries) may even be more severe than in the United States. The primary water problem in developing countries, without doubt, is the contamination of water by untreated human waste. This problem is not just associated with small backwater villages. Large cities with modern industries that employ the latest industrial technologies (such as Rio de Janeiro and Mexico City) also suffer from this problem. In many of these cities, the problem is intensified because of the large slums (completely devoid of any sanitary facilities) filled with migrants from rural areas that have developed around these cities. In addition, in many developing countries and many European countries, sewer systems are merely collection systems, not treatment systems. As collection systems, they merely take the untreated sewage from buildings and funnel it into a recipient water body, such as a river, a lake, an estuary, or the ocean.

A good example occurs in the Po River valley in northern Italy, where many cities (including Milan) dump untreated wastes into the river. Heavy chemical runoff from agriculture further degrades Po River water quality. The Mediterranean Sea, which travel posters depict as paradise, suffers from extreme water pollution problems. These problems are likely to become even worse as increased population growth, urbanization, and industrialization in North Africa leads to more effluents and overwhelm the reductions in pollution that are being undertaken in European countries (Box 15-4).

Transfrontier Externalities

A major problem associated with water extraction and water pollution in Europe, Asia, Africa, and Latin America is the transfrontier externality. The water consumption or waste disposal activities in one country affect water availability and water quality in neighboring countries. This effect occurs particularly in areas such as the Middle East, where geographically small countries overlie common aquifers and where rivers such as the Jordan and the Tigris-Euphrates drain several countries. In addition, political hostility in the region exacerbates the problem and makes it more difficult to develop solutions to prevent the deterioration of water resources.

These transfrontier externalities cannot be internalized without international agreement. One hopeful note is that international commissions, sometimes sponsored by the United Nations and sometimes developed regionally, are being initiated to solve these problems. Although different countries have different perspectives, different needs, and different institutions, the countries are recognizing that if they do not cooperate, all will suffer.

The United States has had long-standing agreements with Canada concerning water use and water quality in boundary areas and a special commission to deal with Great Lakes issues. Agreements with Mexico are being developed at the current time.

Agriculture and Water Quality in Developing Countries

In addition to untreated sewage, agricultural pollution is extremely important in affecting water quality in developing countries. Problems with deforestation, overtillage, tillage of hillsides, heavy use of dangerous pesticides, and runoff of fertilizer (including human and animal waste as fertilizers) has seriously affected water quality in many developing nations.

One of the most degrading uses of water is the irrigation of agricultural fields. Not only may irrigation lead to the rapid depletion of groundwater and

Box 15.4 Privatization of Water in the Third World

As the political and economic climate in the late 1980s and 1990s evolved toward an emphasis on markets, many countries moved to privatize utility services such as water, electricity, and telecommunications. The underlying premise was that the publicly owned water companies (and other utilities) were inefficient because they faced no competition. Privatizing them (selling the enterprises to private firms) would make them more efficient. It was also believed that services would be improved, especially to the urban poor. Price would also rise appropriately to reflect the scarcity value of water, eliminating shortages.

Although the hypothesis seems well-founded in economic theory, the implementation of the policy has left much to be desired. First, the privatization often occurred without creating competition. Therefore, a public monopoly was converted into a private, unregulated monopoly. As discussed in Chapter 2, unregulated monopolies create monopoly profits by restricting output to raise price, causing losses in social welfare. Second, price increased and service often did not improve, causing dissatisfaction. Third, because many of the sales occurred to foreign firms (primarily European and North American), there was often resentment by the public because of the belief that national assets were being sold to foreign firms at bargain basement prices, transferring national wealth out of the developing country into a developed country. See Bjornlund and McKay (2002) and Johnstone and Wood (2001) for more discussion of privatization of water supply services.

reduced flows in rivers, but the irrigation causes major changes in the water that flows out of the agricultural fields and also degrades soils.

A major problem with irrigation is that the repeated soaking of the soil and the evaporation of the water in the soil draws salts from lower levels of the soil and deposits them in the top layers of the soil, where they adversely affect many of the crops that farmers are trying to grow. In addition, the salts wash into nearby streams and rivers, causing ecological damage and reducing the quality of water for downstream water users.

Another major problem with irrigation is that it often diverts so much water out of the river systems that there is massive ecological degradation of the aquatic systems. The premier example of this is a set of irrigation projects in Kazakhstan and Uzbekistan, which has so reduced river flow that the Aral Sea (into which the rivers drain) has been reduced to a fraction of its former size, with the loss of an important commercial and subsistence fishery. This problem has been intensified by the fragmentation of the former Soviet Union, because the rivers flowing into the Aral Sea flow through several now-independent republics, increasing the difficulty of developing a solution to the problem.

A World Resources Institute study cites the damage from irrigation as a major threat to the ability of the planet to produce food in the future. According to this study, irrigated areas constitute 5.4 percent of global agricultural land and 15.7 percent of cropland. The area of irrigated land is currently increasing at 1.6 percent per year, implying a doubling time of approximately 43 years. (Wood, Sebastian, and Sherr, 2001, p. 11).

Summary

Although three-quarters of the earth's surface is covered by water, uncontaminated freshwater is a scarce resource. Many market failures, including externalities, nontransferable property rights, and poorly conceived regulatory practices, exacerbate the scarcity. These market failures adversely affect the quantity of water that is available for use as well as diminishing its quality. This diminished water quality has important effects for social and ecological systems that are dependent on water resources.

From a U.S. and international perspective, one critically important policy change would be to price water so that it included its full opportunity cost. Such pricing would include the opportunity cost of both current and future uses of water as well as the costs associated with reductions in the quality of water resources.

Water scarcity problems are critically important internationally, particularly in developing countries. This chapter has identified some of these problems, but has not extensively discussed solutions, as different institutional, economic, social, and environmental factors imply differences between U.S. policies and the policies that would be most appropriate in a developing country context. These policies and the factors that determine their structure are discussed in depth in Chapter 18.

Review Questions

1. What market failures are associated with the use of water for consumption?
2. How does average cost pricing of water affect social efficiency?
3. Assume that the inverse demand function for water in a town can be described as $D = 25 - 0.04Q$, with $AC = 0.5Q$ and $MC = Q$. If the town prices water at average cost, consumers' and producers' surplus will be lower than if priced at marginal cost. Calculate the loss in this example.
4. What are the strengths and weakness of the Clean Water Act and its amendments?
5. Why is the elimination of all discharges an ill-founded goal for water policy?

Questions for Further Study

1. What extra difficulties are involved with devising water quality policy for internationally shared waters?
2. What are the equity issues involved with rapid consumption of fossil water?
3. Should California farmers be forced to pay full social cost for the water they use?
4. How do Third World water issues differ from those in the United States?
5. How should property rights to water be defined? Does it make any difference if the resource in question is a resource flow or an exhaustible resource?

Suggested Paper Topics

1. Investigate the controversy over Native American water rights. Start with the references by Dumars (1984) and Burton (1991). Search bibliographic databases using Indian water rights and Native American water rights as keywords. Also search government documents databases, paying particular attention to the Bureau of Indian Affairs (Department of the Interior) and congressional committees on Interior and Indian Affairs.
2. Investigate the benefits of water quality improvements in the United States or another country. Also look at recent issues of the *Journal of Environmental Economics and Management, Land Economics,* and *Water Resources Research*. Search the internet and EconLit for current references.
3. Investigate a water quality issue in your area. Is it caused by a pollution externality or a lack of property rights to consumptive uses of the water? What is current policy toward this issue? Use your knowledge of economics to develop an improved set of policies.
4. Investigate the development of policy to manage internationally shared water resources. Start with the *Natural Resource Journal*, which has been active in publishing articles in this area. Search bibliographic databases on international water issues, the Great Lakes Commission, boundary waters, the Colorado River, and the Rio Grande.

Works Cited and Selected Readings

Anderson, T. L. *Water Rights: A Scarce Resource Allocation, Bureaucracy, and the Environment.* Cambridge, MA: Ballinger, 1983.

Becker, N., N. Zeitouni, and D. Zilberman. Issues in the Economics of Water Resource. Pages 55–99 in *The International Yearbook of Environmental and Resource Economics: 2000/2001: A Survey of Current Issues* edited by T. Tietenberg, and H. Folmer. Cheltenham, UK and Northampton, MA: Edward Elgar, 2000.

Bergstrom, J. C., K. J. Boyle, and G. L. Poe (eds.). *The Economic Value of Water Quality.* Cheltenham, UK, and Northampton, MA: Edward Elgar, 2001.

Bjornlund, H., and J. McKay. Aspects of Water Markets for Developing Countries: Experiences from Australia, Chile, and the U.S. *Environment and Development Economics 7*, no. 4 (October 2002): 769–795.

Boris, C. *Water Rights and Energy Development in the Yellowstone River Basin: An Integrated Analysis.* Washington, DC: Resources for the Future, 1980.

Boyd, J. Water Pollution Taxes: A Good Idea Doomed to Failure? *Public Finance and Management 3*, no.1 (2003): 34–66.

Brookshire, D. S., S. Burness, J. Chermak, and K. Krause. Western Urban Water Demand. *Natural Resources Journal 42*, no. 4 (Fall 2002): 873–898.

Burton, L. *American Indian Water Rights and the Limits of Law.* Lawrence: University of Kansas Press, 1991.

Carriker, R. R. *Water Law and Rights in the South*. Starkville: Mississippi State University, Southern Rural Development Center, 1985.

Dewsnup, R. L., and D. W. Jensen. *A Summary Digest of State Water Laws*. Arlington, VA: National Water Commission, 1973.

Doughman, P. M., J. Blatter, and H. Ingram (eds.). *Reflections on Water: New Approaches to Transboundary Conflicts and Cooperation*. Cambridge, MA: MIT Press, 2001.

Dumars, C. T. *Pueblo Indian Water Rights: A Struggle for a Precious Resource*. Tucson: University of Arizona Press, 1984.

Fernandez, L. Solving Water Pollution Problems Along the U.S.-Mexico Border. *Environment and Development Economics 7*, no. 4 (October 2002): 715–732.

Foster, H. *The Emerging Water Crises in Canada*. Toronto: J. Lorimar, 1981.

Frederick, K. D. Water Resources and Climate Change. Pages 67–74 in *Climate Change, Economics and Policy: An RFF Anthology*, edited by M. Toman. Washington, DC: Resources for the Future, 2001.

Freeman, A. M., III. *The Measurment of Environmental and Resource Values*. Washington, DC: Resources for the Future, 1993.

Freeman, A. M., III. Water Pollution Policy. Pages 169–213 in *Public Policies for Environmental Protection* edited by P. R. Portney, and R. N. Stavins. Washington, DC: Resources for the Future, 2000.

Johnstone, N., and L. Wood, (eds.). *Private Firms and Public Water: Realising Social and Environmental Objectives in Developing Countries*. Cheltenham, UK, and Northampton, MA: Edward Elgar, 2001.

Kanazawa, M. Origins of Common-Law Restrictions on Water Transfers: Groundwater Law in Nineteenth-Century California. *Journal of Legal Studies 32*, no. 1 (January 2003): 153–180.

Krause, K., J. M. Chermak, and D. S. Brookshire. The Demand for Water: Consumer Response to Scarcity. *Journal of Regulatory Economics 23*, no. 2 (March 2003): 167–191.

Olcay Unver, I. H., R. K. Gupta, and A. Kibaroglu (eds.). *Water Development and Poverty Reduction*. Boston: Kluwer Academic, 2003.

Organization for Economic Cooperation and Development. *Financing Strategies for Water and Environmental Infrastructure*. Paris: OECD, 2003.

Organization for Economic Cooperation and Development. *Improving Water Management: Recent OECD Experience*. Paris: OECD, 2003.

Pitman, G. K. *Bridging Troubled Waters: Assessing the World Bank Water Resources Strategy*. Washington, DC: World Bank, 2002.

Raje, D. V., P. S. Dhobe, and A. W. Deshpande. Consumer's Willingness to Pay More for Municipal Supplied Water: A Case Study. *Ecological Economics 42*, no. 3 (September 2002): 391–400.

Raven, P. H., L. R. Berg, and G. B. Johnson. *Environment*. Philadelphia: Saunders, 1993.

Reiser, M. *Cadillac Desert: The American West and its Disappearing Water*. New York: Viking, 1986.

Saleth, R. M. (ed.). *Water Resources and Economic Development*. Cheltenham, UK, and Northampton, MA: Edward Elgar, 2002.

Shirley, M. M., (ed.). *Thirsting for Efficiency: The Economics and Politics of Urban Water System Reform*. Amsterdam, London, and New York: Elsevier Science, 2002.

Trawick, P. Against the Privatization of Water: An Indigenous Model for Improving Existing Laws and Successfully Governing the Commons. *World Development 31*, no. 6 (June 2003): 977–996.

Turner, R. K., and I. J. Bateman, (eds.). *Water Resources and Coastal Management*. Cheltenham, UK, and Northampton, MA: Edward Elgar, 2001.

Turner, T. Water and Environment Issues in the Black, Caspian, and Aral Seas. *Problems of Economic Transition 46*, no. 4 (August 2003): 6–77.

Wahl, R. W. *Markets for Federal Water: Subsidies, Property Rights and the Bureau of Reclamation*. Washington, DC: Resources for the Future, 1989.

Waite, G. G. *A Four-State Comparison of Public Rights in Water*. Madison: University of Wisconsin Law Extension, 1967.

Weinberg, M. Assessing a Policy Grab Bag: Federal Water Policy Reform. *American Journal of Agricultural Economics 84*, no. 3 (August 2002): 541–556.

Wood, S., K. Sebastian, and S. J. Scherr. Pilot Analysis of Global Ecosystems: Agroecosystems. Washington, DC: World Resources Institute, 2001. Online: http://www.ifpri.org/pubs/books/page.htm#about.

World Resources Institute. *World Resources 1992–93*. Washington, DC: World Resources Institute, 1993.

PART IV

further topics

Part IV examines important environmental and resource issues that do not relate directly to either exhaustible or renewable resources. Toxic substances, agriculture and the environment, and Third World issues receive special treatment in Chapters 16 through 18. The concluding chapter, Chapter 19, looks at how the interactions among the economic system, the environment, and social policy determines the prospects for the future.

chapter 16
Toxins in the Ecosystem

The chemicals to which life is asked to make its adjustment are no longer merely the calcium and silica and copper and all the rest of the minerals washed out of the rocks and carried in rivers to the sea; they are the synthetic creations of man's inventive mind, brewed in his laboratories, and having no counterparts in nature.

Rachel Carson, Silent Spring

Introduction

In 1962, Rachel Carson alerted the world to the problems associated with Western society's increasing dependence on chemicals. Although her important book, *Silent Spring*, was couched mostly in terms of the increasing use of pesticides, it alerted the public to the ecological and human health consequences of the increasing presence of toxic chemicals in the environment.

In subsequent years, public attention has been refocused on toxic substances. As events such as Love Canal, Times Beach, and the kepone contamination of the James River unfolded during the 1960s and 1970s, the

American public became aware that toxic substances are a critically important environmental problem.[1]

One way of categorizing the toxic problem is to distinguish between exposure as a result of toxic substances being present in economic processes and exposure as a result of wastes that result from economic processes. The first category of exposure would include on-the-job exposure to toxic substances, pesticide residues on fruits and vegetables, and radon exposure in people's homes. The second category of exposure would include environmental exposure to humans and ecosystems, such as through toxic contamination of lakes and rivers. There is little ecosystem exposure in the first category (which is primarily human health-oriented); the primary ecosystem exposure is from the wastes that generate the second category of exposure. The toxic waste part of the problem can be further dichotomized into separate policy dimensions. The first dimension of the problem is to develop solutions to deal with past releases of toxic substances into the environment. The second dimension of the problem is to develop policies to control new sources of exposure to toxic substances.

Before discussing the issues involving toxic wastes, it is necessary to define exactly what is meant by toxic wastes and the implication of toxic waste for ecosystem and human health. A toxin is a poison produced by the metabolic processes of an organism, but when *toxic* is used as an adjective to describe wastes or substances, it generally means a waste or substance that is poisonous and is of inorganic origin. Because almost any substance can be poisonous at some level of exposure, it is necessary to derive a more operational definition of toxic wastes and toxic substances. Toxic wastes are those wastes that have the following properties:

1. Exposure to small amounts of the waste generates adverse health effects in living organisms. These effects include interference with a variety of life processes, including reproduction and often include carcinogenic and tetragenic (creating mutations such as birth defects) effects.
2. The wastes are generally of synthetic or inorganic origin and persist in the environment for long periods of time (many generations of human life).
3. A variety of mechanisms exist for the waste to move through both the physical environment and the ecosystem.

---

[1] Love Canal is a site in Niagara Falls, New York, where a variety of toxic substances were secretly buried in an area upon which homes and a public school were later built. Health problems surfaced and the extent of the toxic contamination became apparent. Love Canal is the "textbook" example of illegal and unethical disposal of toxic substances by a chemical-producing firm.

Times Beach, Missouri, is a small rural town in which dioxin-laden waste oil was dumped on dirt roads to control dust. Although many critics say the government overreacted, the federal government bought the town and forced residents to move to other locations.

The kepone problem in the James River was due to waste products in the manufacture of pesticides in a town near Richmond, Virginia. The kepone releases led to nervous system problems of people who were exposed to the kepone, and it contaminated the fish in the river so badly that commercial fishing was banned until 1989, and there are still health advisories about eating fish that are caught in this section of the river.

The first property is one that makes toxic wastes a particularly important problem. Exposure to toxic waste can kill an organism or stress the organism to the extent that it succumbs to other stresses. From a human perspective, one of the most important health consequences of exposure to toxic waste is that this exposure can lead to an increased risk of cancer.

The second property is important because synthetic materials that do not exist in nature will persist for long periods. Because these substances do not exist in nature, nature has no mechanisms for breaking them down into simpler compounds that are less toxic. Examples of synthetic toxic compounds include PCBs, DDT, benzene, dioxin, and radioactive substances such as plutonium or uranium. There is also a problem with naturally occurring inorganic compounds that are collected and concentrated by economic activity. Among the most important of this class of chemicals are the heavy metals (such as mercury, lead, cadmium, and arsenic).

The third property is important because it provides a mechanism for exposure. Toxic chemicals are transported through physical means, such as the movement of groundwater and surface waters. They are also transported by movement through the food web. For example, algae may absorb toxic substances in a body of water to which toxic waste has been transported. The algae are then eaten by zooplankton that absorb the toxic substance. The zooplankton are eaten by small fish, which are in turn eaten by large fish, which are eaten by piscivorus birds, such as eagles, herons, and ospreys. As the toxic substance passes through the food web, the concentration of the toxic substance in the organism increases. For example, a DDT concentration of 0.00005 ppm (parts per million) in water would lead to a DDT concentration in plants and algae of 0.04 ppm. This concentration would, inturn, lead to a concentration of 0.2 to 1.2 ppm in plant-eating fish and 1 to 2 ppm in larger fish. The DDT concentration in fish-eating birds may be as much as 76 ppm, which is 1 million times greater than the DDT concentration in the water (Raven, et al., 1993). Of course, this increase in concentration has extremely important implications for humans, who are at a terminus on the food web.

The Nature of the Market Failure

As with all of our pollution problems, the toxic substance problem originates in market failure. Since these market failures are different than those associated with conventional pollutants, they merit further discussion.

Market Failures in Exposure to Toxic Substances in Consumption and Production

Toxic substances are present in the production processes that create economic goods and in the economic goods themselves. For example, in agriculture, pesticides are used to reduce the negative impact of pests on agricultural yields. People may receive exposure to these toxic substances in their role as laborers and in their role as consumers. Workers who apply the pesticides and who do other work in the fields on subsequent days may absorb pesticides through their respiratory systems or through contact with their skin. Consumers may be exposed through ingestion of pesticide residues, which may remain on fruits and vegetables even after washing. A variety of economic goods contain toxic substances to which either workers, consumers, or both may be exposed. These substances include solvents, paints, inks, cleaners, fuels, plastics, electronics, pharmaceuticals, pesticides, fungicides, and herbicides. In addition, a variety of foods have additives in them that are suspected to be harmful.

There is considerable discussion of whether this type of exposure represents a market failure, because it can be argued that the people who receive the exposure are a part of the market transaction and *choose* their level of exposure. Even if this type of exposure does not constitute an externality because the people choose their level of exposure, however, it does not mean that the level of exposure is socially optimal. There may be other market failures.

The first potential market failure concerns imperfect information. For the choices of individuals to promote optimal social welfare, they must be aware of the risks that they are facing as a result of their choices. Most consumers probably do not adequately understand the risks associated with using solvents, consuming additives in their hot dogs, or consuming pesticide residues on their fruit. The government can rely on two types of policies to mitigate this problem. The first is to provide information about the hazard on the product label in a fashion that is understandable by the consumer. A good example of this policy is the rotating warning system on cigarette packages and cigarette advertisements. The second is to use direct controls, limiting the use of certain substances in certain applications. For example, certain pesticides can only be applied by licensed applicators and are not available for home use.

An important dimension of the imperfect information problem is that the general public does not adequately understand risk in general. Part of this misunderstanding is due to a lack of understanding of probability. Many people argue that if a coin flips to "heads" three times in a row, then there is a greater than 50 percent chance that it will be "tails" on the next flip. Many people believe that low-probability events such as a house fire or flood are simply events that only happen to other people and could not possibly happen to them. There is also a serious problem of lack of comprehension of very small probabilities (1 in 1 million versus 1 in 100 million) associated with exposure to toxic substances. For example, what does it mean to the average consumer if he or she is told that switching from conventionally produced vegetables (with pesticide applications) to organically produced vegetables (free of all agrichemicals) reduces his or her probability of contracting cancer by 1 in 10,000, 1 in 100,000, or 1 in 1,000,000? It is quite likely that the average consumer cannot distinguish the implications of these probabilities and make an informed decision about whether to pay the price premium associated with organic produce.

Policy makers also have to deal with the problem that many of the risks cannot be perceived by a person's senses. Radon gas, for example, is odorless and colorless and does not stem from a visible hazard such as a waste dump or a weapons facility (see Box 16.1). In addition, many of the risks are of future consequences. This factor is particularly true of exposure to carcinogens, which increases the probability of contracting cancer, but this increased risk may lag behind exposure by several decades.

Finally, it is not necessarily possible to look at voluntary exposure to risk to determine the way that the public values reductions or increases in risk. People may not regard voluntarily accepted risk as being the same good as externally imposed risk. People regard exposing themselves to risk (that is, not wearing a seatbelt, smoking, mountain biking, bungee jumping, and so on) as a basic right. They also believe that they have a basic right to be free of externally imposed risks (for example, secondhand cigarette smoke, toxic waste, violent

Box 16.1 Radon Exposure in Homes

One of the most interesting exposure issues facing policy makers is exposure to radon. Radon is a naturally occurring radioactive gas that percolates up through the soil as small amounts of uranium decay in the soil. This exposure is not a problem that is limited to uranium-mining areas. Many areas of the country have small amounts of uranium in the soil.

Radon gas infiltrates building foundations through cracks, places where pipes penetrate the foundation, and pores in the cement. As people began to seal their homes more tightly to save energy, the ventilation of the house was limited and indoor concentrations of radon increased. In houses in the most radon-prone areas, the health risks associated with radon are equivalent to those associated with smoking several packs of cigarettes per day. Radon is believed to be the second leading cause of lung cancer in the United States (although many of these cases are associated with uranium miners).

Because radon is a naturally occurring hazard, one might expect that there is no role for public policy. Yet there is a very important market failure. Radon is odorless, colorless, and does not lead to immediate health consequences (it leads to an increased chance of cancer many years in the future), so people do not adequately comprehend the nature of the risk to which their family will be exposed. Thus, information is imperfect, and, as a result, the level of remediation is lower than it would be if people had better information.

There are two major ways to address this market failure. First, one can try to educate the public as to the nature of the risk that they face. Smith et al. (1995) have studied alternative mechanisms for communicating this risk. Second, if it is believed that the imperfect information problem cannot be adequately addressed, then a series of direct controls can be enacted. These controls could include mandatory testing of houses, especially before their sale, and mandatory remediation of houses that exceed safe levels of radon. These remediation procedures would include sealing foundation cracks and installing basement ventilation systems.

crime). Consequently, they view an externally imposed risk as a much greater consequence than a voluntarily accepted risk, even though the two types of risks may have equivalent implications for risk of illness, injury, or death.

The primary piece of legislation that addresses these market failures is the Toxic Substances Control Act of 1976 (TSCA). This legislation gives the U.S. Environmental Protection Agency (EPA) the authority to test existing chemicals, conduct premarket screening of new chemicals, control unreasonable risks of chemicals, and collect and distribute information about chemical production and risks. The EPA has implemented several policies to accomplish this authority, including requiring manufacturers to test the chemicals that they produce, limiting or prohibiting the manufacture of certain chemicals, requiring record keeping and labeling, requiring notification of hazards and consumer recalls, and controlling disposal methods. The TSCA does not apply to pesticides, drugs, and nuclear materials, which are covered by other statutes.

The second source of market failure applies to on-the-job exposures. As stated earlier, one could argue that on-the-job exposures do not constitute a market failure, because people voluntarily expose themselves to the risk. In fact, wages would adjust so that (holding other job characteristics constant) the riskier jobs would have the highest wages, because workers would have to be compensated to accept the additional risk.[2] Of course, the problem of imperfect information immediately comes to mind, and it is apparent that the system will only give the optimal level of risk if people have perfect information as to the exact nature of the risks. Even if perfect information exists, however, there could be another important market failure related to the mobility of labor.

The definition of a perfectly competitive market requires that there be perfect mobility throughout the system. This assumption may be violated in many labor markets, where only one employer or type of employment exists in a region and where a variety of barriers keep the workers from moving to another region for another type of employment. For example, migrant farm workers may not regard their wages as high enough to compensate them for exposure to pesticides, but they have little option except to keep working in the fields.

Again, the provision of information and the utilization of direct controls can help reduce this type of exposure toward a socially optimal level. For example, "right to know" laws require employers to inform their workers of actual or potential exposure to toxic substances. In addition, both the Occupational Safety and Health Administration (OSHA) and the EPA regulate exposure through prohibiting the use of certain chemicals and by requiring safety procedures (for example, protective clothing, respirators, ventilation) for use with toxic chemicals.

Should all toxic substances be banned? Although this step might seem to make sense at first, when the question is examined more closely it can be seen that this resource allocation problem is the same as any resource allocation problem. The marginal social benefits of the toxic substance must be com-

[2] In Chapter 4, this voluntary exposure and adjustment of wages is discussed as a basis for measuring the value of reducing risk.

pared with the marginal social costs to determine the socially optimal level of production and consumption of the toxic substance. For example, smoke detectors contain a radioactive material, but the benefits of reduced risk from dying in a house fire far outweigh the increased risk from exposure to the low-level radioactivity contained in the smoke detector. Similarly, artificial sweeteners reduce obesity and its associated health risks (and reduce health risks for diabetics). Even if artificial sweeteners result in an increase in other types of health risks (such as increased risk of disease), their use may result in a net reduction in risk.

The Delaney Clause

The Delaney clause is a controversial piece of legislation that does not recognize the trade-offs between costs and benefits. The Delaney clause is contained in amendments to the Food, Drug, and Cosmetics Act that were enacted in 1958. The purpose of the Delaney clause is to ban the use of additives in processed food that are shown to cause cancer in animals. In addition to not recognizing cost-benefit trade-offs, other problems are associated with this clause. First, it does not regulate exposure in unprocessed foods, so cancer-causing pesticides are prohibited in tomato sauce but not in fresh tomatoes. Second, many pesticides that have been in use are not covered by the legislation, so new pesticides associated with a smaller risk of cancer are not allowed to replace old pesticides with a higher risk of cancer. For example, fungicides are used to treat hops, which is an ingredient of beer. A fungicide called fosetyl A1 was developed that had a 1 in 100 million additional risk of cancer. Because it was associated with this cancer risk, the EPA prohibited its use. However, the older fungicide (called EBDC) that it would have replaced was estimated to have a risk of cancer that is 1000 times as great, on the order of 1 in 100,000 (Raven et al. 1993, p. 516).

Market Failures in the Generation of Toxic Waste

Market failures related to the generation and illegal disposal of toxic waste are completely analogous to market failures associated with other types of pollution. Firms do not take social costs into account when deciding how much of a toxic substance to produce and use, in deciding the safety features of containment systems (such as underground storage tanks for gasoline and other toxic substances), in deciding the level of safety associated with transportation, and in determining the method of disposal of the waste.

Earlier in the chapter, toxic substances were defined in terms of strong health effects (human or ecosystem) that can be generated by relatively small amounts of the substance. They were also defined in terms of the persistence of the chemical in the environment. These properties, especially the first property, imply that the marginal damages from the first few units of emissions are high. These high initial damages will often imply that the optimal level of pollution is near zero, as illustrated in Figure 16.1. As discussed in Chapter 3, when that is the case, it is probably more efficient to simply ban the release of

Figure 16.1 The Optimal Level of Emissions of Toxic Wastes

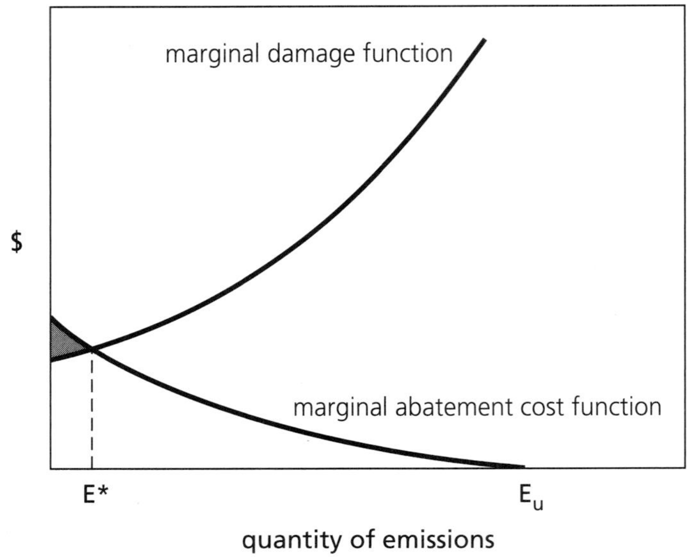

the substance than to try to achieve a level of E* emissions through economic incentives. The reason is that the resource costs of administering the tax or permit system are probably greater than the excess social costs (shaded triangle) that are created when emissions are regulated to zero. Of course, for some toxic substances, the optimal level is zero rather than near zero.

The problem is made even more complex because the damages associated with today's emissions are a function of past emissions, because past emissions linger in the environment and contribute to current concentrations of pollution. Even if initial levels of concentration were to be associated with low levels of damage, as long as the marginal damage function is positively sloped the past emissions that persist in the environment imply that current emissions will have greater marginal damages than past emissions. Rather than simply comparing marginal abatement costs and marginal damages in each period, one must look at the present value of total damages and the present value of abatement costs, and try to minimize the sum of the two. This minimization would be done by choosing an optimal time path of emissions, rather than focusing on each period independently.

When the optimal level of emissions of these toxic pollutants is zero or near zero, economic incentives, such as taxes or marketable pollution permits, are not often discussed as a means for preventing the release of toxic substances into the environment. Direct controls that prohibit the release of toxic substances and that mandate required disposal techniques have been implemented for many classes of toxic substances, along with "cradle to grave" manifest systems that create a written record of the movement of the toxic substances from the time they were manufactured to the time they are disposed of in a licensed toxic waste disposal facility. Other extremely hazardous materials have been banned from some or all types of use. For example, the use of DDT, asbestos, PCB, benzene, and a host of other toxic chemicals has been banned.

Although direct controls have played and should play an important role in the control of toxic substances, there is a role for economic incentives, but not the per unit emissions taxes and marketable pollution permits that economists advocate for conventional types of pollution emissions. The development of deposit-refund systems, performance bond systems, and liability systems can help reduce the release of toxic substances into the environment.

Deposit-Refund Systems

Deposit-refund systems can help reduce the release of toxic substances, particularly releases by households. Consumers use a variety of toxic substances in products such as batteries, solvents, and pesticides. The government could impose direct controls that specify exact procedures for the disposal of these products. Because there are so many millions of households, however, each of which is disposing a small amount of toxic substances, the monitoring cost of administering such a system would be relatively high. One way of avoiding this monitoring problem is to make the households pay for improper disposal "up front" in the form of a deposit. When the product (or product container) is properly disposed of, the deposit is refunded. The deposit-refund system establishes an automatic penalty for improper disposal. Deposit-refund systems could be used for batteries, solvents, paints, pesticides, and other dangerous chemicals. When the battery or container of the toxic chemical is returned to a recycling center, the deposit would be refunded.

A deposit-refund system would be more difficult to establish for large-scale generators of toxic waste such as chemical manufacturers, because with the large-scale generators there is no economic product that has a one-to-one correspondence with the waste, such as a battery or a container of pesticides. Firms assemble a variety of chemical substances as inputs and combine them to produce an economic output and waste outputs (which may be toxic substances). In other words, there is a variable rather than fixed relationship between the inputs and the economic or waste output. Because of this variable relationship, a deposit-refund system could backfire and lead to the generation of more toxic waste than without the system.

Such a deposit-refund system could be based on the law of mass balance.[3] Let the mass of the inputs be equal to X and the mass of the waste output be equal to W. Then the government could require a per unit deposit of δ on each unit of mass of inputs and collect a per unit refund of ρ on each unit of mass of waste outputs. The total deposit would be equal to δX and the total refund would be equal to ρw. Nothing in this system would discourage the production

[3]The law of mass balance states that the mass of the inputs is equal to the mass of the outputs.

of waste, however; it is aimed at ensuring its proper disposal. Firms might even adjust the relationship among outputs and produce more of the waste output (and less of the economic output) just to collect a greater refund.

One possibility for avoiding this undesirable incentive is to rely on the law of mass balance to develop a deposit-refund system, but modify the system presented here. If a firm pays a per unit of input deposit of δ and purchases X weight units of inputs, the firm's total deposit payment will be δX. If the firm simply received a per-unit-weight refund of ρ on each unit of its total legal disposal of waste, it would have a greater incentive to produce more waste output and less economic output. If the per unit refund is constructed by multiplying ρ by X/W, however, the firm cannot increase its total refund payment by producing more waste. The per unit refund would be equal to $\rho(X/W)$, and the total refund would be equal to $\rho(X/W)W$. Although the refund is received per unit of W legally disposed of, the per unit refund is increased by reducing W. The refund is based on W, but it is mathematically equal to ρX.

For example, if the per unit deposit (δ) was equal to \$2 and the firm utilized 2000 pounds of inputs (X), the total deposit it would be required to pay would be \$4000. If the firm produced 1500 pounds of economic output and

Box 16.2 Toxic Waste Sites and Race

The Commission for Racial Justice of the United Church of Christ has investigated the issue of the location of toxic waste facilities with respect to the minority characteristics of the community. Based on anecdotal evidence, this group formulated a hypothesis that minority communities were disproportionately exposed to toxic and hazardous waste. In 1987, the commission released a comprehensive cross-sectional study that provided a statistical examination of toxic sites across the country.

Their study (Commission for Racial Justice, 1987) found that race was the most significant of the variables tested to explain the location of commercial hazardous waste facilities. Socioeconomic status also mattered, but race proved to be more significant, even after controlling for urbanization and regional differences. The study also examined uncontrolled toxic waste sites and found that blacks were heavily overrepresented in the cities with the most uncontrolled toxic wastes sites (Memphis, Tennessee: 173 sites; St Louis, Missouri: 160 sites; Houston, Texas: 152 sites; Cleveland, Ohio: 106 sites; Chicago, Illinois: 103 sites; Atlanta, Georgia: 94 sites).

Additional studies have confirmed these results, Mennis (2002), Pastor et al. (2002), Kriesal et al. (1996). These studies have served as an impetus for increased concern over environmental equity and environmental justice. Current policies call for an examination of the environmental equity and justice provisions of EPA actions. For more information, search the web for environmental justice.

500 pounds of waste output (W) and if the per unit refund (ρ) was \$2 per pound, then if the firm legally disposed of its 500 pounds of waste, it would receive a total refund of \$2(2000/500)(500) = \$4000. Note that the firm cannot increase its refund by producing more waste. If it increased its waste production to 1000 pounds (holding constant the 2000 pounds of input), then its total refund would equal \$2(2000/1000)(1000), which still equals \$4000.

Although such a deposit-refund system has some desirable properties in that it could reduce the amount of waste that was actually produced, it would require more information and monitoring than the types of command and control regulations currently in place. The high information requirements of this type of deposit-refund plan probably indicate that the role of deposit-refunds in toxic waste management may be more for household disposal of toxic waste than for large-scale waste generators.

Performance Bond Systems

Performance bonds are another type of policy that can give firms an economic incentive to properly dispose of toxic waste, and they have less of an information and monitoring requirement than deposit-refund systems. Firms engaged in the production, storage, transportation, or disposal of toxic waste could be required to post a performance bond, which is only returned upon compliance with appropriate standards. The performance bond system is different from the deposit-refund system in that the latter is a "per unit of waste" incentive, whereas the former gives an incentive for complying with environmental standards. In other words, the performance bond system is based on regulating the type of behavior, not the quantity of waste. Performance bond systems are discussed more fully in the context of forestry (Chapter 13) and mining (Chapter 10).

Liability Systems

Although deposit-refund systems may not be effective for large-scale generators, another type of economic incentive is being used that has important incentive effects. This incentive is a liability system that requires toxic waste generators, transporters, and disposal site operators to pay for the damages associated with any release of any waste for which they were responsible. If people who use toxic substances or generate toxic wastes are required to pay any damages that they generate, then this requirement will increase their incentives to provide the appropriate amount of safety in utilizing and disposing of these substances.

This rationale was behind the Comprehensive Environmental Response, Compensation and Liability Act of 1980 (CERCLA), which creates several different types of liabilities for toxic waste generators and transporters. In particular, it establishes liability for wastes that are disposed of improperly and allows the government to force the waste generators, transporters, or disposal site operators (jointly or separately) to clean up a site into which any of these parties were responsible for the release of hazardous substances. Under this legislation, the generator of the waste is responsible for future damages from improper disposal of the waste, even if the generator of the waste contracts the disposal to a licensed transport and disposal firm. Firms that spill chemicals may also be sued for the environmental damage that they generate, with local, federal, state, and Native American government agencies acting as the trustees of these public environmental resources.

The combination of high fines and prison terms for accidental release—extremely high fines ($250,000) and up to 15 years in jail for "knowing endangerment"—liability for damages, and liability for cleanup are strong incentives for firms to comply with laws governing the treatment and disposal of toxic substances. These penalties, combined with adequate record keeping and strict enforcement, may be sufficient to control the generation of new toxic sites. The United States, however, is faced with an incredibly large legacy of existing toxic sites, where wastes have been accidentally released or intentionally dumped in the past. Surprisingly, the federal government is one of the primary culprits in generating this toxic legacy.

The CERCLA legislation also set up the "Superfund." The Superfund was created with required payments of money from firms that were involved in the production and use of toxic substances. Existing toxic waste legacies for which a "responsible party" could not be identified would have their remediation paid out of the Superfund. Sites were placed on a National Priority List and addressed in order of their threat to local communities (with a little bit of politics thrown in). Unfortunately, the money in the Superfund has been almost entirely spent, it is not being replenished, and there remain many toxic waste sites that are generating exposure and threats of future exposure to humans and ecosystems.

Liability and the Creation of Brownfields

Well-intentioned and beneficial policies often have negative indirect impacts, and our liability-oriented toxic waste policy is no exception. Although defining strict liability rules creates financial responsibility to clean up old sites and to avoid new releases of toxic waste, it also creates an economic disincentive to undertake new economic activities on old and abandoned industrial sites.

A series of changes in economic forces has led to industry moving out of city centers and moving to smaller towns, outer suburbs, rural locations, or foreign sites. Many of these old industrial sites may be contaminated, because the old facility manufactured toxic products (such as chemicals or batteries), because the facility used toxic substances in its production processes (such as solvents or heavy metals), or because illegal dumping occurred on the site after it was abandoned. These abandoned sites are not purchased and used for new economic activities because potential purchasers are afraid they will become liable for the cleanup of toxic substances that may be on or beneath the site. The sites remain abandoned and have very negative external effects on the urban neighborhoods in which they exist. The unsightly sites were often used for activities related to illegal drugs, and they simply created barriers which separated parts of communities. Moreover, they could not become sources of new jobs in poor urban areas that have suffered from losses of jobs as manufacturing and retail activities moved out of the inner city. These sites became known as "brownfields," a name chosen to reflect the desolation they created in the communities in which they existed. Attention to brownfields began to increase as the Superfund diminished in magnitude and as the environmental justice[4] implications of the impacts of these sites on low-income and minority neighborhoods began to be recognized. Also, as society became more aware of the need to protect natural areas and green spaces, it recognized that utilizing these abandoned city sites would eliminate the need to convert natural areas to industrial, commercial, or retail sites.

As a consequence, new laws were enacted to give developers economic incentives to convert brownfields into productive economic sites. In recent years, brownfields have been converted to manufacturing, commercial, and retail sites. The first step the United States took to address this problem was the Brownfield Initiative undertaken by the EPA in 1995. The focus of the initiative was to assess brownfields with the potential for past contamination and certify those that were found to be free of contamination. This step eased developers fears of potential liability for someone else's past dumping. In 2002, the Small Business Liability and Brownfields Revitalization Act was signed into law. This legislation codified existing EPA brownfields programs but, more important, it eliminated CERCLA liability for those who attempted to resurrect brownfields and were not responsible for the original contamination. (Up-to-date information can be found at the EPA's brownfields web site at http://www.epa.gov/brownfields.)

The Government and Improper Waste Disposal

Readers may be surprised to find that the U.S. government is responsible for many of the most severely contaminated toxic sites. Defense-related activity is the primary culprit in this problem, with horrendous contamination at many Department of Defense and Department of Energy weapons sites. Contamination with heavy metals, radioactive waste, carcinogenic solvents, ammunition and other ordnance, nerve gas, and other substances is a legacy of the cold war. Tables 16.1 and 16.2 show examples of the magnitude of the militarily generated toxic sites.[5]

If one views the purpose of government as promoting social welfare, it may seem surprising that the government is a primary source of toxic contamination problems. The people who actually make the decisions in government,

---

[4]See Chapter 5 and Box 16.1 for more discussion of environmental justice.

[5]The U.S. military is also responsible for other toxic substance-related problems as a result of military activity. For example, Vietnam veterans suffer a variety of medical effects from exposure to the defoliant "Agent Orange," of which the primary component is dioxin.

Table 16.1 United States Military Hazardous Waste Sites

Location	Observation
Otis Air Force Base, Massachusetts	Groundwater contaminated with trichloroethylene (TCE), a known carcinogen, and other toxins. In adjacent towns, lung cancer and leukemia rates 80 percent above state average.
Picatinny Arsenal, New Jersey	Groundwater at the site shows TCE levels at 5000 times EPA standards; polluted with lead, cadmium, polychlorinated biphenyls (used in radar installations and to insulate equipment), phenols, furans, chromium, toulene, and cyanide. Region's major aquifer contaminated.
Aberdeen Proving Ground, Maryland	Water pollution could threaten a national wildlife refuge and habitats critical to endangered species.
Norfolk Naval Shipyard, Willoughby, Maryland	High levels of copper, zinc, and chromium discharges. Contamination of Elizabeth River and Chesapeake bays.
Tinker Air Force Base, Oklahoma	Concentrations of tetrachloroethylene and methyl chloride in drinking water at levels far exceeding EPA limits. Also, TCE concentration highest ever recorded in U.S. surface waters.
Rocky Mountain Arsenal, Colorado	Approximately 125 chemicals dumped over 30 years of nerve gas and pesticide production. The largest of all seriously contaminated sites, called, "the most contaminated square mile on earth" by the Army Corps of Engineers.
Hill Air Force Base, Utah	Heavy on-base groundwater contamination, including volatile organic compounds up to 27,000 parts per billion (ppb), TCE up to 1.7 ppb, chromium up to 1900 ppb, lead up to 3000 ppb.
McClellan Air Force Base, California	Unacceptable levels of TCE, arsenic, barium, cadmium, chromium, and lead found in municipal well system serving 23,000 people.
McChord Air Force Base, Washington	Benzene, a carcinogen, found on-base in concentrations as high as 503 ppb, nearly 1000 times the state's limit of 0.6 ppb.

Source: From *State of the World, 1991: A Worldwatch Institute Report on Progress Toward a Sustainable Society*, by Lester R. Brown et al, eds. Copyright ©1991 by Worldwatch Institute. Reprinted by permission of W. W. Norton & Company, Inc.

however, have objectives that include other factors. In the pursuit of these other objectives, they incur costs to their programs and costs to society. Just as with corporate managers, these program managers compare private costs and private benefits (program costs and program benefits) rather than social costs and social benefits. Because program costs and program benefits do not constitute the full spectrum of social costs and social benefits, a disparity arises between private values and social values; and an excessive level of toxic releases occurs.

For example, many toxic contamination problems are a result of nuclear weapons manufacture at Department of Energy and Department of Defense facilities. The managers in charge of developing these weapons systems looked toward optimizing values associated with the weapons systems. For example, they might try to produce the maximum defense from a given-sized

Table 16.2 United States Radioactive and Toxic Contamination at Major Nuclear Weapons Production Facilities

Facility (task)	Observation
Feed Materials, Production Center, Fernald, Ohio (converts uranium into metal ingots)	Since plant's opening, at least 250 tons of uranium oxide (and perhaps six times as much as that) released into the air. Off-site surface and groundwater contaminated with uranium, cesium, and thorium. High levels of radon gas emitted.
Hanford Reservation, Washington (recycles uranium and extracts plutonium)	Since 1944, 760 billion liters of contaminated water (enough to create a 12-meter-deep lake the size of Manhattan) have entered the groundwater and Columbia River; 4.5 million liters of high level radioactive waste leaked from underground tanks. Officials knowingly and sometimes deliberately exposed the public to large amounts of airborne radiation in 1943–1956.
Savannah River, South Carolina (produces plutonium)	Radioactive substances and chemicals found in the Tuscaloosa aquifer at levels 400 times greater than government considers safe. Released millions of curies of tritium gas into atmosphere since 1954.
Rocky Flats, Colorado (assembles plutonium triggers)	Since 1952, 200 fires have contaminated the Denver region with unknown amounts of plutonium. Strontium, cesium, and cancer-causing chemicals leaked into underground water.
Oak Ridge Reservation, Tennessee (produces lithium-deuteride and highly enriched uranium)	Since 1943, thousands of pounds of uranium emitted into atmosphere. Radioactive and hazardous wastes have severely polluted local streams flowing in to the Clinch River. Watts Bar Reservoir, a recreational lake, is contaminated with at least 175,000 tons of mercury and cesium.

Primary Sources: "Status of Major Nuclear Weapons Production Facilities: 1990," *PSR Monitor*, September 1990; Robert Alvares and Arjum Makhijani, "Hidden Legacy of the Arms Race: Radioactive Waste," *Technology Review*, August/September 1988.

Secondary Source: Michael Renner, "Assessing the Military's War on the Environment," in *State of the World*, 1991, ed. Lester R. Brown, taken from table 8.7 on p. 148.

budget (of course, they will also be working to increase the size of the budget), or they might try to minimize the cost of each system so that they can produce more systems. Because every dollar of budget devoted to environmental protection reduces their ability to meet other goals, they devote insufficient attention to environmental protection. This behavior is no different than how a profit-maximizing firm would behave, except, until very recently, the Department of Defense and Department of Energy facilities were not subject to the oversight of the EPA or to corresponding state agencies. The urgency (real or imagined) of the Cold War and the perceived objective of preventing world domination by communism exacerbated the narrowness of the objectives of these activities. It is interesting to note that this disparity between the private cost and social cost associated with government activities is the fundamental reason that Eastern Europe and the former Soviet Union are so horribly polluted. For example, a manager of a steel factory (which is a government enterprise) in a socialist country was rewarded based on meeting production quotas and containing costs. Environmental protection was not the charge of the steel factory manager, so even though the steel plant was a government enterprise, it led to socially inefficient levels of pollution.

How Much Should We Pay for Cleanup?

Although the prevention of further toxic contamination is an extremely important policy question, it is not the only dimension of toxic substance policy that must be considered. There remains the immensely important policy question of how much to spend to clean up the contaminated sites that currently exist. This question is important because there are over 50,000 contaminated sites in the United States, and when potentially leaking underground storage tanks are factored into the question, the number of potential sites may be greater than 2.5 million.

Two important questions must be addressed in developing a cleanup or remediation policy. The first question is, Which sites should be cleaned and in what order? The second question is, To what extent should each site be cleaned? A third question might be, Who should pay for the cleanup? This last question, however, is more a question of equity than efficiency, although who pays for cleanups could have an effect on the level of safety that firms choose.

Russell and colleagues (1992) discuss five major programs that deal with past contamination. These programs include the Superfund program of CERCLA, the Resource Conservation and Recovery Act (RCRA), a program established under the RCRA to deal with underground storage tanks, the federal facility program, and state and private programs. The Superfund program charges the EPA with identifying, evaluating, and remediating hazardous waste sites in the United States. These sites include landfills, manufacturing facilities, mining areas, and illegal hazardous waste dumps. According to Russell and colleagues, more than 1200 sites have been placed on the national priority list of hazardous waste sites that are eligible for CERCLA funding, but the total number of sites that belong on the list may be from 2000 to 10,000.

Subtitle C of the RCRA regulates facilities that treat, store, and dispose of hazardous wastes. These facilities are required to obtain permits from the EPA, and corrective action to deal with past or potential releases may be required to obtain permits. According to Russell and colleagues (1992), there are approximately 2500 nonfederal facilities of this sort in the United States.

An additional program established under the RCRA deals with underground storage tanks. There are an incredible number of underground storage tanks in the United States (approximately 1.7 to 2.7 million, according to Russell et al., 1992), such as tanks at gasoline stations, vehicle fleet facilities, and chemical manufacturing companies. Many have been in place since the post-World War II boom in highway transportation and have developed or will develop leaks that allow the release of toxic substances.

The fourth program described by Russell and colleagues (1992) is the federal facility program. As mentioned previously and listed in Tables 16.1 and 16.2, many federal facilities, such as Department of Defense and Department

Table 16.3 Estimated Costs of U.S. Hazardous Waste Remediation from 1990 to 2020

Remediation program	Range points	Cost (updated to billions of 2004 dollars)		
		Less stringent scenario	Current policy	More stringent scenario
Superfund	Plausible upper bound	258	433	1009
	Best guess	129	216	505
	Plausible lower bound	70	151	353
Resource Conservation and Recovery Act	Plausible upper bound	453	540	606
	Best guess	285	335	370
	Plausible lower bound	215	244	270
Underground storage tanks	Plausible upper bound	*	*	*
	Best guess	96	96	96
	Plausible lower bound	46	46	46
Federal facilities	Plausible upper bound	*	*	*
	Best guess	157	357	616
	Plausible lower bound	*	201	*
State and private programs	Plausible upper bound	*	*	*
	Best guess	26	43	100
	Plausible lower bound	*	*	*
Total	Plausible upper bound[a]	990	1499	2429
	Best guess	693	1078	1687
	Plausible lower bound[a]	534	685	1385

Source: *Environment*, "The U.S. Hazardous Waste Legacy," by M. Russell, E. W. Colglazier, and B. E. Tonn, 34: 36, July/August 1992. Reprinted with permission of the Helen Dwight Reid Educational Foundation. Published by Heldref Publications, 1319 18th Street, NW, Washngton, DC 20036-1802. http://www.heldref.org. Copyright © 1992.

*Substantial data limitations and program uncertainties preclude the determination of plausible cost bounds.

[a]In cases where there are no plausible upper and lower bounds for the program's cost estimate, the best guess was added to the total.

of Energy sites, have released toxic waste into the environment. In addition, a large amount of waste is currently stored at these facilities.

The final program examined by these authors is a catchall for state and private programs that do not fall under the other four categories. It is estimated that there are 40,000 sites in the United States in this category. As the numbers of sites and complexity of cleanup would indicate, the cleanup of contaminated sites in the United States will be a tremendously expensive task. Russell and colleagues estimate these costs, which are listed in Table 16.3[6].

[6]More recent cost estimates are not available.

The current policy emphasizes destruction of the waste and a complete cleanup of the contaminated sites. A less stringent set of policies would look toward the containment and isolation of wastes at contaminated sites to prevent their spread into groundwater or into ecosystems. The less stringent policy would not have significantly different impacts on human or ecosystem health. It would, however, push cleanup costs to future generations if they decide that more complete remediation is desirable.

As can be seen in Table 16.3, these cleanup costs are not trivial. For example, Russell and colleagues (1992) point out that the $752 billion ($1.078 trillion in 2004 dollars) best-guess estimate for current policy is approximately equal to 1 year of all nondefense federal expenditures or to 10 years of total public and private spending on all other environmental quality objectives. Table 16.4 lists key factors that could affect those cost estimates.

Table 16.4 Key Factors Affecting Hazardous Waste Remediation Cost Estimates

Program	Factors which may lead to higher costs	Factors which may lead to lower costs
All	States may hinder transport of hazardous wastes. Contamination thresholds may be tightened.	Improvements in remediation technology may occur. Definitions of hazardous waste may narrow.
Superfund	Pumping and treatment may take longer than expected.[a] National priorities list sites could reach or exceed 6000.	Incineration costs may be overestimated.[b]
Resource Conservation and Recovery Act	The number of solid waste management units may have been underreported.	Economies of scale were not considered.
Underground storage tanks	The Clean Air Act may restrict emissions of volatile organic compounds.	The percentage of registered tanks may be higher than is estimated.
Federal facilities	Contamination from mixed and radioactive wastes may be more widespread than was anticipated.	The public may allow more institutional controls than is expected.
State and private programs	The number and average cost of sites may be underestimated.	Sites may eventually fall under other programs.

Source: *Environment*, "The U.S. Hazardous Waste Legacy,' by M. Russell, E. W. Colglazier, and B. E. Tonn, 34: 37, July/August 1992. Reprinted with permission of the Helen Dwight Reid Educational Foundation. Published by Heldref Publications, 1319 18th Street, NW, Washngton, DC 20036-1802. http://www.heldref.org. Copyright © 1992.

[a]C. B. Doty and C. C. Travis, *The Effectiveness of Groundwater Pumping as a Restoration Technology*, ORNL/TM-11849, Oak Ridge, TN: Oak Ridge National Laboratory, 1991.

[b]C.B. Doty, A. G. Crotwell, and C. C. Travis, *Cost Growth for Treatment Technologies at NPL Sites*, ORNL/TM-11849, Oak Ridge, TN: Oak Ridge National Laboratory, 1991.

The big policy question is whether we should spend all this money to clean up every toxic site. This larger policy question can be broken down into smaller policy questions, such as the following:

1. What sites should be cleaned up first?
2. Should they be restored to pristine levels, or should we merely contain the wastes in place to limit their potential for damage?

The second question is particularly intriguing because many of the federal facilities are extremely large and geographically isolated from population centers. It might make sense to contain the wastes on the site and isolate the site from human and animal exposure.

Of course, the answers to these questions and other questions, such as whether we should spend our limited resources on completely cleaning all the sites, on mitigating other environmental problems (such as global warming and preserving habitat), on other social objectives (such as education, AIDS research, and homelessness), or on reducing the budget deficit, have to be answered. Unfortunately, it is extremely difficult to answer these questions at this point because the benefits of different levels of cleanup have not been estimated.

Summary

The toxic waste problem is very different from many of the other environmental problems we face. Toxic substances may persist for long periods and can pervade the ecosystem as they are transported by physical means and through the food web. Another important difference between toxic waste and other types of pollution is that we have to deal with past actions as well as controlling present emissions.

Also associated with toxic substances is that exposure to risk comes not just from release of wastes but from the presence of toxic substances in economic processes and in goods. Both workers and consumers are exposed to toxic substances. Although this factor is not necessarily an externality, market failures may exist as imperfect information and the immobility of labor may imply that this type of exposure to toxic substances is greater than socially optimal.

Intentional or accidental release of toxic substances into the environment is a different type of problem, because it is a traditional environmental externality. Familiar command and control methods as well as economic incentives such as deposit-refund and liability systems can be used to deal with this problem.

Although it is conceptually possible to develop effective policies for dealing with present and future releases, the problem of dealing with our waste legacy may be much more complex. To what extent should we clean up existing toxic waste? Should we clean all sites? Should we restore sites to complete cleanliness, or should we merely try to isolate and contain the waste to keep it from spreading to other areas? These questions are made even more pressing by the huge price tag associated with remediating our legacy of toxic waste.

Review Questions

1. What market failures are associated with toxic waste?
2. Why do past levels of toxic emissions matter for current policy?
3. What policy options exist for dealing with previously contaminated sites?
4. Why is the optimal level of toxic pollutants likely to be at or near zero?
5. Under what circumstances are deposit-refund systems most likely to work with toxic substances?

Questions for Further Study

1. Why might people value the reduction of an externally opposed risk more than the reduction of a voluntarily accepted risk?
2. What, if anything, is wrong with the Delaney clause? Would you change the legislation to improve it? How?
3. How would you define the optimal time path of emissions of a toxic substance?
4. Do we need public regulation of workplace exposure to toxic substances? Why or why not?
5. How should we control public exposure to toxic substances through consumer goods, including food?
6. Compare the potential effectiveness of deposit-refund systems, performance bonds, and liability systems in preventing future releases of toxic substances into the environment.

Suggested Paper Topics

1. The problem of where to locate facilities to store or process hazardous waste is extremely difficult. We need the facilities, but everyone wants to place the facilities somewhere else. This dilemma leads to the "not in my backyard" or NIMBY syndrome. Investigate the NIMBY syndrome, focusing on methods of turning potential Pareto improvements into actual Pareto improvements. Start with the AAAS (1984) book in the references and search bibliographic databases on waste and policy. See if you can devise your own creative solutions.
2. The oceans have been used as a dumping ground for hazardous wastes. The development of policy is even more complex due to the lack of sovereignty outside the 200-mile economic exclusion zone. Look at the global market failures associated with ocean dumping. Start with the U.S. Congress report (1993) in the references and search bibliographic databases on ocean and dumping, law and oceans, and waste and international policy.
3. Investigate the question of whether toxic waste policy is discriminatory. Start with the works by Bullard (1990), Bunyan and Mohai (1992), and the Commission for Racial Justice (1997). Search bibliographic databases and search on race and waste, environmental equity, equity and waste, and environmental justice. Use your knowledge of economics to develop potential policies that address both efficiency and equity.
4. Write a survey paper on methods to value the reduction in risk, paying particular attention to risks associated with toxic substances. Start with the book by Freeman (1993) for a general treatment and for further references.

Works Cited and Selected Readings

Alberini, A., and D. H. Austin. Strict Liability as a Deterrent in Toxic Waste Management: Empirical Evidence from Accident and Spill Data. Resources for the Future Discussion Paper, 1998. Online: http://www.rff.org/rff/Publications/Discussion_Papers.cfn.

Alberini, A.,and D. H. Austin. Accidents Waiting to Happen: Liability Policy and Toxic Pollution Releases. Resources for the Future Discussion Paper, 1999. Online: http://www.rff.org/rff/Publications/Discussion_Papers.cfn.

Alvares, R., and A. Makhijani. Hidden Legacy of the Arms Race: Radioactive Waste. *Technology Review* (August/September 1988): 42–51.

American Association for the Advancement of Science (AAAS). *Hazardous Waste Management: In Whose Backyard?* Boulder, CO: Westview Press, 1984.

Anonymous. "Status of Major Nuclear Weapons Production Facilities: 1990." *PSR Monitor* (September 1990).

Bullard, R. D. *Dumping in Dixie: Race, Class, and Environmental Quality*. Boulder, CO: Westview Press, 1990.

Bunyan, B., and P. Mohai, (eds.). *Race and the Incidence of Environmental Racism*. Boulder, CO: Westview Press, 1992.

Carson, R. *Silent Spring*. New York: Houghton Mifflin, 1962.

Carter, L. *Nuclear Imperatives and Public Trust: Dealing with Radioactive Waste*. Washington, DC: Resources for the Future, 1987.

Commission for Racial Justice, United Church of Christ. *Toxic Wastes and Race in the United States*. 1987. New York: Public Data Access, Inc.

Davis, C. E., and J. P. Lester. *Dimensions of Hazardous Waste Politics and Policy*. New York: Greenwood Press, 1988.

Dewees, D. N. Insurance, Information, and Toxic Risk. Pages 187–222 in *Cutting Green Tape: Toxic Pollutants, Environmental Regulation, and the Law*, edited by R. Stroup, and R. E. Meiners, 2000.

Doty, C. B., A. G. Crotwell, and C. C. Travis. *Cost Growth for Treatment Technologies at NPL Sites*. ORNL/TM-11849. Oak Ridge, TN: Oak Ridge National Laboratory, 1991.

Doty, C. B., and C. C. Travis. *The Effectiveness of Groundwater Pumping as a Restoration Technology*. ORNL/TM-11849. Oak Ridge, TN: Oak Ridge National Laboratory, 1991.

Freeman, A. M., III. *The Measurement of Environmental and Resource Values*. Washington, DC: Resources for the Future, 1993.

Haggerty, M., and S. A. Welcomer. Superfund: The Ascendance of Enabling Myths. *Journal of Economic Issues 37* (2000): 451–459.

Herzik, E. B., and A. H. Mushkatel. *Problems and Prospects for Nuclear Waste Disposal Policy*. Westport, CT: Greenwood Press, 1993.

Hird, J. A. Environmental Policy and Equity: The Case of Superfund. *Journal of Policy Analysis and Management 12* (1993): 323–343.

Jacob, G. *Site Unseen: The Politics of Siting a Nuclear Waste Repository*. Pittsburgh: University of Pittsburgh Press, 1990.

Kohlhase, J. E. The Impact of Toxic Waste Sites on Housing Values. *Journal of Urban Economics 30*, no. 1 (July 1991): 1–26.

Kriesel, W., T. J. Centner, and A. G. Keeler. Neighborhood Exposure to Toxic Releases: Are There Racial Inequities? *Growth and Change 27*, no. 4 (Fall 1996): 479–499.

Macauley, M. K., M. D. Bowes, and K. L. Palmer. *Using Economic Incentives to Regulate Toxic Substances*. Washington, DC: Resources for the Future, 1992.

Mennis, J. Using Geographic Information Systems to Create and Analyze Statistical Surfaces of Population and Risk for Environmental Justice Analysis. *Social Science Quarterly 83* (2002): 281–297.

Montgomery, M., and M. Needelman. The Welfare Effects of Toxic Contamination in Freshwater Fish. *Land Economics 73* (1997): 211–231.

Pastor, M., J. L. Sadd, and R. Morello-Frosch. Who's Minding the Kids: Pollution, Schools and Environmental Justice in Los Angeles. *Social Science Quarterly 83* (2002): 263–280.

Portney, P. R., and K. N. Probst. Cleaning Up Superfund. Pages 105–110 in *The RFF Reader in Environmental and Resource Management*, edited by W. E. Oates. Washington, DC: Resources for the Future, 1999.

Probst, K. N., D. Fullerton, R. E. Litan, and P. R. Portney. Footing the Bill for Superfund Cleanups: Who Pays and How? Washington, DC: Brookings Institution and Resources for the Future, 1995.

Raven, P. H., L. R. Berg, and G. B. Johnson. *Environment*. New York: Saunders, 1993.

Renner, M. Assessing the Military's War on the Environment. Pages 132–152 in *State of the World*, edited by Lester Brown. New York: W. W. Norton, 1991.

Russell, M., E. W. Colglazier, and B. E. Tonn. The U.S. Hazardous Waste Legacy. *Environment 34* (1992): 12–39.

Sigman, H. Hazardous Waste and Toxic Substance Policies. Pages 215–259 in *Public Policies for Environmental Protection*, 2nd ed., edited by P. R. Portney, and R. N. Stavins. Washington, DC: Resources for the Future, 2000.

Smith, V. K., W. H. Desvousges, and J. W. Payne. Do Risk Information Programs Promote Mitigatory Behavior. *Journal of Risk and Uncertainty 10* (1995): 203–221.

Tietenberg, T. H. Indivisible Toxic Torts: The Economics of Joint and Several Liability. Pages 217–231 in *Economics and Environmental Policy*, edited by T. H. Tietenberg. Aldershot, UK: Edward Elgar, 1994.

U.S. Congress, House Committee on Energy and Commerce. *Radon Awareness and Disclosure Act of 1992: Report Together with Dissenting Views*. (to accompany H. R. 3258). Washington, DC: U.S. Government Printing Office, 1992.

U.S. Congress, House Committee on Merchant Marine and Fisheries, Subcommittee on Oceanography, Gulf of Mexico, and the Outer Continental Shelf. *Ocean Disposal of Contaminated Dredge Material: Hearing before the Subcommittee on Oceanography, Gulf of Mexico, and the Outer Continental Shelf of the Committee on Merchant Marine and Fisheries*. Washington, DC: U.S. Government Printing Office, 1993.

U.S. Congress, House Committee on Science, Space, and Technology, Subcommittee on Energy. *Overview of the DOE's Environmental Restoration and Waste Management Program: Hearing before the Subcommittee on Energy of the Committee on Science, Space, and Technology*. Washington, DC: U.S. Government Printing Office, 1993.

U.S. Department of Energy. *Reassessment of the Civilian Radioactive Waste Management Program: Report to the Congress*. Washington, DC: U.S. Department of Energy, Office of Civilian Radioactive Waste Management, 1989.

chapter 17

Agriculture and the Environment

Of all the occupations from which gain is secured, there is none better than agriculture, nothing more productive, nothing sweeter, nothing worthier of a free man.

Cicero, *De Officiis*

Introduction

Although our society tends to view agriculture as both a noble and a "green" lifestyle, the agricultural industry has profound environmental impacts. Agricultural practices often lead to environmental degradation that has myriad effects. Initially, society's focus was on the effect of this degradation on agriculture itself. Soil erosion has been of historical concern in the United States, and the loss of soil productivity has become a life-threatening condition in many developing countries. The importance of this loss of agricultural productivity, and its implications for feeding the world, cannot be overstated.

More recently, attention has also been devoted to other environmental consequences of agriculture. For example, agriculture is a major contributor to diminished water quality, where runoff from agriculture contains soil and agrochemicals such as fertilizers, pesticides, and herbicides. Irrigation also increases the salinity of surface waters, as discussed in Chapter 15. In addition to the effect on water quality, agriculture has other important environmental effects. The conversion of forest, prairie, and wetlands to farmland reduces habitat, impairs the production of ecological services, and threatens biodiversity. In addition, livestock production and rice paddy culture generate significant amounts of methane, an important greenhouse gas.

Although agriculture is an important source of environmental degradation, environmental degradation also has negative impacts on agriculture. In addition to the environmental degradation generated by agriculture that affects soil productivity, numerous other types of environmental change hurt agricultural productivity. For example, tropospheric ozone reduces the growth of crops and trees. The increased ultraviolet radiation associated with the depletion of stratospheric ozone inhibits a plant's ability to photosynthesize. Potential global warming is likely to have both negative and positive effects on agriculture.

This chapter proceeds with a short discussion of the impacts of environmental degradation on agricultural productivity. Then the impacts of agricultural activity on environmental quality are examined, along with the nature of the market failures that lead to these impacts. Finally, current policies to deal with the environmental externalities of agriculture are discussed and new policies are suggested.

The Effect of Environmental Quality on Agriculture

The environmentally degrading activity that has the strongest effect on agriculture is probably agriculture itself, which is examined in the next section. This section focuses on external activities that degrade the environment and have negative effects on agriculture.

An activity generating an effect that adversely affects agriculture will generally reduce the yield per acre of a crop or group of crops. This reduction will shift the supply curve upward, generating a direct loss of benefits equal to the shaded area in Figure 17.1. For example, if tropospheric ozone affects soybean production in Iowa, this model can be used to measure the direct loss in welfare.

In the case of agriculture, however, it is especially important to move past a partial equilibrium analysis (which holds conditions constant in related markets) and look at the indirect effects on other markets. The reason this viewpoint is important is that agricultural markets are very connected, because crops are good substitutes for each other, both in production and consumption. For example, the farmer in Iowa whose soybeans are affected by ozone could choose to plant another crop, such as corn, which will not be as badly affected. In addition, soybean farmers in another area, such as Tennessee, might plant more soybeans as a result of the higher price. Similarly, consumers can choose options other than soybeans. Other grains can be used in animal feed and food products.

Table 17.1 shows selected pollutants. The table reports increases in crop yields generated by reductions in tropospheric ozone associated with the 1990 Clean Air Act Amendments, as well as increases associated with other pollutants.

When economists measure the effects of impacts on agriculture, they model both the farmers' and the consumers' decisions, and they look at the demand and supply for all substitute crops throughout the United States.

Figure 17.1 **Partial Equilibrium Analysis of the Effect of Pollution on Agriculture**

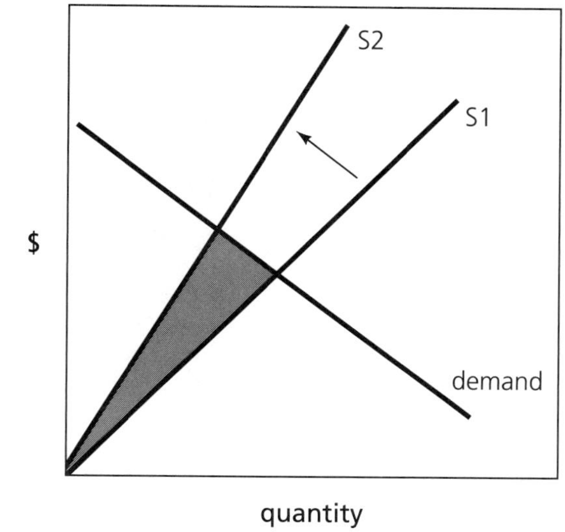

Table 17.1 **Percent Yield Increases Associated with the 1990 Clean Air Act Amendments, 1990–2010**

		Corn	Cotton	Peanuts	Sorghum	Soybeans	Winter wheat
2000	Minimum response	0.01%	1.66%	0.61%	0.01%	0.26%	0.20%
	Maximum response	0.05%	3.79%	0.61%	0.01%	2.75%	5.07%
2010	Minimum response	0.01%	2.84%	1.36%	0.02%	0.42%	0.39%
	Maximum response	0.10%	6.58%	1.36%	0.02%	4.38%	9.11%

Source: Adapted from Table F-2, *The Benefits and Costs of the Clean Air Act, 1990–2010*, EPA Report to Congress, November 1999, EPA 410-R99-01. Online: http://www.epa.gov/air/sect812/1990-2010/fullrept.pdf.

Then, as a change in the supply function of one crop affects its price, the effect of this price change on the consumers' and producers' surplus in all other markets can be examined. For example, an upward shift in the supply curve for soybeans will have many effects on other markets. The higher market price for soybeans will increase the demand for other grains, increasing the equilibrium price and quantity of these grains. For example, in Figure 17.2, the left-hand panel shows the reduction of consumers' and producers' surplus (dark shaded area) in the soybeans that are affected by pollu-

Figure 17.2 **Direct and Indirect Effects of a Pollutant That Reduces Soybean Yields**

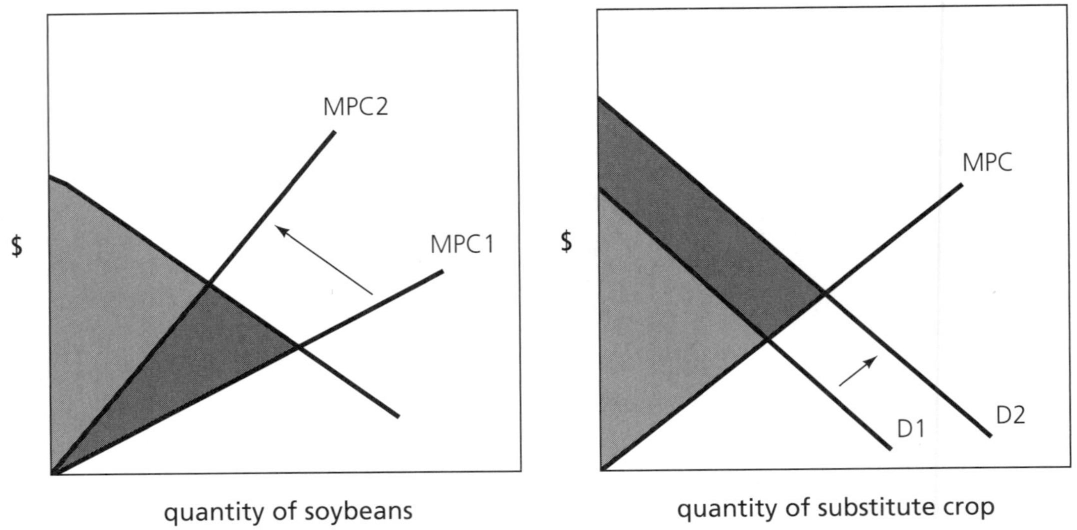

tion. The indirect effects through related markets are represented by the right-hand panel, which shows the increase in consumers' and producers' surplus in the market for a substitute crop. In addition, farmers in affected areas may switch to other crops, which will shift supply curves as well as demand curves. In addition, the problem becomes even more complicated because price supports exist for many crops.

Estimates of this type of change in producers' and consumers' surplus are presented in Table 17.2 and 17.3, which contains estimates of the effects of tropospheric ozone on agricultural activity. Table 17.2 contains older estimates that show changes in ozone concentrations above and below the actual levels in the 1980s, before the Clean Air Act Amendments were implemented. Table 17.3 shows actual and predicted changes associated with the reductions in concentrations generated by these amendments. Note that more pollution actually helps farmers, because the price increases associated with the reduction in supply more than compensate for the loss in quantity supplied. In both tables, consumers are unambiguously better off with higher environmental quality, and the net social benefit of the agricultural impacts or reductions in ozone concentrations is positive. If price supports did not exist, then the initial increases in pollution would hurt both producers and consumers.

Global warming and the increase in carbon dioxide emissions that will generate the global warming problem also have both positive and negative effects on agriculture. Increased temperature and the increased rainfall that accompany global warming will generally have beneficial effects on agriculture, although specific effects may be negative, and the specific negative

Table 17.2 **Effect on Agricultural Sector of Changes in Tropospheric Ozone**

% Changes in ozone	Change in surplus (updated to billions of 2004 dollars)		
	Consumers	Producers	Total
−10	1.186	−0.08	1.116
−25	2.48	0.15	2.61
+10	−1.57	0.324	−1.25
+25	−4.018	0.684	−3.34

Source: NAPAP, *1990 Integrated Assessment Report*, p. 401–402.

Table 17.3 **Changes in Net Crop Income, Consumers' Surplus, and Net Surplus Associated with the 1990 Clean Air Act Amendments, 1990–2010 (updated to millions of 2004 dollars)**

	Change in net crop income		Change in consumers' surplus		Change in net surplus	
	Minimum	Maximum	Minimum	Maximum	Minimum	Maximum
1990	$0	$0	$0	$0	$0	$0
2000	−471	−2726	562	3961	66	1240
2010	−1055	−6531	1080	8691	108	1551

Source: Adapted from Table F-3, *The Benefits and Costs of the Clean Air Act, 1990–2010*, EPA Report to Congress, November 1999, EPA 410-R99-01. Online: http://www.epa.gov/oar/sect812/.

effects could outweigh the general positive effects. For example, although rainfall will increase in general, its distribution will change. Some areas will receive less rainfall and other areas will receive more rainfall. If the areas that lose precipitation are the fertile soil areas and the areas that gain rainfall are the infertile areas, then the net effect on agriculture could be extremely negative. At this point in time, there is considerable scientific uncertainty over how the distribution of rainfall will change. Increased temperature can also generate costs, because areas become too hot for existing cropping patterns and new crops must be introduced. In addition, higher temperature may increase pest populations. Similarly, increased atmospheric concentrations of carbon dioxide will stimulate both crop and weed growth.

The Effect of Agriculture on the Environment

Agriculture has several important effects on the environment. Soil erosion reduces the productivity of soil and leads to water quality problems. Runoff from agricultural fields leads to transportation of fertilizer, pesticides, and herbicides into ground and surface water. Irrigation reduces river flow, depletes aquifers, and increases the salinity of surface water. In addition, conversion of habitat to agricultural areas has led to reductions in biodiversity and losses of some of the world's ecological treasures.

Soil Erosion

The environmental degradation associated with agriculture was blown into public consciousness with the dirt laden winds of the Dust Bowl, which drove many farmers from the land during the 1930s. Intensive plowing and cropping of the land led to the soil being exposed to water and (especially) wind, which led to massive loss of topsoil.[1] Much of this land is still barren.

Soil erosion is a problem for two major reasons. First, the top layers of the soil contain organic matter, which is the source of nutrients for plants. Lower layers of soil tend to be mineral soil or clay and have no organic content. As topsoil is lost, nutrients are lost and the soil becomes less productive. Second, the roots of most crops extend about 1 meter into the soil. If the topsoil layer does not extend very far into the soil, then the roots quickly penetrate into the infertile underlying soil and crop productivity declines at a rapid rate (Heimlich, 1991). In addition, if the topsoil is completely removed or if massive gullying occurs, it is impossible to profitably engage in agriculture, regardless of the input of synthetic fertilizers.

The early public concern with soil erosion was with its internal (on-site) effect, not its external (off-site) effect. That is, public policy was concerned that if a farmer used inappropriate techniques, the farmer would lose the topsoil on his or her farm and the farm would not be as productive. Public policy was not concerned with the external effects, such as the effect of soil erosion on water quality.

This focus on internal effects may seem strange to reader's of this book who have devoted hundreds of pages to reading about the importance of public policy concerning external effects generated by market failures and lack of property rights. One question immediately arises: If the farmer has property rights to his or her farm, should not the market automatically generate the appropriate rate of soil erosion? The answer to this question is that even though there may not be an externality, there may be other market failures.

[1]There are two major types of water-related soil erosion. Sheet erosion is when water moves across the land in a uniform fashion, in a thin sheet. This water movement removes a very thin layer of soil from the land. Rill erosion occurs when the path of the water is more concentrated and cuts gullies through the land. These gullies then capture more of the rainwater and the gullying is intensified.

The first potential market failure is that of imperfect information. The farmer may not know the importance of conserving soil or may not know of, or understand how to implement, agricultural techniques that are more conserving of the soil.

The second problem has to do with the constrained optimization problem that the farmer faces. The farmer may not be free to pursue all agricultural strategies, especially if a strategy involves current sacrifice for future gain. This lack of freedom is because the farmer has limited ability to support his or her family in the short run and may make decisions based on current cash flow rather than on long-term profit maximization, particularly if the farmer does not have access to capital markets (because the farmer is already overextended, for example). The need to meet short-term needs will lead the farmer to have a much higher rate of time preference than society at large. The higher the rate of time preference, the less weight future costs and benefits have and the less important the preservation of the soil for the future becomes.

These two factors exist both in developed countries, such as the United States, and in developing countries, such as many countries in Latin America, Africa, and Asia. In fact, the problem of soil erosion and loss of soil productivity is probably worse in developing countries. Both the imperfect information and the short-run constraints may be more severe in developing countries than in developed countries.

There are two basic reasons the imperfect information problem may be more severe in developing countries. First, it may be harder to get information into the hands of farmers. A greater percentage of the farming population is illiterate in developing countries than in developed countries; farmers are isolated by a lack of good roads and transportation; and mass communication media, such as television, radio, the Internet, and newspapers, are less available. In addition, in countries such as the United States, government agencies (for example, Cooperative Extension, land grant universities, and the National Resources Conservation Service) provide information on less-erosive agricultural techniques. Corresponding agencies do not exist in most developing countries, particularly the very low-income developing countries. Second, the imperfect information problem is exacerbated by population pressures that lead to the cultivation of types of land that have not previously been intensively cultivated and should not be intensively cultivated, such as steep hillsides and rain forest. The cultivation techniques that are acceptable in more conventional settings may be extremely degrading in these new settings, but the uneducated farmers are usually unaware of less erosive alternatives. For example, newly arrived farmers in the Amazon clear cut forests to plant conventional crops rather than engaging in less destructive and more sustainable agroforestry (see Chapter 13).

The short-run constraints also may be more severe in developing countries as well. The banking system is more developed in countries such as the United States, and it is easier for farmers to obtain credit and store the surplus that is generated in good years. In addition, average consumption levels are much greater in the United States and it is easier for farming families to meet basic needs, so they have a less pressing need to sacrifice the future to meet current consumption requirements. The problem is also mitigated by the existence of a "social safety net" in the United States (for example, food stamps, Medicaid, welfare, unemployment insurance) that helps people meet minimum current consumption needs. Of course, in the United States much of the agriculture is industrial in nature, rather than taking place on small family farms.

In addition to the internal (on the farm or on-site) effects of soil erosion, there are external (off-site) effects as well. Soil erosion has very detrimental effects on water quality. The soil is transported to rivers and lakes, where it becomes suspended in the water column. These suspended soil particles have several detrimental effects on aquatic ecosystems. The suspended sediment particles block light from reaching aquatic plants, they generate bottom sed-

Box 17.1 Agriculture and the Florida Everglades

One of the most pronounced environmental effects of agriculture on U.S. ecosystems is the effect of agriculture on the Everglades, the largest wetland system in the United States and one of the nation's greatest ecological treasures.

Agriculture has affected these wetlands in two important ways. First, canals have been dredged to drain areas for cattle ranching and other agricultural activities. This process has interfered with the flow of water into the Everglades and caused them to become drier and smaller. The canals also provide pathways for nonnative species (such as the cattail and melalucca tree) to invade these wetlands and displace native species. Second, excess nutrient loadings from sugar plantations and cattle ranching has degraded water quality in the Everglades and related surface water bodies (Kissimmee River and Lake Okeechobee). These problems were discussed as early as 1947 (Douglas, 1947). In addition to the problems that are occurring directly in the Everglades, the ecological changes in the Everglades are leading to increased water scarcity in southern Florida and environmental degradation of the saltwater areas surrounding the Florida Keys. Increases in groundwater and surface water withdrawals by cities and suburbs in southern Florida is compounding these problems.

The federal government and the state of Florida have embarked on a large-scale project to reengineer the landscape surrounding the Everglades to restore the integrity of the wetlands. Although the plans have not been completely finalized, they focus more on engineering solutions and water storage to treat the symptoms of the problems rather than on direct causes of the problem, such as

(continues)

Box 17.1 (continued)

damaging agricultural activity that occurs upstream of the Everglades. This problem of agricultural pollution and water diversions from the Everglades is a good example of how political considerations interfere with the implementation of good policy.

The sugarcane industry in this region is only economically viable because of quotas on imports of sugar from other nations. The protection from foreign competition increases the domestic price of sugar, and it creates profits that otherwise would not exist for the sugar industry in Florida. The higher prices hurt consumers, however, who pay more for sugar and food products made with sugar. In addition, sugar production leads to the continued degradation of one of the nation's greatest ecological treasures. The sugar quotas would fail any cost-benefit analysis, because they lead to huge net losses in social welfare, but they continue to exist because of the political power of the sugar industry. Although the Everglades restoration program has the objective of preserving this ecosystem, it is unlikely to be successful as long as the agricultural interests are able to protect their position. The same thing can be said for the water withdrawals by cities and communities in southern Florida.

For current information, search bibliographic databases and the Internet, using the following keywords in tandem with the keyword Everglades: agriculture, sugar, restoration, cattle, environmental policy, nutrients, pollution, and hydrological cycle.

iments that change the nature of the stream or lake bottom and suffocate bottom life, and they interfere with the respiratory function of fish and other aquatic animals. In addition, the sediments lower the quality of drinking water and necessitate additional treatment before the water can be used in industrial processes. Another important problem is that the suspended sediments precipitate to the bottom of the stream or lake, where they have a series of undesirable effects, including clogging harbors and filling reservoirs with silt (reducing their ability to generate hydroelectric power and provide drinking water).

A major environmental problem associated with soil erosion is that nutrients, pesticides, and herbicides are carried into surface water bodies along with the soil particles. Pesticides and herbicides are toxic substances and interfere with aquatic life processes in a variety of ways (see Chapters 15 and 16). Nutrients from fertilizer and animal wastes have a number of important ecological effects, but the primary concern is their effect on dissolved oxygen levels in the water. The nutrients lead to growth of algae, which die, decay, and remove dissolved oxygen from the water. The increased algae also blocks sunlight from reaching submerged plants.

Agriculture, Habitat, and Biodiversity

The establishment of agricultural land is generated through conversion of land from other uses. An important ecological problem arises when the land that is converted to agriculture has important ecological values. Although both agricultural areas and natural habitats (such as forests, wetlands, prairies, and other ecosystems) are green, they are not equivalent. They contribute to wildlife habitat, biodiversity, recreation, watershed protection, and existence values in very different ways. In other words, natural ecosystems are much more effective in providing ecological services than engineered ecosystems such as agricultural systems. The farmer who is contemplating converting the land only compares the private costs and benefits of converting the land and does not consider the social costs. This problem is discussed in detail in Chapter 14 and is responsible for the loss of important habitat in developed countries and particularly in developing countries, where deforestation from agricultural activity (see Chapter 13) is an immense ecological problem.

Agriculture and Greenhouse Gases

Another important ecological effect of agriculture is its contribution to increases in the atmospheric concentrations of greenhouse gases. Agricultural activities lead to increases in carbon dioxide, methane, and nitrous oxide emissions.

Methane comes from a variety of agricultural sources, including manure piles and lagoons, wet rice cultivation, and the digestive processes of ruminants such as sheep, goats, and cattle. Carbon dioxide originates in the combustion of fossil fuels used in farm machinery and from the cutting and burning of forests to clear them for agricultural uses (particularly in tropical countries). Nitrous oxides are released by chemical and organic fertilizers.

Agriculture and Public Policy

Although the types of ecological problems (water pollution, generation of greenhouse gases, habitat loss) generated by agriculture are analogous to those generated by other types of activities, there are some very important differences, particularly with respect to water pollution. The most important difference is that most agricultural pollution of surface water and groundwater originates from nonpoint sources rather than from point sources, although large livestock operations, such as feedlots, are an important point source of pollution.

Point sources are sources of pollution where the pollution is released into the environment at a distinct location, such as the end of an effluent pipe. For example, paper and pulp manufacturing plants and municipal sewage treatment plants are point sources of water pollution, because the effluent flows into the rivers from a discharge pipe.

In contrast, agricultural pollution tends to be a nonpoint source of pollution. Rather than entering at a specific location, the pollution flows into the environment over a large area. For example, soil, nutrients, pesticides, and herbicides are carried by rainwater runoff into lakes and rivers. The runoff

Box 17.2 Agriculture and Fisheries

One of the most damaging effects of agricultural pollution is its effect on fisheries. This problem occurs in both developed and developing countries.

In the United States, many of the most important estuaries are degraded by upstream agricultural activities generating pollution that is carried downstream to the estuaries. Sediments, nutrients, pesticides, herbicides, and salinity are generated by agricultural activity. Many important fisheries in the United States have been affected by this type of pollution, including striped bass in the Chesapeake Bay, Atlantic salmon in many northeast rivers, and Pacific salmon in many Northwest rivers. It is also a problem in developing countries, where siltation of rivers, estuaries, lagoons, and coral reefs has substantially affected fish populations that are critically important in feeding people in these areas.

Ulf Silvander and Lars Drake (1991) conducted a study of nitrogen from agricultural fertilizers affecting water quality and fisheries in Sweden (southern Baltic Sea). Not only has this pollution affected commercial and recreational fisheries that rely on wild fish stocks, but it has also affected the aquaculture of mussels and other shellfish. Silvander and Drake conduct empirical analysis of recreational and commercial fishing and of the willingness to pay to prevent nitrate contamination of groundwater. They found that the losses generated by agricultural sources of nitrogen are $22 million in recreational fishing, $93 million to $102 million in commercial fishing, and $140 million for impacts to drinking water.

For more information about the impact of agricultural pollution on fisheries, search bibliographic databases on fisheries, fisheries management, fishery policy, and fish in combination with pollution, environmental policy, agriculture, nutrients, and pesticides. Also visit the National Marine Fisheries Service web site at http://kingfish.ssp.nmfs.gov/, the American Fisheries Society homepage at http://www.esd.ornl.gov/societies/AFS/afshot.html, and the USDA National Resources Conservation Service at http://www.ncg.nrcs.usda.gov/.

enters the lakes and rivers along the entire length of the interface between land and water.

The significance of the pollution being generated by nonpoint sources is that it is much more difficult to monitor and measure the release of pollution by a particular polluter (in this case, the farmer). Thus, it is much more difficult to implement economic incentives, such as per unit pollution taxes or marketable pollution permits. Policy incentives could focus on command and control techniques (such as requiring best available farming techniques) or on economic incentives that are oriented toward inputs (such as fertilizer or pesticide taxes) rather than waste outputs. Another possibility is for the government to encourage research and development of new agricultural techniques combined with programs to disseminate information about these techniques and encourage their use.

Another difference between agriculture and other polluting activities is that agriculture is often a price-supported industry. Price supports serve to raise price above marginal social cost. These can take one of two major forms. In Figure 17.3, for example, if the government wanted to increase price from the market price (P_m) to P_1, it could either buy Q_2 minus Q_1 units of the crop or it could pay farmers not to grow Q_2 minus Q_1 units of the crop. For the purposes of this discussion, the former type of price support will be called a purchase-based price support, whereas the latter will be called a quantity-based price support. In the absence of any pollution or other market failures, the social losses associated with the price support that raises prices from P_m to P_1 are equal to the lightly shaded triangle in Figure 17.3. The heavily shaded trapezoid shows the net benefits of the Q_1 units of the crop that consumers purchase at the supported price of P_1. In this context, there are no differences between the types of price support in terms of the inefficiency (lightly shaded triangle) generated by the price supports.

There will, however, be a big difference between the two types of price supports in the presence of a pollutant. Pollution generates the disparity between the marginal private cost curve and the marginal social cost curve observed in Figures 17.4 and 17.5. In Figure 17.4, the price is supported at P_1 with a purchase-based price support system. Although consumers only buy

Figure 17.3 **Welfare Losses from Quantity- or Purchase-Based Price Supports (no pollution)**

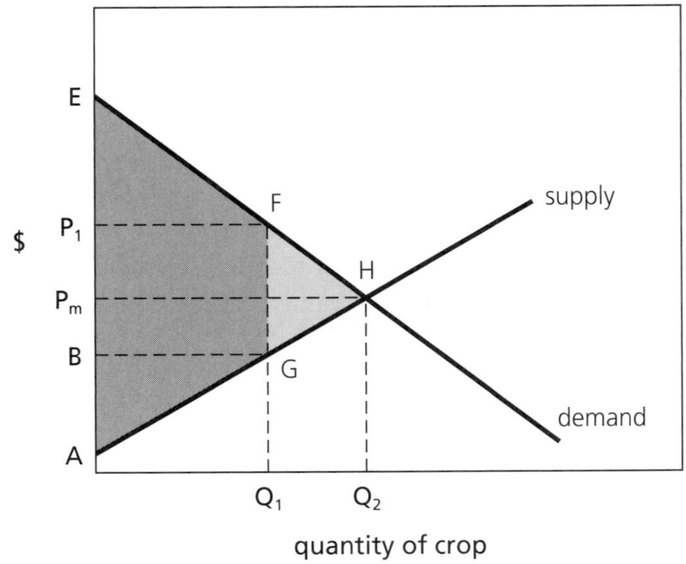

Figure 17.4 **Welfare Losses with Pollution and Purchase-Based Price Supports**

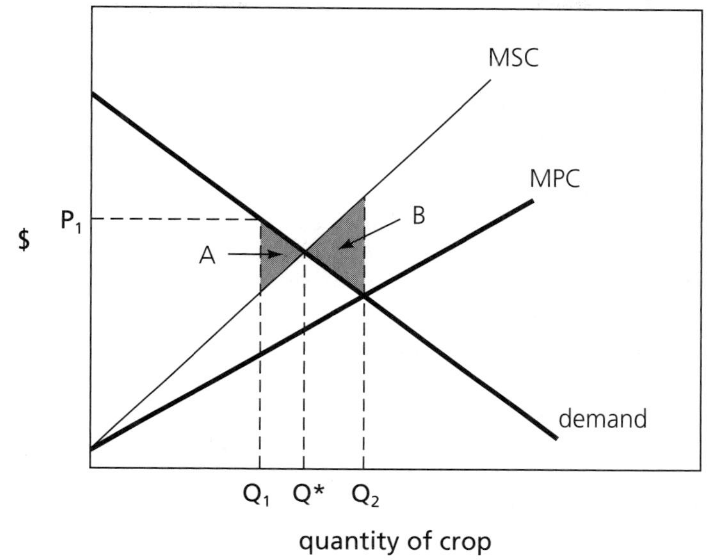

Figure 17.5 **Welfare Losses with Pollution and Quantity-Based Price Supports**

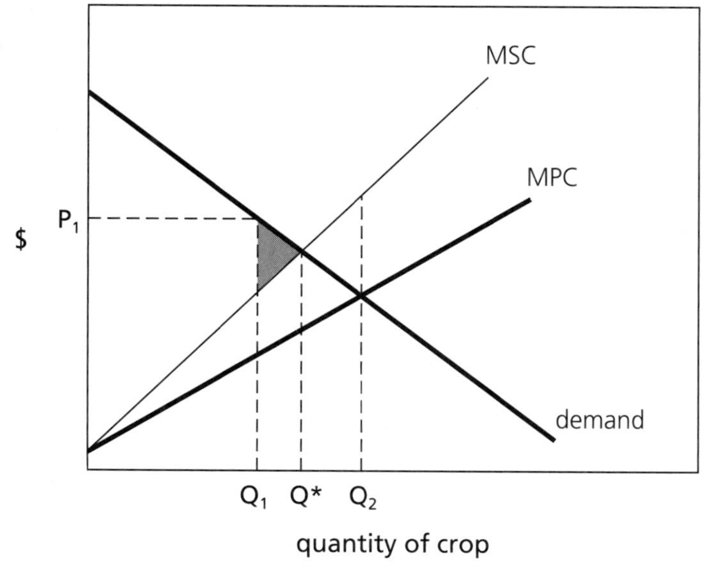

Q_1 units, Q_2 units are produced (with the difference purchased by the government).[2] Neither Q_1 nor Q_2 are optimal in this case; the optimal level of output occurs at Q^*, where marginal social costs are equal to marginal social benefits. Because Q_2 units are produced, there are excess social costs generated by the amount of shaded triangle B, because marginal social costs are higher than marginal social benefits (given by the demand function) in this region. In addition, because consumers only consume Q_1 units, they lose consumers' surplus equal to the upper half of shaded triangle A, whereas producers lose producers' surplus equal to the lower half of triangle A. Thus, the losses from pollution in combination with a purchase-based price support system are equal to the areas of triangles A and B.

In contrast, Figure 17.5 shows the social losses in the context of both pollution and a quantity-based price support system. Because the area between Q_1 and Q_2 is not produced (farmers are paid to take this amount out of production), there is no pollution and no extra social costs associated with that nonexistent production. The social loss is equal only to the area of the shaded triangle, which is the lost consumers' surplus and producers' surplus associated with consuming below the optimal level.

The important point to this discussion is that the type of price support system employed has an effect on pollution and other environmental effects associated with agriculture. If price supports are generated by taking land out of production, then the environmental externalities will be less severe than a price support system that relies on government purchases of crops.

More recently, some agricultural subsidies have taken the form of income supports. These supports take the form of a payment based on the difference between a target price and the market clearing price. This per unit payment is issued over a quantity quota that is based on historical production levels for each participating farmer. Although an exact graphical representation of this program is quite complex, the most important effects are illustrated in Figure 17.6. If the primary effect of the income subsidy is to act as a lump-sum payment, then the number of farmers will increase above the free-market level (some farmers would have dropped out of farming without the income support). The increase in the number of farmers will increase supply and shift the MPC curve rightward, although marginal social cost does not change. Because the shift of the supply function encourages more output in a range of output where marginal social cost is above the demand curve (MSC = MSB), the policy increases welfare losses, which are measured as the shaded triangle in Figure 17.6.

Of course, the price support system itself is a source of inefficiency, but it is something that has been a part of modern public policy. The presence of price supports and associated welfare effects should be kept in mind when analyzing the efficiency of potential environmental policies for agriculture.

[2]Market equilibrium occurs at the point where MPC = MPB, or where the MPC curve intersects the demand curve.

Tuscan Beauty

...ON 9/10THS OF AN ACRE NEAR BOULDER

*TIMELESS STONE & WOOD *SPACIOUS, AIRY VOLUME
*SUNLIGHT & COLOR-DRENCHED *1850 s.f. LOFT
*GARDEN & GAME SPACE *4-CAR TANDEM GARAGE
*DETACHED OFFICE

$1,200,000

Nancy Stocker
303-497-0627

nancystocker@mockrealty.com

MOCK REALTY

"Helping you find your way home."

Trusted since 1965.

NORTH RIM/ LAKE VALLEY GOLF COURSE HOME SO CLOSE TO BOULDER, BUT AT 1/2 THE COST YOU CAN AFFORD IT WITH JUST ONE INCOME!

Gorgeous home centered in the back of the subdivison with almost NO drive-by traffic. Quiet and safe Golf Course neighborhood, Backs to a private park with playground! Out the front door to the sled hill and private swimming lake! 5 beds, 4 baths, and 2 studys from this contemporary 2 story with a finished walkout basement. 3 car garage, central air conditioning, vaulted ceilings, This is a great value and a great neighborhood! **$625,000**

MOCK REALTY

"Helping you find your way home."

Trusted since 1965.

ikpark@mockrealty.com
kPark.HomesAndLand.com

Figure 17.6 **Welfare Losses with Pollution and Farmer Income Supports**

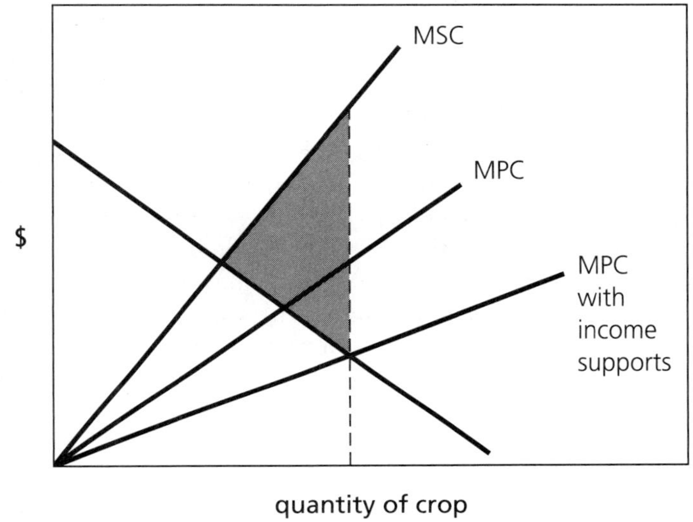

Before analyzing future policy options, past and currently employed policies are discussed.

Past and Currently Employed Policies

Past environmental policy in agriculture has been almost entirely directed at the internal effects of soil erosion. Policies have been developed to attempt to slow the rate at which soil is lost through wind and water erosion.

Modern awareness of the problems associated with soil erosion emerged in 1928, when Hammond Bennett published a U.S. Department of Agriculture report entitled "Soil Erosion: A National Menace." Shortly after, Congress initiated a study of the causes of erosion and the means for its control. Of course, shortly after this study, the dust storms and massive erosion of the 1930s began, which led portions of the western United States to become known as the Dust Bowl. In 1935, Congress established a permanent program of direct soil conservation aid under the auspices of the Soil Conservation Service of the U.S. Department of Agriculture (Heimlich, 1991).

These initial conservation programs were designed to reduce erosion out of concern for the on-site impacts of soil erosion. They were designed to provide information on less-erosive agricultural techniques (contour plowing, windbreaks, and so on) and to provide cost sharing for employment of antierosion measures. One barrier to developing appropriate public policy was that, until very recently, the extent of soil erosion was not known.

The focus of agricultural environmental policy on the on-site impacts of erosion has continued until very recently, when major environmental programs were designed almost solely to eliminate soil loss. Although the initial programs also reduced impacts on water quality, other programs were needed to more specifically target water quality, habitat preservation, and biodiversity.

A good case in point is the Conservation Reserve Program (CRP), which until the mid-1990s was designed primarily to take highly erodible land out of tillage and establish vegetative cover to control erosion. Under the CRP, the U.S. government pays farmers to take land out of crop production and plant protective vegetation on the land. Although improved water quality is an important goal (and result) of this program, water quality objectives may be better met with a program that is structured differently. For example, one of the best ways to improve water quality is to allow buffer strips of land near water bodies to become heavily vegetated with woody and nonwoody plants. These buffer strips trap much of the soil particles and absorb nutrients that would have run off the cultivated land.

The CRP also did not promote low-tillage or no-tillage agricultural techniques. These techniques do not plow the soil or remove the previous season's crop residues, so erosion is diminished. In addition, the CRP did not attempt to preserve areas of important ecological significance. Although the program was not a comprehensive environmental program, it did generate net benefits for society. In addition to reducing erosion and improving surface water quality, the program provides support for participating farmers in a more efficient fashion than price-support payments. Table 17.4 lists the costs and benefits of the CRP, under the older version of the CRP that focused primarily on erosion control.

A program that promotes habitat restoration is found in the Wetlands Reserve Program, which provides incentives for farmers to restore wetlands that were converted to agriculture before this type of conversion became restricted. Several other programs restrict the conversion of existing wetlands (see Chapter 14).

The 1996 Farm Bill generated a very important change in the orientation of the CRP and the policy of the U.S. Department of Agriculture (USDA) toward general environmental programs. The 1996 Farm Bill directed USDA programs in general (and the CRP specifically) to more directly target the off-site environmental benefits associated with farm programs. For example, farms are now chosen for participation in the CRP based on more broadly defined environmental impacts, including potential impacts on habitat, water quality, and biodiversity. This choice is based on the farm's score on an environmental index. This index reflects a wide variety of environmental goals; the higher the score on the index, the greater the priority for including the land in the CRP. Table 17.5 lists acreage that is protected under the CRP and under a related program, the Conservation Reserve Enhancement Program, or CREP.

An interesting example of a comprehensive environmental policy for agriculture is the plan that has been developed to protect the Chesapeake Bay.

Table 17.4 Costs and Benefits of 45 Million Acre CRP Enrollment, United States 1986–1999

National income	Present value (billions of dollars) (negative values in parenthesis)
Gains	
Landowners	
net farm income	9.2–20.3
timber production	4.1–5.4
Natural resources	
productivity	0.8–2.4
water quality	1.9–5.6
wind erosion	0.4–1.1
wildlife habitat	3.0–4.7
Losses	
Consumer costs	(12.7–25.2)
Cover crop establishment	
landowner share	(1.6)
government share	(1.6)
Technical assistance cost	(0.1)
Net Benefit	3.4–11.0
Federal Budget	
Government cost savings	
direct CCC savings	10.2–12.2
indirect (price effects)	6.0–7.3
Government expenses	
CRP rental payments	(19.5–20.8)
corn bonus payments	(0.3)
cover crop establishment	(1.6)
technical assistance	(0.1)
Net Government Expense	(0.2–6.6)

Primary Source: Young and Osborn, 1990.

Secondary Source: Table 5.5 of Ralph E. Heimlich, 1991.

Table 17.5 **Conservation Practices Installed on Conservation Reserve Program by Signup Type (as of end of fiscal year 2002) in Acres**

PRACTICE NAME	PRACTICE CODE	GENERAL SIGNUP	CONTINUOUS NON-CREP[a]	CONTINUOUS CREP	FARMABLE WETLAND	TOTAL
INTRODUCED GRASSES AND LEGUMES	CP01	4,208,448	71,369	49,177	0	4,328,994
NATIVE GRASSES	CP02	6,208,521	17,440	21,785	0	6,247,746
TREE PLANTING	CP03	1,162,354	974	6669	0	1,169,997
WILDLIFE HABITAT W/ WOODY VEG	CP04	2,251,386	2998	28,823	0	2,283,207
FIELD WINDBREAKS	CP05	1068	39,846	1586	0	42,501
DIVERSIONS	CP06	898	0	0	0	898
EROSION CONTROL STRUCTURES	CP07	759	0	1	0	760
GRASS WATERWAYS	CP08	1316	74,093	264	0	75,673
SHALLOW WATER AREAS FOR WILDLIFE	CP09	3649	36,667	1639	0	41,956
EXISTING GRASSES AND LEGUMES[b]	CP10	14,922,612	36,881	4537	0	14,964,029
EXISTING TREES	CP11	1,038,187	0	327	0	1,038,513
WILDLIFE FOOD PLOTS	CP12	68,371	0	792	0	69,163
VEGETATIVE FILTER STRIPS	CP13	31,830	0	0	0	31,830
CONTOUR GRASS STRIPS	CP15	327	60,444	96	0	60,867
SHELTERBELTS	CP16	494	20,362	233	0	21,089

PRACTICE NAME	PRACTICE CODE	GENERAL SIGNUP	CONTINUOUS NON-CREP[a]	CONTINUOUS CREP	FARMABLE WETLAND	TOTAL
LIVING SNOW FENCES	CP17	10	2507	0	0	2516
SALINITY REDUCING VEGETATION	CP18	3202	272,175	0	0	275,377
ALLEY CROPPING	CP19	52	0	0	0	52
ALTERNATIVE PERENNIALS	CP20	15	0	0	0	15
FILTER STRIPS (GRASS)	CP21	0	726,997	81,250	0	808,247
RIPARIAN BUFFERS (TREES)	CP22	0	343,572	83,543	0	427,115
WETLAND RESTORATION	CP23	1,577,425	0	61,889	0	1,639,314
CROSS WIND TRAP STRIPS	CP24	0	522	0	0	522
RARE AND DECLINING HABITAT	CP25	353,797	0	20,968	0	374,766
SEDIMENT RETENTION	CP26	0	0	0	0	0
FARMABLE WETLAND -- WETLAND	CP27	0	0	0	17,271	17,271
FARMABLE WETLAND -- UPLAND	CP28	0	0	0	41,969	41,969
TOTAL		31,834,719	1,766,087	363,579	59,240	33,964,386

Source: Taken from Farm Service Agency, Conservation Reserve Program 2002 Statistics, p. 14. Online: http://www.fsa.usda.gov/dafp/cepd/stats/FY2002.pdf.
[a]Includes approximately 150,000 acres in designated wellhead protection areas.

[b]Includes both introduced grasses and legumes and native grasses.

Additional details on CRP contracts currently entered in USDA Service Center data files are available on FSA's CRP web site (http://www.fsa.usda.gov/dafp/cepd/crp.htm) For more information about this summary, contact Alex Barbarika at 202-720-7093 or at Alexander.Barbarika@usda.gov.

The Chesapeake Bay, the largest estuary in the United States, is heavily polluted with nutrients from municipal treatment plants and agriculture. Although progress has been made in upgrading sewage treatment plants, water quality did not improve substantially because of nutrient loadings from agriculture. The problem is compounded because two states (Maryland and Virginia) have jurisdiction over the Chesapeake Bay, but six states (New York, Pennsylvania, West Virginia, Delaware, Virginia, and Maryland) and the District of Columbia contribute to the pollution of the Chesapeake Bay through their pollution of rivers (Susquehanna, Potomac, and James, among others) that flow into the Chesapeake Bay.

Maryland, Virginia, Washington, DC, Pennsylvania, the U.S. EPA, and the Chesapeake Bay Commission are signatories to the Chesapeake Bay Agreement, which has a substantial nutrient reduction strategy. Thousands of projects covering hundred of thousands of acres of agricultural land have been implemented to encourage farming practices to control nutrients and erosion. These farming practices include no-till farming, contour plowing, manure storage facilities, and other best management practices (Raven et al., 1993).[3]

A Comprehensive Set of Environmental Policies for Agriculture

Environmental policy for agriculture should attempt to accomplish several goals. First, it should seek to discourage erosion and the on-site and off-site impacts of erosion. Second, it should discourage the excessive use of fertilizers and pesticides. Third, it should increase food safety. Fourth, it should restore marginal farmland to natural habitat and protect existing habitat. While accomplishing all these environmental goals, these policies should also help ensure the adequacy of food supplies, the well-being of consumers, and the profitability of farmers. Obviously, these tasks are extremely complex, but steps can be begun in these directions.

Fertilizer and Pesticide Taxes

The economic theory developed in Chapter 3 suggests that the efficient way of dealing with a pollution externality is to impose a per unit pollution tax or implement a system of marketable pollution permits. Because the fertilizer and pesticide runoff associated with agriculture is nonpoint source pollution, however, implementing such a system cannot be easily done. The amount of pollution per farm per unit time cannot be easily measured, so it is difficult to implement taxes or marketable permit systems.

Although this pollution cannot be taxed easily, economic theory suggests that fertilizer and pesticide applications will be excessive, because the farmer

[3]For more details about this program, visit the web sites of the Alliance for the Chesapeake Bay (http://www.acb-online.org) and the Chesapeake Bay Program, http:www.chesapeakebay.net/index.cfm.

chooses application levels by comparing private costs and private benefits rather than social costs and social benefits. At the margin, discouraging fertilizer and pesticide applications will increase social welfare.

Reductions in fertilizer and pesticide applications will be forthcoming if fertilizer and pesticides are taxed. Although some states have fertilizer taxes, they tend to be token taxes (from fractions of a percent of price to several percent of price) and are designed to raise revenues to fund farm programs rather than to internalize the full social cost of pesticide and fertilizer use (Carlin, 1992, pp. 3–5).

One advantage of pesticide and herbicide taxes is that they will encourage a practice called integrated pest management to control insects and other agricultural pests. Integrated pest management is a full portfolio of techniques to control pests, including the use of biological controls such as insect predators. If it becomes more expensive to rely totally on pesticides, then more farmers will move to integrated pest management. Pesticide and herbicide taxes also will have the benefit of increasing food safety. If pesticide and herbicide applications decrease as a result of taxes, less toxic residues will be found in food, *ceteris paribus*.

Although economic theory suggests that pesticide and fertilizer taxes could improve social welfare by mitigating the market failure, taxes that were too high would over control applications of these chemicals and lead to social losses from over control. To determine the appropriate tax levels for these agrochemicals, estimates of the marginal benefits to farmers and the marginal damages to the environment must be conducted.

Pesticide and fertilizer taxes can reduce applications and therefore reduce the release of these substances into the ecosystem, but they do not encourage the full range of pollution-mitigating actions. The reason is that even though they reduce applications, they do nothing to reduce the pollution associated with a given level of application. For example, if the farmer leaves buffer strips of vegetation around the fields and between the creeks and the fields, the amount of fertilizer and pesticides that reach the creeks will be much less than if those buffer strips do not exist.

Promoting "Green" Farming Methods

In addition to input taxes, policies could be established to encourage "green" farming techniques. One of the most important ways of promoting these methods is to provide information on how to engage in these methods. Because the methods often reduce soil erosion and the need for fertilizer and pesticide inputs, they often reduce farmers' costs in the long run. Many agricultural extension agents are trained in conventional agricultural techniques and do not have the appropriate knowledge to pass on to farmers. The agricultural support services, such as the extension program, must become more oriented toward green methods if these methods are to be passed on to farmers. This reorientation of the focus of agricultural support services toward greener methods has accelerated during the past several years.

Some green methods are privately more efficient than other farming methods, but others may reduce farmers' benefits even though they increase social benefits. Farmers have no incentive to adopt these methods, even if they have full information about them. Both command and control regulations and economic incentives can be used to induce farmers to adopt these methods.

Command and control regulations can be used to require or prohibit certain agricultural methods. For example, cultivating within a certain distance of a water body and filling of wetlands can be prohibited. In the same vein, a certain percentage of the farm area can be required to be covered by natural vegetation. Low-tillage methods, holding ponds to contain runoff, and buffer strips surrounding fields can also be required.

Alternatively, farmers can be compensated for engaging in these techniques. Eligibility for price support payments can be made contingent upon using best available farming methods on the land that is under cultivation. In addition, farmers can be paid for leaving critically important natural habitats undisturbed. In fact, basing income support to farmers on environmental performance rather than the traditional factors, would eliminate many of the distortionary impacts of farm subsidies. Environmental subsidies would result in the protection and provision of environmental public goods, rather than reducing consumers' surplus so as to provide more income for farmers. Traditional subsidy programs in high-income countries such as the United States would also have negative impacts on the agricultural sectors of developing countries. Because environmental subsidies would be independent of the quantity of crops produced, they would not generate subsidized competition for developing countries and therefore would not reduce farm income in developing countries.

In some ways, it is easy for consumers to make market decisions that support green agriculture, but in other ways, it is difficult. For example, stringent labeling requirements have been developed in terms of whether a farm product can be called "organic." Organic produce must be cultivated without the use of pesticides, fertilizers, hormones, antibiotics, and synthetic fertilizers. In addition, the land on which the produce is cultivated must be free of applications of these substances for at least 3 years. In this way, consumers can "vote with their pocketbook" for more environmentally sound agriculture.

Although there are strict requirements for calling a product organic, there are no rules about labeling a product eco-friendly in other dimensions. So for example, there is no eco-certification for products grown without irrigation, with adequate riparian buffers, with maintaining habitat, and so on. Thus, it is not possible for consumers to make food consumption decisions that support agricultural methods that improve environmental quality in these other dimensions.

Adequately Priced Water

One of the biggest environmental impacts of agriculture is its effects on water scarcity, particularly in the western United States. The use of water in irrigation depletes aquifers at a much faster rate than they are being replenished, reduces stream flow, and increases the salinity of water. As extensively discussed in Chapter 14, this problem is caused by water being priced at a fraction of its true social cost. The problem can largely be eliminated by requiring farmers (and other water users) to pay the full social cost for the water they consume and by making water rights fully transferable.

Protecting Habitat and Biodiversity

There is an inherent conflict between farmers' profit objectives and the preservation of critical habitat and biodiversity. Because the cultivation of land requires a conversion from natural habitat, farmers' profit incentives lay toward clearing habitat. Again, policy to protect habitat and biodiversity can be undertaken using either direct controls or economic incentives. Conversion of certain types of habitat can be banned (such a ban is already in existence for certain classes of wetlands and for habitat that supports endangered species). As a society, it makes sense for our food to be grown on ground that is already cleared, rather than clearing new natural habitat. Generating this protection by banning agricultural activities in these areas, however, places the financial burden of meeting this social goal entirely on the backs of farmers. Many people argue that in these cases, compensation must take place for these policies to be equitable. Government agencies or NGOs could buy critical habitat from farmers, or farmers could retain ownership but could be paid to leave these areas undisturbed. In fact, many NGOs are already engaging in this practice (see Chapter 14), and new government programs, such as the Wetlands Reserve Program, are contributing to the preservation of important habitat.

In addition, many people suggest that abandoned or marginal agricultural land should be restored to natural habitat. Farmers could be paid to reintroduce native species on former farmland, or the government could purchase this land, restore it, and turn it into parkland or a wildlife sanctuary. As discussed in Chapter 14, the use of conservation easements and other tax incentive programs is being implemented in many regions. These economic incentive programs may ultimately generate more preservation and restoration than is possible with traditional command and control policies. For example, there is broad, grassroots support for the conversion of a large proportion of failed and marginal Great Plains farmland into natural prairie.

Summary

Agriculture is impacted by environmental degradation, but it is also a significant source of environmental degradation. Agriculture is adversely affected by air pollution, by global warming, and by agricultural activity itself. Agriculture generates many environmental problems, including soil erosion, degradation of water quality, increased water scarcity, contributions to global warming, toxic substances in the ecosystem and food supply, and loss of habitat and biodiversity.

Past agricultural policy toward the environment has focused on soil erosion, but this policy needs to be broadened to reduce other types of environmental degradation. The development of new policy is complicated, because many agricultural pollutants are nonpoint source pollutants. An important component of policy could be the development of taxes on agricultural inputs, such as fertilizers and pesticides. Because these taxes do not encourage the full portfolio of pollution-reducing responses, however, other techniques need to be implemented to reduce the release of pollutants into the ecosystem. A combination of direct controls and economic incentives could be used to promote the utilization of greener agricultural methods. In addition, policies must also be developed to promote the protection of habitat and biodiversity and to adequately price water.

Review Questions

1. How do subsidy programs affect the net benefits from agriculture?
2. How do subsidy programs exacerbate social losses generated by the environmental externalities associated with agriculture?
3. Assume that an agricultural crop has an inverse demand function (marginal willingness to pay function) of MWTP = 10 − 2Q. Assume that MPC = Q and MSC = 1.5Q. Find the social losses from the externality, given the market clearing price and quantity. Now assume that price is supported at $7 by government purchases of the crop sufficient to drive P to $7. Find the losses in consumers' and producers' surplus associated with the pollution and the subsidy.
4. How does nonpoint source pollution differ in policy options from point source pollution?
5. What is the difference between on-site and off-site impacts of soil erosion? Identify the market failures associated with each type of impact.
6. How can the private sector promote environmental quality in agricultural areas?

Questions for Further Study

1. Should agricultural activity be subsidized?
2. What type of subsidy program would best achieve environmental goals?
3. What are the strengths and weaknesses of the Conservation Reserve Program?
4. Is food safety adequately protected by current policies? Explain your answer.
5. Should pesticides be banned? Why or why not?

Suggested Paper Topics

1. Look at the economic rationale underlying integrated pest management. How does it affect private costs, social costs, and benefits from agriculture? Look in the *Journal of Environmental Economics and Management* and the *American Journal of Agricultural Economics* for current references.
2. Look at the costs and benefits of the Wetlands Reserve Program. Start with the article by Heimlich (1991) and find more current information at the CRP web site (http://www.nrcs.usda.gov/programs/CRP).
3. Should agricultural and environmental policy be more closely coordinated? Examine this question from an economic perspective. Start with OECD publications for initial perspectives. Search bibliographic databases on agriculture, environment, and policy.
4. Many studies have been done that look at the effect of pollution on agriculture. Start with the U.S. National Acid Precipitation and Assessment Program (1991) report for references and critically examine studies that estimate the economic costs to agriculture of increased air pollution. Other good references include the EPA reports on the Benefits and Costs of the Clean Air Act, available at http://www.epa.gov/oar/sect812. Where would the agricultural sector most greatly benefit from reducing pollution?

Works Cited and Selected Readings

Abler, D. G., and D. Pick, NAFTA, Agriculture, and the Environment in Mexico. *American Journal of Agricultural Economics 75*, no. 3 (August 1993): 794–798.

Alauddin, M., and M. Hossain. *Environment and Agriculture in a Developing Economy: Problems and Prospects for Bangladesh*. Cheltenham, UK, and Northampton, MA: Edward Elgar, 2001.

Antle, J. M., J. N. Lekakis, and G. P. Zanias (eds.). *Agriculture, Trade and the Environment: The Impact of Liberalization on Sustainable Development*. Cheltenham, UK and Northampton, MA: Edward Elgar; 1998.

Batie, S. S., and D. E. Ervin. Transgenic Crops and the Environment: Missing Markets and Public Roles. *Environment and Development Economics 6*, no. 4 (October 2001): 435–457.

Bonnieux, F., and P. Rainelli. Agricultural Policy and Environment in Developed Countries. *European Review of Agricultural Economics 15* (1988): 263–280.

Bowers, J. K. *Agriculture, the Countryside, and Land Use: An Economic Critique*. New York: Methune, 1983.

Carlin, A. *The United States Experience with Economic Incentives to Control Environmental Pollution*, EPA-230-R-92-001. Washington, DC: U.S. Environmental Protection Agency, 1992.

Cleaver, K. M., and G. A. Schreiber. *Reversing the Spiral: The Population, Agriculture, and Environment Nexus in Sub-Saharan Africa*. Directions in Development series. Washington, DC: World Bank, 1994.

Douglas, M. S. *The Everglades: River of Grass*. New York: Rinehart, 1947.

Dragun, A. K., and C. Tisdell (eds.). *Sustainable Agriculture and Environment: Globalisation and the Impact of Trade Liberalization*. Cheltenham, UK and Northampton, MA: Edward Elgar, 1999.

Edwards, G. Trade, Agriculture and the Environment. Pages 137–148 in *World Agriculture in a Post-GATT Environment: New Rules, New Strategies*, edited by R. Gray, T. Becker, and A. Schmitz. Proceedings of a symposium organized by Saskatchewan Wheat Pool and the University of Saskatchewan. Saskatoon: University of Saskatchewan, University Extension Press, 1995.

Ervin, D. E. Toward GATT-Proofing Environmental Programmes for Agriculture. *Journal of World Trade 33*, no. 2 (April 1999): 63–82.

Ervin, D. E. Taking Stock of Methodologies for Estimating the Environmental Effects of Liberalised Agricultural Trade. Pages 117–132 in *Assessing the Environmental Effects of Trade Liberalisation Agreements: Methodologies*, OECD Proceedings. Paris: OECD, 2000.

Ervin, D. E. Trade, Agriculture, and Environment. Pages 84–113 in *International Environmental Economics: A Survey of the Issues*, edited by G. G. Schulze, and H. W. Ursprung. Oxford and New York: Oxford University Press, 2001.

Ervin, D. E., and V. N. Keller. Agriculture, Trade, and the Environment: Discovering and Measuring the Critical Linkages: Key Questions. Pages 281–294 in *Agriculture, Trade, and the Environment: Discovering and Measuring the Critical Linkages*, edited by M. E. Bredahl, J. C. Dunmore, and T. L. Roe. Boulder, CO, and London: Westview Press, HarperCollins, 1996.

Ervin, D. E., and A. Schmitz. A New Era of Environmental Management in Agriculture? *American Journal of Agricultural Economics 78*, no. 5 (December 1996): 1198–1206.

Gutman, G. Agriculture and the Environment in Developing Countries: The Challenge of Trade Liberalization. Pages 33–51 in *The Environment and International Trade Negotiations: Developing Country Stakes*, edited by D. Tussie. New York: St. Martin's Press, 2000.

Hallam, A. Climate Change, Agriculture and the Environment: Some Economic Issues. Pages 458–461 in *Sustainable Agricultural Development: The Role of International Cooperation*, Proceedings of the Twenty-First International Conference of Agricultural Economists, edited by G. H. Peters, and B. F. Stanton. Aldershot, UK: Ashgate, 1992.

Hanley, N., (ed.). *Farming and the Countryside: An Economic Analysis of External Costs and Benefits*. London: CAB International, 1991.

Harris, J. M. *World Agriculture and the Environment*. New York and London: Garland, 1990.

Hazell, P. Agriculture and the Environment. *Environment and Development Economics 6*, no. 4 (October 2001): 516–521.

Heimlich, R. E. Soil Erosion and Conservation Policies in the United States. Pages 59–90 in *Farming and the Countryside: An Economic Analysis of External Costs and Benefits*, edited by N. Hanley. London: CAB International, 1991.

Heimlich, R. E. Costs of an Agricultural Wetland Reserve. *Land Economics 70* (1994): 234–246.

Markandya, A. Technology, Environment, and Employment in Third World Agriculture. Pages 69–93 in *Beyond Rio: The Environmental Crisis and Sustainable Livelihoods in the Third World*, edited by I. Ahmed, and J. A. Doeleman. New York: St. Martin's Press, 1995.

Organization for Economic Cooperation and Development. *Agricultural and Environmental Policies: Opportunities for Integration*. Paris: OECD, 1989.

Organization for Economic Cooperation and Development. *Agricultural and Environmental Policy Integration: Recent Progress and New Directions*. Paris: OECD, 1993.

Raven, P. R., L. R. Berg, and G. B. Johnson. *Regional Issues Sampler for Environment*. Philadelphia: Saunders, 1993.

Shortle, J. S., and D. G. Abler. Agriculture and the Environment. Pages 159–176 in *Handbook of Environmental and Resource Economics*, edited by J. C. J. M. van den Bergh. Cheltenham, UK, and Northampton, MA: Edward Elgar, 1999.

Shortle, J. S., and J. W. Dunn. The Economics of the Control of Non-Point Pollution from Agriculture. Pages 29–47 in *Farming and the Countryside: An Economic Analysis of External Costs and Benefits*, edited by Nicholas Hanley. London: CAB International, 1991.

Siamwalla, A. The Relationship between Trade and Environment, with Special Reference to Agriculture. Pages 103–118 in *Sustainability, Growth, and Poverty Alleviation: A Policy and Agroecological Perspective*, edited by S. A. Vosti and T. Reardon. Baltimore and London: Johns Hopkins University Press for the International Food Policy Research Institute, 1997.

Silvander, U., and L. Drake. Nitrate Pollution and Fisheries Protection in Sweden. Pages 159–178 in *Farming and the Countryside: An Economic Analysis of External Costs and Benefits*, edited by N. Hanley. London: CAB International, 1991.

Tobey, J. A., and H. Smets. The Polluter-Pays Principle in the Context of Agriculture and the Environment. *World Economy 19*, no. 1 (January 1996): 63–87.

U.S. Environmental Protection Agency. *The Benefits and Costs of the Clean Air Act, 1990–2010*, EPA Report to Congress, EPA 410-R99-01. November, 1999. Online: http://www.epa.gov/oar/sect812.

U.S. National Acid Precipitation and Assessment Program (NAPAP). *1990 Integrated Assessment Report*. Washington, DC: U.S. Government Printing Office, 1991.

Young, C. E., and C. T. Osborn. *The Conservation Reserve Program: An Economic Assessment*. AERO-626, EARS. Washington, DC: U.S. Department of Agriculture, 1990.

Zilberman, D., S. R. Templeton, and M. Khanna. Agriculture and the Environment: An Economic Perspective with Implications for Nutrition. *Food Policy 24*, no. 2–3 (April–June 1999): 211–229.

chapter 18

The Environment and Economic Growth in Third World Countries

The achievement of sustained and equitable development is the greatest challenge facing the human race. . . . Economic development and sound environmental management are complimentary aspects of the same agenda. Without adequate environmental protection, development will be undermined; without development, environmental protection will fail.

World Bank, World Development Report 1992: Development and the Environment

Introduction

The focus of environmental attention has been shifting in recent years from one that centers on developed countries to one that focuses on developing countries as well.[1] In fact, many who study environmental issues believe that addressing environmental degradation in developing countries should be the primary focus of environmental policy. A quick inventory of environmental problems associated with devel-

[1]Many terms are used to signify countries that have not yet achieved the standard of living of countries such as the United States, Western European countries, and Japan. In this chapter, the term *developing countries* rather than *less developed countries* is used to emphasize the concept that a stage of development is not a permanent status, but a process of change. Occasionally, the term *Third World countries* will be used, where the term was originally conceived to differentiate developing countries from developed capitalistic/democratic countries (First World) and from socialist/communist countries (Second World). Since the fall of the Iron Curtain and the end of the Cold War, however, these distinctions have less meaning. When the term *Third World countries* is used in this chapter, it will be assumed to be synonymous with *developing countries* and includes those former Soviet republics and former Warsaw Pact countries whose economic status places them in the "low" (under $735 of annual per capita GDP) or "lower middle" ($736–$2935 of annual per capita GDP) or "upper middle" ($2936–$9075) of annual per capita GDP) income designation of the World Bank.

oping countries includes includes the massive environmental degradation in Eastern Europe and former Soviet republics, tropical deforestation, desertification, contamination of drinking water, soil erosion, loss of habitat of all types (including wetlands, grasslands, coral reefs, a variety of aquatic habitats, and forests), loss of biodiversity, and depletion of fisheries.

In the 1970s and early 1980s, many people argued that environmental quality was a luxury that only the rich nations could afford (see Box 18.1). Beginning in the 1980s, however, it became apparent that deteriorated environmental quality was interfering with the economic development of many

Box 18.1 The Lawrence Summers Memo

In December 1991, economist Lawrence Summers, vice president of the World Bank, wrote an internal memo to his colleagues at the World Bank that shocked the world. In this memo, he talked about the desirability of increasing pollution in developing countries, particularly the poorest developing countries. The memo was leaked from the World Bank and has been reproduced in a number of places, including here. (One of the places that this memo is reproduced and from which this book has taken it is http://www.whirledbank.org/ourwords/summers.html.) GEP refers to a report produced by the World Bank entitled Global Economic Prospects.

Of course, environmental justice and equity concerns leap out immediately when reading this memo. It is based on the idea that economic efficiency is the only relevant decision-making criteria, so willingness to pay should completely determine policy. Of course, because willingness to pay is based on ability to pay, important equity and ethical considerations are created.

In addition, Summers's memo is based on a false premise that environmental quality is a luxury good. The examples chosen by Summers such as chemicals that cause cancer after long temporal lags and visibility problems from air pollution, are not representative of the effect of environmental degradation on inhabitants of developing countries. In fact, China has moved aggressively to curtail air pollution because of its affect on human health. Health authorities in China found that most children in large cities suffered respiratory illness and distress as a result of the high levels of air pollution. Changhua Wu (2002) (http://www.peopleandplanet.net/doc.php?id=1494). This pollution not only causes children to suffer, but causes resources to be devoted to their health care, interferes with their ability to learn, and lowers their future productivity. Similar impacts occur to adult populations.

Similarly, the examples chosen by Summers neglect the importance of ecological services to primary productivity, pollution of drinking water (which leads to the high infant mortal-

(continues)

Box 18.1 (continued)

ity rate), impact of air pollution on agricultural productivity, and so on. The memo illustrates the danger of looking at environmental economics issues with a strong background in economics but a lack of understanding of the environment and environmental problems.

DATE: December 12, 1991
TO: Distribution
FR: Lawrence H. Summers
Subject: GEP

'Dirty' Industries: Just between you and me, shouldn't the World Bank be encouraging MORE migration of the dirty industries to the LDCs [Less Developed Countries]? I can think of three reasons:

1) The measurements of the costs of health impairing pollution depends on the foregone earnings from increased morbidity and mortality. From this point of view a given amount of health impairing pollution should be done in the country with the lowest cost, which will be the country with the lowest wages. I think the economic logic behind dumping a load of toxic waste in the lowest wage country is impeccable and we should face up to that.

2) The costs of pollution are likely to be non-linear as the initial increments of pollution probably have very low cost. I've always though that under-populated countries in Africa are vastly UNDER-polluted, their air quality is probably vastly inefficiently low compared to Los Angeles or Mexico City. Only the lamentable facts that so much pollution is generated by non-tradable industries (transport, electrical generation) and that the unit transport costs of solid waste are so high prevent world welfare enhancing trade in air pollution and waste.

3) The demand for a clean environment for aesthetic and health reasons is likely to have very high income elasticity. The concern over an agent that causes a one in a million change in the odds of prostrate cancer is obviously going to be much higher in a country where people survive to get prostrate cancer than in a country where under 5 mortality is 200 per thousand. Also, much of the concern over industrial atmosphere discharge is about visibility impairing particulates. These discharges may have very little direct health impact. Clearly trade in goods that embody aesthetic pollution concerns could be welfare enhancing. While production is mobile the consumption of pretty air is a non-tradable.

The problem with the arguments against all of these proposals for more pollution in LDCs (intrinsic rights to certain goods, moral reasons, social concerns, lack of adequate markets, etc.) could be turned around and used more or less effectively against every Bank proposal for liberalization.

Source: World Bank, *World Development Report 1992: Development and the Environment*, New York: Oxford University Press, 1992.

countries and that economic development cannot take place without environmental improvement.[2]

Income, Growth, and the Environment

In the 1960s, the field of development economics, which looks at how countries can increase their economic well-being, took on increasing importance as former colonies in Africa and Asia became independent. They began independence at a low level of development, and researchers and policy makers sought ways in which to increase the economic well-being of the people of these countries. The definition of well-being that people tended to focus on was per capita gross domestic product (GDP), with capital accumulation as the primary tool to increase per capita GDP.[3]

The focus was on capital accumulation because of how people viewed the economic process. Developing countries tended to have a low productivity of labor, which implied low per capita income. Because income was low, much or all of income was needed for consumption purposes, leaving little for saving and consequently little for investment. The lack of investment meant little capital accumulation, and because increasing capital is one way to increase the marginal product of labor, the lack of investment meant continued low productivity of labor. This process, which was viewed as keeping income low, was called the vicious cycle of poverty. Note that the vicious cycle of poverty, as depicted in Figure 18.1, does not necessarily imply declining income; it just emphasizes the difficulty of increasing income due to the problems associated with a lack of capital formation.

The development projects initiated in the 1960s, 1970s, and early 1980s focused on capital formation.[4] Large, capital-intensive projects involving dams, factories, energy facilities, and large-scale agriculture were initiated, but these projects were not really successful in improving the productivity of the economy. Many countries in sub-Saharan Africa have a lower standard of living than 1980, and in many parts of the world poverty has increased. Many believe that an important reason for the continued low—even worsening—standard of living in many developing countries is the continuing environmental degradation.

Table 18.1 shows how the standard of living has fallen in many African countries (and some other countries) over the last several decades. The indi-

---

[2] The World Bank's *World Development Report 1992* focuses on the interaction between the environment and economic development. It is an excellent first reference for detailed examination of these issues.

[3] Until the 1980s, the primary statistic used for national income was gross national product (GNP). It differs from gross domestic product in the way income and expenditures are credited. For example, the income of a Peruvian soccer player who plays in U.S. Major League Soccer is part of the GNP of Peru, but part of the GDP of the United States.

[4] Since the Brundtland Commission report (World Commission on Environment and Development [1987]) more attention has been focused on the environment, but many projects still focus on human-made capital to the detriment of environmental capital.

Figure 18.1 **Traditional View of Vicious Cycle of Poverty**

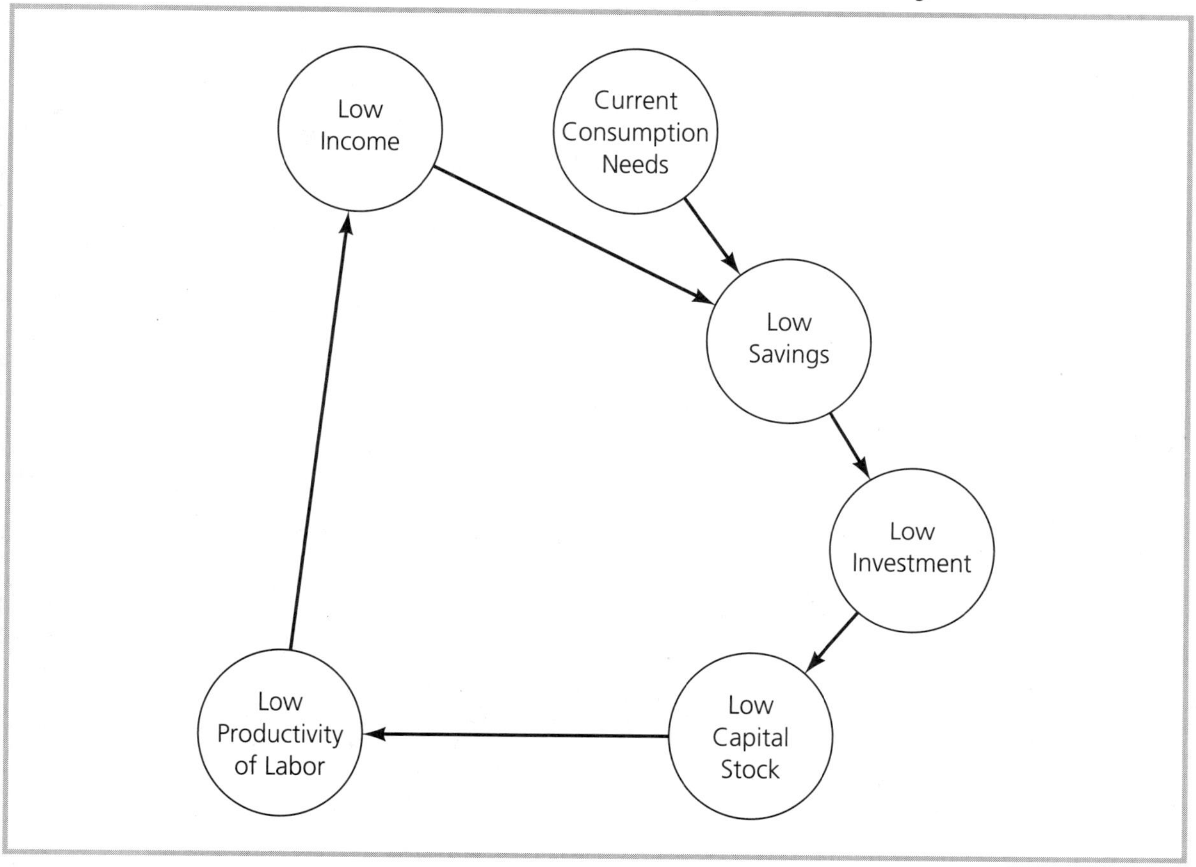

cator used to measure the standard of living is the United Nation's human development index, which incorporates variables related to the health of the population, its educational level, and its per capita income. [5]

At first, the argument that environmental deterioration is lowering income and standard of living may seem to be strange, because people from high-income countries tend to view environmental quality as an amenity or even as a luxury good. Environmental quality, however, is not only a consumption good, it is an input to production processes (see Chapter 6 for further discussion of this point). As an input, the environment may be even more important in developing countries that are more dependent on primary production activities, such as agriculture, forestry, and resource extraction.

[5] More information on the human development index can be obtained from the *Human Development Report 2001* (http://hdr.undp.org/reports/global/2001/en/).

Table 18.1 **Countries Suffering Setbacks in the Human Development Index (HDI), 1999**

HDI lower than in 1975	HDI lower than in 1980	HDI lower than in 1985	HDI lower than in 1990	HDI lower than in 1995
Zambia	Romania Russian Federation Zimbabwe	Botswana Bulgaria Burundi Congo Latvia Lesotho	Belarus Cameroon Kenya Lithuania Moldova, Rep. of South Africa Swaziland Ukraine	Malawi Namibia

Source: Taken directly from the United Nations' *Human Development Report 2001*, Chapter 1. Online: http://hdr.undp.org/reports/global/2001/en/; http://hdr.undp.org/reports/global/2001/en/pdf/chapterone.pdf.

The Effect of Environmental Quality on Economic Productivity

Environmental quality can affect economic productivity in two major ways. First, environmental degradation can drastically affect human health, which can affect the productivity of labor and consume resources in dealing with the adverse health effects. For example, intestinal disorders (cholera, dysentery, and so on) from contaminated drinking water are the leading causes of death of young children in many developing countries. Malaria is an important source of missed workdays in agricultural areas, and its prevalence is increased by deforestation and other environmental changes (see Box 18.2). Second, environmental resources are a direct input into many production processes, and environmental degradation interferes with these production activities. A good example of this type of degradation is deforestation, which leads to soil erosion (which inhibits agriculture), causes the siltation of rivers and embayments (which leads to diminished fishery output), and can lead to changes in the abundance of groundwater and surface waters. The loss of the forests also precludes future economic activity that would directly use forest resources, such as timber and wood product industries, agroforestry, and the production of nontimber forest products.

The Effect of Poverty on the Environment

Much of the environmental degradation is due to the low standard of living that currently exists in developing countries. Current low income makes it very difficult to meet current consumption needs, so environmental resources are unwisely exploited to produce current income. Forests, which could produce a steady stream of income, are decimated so as to provide a temporary burst of current income to meet current consumption needs. Similarly, agricultural areas are cultivated too intensely so as to produce food for the short

Box 18.2 Malaria and Environmental Policy

Malaria is a tropical disease that has important impacts in the Amazonian rain forest and other tropical areas. The malarial season coincides with the beginning of the planting season; when farmers contract debilitating malaria, it has important impacts on their ability to produce the entire year's crop.

Although malaria might be viewed as a natural phenomenon, it is profoundly affected by human activity. The construction of fieldside and roadside ditches provides habitat for malarial mosquitos to breed. Deforestation reduces shading of surface waters, which also increases mosquito abundance. In addition, greater population densities allow the disease to spread more easily.

Donald Jones and Robert O'Neill (1993) examined the economic decisions of farmers who must allocate their labor between producing crops and engaging in preventative ecological activities (draining swamp areas, and so on). They looked at two government policies, one that provides information on preventative ecological actions and one that provides medicine to suppress the effects of malaria. They found that both sets of policies are effective in improving agricultural productivity (because farmers are healthier), but the medication policy exacerbates deforestation, whereas the information policy restrains it.

run, which leads to soil erosion and declines in soil fertility that diminish the long-term ability to produce food. Current needs for food lead to large livestock herds, and the livestock overgraze rangeland, diminishing the productivity of the rangeland to the point that it can support fewer animals in the future. Both deforestation and overgrazing are significant factors in the process of desertification, whereby deserts expand into areas that were formerly vegetated.

This process of degradation is not simply limited to agricultural processes. In many countries, particularly in Eastern Europe and populous developing countries (India, Brazil, Mexico, China, Indonesia), high levels of pollution are produced from industrial activity. Governments do not implement policies to correct market failure, and hesitate to devote resources to pollution control, because these resources are needed to meet current consumption needs. Unfortunately, high levels of air and water pollution degrade public health; reduce the productivity of agriculture, industry, fisheries, and forestry; and generate other social costs that reduce the future ability to produce income.

Figure 18.2 shows how the vicious cycle of poverty should be visualized with an environmental component. Low income leads to both low investment and high environmental degradation. Both the lack of investment and the environmental degradation lead to low productivity. Taken by itself, the

Figure 18.2 **Current View of Vicious Cycle of Poverty**

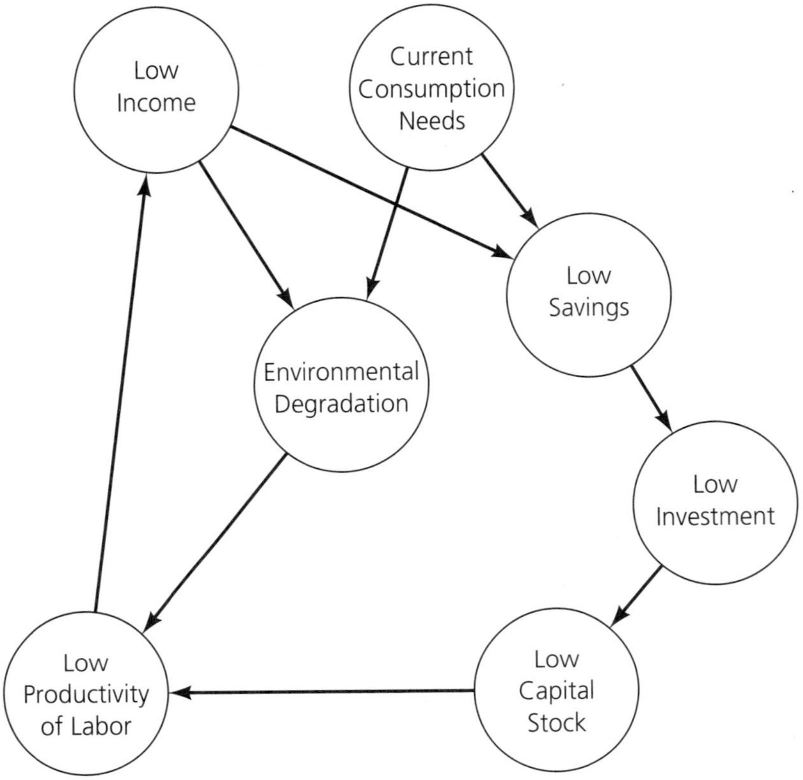

decline in environmental quality can actually lead to a decline in the productivity of labor and a decline in income. In combination with the lack of investment, the decline in environmental quality will almost certainly lead to a decline in income.

The Role of Population Growth in Environmental Degradation and Economic Development

Population growth is portrayed in the popular media as the root of all evil in the sense that it is suggested as the primary cause of both the environmental degradation and the poverty that exists in many developing countries. This conclusion is allegedly supported by the high degree of negative correlation between the growth of income and the growth of population and the high degree of positive correlation between environmental degradation and the growth of population. Correlation, however, does not imply causation.

Rather than rapid population growth leading to slow or negative growth in income, might the low income be leading to the high population growth? Or might the causation actually run in both directions (population growth affects income, and income affects population growth)? Because income and population growth are correlated, might the observed relationship between population growth and environmental degradation actually represent a relationship between income and environmental degradation, which runs in either or both directions? To fully understand the options that are available with which to raise the standard of living in developing countries, it is necessary to have a comprehensive understanding of the interrelationships among population, income, and environmental degradation.

The Effect of Population Growth on Income

In 1798, Thomas Robert Malthus authored *An Essay on the Principle of Population*, which still has a profound effect on the way society thinks about the relationship between population growth and income. In this essay, Malthus argued that the productivity of labor grows at a slower rate than population, because the increased population produces food in conjunction with a fixed amount of land, which implies a diminishing marginal product of labor.

Because Malthus argued that population grows at a faster rate than labor productivity, he concluded that population will grow faster than the amount of food that people can produce. As a result, he postulated that population will only be constrained by the food supply. That is, population will grow until the lack of food keeps population from growing any further. Moreover, each individual will have just enough food to stay alive and therefore, will always be hungry and always be at the brink of starvation. Incidently, because of the dismal outcome it predicted for humankind, this argument is why economics was given the nickname of the "dismal science."

Even though there is much hunger and starvation in the world, Malthus's prediction has not come true (as of yet). Population has continually grown throughout history, and much of the world's population has a standard of living far in excess of the subsistence level. Why did his prediction not come true?

One possible explanation for the lack of fulfillment of this prediction is provided by Barnett and Morse (1963), who suggest that because Malthus only considered a two-input world (labor and land), his results are not truly generalizable to the real world. The reason is that the law of diminishing returns implies that if all other inputs are held constant and only one input is increased, then there must be diminishing returns to that input. If the only two inputs in the production process are land (which is fixed) and labor, then one would expect diminishing returns to increasing labor. If capital, energy, materials, renewable resources, knowledge, and human skills are important inputs in the production process, however, then holding land fixed (but allowing the capital and other inputs to increase) does not imply that there must be diminishing returns to labor. Also, when one considers capital, then there are prospects for technological innovation that can serve to increase both the marginal product of labor and the marginal product of capital. It is somewhat surprising that Malthus did not consider capital, because his work was written as the Industrial Revolution was speeding through England and other parts of Europe. Although there are some countries where the bulk of the population faces Malthusian living conditions (existence on the brink of starvation), the simple version of the Malthusian law does not necessarily hold and does not necessarily imply a bleak existence for humankind.

Yet even if one considers the other inputs, it is possible that population growth may reduce income in another fashion. This potential for income reduction is because faster population growth implies greater current consumption needs, which inhibit the ability to invest and may lead to the destructive overexploitation of environmental resources. This possibility is especially true when population growth leads to a greater percentage of children and a lower percentage of workers in the population.[6] Population growth may also exacerbate the negative effects on income of inefficient government policies and market failures, such as poorly defined property rights. This phenomenon was discussed with respect to the decline in tropical forests in Chapter 13 and is revisited in the discussion of current policies later in this chapter.

Furthermore, population growth tends to exacerbate income inequality for several reasons. First, as population grows, the land available for the poorest elements of society remains constant. Because population growth tends to be highest among poor agrarian families, it tends to shrink the average size of an agrarian family's plot. This shrinkage not only reduces their productive capacity, but also tends to lead to overly intense exploitation of the land. For example, with small landholdings, families do not have the luxury to leave parts of their land fallow so that it can renew its productivity. Overusage leads to soil erosion and declining soil fertility, which will obviously increase the poverty of these poorest families.

The Effect of Income on the Growth of Population

The effect of income on population growth has been characterized by a model known as the demographic transition. The basic premise behind this model is that population growth is related to the stages of development. In the traditional conception of the model, there are three stages of economic development: the traditional agrarian society, the beginning of industrialization, and the industrialized society. These three stages are labeled Stage I through Stage III on the horizontal axis of Figure 18.3, which represents time. The vertical axis measures the birthrate and the death rate.

In the first stage, both birthrates and death rates are relatively high, but birthrates are only slightly higher than death rates, so population grows slowly. As the society begins to become developed, death rates fall due to improvements in public health (vaccinations, pest control, availability of

[6] In 2000, in low-income countries an average of 36.9 percent of the population was less than 15 years of age, whereas the corresponding figure for high-income countries was 18.4 percent. United Nations Development Program, Human Development Report: Deepening Democracy in a Fragmented World. New York: Oxford University Press, 2002.

Figure 18.3 **Demographic Transition**

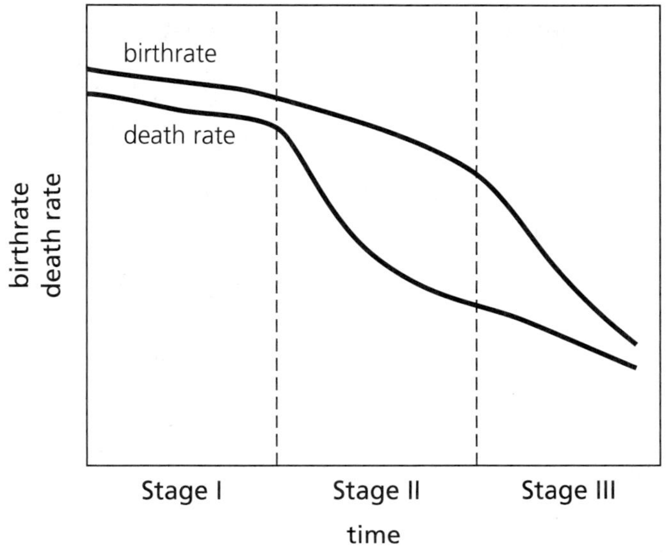

antibiotics, improved sanitation, and so on). Birthrates, however do not fall commensurately, so population growth accelerates. In the third stage, as the countries become industrialized, the demographic transition occurs and birthrates fall to more closely parallel death rates. Once again, population growth slows. This model does not provide an explanation of the determinants of birth and death rates, but a way of organizing past observations on population growth rates. It fits the historical record of population growth in Europe and North America very well. It also seems to fit the rapidly industrializing countries of East Asia fairly well. For example, the average annual population growth rate in East Asia and the Pacific was 2.2 percent for the period 1965–1980, but fell to 1.6 percent for the period 1980–1990. The Republic of Korea (South Korea) had a population growth rate of 2.0 percent for the period 1965–1980, which fell to 1.1 percent in the period 1980–1990 and continued its decline to 1 percent in the period 1990–2001. Corresponding figures for Hong Kong were 2.0 percent and 1.4 percent. In contrast, countries that have been industrialized for some time (high-income OECD countries) had a growth rate of 0.9 percent during the 1965–1980 period and 0.6 percent during the period 1980–1990.[7] Another encouraging

[7] OECD (Organization for Economic Cooperation and Development) high-income member countries include Ireland, Spain, New Zealand, Belgium, United Kingdom, Italy, Luxembourg, Australia, Netherlands, Austria, France, Canada, United States, Denmark, Germany, Norway, Sweden, Japan, Iceland, Finland, and Switzerland. Middle-income OECD countries include Portugal, Greece, and Turkey. OECD member countries include all high-income countries except Israel, Hong Kong, Singapore, United Arab Emirates, and Kuwait.

region is South America. For example, Brazil's population growth rate fell from 2.4 percent in 1985–1990 to 1.4 percent in 1995–2000. In sharp contrast, the corresponding figures for sub-Saharan Africa were 2.7 percent and 3.1 percent, indicating both rapid and increasing population growth. These trends continued in the 1990s. For example, 15 out of 40 African countries had higher population growth rates in the period 1995–2000 in comparison with 1975–80 (World Resources Institute, 2002).

There is evidence that there may be a fourth stage, that as industrialized countries mature, population growth falls to equal or below the replacement rate and zero population growth or negative population growth occurs. For example, in 1990 the total fertility rate (average number of children that a woman has during her lifetime) in high-income OECD countries averaged 1.7 (World Bank, 1992). This rate means that once the effect of the post-World War II baby boomers (which includes the grandchildren of the baby boomers) works its way through the population, the population of this group of countries will stop growing and will probably even shrink. Based on current trends, this shrinkage will not happen until about 2030 (World Bank, 1992), and the amount of immigration from developing countries to developed countries could affect this trend, because immigrant families tend to have higher birth rates than families in developing countries.

Because the model of the demographic transition is a model of what has been observed and not a model of underlying factors of causation, it cannot be conclusively stated that countries in Africa, Latin America, and South Asia will eventually undergo a demographic transition. In particular, environmental and cultural factors that were not present in Western Europe and North America may prevent population growth from slowing in developing countries in a manner analogous to the demographic transition that was observed in Western Europe and North America.

The Microeconomics of Reproduction

There are many factors that affect birthrates, including economic, cultural, social, and religious factors. The religious, social, and cultural factors are quite complex and vary significantly from one society to another. This section focuses on economic factors that affect birthrates. Although the effect of economic factors on birthrates will generally hold, it is often difficult to modify birthrates through policies that are solely economic, because social, cultural, and religious factors also affect outcomes.

Economists like to explain the decision to have children as a microeconomic utility maximizing decision, where the household (both parents) weigh the costs and benefits of having an additional child.[8] Figure 18.4 contains a graphical representation of this process, with the marginal benefits of children declining with the number of children and the marginal costs of

[8] See Becker and Lewis (1973) for a discussion of this decision in a more general context.

Figure 18.4 The Marginal Costs and Demand for Children

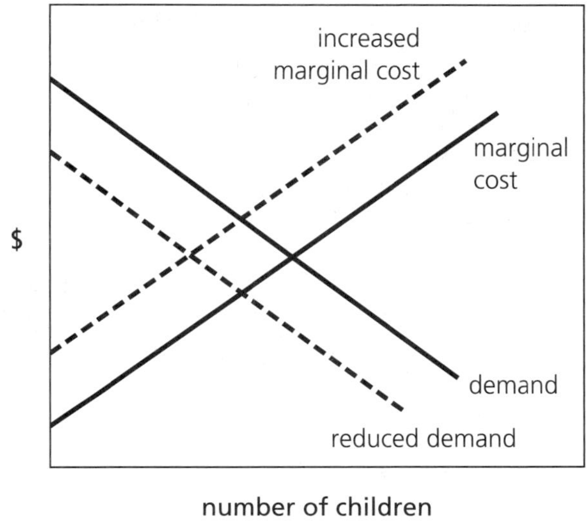

children increasing with the number of children.[9] The optimal number of children occurs where marginal costs are equal to marginal benefits. Any factors that serve to shift the marginal benefit function downward will reduce the number of children per family, and any factors that shift the marginal cost function upward will also reduce the number of children per family. It is enlightening to use this economic model to explain the economic behavior that may be underlying the demographic transition.

Factors that Affect the Marginal Benefits of Having Children. There are many benefits to having children, including the joy of having and raising children. Here, however, the focus is on the economic benefits and how they change as a society undergoes economic development. Economic benefits of children include the following: (1) Children are labor inputs to production processes and (2) Children can provide for their parents in their parents' old age.

It is relatively easy to see how having more children can increase total agricultural production (although if environmental degradation occurs as a result of increasing intensity of cultivation, this effect may be short term). In a preindustrial agrarian society, children virtually always have a positive

[9]The marginal cost function need not be upward sloping for this analysis to hold. The marginal cost function may be downward sloping, as long as it is less steeply sloped than the demand function. If the marginal cost function is more steeply sloped than the demand function, then the equilibrium number of children must be either zero or where the demand curve intersects the horizontal axis. Proof of this point is left as an exercise.

marginal product. Even very young children can help gather firewood and water, weed gardens, scare away pests, tend livestock, and watch the even younger children.

As a society becomes more industrialized and urbanized, the importance of children as an economic input diminishes. Modern manufacturing processes require an adult labor force with some degree of education. Child labor laws are established, and children are generally unproductive until they enter their middle to late teens. Although some urban children can produce income through sweatshop labor or through scavenging and other underground activities, these activities obviously have limited potential.

One interesting feature of the industrial/urban economy is that the importance of classroom learning increases. In a preindustrial agricultural society, education takes place by observing the parents' and siblings' activities in the field. In the industrial/urban society, however, classroom education becomes a much more important component of human capital. As the returns to education grow, an income-maximizing strategy might be to increase the investment in each child (better education, nutrition, and so on) and to have fewer children. In many developing countries, all, or a significant part, of the cost of educating a child is the family's responsibility, particularly at the secondary level.

It is less easy to see the importance of children as a "social security system" for their parents, but that is certainly the case in preindustrial agrarian societies. There are limited options available in agrarian societies to store wealth for the future, because most wealth is in the form of perishable foodstuffs or livestock that has high maintenance costs. The ability to sell products and store the money for the future is limited by the lack of development of financial institutions. Similarly, because much of the economy is subsistence agriculture, it is virtually impossible to raise the tax money to implement a true social security system. Consequently, the best way for a husband and wife to ensure that their old age is not a completely bleak and miserable experience is to have a lot of children to provide for them when they are no longer capable of providing for themselves.

As an economy develops, it becomes easier to store wealth, and public social support systems (social security systems, public hospitals, and so on). Consequently, the need to have children to support one in old age diminishes.

Factors That Affect the Cost of Having Children. A variety of factors affect the marginal costs associated with increasing family size. They include the following:

1. The costs of education
2. The costs of food and housing
3. The opportunity costs of the mother's time

As an economy becomes more urbanized and industrialized, all those factors tend to increase the marginal costs associated with increasing family size. As classroom education becomes more important, the costs of making a child more productive increase. Similarly, as one moves from an agrarian to an urban society, the costs of food and housing increase. Both of these effects are rather straightforward and require little elaboration. The role of the opportunity costs of the mother's time is more complicated and requires detailed explanation.

The Economic Role of Women, Population Growth, and the Environment. In most rural economies in developing countries, women supply the bulk of the labor to the subsistence agricultural economy. Women (and their children) are responsible for preparing the fields, planting the seeds, weeding and protecting the crops from pests, harvesting the crops, gathering drinking water, gathering fuelwood, preparing meals, and sometimes herding the livestock (the livestock responsibilities are usually taken by adult and near-adult males). In such a society, women work at hard labor for the entire daylight period and into the night.

Under this type of economic system where women work so hard and long, it might seem strange to suggest that as a society moves from a rural/agrarian society to an urban/industrial society, the opportunity costs of having children increase. Yet that is exactly the case, because in the agrarian economic system, children are not a hindrance to the mother accomplishing her agricultural chores. Very small babies are strapped to the mother's breast while she works, and older children accompany the mother and are actually assigned some of her responsibilities. In an urban economy where the woman might have a service, manufacturing, clerical, or professional job, the presence of children on the work site is not allowed. Consequently, having children interrupts a woman's employment (especially where child care is not readily available and in societies in which men do not share these responsibilities) and reduces her productivity, development of her human capital, and chances for advancement. Thus, as equality of treatment for women increases, and as women's roles in the monetary economy increase one would expect birthrates to fall.

This expectation, however, is not a reason to be optimistic about further reductions in birthrates, because the integration of women into the market economy and the development of equal opportunity must first occur. Economic development does not guarantee that these conditions will be met, but the lack of fulfillment of these conditions may limit economic development.

For example, many women do not have access to birth control measures. In some cases, it is because of their lack of availability (as many as 300 million women would like to prevent pregnancies, but have no access to birth control methods) (According to the U.N. Population Fund, as cited by Jacobsen, 1992). In other cases, birth control measures are available, but many women cannot employ them because of religious and social pressures.

Traditional Development Models and Their Flaws

Traditional models of development tend to focus on increasing GDP or per capita GDP by increasing capital, by transferring new technology to developing countries, and through increasing human capital. This process of increasing GDP is hypothesized to trigger other changes that will lead to the overall development of these societies. Although these methods seem very appropriate at first glance, important exclusions imply that relying solely on these methods will lead to less developmental progress than desired. To discuss whether or not these traditional methods work, it is necessary to state exactly what is meant by *development*. Michael Todaro's definition of development (1989, pp. 90–91) suggests that it is

> both a physical reality and state of mind in which society has, through some combination of social, economic, and institutional process, secured the means for obtaining a better life. Whatever the specific components of this better life, development in all societies must have at least the following three objectives:
>
> 1. To increase the availability and widen the distribution of basic life-sustaining goods such as food, shelter, health and protection.
> 2. To raise levels of living including, in addition to higher incomes, the provision of more jobs, better education, and greater attention to cultural and humanistic values, all of which will serve not only to enhance material well-being but also to generate greater individual and national self-esteem.
> 3. To expand the range of economic and social choices available to individuals by freeing them from servitude and dependence not only in relation to other people and nation-states but also to the forces of ignorance and human misery.

Despite the articulation by Todaro and others of the more multidimensional aspects of development, development efforts tend to focus on GDP. In particular, both commercial banks and international loan agencies focus on GDP measures as an indicator of creditworthiness, which has several important ramifications. It is understandable that private banks should focus on this measure, because their primary responsibility is to their stockholders. It is less clear, however, that international loan and development agencies should focus on this measure, for the following reasons. Remember that GDP represents total value of market goods produced in a country. In addition to GDP not being directly related to many of the development objectives categorized previously, the pursuit of GDP detracts from many development efforts. Obviously, more GDP is good, but policies that promote the development of GDP may do unintentional harm for two reasons. First, because subsistence crops are grown for the farmers' consumption and are not traded in markets, GDP does not include the subsistence agricultural sector. Because the subsistence agricultural sector provides for the basic needs of the majority of the population in many developing countries, its exclusion is significant. Second, although the measure of GDP is reduced to take into account the depreciation of human-made capital, it does not consider natural capital (see Chapter 6 for a discussion of this point). Consequently, when soils are exhausted and forests depleted, future GDP-producing and subsistence-producing assets are lost.

The Impact of the Exclusion of Subsistence Agriculture from Measures of GDP

The exclusion of subsistence agriculture from measures of GDP and the implementation of policies that are oriented to maximizing the growth of GDP have two major impacts on developing countries. First, they encourage a set of policies that favor cash crops (crops grown for sale, particularly in export markets, such as coffee, tea, sugar, bananas, cocoa, palm oil, and tobacco). Second, they may favor a set of policies that enhance the economic well-being of men at the expense of women.

Because the sale of coffee to the United States increases a country's GDP but the production of corn for consumption by the farmer's family does not, a variety of policies have developed to encourage cash crops over subsistence crops. Also, because export crops bring foreign exchange (desirable foreign currency such as U.S. dollars, British pounds, euros, and Japanese yen) that can be used to purchase imports or repay debt, there is even more incentive for governments to encourage the production of export crops. The policies that encourage these crops include fertilizer subsidies, agricultural extension activities, export loan programs, the development of export infrastructure, and price ceilings on food crops. Although the encouragement of export crops is not inherently bad (after all, holding everything else constant, higher GDP is good), it has several spillover effects that are very detrimental.

One of the most important spillovers is that more land is devoted to cash crops, at the expense of land devoted to subsistence crops and at the expense of land devoted to natural habitats such as forests. The loss of forests and other habitat has two primary impacts. To begin with, it leads to environmental problems, such as soil erosion and the loss of other ecological services. The problems are exacerbated because the productivity of the land in cash crops is often very short (a matter of several years) owing to losses in soil fertility and due to environmental problems associated with the development of monocultures. Because monocultures are very susceptible to pests and diseases in tropical climates, they require tremendous chemical applications to maintain their productivity. For example, the pesticide applications to banana plantations are very large and create toxic exposures for workers and downstream populations, as well as profound ecosystem effects as the pesticides work their way through the food chain. In addition to these environmental degradation effects, there is the loss of common-property resources, such as forests and savannas. These commons provide important resources (food, fuel, and fodder) and contribute to the subsistence agriculture that is managed primarily by women.

The loss of these commons, the environmental degradation of land in general, and the conversion of land from subsistence farming to cash crops may serve to increase the economic hardship and continued impoverishment of women in developing countries. Initially, when development agencies focused on market activities (which are the province of men), they believed that the economic benefits would trickle down to women. Jacobsen (1993),

Box 18.3 Environmental Policies for the Subsistence Sector

This book has devoted much time to the development of policies such as economic incentives (pollution taxes, marketable pollution permits, deposit-refund systems, and so on). An interesting question is whether these systems can work in the non-cash subsistence sectors of developing countries. For example, although performance bonding systems or liability systems may protect tropical forests from damage by commercial logging, can they be used to stop peasant farmers from cutting the forests to create cropland and to promote conservation of renewable resources among traditional forest dwellers who practice a combination of hunting, fishing, and agriculture? Use of a system can be difficult because the subsistence inhabitants have no assets upon which to base a performance bond or liability system or to confiscate as the penalty associated with a command and control system.

This problem arose in the state of Amazonas, Brazil, where the range of a rare primate, the uakari, coincided with the area in which forest dwellers (of mixed indigenous and European ancestry) had established villages and engaged in hunting, fishing, and agriculture for many generations. It was feared that habitat would be lost to the agricultural activities of the local population, which could cause the extinction of the uakari. It would have been difficult to enforce removing the people from the land (and it would have created a hardship for these people) to establish a sanctuary for the uakari, yet it would be difficult to protect the habitat of the uakari through either economic incentives or command and control.

The solution that was developed was to conduct scientific research on the fish and animals upon which the local people depended for a portion of their subsistence. The scientific findings were translated into practical guidelines on hunting and fishing practices, which increased both the abundance of the animals and the harvest of the people. This increase in hunting and fishing harvest lessened the need to create cropland, and the increase in the standard of living created credibility for the scientists in the eyes of the local people; additional conservation measures since have been implemented. As with the examples of gold mining and mercury (discussed in Box 10.3) and agroforestry and the rain forest (discussed in Chapter 13), solutions to environmental problems in the subsistence sector may be best developed by finding ways to make conservation and environmental protection economically beneficial and then educating the local people in these methods.

however, argues that this has not been the case. She believes that development programs need to be specifically oriented toward promoting the economic activity of women and that given the social, cultural, and economic structures in many developing countries, one cannot expect a flow of benefits from the male-dominated market economy to the female-dominated subsistence economy.

Given that women are more closely tied to the land (although not often as owners) and that they are the exploiters/managers of common-property resources, it is not surprising to find that environmental movements in many Third World countries are dominated by women. For example, in Kenya, two of the most important grassroots environmental organizations, the Kenya Water for Health Organization (KWAHO) and the Green Belt Movement, were founded by women and have their activities implemented mainly by women. KWAHO was founded as a women's cooperative to train women to build and maintain simple water systems. The Green Belt Movement was founded by women's rights and environmental advocate Wangari Maathiai. Its purpose is to encourage people to find public areas and plant trees on these areas. As of March 2004, more than 25 million trees had been planted in 1000 tree belts by more than 30,000 Kenyan women (http://www.greenbeltmovement.org/Achievements.htm).

Several decades ago, there was a feeling among those involved in international development that development efforts had to take place entirely within the cultural context of the developing country. It was considered to be interventionist to try to change aspects of the current cultures of these countries. Although there is a lot of merit to these arguments in many contexts, many believe that it no longer applies in some contexts, particularly with respect to the role of women in developing countries. In the opinion of this author, when basic human rights for women conflict with current cultural norms, the development process should be constructed to help women obtain these rights. The same argument can be made about caste systems and other social structures that lead to discrimination against minority groups. Jacobsen (1993, pp. 76–77) argues that

> improving the status of women, and thereby the prospects for humanity, will require a complete reorientation of development efforts away from the current overemphasis on limiting women's reproduction. Instead, the focus needs to be on establishing an environment in which women and men together can prosper. This means creating mainstream development programs that seek to expand the women's control over income and household resources, improve their productivity, establish legal and social rights, and increase the social and economic choices they are able to make.

Sustainable Development

The focus on GDP also tends to promote activities that lead to the increase of current GDP at the expense of future GDP. For example, the cutting of forests to raise current income destroys a natural asset that could produce future income through a variety of activities (see Chapter 13) that do not destroy the forest. Monoculture agriculture is another example of an economic activity that can produce current income, but it has a limited productive life and destroys a productive natural asset. The central point is that development policies that promote activities that are not environmentally sustainable do not really contribute to the economic development of the nation, because future possibilities are eroded by the current economic activities. The potential of ecotourism for sustainable development is discussed in Box 18.4.

Box 18.4 Wildlife, Ecotourism, and Economic Development

The natural resources of many developing countries provide an opportunity to earn income and preserve the resources at the same time. For example, tourism is the leading earner of foreign exchange in Kenya, where tourists participate in photographic safaris and tropical beach vacations.

Ecotourism is growing rapidly in the Amazon region, the Galapagos Islands, parts of Africa, and many Caribbean and Central American countries. Many people with high incomes from Western Europe, North America, and Japan are willing to pay large amounts of money to see these ecological wonders. This type of activity is often viewed as a way to "have your cake and eat it too" in the sense that it is possible to generate income and maintain resources at the same time.

Yet one must be cautious in the development of these tourist activities for two reasons. First, it is possible that the tourism takes a form where it generates environmental degradation that destroys the very resources the people are traveling to see. For example, in the fragile semiarid grassland areas of Kenya, vehicles that take tourists to see the wildlife spectacles can compress the soil and permanently render it unable to support vegetation. Sewage and solid wastes generated by hotels and resorts can pollute the water resources that tourists come to see. Second, care must be taken to ensure that the revenue that tourism generates raises the quality of life of the local inhabitants in the tourism areas. This factor is important for several reasons. If tourism does not raise the quality of life, then it does little to enhance the development process. For example, much of a tourist's total tourism expenditure accrues to international airlines, because airfare is usually the largest component of expenditure. That obviously, does little to aid in the development process. Care must be taken that other expenditures benefit the tourism region and lead to improvements in the quality of life in that region. In addition, unless the local populations benefit from the tourism, they have little incentive to preserve the resource upon which the tourism is based. Because there is a scarcity of agricultural land in many of these areas, it is important that local residents see the benefits of preserving the resources. Giving local residents a financial stake in the preservation of the environment is a very positive step toward environmental preservation. Instead of wild animals being seen as competitors to the residents' livestock,

(continues)

Box 18.4 (continued)

they are seen as a source of jobs and other benefits (schools, hospitals, and so on). Under these circumstances, local residents will often take positive steps to inhibit the operation of poachers (hunters who illegally take game to sell body parts, such as tusks, skins, horns, and internal organs, in illegal overseas markets).

A simple way to summarize the policies that must be taken to preserve these ecological treasures is to see that a global potential Pareto improvement must be made into an actual Pareto improvement for those who have a stake in the environmental resources. The world as a whole benefits from the preservation of these environmental resources, but the country that contains the resource and the communities that are in proximity to the resource pay the opportunity costs (lost economic opportunities) of preserving the resource. If the world's willingness to pay for preservation can be translated into increased economic opportunities for those who are in proximity to the resources, then preservation can be achieved.

To maximize the development benefits of ecotourism, more research needs to be conducted into what tourists value in an "ecotourism" vacation and how to structure ecotourism to preserve the ecological resources and improve the quality of life of local populations. If these questions can be answered and if ecotourism can be properly structured, then it can play a substantial role in the sustainable development of tropical countries. For more information on ecotourism, see the tourism web site of the United Nations Environmental Programme (http://www.uneptie.org/pc/tourism/home.htm).

To emphasize the importance of the concept of sustainability in development, a considerable literature has developed that diagrams the objectives of and the conditions for sustainable development. Pearce and colleagues (1990) list the following set of development objectives that are similar to those defined by Todaro:

1. Increases in real per capita income
2. Improvements in health and nutritional status
3. Educational achievement
4. Access to resources
5. A "fairer" distribution of income
6. Increases in basic freedoms

Pearce and his coauthors suggest that sustainable development be defined as a process whereby the above objectives of development (or a modified version of this list) be nondecreasing over time. The World Commission on Environment and Development (1987, p. 1) defines sustainable development as a process by which current generations can "meet their needs without compromising the ability of future generations to meet their needs." Although either of these may constitute a suitable definition of sustainable development, Pearce and colleagues point out that a definition of sustainability and the conditions for achieving sustainability are very different.

In Chapters 5 and 6, the role of capital in sustainable development was discussed. This discussion emphasized the role of environmental resources that generate environmental services in sustainable development. Maintaining these environmental resources has been a particular problem for many developing countries, because their lack of current income forces them to treat renewable resources as exhaustible resources, degrading the ability of the environmental resources to regenerate and to provide ecological services. Examples include intensive cultivation that leads to soil erosion, deforestation, intensive grazing that leads to desertification, destruction of coral reefs, and overexploitation of fish stocks. How can sustainable growth of income be generated? The conceptual answer to this question can be developed by looking back at Figure 18.2. The marginal product of labor and current income must be increased while maintaining the integrity of environmental resources. In other words, a way must be found to meet current consumption needs, increase all types of capital (human-made, human, natural, and environmental), and protect the environment from degradation. Although each individual policy or development program might not be able to address all these problems simultaneously, the total package of development programs in a country must address all four. In addition, the other dimensions of development such as human health, education, and basic freedoms must be simultaneously addressed.

Sustainable Development Policy

Many past development projects emphasized the creation of human-made capital such as dams, roads, and factories. As originally conceived, these projects may have been thought to be sustainable, but they interact with the environment in a way that reduces the sustainability of other productive activities. For example, a hydroelectric dam seems like the epitome of a renewable, sustainable resource. Yet even under ideal conditions, the dam will eventually fill with silt, which reduces its capacity to produce electricity. If the dam also encourages the agricultural development of the surrounding hillsides (because people move along the road that is built to the dam or because factories are built near the dam to take advantage of cheap electricity), then the destruction of the hillside forests and exposure of the soil resulting from agriculture will lead to even faster siltation of the dam. Another example is the creation of factories that do not control their pollution emissions, with the pollution emissions adversely affecting human health and agricultural productivity and the ability of ecosystems to provide ecological services.

Government development policies often create incentives for environmental degradation. In Chapter 13, inefficient forestry policies were discussed in great detail. These policies include poorly constructed concessionaire agreements, poorly defined property rights, and poorly defined incentives such as subsidizing cattle ranching. These poorly defined policies are not limited to forests. The World Bank (1992, p. 65) lists several types of inefficient government development policies, including

1. Subsidization of agricultural inputs, such as fertilizer
2. Subsidization of energy inputs
3. Subsidization of logging and cattle ranching
4. Nonaccountability of public-sector polluters
5. Provision of services, such as water and electricity, at subsidized prices
6. Inefficient management of public lands

Therefore, a first step toward a well-constructed development plan is the elimination of these policy negatives. In addition, positive steps must also be initiated. The World Bank (1992) lists three classes of development policies that can increase the quality of life of developing countries, that will minimize environmental degradation, and that can be sustainable. These three classes are the elimination of inefficient policies, the provision of public and private investments that have net benefits independent of environmental benefits, and the correction of market failures that lead to reduced environmental quality.

Inefficient government policies that lead to the loss of GDP and the deterioration of the environment include subsidies for production inputs, subsidies for certain extractive activities such as cattle ranching and logging, and poorly defined property rights to land for farmers. Each of these policies lead to a misallocation of the country's productive resources and to an inefficiently high level of environmental degradation.

Many governments subsidize the use of certain inputs in selected production activities so as to increase output in these activities. For example, energy, fertilizer, and irrigation water are often provided at subsidized prices. These subsidies encourage the excess use of these inputs and distort the economy in favor of those activities that use those inputs. For example, in the former Soviet Union, a massive irrigation program was developed using waters from rivers that flowed into the Aral Sea. The agricultural production never came close to meeting project goals and resulted in both environmental and economic damage. With so much water diverted to irrigation where evaporation takes place at a higher rate than in rivers, the Aral Sea shrank to a fraction of its former size.[10] This shrinkage caused immense ecosystem damage and destroyed a valuable commercial fishery that supplied both nutrition and income to the region. If the irrigation water had been priced at its true social cost, the project would never have been viewed as having any economic benefits.

Similar arguments can be made with respect to both energy and fertilizer.[11] In fact, the artificially low price at which energy was traded in Eastern Europe was one of the major factors that led to the abominably high levels of air pollution in that region.

It is relatively easy to see the importance of the elimination of policies that subsidize and encourage activities such as logging and cattle ranching. In

---

[10]See Chapters 16 and 17 for more discussion of the environmental problems associated with irrigation.

[11]See Chapters 9 and 10 for a discussion of the environmental problems associated with energy use and Chapters 15 and 17 for a discussion of the environmental problems associated with fertilizer use.

many cases, these activities were only privately profitable because of the subsidies and resulted in net costs to the economy without even taking into consideration the environmental effects. A consideration of environmental costs implies that the subsidization of these activities leads to large social losses. Finally, it is critically important that farmers' property rights to land be carefully defined. If property rights are appropriately defined, then farmers have an incentive to treat their land as a long-term asset and to protect their land from degradation. Notice that this process does not always imply the creation of private property rights. Many lands, particularly forestlands and rangelands, may be most effectively used when maintained as a commons. Property rights, however, must still be defined to protect the land from open-access exploitation. If property rights to common land are given to local social organizations (such as villages, clans, tribes, or farmers' cooperatives), then the local social organizations can develop socially enforceable rules governing the use of these communal resources. This form of property rights is, in fact, the predominant form that existed among indigenous peoples of the world before they were incorporated into colonies or independent nation-states.

Policies that initiate public investment and that encourage private investment can also lead to important developmental benefits. The World Bank (1992) cites several investments that are representative of this type. They include investment in water supply and sanitation, soil conservation, and the education of women.

In addition, it is important to address market failures that cause a divergence between the marginal social costs and marginal private costs of market activities. These market failures were addressed in a general application in Chapter 3. Government policies to address these market failures could include taxes on emissions and wastes, regulation on the disposal of toxic and hazardous waste, and appropriately structured fees for timber and mineral extraction (World Bank, 1992).

An important market failure that needs to be addressed is the existence of imperfect information. For example, techniques often exist for sustainable agroforestry and other sustainable activities, but they are not implemented by subsistence farmers because of lack of knowledge about the technique and uncertainty about the outcome. Box 18.5 contains a discussion of the importance of information in the decision to use sustainable agroforestry techniques in rural Mexico.

The Role of Developed Nations

Figure 18.2 provides considerable insight as to how developed countries can help developing countries protect their environmental resources and improve both their short- and long-term prospects for economic development. The problem, as illustrated in Figure 18.2, is that short-term needs and low current income lead to environmental degradation and slow growth of capital stocks. The obvious way that developed nations can help in the development process is to work to help developing nations reduce the short-

Box 18.5 The Role of Information in Sustainable Development

Economists often focus on the lack of properly defined property rights as a reason subsistence farmers do not engage in sustainable activities. The hypothesis is that although sustainable techniques may exist, farmers have little incentive to engage in them if they have insecure rights to their land. Under these conditions, a better strategy for farmers might be to clear forests and plant field crops, yielding current income but destroying the productivity of the land in the future.

Recent research, however, has shown that even with secure property rights, farmers often make the seemingly irrational decision to engage in clearing and planting of field crops, rather than in more sustainable agroforestry techniques. One of these studies, by James Casey of Washington and Lee University, looks at this problem in the Campeche region of Mexico. Casey examined farming families who are members of farmers' cooperatives and have both private and collective property rights to land. He collected data on a variety of farm and farmer characteristics through questionnaires that were administered to farming families. He then estimated the determinants of the choice of sustainable agroforestry techniques, or less sustainable field agriculture.

Casey found that information about sustainable techniques is the primary determinant of whether they are adopted. He theorizes a causal link that uncertainty about outcomes of untried techniques keeps farmers from adopting them. Information that reduces this uncertainty increases the probability of farmers adopting these techniques. Similar results have been found in Brazil and other areas.

term income gap, help them accumulate more and better human-made capital, help them improve their human capital, and help them with the preservation of their environmental resources.

The immediate and pressing problem of high short-term needs and low income can be addressed in several ways. First, developed nations can provide debt relief for developing nations. As mentioned in Chapter 13, the debt burden of some nations is very high, causing them to spend a high portion of current income just to service their debt. If developed nations (and international lending agencies) were to forgive all or a portion of the debt, there would be less pressure on current income and greater ability to meet current needs with current income. Similarly, if developed nations truly opened their markets to the imported goods of developing countries, it would increase the income of developing countries. That would mean the elimination of subsidies, tariffs, and quotas that protect the domestic industry of developed countries. Finally, increased development aid would also aid in the process of meeting current needs without jeopardizing the future. The development aid would also help in the process of investing in human capital and human made capital, as well as help with the maintenance of environmental capital.

Other steps to help make protection of environmental capital viable in the short-term for developing countries could also be taken. An important part would be to help develop markets for products that were produced in harmony with the ecosystem rather than by destroying the ecosystem. A global climate treaty could be written that rewarded developing nations for carbon sequestration in pristine ecosystems. Sewage treatment and other technologies could be provided for developing countries. In addition, developing countries do not have adequate resources to monitor their environmental resources and enforce their domestic environmental law, so assistance could be provided to help provide these important functions.

Summary

Many Third World countries find themselves in a poverty trap that is partially generated by environmental degradation. Poverty leads to overexploitation of environmental resources in an effort to generate current income, and the degradation of environmental resources lowers productivity and income. Population growth may exacerbate these pressures and lead to increased poverty and environmental degradation. In addition, population growth may make market failures more severe and make it more difficult to correct market failures.

Current development policies must be aimed at breaking this vicious cycle of poverty and environmental degradation by maintaining current income with environmentally sustainable development projects such as agroforestry. In addition, direct government action aimed at eliminating inefficient government programs, stimulating appropriate investments, and addressing market failures are key components of a development program. Development policies must also ensure that development benefits the entire population. Consequently, development policies must not ignore the role of women in the economy of developing nations and must seek to eliminate practices that relegate women to second-class status. Although there is no "magic formula" or specific recipe for development, much progress has been made in recent years in more properly conceptualizing the development process, which can provide guidance for more enlightened policies. A key aspect would be for developed nations to open their markets to developing nations, reduce their subsidies to industries that compete with industries in developing nations, and increase the flow of wealth and technology from developed nations to developing nations.[12]

---

[12]For current information on the environment and development, investigate the web sites of the World Bank (http://www.worldbank.org/), the United Nations Development Programme (http://www.undp.org/), and the *1997 Global State of the Environment Report* of the United Nations Environment Programme (http://www.grid2.cr.usgs.gov/geo1/).

Review Questions

1. What is the "vicious cycle of poverty," and how does environmental quality affect it?
2. What is the effect of income on population growth?
3. What is the effect of population growth on the environment and income?
4. What factors affect the costs of having children?
5. What factors affect the benefits of having children?
6. Prove footnote 8.
7. What is meant by "sustainable development"?

Questions for Further Study

1. Can population growth be limited without redefining the role of women in society? Why or why not?
2. Should countries that provide development aid insist on increased rights for women and minorities, even if such rights conflict with the developing countries' cultural norms?
3. How does a focus on GDP affect the development process?
4. Why should the focus of development be on sustainable development rather than on maximizing the present value of the time path of GDP? (*Hint*: How do the two alternates treat the future differently?)
5. Why do property rights matter for the development process?
6. How does government subsidization of export crops affect the development process?
7. Is environmental quality a luxury that should be the concern of only wealthy nations?

Suggested Paper Topics

1. Investigate the economic paradigm of sustainable development. How does it differ from the neoclassical economic paradigm? Start with the book by Pearce and Warford (1993). Also check the web sites cited in footnote 10.
2. Conduct an empirical analysis of the relationship between economic (or social variables) and environmental variables. *World Resources 1992–93* and *World Development Report 1992* are excellent sources of data on this subject.
3. Look at the problem of contaminated drinking water in Third World countries. What economic factors (market failures, for example) lead to this problem? How do these economic factors affect the ability to develop solutions? Go to the *World Development Report* web site (http://worldbank.org/poverty/wdrpoverty) for an excellent set of resources.

Works Cited and Selected Readings

Ahmed, B. Role of the Environment in the Sustainable Development of the Caribbean. *Social and Economic Studies 47*, no. 4 (December 1998): 83–97.

Barbier, E. B. Development, Poverty, and Environment. Pages 731–744 in *Handbook of Environmental and Resource Economics*, edited by J. C. J. M. van den Bergh. Cheltenham, UK, and Northampton, MA: Edward Elgar, 1999.

Barnett, H. J., and C. Morse. *Scarcity and Growth*. Baltimore: Johns Hopkins University Press, 1963.

Becker, G. S., and H. G. Lewis. On the Interaction between the Quantity and Quality of Children. *Journal of Political Economy 81* (1973): 279–288.

Brown, L. R., C. Flavin, and H. Kane, (eds.). *Vital Signs, 1992*. New York: W. W. Norton, 1992.

Brown, L. R., C. Flavin, and S. Postel, (eds.). *State of the World 1993*. New York: W. W. Norton, 1993.

Calvert, P. Deforestation, Environment, and Sustained Development in Latin America. Pages 155–172 in *Deforestation, Environment, and Sustainable Development: A Comparative Analysis*, edited by D. D. Vajpeyi. Westport, CT, and London: Greenwood, 2001.

Casey, J., Agroforestry Adoption in Mexico: Using Keynes to Better Understand Farmer Decision-making, *Journal of Post-Keynesian Economics*, in press 2004, 26, no. 3.

Coxhead, I. Development and the Environment. *Asian-Pacific Economic Literature 17*, no. 1 (May 2003): 22–54.

Coxhead, I., and S. Jaysuariya. *The Open Economy and the Environment: Development, Trade and Resources in Asia*. Cheltenham, UK, and Northampton, MA: Edward Elgar, 2003.

Faucheux, S., I. Nicolai, and M. O'Connor. Globalization, Competitiveness, Governance and Environment: What Prospects for a Sustainable Development? Pages 13–39 in *Sustainability and Firms: Technological Change and the Changing Regulatory Environment*, edited by S. Faucheux, J. Gowdy, and I. Nicolai. Cheltenham, UK, and Northampton, MA: Edward Elgar, 1998.

Gutner, T. L. *Banking on the Environment: Multilateral Development Banks and their Environmental Performance in Central and Eastern Europe Global Environmental Accord: Strategies for Sustainability and Institutional Innovation*. Cambridge, MA: MIT Press, 2002.

Jacobsen, J. L. Coerced Motherhood Increasing. *Vital Signs, 1992*, edited by L. R. Brown, C. Flavin, and H. Kane. New York: W. W. Norton, 1992.

Jacobsen, J. L. Closing the Gender Gap in Development. *State of the World 1993*, edited by L. R. Brown et al. New York: W. W. Norton, 1993.

Jones, D. W., and R. V. O'Neill. A Model of Neotropical Endogenous Malaria and Preventative Ecological Measures. *Environment and Planning 25* (1993): 1677–1687.

Kettel, B. Women, Environment and Development: From Rio to Beijing. Pages 220–239 in *Political Ecology: Global and Local*, edited by R. Keil et al. London and New York: Routledge, 1998.

Malthus, T. R. An Essay on the Principle of Population. Pages 15–129 in *An Essay on the Principle of Population, Text, Sources and Background, Criticism*, edited by P. Appleman. New York: W. W. Norton, 2003.

Markandya, A. Poverty, Environment and Development. Pages 192–213 in *Frontiers of Environmental Economics*, edited by H. Folmer et al. Cheltenham, UK, and Northampton, MA: Edward Elgar, 2001.

Pearce, D., E. Barbier, and A. Markandya. *Sustainable Development*. London: Gower, 1990.

Pearce, D. W., and J. J. Warford. *World without End*. Washington, DC: Oxford University Press for the World Bank, 1993.

Perman, R., and P. B. Anand. Development and the Environment: An Introduction.

Journal of Economic Studies 27, nos. 1–2 (2000): 7–18.

Redclift, M. Global Equity: The Environment and Development. Pages 98–113 in *Global Sustainable Development in the Twenty-First Century*, edited by K. Lee, A. Holland, and D. McNeill. Edinburgh: Edinburgh University Press; distributed by Columbia University Press, New York, 2000.

Repetto, R. *World and Enough Time*. New Haven, CT: Yale University Press, 1986.

Salih, T. M. Sustainable Economic Development and the Environment. *International Journal of Social Economics 30*, nos. 1–2 (2003): 153–162.

Soderbaum, P. *Ecological Economics: A Political Economics Approach to Environment and Development*. London: Earthscan, 2000.

Strong, M. Environment and Sustainable Development in Africa. Pages 151–164 in *Renewing Social and Economic Progress in Africa: Essays in Memory of Philip Ndegwa*, edited by G. Dharam. New York: St. Martin's Press, 2000.

Tisdell, C. *Tourism Economics, the Environment and Development: Analysis and Policy*. Cheltenham, UK, and Northampton, MA: Edward Elgar, 2001.

Todaro, M. P. *Economic Development in the Third World*. 4th ed. New York: Longman, 1989.

Verbruggen, H. Environment, International Trade, and Development. Pages 449–460 in *Handbook of Environmental and Resource Economics*, edited by J. C. J. M. van den Bergh. Cheltenham, UK, and Northampton, MA: Edward Elgar, 1999.

World Bank. *World Development Report 1992: Development and the Environment*. New York: Oxford University Press, 1992.

World Commission on Environment and Development. *Our Common Future: The Brundtland Report*. New York: Oxford University Press, 1987.

World Resources Institute. *World Resources 1992–93*. New York: Oxford University Press, 1992.

World Resources Institute. *World Resources 1994–95*. New York: Oxford University Press, 1994.

World Resources Institute. *World Resources 1996–97*. New York: Oxford University Press, 1996.

chapter 19

Prospects for the Future

The optimist proclaims that we live in the best of all possible worlds; and the pessimist fears this is true.

James Branch Cabell (1879–1958), The Silver Stallion

Introduction

This quotation by James Branch Cabell emphasizes that reality is a matter of perspective. The optimist looks at the good that has been accomplished, whereas the pessimist looks at the problems that remain.

One can look at the "environmental crises" facing planet Earth in much the same fashion. We have made much progress in dealing with some environmental problems, particularly in developed countries. In such countries, conventional air and water pollutants have been regulated, birthrates have declined to the point where zero population growth will be realized in the near future, the ozone depletion problem has been addressed, most developed countries are committed to reducing emissions of greenhouse gases, and many national governments are developing policies based on principles of sustainability. There is a general recognition of the importance of protecting the environment. Although many problems remain to be solved in developed countries, one can point to significant progress. Yet once we leave the borders of selected developed countries, the situation in much less rosy.

The depletion of the global commons continues unabated, and developed countries play a major role in this. For example, high-income countries are primarily responsible for the depletion of global fisheries, the pollution of the oceans, and the accumulation of greenhouse gases in the atmosphere. No effective policies to control these problems have yet been implemented, and no progress appears to be on the horizon.

For all the reasons to be optimistic about the situation in developed countries, there are reasons to be pessimistic about the situation in many developing countries. First and foremost, population growth is far from being under control. Second, environmental degradation is taking place at a massive and unprecedented rate, which is leading to the loss of much of the world's renewable resource base, including loss of tropical forest, desertification, fisheries depletion, and soil loss. Water pollution is a leading cause of death in many developing countries, leading to infant diarrhea and other intestinal problems. Third, the economic situation in many developing countries prevents the people from having a long-term perspective. This short-term perspective and a lack of understanding of the long-term economic importance of maintaining environmental quality imply that many developing nations have not recognized the need to take immediate steps to preserve the environment.

Will environmental degradation lead to a collapse of the world's ability to support its population, or will social responses mitigate environmental degradation and move us to a sustainable future? Obviously, this question cannot be answered in this short, concluding chapter to this book. Rather, this chapter attempts to summarize some of the debate on this issue. Because it is not possible to test to see if the pessimistic or optimistic forecast (or some forecast in the middle) is correct, this chapter presents alternative outlooks on the issue, with a focus on choices.

Absolute Scarcity

The concept of absolute scarcity has shaped much of the debate about scarcity and the ability of the earth and its resources to sustain humankind. This concept originated in the work of Thomas Malthus, who argued that because there was a fixed amount of land, scarcity was an inevitability. He argued that the law of diminishing returns implies that if land is held constant, increased labor must ultimately be faced with diminishing marginal productivity. Thus, population will grow faster than the marginal product of labor, so population will grow faster than the food supply. Because Malthus believed that the only constraint on the growth of population is the availability of food, population will continually grow until it reaches the limits of the food supply. At this point, each individual will be at a subsistence level of consumption (just enough food to survive), and increased population growth will be limited by starvation.

Obviously, Malthus's prediction of nearly two centuries ago has not taken place. In some areas of the world, the population is at a subsistence level of consumption, but population growth has been continual and exponential. It is not likely that the food supply or other constraints on population will serve to limit population growth in the near future. In addition, when developed nations are also considered, there has been a large increase in the amount of consumption (both food and goods) per capita.

The idea of absolute scarcity has been revisited in modern times. In the 1960s and 1970s, as world population exploded, pollution intensified, hunger increased, and shortages of energy and other resources materialized, absolute scarcity was seriously considered in public debate. Many scholars, citing the finite nature of the world and its resources, argued that scarcity was inescapable. Because these scholars viewed the finiteness of resources as a limit on the growth of population and economic activity, they have come to be known as neo-Malthusians.

Entropy and Economics

Nicholas Georgescu-Roegen (1971, 1975) has argued that entropy is the source of ultimate scarcity. Entropy refers to the amount of disorder in a system. The higher the entropy, the higher the state of disorder; the lower the entropy, the greater the state of order. The third law of thermodynamics (the entropy law) states that the universe (or a subsystem of the universe) is in a constant state of entropic degradation. A simpler way of phrasing this principal is that as time and the physical forces of the universe progress, energy and materials tend to dissipate and become more difficult to access. The relevance of the entropy law for economic activity and prospects for the future is that useful goods and resources tend to be low entropy, and the economic process increases their entropy. Although we can switch from coal to oil to uranium and we can substitute plastic for steel, we cannot substitute away from low-entropy matter. According to Georgescu-Roegen, it is the ultimate source of scarcity.

For example, a fossil fuel, such as coal or oil, is characterized by low entropy. It is a relatively homogenous substance, with a much higher concentration of carbon than the environment as a whole. When the coal is burned in the economic process, however, the carbon is scattered throughout the atmosphere. The heat that is initially highly concentrated becomes highly dispersed. The process of using the coal increases its entropy and reduces its usefulness.

Because the amount of low entropy on the earth is fixed and because entropic degradation is irreversible, it will be the ultimate constraint on the human species.[1] Not only does the law of entropy limit the size of the social system, Georgescu-Roegen argues, but it constrains the life span of the human species as well. Entropic degradation implies that the time span of human existence is limited because we will eventually run out of low-entropy matter to support life.

---

[1] Entropic degradation is not irreversible if energy is available to reverse it. This energy, however, must come from somewhere, so the entropic degradation of a system can be reversed, but only at the expense of the entropy of another system. For example, a person can increase his or her low entropy (grow), but only at the expense of the entropy of the rest of the system.

There are two basic criticisms of the work by Georgescu-Roegen. First, because we do not really know the initial stock of low-entropy matter, we do not know if our rate of consumption is high relative to the stock. Second, we receive constant infusions of energy from the sun, and this energy can be used to slow the process of entropic degradation.

Although the entropy constraint might not be binding in the foreseeable future, the relationship between entropy and the economic process provides some guidelines for policy. Activities should be encouraged that are less degrading of low entropy, because these activities impose less costs on the future. Of course, the current cost of encouraging these activities must be compared with the future costs of entropic degradation. Conserving low entropy is conceptually equivalent to saying that we should minimize use of inputs and minimize waste, which is what Daly calls for in his examination of the necessity and feasibility of moving our economic system to a steady state.

Doomsday Models

As the fields of computer science, systems science, and operations research began to develop in the 1960s and early 1970s, these tools began to be applied to the questions of overall scarcity and environmental degradation. *The Limits to Growth* model of Meadows, Meadows, and Behrens (1972) was the most widely cited of this class of models.

The basic premise of these models was to specify initial conditions (of population, wealth, arable land, capital, natural resources, and so on) and then allow these variables to grow. The implications of growth are computed (that is, more output implies more pollution, more output implies faster resource depletion, more people means more food cultivation and more soil erosion). What these models found was that in a rather short period of time (20–50 years), some sort of constraint interfered with the ability of the economic system to support population. Depending on the scenario that was examined, resources were depleted, food shortages developed, or massive pollution developed. These constraints interfered with growth and implied collapse. Output per capita and food consumption per capita declined in these models and eventually was severe enough to constrain population growth. Because these models predicted such a dismal outcome for human society, they came to be known as doomsday models. And because they were similar to Malthus's work in having scarcity constraints limit population and impoverish the human condition, they were also known as neo-Malthusian models.

These models caused considerable excitement for two reasons. First, society was just beginning to become aware of the problems of environmental degradation and population growth, as books such as Rachel Carson's *Silent Spring* (1962) and Paul Ehrlich's *Population Time Bomb* (1968) were published. Second, the public was enthralled by (and did not really understand the nature of) computers and computer models. Many people believed that if a computer predicted the collapse of humankind, this prediction must be taken seriously.

There are two criticisms of these doomsday models. First, they are tremendously sensitive to the assumed rates of exponential growth. Second, there is no endogeniety or positive feedback in the model, including the effect of scarcity on prices and prices on scarcity. The sensitivity to growth rates can be illustrated by example. If population is increasing at 2 percent per year, it will double in 35 years, and if it is increasing at 3 percent a year, it will double every 23 years. If we start with a population of around 5 billion at the present, a population that grows at 2 percent for 100 years will be 30 billion and a population that grows at 3 percent will be approximately 100 billion. The importance is apparent even for smaller growth rates and smaller differences between growth rates. For example, if the population is growing at 1.4 percent per year, it will double every 50 years, and if it is growing at 1.5 percent, it will double every 47 years. This difference might seem insignificant, but if we start at 5 billion people, there will be 20.3 billion in 100 years with a 1.4 percent growth rate, and 22.4 billion with a 1.5 percent growth rate. The 2 billion person differential does not seem as insignificant as the difference between 1.4 and 1.5 percent. The other major criticism is that there is no endogeniety or feedback in the system. There is no mechanism for increasing scarcity, pollution, or population to affect behavior in these models. In other words, even as we are forced to wear gas masks because of the hideous pollution, we take no steps to reduce the level of pollution.

A major absence of feedback is that market prices are not included in these models. As scarcity increases, price will increase, which will trigger a full set of market responses that tend to lesson the scarcity problem. Because environmental resources are not traded in markets, however, prices cannot alleviate their scarcity. These effects are discussed more fully in the next section.

Before leaving this section, a comment on the importance of the neo-Malthusian models should be made. The people who developed these models did so to create a new intellectual paradigm that addresses the role of scarcity and the long-term prospects for humankind. It is easy to criticize these models for omissions and shortcomings retrospectively, because new ideas had not yet had a chance to be tested and perfected. These models served an important purpose in encouraging economists and other scientists to think about the issues of scarcity and the future of the planet, and they are the intellectual foundation for the models of sustainability that are discussed later in the chapter.

Price, Scarcity, and Neoclassical Economics

The work of Hotelling (1931) (who identified user cost as the mechanism that makes price reflect scarcity) forms the basis of the neoclassical (modern microeconomic) economic approach to scarcity. This approach is epitomized by the work of Barnett and Morse, who investigated the scarcity question in the 1960s.

One of the most important contributions of Barnett and Morse (1963) is that they discussed mechanisms through which price mitigates scarcity. This aspect is extremely important because as price increases to reflect scarcity, it sets into motion mechanisms that reduce scarcity.[2] For example, if oil becomes scarcer, then the price will rise. This higher price has several important effects. First, it generates added incentives for exploration of new sources of oil. Second, it makes it more profitable to remove oil from more difficult places. Third, it gives added incentives for research and development into new technologies for finding, extracting, and utilizing oil (more efficient engines, and so on). The higher price also discourages current consumption of oil. Finally, it encourages the development of substitutes for oil, such as solar energy.

There are many historical examples of what appears to be shortage that is mitigated by scarcity-induced forces, such as higher prices. The whole history of oil exploration and development is seeming scarcity mitigated by new discoveries. When it looked like the Pennsylvania oil fields were being depleted, more and larger fields were found in Texas and Oklahoma. Then, as oil became more expensive, new discoveries were found in North Africa and the Persian Gulf. As oil became apparently scarce and very expensive in the 1970s, new fields came on line in Alaska, Mexico, and the North Sea. Although the price of oil is constantly fluctuating, the trend has been lower prices (inflation adjusted) since World War II. When oil again becomes scarcer and more expensive, new adjustments will occur. These adjustments could include development of more oil producing areas or the development of alternatives to oil.

Although these mechanisms can tend to mitigate scarcity, they may not necessarily eliminate it or prevent it from impacting per capita output. Consequently, Barnett and Morse (1963) further investigated the question of scarcity. The first step was to develop conceptual models of scarcity, and the second step was to conduct empirical tests to determine if scarcity is increasing or decreasing.

The first step in their conceptual discussion of scarcity was to examine the Malthus hypothesis that the law of diminishing returns implies that as labor increases, the marginal product of labor must decline. As discussed in Chapter 17, Barnett and Morse (1963) point out that although Malthus correctly applied the law of diminishing returns to an economy in which the only inputs are labor and land, Malthus's conclusion does not necessarily hold when one moves to an economy of more than two inputs. The law of diminishing returns states that if all but one input is held constant, the remaining input will exhibit diminishing returns. In a two-input economy, holding land constant while labor increases is equivalent to holding all inputs equivalent while labor increases. If, however, one considers an economy with more than two outputs (such as land, labor, capital, or energy), increasing labor while only land is held constant does not imply that the marginal product of labor must be declining. Increases in capital (either quantitative or qualitative) can generate an increasing marginal product, even if land is held constant. The importance of this concept is that a finite amount of land (or natural resources) does not necessarily imply declining marginal product of labor.

[2] See Chapters 2, 3, 7, 8, and 9 for discussions of price, user cost, and scarcity.

According to this discussion, the existence of scarcity is an empirical question that can only be answered by looking at real world phenomenon.

Barnett and Morse (1963) suggest two types of tests for the existence of scarcity and two methods for conducting each test. First, they stress that it is important to examine the scarcity of individual resources and scarcity of resources in general. It is important to examine resources in general because as a particular resource becomes scarcer, other resources could be substituted for it. Both the scarcity of individual resources and the scarcity of substitution possibilities must be examined.

In examining these types of scarcity, they suggest two hypotheses on which to build empirical tests. Both hypotheses are based on the supposition that if resources become more scarce, then their opportunity cost should rise. Barnett and Morse's strong scarcity hypothesis looks at whether the costs of extracting resources (labor and capital costs) have increased over time. Their weak scarcity hypothesis looks at whether the price of extractive materials has been rising relative to the price of other goods. Both hypotheses are tested using historical data, and their general conclusion is that scarcity is not increasing. This conclusion holds for most extractive resources when viewed separately and for extractive resources as a whole. The two major criticisms of this conclusion are discussed next.

First, it is difficult to make predictions into the future by looking at past trends, particularly when the forces underlying the trends are not included in the analysis. For example, the Barnett and Morse study looks at the change in extraction costs over time, but it does not look at the factors that affect extraction cost, such as the characteristics of resource reserves, technological innovation, and the availability of cheap energy. Second, Barnett and Morse choose a monotonic specification for their empirical tests. A monotonic function is one that is always increasing or always decreasing. If one fits a monotonic function through a long time series of data, then recent changes in the data may not be reflected in the sign of the slope of the function because the preceding data outweigh the more recent change. This relationship is illustrated in Figure 19.1, where a stylized line-fitting will have a negative slope and not reflect the increases in costs in recent years. Slade (1982) reestimated some of these functions for selected minerals with a quadratic (U-shaped) function and found that we are now on the upward sloping part of the "U."

Second, the measure employed by Barnett and Morse might not be the best indicator of scarcity. Different properties of scarcity indicators are discussed in Smith (1979). For the purpose of this chapter, the most important missing dimension is that, because they exclude environmental costs, these measures do not include the full social cost of removing extractive resources. The labor and capital cost associated with removing extractive resources could be falling at the same time that environmental costs are rising. This increase in environmental costs is likely to come about for three reasons, all because the resources that are easiest to extract (closest to the surface, highest concentration, closest to market areas, etc.) are extracted first. First, as lower and lower grades of ore are extracted, the amount of waste material

Figure 19.1 **Fitting a Monotonic Function to Nonmonotonic Data**

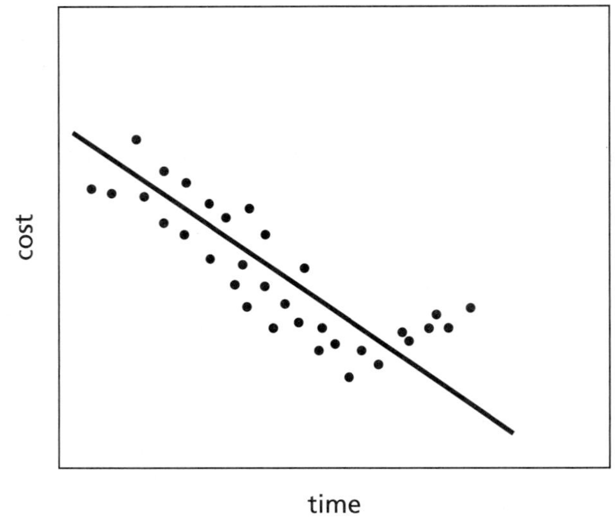

increases. Second, as lower-grade ores and deeper deposits are extracted, the use of more energy is required. Third, as environmental degradation increases (from both extractive and nonextractive activities), the marginal social damages of degradation may be increasing. This increase is particularly true with the loss of unique natural areas, such as wilderness areas that are diminishing in number as more and more natural areas are lost to extractive activity and other development.

One might argue that if the price of the extractive good includes its environmental cost, then price would still serve as a good signal of resource scarcity. In fact, it is often argued that the current environmental regulations in the United States fully internalize the environmental cost of goods. Even if one accepted this argument, however, one could not use it as a basis for measuring scarcity, because the strict environmental regulations have only been in place for a short period of time (less than two decades), which is insufficient time to conduct a time series analysis. Because empirical tests of the change in total social costs are not available, however, it is difficult to say whether scarcity is increasing or decreasing.

Systemwide Change and Sustainability

Recent concern with scarcity is not that we are running out of individual materials in general, but that economic activity is fundamentally changing the ecosystem and physical environment. This systemwide change, it is argued, interferes with the long-term ability of the planet to support human population because it impairs the ability of ecosystems to provide ecological services. Global warming, acid rain, ozone depletion, deforestation, soil loss, water availability and quality problems, and the loss of biodiversity reflect this systemwide change. Current work by past neo-Malthusians (such as Meadows and colleagues, 1972, 1992) and by other authors, such as Gore (1992) and Brown (1991), cite this fundamental systemwide change as the potential source of limitations of future prospects.

These authors all argue that the current methods of economic production are not sustainable in that they generate this systemwide change. Because environmental resources and the state of the environment are fundamental to both life processes and economic production processes, systemwide decline could lead to a great future loss of productive ability and severely limit the prospects of future generations in many dimensions. Not everyone accepts the hypothesis that systemwide change is imminent or significant even if it were to occur, and this debate has become fundamental in political discussions on environmental policy. This controversy over whether or not systemwide change exists leads to an extremely important policy question, and one that has not been adequately addressed: What level of proof is required before one acts?

The scientific method requires rigorous proof before claiming that a result holds. Typically, 95 percent or 99 percent confidence is required before rejecting a null hypothesis.[3] This high degree of burden of proof has been passed forward to the policy arena. For example, skeptics of global warming argue that there is not sufficient proof that global warming exists. Yet do we wait for 99 percent confidence before taking action? For example, if we are 90 percent sure that there will be global warming as a result of carbon dioxide emissions and 70 percent sure that there will be significant negative consequences, do we act now, or do we wait?

A risk-adverse posture would be to begin to take actions now to limit system-wide change in the future. People such as Brown (1991), Gore (1992), Meadows and colleagues (1992), and Pearce and Warford (1993) argue that the criterion of sustainability be used to evaluate present decisions. According to the criterion of sustainability, we do not need to prohibit economic growth, but we need to constrain growth and pursue growth paths that are sustainable and in which the change that the economic activity engenders does not undermine the ability to engage in that activity or alternative economic activities in the future.

The concept of sustainable development is fundamentally different from the idea of Malthusian limits to growth. The concept of sustainable development implies that some growth paths are possible, whereas Malthusian con-

---

[3] A null hypothesis is the supposition that the researcher attempts to disprove, so as to accept the alternative hypothesis. In the global climate change area, the null hypothesis is that carbon dioxide emissions are not causing global warming.

cepts say that growth is fundamentally limited. It is rather interesting to note that some of the most noted neo-Malthusians have now become advocates of sustainability and have backed away from their predictions of societal collapse. In *Beyond the Limits: Confronting Global Collapse, Envisioning a Sustainable Future*, Meadows and coauthors (1992) use computer models to contrast sustainable paths to nonsustainable paths. Sustainable paths include such policies as controlling greenhouse gas emissions, limiting soil erosion, and limiting population growth.

The current work on sustainability and the past work in traditional economics, which shows that price can limit scarcity, are not inconsistent. Their relationship can be traced to John Krutilla's 1967 call to reconsider the concept of conservation. Krutilla argued that we need to refocus our old concern with the conservation of extractive resources and be more concerned with the conservation of unique natural environments. A current extension of his reconsideration argument would be to extend the concern with conservation to the viability and sustainability of entire environmental systems. This need to focus on systems and not on individual resources or sites is the fundamental premise that underlies the concept of sustainable growth: *Growth that is conserving of environmental systems is sustainable, even though individual resources may be depleted; growth that degrades systems is fundamentally unsustainable.*

People who argue for movement toward a theory of sustainable economics do not argue that price is incapable of mitigating the types of scarcity that Hotelling (1931) and Barnett and Morse (1963) were concerned about. Rather, they would argue that systemwide environmental degradation will not be incorporated into market prices, so public policy is necessary.

The advocacy of sustainable economics is also not inconsistent with cost-benefit analysis. Costs and benefits, however, are treated much differently in the sustainability paradigm than in the traditional economics paradigm, because future costs and benefits are not necessarily discounted to present values in the sustainability paradigm. As discussed in (Appendix 2.A and Chapter 5), discounting reduces costs that are in the distant future to insignificant levels. The sustainability paradigm implies that these future costs and benefits should be more fully incorporated into current decision making.

Many scholars have developed plans to move the global economy onto a sustainable path. For example, Brown (1991), Gore (1992), Meadows and coauthors (1992), and others have developed point-by-point plans. These plans share many elements, including operational goals and attitudinal goals.

Attitudinal goals may be more important than operational goals. Advocates of sustainable growth argue that sustainability will not occur unless values change. They state that we have to be more concerned with equity, both intratemporal and intertemporal, and be more willing to accept short-term sacrifice for long-term gain. Of course, because these attitudes are not synchronized with the way political systems have developed, political systems will have to change to be more future oriented. Such change would require leadership in this direction by both political leaders and citizens' groups. Meadows and coauthors (1992) speak of this change as a revolution and discuss past revolutions in economic systems. The first was the agricultural revolution, when people moved from a hunting/gathering existence to domesticated agriculture. The second revolution that dramatically changed human existence was the Industrial Revolution. Meadows and coauthors argue that it is time for a new economic revolution, a sustainability revolution, when we fundamentally change our economic activity from attempting to maximize short-term output and focus on sustainable growth.

Although each author has suggested a different set of operational goals that must be met for sustainability to occur, there are some common threads. The reader is referred to the original books for complete descriptions of each author's plans. The common threads include the following goals:

1. Control population growth.
2. Eliminate reliance on fossil fuels.
3. Reduce pollution emissions and waste.
4. Eliminate the pressing Third World poverty that is the source of so much degradation.
5. Slow deforestation, desertification, soil erosion, overexploitation of fisheries, and other assaults on our renewable resource base.
6. Eliminate military conflict and the devotion of resources to military hardware.
7. Develop new "appropriate" technology that is capable of meeting economic needs at minimal environmental costs, particularly in developing countries.

Summary

It is relatively easy to read a book like this one and become depressed. Severe problems have been identified, and often little has been done to rectify these problems. Pollution, environmental degradation, global warming, loss of biodiversity, and other problems have been shown to have the potential to drastically affect the quality of life in the future. Many people speak of apocalyptic outcomes, and few are sanguine about the future.

Yet the future is not already determined; the future is a choice, and our actions today will determine the future. If we refuse to act today, then environmental systems will continue to collapse and the prospects for the future will be limited. Sound policies and individual actions can make an important difference in the viability of our future. Through an understanding of scientific relationships, social institutions, and economic principles that determine people's behavior, we can understand the forces that govern environmental change and choose a set of policies that move us toward a sustainable future.

Review Questions

1. What is meant by "absolute scarcity"?
2. What is the entropy law, and what is its relevance for environmental policy?
3. What are the primary criticisms of the "doomsday models"?
4. What does the empirical work of Barnett and Morse say about resource scarcity?
5. How can the invisible hand of the market mitigate scarcity? What are its shortcomings in this regard?

Questions for Further Study

1. What are the shortcomings of Barnett and Morse's scarcity measures?
2. Why is the environmental cost of extracting resources increasing?
3. What are the necessary conditions for sustainability?
4. How do the sustainability paradigm and cost-benefit analysis differ in their treatments of costs?
5. How would you change political systems to make them more future oriented?

Suggested Paper Topics

1. Take a plan for sustainability from an author, such as Gore; Meadows, Meadows, and Randers; or Brown. Evaluate each point in the plan using the environmental economics concepts discussed in this book.
2. Look at studies such as Barnett and Morse (1963) and Smith (1978, 1979) that develop empirical measures of resource scarcity. Compare and contrast the different measures and their methods of implementation. See current issues of the *Journal of Environmental Economics and Management* and other resource journals for the most recent studies.

Works Cited and Selected Readings

Barnett, H., and C. Morse. *Scarcity and Growth*. Washington, DC: Resources for the Future, 1963.

Brown, L. *Eco-Economy: Building an Economy for the Earth*. New York: W. W. Norton, 2001.

Brown, L. Global Resource Scarcity Is a Serious Problem. Pages [[page]] in *Global Resources: Opposing Viewpoints*, edited by M. Poletsky. San Diego: Greenhaven Press, 1991.

Brown, L. R., C. Flavin, and S. Postel. *Saving the Planet: How to Shape an Environmentally Sustainable Global Economy*. New York: W. W. Norton, 1991.

Carson, R. *Silent Spring*. New York: Houghton Mifflin, 1962.

Daly, H. *Beyond Growth: The Economics of Sustainable Development*. Boston: Beacon Press, 1997.

Daly, H. *Steady State Economics: The Economics of Biophysical Equilibrium and Moral Growth*. San Francisco: Freeman, 1977.

Costanza, R., and S. E. Jorgenson, (eds.). *Understanding and Solving Environmental Problems in the 21st century*. Elsevier Science, 2002.

Ehrlich, P. H. *The Population Time Bomb*. New York: Ballantine, 1968.

Ehrlich, P. R., and A. H. Ehrlich. Population Growth Threatens Global Resources. Pages [[page]] in *Global Resources: Opposing Viewpoints*, edited by M. Poletsky. San Diego: Greenhaven Press, 1991.

Georgescu-Roegen, N. *The Entropy Law and the Economic Process*. Cambridge, MA: Harvard University Press, 1971.

Georgescu-Roegen, N. Energy and Economic Myths. *Southern Economic Journal 41* (1975): 347–381.

Gore, A. *Earth in the Balance*. New York: Houghton Mifflin, 1992.

Hotelling, H. The Economics of Exhaustible Resources. *Journal of Political Economy 39* (1931): 137–175.

Kaufman, D. G., and C. M. Franz. Biosphere 2000: Protecting our Global Environment. New York: Kendall/Hunt Publishing Co., 2000.

Krutilla, J. Conservation Reconsidered. *American Economic Review* (1967): 777–787.

Malthus, T. R. An Essay on the Principle of Population. Pages 15–129 in *An Essay on the Principles of Population, Text Sources and Background, Criticism*, edited by P. Appelman. New York: W. W. Norton, 2003.

Meadows, D. H., D. L. Meadows, and W. W. Behrens. *The Limits to Growth*. New York: Universe Books, 1972.

Meadows, D. H., D. L. Meadows, and J. Randers. *Beyond the Limits: Confronting Global Collapse, Envisioning a Sustainable Future*. Post Mill, VT: Chelsea Green, 1992.

Pearce, D. W., and J. J. Warford. *World without End*. New York: Oxford University Press, 1993.

Ray, D. L., and L. Guzzo. *Trashing the Planet: How Science Can Help Us Deal with Acid Rain, Depletion of Ozone, and Nuclear Waste (Among Other Things)*. Washington, DC: Regnery Gateway, 1990.

Simon, J. L., and H. Kahn, (eds.). *The Resourceful Earth: A Response to Global 2000*. Oxford: Basil Blackwell, 1984.

Slade, M. E. Trends in Natural Resource Commodity Prices: An Analysis of the Time Domain. *Journal of Environmental Economics and Management 9* (1982): 122–137.

Smith, V. K. Measuring Natural Resource Scarcity. *Journal of Environmental Economics and Management 5* (1978): 150–171.

Smith, V. K. *Scarcity and Growth Reconsidered*. Washington, DC: Resources for the Future, 1979.

World Bank, World Development Report: Sustainable Development in a Dynamic World: Transforming Institutions, Growth and Quality of Life. Washington DC: World Bank, 2002.

name index

subject index